20th Century®
Bookkeeping & Accounting

TWENTY-FIRST EDITION

PAUL A. CARLSON

Director, Division of Business Education
Wisconsin State College
Whitewater, Wisconsin

HAMDEN L. FORKNER

Chairman, Department of Business Education
Teachers College, Columbia University
New York, New York

LEWIS D. BOYNTON

Chairman, Department of Business Education
Teachers College of Connecticut
New Britain, Connecticut

South-Western Publishing Company

Cincinnati 27 | Chicago 5 | San Francisco 3 | Dallas 2 | New Rochelle, N. Y.

B65

Preface

Why study bookkeeping and accounting?

Bookkeeping as general education. The principles and practices of bookkeeping and accounting are related to the daily lives of all of us. Even the simplest business transaction affects the financial records of some business. A person who rides on a bus, gets a check for work he has done, buys a pair of shoes, or performs any other of the numerous common business activities of everyday living starts a chain of bookkeeping and accounting records. The study of bookkeeping will help us understand how business functions in our everyday life and what business contributes to our society.

The principles and practices of bookkeeping and accounting make our personal lives more effective. If we keep records of our finances, we can use our income more wisely. Spending can be planned to include not only the purchase of the necessities of life, but also recreational activities and provision for the future. Personal records, too, are now needed for income tax purposes.

Knowing the place of business in our society and knowing how to manage wisely our own personal business affairs makes for good citizenship. The study of bookkeeping and accounting, therefore, contributes to everyone's general education.

Bookkeeping as vocational education. The study of bookkeeping prepares people for employment in business. The bookkeeper is a valuable citizen. He is an important member of the office workers of the country — the second largest working force in the nation. He is at the hub of the big wheel of business. All business activities revolve around his work. He is in a vital position and his work is essential to the success of business enterprises. Upon the basis of the accurate work of the bookkeeper, many far-reaching decisions are made concerning business activity.

Businessmen and individuals keep more records than formerly. Many laws have been passed relating to keeping records about such things as social security, wages and hours of employment, workmen's compensation, income taxes, sales taxes, and so on. These laws have added to the volume and the detail of bookkeeping procedures. Many businesses that had not kept books previously must now do so.

Bookkeeping as a field of work. "Bookkeeping" is a term that covers a wide area of work in business. It is the practice of keeping a systematic record of business transactions. In many businesses the task of keeping the books is so large that it is divided among many people.

There are record keepers. Record keepers include posting clerks, entry bookkeepers, payroll clerks, clerks who fill out forms, and bookkeeping machine operators. These workers deal with parts of the total bookkeeping work. We might call them junior bookkeepers. Machines may be used to keep some of the records. They are tools to work with and are no substitute for the knowledge of bookkeeping.

There are bookkeepers. Those who keep the records are often required to understand the effects of a firm's business transactions. They keep the records and make the reports that reflect the condition of the business. They are senior bookkeepers. The material in this textbook gives specific training for work in both bookkeeping and record keeping.

There are accountants. The accountant is a professional person who is trained to *interpret* the meaning of business records, to *audit* accounts and records, and to *advise* businessmen and individuals in accounting matters. Accounting is one of the highest paid professions. A study of bookkeeping in high school will aid each student to discover if he has the aptitude, the interest, and the ability to become an accountant.

Bookkeeping as a help to workers. Bookkeeping is useful to many kinds of workers in business. A *typist* prepares statements and other reports dealing with bookkeeping work. A *secretary* takes dictation or transcribes information dealing with bookkeeping terms, transactions, and records. She may also keep bookkeeping records for her employer. A *salesperson* records cash and charge transactions, and is often required to assist in inventory work. Bookkeeping helps *junior executives* understand the problems of business. The material in this text will help all business workers perform their tasks with greater confidence and efficiency.

Bookkeeping necessary to small business owners. Bookkeeping is essential to the person planning to operate his own service station, beauty parlor, farm, restaurant, or store. Lack of proper records and the understanding of such records is one of the most frequent causes of business failure. This book will help a person who plans to own his own business keep the records necessary to assure success.

Organization of this textbook

Progress brings change. Changes in government regulations, in laws, and in taxes bring about changes that affect business and bookkeeping. New business practices and new business terms replace old ones. Teaching methods bring new, improved, and simpler ways of presenting a subject. Today's students should experience the benefit of these changes and improvements. That is the reason for and the purpose of this 21st Edition of *20th Century Bookkeeping and Accounting.* The general pattern of its eminently popular predecessor has been retained, but the contents of each chapter have been brought up to date.

The place of research in this revised edition. Three important groups of people have played a vital part in the revision of this textbook. The recommendations of many *practicing accountants* have been solicited and considered. Published surveys and research of The American Institute of Certified Public Accountants have been studied. The nation's leading *manufacturers of accounting forms and bookkeeping systems* have been consulted. As a result, the forms used in this revision conform to the latest business practices and standards. Hundreds of *bookkeeping teachers* in both large and small schools have responded to inquiries about the teaching of bookkeeping. Personal interviews have also been held with many bookkeeping teachers.

Spiral development. Psychologists have quite generally agreed that the best way to learn a process is to see the whole picture as quickly as possible. After the whole process is seen, the learner proceeds to study and expand the details and the fine points that make up the picture. A quick overview of the complete bookkeeping cycle in its simplest form is therefore presented in Part 1. Each time the bookkeeping cycle is repeated, it is expanded just as a spiral is expanded. The one book of original entry in Part 1 is expanded in Part 2 to include special journals, and in Part 3 a combination journal with many amount columns is used. The single ledger in Part 1 is expanded in Part 2 to include the use of a general ledger and two subsidiary ledgers. The simple six-column work sheet without adjusting entries in Part 1 is expanded in Part 2 into an eight-column work sheet with adjusting entries.

Step-by-step illustrations and development. Each chapter of the textbook takes up a specific bookkeeping principle and develops it in a manner that makes learning effective. First, a business situation is presented.

Second, a step-by-step analysis is made of the recording required by the situation. Third, an illustration is given showing step-by-step what is done by the bookkeeper.

Drills for understanding. Bookkeeping requires an understanding of the reasons for what is done and skill in doing it. Such understanding and skill are acquired through practice and drill. Special consideration has been given in this edition to meaningful drills for understanding at the end of many chapters. A liberal number of these drill exercises are available for classroom use or for homework assignments.

Chapter organization. Special attention has been given to the organization of each chapter for the purpose of making the teaching and the learning as effective as possible. Each chapter concludes with review and summary material for testing and reinforcing the students' understanding and application of the material covered by the chapter. These end-of-chapter materials include: (1) *Chapter Questions* to review the information presented in the chapter; (2) *Increasing Your Business Vocabulary* to assist students in mastering the new business words embodied in the chapter; (3) *Cases for Discussion* to challenge students to apply the principles they have learned; (4) *Drills for Understanding* to aid in helping to fix learnings; and (5) *Application Problems* to give students ample opportunity to apply and reinforce new and previous learnings.

Projects and practice sets. The learning of any knowledge or skill requires application. Directed practice through carefully planned projects and practice sets at frequent intervals throughout the textbook gives the student practice in performing the bookkeeping tasks commonly found in business. The workbook that accompanies this textbook provides ruled paper for the written exercises and projects. Ordinary bookkeeping paper may be used if the teacher prefers. Bookkeeping practice sets with or without business papers are also available. The sets with business papers give the student an actual contact with commonly used business forms.

Acknowledgments. There have been many people who have contributed to the continual improvement of *20th Century Bookkeeping and Accounting:* the innumerable students and teachers who have used the previous editions, those who have given freely of their professional knowledge, and those who have worked directly on the production of the book itself. To all of these, the authors wish to express their great appreciation and sincere thanks.

The Authors

Contents

Part 3 Problems in recording bookkeeping transactions
(Applied with combination journal and cash register)

Part 4 Adapting bookkeeping methods to the business
(*Applied with columnar special journals*)

Part 5 Bookkeeping systems for special purposes
(*Applied to personal, social, professional, and farm records*)

The bookkeeping process

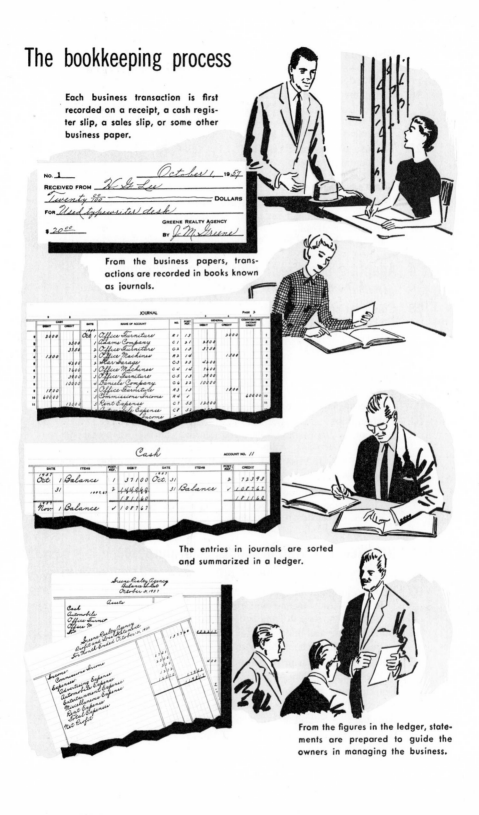

Each business transaction is first recorded on a receipt, a cash register slip, a sales slip, or some other business paper.

From the business papers, transactions are recorded in books known as journals.

The entries in journals are sorted and summarized in a ledger.

From the figures in the ledger, statements are prepared to guide the owners in managing the business.

Starting a bookkeeping system CHAPTER 1

Importance of bookkeeping records. The key to good business management is good bookkeeping records. Bookkeeping records can show whether a business operates at a profit or at a loss. Studies show that the success or the failure of a business may often be traced to the kind of records that are kept.

The work of the bookkeeper. One who records all the business affairs of a business in an orderly manner is called a *bookkeeper*. A bookkeeper must (a) be accurate, (b) understand what he is to do and how he should do it, and (c) be systematic, neat, and rapid in his work. A person who knows bookkeeping can manage his own business affairs better than one who does not, and he can also secure well-paying positions in business.

Starting a bookkeeping system. Before a person starts a bookkeeping system for himself, he should know how much he is worth. What he is worth is the difference between what he owns and what he owes.

For example, Charles Jones is starting a personal bookkeeping system. As the first step he finds:

What he owns:		*What he owes:*	
Cash on hand.....	$ 250.00	To Hackett Grocery...$ 58.00	
Government bonds	1,000.00	To Johnson Market....	37.00
Automobile.......	1,200.00	To Webster Garage....	144.00
Furniture........	3,500.00	Total owed..........$239.00	
House and lot.....	15,000.00		
Total owned.....	$20,950.00		

Charles Jones can now find what he is worth by subtracting what he owes from what he owns.

What he owns.....................................	$20,950.00
What he owes.....................................	239.00
What he is worth.................................	$20,711.00

1

The balance sheet. In bookkeeping, a business form showing what is owned, what is owed, and what the proprietor is worth is called a *balance sheet*. The balance sheet of Charles Jones prepared from the information on page 1 is as follows:

Assets		Liabilities	
		Charles Jones	
		Balance Sheet	
		December 31, 1957	
Cash	250 00	Hackett Grocery	58 00
Government Bonds	100 00	Johnson Market	37 00
Automobile	1 200 00	Webster Garage	144 00
Furniture	350 00	Total Liabilities	239 00
House and Lot	15 000 00		
		Proprietorship	
		Charles Jones, Capital	20 711 00
Total Assets	20 950 00	Total Liabilities and Prop.	20 950 00

Beginning balance sheet of an individual

Heading of the balance sheet. The heading of Charles Jones's balance sheet is written on three lines. Each of the three lines gives important information about the form as follows:

Line 1. Who? — the name of the person   *Charles Jones*
Line 2. What? — the name of the business form   *Balance Sheet*
Line 3. When? — the date of the balance sheet   *December 31, 1957*

Body of a balance sheet. The body of a balance sheet has three sections: (1) Assets, (2) Liabilities, and (3) Proprietorship. The Assets section is placed on the left-hand side of the balance sheet; the Liabilities section and the Proprietorship section are placed on the right-hand side.

1. Assets. Anything of value that is owned is called an *asset*. Charles Jones's assets are cash on hand, government bonds, automobile, furniture, and house and lot. Assets are listed on the left-hand side of the balance sheet. Each asset is given a brief title that describes it. For example, cash on hand is listed as *Cash.*

2. Liabilities. An amount owed is called a *liability*. The one to whom an amount is owed is known as a *creditor*. Charles Jones has three liabilities. Liabilities are listed on the right-hand side of the balance sheet. The title of each liability is the name of the creditor. For example, "Owed to Hackett Grocery" is listed simply as *Hackett Grocery.*

3. Proprietorship. The amount that would remain if all of the liabilities were paid is known as *proprietorship*. The amount of the proprietorship is obtained by subtracting the total liabilities from the total assets. The proprietorship is listed on the right-hand side of the balance sheet. The word *Capital* is written after the name of the owner. Charles Jones lists his proprietorship by writing *Charles Jones, Capital.*

Beginning a bookkeeping system for a social organization. On August 1, the athletic director and the student council of the local high school decide to start a new bookkeeping system for the high school athletic department. Before the books can be started, the bookkeeper needs to know what the department owns, what it owes, and what it is worth. This information in balance sheet form is shown below.

High School Athletic Department
Balance Sheet
August 1, 1957

Assets		Liabilities	
Cash	1 2 7 0 0	Athletic Supply Co.	3 7 0 0 0
Basketball Equipment	8 5 0 0 0	Coe Printing Co.	3 5 0 0
Football Equipment	3 1 6 4 0 0	Quaker Drug Co., Inc.	8 6 0 0
Therapy Equipment	3 0 6 0 0	Total Liabilities	4 9 1 0 0
Track Equipment	4 8 3 0 0		
		Proprietorship	
		H.S. Athletic Dept. Capital	4 4 3 9 0 0
Total Assets	4 9 3 0 0 0	Total Liabilities and Prop.	4 9 3 0 0 0

Beginning balance sheet of a school organization

Analyzing the balance sheet. This balance sheet is similar to the balance sheet of an individual illustrated on page 2. Note that:

1. The heading has three lines showing the name, High School Athletic Department, the name of the form, and the date.
2. The assets are listed in the Assets section on the left-hand side of the balance sheet.
3. The liabilities are listed in the Liabilities section on the right-hand side of the balance sheet.
4. The amount that the athletic department is worth is shown in the Proprietorship section on the right-hand side of the balance sheet. It is given the title *High School Athletic Department, Capital.*
5. The total of the liabilities is added to the proprietorship. The total of the liabilities plus the proprietorship equals the total of the assets.

Beginning a bookkeeping system for a business. J. M. Greene is the owner of a real estate business known as the Greene Realty Agency. He has decided to start a new bookkeeping system that will give him better information about the operations of his business. Before he can start his new system, he needs to know:

1. What he owns — his assets.
2. What he owes — his liabilities.
3. What he is worth — his proprietorship.

The balance sheet of the Greene Realty Agency. When Mr. Greene has the necessary information, he prepares a balance sheet as the first step in starting the new bookkeeping system. The balance sheet is shown below.

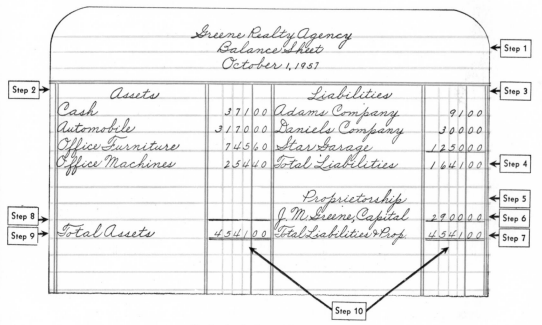

Beginning balance sheet of a business

Steps in preparing a balance sheet. In preparing a balance sheet use the following steps. As you study each step, check it with the illustration of the balance sheet of the Greene Realty Agency.

Step 1. Write the heading on three lines; center each line.

Step 2. Write the word *Assets* in the center of the first line of the wide column on the left-hand side of the balance sheet. Then, list the name and the amount of each asset.

When amounts are written in ruled columns, the dollar signs and the decimal points are not written. The red ruling in the amount column separates dollars and cents and serves as the decimal point. When an amount is in even dollars, two zeros are written in the cents column.

Step 3. Write the word *Liabilities* in the center of the wide column on the right-hand side of the balance sheet. Then, list the name of each creditor and the amount owed to him.

Step 4. Draw a single ruled line under the last liability amount, add the column, and write the total on the next line. Write the words *Total Liabilities* on the same line as the total.

Step 5. Skip one line after *Total Liabilities* and write the word *Proprietorship* in the center of the wide column. The blank line separates the Proprietorship section from the Liabilities section.

Step 6. Write the *name of the proprietor* and the word *Capital* on the next line under the heading *Proprietorship*. Then on a separate sheet of paper, find the amount of the proprietorship by subtracting the total liabilities from the total assets. Write the amount of the proprietorship in the amount column after the word *Capital*.

Step 7. Draw a single ruled line across the amount column under the amount of the proprietorship. Add the total liabilities and the amount of the proprietorship and write the total immediately below the single ruled line. Write the words *Total Liabilities and Proprietorship* on the same line as the total. If necessary, the words may be abbreviated. For example: *Total Liabilities & Prop.*

Step 8. Draw a single ruled line across the amount column on the left-hand side of the balance sheet on the same line as the last single ruled line on the right-hand side. This is done in order to place the final totals of the balance sheet on the same line on both sides.

Step 9. Add the assets amount column on the left-hand side of the balance sheet and write the total immediately under the single ruled line. Write the words *Total Assets* on the same line as the amount of the total.

Step 10. Compare the final total of the left-hand side of the balance sheet with the final total of the right-hand side. The two totals should be the same. If the two final totals are the same, draw double ruled lines across the amount columns immediately under the totals on both sides. If the final totals are not the same, find and correct the error in addition or subtraction before drawing double ruled lines.

Double ruled lines are drawn to show that all work has been completed and that the balance sheet is believed to be accurate.

The fundamental bookkeeping equation. On any balance sheet, the total amount of the assets is equal to the total amount of the liabilities plus the amount of the proprietorship. This important principle of bookkeeping may be stated in the form of the following simple equation:

$$\text{ASSETS} = \text{LIABILITIES} + \text{PROPRIETORSHIP}$$

This equation is true of all balance sheets. It is therefore known as the *fundamental bookkeeping equation.*

$$\text{Assets} = \begin{cases} \text{Liabilities} \\ + \\ \text{Proprietorship} \end{cases}$$

CHAPTER QUESTIONS

1. What is the first step in starting a new bookkeeping system?
2. What is written on each of the three lines of the heading at the top of a balance sheet?
3. What word did Charles Jones write immediately after his name in the Proprietorship section of his balance sheet in order to show that he is worth $20,711.00?
4. What is the heading of the section of the balance sheet that appears on the left-hand side of each of the three balance sheets in this chapter?
5. What are the headings of the two sections of the balance sheet that are on the right-hand side of each of the balance sheets in this chapter?
6. Why are double lines drawn on the balance sheet?
7. State the fundamental bookkeeping equation that summarizes the contents of any balance sheet.

INCREASING YOUR BUSINESS VOCABULARY

What is the meaning of each of the following:

(a) bookkeeper
(b) balance sheet
(c) asset
(d) liability
(e) creditor
(f) proprietorship

CASES FOR DISCUSSION

1. The Future Business Leaders of America chapter of the local high school has a bank balance of $83.64 and no other assets. The association has no unpaid bills. What is the amount of proprietorship?

2. The Caldwell Shoe Company has property worth $45,000. The debts of the Caldwell Shoe Company amount to $25,000. What is the amount of proprietorship?

DRILL FOR UNDERSTANDING

Drill 1-A. This drill is planned to give you skill in classifying items as assets, liabilities, and proprietorship.

Instructions: 1. If you do not have a workbook, copy on a sheet of paper the list of items shown at the right. Then rule a one-inch Answers column at the right of the list. Write the heading *Answers* at the top of this column.

2. Classify each item on your list as an asset, a liability, or proprietorship by writing in the Answers column a capital *A* for asset, a capital *L* for liability, or a capital *P* for proprietorship. The first item, cash on hand, is given as an example.

3. Now cover your answers and see how rapidly you can do this orally without looking at your answers. Repeat this drill orally several times for increased speed and accuracy.

Items to be Classified	Answers
1. Cash on hand	A
2. Owed to grocery	
3. Automobile	
4. Unpaid meat bill	
5. Furniture	
6. Owed to dairy	
7. House and lot	
8. Amount person is worth	
9. Government bonds	
10. Any item owned	
11. Any amount owed	

APPLICATION PROBLEMS

Problem 1-1. Balance sheet for an individual

George Lane plans to set up a personal bookkeeping system. He has prepared the following lists of things owned and amounts owed:

Things owned:

Cash on hand..............	$ 380.00
Government bonds........	2,000.00
Automobile valued at......	1,600.00
Furniture valued at........	4,200.00
House and lot valued at....	15,500.00
Total value of items owned.	**$23,680.00**

Amounts owed:

Owed to Dr. S. H. Ambrose	$ 250.00
Owed to Barty's Store......	147.00
Owed to Slowey's Market..	86.00
Total amount owed........	**$ 483.00**

Instructions: Prepare a balance sheet for George Lane dated June 30 of the current year. Follow the steps for preparing a balance sheet given on pages 4 and 5. Use the illustration of the balance sheet on page 2 as your model. Strive for accuracy and neatness.

Self-checking: Check the accuracy and the completeness of your work by asking yourself the following questions:

(a) Did you center each of the three sectional headings in the body of your balance sheet?

(b) On the right-hand side of your balance sheet did you leave a blank line between the Liabilities section and the Proprietorship section?

(c) Is the amount of the total assets at the bottom of the left-hand side of your balance sheet on the same line as the amount of the total liabilities and proprietorship at the bottom of the right-hand side?

(d) Are the two totals at the bottom of your balance sheet the same amount?

(e) Did you draw single and double lines across the amount columns only?

Problem 1-2. Balance sheet for a school organization

The High School Athletic Department has the following assets and liabilities:

Cash and other property:		*Unpaid bills:*	
Cash on hand..............	$ 216.00	Athletic Supply Company...	$ 937.00
Football equipment........	1,965.00	Collins Printing Company...	46.00
Basketball equipment.......	750.00	Martin Pharmacy..........	52.00
Baseball equipment........	687.00	Total unpaid bills..........	$1,035.00
Track equipment..........	243.00		
Total cash and other property	$3,861.00		

Instructions: Prepare a balance sheet for the High School Athletic Department dated August 31 of the current year. Use as your model the illustration of a balance sheet on page 3.

Self-checking: Check your work by asking yourself the questions that are listed under Problem 1-1.

Problem 1-3. Balance sheet for a small business

The following are the assets and the liabilities of the Shorewood Laundry, owned and operated by E. S. Thompson.

ASSETS		LIABILITIES	
Cash......................	$ 486.25	Allied Machinery Co.........	$711.50
Office Equipment...........	363.80	National Equipment Co.......	252.75
Delivery Equipment........	1,792.00		
Machinery.................	5,630.00		

Instructions: Prepare a balance sheet for the Shorewood Laundry dated September 30 of the current year. Use as your model the balance sheet on page 4.

Self-checking: Check your work by asking yourself the questions that are listed under Problem 1-1.

Recording the opening entry in a journal

Recording the beginning balance sheet in a book. The beginning balance sheet is prepared on a sheet of paper. It should be made a part of the permanent record and should therefore be recorded in the books of the business. A book in which any of the records of a business are first written is called a *journal*. An entry in a journal to record a beginning balance sheet is known as an *opening entry*.

The journal. There are many kinds of journals. A journal may have one or more amount columns. The Greene Realty Agency uses two amount columns in recording its opening entry.

	DATE	NAME OF ACCOUNT	POST. REF.	DEBIT	CREDIT	
1						1
2						2

JOURNAL   **PAGE**

A journal with two amount columns

Making the opening entry. The opening entry in the journal is made from the information on the balance sheet. The balance sheet of the Greene Realty Agency from which an opening entry is made is illustrated below.

Greene Realty Agency
Balance Sheet
October 1, 1951

Assets		Liabilities	
Cash	37 00	Adams Company	9 00
Automobile	3170 00	Daniels Company	30 00
Office Furniture	745 60	Star Garage	125 00
Office Machines	254 40	Total Liabilities	164 00
		Proprietorship	
		J. M. Greene, Capital	2900 00
Total Assets	4541 00	Total Liabilities & Prop.	4541 00

Beginning balance sheet of Greene Realty Agency

9

The following are the steps in making the opening entry in the journal:

Step 1. Write the date of the opening entry — year, month, and day — under the heading *Date* as shown below.

	DATE		NAME OF ACCOUNT	POST. REF.	DEBIT	CREDIT	
	1957 Oct.	*1*					1
2							2
3							3

JOURNAL   PAGE *1*

The date of an entry consists of three parts: (1) the year, (2) the month, and (3) the day of the month. The year is written in small figures at the top of the first column. The month is written immediately below the year on the first line in the first column. The day of the month is written on the first line in the second column. The day is written once for each entry, but only once, regardless of the number of items in the entry.

Step 2. Write the *names* of the assets in the Name of Account column of the journal and the *amounts* of the assets in the Debit column.

In recording the balance sheet in the journal, the amounts on the left-hand side of the balance sheet are recorded in the left-hand amount column, the Debit column, of the journal. The amounts on the right-hand side of the balance sheet are recorded in the right-hand amount column, the Credit column, of the journal.

The journal, after the left-hand side of the balance sheet has been recorded, appears as follows:

JOURNAL   PAGE *1*

	DATE		NAME OF ACCOUNT	POST. REF.	DEBIT	CREDIT	
1	*1957* Oct.	*1*	Cash		371 00		1
2			Automobile		3170 00		2
3			Office Furniture		745 60		3
4			Office Machines		254 40		4
5							5
6							6
7							7

The names of the assets, which appear on the left-hand side of the balance sheet, are written at the extreme left edge of the Name of Account column of the journal. The amounts of these assets are written in the Debit column of the journal.

Step 3. Write the *names* of the liabilities and the *name* of the proprietor in the Name of Account column of the journal. Write the word *Capital* after the proprietor's name. Record the *amounts* of these items in the Credit column of the journal.

After the credit items have been recorded, the journal appears as follows:

	DATE	NAME OF ACCOUNT	POST. REF.	DEBIT	CREDIT	
	1957					
1	Oct. 1	Cash		37 1 00		1
2		Automobile		3 1 7 0 00		2
3		Office Furniture		7 4 5 60		3
4		Office Machines		2 5 4 40		4
5		Adams Company			9 1 00	5
6		Daniels Company			3 00 00	6
7		Star Garage			1 2 5 0 00	7
8		J. M. Greene, Capital			2 9 0 0 00	8
9						9
10						10
11						11
12						12
13						13
14						14
15						15

JOURNAL — PAGE 1

The names of the liabilities and the name of the proprietor are on the right-hand side of the balance sheet. In the journal these names are written in the Name of Account column about one-half inch to the right of the vertical red line. In this way the credit items are distinguished from the debit items. The amounts of the liabilities and the amount of the proprietorship are written in the right-hand or Credit column of the journal.

Step 4. Write a brief explanation of the complete journal entry in the Name of Account column immediately below the last credit item. The explanation is indented about one-half inch farther than the credit items to distinguish between the explanation and the credit items. If more than one line is needed for the explanation, the second line of the explanation begins with the same indentation as the first line.

The purpose of the explanation is to make the journal entry clear whenever later reference is made to it. The explanation should therefore add any desirable information that is not indicated in the debit and credit lines of the journal entry. The explanation should be brief.

The complete opening entry in the journal then appears as shown on the following page.

DATE	NAME OF ACCOUNT	POST. REF.	DEBIT	CREDIT	
1957 Oct. 1	Cash		371 00		1
	Automobile		3170 00		2
	Office Furniture		745 60		3
	Office Machines		254 40		4
	Adams Company			91 00	5
	Daniels Company			300 00	6
	Star Garage			1250 00	7
	J. M. Greene, Capital			2900 00	8
	To record October 1 balance				9
	sheet.				10
					11
					12
					13
					14
					15
					16

An opening entry in a journal

Analyzing the opening entry. Every journal entry has two parts: the debit part and the credit part. In a journal with two amount columns, the left-hand amount column is called the *Debit column;* the right-hand amount column is called the *Credit column.* Assets that have amounts recorded in the Debit column are said to be *debited.* Liabilities and proprietorship that have amounts recorded in the Credit column are said to be *credited.*

The journal entry to record the balance sheet of the Greene Realty Agency shows that all of the asset accounts were debited. These debits are the same as the items on the left-hand side of the balance sheet. The entry shows that all liabilities and the proprietorship were credited. These credits are the same as the items on the right-hand side of the balance sheet.

In every journal entry, the total of the debit amounts must equal the total of the credit amounts. The total of the debits in the journal entry, $4,541.00, is the same as the total of the assets on the balance sheet. The total of the credits, $4,541.00, is the same as the total of the liabilities and proprietorship on the balance sheet. Since the totals are the same, the journal entry is considered correct.

Post. Ref. column. The heading of this column is an abbreviation of "Posting Reference." The use of this narrow column will be explained when posting is explained in Chapter 3.

CHAPTER QUESTIONS

1. What is the relationship between the balance sheet and the opening entry?
2. Why should the information on the beginning balance sheet be recorded in a journal?
3. What is the heading of the left-hand amount column of the two-column journal on page 12?
4. What is the heading of the right-hand amount column of the two-column journal on page 12?
5. Where is the date of the opening entry written in the journal?
6. What kind of balance sheet items are recorded in the Debit column in the journal on page 12?
7. Where are the names of the debit items written in the journal on page 12?
8. What two kinds of balance sheet items are recorded in the Credit column of the journal on page 12?
9. Where are the names of the credit items written in the journal on page 12?
10. What is the purpose of the written explanation?
11. How far should the first word of the first line of the explanation be indented?
12. If there are two lines of explanation, how far should the first word of the second line of the explanation be indented?

INCREASING YOUR BUSINESS VOCABULARY

What is the meaning of each of the following:

        (a) journal   (c) debit column
        (b) opening entry   (d) credit column

CASES FOR DISCUSSION

1. Paul Baker is the proprietor of a small business in your neighborhood. He has decided that his record keeping is incomplete. He desires to install a complete bookkeeping system.
   (a) What types of information about his business must he list as the first step in the preparation for opening a new set of books?
   (b) What bookkeeping form should he prepare from this information?
   (c) What will be his second step in starting a new bookkeeping system?
2. Ralph Brown desires to start a new bookkeeping system for the business that he operates. His assets consist of cash and office furniture. His only liability is to the Hickey Furniture Company.
   (a) What two items will be listed as debits in the opening entry?
   (b) What two items will be listed as credits in the opening entry?

Drill 2-A. This drill is planned to give you skill in classifying balance sheet items as either debits or credits when recorded in a journal.

Instructions: 1. If you do not have a workbook, copy on a sheet of paper the balance sheet items shown at the right. Then rule two narrow columns at the right of your list. Write *Debit* above your left-hand column and *Credit* above your right-hand column.

Balance Sheet Items
1. Automobile
2. Cash
3. Daniels Co. (creditor)
4. J. M. Greene, Capital
5. Office Furniture
6. Office Machines
7. Star Garage (creditor)

2. If the amount of the balance sheet item will be debited in the journal entry, make a check mark in the Debit column; if it will be credited, make a check mark in the Credit column. The first item, Automobile, is given below as an example.

Balance Sheet Items	Debit	Credit
1. *Automobile*	√	

3. Now cover your answers and see how rapidly you can do this orally without looking at your written answers. Repeat this drill orally several times for increased speed and accuracy.

APPLICATION PROBLEMS

Problem 2-1. Opening entry for an individual

Instructions: Prepare an opening entry in a journal from the following balance sheet. Use May 1 of the current year as the date of the entry.

STEPHEN CROCKER
Balance Sheet
May 1, 19--

Assets			Liabilities		
Cash..........................	675	00	Marshall's.....................	45	00
Government Bonds..............	500	00	Second National Bank..........	1,200	00
Automobile....................	2,400	00	Total Liabilities.............	1,245	00
Furniture.....................	4,250	00			
House and Lot.................	17,500	00	Proprietorship		
			Stephen Crocker, Capital......	24,080	00
Total Assets.................	25,325	00	Total Liabilities and Prop....	25,325	00

Self-checking: Compare your journal entry with the illustration on page 12, and check the accuracy of form by asking yourself the following questions:

(a) Did you write the date at the top of the Date column of the journal, showing the year, the month, and the day?

(b) Does the first letter of each debit item in the Name of Account column touch the vertical red line?

(c) Is each credit item in the Name of Account column indented the same so that the credits do not zigzag back and forth?

(d) Did you write the explanation so that the first word of the explanation is indented about twice as much as the credit items?

Problem 2-2. Opening entry for a beauty shop

Instructions: Prepare an opening entry from the following balance sheet. Use August 1 of the current year as the date of this entry.

UPTOWN BEAUTY SHOP
Balance Sheet
August 1, 19--

Assets			Liabilities		
Cash.........................	541	20	Beauty Supply Co.............	246	76
Supplies.....................	103	00	Gibson Equipment Company......	528	25
Furniture....................	1,500	00			
Equipment....................	2,780	00	Total Liabilities............	775	01
			Proprietorship		
			Sandra Weston, Capital........	4,149	19
Total Assets.................	4,924	20	Total Liabilities and Prop....	4,924	20

Self-checking: Check the accuracy of your journal entry by asking yourself the questions given at the end of Problem 2-1.

Problem 2-3. Balance sheet and opening entry for a parking lot

The Eastwood Parking Lot is owned and operated by R. D. Miller. He desires to install a new bookkeeping system. His assets and liabilities are:

Assets		Liabilities	
Cash.....................	$ 172.00	Doyan Lumber Company...	$ 175.00
Office Equipment..........	350.00	Webster Equipment Co.....	64.50
Building.................	1,000.00	Total Liabilities...........	$ 239.50
Land.....................	9,000.00		
Total Assets.............	$10,522.00		

Instructions: 1. Prepare a balance sheet for the Eastwood Parking Lot dated September 1 of the current year.

2. From this balance sheet record an opening entry in a journal, using September 1 of the current year as the date.

Self-checking: Check the accuracy of your journal entry by asking yourself the questions given at the end of Problem 2-1.

Problem 2-3 will be continued in the next chapter. If it is collected by your teacher at this time, it will be returned to you before it is needed in Problem 3-1.

CHAPTER 3

Posting the opening entry

Relationship of the balance sheet, the opening entry, and the ledger accounts. The diagram at the right shows:

1. The balance sheet is a sheet of paper that lists the assets, the liabilities, and the proprietorship of the business.

2. In starting a new bookkeeping system, the balance sheet is recorded in a journal. The assets on the balance sheet are recorded in this journal as debits, and the liabilities and the proprietorship are recorded as credits.

3. The items recorded in the opening entry in the journal are transferred to a ledger. A ledger is made up of accounts, each of which is on a separate page. It is the purpose of this chapter to explain the use of accounts and the ledger.

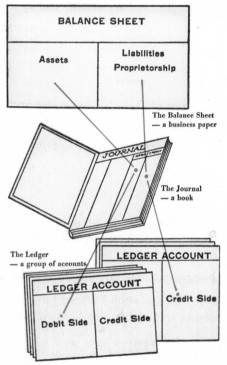

Need for accounts. The opening entry in the journal provides a complete record of the assets, the liabilities, and the proprietorship at the time the books are opened. As business is transacted, there will be changes in these assets, liabilities, and proprietorship. Entries will have to be made in the journal to record these changes.

The entries in the journal do not bring together in one place all the information about one item, such as cash or office furniture. For this reason, the items in journal entries are sorted into forms known as accounts. An *account* is a device for grouping and summarizing the changes caused by transactions. Transferring journal entries to the proper accounts is known as *posting*.

A group of accounts is known as a *ledger*. A ledger is often a bound book or a loose-leaf book. It may also be a group of ledger sheets or cards kept in a tray or a filing cabinet.

Form of the account. Accounts are ruled in various ways, but a common form is that shown below. This form of account is called the standard form.

(Account Title)								ACCOUNT NO.
DATE	ITEMS	POST. REF.	DEBIT	DATE	ITEMS	POST. REF.	CREDIT	
	(Debit Side)					(Credit Side)		

Standard form of account

The account is divided into two halves, each with the same ruling. The left half of an account is known as the *debit side* and is for debit entries. The right half of an account is known as the *credit side* and is for credit entries. The amount column on the debit side is headed *Debit;* the amount column on the credit side is headed *Credit*. The headings of the other columns are the same on both sides of the account.

Posting. In posting the opening entry recorded in the preceding chapter, use the method described in the following paragraphs.

Step 1. Open the journal to the page on which the opening entry is recorded. The entry below is the same as that illustrated on page 12.

	DATE	NAME OF ACCOUNT	POST. REF.	DEBIT	CREDIT	
	JOURNAL				PAGE 1	
1	1951 Oct. 1	Cash		37 1 00		1
2		Automobile		3 1 70 00		2
3		Office Furniture		7 45 60		3
4		Office Machines		2 54 40		4
5		Adams Company.			9 1 00	5
6		Daniels Company			3 00 00	6
7		Star Garage			1 25 00	7
8		J. M. Greene, Capital			2 9 00 00	8
9		To record October 1 balance				9
10		sheet.				10
11						11
12						12
13						13

Step 2. Open the ledger to its first page. Indicate the account number by writing *11* in the upper right-hand corner of the page.

The method used in numbering accounts is explained on page **51**.

DATE	ITEMS	POST. REF.	DEBIT	DATE	ITEMS	POST. REF.	CREDIT

ACCOUNT NO. *11*

Step 3. Write the name of the first debit item, which is *Cash*, on the first line as follows:

Cash — ACCOUNT NO. *11*

DATE	ITEMS	POST. REF.	DEBIT	DATE	ITEMS	POST. REF.	CREDIT

The name given to an account is known as the *account title*. It indicates the nature of the items recorded in the account. *Cash*, the title of the first account, is centered on the line at the top of the account. Writing the title of an account and the account number for the first time in the ledger is known as *opening the account*. In Step 3, the cash account has been opened.

Step 4. Transfer the amount of the cash item in the journal, $371.00, to the *left* or *debit* side of the cash account. Write the amount of the debit item in the amount column on the debit side of the cash account as shown below:

Cash — ACCOUNT NO. *11*

DATE	ITEMS	POST. REF.	DEBIT	DATE	ITEMS	POST. REF.	CREDIT
			371 00				

The amount is recorded in the Debit column because the journal entry shows this amount as a debit.

18 *20th Century Bookkeeping and Accounting*

Step 5. Write the date of the opening entry, as found in the journal, in the Date column on the debit side of the cash account as shown below:

DATE		ITEMS	POST. REF.	DEBIT		DATE	ITEMS	POST. REF.	CREDIT
1957									
Oct.	1			3 7 1	0 0				

Cash   ACCOUNT NO. *11*

The date of the entry consists of the year, the month, and the day. Write the date as follows:

(a) Write the year at the top of the Date column. The year is written only once on each side of each account until the year changes or the account is closed or balanced. The year is not written on the side of the account that has no entries.

(b) Write the month in the first column under the heading *Date* on the same line as the amount. If the name of the month is long, such as October, it may be abbreviated. The name of the month is written only once on each side of the account that is used during the month. The month is not written on the side of the account that has no entries.

(c) Write the day of the month in the second column under the heading *Date*.

Step 6. Write in the Items column of the account any special information that may be of value to anyone who later examines this account.

DATE		ITEMS	POST. REF.	DEBIT		DATE	ITEMS	POST. REF.	CREDIT
1957									
Oct.	1	*Balance*		3 7 1	0 0				

Cash   ACCOUNT NO. *11*

Bookkeepers distinguish between the beginning amounts in an account and the amounts recorded later as a result of business transactions. The beginning balance in the cash account is, therefore, labeled with a single word *Balance* in the Items column.

Step 7. Write in the column headed *Post. Ref.* in the cash account the number of the page in the journal from which the entry comes. (Post. Ref. is the abbreviation for Posting Reference; it shows the page of the journal from which the entry in the ledger was posted.)

DATE	ITEMS	POST. REF.	DEBIT	DATE	ITEMS	POST. REF.	CREDIT
1957 Oct. 1	Balance	1	371 00				

Cash ACCOUNT NO. 11

Since the opening entry is recorded on page 1 of the journal of the Greene Realty Agency, the figure *1* is written in the Post. Ref. column of the ledger account.

Step 8. Return to the journal and write in the Post. Ref. column of the journal the account number of the account to which the item was transferred. The account number, 11, is written in the Post. Ref. column of the journal on the same line as the cash item. This number in the Post. Ref. column of the journal shows that the posting of this line has been completed. For this reason it is always written as the last step in posting. The journal with the account number, 11, written in the Post. Ref. column is shown below.

JOURNAL PAGE 1

	DATE	NAME OF ACCOUNT	POST. REF.	DEBIT	CREDIT	
1	1957 Oct. 1	Cash	11	371 00		1
2		Automobile		3170 00		2
3		Office Furniture		745 60		3
4		Office Machines		254 40		4
5		Adams Company			91 00	5
6		Daniels Company			300 00	6
7		Star Garage			1250 00	7
8		J. M. Greene, Capital			2900 00	8
9		To record October 1 balance				9
10		sheet.				10
11						11
12						12
13						13
14						14
15						15
16						16

Posting the remaining debits of the opening entry. The same procedure is followed in posting the three other debit items in the opening entry. Each account is placed on a separate page. After these items have been posted, the accounts appear as follows:

Cash — ACCOUNT NO. 11

DATE		ITEMS	POST. REF.	DEBIT	DATE	ITEMS	POST. REF.	CREDIT
1957 Oct.	1	Balance	1	37 00				

Automobile — ACCOUNT NO. 12

DATE		ITEMS	POST. REF.	DEBIT	DATE	ITEMS	POST. REF.	CREDIT
1957 Oct.	1	Balance	1	3170 00				

Office Furniture — ACCOUNT NO. 13

DATE		ITEMS	POST. REF.	DEBIT	DATE	ITEMS	POST. REF.	CREDIT
1957 Oct.	1	Balance	1	745 60				

Office Machines — ACCOUNT NO. 14

DATE		ITEMS	POST. REF.	DEBIT	DATE	ITEMS	POST. REF.	CREDIT
1957 Oct.	1	Balance	1	254 40				

The journal after posting the four debit items is shown below. It is the same as the journal on page 17 except that the completion of posting of the additional debits in the journal has been indicated by placing the account numbers in the posting reference column.

JOURNAL — PAGE 1

	DATE		NAME OF ACCOUNT	POST. REF.	DEBIT	CREDIT	
1	1957 Oct.	1	Cash	11	37 00		1
2			Automobile	12	3170 00		2
3			Office Furniture	13	745 60		3
4			Office Machines	14	254 40		4
5			Adams Company			91 00	5
6			Daniels Company			300 00	6
7			Star Garage			1250 00	7
8			J. M. Greene, Capital			2900 00	8
9			To record October 1 balance				9
10			sheet.				10
11							11
12							12

Posting the credits of the opening entry. The procedure for posting the credits is the same as that for posting the debits except that the credits are posted to the *right* or *credit* side of the accounts. After the credits are posted, the liability and proprietorship accounts appear as follows:

Adams Company — ACCOUNT NO. 21

DATE	ITEMS	POST. REF.	DEBIT	DATE	ITEMS	POST. REF.	CREDIT
				1957 Oct. 1	Balance	1	9 1 00

Daniels Company — ACCOUNT NO. 22

DATE	ITEMS	POST. REF.	DEBIT	DATE	ITEMS	POST. REF.	CREDIT
				1957 Oct. 1	Balance	1	3 00 00

Star Garage — ACCOUNT NO. 23

DATE	ITEMS	POST. REF.	DEBIT	DATE	ITEMS	POST. REF.	CREDIT
				1957 Oct. 1	Balance	1	1 2 5 0 00

J. M. Greene, Capital — ACCOUNT NO. 31

DATE	ITEMS	POST. REF.	DEBIT	DATE	ITEMS	POST. REF.	CREDIT
				1957 Oct. 1	Balance	1	2 9 00 00

After the credits have been posted, the Post. Ref. column in the journal appears as follows:

JOURNAL — PAGE 1

	DATE	NAME OF ACCOUNT	POST. REF.	DEBIT	CREDIT	
1	1957 Oct. 1	Cash	11	3 7 1 00		1
2		Automobile	12	3 1 7 0 00		2
3		Office Furniture	13	7 4 5 60		3
4		Office Machines	14	2 5 4 40		4
5		Adams Company	21		9 1 00	5
6		Daniels Company	22		3 00 00	6
7		Star Garage	23		1 2 5 0 00	7
8		J. M. Greene, Capital	31		2 9 00 00	8
9		To record October 1 balance				9
10		sheet.				10

The numbers in the Post. Ref. column for all items in the opening entry show that the posting of the opening entry has been completed.

The figures in the posting reference columns of the journal and of the ledger not only indicate that the posting has been completed, but also are useful for cross reference. Anyone looking at the opening entry in the journal can find the number of the account in the ledger to which each item was posted. Similarly, anyone looking at any account in the ledger can find the page number of the journal from which the posting was made. This information is useful if the accuracy of the posting is being checked or if information about the complete transaction is desired.

Account balance. The difference between the two sides of an account is known as the *account balance.* If an account contains only one entry, this single amount is the account balance. If a balance is on the left-hand side of the account, it is called a *debit balance;* if it is on the right-hand side of the account, it is called a *credit balance.* Note on page 21 that the balance of each asset account is a *debit* balance. Note on page 22 that the balance of each liability account is a *credit* balance and that the balance of the proprietor's capital account is also a *credit* balance. These fundamentals may be remembered easily if the illustrations at the right are studied carefully.

ANY ASSET ACCOUNT	
Debit Balance	

ANY LIABILITY ACCOUNT	
	Credit Balance

ANY PROPRIETOR'S CAPITAL ACCOUNT	
	Credit Balance

CHAPTER QUESTIONS

1. What are the printed headings on the *debit* side of the standard form of ledger account?
2. How do the headings on the *credit* side of the standard form of ledger account differ from the headings on the debit side?
3. What are the steps followed in posting the first debit item of the opening entry?
4. Why is the word *Balance* written in the Items column of the ledger account in posting the opening entry?
5. How does posting a credit item differ from posting a debit item?
6. Why is it advisable to indicate posting reference pages in the ledger?
7. What are the two reasons for recording the account number in the posting reference column of the journal?
8. After an opening entry has been posted:
    (a) Does each asset account have a debit balance or a credit balance?
    (b) Does each liability account have a debit balance or a credit balance?
    (c) Does each proprietorship account have a debit or a credit balance?

INCREASING YOUR BUSINESS VOCABULARY

What is the meaning of each of the following:

(a) account   (e) debit side   (h) account balance
(b) posting   (f) credit side   (i) debit balance
(c) ledger   (g) opening the account (j) credit balance
(d) account title

CASES FOR DISCUSSION

1. The bookkeeper for the Clark Real Estate Agency, in preparing the opening entry for the agency, finds the following items on the beginning balance sheet: Cash, Automobile, Office Furniture, Culver Company (a creditor), and Robert C. Clark, Capital. (a) Which of the items on the beginning balance sheet should be recorded in the opening entry as debits? (b) Which of the items should be recorded as credits?
2. Cooper Real Estate Agency uses a loose-leaf form of ledger book. Rogers Real Estate uses a permanently bound ledger book. What are the advantages of each kind of ledger?
3. Henry Collins is interrupted by a telephone call while in the midst of posting his opening entry. If he has been following correct bookkeeping procedure in his posting, how can he tell quickly where he left off in the journal at the time that his work was interrupted?

DRILLS FOR UNDERSTANDING

Drill 3-A. This drill will give you additional skill in classifying accounts quickly as assets, liabilities, and proprietorship. You need this skill in journalizing and in posting.

Instructions: 1. If you do not have a workbook, on a sheet of paper copy the ledger account titles that are given at the right. Rule a one-inch column at the right of the list. Write the heading *Answers* at the top of this column.

(1) Cash
(2) Adams Company (creditor)
(3) Automobile
(4) Daniels Company (creditor)
(5) J. M. Greene, Capital
(6) Office Furniture
(7) Office Machines
(8) Star Garage (creditor)

Instructions: 2. Classify each account on your list as an asset, a liability, or a proprietorship account by writing in the Answers column a capital *A* for Assets, a capital *L* for Liabilities, or a capital *P* for Proprietorship. The first item is given as an example.

Account Titles	Answers
(1) Cash...............	*A*

3. Now cover your answers and see how rapidly you can do this orally without looking at your answers. Repeat this drill orally several times for increased speed and accuracy.

24 *20th Century Bookkeeping and Accounting*

Drill 3-B. This drill will give you additional skill in remembering that:

Asset account balances are always debit balances.

Liability account balances are always credit balances.

Proprietorship account balances are always credit balances.

Instructions: An outline of an account may be prepared in the form shown at the right. This form is commonly called a T account because it looks like a capital T.

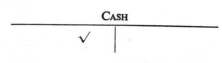

If you do not have a workbook, prepare T accounts for the eight accounts listed below. Then make a check mark on the proper side of each account to show where the balance should appear in that account.

Cash	Adams Company (Creditor)
Automobile	Daniels Company (Creditor)
Office Furniture	Star Garage (Creditor)
Office Machines	J. M. Greene, Capital

APPLICATION PROBLEMS

Problem 3-1. Posting the opening entry of a parking lot

The opening entry completed in Problem 2-3 of the preceding chapter is required for this problem. If Problem 2-3 has not been returned to you, complete Exercise 3-A in the Appendix.

Instructions: 1. Open the accounts in the ledger that are required for posting the journal entry that you prepared in Problem 2-3. Allow one fourth of a page for each account. Use the account titles and numbers shown below.

Account Title	Account Number	Account Title	Account Number
Cash......................	11	Doyan Lumber Company.....	21
Office Equipment............	12	Webster Equipment Company.	22
Building...................	13	R. D. Miller, Capital.........	31
Land......................	14		

2. Post the opening entry that you recorded in Problem 2-3.

Self-checking: Compare your work with the illustrations on pages 21 and 22 and ask yourself the self-checking questions given below:

(a) Did you write the year, the month, and the day in each ledger account on the side of the account that was used in posting?

(b) Are all of your postings of debits on the left-hand or debit side of four asset accounts? Are all of your postings of credits on the right-hand or credit side of two liability accounts and one proprietorship account?

(c) Did you write in the Post. Ref. column of each ledger account the journal page number of the entry?

(d) Did you write in the Post. Ref. column of your journal the number of the account to which each line in the journal was posted? •

Problem 3-2.   Recording and posting the opening entry for an auto repair shop

The balance sheet on September 1 of the Lakeland Repair Shop, owned by Thomas Cassidy, is as follows:

LAKELAND REPAIR SHOP
Balance Sheet
September 1, 19--

Assets			Liabilities		
Cash.............................	1,271	00	Auto Supply Company.........	450	80
Parts...........................	1,170	70	Hagen and Company...........	151	70
Office Equipment.............	252	10	Total Liabilities...........	602	50
Shop Equipment.............	6,400	00			
			Proprietorship		
			Thomas Cassidy, Capital......	8.491	30
Total Assets................	9,093	80	Total Liab. and Prop........	9,093	80

Instructions: 1. Record on two-column journal paper the opening entry for the balance sheet of the Lakeland Repair Shop. Use the date of September 1 of the current year.

2. Post the opening entry to ledger accounts. Allow one fourth of a page for each account. Number the accounts as follows: asset accounts, 11 to 14; liability accounts, 21 and 22; and capital account, 31.

Self-checking: (1) Compare your opening entry with the illustration on page 22. Check the accuracy of your journalizing by asking yourself the following questions:

(a) Did you write the date at the top of the Date column of the journal, showing the year, the month, and the day?

(b) Does the first letter of each debit item in the Name of Account column touch the vertical red line?

(c) Is each credit item in the Name of Account column indented the same so that the credits do not zigzag back and forth?

(d) Did you write the explanation so that the first word of the explanation is indented about twice as much as the credit items?

Self-checking: (2) Compare your ledger accounts with the illustrations on pages 21 and 22. Check the accuracy of your posting by asking yourself the following questions:

(a) Did you write the year, the month, and the day in each ledger account on the side of the account that was used in posting?

(b) Are all of your postings of debits on the left-hand or debit side of four asset accounts? Are all of your postings of credits on the right-hand or credit side of two liability accounts and one proprietorship account?

(c) Did you write in the Post. Ref. column of each ledger account the journal page number of the entry?

(d) Did you write in the Post. Ref. column of your journal the number of the account to which each line in the journal was posted?

Recording changes in
asset and liability accounts

Business transactions. The amounts shown in all the accounts in Chapter 3 were recorded as balances. In this chapter you will learn that account balances are changed by the activities of the business. In business any exchange of one value for another is known as a *business transaction.* Some examples of the most common business transactions are: receiving cash, paying cash, buying anything, selling anything.

Transactions change account balances. Every business transaction increases or decreases the balance of *two or more* accounts in the ledger. In this chapter and the next chapter you will learn how these changes are recorded in a journal.

The immediate record of a cash received transaction. Mr. J. M. Greene is the owner of the Greene Realty Agency. Each time Mr. Greene receives cash, he records the transaction in a receipt book. As he writes each receipt, he makes a carbon copy of it. The original copy is removed from the receipt book and is given to the person from whom the cash is received. The carbon copy of the receipt is kept in the receipt book as an immediate record of the transaction. A carbon copy of the first receipt issued by the Greene Realty Agency is illustrated below.

Carbon copy of a receipt

NO. 1   *October 1,* 19 57

RECEIVED FROM *H. G. Lee*

Twenty 00/100 ——————— DOLLARS

FOR *Used typewriter desk*

$ 20 00

GREENE REALTY AGENCY

BY *J. M. Greene*

Transaction No. 1 — Increase in one asset and decrease in another asset

The business transaction represented by Receipt No. 1 may be stated as follows:

October 1, 1957. Received cash, $20.00, for sale of old office furniture. Issued Receipt No. 1.

Journalizing. Every transaction is recorded in a journal to provide complete information about that transaction in one place. Each transaction has two parts: a debit part and a credit part. Both parts of the transaction are recorded in each journal entry. Separating each transaction into its debit part and its credit part and recording them in a journal is called *journalizing*.

The columnar journal. Mr. Greene uses a journal with more than two amount columns in recording his transactions. It saves time in making journal entries. It also saves time in the later posting of these entries from the journal to the ledger. The advantages of using a journal with several amount columns will be developed in the next two chapters.

A journal with more than two amount columns is called a *columnar journal*. The columnar journal used by the Greene Realty Agency is illustrated below.

CASH		DATE	NAME OF ACCOUNT	NO.	POST. REF.	GENERAL		COMMISSIONS INCOME CREDIT
DEBIT	CREDIT					DEBIT	CREDIT	

A columnar journal

Journal Entry No. 1. The journal entry to record Transaction No. 1 was made from the carbon copy of Receipt No. 1. (See the illustration of the receipt on page 27.) This first journal entry for the month of October, 1957, was written as follows:

CASH		DATE	NAME OF ACCOUNT	NO.	POST. REF.	GENERAL		COMMISSIONS INCOME CREDIT
DEBIT	CREDIT					DEBIT	CREDIT	
20 00		1957 Oct 1	Office Furniture	R 1			20 00	

Analyzing Journal Entry No. 1. This entry was made on Line 1 of the journal.

Date. The steps in recording the date of Entry No. 1 were:

Step 1. The bookkeeper obtained the date of this journal entry from the carbon copy of Receipt No. 1 in the receipt book. (See the illustration of Receipt No. 1 on page 27.)

Step 2. The year, 1957, was written at the top of the Date column of the journal as shown in the illustration.

Step 3. The abbreviation of the month, Oct., was written in the month section of the Date column on Line 1 of the journal.

Step 4. The day of the month, 1, was written in the day section of the Date column on Line 1.

Debit part of Entry No. 1. The cash account was debited by writing *$20.00* in the Cash Debit column on Line 1. The reasons why the cash account was debited were as follows:

In this transaction, $20.00 in cash was received. The asset Cash was increased. All increases in any asset account must be recorded on the same side of the account in the ledger as the balance of the account.

The *balances* of asset accounts are *debit* balances. Therefore, all increases in any asset account are debits. The cash account is debited each time cash is received.

Increases in assets are recorded in the journal as debits so that, when posted, they can be added conveniently to the *debit balances* in the ledger.

Special columns. Why does the Greene Realty Agency have a special column in the journal with the heading Cash Debit?

Cash received transactions occur often. There will be many cash debits on each page of the journal. A special column with the heading Cash Debit saves time in journalizing and later in posting. It saves time in journalizing because writing the amount in the Cash Debit column indicates clearly that Cash is to be debited without "Cash" being written in the Name of Account column. It saves time later in posting because it is not necessary to post each amount in the Cash Debit column separately. Only the total of a special column needs to be posted. Posting a columnar journal will be presented in Chapter 6.

Credit part of Entry No. 1. The office furniture account was credited by writing *$20.00* in the General Credit column and the words *Office Furniture* in the Name of Account column. The reasons were as follows:

Office furniture was sold. The asset Office Furniture was *decreased*. The amount of the decrease had to be subtracted from the balance of the office furniture account in the ledger.

An amount to be subtracted from a balance is always placed on the side of the account that is *opposite* the balance. For example, if an amount is to be subtracted in an account that has a *debit* balance, the amount to be subtracted is placed on the opposite or *credit* side of the account.

An asset account balance is a *debit* balance. Consequently a *decrease* in an asset account is always placed on the *credit* side of the asset account.

General columns. Why doesn't the office furniture account have two special columns in the journal with the headings Office Furniture Debit and Office Furniture Credit?

The Greene Realty Agency rarely buys or sells office furniture. If special columns were provided with the heading Office Furniture Debit and Office Furniture Credit, the columns would be used very seldom. It is more efficient to use the General Debit and General Credit columns for such entries. Therefore, special columns for office furniture transactions are not provided.

Use of number column. In Entry No. 1, *R1* was written in the No. column of the journal to show that Receipt No. 1 was the basis of this journal entry.

At a later date, some information not shown in the journal may be desired. For example, the journal entry does not show what item of office furniture was sold or to whom it was sold. The carbon copy of Receipt No. 1 shows all of this information. It shows that a used typewriter desk was sold to H. G. Lee. R1 in the number column of the journal shows that this information may be obtained quickly by locating the carbon copy of Receipt No. 1.

Increase in one asset and decrease in another asset. The effect of all transactions of the type represented by Transaction No. 1 may be summarized as follows:

ONE ASSET ACCOUNT		ANOTHER ASSET ACCOUNT
Debit Side.		*Credit Side.*
Increase Side.		*Decrease Side.*
1. *Increases* in assets are recorded as *debits* in the journal.		1. *Decreases* in assets are recorded as *credits* in the journal.
2. *Increases* in assets are posted to the left-hand or *debit side* of the proper asset account in the ledger.		2. *Decreases* in assets are posted to the right-hand or *credit side* of the proper asset account in the ledger.

Two important parts of every transaction — debit and credit. In every journal entry the two important parts, the *debit* amount and the *credit* amount, are always equal. The basic principle of all journalizing may be stated as follows:

Debit part of a transaction = Credit part of that transaction.

Double-entry bookkeeping. The recording of the two parts in each transaction, debit and credit, is often referred to as *double-entry bookkeeping*. Complete bookkeeping, then, is double-entry bookkeeping.

The immediate record of a cash payment transaction. Each time cash is paid by Mr. Greene, he writes a check. Before writing the check, he first fills out the stub of the check. The check stub is an immediate record of each cash payment transaction. Journal entries for all cash payments are then made from the information on the check stubs.

	DOLLARS	CENTS
NO. **1** $25 00		
DATE *October 1,* 1957		
TO *Adams Co.*		
FOR *On account*		
BAL. BRO'T FOR'D	371	00
AMT. DEPOSITED		
TOTAL		
AMT. THIS CHECK	25	00
BAL. CAR'D FOR'D	346	00

Check stub for Transaction No. 2

Transaction No. 2 — Decrease in a liability and decrease in an asset

The business transaction represented by Check Stub No. 1 may be stated as follows:

October 1, 1957. Paid cash, $25.00, to Adams Company in part payment of the amount owed. Issued Check No. 1.

Journal Entry No. 2. The journal entry to record this transaction was made from the check stub for Check No. 1. The entry to record this cash payment was written on Line 2 of the journal as follows:

CASH DEBIT	CASH CREDIT	DATE	NAME OF ACCOUNT	NO.	POST. REF.	GENERAL DEBIT	GENERAL CREDIT	COMMISSIONS INCOME CREDIT	
20 00		1957 Oct. 1	*Office Furniture*	R 1			20 00		1
	25 00	1	*Adams Company*	C 1		25 00			2
									3
									4

JOURNAL — PAGE 2

Analyzing Journal Entry No. 2. This entry was made on Line 2 of the journal.

Date. The steps in recording the date of Entry No. 2 were:

Step 1. The bookkeeper obtained the date for this entry from Check Stub No. 1.

Step 2. He wrote *1* in the day section of the Date column of the journal. (The year and the month were written at the top of the Date column when the first entry was recorded. The year and the month are written only once on each page of the journal.)

Debit part of Entry No. 2. The Adams Company account was debited by writing *$25.00* in the General Debit column and the words *Adams Company* in the Name of Account column — all on Line 2.

The Adams Company account is a liability account. Liability accounts have credit balances. In this transaction the credit balance of the Adams Company account was *decreased.* A subtraction from the *credit* balance of an account is always shown by *debiting* the account.

Transactions with the Adams Company do not occur often; hence a special column with the heading Adams Company is not desirable. Writing *$25.00* in the General Debit column shows that an account is to be debited for $25.00; writing the words *Adams Company* in the Name of Account column shows what account is to be debited.

Credit part of Entry No. 2. Cash was credited by writing *$25.00* in the Cash Credit column on Line 2. The account title, Cash, was not written in the Name of Account column because the amount was written in the Cash Credit column. The heading of this column shows that Cash was credited.

The cash account was credited in this entry because the asset Cash was decreased by writing Check No. 1. *Decreases* in assets are always shown as *credits.* The cash account is credited each time cash is paid.

Use of number column. *C1* was written in the No. column to show that Check No. 1 was issued in this transaction. The letter *C* in the No. column stands for check and is followed by the number of the check. The proper check number is obtained from the check stub.

The number in the No. column shows which check stub has the additional details about this transaction. Since this information can be located quickly when needed, it is not necessary to record any of these details in the journal entry.

Decrease in a liability and decrease in an asset. The effect of all transactions of this type may be summarized as follows:

ANY ASSET ACCOUNT		ANY LIABILITY ACCOUNT	
Debit Side. *Increase Side.*	*Credit Side.* *Decrease Side.*	*Debit Side.* *Decrease Side.*	*Credit Side.* *Increase Side.*
	1. *Decreases* in assets are recorded as *credits* in the journal.	1. *Decreases* in liabilities are recorded as *debits* in the journal.	
	2. *Decreases* in assets are posted to the right-hand or *credit side* of the proper asset account in the ledger.	2. *Decreases* in liabilities are posted to the left-hand or *debit side* of the proper liability account in the ledger.	

Transaction No. 3 — Increase in one asset and decrease in another asset

October 2, 1957. *Paid cash, $37.50, for purchase of new office desk. Issued Check No. 2.*

Each time a check is issued, the check stub is the immediate record of the transaction. The immediate record of Transaction No. 3 is Check Stub No. 2.

Journal Entry No. 3. The journal entry to record this transaction was made from the check stub for Check No. 2. The entry to record this cash payment was written on Line 3 of the journal as follows:

CASH DEBIT	CASH CREDIT	DATE	NAME OF ACCOUNT	NO.	POST. REF.	GENERAL DEBIT	GENERAL CREDIT	COMMISSIONS INCOME CREDIT	
		1957							
20 00		Oct 1	Office Furniture	R 1			20 00		1
	25 00	1	Adams Company	C 1		25 00			2
	37 50	2	Office Furniture	C 2		37 50			3
									4
									5

JOURNAL   PAGE 2

Analyzing Journal Entry No. 3. This entry was recorded on Line 3 of the journal.

Date. In recording the date of Entry No. 3, Mr. Greene wrote the figure *2* in the day section of the Date column. (As was explained in the analysis of Journal Entry No. 2, the month and the year are written only once on each page of the journal.)

Debit part of Entry No. 3. The amount to be debited, $37.50, was written in the General Debit column. The office furniture account is an asset account. Asset accounts have debit balances. In this transaction, the asset account Office Furniture was increased. Increases in an asset account are recorded on the same side as the debit balance. Office Furniture was therefore debited. As explained previously, transactions involving office furniture occur rarely, and amount columns are not provided for such transactions. The General Debit column was therefore used.

Credit part of Entry No. 3. The amount to be credited, $37.50, was written in the Cash Credit column. (The heading, Cash Credit, shows that the cash account is credited for each amount in this special column. Therefore, it was not necessary to write "Cash" in the Name of Account column for the credit part of this transaction.)

Use of number column. C2 was written in the No. column. It shows that Check No. 2 was written for this cash payment.

Recording additional transactions. The first three transactions recorded in the journal shown below were discussed in the preceding paragraphs. The additional transactions were recorded in a similar manner. Each entry shows a debit or a credit to Cash and a debit or a credit to another asset account or to a liability account.

CASH DEBIT	CASH CREDIT	DATE	NAME OF ACCOUNT	NO.	POST. REF.	GENERAL DEBIT	GENERAL CREDIT	COMMISSIONS INCOME CREDIT	
2000		1957 Oct. 1	Office Furniture	R 1			2000		1
	2500	1	Adams Company	C 1		2500			2
	3750	2	Office Furniture	C 2		3750			3
1500		2	Office Machines	R 2			1500		4
	4200	2	Star Garage	C 3		4200			5
	7600	3	Office Machines	C 4		7600			6
	3900	3	Office Furniture	C 5		3900			7
	10000	4	Daniels Company	C 6		10000			8
1800		5	Office Furniture	R 3			1800		9
									10

Principles of journalizing cash receipts and cash payments. Examine the journal above and note the application of the following principles of journalizing:

1. The complete record of each transaction is written on a single line.
2. For each amount in a *debit column* there is an equal amount in a *credit column.*
3. All cash receipts are increases in the asset Cash and are recorded as debits in the Cash Debit column.
4. All cash payments are decreases in the asset Cash and are recorded as credits in the Cash Credit column.
5. Each time Cash is *debited* in the Cash Debit amount column, the title of the account to be credited is written in the Name of Account column. The amount of the *credit* is then recorded in the General Credit column.
6. Each time Cash is *credited* in the Cash Credit amount column, the name of the account to be debited is written in the Name of Account column. The amount of the *debit* is then recorded in the General Debit column.
7. The journal entry for each cash received transaction is made from the information given on the carbon copy of the receipt in the receipts book.
8. The journal entry for each cash payment transaction is made from the information given on the check stub.

Commissions Income Credit column. In this chapter you have studied selected transactions in which no income was involved. The use of the Commissions Income Credit column will be studied in the next chapter.

1. How do business transactions affect account balances?
2. What form of business paper is used in this chapter as the immediate record of each cash received transaction?
3. What are the two parts of each business transaction?
4. What are the parts of the journal entry illustrated on page 28?
5. What are the steps in writing the date of the first entry in the journal?
6. Is the cash account debited or credited when cash is received? Why?
7. Is the cash account debited or credited when cash is paid? Why?
8. What are the advantages of having special columns in the journal for recording debits and credits to the cash account?
9. What is the meaning of "R1" in the No. column of Line 1 of the journal on page 34? of "C1" in the No. column of Line 2?
10. What business paper is used as the immediate record of each cash payment transaction?
11. What are the two steps in writing the date of the second entry in the journal?
12. Why does not the journal in this chapter have special columns for the Adams Company account? for the furniture account?

INCREASING YOUR BUSINESS VOCABULARY

What is the meaning of each of the following:

    (a) business transaction   (c) columnar journal
    (b) journalizing   (d) double-entry bookkeeping

CASES FOR DISCUSSION

1. Roger Allen uses a receipt book that has a receipt stub record for each receipt issued. Richard West uses a receipt book that has a carbon copy for each receipt issued and no stub record. What are the advantages of West's plan of using a carbon copy of each receipt issued instead of a receipt stub record?

2. John Underwood is very particular about writing the stub of each check before he writes the check. As Charles Wilde is often in a hurry, he writes the check first and fills in the stub later. Why is Wilde's check-writing habit of sometimes writing the check before he fills in the stub not a good habit?

Drill 4-A. For each entry in the journal illustrated on page 34 you are to tell what account is debited and what account is credited.

Instructions: 1. If you do not have a workbook, take a sheet of paper and draw a line through the middle of it from top to bottom. Rule a narrow column at the left edge of your paper as shown below. At the top of your paper, copy the headings of the following form:

Line No.	Title of Account Debited	Title of Account Credited
1	*Cash*	*Office Furniture*

2. Turn to the completed journal of this chapter illustrated on page 34. On the form that you have just prepared or that you find in your workbook, copy the analysis of Line No. 1 of that journal as shown above.

3. Write a similar analysis of each of the remaining entries (Lines 2 to 9) of the journal illustrated on page 34.

Drill 4-B. For each entry in the journal illustrated on page 34 you are to tell whether an asset was increased or decreased, or whether a liability was increased or decreased.

Instructions: 1. If you do not have a workbook, take a sheet of paper and draw a line through the middle of it from top to bottom. Rule a narrow column at the left edge of your paper as shown below. At the top of your paper, copy the headings of the following form:

Line No.	Effect of Debit Entry	Effect of Credit Entry
1	*Increased an asset*	*Decreased an asset*

2. Turn to the completed journal of this chapter illustrated on page 34. On the form that you have just prepared or that you find in your workbook, copy the analysis of Line No. 1 of that journal as shown above.

3. Write a similar analysis of each of the remaining lines (Lines 2 to 9) of the journal illustrated on page 34.

Drill 4-C. *Instructions: 1.* If you do not have a workbook, rule five columns on a sheet of paper and copy the headings of the following form:

Trans. No.	Title of Account Debited	Effect of the Debit	Title of Account Credited	Effect of the Credit
1	*Cash*	*Increased an asset*	*Office Machines*	*Decreased an asset*

2. A series of transactions is given at the top of page 37. Read Transaction 1. Then copy the analysis that is given as an example.

3. Write a similar analysis of Transactions 2 to 9.

Transactions:

1. Received cash from sale of old office machine.
2. Paid cash for purchase of additional office furniture.
3. Paid cash to Hickey Company in partial payment of amount owed to them.
4. Received cash from sale of old office furniture.
5. Paid cash for additional office machines.
6. Paid cash to Burns Garage in full payment of the amount owed to them.
7. Paid cash to Atlas Company in part payment of the amount owed to them.
8. Received cash from sale of old office furniture.
9. Paid cash for additional office machines.

APPLICATION PROBLEMS

Problem 4-1. Journalizing the transactions of a laundry

The Olson Laundry is owned and operated by Donald Olson. Some of the account titles in his ledger are listed below. These are not all of the accounts in his ledger, but they are all of the accounts that you will need to use.

Partial list of accounts in ledger of Olson Laundry

Assets	*Liabilities*
Cash	Atlas Company
Office Furniture	Burns Garage
Office Machines	Hickey Company

Instructions: Record in a five-column journal the selected transactions given below. Use as your guide the model journal that is illustrated on page 34. Use the current year in recording the date.

Transactions:

Oct. 1. Received cash, $30.00, from sale of used office machine. Issued Receipt No. 1.
   1. Paid cash, $84.00, for purchase of new office furniture. Issued Check No. 1.
   1. Paid cash, $550.00, to Hickey Company in part payment of amount owed to them. Issued Check No. 2.
   2. Received cash, $150.00, from sale of used office furniture. Issued Receipt No. 2.
   2. Paid cash, $300.00, for new office machines. Issued Check No. 3.
   2. Paid cash, $85.00, to Burns Garage in full payment of the amount owed to them. Issued Check No. 4.
   2. Paid cash, $25.00, to Atlas Company in part payment of the amount owed to them. Issued Check No. 5.
   3. Received cash, $60.00, from sale of old office furniture. Issued Receipt No. 3.
   3. Paid cash, $194.00, for additional office machines. Issued Check No. 6.

Self-checking: Compare the entries in your journal with the model journal on page 34. Check the accuracy of all details by asking yourself the following questions:

(a) Did you show the date of the first journal entry by writing the year at the top of the Date column and the month and the day on Line 1 of the Date column?

(b) Did you show the date of each succeeding entry by writing only the day in the day section of the Date column?

(c) Do you have an amount recorded in the Cash Debit column for each cash receipt?

(d) Do you have an amount recorded in the Cash Credit column for each cash payment?

(e) Did you write the proper account title in the Name of Account column for each amount in the General columns?

(f) Does the amount in a debit column equal the amount in a credit column on each line of your journal?

(g) Have you indicated in the No. column the correct check number for each cash payment? the correct receipt number for each receipt of cash?

Problem 4-2. Journalizing the transactions of a restaurant

The Green Shutters Restaurant is owned and operated by Arlene Weber. Some of the account titles in her ledger are listed below.

Partial list of accounts in ledger of Green Shutters

Assets	*Liabilities*
Cash	Grant Company
Furniture	Hetzel Company
Kitchen Equipment	Star Garage

Instructions: Record in a five-column journal the selected transactions given below. Use the current year in recording the date.

Transactions:

Nov. 1. Paid cash, $325.00, for new kitchen equipment. Issued Check No. 1.

1. Received cash, $24.00, from sale of used furniture. Issued Receipt No. 1.

1. Received cash, $10.00, from sale of used kitchen equipment being replaced. Issued Receipt No. 2.

2. Paid cash, $728.73, to Grant Company in full payment of amount owed to them. Issued Check No. 2.

2. Paid cash, $850.26, to Hetzel Company in full payment of amount owed to them. Issued Check No. 3.

2. Paid cash, $43.00, to Star Garage in full payment of amount owed to them. Issued Check No. 4.

3. Paid cash, $322.00, for new furniture. Issued Check No. 5.

3. Paid cash, $64.50, for new kitchen equipment. Issued Check No. 6.

Self-checking: Check your work by asking yourself the questions that are listed for Problem 4-1.

Recording income and expenses

Increases and decreases in proprietorship. The business transactions studied in Chapter 4 showed changes in the *assets* and the *liabilities* of the business. In this chapter you will study transactions that cause changes in *proprietorship*.

Some transactions increase proprietorship; some transactions decrease proprietorship. An *increase* in proprietorship that results from a business transaction is called *income*. A *decrease* in proprietorship that results from a business transaction is called *expense*.

Income accounts. Mr. Greene's real estate business has income from commissions earned for sales and rentals of property. All commissions earned are recorded in an income account with the title *Commissions Income*.

In the insurance business a similar account frequently has the title *Premiums Income*. Attorneys and accountants use a similar account that has the title *Fees Income*. These income accounts will be developed later.

Transaction No. 10 — An income transaction

October 5. Received cash, $600.00, as commission for the sale of a house. Issued Receipt No. 4.

Commissions for services rendered in selling property are collected by Mr. Greene at the rate of 5 per cent of the sale price of the property. In this transaction, Mr. Greene sold property for $12,000.00 and collected a commission of $600.00.

The immediate record of an income transaction. Each time Mr. Greene receives cash, he issues a receipt with a carbon copy. He gives the receipt to his customer and keeps the carbon copy in his receipt book. Later, when Mr. Greene returns to his office, he records each receipt in his journal.

Journal entry for Transaction No. 10. From the information on the carbon copy of Receipt No. 4, Mr. Greene made the following journal entry:

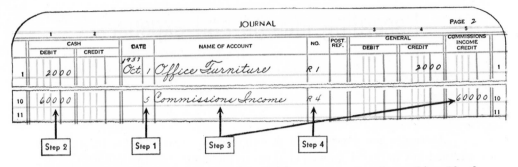

Analyzing Journal Entry No. 10. This entry was made on Line 10 of the journal begun in the preceding chapter. (See the illustration of the journal on page 34.) In this entry Cash was debited and Commissions Income was credited. The steps in recording Transaction No. 10 were:

Step 1 — Date. To record the date of Entry No. 10, Mr. Greene wrote the figure *5* in the day section of the Date column. The year and the month, 1957 and October, had been written previously at the top of the Date column. The year and the month were not repeated on this page.

Step 2 — Debit part of entry. The cash account was debited by writing *$600.00* on Line 10 in the Cash Debit column. The cash account was debited because the transaction increased the asset Cash and all increases in assets are debits.

Step 3 — Credit part of entry. The commissions income account was credited (a) by writing *$600.00* on Line 10 in the Commissions Income Credit column and (b) by writing *Commissions Income* in the Name of Account column. Commissions Income was credited because this transaction caused an increase in income, that is, an increase in proprietorship.

The capital of the owner (proprietorship) is listed on the right-hand side of the balance sheet and is recorded on the right-hand side (credit side) of his *Capital* account. If incomes were recorded directly in the proprietor's capital account, they would be recorded as *credits*. Therefore, when a separate account is kept for income transactions, an income account is credited.

Step 4 — Use of number column. *R4* was written in the number column. It shows that Receipt No. 4 was the immediate record of this cash received transaction.

Why is there a special column for Commissions Income? As explained in Chapter 4, whenever an account in the ledger is debited or credited frequently during the month, a special column in the journal saves labor.

A special column in the journal has as its heading the title of an account in the ledger. This column saves time in posting to the ledger because it is not necessary to post each amount separately. Only the total of the special column needs to be posted.

Since the column heading is Commissions Income Credit, the account title Commissions Income might be omitted from the Name of Account column, but it is ordinarily written. Not every receipt of cash comes from Commissions Income. Writing *Commissions Income* in the Name of Account column shows that the transaction was correctly recorded when the amount was written in the Commissions Income Credit column.

Checking the accuracy of each entry. Note that all of the journal entry for this transaction was placed on one line. Cash was *debited* for $600.00 and Commissions Income was *credited* for $600.00.

In each journal entry the amount of the debit part of the entry must be equal to the amount of the credit part of the entry.

The effect of income transactions. The effect of all transactions of the type represented by Transaction No. 10 may be summarized as follows:

ANY ASSET ACCOUNT		ANY INCOME ACCOUNT	
Debit Side. *Increase Side.*	*Credit Side.* *Decrease Side.*	*Debit Side.* *Decrease Side.*	*Credit Side.* *Increase Side.*
1. *Increases* in assets are recorded as *debits* in the journal. 2. *Increases* in assets are posted to the left-hand or *debit side* of the proper asset account in the ledger.			1. *Increases* in proprietorship are recorded as *credits* in the journal. 2. Incomes are *increases* in proprietorship. 3. Incomes are posted to the right-hand or *credit side* of the proper income account in the ledger.

Transaction No. 11 — An expense transaction

October 5. Paid cash, $120.00, for rent of office for October. Issued Check No. 7.

Immediate record of cash payment. All of the details needed for making a journal entry of this transaction are shown on the check stub for Check No. 7. This check stub is illustrated at the right. It shows that Check No. 7 was issued on October 5 to pay the rent of the office for the month of October.

NO. 7	$ 120 00
DATE October 5 1957	
TO Klein & Co	
FOR Oct. office rent	

	DOLLARS	CENTS
BAL. BRO'T FOR'D	86	50
AMT. DEPOSITED	618	00
TOTAL	704	50
AMT. THIS CHECK	120	00
BAL. CAR'D FOR'D	584	50

Check stub for Check No. 7

Journal entry for payment of rent. From the information given on Check Stub No. 7, Mr. Greene made the following journal entry:

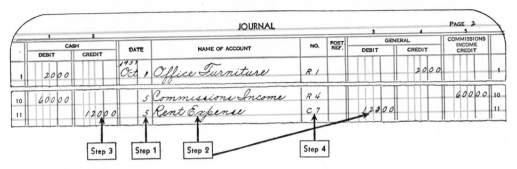

Step 1 — Date of entry. Only the day of the month, 5, was written in the Date column of the journal. This was the date of the check that was issued in this transaction.

Step 2 — Debit part of entry. The rent expense account was debited (a) by writing *$120.00* in the General Debit column and (b) by writing *Rent Expense* in the Name of Account column. The payment of rent occurs only once each month. For this reason, a special column for rent expense would not save labor.

Expenses *decrease* proprietorship. All *decreases* in proprietorship are *debits* to the proper account. If the decrease in proprietorship is the result of expenses in the operation of the business, an *expense* account is debited.

Step 3 — Credit part of entry. The amount to be credited, $120.00, was written in the Cash Credit column. Cash was credited because this asset was decreased.

Step 4 — Use of number column. C7 was written in the number column to show that Check No. 7 was issued in this transaction.

The effect of expense transactions. The effect of all expense transactions may be summarized as follows:

ANY EXPENSE ACCOUNT		ANY ASSET ACCOUNT	
Debit Side. *Increase Side.*	*Credit Side.* *Decrease Side.*	*Debit Side.* *Increase Side.*	*Credit Side.* *Decrease Side.*
1. *Increases* in expenses are recorded as *debits* in the journal. 2. *Increases* in expenses are posted to the left-hand or *debit side* of the proper expense account in the ledger.			1. *Decreases* in assets are recorded as *credits* in the journal. 2. *Decreases* in assets are posted to the right-hand or *credit side* of the proper asset account in the ledger.

Transaction No. 12 — An expense transaction

October 8. Paid cash, $25.00, for gas and oil used in operating the automobile. Issued Check No. 8.

Immediate record of cash payment. All of the details of this transaction were recorded on Check Stub No. 8. The check stub is similar to the one illustrated for Transaction No. 11.

Journal entry for payment of automobile expense. From the information given on Check Stub No. 8, Mr. Greene made the following entry:

	CASH		DATE	NAME OF ACCOUNT	NO.	POST. REF.	GENERAL		COMMISSIONS INCOME CREDIT	
	DEBIT	CREDIT					DEBIT	CREDIT		
1	20 00		Oct. 1	*Office Furniture*	R 1			20 00		1
10	60 00		5	*Commissions Income*	R 4				60 00	10
11		120 00	5	*Rent Expense*	C 7		120 00			11
12		25 00	8	*Automobile Expense*	C 8		25 00			12

Step 3   Step 1   Step 2   Step 4

Step 1 — Date of journal entry. Only the day of the month, 8, was written in the Date column on Line 12 of the journal.

Step 2 — Debit part of entry. Automobile Expense was debited (a) by writing *$25.00* in the General Debit column and (b) by writing *Automobile Expense* in the Name of Account column. Mr. Greene charged every expense incurred in connection with the use of the automobile to Automobile Expense. As was explained in Transaction No. 11, every expense transaction is recorded as a debit to the proper expense account.

Step 3 — Credit part of journal entry. The amount, $25.00, was written in the Cash Credit column because the asset Cash had been decreased by that amount.

Step 4 — Use of number column. *C8* was written in the number column to show that Check No. 8 was issued in this transaction.

Entry No. 13 to Entry No. 26. The transactions for the remainder of October were similar to those discussed. The complete journal of the Greene Realty Agency for October is illustrated on page 44.

The Greene Realty Agency maintains five expense accounts: Advertising Expense, Automobile Expense, Entertainment Expense, Miscellaneous Expense, and Rent Expense. Miscellaneous Expense is debited for all expenses that should not be charged to one of the other accounts.

JOURNAL

CASH DEBIT	CASH CREDIT	DATE	NAME OF ACCOUNT	NO.	POST. REF.	GENERAL DEBIT	GENERAL CREDIT	COMMISSIONS INCOME CREDIT	
		1951							
2000		Oct 1	Office Furniture	R 1			2000		1
	2500	1	Adams Company	C 1		2500			2
	3750	2	Office Furniture	C 2		3750			3
1500		2	Office Machines	R 2			1500		4
	4200	2	Star Garage	C 3		4200			5
	7600	3	Office Machines	C 4		7600			6
	3900	3	Office Furniture	C 5		3900			7
	10000	4	Daniels Company	C 6		10000			8
1800		5	Office Furniture	R 3			1800		9
60000		5	Commissions Income	R 4				60000	10
	12000	5	Rent Expense	C 7		12000			11
	2500	8	Automobile Expense	C 8		2500			12
24000		12	Commissions Income	R 5				24000	13
	17500	12	Office Machines	C 9		17500			14
	763	13	Advertising Expense	C 10		763			15
2500		14	Commissions Income	R 6				2500	16
37500		15	Commissions Income	R 7				37500	17
	450	16	Miscellaneous Expense	C 11		450			18
1000		18	Office Furniture	R 8			1000		19
	5000	18	Star Garage	C 12		5000			20
4200		19	Commissions Income	R 9				4200	21
	500	22	Entertainment Expense	C 13		500			22
	978	22	Advertising Expense	C 14		978			23
	752	25	Miscellaneous Expense	C 15		752			24
4560		29	Commissions Income	R 10				4560	25
5000		30	Commissions Income	R 11				5000	26
144060	72393	31	Totals			72393	6300	137760	27
									28

Journal of Greene Realty Agency for October

Footing the journal. At the end of the month all amount columns of the journal were added. The total of each amount column was written in small pencil figures immediately under the last entry. Pencil totals are commonly called *footings*.

Checking the accuracy of journal entries and footings. On a separate sheet of paper the footings of the debit columns were listed and added. The footings of the credit columns were also listed and added. The calculations are shown below:

Cash Debit Footing.........	$1,440.60	Cash Credit Footing........	$ 723.93
General Debit Footing......	723.93	General Credit Footing......	63.00
		Commissions Income Credit Footing.................	1,377.60
Total Debits...............	$2,164.53	Total Credits..............	$2,164.53

The sum of the totals of the *two debit* columns should equal the sum of the totals of the *three credit* columns. If the total of the debits does not equal the total of the credits, it shows that one or more errors have been made. The error or errors should be located and corrected.

Ruling the journal. After the equality of debits and credits was proved, a single line was drawn across all amount columns under the last entry. The totals of the columns were then entered in ink. The last day of the month was written in the Date column on the line with the totals. The word "Totals" was written in the Name of Account column. A double line was drawn across all columns except the Name of Account column. A ruler should always be used in drawing lines. Either red or black ink may be used.

The foregoing instructions apply to situations such as the one illustrated on page 44, where the journal page is not filled at the end of the month.

When a page that is filled is totaled, the printed rulings at the bottom of the page are used and ruling with a pen is unnecessary. If a page that is almost full is totaled, the printed rulings at the bottom of the page may also be used. In this case the spaces between the last entry and the printed rulings are canceled with a diagonal line drawn from the Date column to the Post. Ref. column.

Examine carefully the footings, totals, and rulings of the journal of the Greene Realty Agency on page 44.

Correcting errors as they are found in the journal. An error may be made in recording a transaction in the journal. If an error is in the amount, the incorrect amount should be canceled by drawing a line through it. The correct amount should then be written immediately above the canceled amount.

An error in an account title is corrected by drawing a line through the incorrect title and writing the correct title immediately above the canceled title.

Corrections of an error in an amount and of an error in an account title are shown in the illustration below.

	CASH		DATE	NAME OF ACCOUNT	NO.	POST. REF.	GENERAL		COMMISSIONS INCOME CREDIT	
	DEBIT	CREDIT					DEBIT	CREDIT		
1	2000		*1957* Oct 1	Office Furniture	R 1			2000		1
24		~~752~~ ~~725~~	25	~~Miscellaneous~~ Advertising Expense	C 15		752			24
25	4560		29	Commissions Income	R 10				4560	25

CHAPTER QUESTIONS

1. What form of business paper does Mr. Greene use as the immediate record of each income transaction?
2. What effect does cash received for commissions income have on Mr. Greene's proprietorship?
3. Why does Mr. Greene have a special column in his journal for Commissions Income Credit?
4. Why is it customary to write the words *Commissions Income* in the Name of Account column of Mr. Greene's journal when recording a commission transaction?
5. What form of business paper does Mr. Greene use as his immediate record of each expense transaction?
6. Why doesn't Mr. Greene have a special column in his journal for each expense account?
7. Why is it necessary to write the name of the expense account in the Name of Account column each time an expense account is debited in Mr. Greene's journal?
8. If an amount in the journal is recorded incorrectly, how is the error corrected?

INCREASING YOUR BUSINESS VOCABULARY

What is the meaning of each of the following:

(a) income   (c) special column

(b) expense   (d) footings

CASES FOR DISCUSSION

1. Both William Myers and John Cole use columnar journals similar to the one illustrated on page 44. When William Myers records Commissions Income, he records the debit in the Cash Debit column and the credit in the Commissions Income Credit column and makes a check mark in the Name of Account column. John Cole follows the same procedure except that he writes the account title, Commissions Income, in the Name of Account column. Which person do you believe follows the better plan? Why?

2. John Cole refers to all of his cash payments as "my expenses." William Myers tells him that some cash payments increase the value of assets and that others decrease the amount of liabilities. Refer to the journal on page 44 and indicate which of the cash payments are not payments of expenses.

The following drills are planned to give you additional skill, accuracy, and speed in selecting proper account titles for business transactions and in analyzing the effect of the transactions.

Drill 5-A. For the entries on Lines 10 to 26 of the journal illustrated on page 44 you are to tell what account title is debited and what account title is credited.

Instructions: **1.** If you do not have a workbook, take a sheet of paper and draw a line down through the middle of it from top to bottom. Rule a narrow column at the left of your paper. At the top of your paper, copy the following headings:

Line No.	Title of Account Debited	Title of Account Credited
10	*Cash*	*Commissions Income*

2. Turn to the completed journal of this chapter illustrated on page 44. On the form that you have just prepared or that you found in your workbook, copy the analysis of Line 10 of that journal in the manner shown above.

3. Write a similar analysis of each of the remaining entries (Lines 11 to 26) of the journal illustrated on page 44.

Drill 5-B. For the entries on Lines 10 to 26 in the journal illustrated on page 44 you are to tell whether an asset, a liability, or the proprietorship was increased or decreased.

Instructions: **1.** If you do not have a workbook, take a sheet of paper and draw a line through the middle of it from top to bottom. Rule a narrow column at the left edge of your paper. At the top of your paper, copy the following headings:

Line No.	Effect of Debit Entry	Effect of Credit Entry
10	*Increased an asset*	*Increased proprietorship*

2. Turn to the completed journal of this chapter illustrated on page 44. On the form that you have just prepared or that you found in your workbook, copy the analysis of Line 10 of that journal in the manner shown above.

3. Write a similar analysis of each of the remaining lines (Lines 11 to 26) of the journal illustrated on page 44. If the debit is an expense account, write "Decreased proprietorship"; if the credit is an income account, write "Increased proprietorship."

Drill 5-C. For each of the transactions given below you are to indicate the account debited and the account credited and the effect of each debit and each credit.

Instructions: 1. If you do not have a workbook, rule five columns on a sheet of paper and copy the headings of the following form. Also copy the analysis of Transaction 1, which is given as an example.

1	2	3	4	5
Trans. No.	Title of Account Debited	Effect of the Debit	Title of Account Credited	Effect of the Credit
1	*Cash*	*Increased an asset*	*Commissions Income*	*Increased proprietorship*

2. Write a similar analysis of Transactions 2 to 15, using the following account titles in Columns 2 and 4:

Account Titles:

Cash	Commissions Income
Automobile	Advertising Expense
Office Furniture	Automobile Expense
Office Machines	Electricity Expense
Atlas Company	Rent Expense
Thompson Garage	Stationery Expense
	Telephone Expense

Transactions:

1. Received cash as commission from sale of a house. (You have copied this answer.)
2. Received cash from sale of old office furniture.
3. Paid cash for rent of office for October.
4. Paid cash for gas and oil used in operating the automobile.
5. Received cash from sale of old office machine.
6. Paid cash to Atlas Company in partial payment of the amount owed.
7. Paid cash for purchase of new office furniture.
8. Paid cash to Thompson Garage in partial payment of amount owed.
9. Paid cash for purchase of new office machine.
10. Received cash as commission from sale of a house.
11. Paid cash for office stationery.
12. Paid cash for advertising.
13. Received cash as commission for renting a house.
14. Paid cash for telephone bill.
15. Paid cash for electric bill.

Problem 5-1.   Journalizing transactions of a real estate business

Instructions: 1. Record the following transactions of the Hackett Realty Agency in a five-column journal. Use as your model the five-column journal form illustrated on page 44. In the Name of Account column of your journal, use the account titles listed in Drill 5-C.

Transactions:

Oct. 1. Received cash, $200.00, as commission from sale of a house. Issued Receipt No. 1.
  2. Received cash, $16.00, from sale of old office furniture. Issued Receipt No. 2.
  2. Paid cash, $75.00, for rent of office for October. Issued Check No. 1.
  4. Paid cash, $5.50, for gas and oil for automobile. Issued Check No. 2.
  5. Received cash, $36.00, from sale of old office machine. Issued Receipt No. 3.
  7. Paid cash, $95.50 to Atlas Company in part payment of account. Issued Check No. 3.
  10. Paid cash, $114.00, for new office furniture. Issued Check No. 4.
  12. Paid cash, $32.50, to Thompson Garage in part payment of amount owed them. Issued Check No. 5.
  15. Paid cash, $125.00, for a new office machine. Issued Check No. 6.
  17. Received cash, $120.00, as commission from sale of a house. Issued Receipt No. 4.
  19. Paid cash, $6.00, for office stationery. Issued Check No. 7.
  23. Paid cash, $2.50, for advertisement in paper. Issued Check No. 8.
  25. Received cash, $55.00, as commission from renting a house. Issued Receipt No. 5.
  29. Paid cash, $10.00, for telephone bill. Issued Check No. 9.

Instructions: 2. Foot each of the five columns of your journal, using small pencil figures. Place these tiny pencil figures close to the line above so that they seem to hang from it. Study the model journal on page 44.

3. Prove the equality of debits and credits in your journal by finding the sum of all the debit totals and then the sum of all the credit totals. The sum of the two debit columns should equal the sum of the three credit columns.

4. If the sum of the totals of the debits in your journal is equal to the sum of the totals of the credits, rule a single line across all amount columns of your journal. Compare your work with the journal on page 44.

5. Write the totals of each column in ink. Label these totals by writing the word *Totals* in the Name of Account column. All of these totals should be on the same line. Compare your work with the journal on page 44.

6. Rule double lines across all columns except the Name of Account column immediately below the totals. Use as your model the completed journal on page 44.

Problem 5-2. Journalizing transactions of a public accountant

Robert Pepper is a public accountant and obtains his income from fees for professional accounting services. The title he uses for his income account is *Fees Income*.

Instructions: 1. Record on page 2 of a five-column journal the selected transactions given below. Use the following account titles:

Account Titles in Robert Pepper's Ledger

Assets	*Liabilities*	*Income*
Cash	Metcalf Company	Fees Income
Automobile	O'Brien Company	*Expenses*
Office Furniture	*Proprietorship*	Automobile Expense
Professional Library	Robert Pepper, Capital	Miscellaneous Expense
		Rent Expense

Transactions:

Oct. 1. Paid cash, $100.00, for rent of the office for October. Issued Check No. 1.

1. Paid cash, $8.00, for parking space for the automobile for October. This is automobile expense. Issued Check No. 2.

2. Received cash, $15.00, from sale of old office desk. This is office furniture. Issued Receipt No. 1.

2. Received cash, $185.00, for accounting services. This is fees income. Issued Receipt No. 2.

2. Paid cash, $5.00, for gas and oil for automobile. Issued Check No. 3.

3. Paid cash, $240.00, for a new desk and a bookcase. Issued Check No. 4.

4. Received cash, $270.00, for accounting services. Issued Receipt No. 3.

10. Received cash, $175.00, for accounting services. Issued Receipt No. 4.

14. Paid cash, $8.50, for a new book on accounting. This is professional library. Issued Check No. 5.

15. Received cash, $250.00, for accounting services. Issued Receipt No. 5.

19. Received cash, $110.00, for accounting services. Issued Receipt No. 6.

22. Paid cash, $160.00, to the O'Brien Company for amount owed on account. Issued Check No. 6.

25. Paid cash, $30.00, to the Metcalf Company for amount owed on account. Issued Check No. 7.

29. Received cash, $190.00, for accounting services. Issued Receipt No. 7.

31. Paid cash, $15.00, for the electric bill for October. This is miscellaneous expense. Issued Check No. 8.

31. Paid cash, $9.50, for the telephone bill for October. This is miscellaneous expense. Issued Check No. 9.

Instructions: 2. Foot each of the five columns of your journal.

3. Prove the equality of debits and credits in your journal.

4. Record the column totals.

5. Rule the journal.

This problem will be continued in the next chapter. If it is collected by your teacher at this time, it will be returned to you before it is needed in Problem 6-1.

Posting

Need for posting transactions. The journal of the Greene Realty Agency on page 44 is a record of all transactions for the month of October. Each journal entry has changed the balance of two accounts. To provide a clear picture of the effect of these changes on account balances, it is now necessary to post all the journal entries to Mr. Greene's ledger.

Order of arrangement of accounts in the ledger. All accounts of one kind are grouped together in the ledger. It is customary to have separate groups for assets, liabilities, proprietorship, income, and expenses. Each of these groups is called a division of the ledger.

Some businesses have more than five divisions in the ledger. These variations will be developed in later chapters. For example, the ledger on page 229 has six divisions.

A list of accounts that shows the arrangement of the accounts in the ledger is called a *chart of accounts*. The chart of accounts of the Greene Realty Agency ledger is arranged as follows:

Chart of accounts

(1) ASSETS	(3) PROPRIETORSHIP	(5) EXPENSES
ACCT. No.	ACCT. No.	ACCT. No.
11 Cash	31 J. M. Greene, Capital	51 Advertising Expense
12 Automobile		52 Automobile Expense
13 Office Furniture	(4) INCOME	53 Entertainment Expense
14 Office Machines	41 Commissions Income	54 Miscellaneous Expense
		55 Rent Expense
(2) LIABILITIES		
21 Adams Company		
22 Daniels Company		
23 Star Garage		

Numbering accounts in the ledger. Note that each account number has two digits. The first digit indicates the division of the ledger; the second digit indicates the number of the account within that division. For example, the office machines account is numbered 14. The first digit, 1, indicates that the office machines account is an asset account. The second digit, 4, indicates that the office machines account is the fourth account in the asset division.

The number of each asset account starts with the figure 1; the number of each liability account, with the figure 2; the number of each proprietorship account, with the figure 3; the number of each income account, with the figure 4; and the number of each expense account, with the figure 5. Within each division the accounts are numbered consecutively.

Posting the journal of the Greene Realty Agency. Each individual amount in the General Debit and the General Credit columns of the journal must be posted separately because these amounts apply to many different accounts. Each amount in the General columns is posted to the account named in the Name of Account column. Only the totals of the three special columns in the journal are posted.

Steps in posting the journal. The first entry on page 2 of the journal of the Greene Realty Agency is shown below.

	CASH		DATE	NAME OF ACCOUNT	NO.	POST. REF.	GENERAL		COMMISSIONS INCOME CREDIT	
	DEBIT	CREDIT					DEBIT	CREDIT		
1	2000		*1957* Oct. 1	Office Furniture	R 1			2000		1
2										2
3										3

This entry shows a debit to Cash and a credit to Office Furniture. The debit to Cash in the Cash Debit column is not posted separately. At the end of the month the column will be added and the total will be posted as one amount.

To post the credit part of this entry, proceed as follows:

Step 1. Open the ledger to the account named on the first line of the journal, Office Furniture. This account contains a debit balance, which was recorded when the opening entry was made.

Office Furniture   ACCOUNT NO. 13

DATE	ITEMS	POST. REF.	DEBIT	DATE	ITEMS	POST. REF.	CREDIT
1957 Oct. 1	Balance	1	74560				

Step 2. Transfer the amount in the General Credit column of the journal to the credit side of the Office Furniture account in the ledger. Write the amount of the credit, $20.00, in the Credit amount column of the office furniture account.

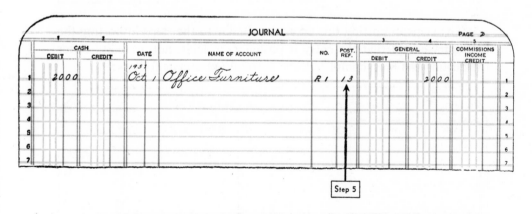

Step 3. Write the date of this journal entry, as found in the journal, in the Date column on the credit side of the office furniture account.

Since this is the first entry on the credit side of the office furniture account, it is necessary to write the complete date: 1957, Oct. 1.

Step 4. Write the figure 2 in the Post. Ref. column of the account to show that this entry was posted from page 2 of the journal.

Step 5. Return to the journal and write in the Post. Ref. column of the journal the number of the ledger account, 13.

A figure in the Post. Ref. column of the journal shows that all details of posting this line have been completed. For this reason the Post. Ref. figure is always written in the journal as the last step in posting.

Steps in posting the second entry. The journal of the Greene Realty Agency, including the first two transactions for the month of October, is shown below.

CASH		DATE	NAME OF ACCOUNT	NO.	POST. REF.	GENERAL		COMMISSIONS INCOME CREDIT	
DEBIT	CREDIT					DEBIT	CREDIT		
		1957							
2000		Oct. 1	*Office Furniture*	R 1	13		2000		1
	2500	1	*Adams Company*	C 1		2500			2
									3
									4
									5

The second entry in the journal shows a debit to Adams Company and a credit to Cash. The credit to Cash in the Cash Credit column will be posted at the end of the month. At that time, the column will be added and the total will be posted as one amount.

Before the debit is posted to the account of the Adams Company, the account appears as follows:

Adams Company   ACCOUNT NO. 21

DATE	ITEMS	POST. REF.	DEBIT	DATE	ITEMS	POST. REF.	CREDIT
				1957			
				Oct. 1	*Balance*	1	9100

The steps in posting this entry are similar to the steps in posting the first entry except that the entry is posted as a debit, not a credit. After the posting has been completed, the account appears as follows:

Adams Company   ACCOUNT NO. 21

DATE	ITEMS	POST. REF.	DEBIT	DATE	ITEMS	POST. REF.	CREDIT
1957				*1957*			
Oct. 1		2	2500	Oct. 1	*Balance*	1	9100

The number of the Adams Company account, 21, is written in the Post. Ref. column of the journal. The journal then appears as follows:

CASH		DATE	NAME OF ACCOUNT	NO.	POST. REF.	GENERAL		COMMISSIONS INCOME CREDIT	
DEBIT	CREDIT					DEBIT	CREDIT		
		1957							
2000		Oct. 1	Office Furniture	R 1	13		2000		1
	2500	1	Adams Company	C 1	21	2500			2
									3
									4
									5

Completing the posting of individual entries in the General columns. Each amount in the General Debit column of the journal is posted to the debit side of the account named in the Name of Account column. Each amount in the General Credit column of the journal is posted to the credit side of the account named in the Name of Account column.

Posting the totals of special columns in the journal. Nothing is posted from a special column until the end of the month; then it is necessary to post only the total of the column. The total of each special column is posted to the account named in the heading of the column. For example, the total of the Cash Debit column, $1,440.60, of the journal on page 58 is posted to the debit side of the cash account in the ledger. The total of the Cash Credit column, $723.93, is posted to the credit side of the cash account. The total of the Commissions Income Credit column, $1,377.60, is posted to the credit side of the commissions income account.

Totals of the General columns of the journal are not posted. Each individual amount in both of the General columns has been posted separately. Therefore, the totals of these two columns must not be posted. A check mark in parentheses is placed below the totals of each of the two General columns to indicate that no further posting is required. Note how the check marks appear in the illustration on page 58.

Posting the total of the Cash Debit column of the journal. To post the total of the Cash Debit column of the journal, proceed as follows:

Step 1. Open the ledger to the account named by the heading of the first special column in the journal, Cash. The cash account in the ledger appears as follows:

Cash   ACCOUNT NO. 11

DATE	ITEMS	POST. REF.	DEBIT	DATE	ITEMS	POST. REF.	CREDIT
1957							
Oct. 1	Balance	1	371 00				

Step 2. Transfer the total of the Cash Debit column of the journal, $1,440.60, to the cash account in the ledger. Write the amount of the debit, $1,440.60, in the Debit Amount column of the cash account.

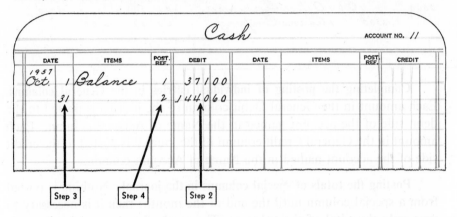

Step 3. Write the day found on the total line of the journal, 31, in the Date column on the debit side of the cash account.

> This is the second entry on the debit side of the cash account. The date of the first entry in the cash account is 1957, Oct. 1. The date of the second entry is also the same year and the same month; therefore, it is not necessary to repeat 1957 and Oct. on the debit side of the cash account.

Step 4. Write the figure *2* in the Post. Ref. column of the cash account to show that this entry was posted from page 2 of the journal.

Step 5. Return to the journal and write *11*, the account number of the cash account, immediately under the total of the Cash Debit column. Place parentheses around the account number.

Posting the total of the Cash Credit column of the journal. The total of the Cash Credit column of the journal is posted in the same manner as the total of the Cash Debit column with two exceptions:

1. The posting is made to the credit side of the cash account.

2. The complete date (the year, the month, and the day) is written in the cash account because this is the first entry on the credit side of that account.

Cash account after posting journal totals. After the totals of the Cash Debit and the Cash Credit columns of the journal are posted, the cash account in the ledger appears as follows:

				Cash				ACCOUNT NO. 11
DATE	ITEMS	POST. REF.	DEBIT		DATE	ITEMS	POST. REF.	CREDIT
1957 Oct. 1	Balance	1	371 00		1957 Oct. 31		2	723 93
31		2	1440 60					

Posting the total of the Commissions Income Credit column of the journal. The steps in posting the total of the Commissions Income Credit column of the journal are similar to the steps used in posting the total of the Cash Credit column. The final step in posting the total of the Commissions Income Credit column is the writing of the account number, 41, in parentheses immediately below the total of the Commissions Income Credit column in the journal. Writing the number of the commissions income account, 41, below the column total shows that the posting of this column total has been completed.

The commissions income account in the ledger now appears as follows:

				Commissions Income				ACCOUNT NO. 41
DATE	ITEMS	POST. REF.	DEBIT		DATE	ITEMS	POST. REF.	CREDIT
					1957 Oct. 31		2	1377 60

A check mark is placed in the Post. Ref. column for each entry in the Commissions Income Credit column. This check mark shows that no further posting is required for the item on this line. (See illustration on page 58.) Many experienced bookkeepers prefer to insert a check mark in the Post. Ref. column at the time each amount in the Commissions Income column is recorded. Such a procedure indicates in advance of posting that each of these amounts will not be posted individually.

CASH DEBIT	CASH CREDIT	DATE	NAME OF ACCOUNT	NO.	POST. REF.	GENERAL DEBIT	GENERAL CREDIT	COMMISSIONS INCOME CREDIT	
		1957							
20 00		Oct 1	Office Furniture	R 1	13		20 00		1
	25 00	1	Adams Company	C 1	21	25 00			2
	37 50	2	Office Furniture	C 2	13	37 50			3
15 00		2	Office Machines	R 2	14		15 00		4
	42 00	2	Star Garage	C 3	23	42 00			5
	76 00	3	Office Machines	C 4	14	76 00			6
	39 00	3	Office Furniture	C 5	13	39 00			7
	100 00	4	Daniels Company	C 6	22	100 00			8
18 00		5	Office Furniture	R 3	13		18 00		9
600 00		5	Commissions Income	R 4	✓			600 00	10
	120 00	5	Rent Expense	C 7	55	120 00			11
	25 00	8	Automobile Expense	C 8	52	25 00			12
240 00		12	Commissions Income	R 5	✓			240 00	13
	175 00	12	Office Machines	C 9	14	175 00			14
	7 63	13	Advertising Expense	C 10	51	7 63			15
25 00		14	Commissions Income	R 6	✓			25 00	16
375 00		15	Commissions Income	R 7	✓			375 00	17
	4 50	16	Miscellaneous Expense	C 11	54	4 50			18
10 00		18	Office Furniture	R 8	13		10 00		19
	50 00	18	Star Garage	C 12	23	50 00			20
42 00		19	Commissions Income	R 9	✓			42 00	21
	5 00	22	Entertainment Expense	C 13	53	5 00			22
	9 78	22	Advertising Expense	C 14	51	9 78			23
	7 52	25	Miscellaneous Expense	C 15	54	7 52			24
45 60		29	Commissions Income	R 10	✓			45 60	25
50 00		30	Commissions Income	R 11	✓			50 00	26
1440 60	723 93	31	Totals			723 93	63 00	1377 60	27
(11)	(11)					(✓)	(✓)	(41)	28

Journal of Greene Realty Agency after posting

The journal and the ledger after posting. The journal after all posting has been completed is illustrated above. The amounts recorded in the General Debit and the General Credit columns are usually posted at intervals during the month so that there will not be too much work at the end of the month. In some businesses these amounts are posted daily.

The ledger after all posting has been completed is illustrated on pages 59 and 60.

Cash
ACCOUNT NO. 11

DATE		ITEMS	POST. REF.	DEBIT	DATE		ITEMS	POST. REF.	CREDIT
1957 Oct.	1	Balance	1	3 7 1 0 0	1957 Oct.	31		2	7 2 3 9 3
	31		2	1 4 4 0 6 0					

Automobile
ACCOUNT NO. 12

DATE		ITEMS	POST. REF.	DEBIT	DATE	ITEMS	POST. REF.	CREDIT
1957 Oct.	1	Balance	1	3 1 7 0 0 0				

Office Furniture
ACCOUNT NO. 13

DATE		ITEMS	POST. REF.	DEBIT	DATE		ITEMS	POST. REF.	CREDIT
1957 Oct.	1	Balance	1	7 4 5 6 0	1957 Oct.	1		2	2 0 0 0
	2		2	3 7 5 0		5		2	1 8 0 0
	3		2	3 9 0 0		18		2	1 0 0 0

Office Machines
ACCOUNT NO. 14

DATE		ITEMS	POST. REF.	DEBIT	DATE		ITEMS	POST. REF.	CREDIT
1957 Oct.	1	Balance	1	2 5 4 4 0	1957 Oct.	2		2	1 5 0 0
	3		2	7 6 0 0					
	12		2	1 7 5 0 0					

Adams Company
ACCOUNT NO. 21

DATE		ITEMS	POST. REF.	DEBIT	DATE		ITEMS	POST. REF.	CREDIT
1957 Oct.	1		2	2 5 0 0	1957 Oct.	1	Balance	1	9 1 0 0

Daniels Company
ACCOUNT NO. 22

DATE		ITEMS	POST. REF.	DEBIT	DATE		ITEMS	POST. REF.	CREDIT
1957 Oct.	4		2	1 0 0 0 0	1957 Oct.	1	Balance	1	3 0 0 0 0

Star Garage
ACCOUNT NO. 23

DATE		ITEMS	POST. REF.	DEBIT	DATE		ITEMS	POST. REF.	CREDIT
1957 Oct.	2		2	4 2 0 0	1957 Oct.	1	Balance	1	1 2 5 0 0
	18		2	5 0 0 0					

Ledger of Greene Realty Agency after posting all transactions for October

J. M. Greene, Capital — ACCOUNT NO. 31

DATE	ITEMS	POST. REF.	DEBIT	DATE	ITEMS	POST. REF.	CREDIT
				1957 Oct. 1	Balance	1	2900 00

Commissions Income — ACCOUNT NO. 41

DATE	ITEMS	POST. REF.	DEBIT	DATE	ITEMS	POST. REF.	CREDIT
				1957 Oct. 31		2	1377 60

Advertising Expense — ACCOUNT NO. 51

DATE	ITEMS	POST. REF.	DEBIT	DATE	ITEMS	POST. REF.	CREDIT
1957 Oct. 13		2	7 63				
22		2	9 78				

Automobile Expense — ACCOUNT NO. 52

DATE	ITEMS	POST. REF.	DEBIT	DATE	ITEMS	POST. REF.	CREDIT
1957 Oct. 8		2	25 00				

Entertainment Expense — ACCOUNT NO. 53

DATE	ITEMS	POST. REF.	DEBIT	DATE	ITEMS	POST. REF.	CREDIT
1957 Oct. 22		2	5 00				

Miscellaneous Expense — ACCOUNT NO. 54

DATE	ITEMS	POST. REF.	DEBIT	DATE	ITEMS	POST. REF.	CREDIT
1957 Oct. 16		2	4 50				
25		2	7 52				

Rent Expense — ACCOUNT NO. 55

DATE	ITEMS	POST. REF.	DEBIT	DATE	ITEMS	POST. REF.	CREDIT
1957 Oct. 5		2	120 00				

Ledger of Greene Realty Agency after posting all transactions for October (concluded)

Recording increases in account balances. Assets are found on the left-hand side of the balance sheet; therefore, when an asset is recorded or is increased, the entry is made in a *debit* column of the journal and is posted to the left-hand or debit side of the account.

ANY ASSET ACCOUNT	
Debit Side	*Credit Side*
Balance Side	
Increases in an asset are entered on the left-hand or debit side.	

Liabilities are found on the right-hand side of the balance sheet; therefore, when a liability is recorded or is increased, the entry is made in a *credit* column of the journal and is posted to the right-hand or credit side of the account.

ANY LIABILITY ACCOUNT	
Debit Side	*Credit Side*
	Balance Side
	Increases in a liability are entered on the right-hand or credit side.

Proprietorship is found on the right-hand side of the balance sheet; therefore, when proprietorship is recorded for the first time or is increased, the entry is made in a *credit* column of the journal and is posted to the right-hand or credit side of the account.

ANY PROPRIETORSHIP ACCOUNT	
Debit Side	*Credit Side*
	Balance Side
	Increases in proprietorship are entered on the right-hand or credit side.

Incomes increase proprietorship and are always recorded in the journal in a *credit* column. Income items are posted to the right-hand or credit side of the account in the ledger.

ANY INCOME ACCOUNT	
Debit Side	*Credit Side*
	All incomes are entered on the right-hand or credit side.

Expenses decrease proprietorship and are always recorded in the journal in a *debit* column. Expense items are posted to the left-hand or debit side of the account in the ledger.

ANY EXPENSE ACCOUNT	
Debit Side	*Credit Side*
All expenses are entered on the left-hand or debit side.	

Recording decreases in account balances. In bookkeeping, subtraction in a ledger account is always indicated by "opposite position." The amount to be *subtracted* from an account balance is always placed on the side of the account that is *opposite* the balance from which it is to be subtracted. For example, if an amount is to be subtracted from an asset account *debit* balance, the amount to be subtracted is placed on the *credit* side of the asset account. Similarly, if an amount is to be subtracted from a liability account *credit* balance, the amount to be subtracted is placed on the *debit* side of the liability account.

A decrease in an asset account, therefore, is always placed in a *credit* column in the journal and is posted to the right-hand or credit side of the account in the ledger.

ANY ASSET ACCOUNT	
Debit Side	*Credit Side*
Balance Side	Decreases in an asset are entered on the right-hand or credit side.

A decrease in a liability account is always placed in a *debit* column in the journal and is posted to the left-hand or debit side of the account in the ledger.

ANY LIABILITY ACCOUNT	
Debit Side	*Credit Side*
Decreases in a liability are entered on the left-hand or debit side.	*Balance Side*

A decrease in proprietorship is always placed in a *debit* column in the journal and is posted to the left-hand or debit side of the account in the ledger.

ANY PROPRIETORSHIP ACCOUNT	
Debit Side	*Credit Side*
Decreases in proprietorship are entered on the left or debit side.	*Balance Side*

CHAPTER QUESTIONS

1. What are the five divisions of the chart of accounts of the Greene Realty Agency?
2. Explain the numbering system used by the Greene Realty Agency in numbering ledger accounts.
3. Why must each amount in the two General columns of the journal be posted separately?
4. What are the five steps in posting an amount from the General Debit column of the journal?
5. How can you tell whether a journal entry has been posted?
6. What are the five steps in posting the total of the Cash Debit column of the journal?
7. How does the posting of the total of the Cash Credit column differ from the posting of the total of the Cash Debit column?
8. How do you show in the journal that the totals of the General columns are not posted?

CASES FOR DISCUSSION

1. Mr. Leslie Babcock posts from both General columns of the journal in the order in which the transactions appear. Mr. John Devine posts all of the amounts in the General Debit column first and then posts all of the amounts in the General Credit column.

   (a) What are the advantages of the procedure used by Mr. Babcock?
   (b) What are the advantages of the procedure used by Mr. Devine?

2. Mr. Neels writes the account number of the ledger account to which the journal entry was transferred as the last step in the process of posting. Mr. Kissinger reverses this procedure and begins the posting process by writing the ledger account number in the Post. Ref. column of the journal as the first step in posting. What are the advantages of Mr. Neels's procedure?

3. J. R. Gammon has dozens of accounts in his ledger and numerous pages in his journal. While examining one of his ledger accounts, he becomes interested in getting some additional information about one of the amounts. He wants to trace this ledger entry back to the journal entry from which it was posted. How can he quickly determine the exact page of the journal to which to refer?

DRILLS FOR UNDERSTANDING

You have learned that the proper sequence in bookkeeping is: (1) the immediate record, (2) the journal entry, and (3) posting to the proper ledger account. But a bookkeeper plans his entry before recording it in the journal. The experienced bookkeeper does this mentally. The inexperienced bookkeeper may use a form known as a T account, so called because it resembles the capital letter T. For example, he would record the first transaction on page 58 in the following form:

Sample transaction: *Sample T account solution:*

Received cash, $20.00, from sale of old office furniture.

CASH	OFFICE FURNITURE
20.00	20.00

Drill 6-A. *Instructions: 1.* Read Transaction No. 1 given below. Draw two T accounts and write the proper account titles for each, one for the debit part of the transaction and one for the credit part. Then indicate the amount of the debit in one T account and the amount of the credit in the other T account. When this transaction is recorded, your accounts should be similar to those shown in the sample transaction above.

2. Record the additional transactions in T accounts. Use two T accounts for each transaction.

If these were complete accounts, they would have beginning balances; but it is not necessary to show balances in T accounts that are used merely for planning the debit and the credit for each entry.

Transactions:
1. Received cash, $20.00, from the sale of old office furniture.
2. Paid cash, $25.00, to Adams Company in part payment of the amount owed.
3. Paid cash, $37.50, for purchase of new office desk.
4. Received cash, $15.00, from sale of office machine.
5. Paid cash, $42.00, to Star Garage in part payment of the amount owed.

Drill 6-B. *Instructions:* Plan the recording of the following transactions by the use of T accounts as you did in Drill 6-A.

Transactions:

1. Received cash, $600.00, as commission from sale of a house.
2. Paid cash, $76.00, for purchase of office machine.
3. Paid cash, $39.00, for purchase of office furniture.
4. Paid cash, $100.00, to Daniels Company in part payment of the amount owed.
5. Received cash, $18.00, from sale of office furniture.

Drill 6-C. *Instructions:* Plan the recording of the following transactions by the use of T accounts as you did in Drill 6-A.

Transactions:

1. Received cash, $500.00, as commission from sale of a house.
2. Paid cash, $120.00, for rent for October.
3. Paid cash, $5.00, for gas and oil for automobile.
4. Received cash, $240.00, as commission from sale of a house.
5. Paid cash, $4.50, for telephone bill. (Miscellaneous Expense)
6. Paid cash, $20.00, for repairs on automobile.
7. Paid cash, $7.52, for electric bill. (Miscellaneous Expense)

APPLICATION PROBLEMS

Problem 6-1. Posting the journal of a public accountant

The journal completed in Problem 5-2 of Chapter 5 is required for this problem. If Problem 5-2 has not been returned to you, complete Exercise 6-A in the Appendix.

Instructions: **1.** Prepare the Pepper ledger by opening the accounts listed below. Place six accounts on each page of the ledger. Use the account numbers shown in the following list. Be sure to write the proper account number after the title of each account.

ACCOUNT	ACCT. No.	ACCOUNT	ACCT. No.
Cash	11	Robert Pepper, Capital	31
Automobile	12	Fees Income	41
Office Furniture	13		
Professional Library	14	Automobile Expense	51
Metcalf Company	21	Miscellaneous Expense	52
O'Brien Company	22	Rent Expense	53

Instructions: **2.** The asset accounts have *debit* balances as follows:

Cash	$1,400.00	Office Furniture	$560.00
Automobile	$2,750.00	Professional Library	$240.00

Copy these balances in the ledger that you have just prepared. Use the date October 1 of the current year.

Whenever a balance is copied in a ledger account, place a check mark in the posting reference column.

Instructions: 3. The liability and proprietorship accounts have *credit* balances as follows:

| Metcalf Company | $ 30.00 | Robert Pepper, Capital | $4,760.00 |
| O'Brien Company | $160.00 | | |

Copy these balances in the ledger. Use the date October 1 of the current year.

Instructions: 4. Turn to the journal you completed for Problem 5-2. Post each amount that is recorded in the General Debit and the General Credit columns of your journal.

5. Place a check mark in the Post Ref. column for each entry crediting Fees Income. This check mark shows that this entry is not posted individually.

6. Post the totals of the three special columns of your journal to the proper accounts in your ledger. Place a check mark under the columns General Debit and General Credit to indicate that these totals are not posted.

Problem 6-2. Journalizing and posting the transactions of a lawyer

You will need to prepare the ledger of James N. Henderson, a lawyer, before you can do the work in this exercise.

Instructions: 1. Open the twelve accounts in the ledger that will be needed for this exercise. Place six accounts on each page of your ledger. A list of the account titles with account numbers is given below.

ACCOUNT TITLE	ACCT. No.	ACCOUNT TITLE	ACCT. No.
Cash	11	Fees Income	41
Automobile	12	Automobile Expense	51
Office Furniture	13	Miscellaneous Expense	52
Professional Library	14	Rent Expense	53
Cumming's Garage	21	Stationery Expense	54
Hoffman Company	22		
James N. Henderson, Capital	31		

Instructions: 2. Copy the balances given below in the proper accounts of the ledger prepared in Instruction 1. Date each account balance October 1 of the current year.

Assets (Debit Balances)
Cash, $1,313.00
Automobile, $2,800.00
Office Furniture, $450.00
Professional Library, $645.00

Liabilities and Proprietorship (Credit Balances)
Cumming's Garage, $139.00
Hoffman Company, $184.50

James N. Henderson, Capital, $4,884.50

(Note that the only accounts that have balances are the accounts for assets, liabilities, and proprietorship. The reason will be explained in a later chapter.)

Instructions: 3. On page 2 of a journal similar to the model journal on page 58, journalize the transactions for October given below.

Transactions:

Oct. 1. Paid cash, $125.00, for rent for October. (Check No. 1)
2. Received cash, $54.00, from J. E. Clem for professional fees. (Receipt No. 1)
3. Paid cash, $45.00, for office furniture. (Check No. 2)
5. Paid cash, $14.00, for stationery. (Check No. 3)
7. Paid cash, $116.00, to Cumming's Garage on account. (Check No. 4)
9. Received cash, $32.50, from R. L. Brimer for professional fees. (Receipt No. 2)
11. Received cash, $94.00, from sale of old office furniture. (Receipt No. 3)
15. Paid cash, $5.00, for gas and oil. (Check No. 5)
17. Paid cash, $5.00, for postage stamps. This is miscellaneous expense. (Check No. 6)
18. Paid cash, $21.50, for new tire for automobile. (Check No. 7)
21. Paid cash, $4.50, for envelopes. (Check No. 8)
24. Received cash, $44.00, from J. P. Mullane for professional fees. (Receipt No. 4)
25. Paid cash, $23.00, to Cumming's Garage on account. (Check No. 9)
26. Received cash, $111.10, from Jack Burant for professional fees. (Receipt No. 5)
29. Received cash, $81.00, from H. R. Sinner for professional fees. (Receipt No. 6)
30. Paid cash, $14.00, for telephone service for month. This is miscellaneous expense. (Check No. 10)
30. Paid cash, $24.00, for electricity for month. This is miscellaneous expense. (Check No. 11)
31. Paid cash, $133.00, to Hoffman Company on account. (Check No. 12)

Instructions: 4. Post the individual amounts in the General Debit and the General Credit columns to the accounts in the ledger.

5. Place a check mark in the Post Ref. column for each entry crediting Fees Income to show that this entry is not posted individually.

6. Foot each amount column with small pencil figures. Prove the equality of debits and credits in your journal. The sum of the totals of the two debit columns should equal the sum of the totals of the three credit columns.

7. Draw single lines across all amount columns. Use as your guide the model journal on page 58.

8. Write the column totals on the total line. Write the word *Totals* in the Name of Account column.

9. Rule your journal with double lines.

10. Post the totals of the three special columns. Place a check mark under the General Debit and General Credit columns to indicate that these totals are not posted.

Proving the accuracy of posting

Accuracy in bookkeeping. Bookkeeping records are valuable only to the extent that they are accurate. The bookkeeper should be careful to avoid errors. He should also use methods that will help him to detect promptly any errors that do occur. Two methods of checking the accuracy of bookkeeping records will be discussed in this chapter: (1) proving cash and (2) taking the trial balance.

Proving cash. In the Greene Realty Agency, every transaction is a cash transaction. If the amount of cash on hand is the same as the balance of the cash account in the ledger, it is probable that the cash part of each transaction has been recorded and posted correctly. Determining that the amount of cash on hand agrees with the balance of the cash account in the ledger is known as *proving cash*. The method of proving cash includes:
1. Finding the amount of cash on hand.
2. Finding the balance of the cash account.
3. Comparing the amount of cash on hand with the balance of the cash account.

Finding the amount of cash on hand. When all cash that has been received has been deposited in the bank, the total cash on hand is the balance in the checkbook. If some cash that has been received has not yet been deposited, the cash on hand is the sum of the undeposited cash plus the balance in the checkbook.

Mr. Greene deposits all cash received; his check-stub balance, $1,087.67, was therefore the amount of cash on hand on October 31.

Finding the balance of the cash account. The cash account of the Greene Realty Agency, after the balance has been found, appears as follows:

\u200b					*Cash*			ACCOUNT NO. *11*	
DATE	ITEMS	POST. REF.	DEBIT	DATE	ITEMS	POST. REF.	CREDIT		
1957 Oct. 1	*Balance*	*1*	3 7 1 00	*1957* Oct. 31		2	7 2 3 93		
31		*1087.67*	2 1 4 4 0 60						

67

In finding the balance of the cash account proceed as follows:

Step 1. Add the amounts in the Debit column; write the total in small figures immediately under the last amount in that column. Use a sharp, firm pencil.

A soft lead pencil may blur, and a dull pencil point will not make small figures. The footing is written very small so the next line can be used for another entry.

Step 2. If there were several entries in the Credit column, you should add them and record the footing the same as you did in the Debit column. Since there is only one entry on the credit side of this account, it is not necessary to make a pencil footing.

Step 3. Find the difference between the totals of the two sides of the cash account:

Total of debit side of cash account......................	$1,811.60
Total of credit side of cash account......................	723.93
Difference between two sides.........................	$1,087.67

The difference between the two sides of the cash account, $1,087.67, is known as the *balance* of the account.

Step 4. Write the amount of the balance in the Items column on the side with the larger total even with the column footing.

Comparing the amount of cash on hand with the balance of the cash account. On October 31, the Greene Realty Agency had cash on hand amounting to $1,087.67. The balance of the cash account was also $1,087.67. Since the cash on hand is found to agree with the balance of the cash account, cash is said to be *proved*.

A disagreement between the cash account balance and the amount of cash on hand would have indicated that one or more errors had been made either in handling the cash or in the bookkeeping records. When the cash account does not prove, the error should be found and corrected.

The trial balance. The debits in the journal were found in Chapter 5 to be equal to the credits. If no errors were made in posting, the total of all debit amounts in the ledger should equal the total of all credit amounts in the ledger. It follows, then, that a method of testing the accuracy of posting is to prove the equality of the debits and the credits in the ledger.

The proof of the equality of the debits and the credits in the ledger is called a *trial balance*. It consists of a list of the account titles with their balances arranged in a debit column and a credit column and each column totaled. (See the illustration of a trial balance on page 72.)

If the two totals of the trial balance are equal, the posting of the journal is assumed to be correct.

Footing the accounts. Since account balances are recorded on the trial balance, all accounts should be footed before the preparation of the trial balance is started. The cash account was footed in connection with the proving of cash. The method of footing other accounts depends on the number of entries in each account.

When an account has only one entry, it is not necessary to write a footing or a balance. The one amount in the account is the footing and the balance. Such an account is Account No. 12, Automobile, illustrated in the ledger below.

When an account has several entries on each side, both the Debit column and the Credit column are footed. The footing of the smaller side is subtracted from that of the larger side. The difference between the two footings is written in the Items column on the side of the account that has the larger total. This amount is the balance of the account. Account No. 13, Office Furniture, in the ledger on page 70 shows this method of footing.

When an account has only one debit entry and one credit entry, footings are not needed in the Debit and the Credit columns because the amounts are the footings. The balance is written in the Items column on the side that has the larger amount. Account No. 21, Adams Company, illustrates this method.

When an account has two or more entries on one side only, that side is footed, but the balance is not written in the Items column because the footing is the balance. Account No. 51, Advertising Expense, illustrates this method of footing.

A complete ledger containing the necessary footings for all accounts is illustrated below and on pages 70 and 71.

Cash   ACCOUNT NO. *11*

DATE		ITEMS	POST. REF.	DEBIT	DATE	ITEMS	POST. REF.	CREDIT
1957 Oct.	*1*	Balance	*1*	37 00	*1957* Oct. 31		*2*	723 93
	31		*1087.67*	1,440 60				

Automobile   ACCOUNT NO. *12*

DATE		ITEMS	POST. REF.	DEBIT	DATE	ITEMS	POST. REF.	CREDIT
1957 Oct.	*1*	Balance	*1*	3170 00				

A ledger with the accounts footed

Office Furniture   ACCOUNT NO. 13

DATE		ITEMS	POST. REF.	DEBIT	DATE		ITEMS	POST. REF.	CREDIT
1957 Oct.	1	Balance	1	745 60	1957 Oct.	1		2	20 00
	2		2	37 50		5		2	18 00
	3	774.10	2	39 00 822 10		18		2	48 00

Office Machines   ACCOUNT NO. 14

DATE		ITEMS	POST. REF.	DEBIT	DATE		ITEMS	POST. REF.	CREDIT
1957 Oct.	1	Balance	1	254 40	1957 Oct.	2		2	15 00
	3		2	76 00					
	12	490.40	2	175 00 505 40					

Adams Company   ACCOUNT NO. 21

DATE		ITEMS	POST. REF.	DEBIT	DATE		ITEMS	POST. REF.	CREDIT
1957 Oct.	1		2	25 00	1957 Oct.	1	Balance 66.00	1	91 00

Daniels Company   ACCOUNT NO. 22

DATE		ITEMS	POST. REF.	DEBIT	DATE		ITEMS	POST. REF.	CREDIT
1957 Oct.	4		2	100 00	1957 Oct.	1	Balance 200.00	1	300 00

Star Garage   ACCOUNT NO. 23

DATE		ITEMS	POST. REF.	DEBIT	DATE		ITEMS	POST. REF.	CREDIT
1957 Oct.	2		2	42 00	1957 Oct.	1	Balance 1158.00	1	1250 00
	18		2	50 00					

J. M. Greene, Capital   ACCOUNT NO. 31

DATE		ITEMS	POST. REF.	DEBIT	DATE		ITEMS	POST. REF.	CREDIT
					1957 Oct.	1	Balance	1	2900 00

A ledger with the accounts footed (continued)

Commissions Income
ACCOUNT NO. 41

DATE	ITEMS	POST. REF.	DEBIT	DATE	ITEMS	POST. REF.	CREDIT
				1957 Oct. 31		2	1377 60

Advertising Expense
ACCOUNT NO. 51

DATE	ITEMS	POST. REF.	DEBIT	DATE	ITEMS	POST. REF.	CREDIT
1957 Oct. 13		2	7 63				
22		2	9 78				

Automobile Expense
ACCOUNT NO. 52

DATE	ITEMS	POST. REF.	DEBIT	DATE	ITEMS	POST. REF.	CREDIT
1957 Oct. 8		2	25 00				

Entertainment Expense
ACCOUNT NO. 53

DATE	ITEMS	POST. REF.	DEBIT	DATE	ITEMS	POST. REF.	CREDIT
1957 Oct. 22		2	5 00				

Miscellaneous Expense
ACCOUNT NO. 54

DATE	ITEMS	POST. REF.	DEBIT	DATE	ITEMS	POST. REF.	CREDIT
1957 Oct. 16		2	4 50				
25		2	7 52				

Rent Expense
ACCOUNT NO. 55

DATE	ITEMS	POST. REF.	DEBIT	DATE	ITEMS	POST. REF.	CREDIT
1957 Oct. 5		2	120 00				

A ledger with the accounts footed (concluded)

Step 1 ▶

Greene Realty Agency
Trial Balance
October 31, 1957

Step 2 ▶

Account	No.	Debit	Credit
Cash	11	1087 67	
Automobile	12	3170 00	
Office Furniture	13	774 10	
Office Machines	14	490 40	
Adams Company	21		66 00
Daniels Company	22		200 00
Star Garage	23		1158 00
J. M. Greene, Capital	31		2900 00
Commissions Income	41		1377 60
Advertising Expense	51	17 41	
Automobile Expense	52	25 00	
Entertainment Expense	53	5 00	
Miscellaneous Expense	54	12 02	
Rent Expense	55	120 00		◀ **Step 3**
		5701 60	5701 60	◀ **Step 4**

▲ **Step 5**

Trial balance

How to prepare a trial balance. In making a trial balance proceed as follows:

Step 1. Write the trial balance heading at the top of a sheet of paper that has two amount columns.

The heading consists of three lines: (1) the name of the business, (2) the words "Trial Balance," and (3) the date. The date is the month, the day, and the year for which the trial balance is prepared.

Step 2. Enter on the trial balance each account in the ledger that has a balance. In each case record the account title, the account number, and the balance. If the balance is a debit, enter it in the left-hand or debit amount column; if the amount is a credit, enter it in the right-hand or credit amount column.

Step 3. Show that each amount column of the trial balance is to be added by ruling a single line across both amount columns under the last amount listed.

Step 4. Add each amount column. Write the totals on the first line below the single ruling.

Step 5. Indicate that the trial balance is correct by ruling a double line under the totals across the amount columns. Note how the totals have been entered and the trial balance has been ruled in the illustration.

In bookkeeping a double ruling indicates that the work has been completed. The double line should not be drawn until the trial balance is in balance. The ruling may be made in red or black. All lines should be drawn with the aid of a ruler.

Proof provided by the trial balance. If the two totals of the trial balance are equal, the trial balance is said to be *in balance.* The person preparing the trial balance can assume that there is equality of debits and credits in the ledger.

But a trial balance that is in balance does not prove the complete accuracy of the bookkeeping records. For example, if the $25.00 debited to the Adams Company account on October 1 had been posted by mistake to the debit side of the Star Garage account, the trial balance would still be in balance. An error of this kind should be discovered when monthly statements of account are received from these two creditors.

If the recording of a transaction is omitted entirely, the ledger will still be in balance and the error will not be indicated by the trial balance. If, however, the omitted transaction affects cash, the error will be shown when the cash balance is proved. The balance of the cash account will not agree with the cash actually on hand.

Finding errors when a trial balance is out of balance. Proceed as follows in checking a trial balance out of balance:

Step 1. Add again each column of the trial balance. (One or both of the columns may have been added incorrectly.)

Step 2. Find the amount of the difference between the debit total and the credit total of the trial balance. Look in the ledger for this amount. The amount of the difference may be the balance of an account that has been omitted from the trial balance. Also look in the journal for this amount. Perhaps this amount was not posted when it should have been.

Step 3. Divide the amount of the difference between the debit total and the credit total of the trial balance by 2. Look in the ledger to see if this amount has been recorded on the wrong side of a ledger account or in the wrong column of the trial balance. This kind of error makes the trial balance off by twice the amount of the error.

Step 4. Divide the difference between the debit total and the credit total of the trial balance by 9. If the difference is divisible by 9, figures in an amount may have been transposed. For example, an amount of $36.00 may have been transposed by writing $63.00, in which case the trial balance would be out of balance $27.00.

Step 5. Compare the balances on the trial balance with the balances in the ledger accounts. An error may have been made in copying the account balance on the trial balance.

Step 6. Verify the pencil footings and the account balances in the ledger. An error may have been made in footing an account or in determining the balance.

Step 7. Verify the posting of each item in the journal. As each posting is verified, place a small check mark ($\sqrt{}$) on the double vertical line at the left of the corresponding amount in both the journal and the ledger. An item may have been (a) posted twice, (b) not posted at all, (c) entered on the wrong side of an account, or (d) copied incorrectly.

Step 8. Examine first the journal and then the ledger to find items not checked or items that have been checked twice.

The error or errors should now be found because all of the work has been retraced.

Correcting errors as they are found in the ledger. If an item has been posted to the wrong side of an account, a line should be drawn through the incorrect posting and the item should then be posted correctly, as follows:

DATE	ITEMS	POST. REF.	DEBIT	DATE	ITEMS	POST. REF.	CREDIT
1951 Oct. 1	Balance	1	2 54 40	*1951* Oct. 2		2	1 5 0 0
3		2	7 6 00	3		2	7 6 0 0

Office Machines — ACCOUNT NO. *14*

Correction of the posting to the wrong side of an account

If an amount has been posted incorrectly, a line should be drawn through the incorrect amount in the account and the correct amount should then be written above it, as follows:

DATE	ITEMS	POST. REF.	DEBIT	DATE	ITEMS	POST. REF.	CREDIT
1951 Oct. 1		2	25 00 / 2 5 0	*1951* Oct. 1	Balance	1	9 1 0 0

Adams Company — ACCOUNT NO. *21*

Correction of the posting of a wrong amount

If an item has been posted to the wrong account, a line should be drawn through the incorrect posting and the item should be posted correctly. If the posting of an item has been omitted, the amount should be posted at once. If an item has been posted twice, a line should be drawn through the second posting in the account.

An error in a pencil footing in the ledger should be erased and the correct pencil footing should be substituted for it.

Correcting errors in the trial balance. If an account balance has been omitted from the trial balance, it should be inserted in its proper position. If an account balance has been placed in the wrong column of the trial balance, the amount should be erased or canceled with a line and the same amount should be written in the correct column. A similar correction should be made for a balance copied incorrectly. The trial balance totals should also be corrected.

CHAPTER QUESTIONS

1. What are the steps that should be followed in proving cash?
2. What are the steps that should be followed in finding the balance of the cash account?
3. Where is the pencil footing of each side of an account written?
4. Why should the pencil footings of an account be written very small?
5. Where is the difference between the pencil footings of the two sides of an account written?
6. What is the purpose of a trial balance?
7. What are the three parts of the heading of a trial balance?
8. What are the steps that should be followed in preparing a trial balance?
9. What are the steps that should be followed in finding errors when a trial balance is out of balance?
10. What kind of errors in journalizing and posting are not detected by a trial balance?
11. How is the posting of an amount to the wrong account in the ledger corrected?
12. How is an incorrect posting of an amount to the ledger corrected?

INCREASING YOUR BUSINESS VOCABULARY

What is the meaning of each of the following:

    (a) proving cash   (d) trial balance in balance
    (b) account balance   (e) trial balance out of balance
    (c) trial balance

CASES FOR DISCUSSION

1. After all posting has been completed, the balance of R. J. Lane's cash account does not agree with the amount of cash on hand. What steps should he take to find the error?
2. Which of the following errors would not be indicated by the trial balance:
   (a) In posting the October journal of the Greene Realty Agency, the debit of $42.00 to the Star Garage account was posted to the debit side of the Daniels Company account.
   (b) On October 16 the debit of $4.50 to the miscellaneous expense account was posted to the credit side of that account.
   (c) The office furniture account balance of $774.10 was not listed on the trial balance.
   (d) The debit balance of $17.41 in the advertising expense account was written in the credit column of the trial balance.
3. Explain the method of correcting each of the errors listed in Case 2.

DRILL FOR UNDERSTANDING

Drill 7-A. *Instructions: 1.* On a sheet of paper, copy in one column the ledger account titles that are given below.

1. Advertising Expense
2. Atlas Company (creditor)
3. Automobile
4. Automobile Expense
5. Cash
6. Commissions Income
7. Drake Company (creditor)
8. Electricity Expense
9. Kenneth Hackett, Capital
10. Office Furniture
11. Office Machines
12. Rent Expense
13. Rolfe Garage (creditor)
14. Stationery Expense

Instructions: 2. Rule three columns at the right of your list of accounts and write in the headings shown in the form below.

Account Titles	Classifi-cation	Trial Balance	
		Debit	Credit
1. Advertising Expense	E	√	

Instructions: 3. Classify each item on your list as an asset, a liability, proprietorship, an income, or an expense by writing in the Classification column a capital: A for Asset
L for Liability
P for Proprietorship
I for Income
E for Expense

Instructions: 4. Indicate whether the balance of each account will appear in the Debit column or the Credit column of the trial balance by making a check mark in the appropriate column.

The first item is given as an example.

5. Now cover your answers and see how rapidly you can classify these accounts orally without looking at your answers. Repeat this drill orally several times for increased speed and accuracy.

APPLICATION PROBLEMS

Problem 7-1. Taking a trial balance

If you are not using the workbook correlating with this textbook, complete Exercise 7-A in the Appendix instead of this problem.

The ledger accounts of G. P. Grant on October 31 of the current year are given in the workbook.

Instructions: 1. Foot the ledger accounts. Write the footings in very small figures with a sharp pencil and place each footing close to the last item. If an account has entries on both sides, write the balance in small pencil figures in the Items column of the larger side.

2. Prove cash. The cash on hand on October 31 of the current year, by actual count, is $740.32. This amount should agree with the balance of the cash account in the ledger.

3. Prepare a trial balance dated October 31 of the current year. If the two totals of the trial balance are equal, rule single and double lines as shown on the model trial balance on page 72.

Self-checking: Compare your ledger with the illustrations on pages 69 to 71 and ask yourself the following questions:

(a) Were the pencil footings written in the ledger in small figures with a sharp, firm pencil?

(b) Was each amount column of an account footed when, and only when, it contained two or more entries?

(c) For each account having one or more entries on both the debit and the credit sides, was the balance of the account written in small pencil figures in the Items column of the larger side?

Problem 7-2. Finding and correcting errors indicated by a trial balance

If you are not using the workbook correlating with this textbook, complete Exercise 7-B in the Appendix instead of this problem.

The journal and the ledger accounts of William Johnson after the posting of the entries for November of the current year are given in the workbook.

Instructions: 1. Foot the ledger accounts. Write the footings in very small figures with a sharp pencil and place each footing close to the last item. If an account has entries on both sides, write the balance in small pencil figures in the Items column of the larger side.

2. Prove cash. The cash on hand on November 30 of the current year, by actual count, is $2,002.96.

3. Prepare a trial balance dated November 30 of the current year. If the two totals of the trial balance are not equal, proceed as you were directed in Steps 1-8, pages 73 and 74, to find the error or errors. Correct any errors in the journal or the ledger, using the methods explained and illustrated on pages 45, 74, and 75. Then complete the trial balance.

Journal, ledger, and trial balance

Purpose of Project 1. This project makes use of all the steps in the book-keeping process that have been developed in the preceding seven chapters. It requires:

(a) Opening the necessary accounts in the ledger.
(b) Journalizing a series of selected transactions.
(c) Posting from the journal.
(d) Preparing a trial balance.

Henry Realty Agency

George Henry is the owner of the Henry Realty Agency. His ledger contains the following accounts with the balances shown:

List of accounts and balances

(1) ASSETS

ACCT.
No.
11. Cash, $375.60
12. Automobile, $3,600.00
13. Office Furniture, $901.00
14. Office Machines, $574.40

(2) LIABILITIES

21. Duffy's Garage, $1,800.00
22. Gates Brothers, $651.00

(3) PROPRIETORSHIP

31. George Henry, Capital, $3,000.00

(4) INCOME

ACCT.
No.
41. Commissions Income

(5) EXPENSES

51. Advertising Expense
52. Automobile Expense
53. Entertainment Expense
54. Miscellaneous Expense
55. Rent Expense

Items are to be charged to the expense accounts as follows:

Advertising Expense is debited for all advertising for the business.

Automobile Expense is debited for the cost of operating the automobile for business purposes.

Entertainment Expense is debited for the cost of entertaining prospective customers.

Miscellaneous Expense is debited for expenses such as postage, stationery, electricity, telephone service, and any expense item not covered by other expense accounts.

Rent Expense is debited for rent.

Instructions: 1. Open the accounts shown in the list on page 78 and copy the balances. Date these balances November 1 of the current year. (If you are not using the workbook correlating with this textbook, allow four lines for each account.) Number the accounts with the numbers shown in the list of accounts.

Recording transactions in the journal

Instructions: 2. Record the following transactions on page 2 of a columnar journal similar to the journal illustrated on page 58.

Nov. 1. Received $700.00 as commission on the sale of a house and lot. (Receipt No. 1)
　　1. Paid $150.00 for rent for November. (Check No. 1)
　　2. Paid $10.00 for dinner for prospective customers. (Check No. 2)
　　4. Paid $10.00 for postage stamps. (Check No. 3)
　　5. Paid $250.00 for a new typewriter. (Check No. 4)
　　6. Paid $32.40 for advertising handbills. (Check No. 5)
　　8. Received $120.00 as commission for the rental of a house. (Receipt No. 2)
　　9. Received $12.00 as commission for renting a garage. (Receipt No. 3)
　　11. Paid $10.80 for gas and oil for the automobile. (Check No. 6)
　　11. Received $200.00 as commission on the sale of a house. (Receipt No. 4)
　　12. Paid $69.18 for advertisements in last week's paper. (Check No. 7)
　　12. Paid $9.60 for gas and oil for the automobile. (Check No. 8)
　　15. Received $800.00 as commission on the sale of a house. (Receipt No. 5)
　　16. Paid $30.00 for additional office furniture. (Check No. 9)
　　20. Received $50.00 as commission on the rental of second-floor apartment. (Receipt No. 6)
　　20. Paid $43.50 for a new chair for the office. (Check No. 10)
　　22. Paid $26.50 for advertisements. (Check No. 11)
　　22. Paid $13.00 for dinner for prospective customers. (Check No. 12)
　　22. Received $33.90 from sale of old office furniture. (Receipt No. 7)
　　23. Received $84.00 as commission for obtaining a tenant for a house. (Receipt No. 8)
　　25. Received $70.00 as commission for the rental of a house. (Receipt No. 9)
　　26. Paid $60.00 to Gates Brothers on account. (Check No. 13)
　　29. Received $170.00 as commission for the rental of a store building. (Receipt No. 10)
　　30. Paid $10.00 for gas and oil for the automobile. (Check No. 14)
　　30. Paid $24.60 for the electric light bill for the month of November. (Check No. 15)
　　30. Paid $14.00 for telephone service for the month. (Check No. 16)
　　30. Paid $500.00 to Duffy's Garage on account. (Check No. 17)

Posting the journal entries to the ledger accounts

Instructions: **3.** Foot all columns of the journal and prove the equality of debits and credits. Total and rule the journal. (See model on page 58.)

4. Complete the posting of the amounts in the General Debit and the General Credit columns of the journal. Make a check mark ($\sqrt{}$) under the totals of the General Debit and the General Credit columns to show that these totals are not to be posted. (See model on page 58.)

5. Post the total of each of the three special columns of the journal: Cash Debit, Cash Credit, and Commissions Income Credit. Write the proper account number under each total after the posting is completed. (See model on page 58.)

Footing and proving the cash account

Instructions: **6.** Foot the cash account and enter the balance. (See model on page 67.)

7. Prove cash. The cash on hand determined by actual count is $1,351.92.

Preparing a trial balance

Instructions: **8.** Foot the accounts that have more than one entry on either side. If an account has entries on both sides, write the balance in small pencil figures in the Items column. (See model on pages 69 to 71.)

9. Prepare a trial balance. (See model on page 72.)

The six-column work sheet

Need for interpreting the trial balance. J. M. Greene, the proprietor of the Greene Realty Agency, is interested in learning at regular intervals whether his transactions have resulted in a profit or a loss. All of the needed information is in the ledger. Since the ledger is summarized in the trial balance, it is possible to calculate the amount of the profit or the amount of the loss directly from the trial balance.

The nature of the trial balance. The trial balance lists accounts in the order in which they appear in the ledger. The accounts in the trial balance of the Greene Realty Agency are arranged as follows:

GREENE REALTY AGENCY
Trial Balance
October 31, 1957

Balance Sheet Items							
(1) *Assets*	Cash	11	1,087	67			
	Automobile	12	3,170	00			
	Office Furniture	13	774	10			
	Office Machines	14	490	40			
(2) *Liabilities*	Adams Company	21			66	00	
	Daniels Company	22			200	00	
	Star Garage	23			1,158	00	
(3) *Proprietorship*	J. M. Greene, Capital	31			2,900	00	
Income and Expense Items							
(4) *Income*	Commissions Income	41			1,377	60	
(5) *Expenses*	Advertising Expense	51	17	41			
	Automobile Expense	52	25	00			
	Entertainment Expense	53	5	00			
	Miscellaneous Expense	54	12	02			
	Rent Expense	55	120	00			
			5,701	60	5,701	60	

Analysis paper. The modern method of analyzing the trial balance is to use a single sheet of paper with six or more amount columns and to distribute the balances among these amount columns. The number of columns used depends on the kind and the size of the enterprise. Accounting paper with a number of amount columns that are used for analysis purposes is known as *analysis paper*.

The work sheet. Analysis paper that provides for the sorting and the interpreting of the trial balance on a single sheet of paper is called a *work sheet*. The work sheet of the Greene Realty Agency for the month ended October 31, 1957, is shown on the next page.

Analyzing the work sheet. The work sheet is a bookkeeper's working paper and is not a part of the permanent bookkeeping record. It may therefore be prepared with a pencil. The chief purpose of the work sheet is to provide a sorting process that makes it possible to calculate the profit (or the loss) with the minimum amount of work. The work sheet also provides a convenient method of summarizing the bookkeeping records and proving the accuracy of all calculations.

Step 1 — Write the heading. The heading is written in three lines at the top of the form. The first line is the name of the business, "Greene Realty Agency"; the second line is the name of the form, "Work Sheet"; and the third line shows the length and the date of the period for which the analysis is made, "For Month Ended October 31, 1957." The period for which an analysis of the operations of the business is made is called an *accounting period* or a *fiscal period*. It may be any length of time desired, such as four weeks, one month, three months, six months, or one year.

Step 2 — Write the column headings. If column headings are not printed on the analysis paper, write the headings shown in the illustration of the work sheet on page 83.

Step 3 — Write the trial balance. The trial balance is written in the columns at the left of the work sheet. The addition of the amounts in the Trial Balance columns (Columns 1 and 2) is indicated by a single ruled line, and the completion of this part of the work sheet is indicated by the double ruled lines immediately below the trial balance totals.

> The information in the Account Titles, Account No., and Trial Balance columns on the work sheet of the Greene Realty Agency is exactly the same as the information in the trial balance on page 72. When a work sheet is prepared at the same time that a trial balance is taken, the trial balance is recorded directly on the work sheet.

Step 4 — Extend the balance sheet items to the Balance Sheet columns. At the end of each fiscal period a report is prepared to show the assets (what is owned), the liabilities (what is owed), and the proprietorship (what the business is worth). The report showing the assets, the liabilities, and the proprietorship on a specified date is known as the *balance sheet*.

Before the balance sheet is typewritten or is prepared in ink, it is desirable to assemble it quickly in pencil on the work sheet. To sort out

	ACCOUNT TITLES	ACCT. NO.	TRIAL BALANCE		P. & L. STATEMENT		BALANCE SHEET		
			DEBIT	CREDIT	DEBIT	CREDIT	DEBIT	CREDIT	
1	Cash	11	108767				108767		1
2	Automobile	12	317000				317000		2
3	Office Furniture	13	77410				77410		3
4	Office Machines	14	49040				49040		4
5	Adams Company	21		6600				6600	5
6	Daniels Company	22		20000				20000	6
7	Star Garage	23		115800				115800	7
8	J. M. Greene, Capital	31		290000				290000	8
9	Commissions Income	41		137760		137760			9
10	Advertising Expense	51	1741		1741				10
11	Automobile Expense	52	2500		2500				11
12	Entertainment Expense	53	500		500				12
13	Miscellaneous Expense	54	1202		1202				13
14	Rent Expense	55	12000		12000				14
15			570160	570160	17943	137760	552217	432400	15
16	Net Profit				119817			119817	16
17					137760	137760	552217	552217	17

Six-column work sheet

the items for the balance sheet, extend the amount of each asset from the Trial Balance Debit column to the Balance Sheet Debit column (Column 5). Then extend the amount of each liability and the amount of the proprietorship from the Trial Balance Credit column to the Balance Sheet Credit column (Column 6).

Step 5 — Extend the income and expense items to the P. & L. Statement columns. At the end of each fiscal period a report is also prepared to show the income earned during the period, the expenses incurred during the period, and the amount of the net profit or the net loss. If the income is larger than the expenses, the amount of the difference is called *net profit*. If the expenses are larger than the income, the amount of the difference is called *net loss*. The report showing the income, the expenses, and the net profit or the net loss is known as the *profit and loss statement*.

The Profit and Loss Statement columns of the work sheet provide the information from which the profit and loss statement is prepared. To sort out the items for this statement, extend the amount of the commissions income, which is in the Trial Balance Credit column, into the P. & L. Statement Credit column (Column 4). Also extend the amounts of the expenses, which are in the Trial Balance Debit column, into the P. & L. Statement Debit column (Column 3).

Step 6 — Find the net profit. After the account balances on the trial balance have been sorted into the P. & L. Statement columns and the Balance Sheet columns, these columns are totaled. A partial work sheet on which these totals have been entered is shown below:

ACCOUNT TITLES	ACCT. NO.	TRIAL BALANCE		P. & L. STATEMENT		BALANCE SHEET		
		DEBIT	CREDIT	DEBIT	CREDIT	DEBIT	CREDIT	
1 *Greene Realty Agency Work Sheet For Month Ended October 31, 1957*								
1 Cash	11	1087 67				1087 67		1
2 Automobile	12	3170 00				3170 00		2
3 Office Furniture	13	774 10				774 10		3
11 Automobile Expense	52	25 00		25 00				11
12 Entertainment Expense	53	5 00		5 00				12
13 Miscellaneous Expense	54	12 02		12 02				13
14 Rent Expense	55	120 00		120 00				14
15		5701 60	5701 60	179 43	1377 60	5522 17	4324 00	15

The net profit made during the period may now be found from the totals of these columns in two different ways. These two ways are:

1. Net profit from profit and loss statement columns

The net profit is the difference between the income and the expenses. The net profit may therefore be found as follows:

Total of P. & L. Statement Credit column (income)............... $1,377.60
Total of P. & L. Statement Debit column (expenses)............. 179.43

Net profit (income minus expenses)............................ $1,198.17

2. Net profit from balance sheet columns

Assets equal liabilities plus proprietorship. If the assets are greater than the liabilities plus the invested capital, the difference is net profit, which is a part of the proprietorship. The net profit may therefore be found as follows:

Total of Balance Sheet Debit column (assets).................... $5,522.17
Total of Balance Sheet Credit column (liabilities plus invested capital) 4,324.00

Net profit (assets minus liabilities and invested capital)............ $1,198.17

If the net profit obtained from the profit and loss statement columns is the same as that obtained from the balance sheet columns, both calculations are assumed to be correct.

*Step 7 — **Balance the columns of the work sheet.*** The amount of the net profit is added to the total of the P. & L. Statement Debit column (Column 3) to prove calculations; the expenses plus the net profit should equal the total income. The same net profit is then added to the Balance Sheet Credit column (Column 6) to prove calculations; the total of the liabilities, the capital, and the profit should equal the total of the assets.

After the net profit has been added to these columns, the footings appear as follows:

Greene Realty Agency
Work Sheet
For Month Ended October 31, 1957

	ACCOUNT TITLES	ACCT. NO.	TRIAL BALANCE		P. & L. STATEMENT		BALANCE SHEET		
			DEBIT	CREDIT	DEBIT	CREDIT	DEBIT	CREDIT	
1	Cash	11	1087 67				1087 67		1
2	Automobile	12	3170 00				3170 00		2
12	Entertainment Expense	53	5 00		5 00				12
13	Miscellaneous Expense	54	12 02		12 02				13
14	Rent Expense	55	120 00		120 00				14
15			5701 60	5701 60	179 43	1377 60	5522 17	4324 00	15
16	Net Profit				1198 17			1198 17	16
17					1377 60	1377 60	5522 17	5522 17	17

Note that the words "Net Profit" are written in the Account Titles column on the line on which the profit is entered. The completion of the columns is indicated by the double ruled lines below the final totals.

CHAPTER QUESTIONS

1. What is the chief purpose of the work sheet?
2. What are the three parts of the heading of the work sheet?
3. To what debit columns in the six-column work sheet are the debit amounts in the trial balance extended?
4. To what credit columns in the six-column work sheet are the credit amounts in the trial balance extended?
5. By what two methods may the net profit be found on the work sheet?
6. In which two columns is the net profit shown on the work sheet?
7. What is indicated when single lines are ruled across amount columns of the work sheet?
8. What is indicated when double lines are ruled under the totals of each double column of the work sheet?

What is the meaning of each of the following:

(a) analysis paper	(d) fiscal period	(g) net loss
(b) work sheet	(e) balance sheet	(h) profit and loss
(c) accounting period	(f) net profit	statement

CASES FOR DISCUSSION

1. The accounts in the ledger of the Greene Realty Agency are arranged in the following order: (1) assets, (2) liabilities, (3) proprietorship, (4) income, (5) expenses.
   (a) What is the purpose of this arrangement?
   (b) Why would it not be desirable to arrange all accounts in the ledger in alphabetic order?

2. The balance of the automobile expense account was transferred by error to the Balance Sheet Debit column of the work sheet.
   (a) Will this error be discovered by the calculation of the net profit on the work sheet?
   (b) What is the effect of this error on the net profit as calculated on the work sheet?
   (c) When is an error of this type likely to be discovered?

DRILL FOR UNDERSTANDING

Drill 8-A. *Instructions: 1.* On the left side of a sheet of paper write *Account Titles* and copy the ledger account titles that are given below. At the top of the right side of the paper write the heading *Classification.*

1. Adams Company	8. Entertainment Expense
2. Advertising Expense	9. J. M. Greene, Capital
3. Automobile	10. Miscellaneous Expense
4. Automobile Expense	11. Office Furniture
5. Cash	12. Office Machines
6. Commissions Income	13. Rent Expense
7. Daniels Company	14. Star Garage

Instructions: 2. You are to show in which section of the work sheet the trial balance amounts will be written. If the account balance is shown in the profit and loss statement section of the work sheet, write *Profit and Loss Statement* after the account name. If the account balance is shown in the balance sheet section of the work sheet, write *Balance Sheet* after the account name. The first item is given as an example.

Account Titles	Classification
1. Adams Company...	*Balance Sheet*

APPLICATION PROBLEMS

Problem 8-1. Work sheet for an insurance agency

The Upham Insurance Agency calculates net profit or net loss for each month. On October 31 of the current year, the account balances in the ledger of the Upham Insurance Agency were as follows:

Cash, $1,469.32

Automobile, $2,500.00

Office Furniture, $650.00

Office Machines, $595.00

Baxter Company (creditor), $495.00

Hale Company (creditor), $798.30

State Garage (creditor), $1,200.34

Ethel Upham, Capital, $2,000.00

Premiums Income, $1,216.00

Advertising Expense, $100.00

Automobile Expense, $75.00

Entertainment Expense, $50.00

Miscellaneous Expense, $150.32

Rent Expense, $120.00

Instructions: Prepare a six-column work sheet for the Upham Insurance Agency, using the account balances given above.

Self-checking: Except for the omission of account numbers, is your work sheet similar in all respects to the model on page 83?

This problem will be continued in the next chapter. If it is collected by your teacher at this time, it will be returned to you before it is needed in Problem 9-1.

Problem 8-2. Work sheet for a theater

The account balances in the ledger of Frank Rimer, proprietor of the Strand Theater, on November 30 of the current year, the end of a fiscal period of one month, were as follows:

Cash, $2,031.12

Air Conditioning Equipment, $3,750.00

Projection Equipment, $9,000.00

Sound Equipment, $542.00

Film Producers, Inc. (creditor), $62.50

International Studios (creditor), $145.00

Majestic Films (creditor), $96.00

Midwest Sound Service (creditor), $34.90

National Supply Co. (creditor), $53.72

Frank Rimer, Capital, $14,290.18

Admissions Income, $1,932.75

Advertising Expense, $108.50

Electricity Expense, $57.50

Film Rental Expense, $837.00

Maintenance Expense, $35.00

Projection Expense, $26.50

Rent Expense, $200.00

Water Expense, $27.43

Instructions: Prepare a six-column work sheet for the Strand Theater, using the account balances given above.

Self-checking: Except for the omission of account numbers, is your work sheet similar in all respects to the model on page 83?

This problem will be continued in the next chapter. If it is collected by your teacher at this time, it will be returned to you before it is needed in Problem 9-2.

The profit and loss statement and the balance sheet

Need for financial statements. If the enterprise is small, the work sheet may be a sufficient analysis for the proprietor. There may, however, be individuals or institutions outside the business that are entitled to some of the information included in the work sheet but not to all of the information. Sometimes these individuals or institutions receive only a report of assets and liabilities, and sometimes they receive only a report of income and expenses. For these reasons, separate financial statements, such as the profit and loss statement and the balance sheet, are commonly prepared from the different sections of the work sheet.

P. & L. Statement section of the work sheet. The profit and loss statement for the Greene Realty Agency is prepared from the P. & L. Statement columns of the work sheet. This section of the work sheet appears as follows:

			1	2	3	4
	ACCOUNT TITLES	ACCT. NO.	TRIAL BALANCE DEBIT	CREDIT	P. & L. STATEMENT DEBIT	CREDIT
9	Commissions Income	41		1377 60		1377 60
10	Advertising Expense	51	17 41		17 41	
11	Automobile Expense	52	25 00		25 00	
12	Entertainment Expense	53	5 00		5 00	
13	Miscellaneous Expense	54	12 02		12 02	
14	Rent Expense	55	120 00		120 00	
15			570 60	570 60	179 43	1377 60
16	Net Profit				1198 17	
17					1377 60	1377 60

Profit and loss statement. The profit and loss statement of the Greene Realty Agency prepared from the P. & L. Statement section of the work sheet is shown on the opposite page.

Heading of the profit and loss statement. Each profit and loss statement covers a definite accounting period. The length of the accounting period is indicated clearly in the heading. The heading of the profit and loss statement for the Greene Realty Agency includes:

1st Line — Name of the business: *Greene Realty Agency*
2nd Line — Name of the form: *Profit and Loss Statement*
3rd Line — {Length of the accounting period: *For Month*
{Date: *Ended October 31, 1957*

The name of the business is written centered on the first line at the top of the profit and loss statement. The name of the form is written centered on the second line of the heading. The length of the accounting period and the date the accounting period ended are written centered on the third line of the heading.

Greene Realty Agency		
Profit and Loss Statement		
For Month Ended October 31, 1957		
Income:		
Commissions Income		1 3 7 7 60
Expenses:		
Advertising Expense	1 7 4 1	
Automobile Expense	2 5 0 0	
Entertainment Expense	5 0 0	
Miscellaneous Expense	1 2 0 2	
Rent Expense	1 2 0 0 0	
Total Expenses		1 7 9 4 3
Net Profit		1 1 9 8 1 7

Profit and loss statement

Income section of the profit and loss statement. The information for preparing the income section of the profit and loss statement is obtained directly from the work sheet P. & L. Statement Credit column.

The heading of the income section is "Income." This heading is written on the first line, beginning at the vertical red rule at the left. The title of the income account, "Commissions Income," is written on the second line, indented about one-half inch. As the Greene Realty Agency receives income from commissions only, the amount of the commissions income is also the amount of the total income. The amount is therefore written in the second column, the column used for totals.

Expense section of the profit and loss statement. The information for preparing the expense section of the profit and loss statement is obtained directly from the work sheet P. & L. Statement Debit column.

The heading of this section is "Expenses." This heading is written at the left margin. The titles of the individual expense accounts are listed

Chapter 9. Profit and loss statement and balance sheet 89

in the same order in which they are given on the work sheet and are indented about one-half inch. The amount of each of these expenses is written in the first amount column, and the total of the expenses is written in the second amount column. The total expenses, $179.43, can then be subtracted conveniently from the total income, $1,377.60.

Net profit. The amount of the net profit has already been calculated on the work sheet. The net profit is calculated also on the profit and loss statement by subtracting the total expenses from the total income. The amount of the net profit shown on the profit and loss statement should agree with the amount of the net profit shown on the work sheet.

Ruling the profit and loss statement. The illustration of the profit and loss statement shows where single lines and double lines should be ruled.

In bookkeeping forms and reports, a single line is drawn across an amount column to indicate either addition or subtraction. In the illustration of the profit and loss statement, a single line is drawn across the first amount column to indicate addition of all of the expense amounts. But a single line is drawn across the second amount column to indicate subtraction of the total expenses from the total income to find the net profit.

Double lines are ruled across the amount columns of a bookkeeping form: (1) after all work has been completed and (2) after all arithmetic has been proved to be accurate. In bookkeeping, double lines are used as a symbol of completion of satisfactory work.

Balance Sheet section of the work sheet. The balance sheet for the Greene Realty Agency is prepared from the Balance Sheet columns of the work sheet. The Balance Sheet section and part of the Trial Balance section of the work sheet are shown below.

			1	2		5	6	
	ACCOUNT TITLES	ACCT. NO.	TRIAL BALANCE			BALANCE SHEET		
			DEBIT	CREDIT		DEBIT	CREDIT	
1	Cash	11	1087 67			1087 67		1
2	Automobile	12	3170 00			3170 00		2
3	Office Furniture	13	774 10			774 10		3
4	Office Machines	14	490 40			490 40		4
5	Adams Company	21		66 00			66 00	5
6	Daniels Company	22		200 00			200 00	6
7	Star Garage	23		1158 00			1158 00	7
8	J. M. Greene, Capital	31		2900 00			2900 00	8
14	Rent Expense	55	120 00					14
15			5701 60	5701 60		5522 17	4324 00	15
16	Net Profit						1198 17	16
17						5522 17	5522 17	17

Heading of the balance sheet. The heading of the balance sheet includes the name of the business, the name of the form, and the date on which it was prepared. Unlike the heading of the profit and loss statement, the heading of the balance sheet does not indicate the length of the fiscal period, because a balance sheet is a picture of the business only at the moment for which it is taken. The heading of the balance sheet of the Greene Realty Agency consists of:

1st Line — Name of the business: *Greene Realty Agency*
2nd Line — Name of the form: *Balance Sheet*
3rd Line — Date for which balance sheet was prepared: *October 31, 1957*

Assets section of the balance sheet. The information for this section is obtained from the Balance Sheet Debit column of the work sheet (Column 5). The account balances are listed in the first amount column. The total of the assets is shown in the second amount column.

Liabilities section of the balance sheet. The information for this section is obtained from the Balance Sheet Credit column of the work sheet (Column 6). The account balances are listed in the first amount column. The total of the liabilities is written in the second amount column.

Greene Realty Agency		
Balance Sheet		
October 31, 1957		
Assets		
Cash	1 087 67	
Automobile	3 170 00	
Office Furniture	7 74 10	
Office Machines	4 90 40	
Total Assets		5 522 17
Liabilities		
Adams Company	66 00	
Daniels Company	2 00 00	
Star Garage	1 158 00	
Total Liabilities		1 424 00
Proprietorship		
J. M. Greene, Capital	2 900 00	
Add Net Profit	1 198 17	
J. M. Greene, Present Capital		4 098 17
Total Liabilities and Proprietorship		5 522 17

Balance sheet in report form

Chapter 9. Profit and loss statement and balance sheet 91

Proprietorship section of the balance sheet. The information for this section is also obtained from the Balance Sheet Credit column of the work sheet (Column 6). The present capital of the proprietor consists of two elements: (1) the balance of the ledger account and (2) the increase in proprietorship caused by net profit. These two amounts are written in the first amount column. The total proprietorship is written in the second amount column.

Ruling the balance sheet. A single line is drawn across an amount column to indicate addition. Double lines are ruled to show that the balance sheet has been completed and proved to be in balance. The double lines are ruled under the totals of the two principal sections of the balance sheet: (1) the assets section and (2) the liabilities and proprietorship section. In the balance sheet of the Greene Realty Agency the two proving totals are $5,522.17. Double lines are ruled under the totals across both amount columns.

Two forms of balance sheet. The balance sheet may be prepared in either of two forms. If the balance sheet items are listed in the ledger account form with the assets at the left and the liabilities and the proprietorship at the right, the arrangement is commonly referred to as the *account form* of balance sheet. If the balance sheet lists the assets, the liabilities, and the proprietorship in a vertical arrangement, with the liabilities and the proprietorship below the assets, the arrangement is known as the *report form* of balance sheet. The report form of balance sheet is illustrated on page 91.

The choice of forms of the balance sheet depends upon the space available. When account titles are long and amounts are large, the account form of the balance sheet requires a very wide form. When the available space is wide, the account form may be used. When the space is narrow, the report form is preferred.

CHAPTER QUESTIONS

1. From what section of the work sheet is the information for construction of the profit and loss statement obtained?
2. What are the parts of the heading of the profit and loss statement?
3. From what section of the work sheet is the information for construction of the balance sheet obtained?
4. What are the parts of the heading of the balance sheet?
5. Why does the amount of the net profit appear on both the profit and loss statement and the balance sheet?
6. How does the account form of balance sheet differ from the report form?

CASES FOR DISCUSSION

1. The heading of the profit and loss statement of the Greene Realty Agency includes the phrase "For Month Ended October 31, 1957." The heading of the balance sheet does not include the words "For Month Ended."
   (a) Which financial statement represents a report covering a period of time?
   (b) Which financial statement represents a report for a given date only?
   (c) Why are the words "For Month Ended" omitted in the heading of the balance sheet?

2. In the profit and loss statement of the Greene Realty Agency the total income is $1,198.17 larger than the total expenses. In the balance sheet of the Greene Realty Agency the total of the assets is $1,198.17 larger than the total of the liabilities plus the beginning proprietorship. Why are these two amounts the same?

DRILL FOR UNDERSTANDING

Drill 9-A. This drill is planned to give you additional skill in determining which ledger account amounts are found on the balance sheet and which ledger account amounts are found on the profit and loss statement.

Instructions: 1. On the left side of a sheet of paper, write the heading *Account Titles.* Then copy the ledger account titles that are given below. Rule two one-inch wide columns at the right of the list. Write the heading *P. & L. Statement* at the top of the first column and *Balance Sheet* at the top of the second column.

1. Cash	13. Automobile Expense
2. Adams Company (creditor)	14. Stationery Expense
3. Automobile	15. Advertising Expense
4. J. M. Greene, Capital	16. Telephone Expense
5. Office Furniture	17. Electricity Expense
6. Office Machines	18. Commissions Income
7. Office Equipment	19. Professional Library
8. Harry Good, Capital	20. Miscellaneous Expense
9. Shop Equipment	21. Entertainment Expense
10. Thomas Cassidy, Capital	22. Premiums Income
11. Kitchen Equipment	23. Supplies Expense
12. Rent Expense	24. Admissions Income

Instructions: 2. If the account title appears on the profit and loss statement, place a check mark in the column headed "P. & L. Statement." If the account title appears on the balance sheet, place a check mark in the column headed "Balance Sheet." The first item is given as an example.

Account Titles	P. & L. Statement	Balance Sheet
1. Cash		✓

Problem 9-1. Financial reports for an insurance agency

The work sheet prepared in Problem 8-1 of Chapter 8 is required for this problem. If Problem 8-1 has not been returned to you, complete Exercise 9-A in the Appendix.

In Problem 8-1 you prepared a work sheet for the Upham Insurance Agency for the month ended October 31 of the current year.

Instructions: 1. Prepare a profit and loss statement, using the profit and loss columns of the work sheet you completed in Problem 8-1.

2. Prepare a balance sheet in report form, using the balance sheet columns of the work sheet you completed in Problem 8-1.

Self-checking: (1) Is your profit and loss statement similar to the model on page 89?

(2) Is your balance sheet similar to the model on page 91?

Problem 9-2. Financial reports for a theater

The work sheet prepared in Problem 8-2 of Chapter 8 is required for this problem. If Problem 8-2 has not been returned to you, complete Exercise 9-B in the Appendix.

In Problem 8-2 you prepared a work sheet for the Strand Theater for the month ended November 30 of the current year.

Instructions: 1. Prepare a profit and loss statement, using the profit and loss columns of the work sheet you completed in Problem 8-2.

2. Prepare a balance sheet in report form, using the balance sheet columns of the work sheet you completed in Problem 8-2.

Self-checking: (1) Is your profit and loss statement similar to the model on page 89?

(2) Is your balance sheet similar to the model on page 91?

Need for bringing the proprietorship section of the ledger up to date. At the time the balance sheet of the Greene Realty Agency was prepared on October 31, 1957, the proprietor's capital account in the ledger appeared as follows:

					J. M. Greene, Capital			ACCOUNT NO. 31
DATE	ITEMS	POST. REF.	DEBIT		DATE	ITEMS	POST. REF.	CREDIT
					1957 Oct. 1	Balance	1	2900 00

But the proprietorship section of the balance sheet on October 31 shows Mr. Greene's present capital to be $4,098.17. The difference between what the ledger account shows and what the balance sheet shows is due to the net profit, $1,198.17. This net profit should be shown in the proprietorship section of the ledger.

Where is the net profit shown in the ledger? Increases in proprietorship during the month are recorded in the commissions income account. Decreases in proprietorship during the month are recorded in several expense accounts. These separate accounts are used in order to make it possible to prepare a profit and loss statement that will have detailed information.

Need for a profit and loss summary account in the ledger. After the profit and loss statement is completed, it is desirable to show the net profit as a single figure in one account. This is done by transferring all of the balances of the income and the expense accounts to a summarizing account. The account to which the balances of all income and expense accounts are transferred at the end of the fiscal period is known as the *profit and loss summary* account.

95

Relationship of profit and loss summary account to income section and expense section of ledger. The balance of the commissions income account and the balances of the several expense accounts are shown in the chart below. The *debit* balances of the expense accounts are transferred to the *debit* side of the profit and loss summary account. The *credit* balance of the commissions income account is transferred to the *credit* side of the profit and loss summary account.

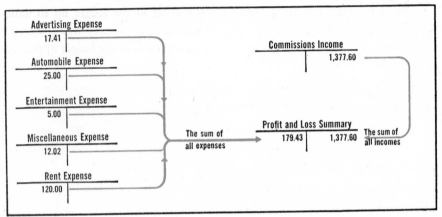

Diagram showing flow of expenses and income to Profit and Loss Summary

When these transfers of account balances have been completed, the profit and loss summary account shows on the debit side the total expenses for the fiscal period and on the credit side the total income for the same period. The difference between the two sides of the profit and loss summary account shows the net increase or the net decrease in proprietorship. For this reason the profit and loss summary account is placed in the proprietorship section of the ledger.

Bookkeeping procedure in transferring account balances. In bookkeeping, all transfers from one account in the ledger to another account should first be recorded in the journal. When these journal entries are posted to the ledger accounts, the income and the expense accounts are in balance and the former balances of these accounts are recorded in the profit and loss summary account.

This procedure of using journal entries to transfer account balances in the ledger is desirable because (1) it helps the bookkeeper to avoid errors and (2) it is easier to audit the work of the bookkeeper if all transfers of account balances are first recorded together in the journal.

An entry in the journal to transfer the balance of one account to another account is referred to as a *closing entry*.

Closing the income account. The information necessary for closing the income and the expense accounts is found in the profit and loss statement columns of the work sheet. The balances of the income and the expense accounts are transferred to the profit and loss summary account in the same order in which they appear on the work sheet. According to the work sheet, the first account in the Greene Realty Agency ledger to be transferred to the profit and loss summary account is the commissions income account. The balance of the commissions income account, $1,377.60, is shown in the P. & L. Statement Credit column of the work sheet as follows:

	ACCOUNT TITLES	ACCT. NO.	TRIAL BALANCE		P. & L. STATEMENT	
			DEBIT	CREDIT	DEBIT	CREDIT
9	Commissions Income	41		1 3 7 7 6 0		1 3 7 7 6 0

All income account credit balances are transferred to the credit side of the profit and loss summary account. There is only one income account, Commissions Income, in the Greene Realty Agency ledger.

Before any closing entry is made, the commissions income account and the profit and loss summary account appear as shown below.

Profit and Loss Summary   ACCOUNT NO. 33

DATE	ITEMS	POST. REF.	DEBIT	DATE	ITEMS	POST. REF.	CREDIT

Commissions Income   ACCOUNT NO. 41

DATE	ITEMS	POST. REF.	DEBIT	DATE	ITEMS	POST. REF.	CREDIT
				1951 Oct. 31		2	1 3 7 7 6 0

Since the balance of the commissions income account is a *credit* before the transfer, it will be a *credit* item in the profit and loss summary account after the transfer. The amount to be *credited* to Profit and Loss Summary is $1,377.60.

To show that the commissions income account has been transferred, it is necessary to reduce the commissions income account balance to zero. This is accomplished by *debiting* the commissions income account for $1,377.60. The journal entry to transfer the credit balance of the commissions income account to the credit side of the profit and loss summary account is shown at the top of the following page.

		CASH		DATE	NAME OF ACCOUNT	NO.	POST. REF.	GENERAL		COMMISSIONS INCOME CREDIT	
		DEBIT	CREDIT					DEBIT	CREDIT		
1					*Closing Entries*						1
2				1957 Oct. 31	Commissions Income	41		1377 60			2
3					Profit and Loss Summary	33			1377 60		3
4											4
5											5
6											6
7											7
8											8
9											9
10											10

The words "Closing Entries" are written in the Name of Account column before the first closing entry is made. This heading explains the nature of the three closing entries, and therefore a separate explanation for each closing entry is unnecessary.

After the journal entry illustrated above has been posted, the two accounts affected by it appear as follows:

Profit and Loss Summary   ACCOUNT NO. 33

DATE	ITEMS	POST. REF.	DEBIT	DATE	ITEMS	POST. REF.	CREDIT
				1957 Oct. 31		3	1377 60

Commissions Income   ACCOUNT NO. 41

DATE	ITEMS	POST. REF.	DEBIT	DATE	ITEMS	POST. REF.	CREDIT
1957 Oct. 31		3	1377 60	1957 Oct. 31		2	1377 60

An income or an expense account with equal debits and credits is said to be a *closed account*. Note that the commissions income account illustrated above is now closed. Note also that the original balance of the commissions income account, which was a *credit* balance of $1,377.60, has now been transferred to the *credit* side of the profit and loss summary account.

If there were other income accounts, their balances would be transferred to Profit and Loss Summary in the same manner as the balance of the commissions income account was transferred.

Closing the expense accounts. The balances of the expense accounts as shown in the P. & L. Statement Debit column of the work sheet are:

	ACCOUNT TITLES	ACCT. NO.	TRIAL BALANCE		P. & L. STATEMENT	
			DEBIT	CREDIT	DEBIT	CREDIT
10	Advertising Expense	51	17 41		17 41	
11	Automobile Expense	52	25 00		25 00	
12	Entertainment Expense	53	5 00		5 00	
13	Miscellaneous Expense	54	12 02		12 02	
14	Rent Expense	55	120 00		120 00	
15			570 60	570 60	179 43	1377 60

All expense account debit balances are transferred to the debit side of the profit and loss summary account.

The expense accounts are closed in the order in which they appear on the work sheet. All of the expense account balances are transferred to the profit and loss summary account in one entry. Since all the expense account balances are *debits* before the transfer is made, the total of all the expense account balances will be a *debit* item in the profit and loss summary account after the transfer is completed. The sum of the expense account balances is $179.43. The amount to be *debited* to Profit and Loss Summary is therefore $179.43.

To show that the balances of the expense accounts have been transferred, it is necessary to reduce each account balance to zero. This is accomplished by *crediting* each expense account with the amount of its balance. The journal entry to transfer the debit balances of the expense accounts to the debit side of the profit and loss summary account is:

CASH		DATE	NAME OF ACCOUNT	NO.	POST. REF.	GENERAL		COMMISSIONS INCOME CREDIT
DEBIT	CREDIT					DEBIT	CREDIT	
		31	Profit and Loss Summary		33	179 43		
			Advertising Expense		51		17 41	
			Automobile Expense		52		25 00	
			Entertainment Expense		53		5 00	
			Miscellaneous Expense		54		12 02	
			Rent Expense		55		120 00	

JOURNAL   PAGE 3

When an entry contains two or more debits or two or more credits that might have been separated into different entries, it is known as a *combined entry*.

The profit and loss summary account and the expense accounts after the entry closing the expense accounts has been posted are shown below:

Profit and Loss Summary — ACCOUNT NO. 33

DATE	ITEMS	POST. REF.	DEBIT	DATE	ITEMS	POST. REF.	CREDIT
1957 Oct. 31		3	179 43	1957 Oct. 31		3	1377 60

Advertising Expense — ACCOUNT NO. 51

DATE	ITEMS	POST. REF.	DEBIT	DATE	ITEMS	POST. REF.	CREDIT
1957 Oct. 13		2	7 63	1957 Oct. 31		3	17 41
22		2	9 78				

Automobile Expense — ACCOUNT NO. 52

DATE	ITEMS	POST. REF.	DEBIT	DATE	ITEMS	POST. REF.	CREDIT
1957 Oct. 8		2	25 00	1957 Oct. 31		3	25 00

Entertainment Expense — ACCOUNT NO. 53

DATE	ITEMS	POST. REF.	DEBIT	DATE	ITEMS	POST. REF.	CREDIT
1957 Oct. 22		2	5 00	1957 Oct. 31		3	5 00

Miscellaneous Expense — ACCOUNT NO. 54

DATE	ITEMS	POST. REF.	DEBIT	DATE	ITEMS	POST. REF.	CREDIT
1957 Oct. 16		2	4 50	1957 Oct. 31		3	12 02
25		2	7 52				

Rent Expense — ACCOUNT NO. 55

DATE	ITEMS	POST. REF.	DEBIT	DATE	ITEMS	POST. REF.	CREDIT
1957 Oct. 5		2	120 00	1957 Oct. 31		3	120 00

The proprietor's drawing account. The net profit represents an increase in proprietorship resulting from the proprietor's services and the use of his capital. Usually the proprietor withdraws much of this profit in order to take care of his living expenses.

The proprietor's capital account is used to show the proprietor's permanent investment in the business. The profits that are earned and the withdrawals that are made are therefore not recorded in the capital account but are recorded in a separate account known as the *proprietor's drawing account.* The title of this account is the proprietor's name followed by the word *Drawing.*

The journal entry to transfer the credit balance of the profit and loss summary account to the credit side of the proprietor's drawing account is as follows:

	CASH		DATE	NAME OF ACCOUNT	NO.	POST. REF.	GENERAL		COMMISSIONS INCOME CREDIT
	DEBIT	CREDIT					DEBIT	CREDIT	
10			31	Profit and Loss Summary	33		1 1 9 8 17		10
11				J. M. Greene, Drawing	32			1 1 9 8 17	11

JOURNAL — PAGE 3

After this entry has been posted, the profit and loss summary account and the proprietor's drawing account are as follows:

J. M. Greene, Drawing — ACCOUNT NO. 32

DATE	ITEMS	POST. REF.	DEBIT	DATE	ITEMS	POST. REF.	CREDIT
				1957 Oct. 31		3	1 1 9 8 17

Profit and Loss Summary — ACCOUNT NO. 33

DATE	ITEMS	POST. REF.	DEBIT	DATE	ITEMS	POST. REF.	CREDIT
1957 Oct. 31		3	1 7 9 43	1957 Oct. 31		3	1 3 7 7 60
31		3	1 1 9 8 17				

The drawing account now shows a credit balance of $1,198.17. This amount represents the net increase in proprietorship and may be transferred to the capital account if the proprietor desires to make this a permanent increase in his investment. Since Mr. Greene plans to withdraw at least a part of this amount in the near future, he leaves the net profit in his drawing account.

At intervals, probably once a year, the proprietor should decide whether the credit balance (or the debit balance) in the drawing account represents a permanent change in proprietorship. Whenever it is decided that the balance of the drawing account does represent a permanent change in proprietorship, the drawing account should be closed to the capital account.

Summary of closing entries. This chapter has explained step by step the three journal entries that are needed to complete the bookkeeping process known as *closing the ledger*. These three journal entries as they appear in the journal of the Greene Realty Agency after being posted are:

| CASH | | DATE | NAME OF ACCOUNT | NO. | POST. REF. | GENERAL | | COMMISSIONS INCOME CREDIT |
DEBIT	CREDIT					DEBIT	CREDIT	
			Closing Entries					
		1957 Oct. 31	Commissions Income	41		1377 60		
			Profit and Loss Summary	33			1377 60	
		31	Profit and Loss Summary	33		179 43		
			Advertising Expense	51			17 41	
			Automobile Expense	52			25 00	
			Entertainment Expense	53			5 00	
			Miscellaneous Expense	54			12 02	
			Rent Expense	55			120 00	
		31	Profit and Loss Summary	33		1198 17		
			J. M. Greene, Drawing	32			1198 17	

Closing entries for the Greene Realty Agency after posting

Note that all these entries should be made from the work sheet illustrated on page 83. Profit and Loss Summary is credited for the total of the P. & L. Statement Credit column, and each income account (in this case Commissions Income only) is debited. Profit and Loss Summary is debited for the total of the P. & L. Statement Debit column, and each expense account is credited. Profit and Loss Summary is then debited for the amount of the net profit, and the proprietor's drawing account is credited for the same amount.

After posting the closing entries to the ledger, a double line is drawn immediately under the last entry and across all the columns of the journal except the Name of Account column. This double line indicates that the work of journalizing and posting the closing entries is completed.

Proprietorship division of the ledger. The accounts in the proprietorship section of J. M. Greene's ledger now show: (1) the investment in the business and (2) the net increase in the investment because of the operations of the business. The investment is shown in the capital account, and the net increase because of the operations of the business is shown in the proprietor's drawing account. If the business had shown a net loss, the net decrease would be shown as a debit entry in the proprietor's drawing account.

The sum of the balances of these two proprietorship accounts (J. M. Greene, Capital and J. M. Greene, Drawing) is the present capital, $4,098.17. The present capital on the balance sheet is also $4,098.17. The closing entries have therefore brought the proprietorship section of the ledger up to date. The entire process of summarizing the income and the expense accounts and transferring the net profit or the net loss to the proprietor's drawing account is known as *closing the ledger*.

Ruling accounts that are closed. As a result of the posting of the closing entries, each income account, each expense account, and the profit and loss summary account are in balance and are said to be closed. The amounts now recorded in these accounts should not be confused with the amounts that are entered during the following fiscal period. In order to show that the amounts now in these accounts have been definitely disposed of, the accounts are ruled. The miscellaneous expense account after ruling is shown below.

DATE	ITEMS	POST. REF.	DEBIT	DATE	ITEMS	POST. REF.	CREDIT
1957 Oct. 16		2	4 50	*1957* Oct. 31		3	12 02
25		2	7 52				
			12 02				12 02

Miscellaneous Expense   ACCOUNT NO. 54

The following steps are usually taken in ruling an income or an expense account:

Step 1. The totals of the debit and the credit sides of the account are written in ink on the same horizontal line.

Step 2. A single line is drawn across only the amount columns on the line above each total. This single line indicates addition and a total.

Step 3. Double lines are drawn on the line under the totals across all columns except the Items columns to indicate that the account is in balance and that the work of closing has been completed.

When an income or an expense account has, after closing, only one debit and one credit, the debit must equal the credit. It is therefore unnecessary to total the amount columns. The account is ruled with double lines across all columns except the Items columns as shown below.

DATE	ITEMS	POST. REF.	DEBIT	DATE	ITEMS	POST. REF.	CREDIT
1957 Oct. 8		2	25 00	1957 Oct. 31		3	25 00

Automobile Expense   ACCOUNT NO. 52

Balancing asset, liability, and proprietorship accounts. It is often desirable to show the balance of an account in the ledger at the beginning of a fiscal period. When an asset, a liability, or a proprietorship account has one or more entries on each side, it may be balanced as follows:

Step 1. The balance of the account is entered on the side having the smaller footing. The word "Balance" is written in the Items column, and a check mark is placed in the Post. Ref. column to show that this item was not posted from a journal. (See the cash account on page 105.)

Step 2. The account is then totaled and ruled in the manner in which an income or an expense account is totaled and ruled when it is closed.

Step 3. The balance is entered below the double ruling on the side originally having the larger footing. The date of the new balance is the first day of the new fiscal period. Below the double ruled line a complete date is used the same as if the date were at the top of a page. The word "Balance" is entered in the Items column, and a check mark is placed in the Post. Ref. column.

The process of determining the balance of an account, writing it on the smaller side, totaling and ruling the account, and bringing the balance into the new section of the account below the double lines is known as *balancing an account.*

On the two following pages the asset and the liability accounts that are balanced are Cash, Office Furniture, Office Machines, Adams Company, Daniels Company, and Star Garage. The asset account Automobile and the proprietorship accounts J. M. Greene, Capital and J. M. Greene, Drawing are not balanced because they have entries on one side of the account only. Some bookkeepers prefer to balance such accounts, especially if numerous entries are made in them.

Ledger that has been balanced and ruled. The ledger of the Greene Realty Agency after the closing entries have been posted and the accounts have been balanced and ruled is shown on pages 105 to 107.

Cash

ACCOUNT NO. 11

DATE		ITEMS	POST. REF.	DEBIT	DATE		ITEMS	POST. REF.	CREDIT
1957 Oct.	1	Balance	1	371 00	1957 Oct.	31		2	723 93
	31		2	1440 60		31	Balance	✓	1087 67
		_1087.67_		1811 60					1811 60
1957 Nov.	1	Balance	✓	1087 67					

Automobile

ACCOUNT NO. 12

DATE		ITEMS	POST. REF.	DEBIT	DATE		ITEMS	POST. REF.	CREDIT
1957 Oct.	1	Balance	1	3170 00					

Office Furniture

ACCOUNT NO. 13

DATE		ITEMS	POST. REF.	DEBIT	DATE		ITEMS	POST. REF.	CREDIT
1957 Oct.	1	Balance	1	745 60	1957 Oct.	1		2	20 00
	2		2	37 50		5		2	18 00
	3	_774.10_	2	39 00		18		2	10 00
				822 10		31	Balance	✓	774 10
				822 10					822 10
1957 Nov.	1	Balance	✓	774 10					

Office Machines

ACCOUNT NO. 14

DATE		ITEMS	POST. REF.	DEBIT	DATE		ITEMS	POST. REF.	CREDIT
1957 Oct.	1	Balance	1	254 40	1957 Oct.	2		2	15 00
	3		2	76 00		31	Balance	✓	490 40
	12	_490.40_	2	175 00					
				505 40					505 40
1957 Nov.	1	Balance	✓	490 40					

Adams Company

ACCOUNT NO. 21

DATE		ITEMS	POST. REF.	DEBIT	DATE		ITEMS	POST. REF.	CREDIT
1957 Oct.	1		2	25 00	1957 Oct.	1	Balance _66.00_	1	91 00
	31	Balance	✓	66 00					
				91 00					91 00
					1957 Nov.	1	Balance	✓	66 00

Ledger of Greene Realty Agency closed, balanced, and ruled

Daniels Company   ACCOUNT NO. 22

DATE	ITEMS	POST. REF.	DEBIT	DATE	ITEMS	POST. REF.	CREDIT
1957 Oct. 4		2	1 0 0 00	1957 Oct. 1	Balance 500.00	1	3 0 0 00
31	Balance	✓	2 0 0 00				
			3 0 0 00				3 0 0 00
				1957 Nov. 1	Balance	✓	2 0 0 00

Star Garage   ACCOUNT NO. 23

DATE	ITEMS	POST. REF.	DEBIT	DATE	ITEMS	POST. REF.	CREDIT
1957 Oct. 2		2	4 2 00	1957 Oct. 1	Balance 1,158.00	1	1 2 5 0 00
18		2	5 0 00				
31	Balance	✓	1 1 5 8 00				
			1 2 5 0 00				1 2 5 0 00
				1957 Nov. 1	Balance	✓	1 1 5 8 00

J. M. Greene, Capital   ACCOUNT NO. 31

DATE	ITEMS	POST. REF.	DEBIT	DATE	ITEMS	POST. REF.	CREDIT
				1957 Oct. 1	Balance	1	2 9 0 0 00

J. M. Greene, Drawing   ACCOUNT NO. 32

DATE	ITEMS	POST. REF.	DEBIT	DATE	ITEMS	POST. REF.	CREDIT
				1957 Oct. 31		3	1 1 9 8 17

Profit and Loss Summary   ACCOUNT NO. 33

DATE	ITEMS	POST. REF.	DEBIT	DATE	ITEMS	POST. REF.	CREDIT
1957 Oct. 31		3	1 7 9 43	1957 Oct. 31		3	1 3 7 7 60
31		3	1 1 9 8 17				
			1 3 7 7 60				1 3 7 7 60

Commissions Income   ACCOUNT NO. 41

DATE	ITEMS	POST. REF.	DEBIT	DATE	ITEMS	POST. REF.	CREDIT
1957 Oct. 31		3	1 3 7 7 60	1957 Oct. 31		2	1 3 7 7 60

Advertising Expense — ACCOUNT NO. 51

DATE	ITEMS	POST. REF.	DEBIT	DATE	ITEMS	POST. REF.	CREDIT
1957 Oct. 13		2	7 63	1957 Oct. 31		3	17 41
22		2	9 78				
			17 41				17 41

Automobile Expense — ACCOUNT NO. 52

DATE	ITEMS	POST. REF.	DEBIT	DATE	ITEMS	POST. REF.	CREDIT
1957 Oct. 8		2	25 00	1957 Oct. 31		3	25 00

Entertainment Expense — ACCOUNT NO. 53

DATE	ITEMS	POST. REF.	DEBIT	DATE	ITEMS	POST. REF.	CREDIT
1957 Oct. 22		2	5 00	1957 Oct. 31		3	5 00

Miscellaneous Expense — ACCOUNT NO. 54

DATE	ITEMS	POST. REF.	DEBIT	DATE	ITEMS	POST. REF.	CREDIT
1957 Oct. 16		2	4 50	1957 Oct. 31		3	12 02
25		2	7 52				
			12 02				12 02

Rent Expense — ACCOUNT NO. 55

DATE	ITEMS	POST. REF.	DEBIT	DATE	ITEMS	POST. REF.	CREDIT
1957 Oct. 5		2	120 00	1957 Oct. 31		3	120 00

Ledger of Greene Realty Agency closed, balanced, and ruled (concluded)

Post-closing trial balance. After the closing entries have been posted and the accounts have been ruled, it is customary to take a trial balance to test the equality of debits and credits in the ledger. The trial balance taken after the closing entries have been posted and the accounts have been ruled is called a *post-closing trial balance.*

The post-closing trial balance of the Greene Realty Agency appears on page 108. No income or expense account appears on this post-closing trial balance because each has been closed. The open asset, liability, and proprietorship accounts (those containing balances) are the only accounts appearing on a post-closing trial balance. The post-closing trial balance is actually a balance sheet in trial balance form.

Greene Realty Agency
Post-Closing Trial Balance
October 31, 1957

Cash	11		1 0 8 7 67			
Automobile	12		3 1 7 0 00			
Office Furniture	13		7 7 4 10			
Office Machines	14		4 9 0 40			
Adams Company	21				6 6 00	
Daniels Company	22				2 0 0 00	
Star Garage	23				1 1 5 8 00	
J. M. Greene, Capital	31				2 9 0 0 00	
J. M. Greene, Drawing	32				1 1 9 8 17	
			5 5 2 2 17		5 5 2 2 17	

Post-closing trial balance of the Greene Realty Agency

CHAPTER QUESTIONS

1. Why is it desirable to close the income and the expense accounts in the ledger at the end of each fiscal period?
2. What account is used for the purpose of summarizing the income and the expense accounts?
3. Give two reasons why it is desirable to use journal entries to transfer account balances in the ledger.
4. What two columns of the work sheet are used as a guide for the closing entries in the journal?
5. In what order are the closing entries in the journal prepared?
6. Why is the net profit or the net loss closed into the proprietor's drawing account instead of into his capital account?
7. After the closing entries have been posted, what kinds of accounts in the ledger have zero balances?
8. Explain the three steps usually taken in balancing and ruling an asset, a liability, or a proprietorship account.
9. What is the purpose of the post-closing trial balance?
10. What kinds of accounts remain open in the ledger after the closing entries have been posted?

INCREASING YOUR BUSINESS VOCABULARY

What is the meaning of each of the following:

(a) profit and loss summary account
(b) closing entry
(c) closed account
(d) combined entry
(e) drawing account
(f) closing the ledger
(g) balancing an account
(h) post-closing trial balance

CASES FOR DISCUSSION

1. The proprietorship section of the Greene Realty Agency has the following three proprietorship accounts:

   J. M. Greene, Capital   J. M. Greene, Drawing   Profit and Loss Summary

   (a) Why are the income and expense accounts in the ledger closed into the profit and loss summary account instead of into the proprietor's drawing account?

   (b) After the closing entries are posted, what kind of accounts are summarized on the debit side of the profit and loss summary account?

   (c) Why is it desirable to have the present capital of the proprietor distributed between the two accounts, Capital and Drawing?

2. The proprietor's drawing account in the Greene Realty Agency ledger after the closing process has been completed is illustrated on page 106.

   (a) From what account was the credit balance in the proprietor's drawing account transferred?

   (b) Does this credit balance in the drawing account represent a net profit or a net loss?

DRILL FOR UNDERSTANDING

Drill 10-A. *Instructions: 1.* On the left side of a sheet of paper, write the heading *Account Titles;* then copy the ledger account titles that are given below. Rule a one-inch wide column at the right of the list. Write the heading *Answers* at the top of the column.

1. Admissions Income
2. Advertising Expense
3. Air Conditioning Equipment
4. Cash
5. Electricity Expense
6. Film Producers, Inc. (creditor)
7. Film Rental Expense
8. International Studios (creditor)
9. Maintenance Expense
10. Majestic Films (creditor)
11. Midwest Sound Service (creditor)
12. National Supply Co. (creditor)
13. Projection Equipment
14. Projection Expense
15. Rent Expense
16. Frank Rimer, Capital
17. Sound Equipment
18. Water Expense

2. If the account is closed after the closing entries are posted, write capital *C* (for "Closed") in the Answers column. If the account remains open after all closing entries are posted, write capital *O* (for "Open") in the Answers column. The first item is given as an example.

Account Titles	Answers
1. Admissions Income	*C*

3. Now cover your answers and see how rapidly you can do this orally without looking at your answers. Repeat this drill orally several times for increased speed and accuracy.

APPLICATION PROBLEM

Problem 10-1. Closing the ledger

If you are not using the workbook correlating with this textbook, complete Exercise 10-A in the Appendix instead of this problem.

Instructions: 1. Foot the ledger accounts of John Norris provided for this problem in the workbook. If an account has entries on both sides, write the balance in small pencil figures in the proper Items column.

2. Prove cash. The cash on hand on November 30, 19--, by actual count is $1,581.62. This amount should agree with the balance in the cash account in the ledger.

3. Prepare a work sheet on six-column work sheet paper.

4. Prepare a profit and loss statement.

5. Prepare a balance sheet in report form.

6. Record the closing entries in a journal.

7. Post the closing entries.

8. Rule the profit and loss summary, the income, and the expense accounts.

9. Balance all asset, liability, and proprietorship accounts that need to be balanced.

10. Prepare a post-closing trial balance.

Self-checking: (1) Were the pencil footings written in your ledger in small figures with a sharp, firm pencil?

(2) Was each amount column of an account footed when, and only when, it contained two or more entries?

(3) Is your work sheet similar to the model on page 83?

(4) Is your profit and loss statement similar to the model on page 89?

(5) Is your balance sheet similar to the model on page 91?

(6) Are your closing entries similar to the model on page 102?

(7) After you have closed, ruled, and balanced your ledger, is it similar to the model ledger on pages 105 to 107?

(8) Is your post-closing trial balance similar to the model on page 108?

The complete bookkeeping cycle

Purpose of Project 2. In this project you will record the transactions for a fiscal period and will do all the work required at the end of the fiscal period. When you have completed this project, you will have demonstrated that you are capable of keeping a simple set of books. Additional accounts and methods will be presented in later chapters, but the basic principles of bookkeeping and accounting will remain the same.

The journal. A businessman may have as many amount columns in his journal as he desires. Amount columns should be added in the journal only when they will bring about a saving in time and effort in posting. The best test as to whether or not a special amount column should be provided is the number of times that the column will be used.

The Town Theater, a motion picture theater in a small community, is owned and operated by Herbert Sherman. In recording his transactions, Mr. Sherman uses a journal with seven amount columns.

JOURNAL   PAGE 9

	1	2					3	4	5	6	7	
	CASH		DATE	NAME OF ACCOUNT	CHK. NO.	P. R.	GENERAL		ADMIS-SIONS INCOME CREDIT	FILM RENTAL EXPENSE DEBIT	ADVER-TISING EXPENSE DEBIT	
	DEBIT	CREDIT					DEBIT	CREDIT				
1		200 00	19— Oct. 1	Rent Expense...	111	56	200 00					1
2		12 50	3	Advertising Exp.	112	√					12 50	2
3	151 65		4	Admissions Inc..		√			151 65			3
4		67 50	4	Film Rental....	113	√				67 50		4
26		7 53	31	Projection Exp...	121	55	7 53					26
27	939 80	646 10	31	Totals..........			313 30	7 00	932 80	285 30	47 50	27
28	(11)	(11)					(√)	(√)	(41)	(52)	(51)	28

The journal of the Town Theater differs from the one used by the Henry Realty Agency in Project 1 in the following respects:

Check No. column. The Check No. column replaces the No. column used in Project 1. The Town Theater receives its income from admissions and does not issue receipts. The Check No. column is used only to record the number of each check written.

Admissions Income Credit. The Town Theater receives its income from the sale of tickets. Each day that the theater is operated, an entry is made debiting Cash and crediting Admissions Income for the total amount received from the sale of tickets. The entry includes a debit in the Cash Debit column and a credit in the Admissions Income Credit column.

Film Rental Expense Debit. As payments for film rental are made each week, a special column is provided for film rental expense. Each payment for film rental is recorded as a debit in the Film Rental Expense column and as a credit in the Cash Credit column.

Advertising Expense Debit. Advertising expenses occur often. Each payment for an advertising expense is recorded in the Advertising Expense Debit column and in the Cash Credit column.

Posting. Each item in the General Debit column and in the General Credit column is posted individually. The amounts entered in the special columns Cash Debit, Cash Credit, Admissions Income Credit, Film Rental Expense Debit, and Advertising Expense Debit are not posted individually. They are posted only as a part of the column totals. A check mark in the Post. Ref. column indicates that neither the debit nor the credit is posted individually.

At the end of the month the accuracy of debits and credits is proved and the journal is ruled. Check marks are then placed under the General Debit column and the General Credit column to indicate that these totals are not to be posted. The posting of the total of each of the other columns is indicated by writing the account number in parentheses below the column total.

Opening the accounts in the ledger

Instructions: 1. Open the accounts in the ledger in the order in which they are listed in the chart of accounts below. Number the accounts in the ledger with the account numbers given in the chart of accounts. (If you are not using the workbook correlating with this textbook, place four ledger accounts on a page.)

Chart of accounts

ACCT.
No.

(1) ASSETS

11 Cash
12 Projection Equipment
13 Sound Equipment

(2) LIABILITIES

21 Morrison Optical Company
22 Phelps Sound Service

(3) PROPRIETORSHIP

31 Herbert Sherman, Capital
32 Herbert Sherman, Drawing
33 Profit and Loss Summary

ACCT.
No.

(4) INCOME

41 Admissions Income

(5) EXPENSES

51 Advertising Expense
52 Film Rental Expense
53 Fuel Expense
54 Maintenance Expense
55 Projection Expense
56 Rent Expense
57 Utilities Expense

Instructions: 2. Copy the following balances in your ledger, using as the date November 1 of the current year. As you copy these balances, write the word *Balance* in the Items column of each ledger account.

	Debit Balances	Credit Balances
Cash	$2,142.23	
Projection Equipment................	9,111.11	
Sound Equipment....................	653.11	
Morrison Optical Co..................		$ 66.67
Phelps Sound Service.................		180.00
Herbert Sherman, Capital.............		11,659.78

Transactions for November

Instructions: 3. Journalize the following transactions completed by Mr. Sherman. He finds it profitable to operate his theater two nights each week.

Nov. 1. Received $140.65 from admissions.

2. Received $105.95 from admissions.

3. Paid $73.32 for film rental. (Check No. 241)

4. Paid $40.00 to Morrison Optical Co. on account. (Check No. 242)

4. Paid $12.50 for advertising. (Check No. 243)

5. Paid $100.00 to Phelps Sound Service on account. (Check No. 244)

6. Paid $200.00 for rent for November. (Check No. 245)

8. Received $158.30 from admissions.

9. Paid $4.39 for new fuses for projector. This is Projection Expense. (Check No. 246)

9. Received $125.40 from admissions.

10. Paid $80.74 for film rental. (Check No. 247)

11. Paid $12.50 for advertising. (Check No. 248)

12. Paid $47.39 for repair of seats. This is Maintenance Expense. (Check No. 249)

15. Paid $43.91 for new sound equipment. (Check No. 250)

15. Received $113.50 from admissions.

16. Received $25.00 from sale of old sound equipment.

16. Received $144.75 from admissions.

17. Paid $75.65 for film rental. (Check No. 251)

18. Paid $12.50 for advertising. (Check No. 252)

20. Paid $13.00 for repair of carpet. This is Maintenance Expense. (Check No. 253)

22. Received $156.10 from admissions.

23. Received $131.10 from admissions.

24. Paid $81.24 for film rental. (Check No. 254)

25. Received $25.00 for old projection equipment.

27. Paid $12.50 for advertisements. (Check No. 255)

Nov. 29. Received $103.40 from admissions.

  30. Paid $47.63 for fuel for November. (Check No. 256)

  30. Paid $53.90 for electricity for November. This is Utilities Expense. (Check No. 257)

  30. Paid $11.67 for water for November. This is Utilities Expense. (Check No. 258)

  30. Received $97.75 from admissions.

  30. Paid $66.22 for film rental. (Check No. 259)

Work at the end of the month

Instructions: **4.** Foot all amount columns of the journal with small pencil figures. Prove the equality of total debits and total credits. The sum of the pencil footings of the debit amount columns should equal the sum of the pencil footings of the credit amount columns.

5. Total and rule the journal.

6. Post each amount in the General Debit and the General Credit columns of the journal individually. Place a check mark in the posting reference column opposite each amount entered in a special column.

7. Post the total of each of the special columns. Place check marks under the total of each General column to show that these two totals are not posted.

8. Foot and prove the cash account. The cash on hand is $2,480.07. The amount of the cash on hand should be the same as the balance of the cash account in the ledger.

9. Foot the remaining accounts in the ledger. If an account has entries on both sides, write the balance of the account in small pencil figures in the proper Items column.

10. Prepare a trial balance on six-column work sheet paper, using the first two amount columns of the work sheet for the trial balance. Note that the name of the business is the Town Theater and that the work sheet is prepared for the month ended November 30 of the current year. (The entire work sheet should be prepared with pencil.)

11. Complete the work sheet.

12. Prepare the profit and loss statement.

13. Prepare the balance sheet in report form.

14. Record the closing entries in the journal.

15. Post the closing entries from the journal to the ledger.

16. Rule the profit and loss summary, the income, and the expense accounts.

17. Balance all asset, liability, and proprietorship accounts that need to be balanced.

18. Prepare a post-closing trial balance.

Recording the buying of merchandise on account

Merchandise. Mr. J. C. Kelly owns and operates a household appliance store known as Kelly Appliances. He carries in stock for sale to his customers household appliances such as refrigerators, stoves, and electric fans. Goods carried in stock for sale to customers are known as *merchandise*.

Buying procedures. Mr. Kelly buys his merchandise from different manufacturers and wholesalers. He may order his merchandise by letter, on an order blank supplied by the wholesaler or the manufacturer, or on a printed form of his own. A business paper prepared by the buyer describing merchandise he wishes to purchase is called a *purchase order*. He keeps a carbon copy of each order that he can later use in checking the quantities received and the amounts charged by the seller.

The immediate record — the invoice. Mr. Kelly receives an invoice from the seller for each order that he has placed. A form showing the goods that have been shipped, the method of shipment, and the cost is known as an *invoice*. An invoice for a purchase made by Mr. Kelly from the Rollo Manufacturing Company is shown below.

	ROLLO MANUFACTURING COMPANY✓		#111
	464 BELT DRIVE		
	DETROIT 8, MICHIGAN	NOV 4 RECD	
SOLD TO	Kelly Appliances 289 Main Street Ann Arbor, Michigan	DATE Nov. 1, 1957	
		NO. 3968	
TERMS 30 days	Purchase Order No. 1864	HOW SHIPPED O K Truck Co.	

QUANTITY	DESCRIPTION	UNIT PRICE	TOTAL
3✓	Model K No. 209 Rollo Pressure Cookers	8.90	26.70✓
6✓	Rollo Rotobroilers #654	22.50	135.00✓
6✓	Rollo Kitchen Exhaust Fans	11.30	67.80✓
			229.50✓

Invoice

Invoices differ in form from business to business. Most invoices, however, include the following:

1. The name and the address of the one from whom the merchandise is purchased.
2. The name and the address of the purchaser.
3. The date of the invoice.
4. The seller's invoice number.
5. The method of shipment.
6. The terms.
7. The buyer's purchase order number.
8. The quantity, description, and unit price of items purchased.
9. The total cost of each item and the total of the invoice.

Checking an invoice. It is important for Mr. Kelly to know that he has been shipped the items he ordered and that he has been charged the proper amount. Therefore, he takes the following steps to prove the correctness of each invoice:

Step 1. He compares the invoice with the purchase order to see that the items on the invoice agree with those on the purchase order.

Step 2. He examines the merchandise to see if it was delivered in good condition. He checks the invoice with the purchase order to see if quantities and prices are correct. The check mark at the right of each amount in the quantity column on the invoice on page 115 shows that these items have been approved.

Step 3. He checks the accuracy of the multiplication on each line and the addition of the total column. Proving the multiplication and the addition on an invoice is known as *verifying the extensions*. The check mark at the right of each item in the Total column on the invoice on page 115 shows that the extensions and the addition have been found to be correct.

The purchases journal. When merchandise is purchased with an agreement that it is to be paid for at a later date, the transaction is a *purchase on account*. Mr. Kelly usually makes his purchases of merchandise on account. He might record these purchases in a columnar journal similar to the journal illustrated in earlier chapters. As he has numerous purchases on account, he finds it more convenient to record them in a separate journal. A special journal for recording purchases of merchandise on account is known as a *purchases journal*.

The purchases journal for Kelly Appliances showing the first entry made in the month of November is illustrated on page 117.

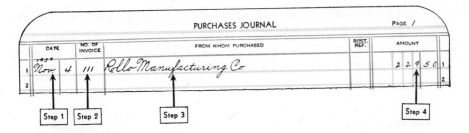

PURCHASES JOURNAL   PAGE *1*

DATE	NO. OF INVOICE	FROM WHOM PURCHASED	POST. REF.	AMOUNT
1957 Nov 4	111	Rollo Manufacturing Co		229 50

Step 1   Step 2   Step 3   Step 4

Recording an invoice in the purchases journal. As each invoice was received, it was recorded on one line in the purchases journal. The steps in recording the invoice illustrated on page 115 were:

Step 1. The date the invoice was received, Nov. 4, 1957, was recorded in the Date column of the purchases journal. Since this was the first entry on the page, the year, month, and day were recorded. The year and the month were not repeated on the same page for additional entries.

The invoice was stamped with the date at the time that it was received. Note on the invoice of the Rollo Manufacturing Company the stamp showing that the invoice was received on November 4.

Step 2. The number of the invoice, 111, was recorded in the No. of Invoice column. Mr. Kelly numbers the invoices he receives. The number is shown in the upper right-hand corner of the invoice on page 115.

Step 3. The name of the business from whom the purchase was made, Rollo Manufacturing Company, was written in the From Whom Purchased column.

Step 4. The amount of the invoice, $229.50, was recorded in the Amount column.

Step 5. A check mark was placed on the invoice at the right of the name to show that the invoice had been recorded. (See the invoice on page 115.) The invoice was then filed so that it could be referred to when necessary.

The accounts payable ledger. Mr. Kelly finds it convenient to have the accounts with creditors in a ledger separate from other accounts. A ledger that contains accounts with creditors only is an *accounts payable ledger.*

The ledger that Mr. Kelly uses for his accounts payable differs from the ledger used heretofore. It provides three amount columns, one for debits, one for credits, and one for credit balances. Such a ruling is known as *balance-column ledger ruling.*

The special column for credit balances in the balance-column ledger ruling enables the bookkeeper to record the balance after each entry. This is desirable because it shows at any time how much is owed to a creditor.

Posting the individual items from the purchases journal. As was explained in Chapter 1, amounts owed are liabilities. Liabilities and increases in liabilities are recorded as credits. Each purchase on account increases the amount owed a creditor and therefore must be posted to the creditor's account as a credit.

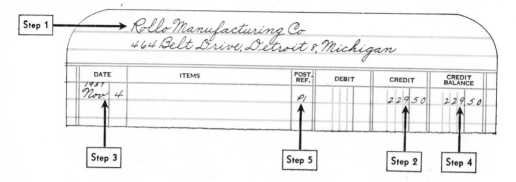

Analyzing the posting to a creditor's account. The posting of the first entry in the purchases journal on page 117 is shown above. The steps in posting this entry were as follows:

Step 1. The name and the address of the creditor were written at the top of the account. As this was a new account, the address was obtained from the invoice.

Step 2. The amount of the invoice, $229.50, was recorded in the Credit column.

Step 3. The year, 1957, was written at the top of the Date column. On the first line of the Date column, the month and the day, Nov. 4, were written.

Step 4. The amount of the invoice, $229.50, was also extended to the Credit Balance column. As there was no previous balance in this account, this credit was also the balance.

Step 5. The letter "P" and the number "1" were written in the Post. Ref. column to show that the entry came from page 1 of the purchases journal.

Step 6. A check mark (√) was placed in the Post. Ref. column of the purchases journal to show completion of the posting. Accounts with creditors are arranged alphabetically so that they can be easily found. When new accounts are opened they are placed in their proper alphabetic position. For this reason creditor accounts are not numbered. As an account number was not available for use in indicating that the posting had been completed, the check mark was used.

The purchases journal after the posting to the Rollo Manufacturing Company account is shown below.

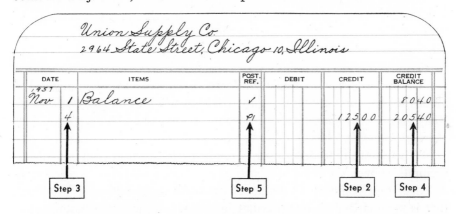

	DATE	NO. OF INVOICE	FROM WHOM PURCHASED	POST. REF	AMOUNT	
1	1957 Nov. 4	111	Rollo Manufacturing Co	✓	2 2 9 50	1
2						2
3						3
4						

PURCHASES JOURNAL — PAGE 1

Step 6

Recording the balance in a creditor's account. Mr. Kelly opened accounts with creditors on November 1 in a new accounts payable ledger. At that time the account of the Union Supply Company had a balance of $80.40. This balance is properly recorded as a credit balance in the account of the Union Supply Company illustrated below.

Note how the date was recorded in the Date column. The word *Balance* was written in the Items column and the credit balance, $80.40, was recorded in the Credit Balance column. To show that this did not come from a journal, a check mark was placed in the Post. Ref. column.

Union Supply Co
2964 State Street, Chicago 10, Illinois

DATE	ITEMS	POST. REF.	DEBIT	CREDIT	CREDIT BALANCE
1957 Nov. 1	Balance	✓			8 0 40
4		P1		1 25 00	2 05 40

Step 3 — Step 5 — Step 2 — Step 4

Analyzing the posting of an additional entry to a creditor's account. The steps in posting the second entry in the purchases journal below to the account of Union Supply Company were as follows:

Step 1. The account of the Union Supply Company was found in the accounts payable ledger. As the account had already been opened, the name and the address did not have to be written.

Step 2. The amount of the invoice, $125.00, was recorded in the Credit column.

Step 3. The date was written in the Date column. As the year and the month had already been entered, the date consisted only of the day. The month and the year are not repeated unless they change.

Step 4. The new credit of $125.00 was added to the credit balance of $80.40. The new credit balance of $205.40 was recorded in the Credit Balance column.

Step 5. The source of the entry, P1, was written in the Post. Ref. column to show that the entry came from page 1 of the purchases journal.

Step 6. A check mark was placed in the Post. Ref. column of the purchases journal to indicate that the posting had been completed.

The purchases journal after the Union Supply Company entry was posted is shown below.

			PURCHASES JOURNAL		PAGE *1*	
DATE	NO. OF INVOICE		FROM WHOM PURCHASED	POST. REF.	AMOUNT	
1957 Nov. 4	111		Rollo Manufacturing Co.	✓	2 2 9 5 0	1
4	112		Union Supply Co.	✓	1 2 5 0 0	2

Step 6

General ledger and subsidiary ledgers. In order to avoid having to list all of the creditors' accounts on the trial balance and on the work sheet, Kelly Appliances maintains one account in the general ledger known as *Accounts Payable.*

When more than one ledger is used, the ledger that contains all the accounts shown on the trial balance is known as the *general ledger.* A ledger that contains a number of accounts with detailed information that is summarized in one account in the general ledger is known as a *subsidiary ledger.* The accounts payable ledger is a subsidiary ledger. An account in the general ledger that summarizes all the accounts in a subsidiary ledger is known as a *controlling account.* The account in the general ledger with the title *Accounts Payable* is a controlling account.

The controlling account Accounts Payable is debited with the total of all amounts posted to the debit of creditors' accounts in the accounts payable ledger. It is credited with the total of all amounts posted to the credit of creditors' accounts in the accounts payable ledger.

When all posting is completed at the end of the fiscal period, the balance of the controlling account is the same as the total of all of the balances of the creditors' accounts in the accounts payable ledger.

Completing the purchases journal. During the month of November, Mr. Kelly made a number of purchases on account. Each of the purchases was recorded in the purchases journal, and each was posted to a creditor's account in the accounts payable ledger. The purchases journal for November showing all the purchases for the month is illustrated below.

	DATE	NO. OF INVOICE	FROM WHOM PURCHASED	POST. REF.	AMOUNT	
1	1957 Nov 4	111	Rollo Manufacturing Co	✓	2 2 9 5 0	1
2	4	112	Union Supply Co	✓	1 2 5 0 0	2
3	6	113	Arco Atlas Company	✓	2 5 2 5 0	3
4	9	114	Metals, Inc	✓	4 5 0 0	4
5	9	115	Union Supply Co	✓	2 0 0 5 0	5
6	16	116	Wills Electric Co	✓	1 2 0 0 0	6
7	18	117	Metals, Inc	✓	1 5 0 0 0	7
8	25	118	Bell Light Fixture Co	✓	4 8 1 5 0	8
9	29	119	Acme Stove Company	✓	1 6 0 0 0	9
10	30		Purchases Dr./Accounts Payable Cr		1 7 6 4 0 0	10
11						11
12						12
13						13

PURCHASES JOURNAL   PAGE 1

Purchases journal totaled and ruled

Analyzing the completion of the purchases journal. At the end of the month the purchases journal was totaled and ruled as follows:

Step 1. A single line was drawn across the amount column immediately under the last entry in that column.

Step 2. The column was totaled and the amount, $1,764.00, was written on the line immediately below the single ruled line.

Step 3. The date was entered in the Date column.

Step 4. The accounts to be debited and credited for the total of the purchases journal were shown by writing *Purchases Dr./Accounts Payable Cr.* on the same line as the total. The two account titles were separated by a diagonal line.

Step 5. A double ruled line was drawn across all of the columns except the From Whom Purchased column to show that all entries for the month had been recorded.

Posting the total of the purchases journal. The total of the purchases journal represented the total cost of the merchandise purchased on account during the month. Merchandise bought for resale is recorded in an account titled *Purchases*. Purchases will make up a part of the cost of merchandise sold. The cost of merchandise sold is a deduction from the income of the business. For this reason the total purchases for the month, as shown in the purchases journal, were recorded as a debit to the account Purchases.

All of the amounts recorded in the purchases journal were purchases on account; therefore, the total amount for the month represented an increase in liabilities. As increases in liabilities are recorded as credits, the total for the month was recorded as a credit to Accounts Payable.

The posting of the total of the purchases journal is shown in the illustration below.

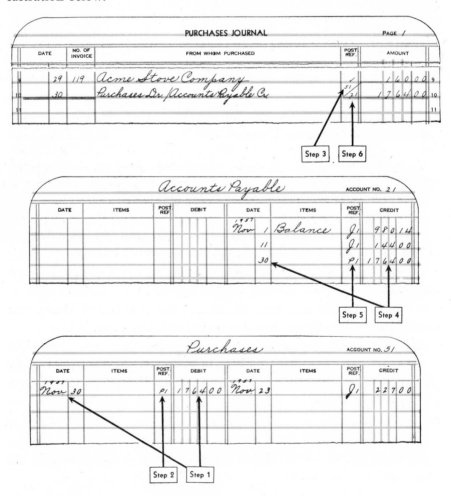

Analyzing the posting of the total of the purchases journal. The steps followed in posting the total of the purchases journal were:

Step 1. The total of the purchases journal, $1,764.00, was posted to the debit of Purchases, Account No. 51 in the general ledger. The date, Nov. 30, 1957, was recorded in the Date column.

> Different businesses use different account numbers. The method of numbering accounts used by Mr. Kelly will be explained later.

Step 2. *P1* was written in the Post. Ref. column of the purchases account to show that this entry came from page 1 of the purchases journal.

Step 3. The purchases account number, 51, was written in the left part of the Post. Ref. column of the purchases journal.

Step 4. The total of the purchases journal, $1,764.00, was also posted to the credit of Accounts Payable, Account No. 21 in the general ledger. The date, 30, was written in the Date column of the account.

Step 5. *P1* was written in the Post. Ref. column of the accounts payable account to show that the entry from page 1 of the purchases journal.

Step 6. The accounts payable account number, 21, was written in the Post. Ref. column of the purchases journal and was separated from the other account number by a diagonal line.

Relationship of the purchases journal, the accounts payable ledger, and the general ledger. The total of the purchases journal is posted as a debit to the purchases account in the general ledger. It is also posted as a credit to the accounts payable account in the general ledger. The equality of debits and credits in the general ledger is therefore maintained, because Purchases is debited and Accounts Payable is credited for the same amount.

Each entry in the purchases journal is posted as a credit to a creditor's account in the accounts payable ledger. The one credit posted to Accounts Payable in the general ledger is therefore equal to the sum of all the credits posted to the individual accounts in the accounts payable ledger. The balance of the accounts payable account is used in the trial balance. The balances of the individual accounts in the subsidiary ledger are not used in the trial balance, but they are useful in showing the amount owed to each individual creditor.

A second method — using purchases invoices as a purchases journal. Some businesses file or bind the purchases invoices together and use them as a purchases journal. When this method is used, the posting is done from the original invoices and the purchases journal is not used.

The method of using the purchases invoices for the purchases journal is not the same in all businesses, but a satisfactory method is as follows:

Step 1. The invoices are numbered consecutively as they are received and are filed together.

Step 2. The amount of each purchases invoice is posted directly to the creditor's account in the accounts payable ledger. The number of the invoice is placed in the posting reference column of the creditor's account to show the source of the entry. A check mark is placed at the right of the name of the creditor printed at the top of the purchases invoice to show that the invoice has been posted.

Step 3. At the end of the month the amounts of all purchases invoices for the month are added. Ordinarily an adding machine is used for this purpose. The invoices for a month, with the adding machine list showing the totals, are illustrated below.

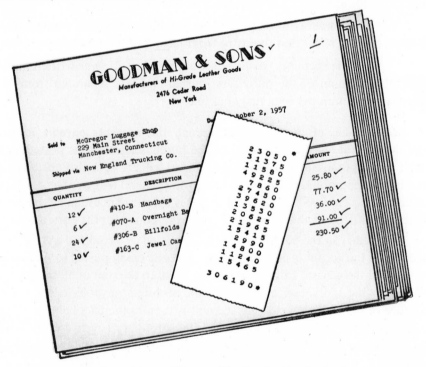

Invoices with an adding machine list showing the total

Step 4. The total of the invoices for the month is recorded in a journal as a debit to Purchases and a credit to Accounts Payable. Such an entry is illustrated at the top of the following page.

	DATE	NAME OF ACCOUNT	POST. REF.	DEBIT	CREDIT	
28	31	*Purchases*		3 0 6 1 9 0		28
29		*Accounts Payable*			3 0 6 1 9 0	29
30		*Purchases on account for*				30
31		*October.*				31
32						32
33						33
34						34

The form of journal illustrated here is the general journal. The use of this journal is discussed and illustrated in Chapter 15.

Step 5. The journal entry is posted to the debit of Purchases and to the credit of Accounts Payable in the general ledger.

A third method — cash method of handling buying of merchandise. A third method of handling purchases is to handle them as cash purchases. The invoices are kept on file and are entered only when they are paid. The method of handling cash purchases will be discussed later.

CHAPTER QUESTIONS

1. What business paper is the basis for each entry in the purchases journal?
2. What three steps are taken after an invoice is received and before it is recorded?
3. In what journal are purchases of merchandise on account recorded?
4. How do you determine what number to record in the Invoice No. column of the purchases journal?
5. How do you indicate on the invoice that the invoice has been recorded?
6. What is the advantage of using balance-column ruling for creditors' accounts?
7. Why is a check mark used in the Post. Ref. column of the purchases journal instead of a number to indicate that the item has been posted?
8. What is the meaning of "P1" in the Post. Ref. column of the creditor's account illustrated on page 118?
9. When the November 1 balance was recorded, why was a check mark used in the Post. Ref. column of the Union Supply Company account illustrated on page 119 instead of a page number?
10. With what total does the balance of the controlling account, Accounts Payable, agree when all of the posting is completed?

Chapter 11. Buying merchandise on account 125

What is the meaning of each of the following:

(a) merchandise	(h) balance-column ledger ruling
(b) purchase order	(i) accounts payable account
(c) invoice	(j) general ledger
(d) verifying extensions	(k) subsidiary ledger
(e) purchase on account	(l) controlling account
(f) purchases journal	(m) purchases account
(g) accounts payable ledger	

CASES FOR DISCUSSION

1. The Arcade Record Shop telephones its orders to a wholesaler. It frequently finds that its orders are incorrectly filled. What suggestions can you make to the owner about placing orders to help avoid these errors?

2. T. R. Nelson paid $300 for an electric typewriter to be used in his office. The bookkeeper recorded this transaction in the purchases journal. Why was that procedure not correct?

3. The bookkeeper for the Arcade Record Shop posted the total of the purchases journal to the credit of the accounts payable account. He failed to post the total to the debit of the purchases account. What effect will this have on the equality of debits and credits in the general ledger?

4. The Arcade Record Shop makes 90 purchases of merchandise on account in the average month. Each purchase is recorded in the purchases journal. The purchases journal is posted to the subsidiary ledger and the general ledger.
   (a) How much work might be saved by posting directly from the purchases invoices according to the method outlined on pages 123 to 125?
   (b) If this method were followed, where and how should the Arcade Record Shop record the total purchases for the month?

5. The bookkeeper for the Arcade Record Shop was interrupted in his work as he was posting from the purchases journal to the creditors' accounts. When he started to post a credit to J. H. Jones, he placed a check mark in the Post. Ref. column of the purchases journal. Because of the interruption he failed to post the amount to Jones's account. What change in posting steps would prevent this kind of incomplete posting?

Drill 11-A. Below is the purchases journal for W. L. Watson with the entries recorded for purchases of merchandise on account during the month of March.

PURCHASES JOURNAL

Date		No. of Invoice	From Whom Purchased	Post. Ref.	Amount	
1957						
March	1	242	A. R. Swanson		247	25
	4	243	John Carson		324	56
	5	244	William Borden		122	48
	8	245	Fred Vincent		266	20
	11	246	Alfred Thompson		42	75
	14	247	James Horton		96	50
	19	248	Mrs. T. H. Loomis		124	69
	20	249	Arthur Kenyon		462	20
	23	250	Alden Wirt		129	60
	27	251	Kenneth Sims		227	62
	30	252	Mary Mathers		59	80
					2103	65

Instructions: Answer the following questions:

(1) To which column in a balance-column accounts payable ledger will each of the individual amounts be posted?

(2) If the creditor's account has a previous balance, will the amount posted to his account from the purchases journal be added to the balance or be subtracted from it?

(3) If the creditor's account has no previous balance, what amount will be extended to the Credit Balance column?

(4) What account in the general ledger will be debited for the total of the purchases journal?

(5) What account in the general ledger will be credited for the total of the purchases journal?

(6) How will the posting of the total be indicated in the purchases journal?

APPLICATION PROBLEMS

Problem 11-1. Opening an accounts payable ledger for a retail dress shop

The names of the businesses from which the Burch Dress Shop buys on account and the amounts owed to them on February 28 of the current year are as follows:

	Account Balances
Adams & Lane, 4660 Fourth Street, City.....................	$781.50
Burton & King, 1216 Main Street, City......................	225.60
Hess Clothing Co., 3975 Clark Street, Chicago...............	335.00
National Dress Co., 2860 Sixth Avenue, New York............	467.50
Parker Bros., 316 Broadway, St. Louis......................	621.25
Todd Apparel Co., 8120 Fifth Avenue, New York.............	197.85

Instructions: Open accounts in an accounts payable ledger with balance-column ruling for the creditors listed. Allow five lines for each account. Record the balance in each account. (Note how the balance was recorded in the account illustrated on page 119 and use this account as a model.)

The ledger accounts opened in this problem will also be used in Problem 11-3.

Problem 11-2. Recording purchases on account of a retail dress shop

The following purchases of merchandise on account were made by the Burch Dress Shop during March of the current year:

Mar. 2. Burton & King	$ 869.40
5. National Dress Co.	1,012.80
8. Todd Apparel Co.	691.25
12. Hess Clothing Co.	285.30
15. Adams & Lane	307.10
18. National Dress Co.	443.20
21. Parker Bros.	561.70
23. Hess Clothing Co.	739.25
26. Burton & King	610.50
29. National Dress Co.	487.75

Instructions: Record each of these purchases on page 3 of a purchases journal similar to the one illustrated on page 121. The invoices are to be numbered consecutively beginning with No. 211 for the invoice from Burton & King.

The purchases journal prepared in this problem will also be used in Problems 11-3 and 11-4.

Problem 11-3. Posting to creditors' accounts in the accounts payable ledger

Instructions: Use the accounts payable ledger accounts opened in Problem 11-1 and post the entries from the purchases journal prepared in Problem 11-2 to the proper accounts.

The accounts payable ledger prepared in this problem will be used also in Problem 12-2.

Problem 11-4. Totaling, ruling, and posting the total of the purchases journal

Instructions: 1. In a general ledger open the following accounts. Record the balance for each account for which a balance is given. Date the balance February 28. Allow four lines for each account.

Acct. No.	Account Title	Balance
11	Cash	$6,335.85 (Dr.)
21	Accounts Payable	2,628.70 (Cr.)
31	Sally M. Burch, Capital	3,707.15 (Cr.)
32	Sally M. Burch, Drawing	
51	Purchases	
63	Miscellaneous Expense	
64	Rent Expense	
65	Salary Expense	

2. Total and rule the purchases journal of Problem 11-2 in a manner similar to that used in the illustration on page 121. Post the total to the purchases account and to the accounts payable account in the general ledger.

The general ledger prepared in this problem will be used also in Problem 12-3.

Recording cash payments

Importance of accurate cash records. Cash payments and cash receipts are among the most frequent of business transactions. Those who own or operate a business should know at all times the amount of cash paid out, the amount of cash received, and the amount of cash on hand. A plan for recording these facts in detail is therefore very important.

Cash payments journal. Mr. J. C. Kelly, owner of Kelly Appliances, follows a plan of recording cash payments and cash receipts that is used in a great many businesses. He uses one journal to record all cash payments and another journal to record all cash receipts.

A special journal in which all cash payments, but only cash payments, are recorded is called a *cash payments journal.*

The immediate record of a cash payment — the check stub. When a cash payment is made by check, the check stub is the immediate record of the entry that is recorded in the cash payments journal. The check stub and the check written by Mr. Kelly in payment for rent for November are illustrated below.

Check and check stub

The check-stub record. The depositor should keep a record of his deposits and his checks on his check stubs. He will then know the amount in his bank account at all times and can avoid writing checks for more than he has on deposit. The method of keeping the record on the check stubs is shown in the illustration above. The amount of each deposit is added to the previous balance. The amount of each check is subtracted from the previous balance plus the deposit if a deposit has been made. The stub, therefore, shows the new bank balance after each check has been written.

On the stub, the drawer also writes the number of the check, the date, the name of the payee, and the purpose for which the check is drawn. This information is needed because the check stub is the source of the book-keeping record. The check stub should always be filled out before the check is written. If this is not done, the details may be forgotten.

Writing a check. An order in writing, signed by the depositor, ordering a bank to pay cash from his account is known as a *check*. The one who orders the bank to pay cash from his account is called the *drawer*. The one to whom the bank is ordered to pay the cash is called the *payee*. In the illustration on the preceding page, Kelly Appliances is the drawer and Modern Realty Company is the payee.

The check should show (1) the date, (2) the name of the payee, (3) the amount, and (4) the signature of the drawer. The amount should be written twice, once in figures and once in words.

If desired, the purpose of the check may be written, preferably in the lower left corner. Some checks have a printed space for writing the purpose of the check.

The three-column cash payments journal. Kelly Appliances records all cash payments in a cash payments journal. The cash payments journal contains columns in which to record:

1. The date of the transaction.
2. The name of the account to be debited for each transaction.
3. The number of the check that was issued.
4. The posting reference.
5. The debit and the credit amounts.

				1	2	3
DATE	ACCOUNT DEBITED	CHK. NO.	POST. REF.	GENERAL DEBIT	ACCOUNTS PAYABLE DEBIT	CASH CREDIT

CASH PAYMENTS JOURNAL — PAGE

Cash Payments Transaction No. 1 — Paying rent expense

November 2. Paid cash, $180.00, for November rent. Issued Check No. 172 in favor of Modern Realty Company.

The entry to record the payment of rent on November 2, as shown on the check stub, is illustrated at the top of the following page.

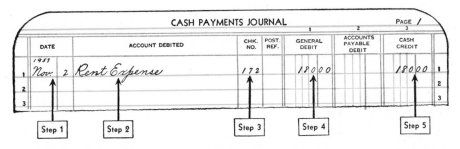

Note that the entire cash payments journal entry is written on one line. The parts of this cash payments journal entry are: (1) the date, (2) the name of the account to be debited, (3) the check number, (4) the amount debited, and (5) the amount credited.

Analyzing the recording of rent expense. The steps in recording Transaction No. 1, the payment of rent, were as follows:

Step 1. The year, 1957, was written at the top of the Date column. On the first line, the month and the day, Nov. 2, were written in the Date column.

Step 2. The words *Rent Expense* were written in the Account Debited column. Rent Expense is debited because payment of rent represents an increase in expenses. Increases in expenses are always debits.

Step 3. The number of the check, 172, was written in the Check No. column.

Step 4. The amount, $180.00, was recorded in the General Debit column. Rent is paid only once each month; therefore a special column would not save time in posting.

Step 5. The amount, $180.00, was also recorded in the Cash Credit column. Cash was credited because the asset Cash was decreased. Every time a cash payment is recorded, the amount will be entered in the Cash Credit column. The word "Cash" was not written because there is a special column for cash credits.

Step 6. A check mark was placed on the check stub after the check number to show that the check had been recorded.

Cash Payments Transaction No. 2 — Paying cash on account
Nov. 7. Paid cash, $96.80, to Acme Stove Company on account. Issued Check No. 173.

Recording cash paid on account. The check stub was the immediate record from which the entry was made. The entry was recorded on the second line of the cash payments journal as shown on page 132.

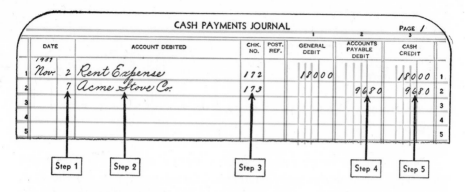

DATE	ACCOUNT DEBITED	CHK. NO.	POST. REF.	GENERAL DEBIT	ACCOUNTS PAYABLE DEBIT	CASH CREDIT	
1951							
Nov. 2	Rent Expense	172		180 00		180 00	1
7	Acme Stove Co.	173			96 80	96 80	2
							3
							4
							5

Step 1   Step 2   Step 3   Step 4   Step 5

Analyzing the recording of a cash payment on account. The steps in recording Transaction No. 2, the payment of cash on account, were:

Step 1. The date, 7, was written in the Date column. It was not necessary to repeat the name of the month.

Step 2. The name of the creditor, Acme Stove Company, was written in the Account Debited column so that the proper account in the accounts payable ledger would be debited.

Step 3. The number of the check, 173, as shown on the check stub, was written in the Check No. column.

Step 4. The amount, $96.80, was recorded in the Accounts Payable Debit column. Accounts Payable was debited because payments to creditors decrease the amount of the liability account Accounts Payable. Entries to the debit of Accounts Payable occur often. The use of a special column for accounts payable in the cash payments journal saves time in posting to the accounts payable account because only the total is posted at the end of the month.

Step 5. The amount of the cash payment, $96.80, was recorded in the Cash Credit column.

Step 6. A check mark was placed on the check stub to show that the check had been recorded.

Cash Payments Transaction No. 3 — Cash withdrawals by the proprietor

Nov. 7. Paid cash, $100.00, to Mr. J. C. Kelly, proprietor, for personal use. Issued Check No. 174.

Cash withdrawals by the proprietor. A person who is sole owner of a business often withdraws cash from the business as he needs it for personal use. Assets taken out of the business by the owner are referred to as *withdrawals.*

Under the Federal Income Tax Law, withdrawals by the proprietor are not deductible expenses. For this reason, withdrawals of cash or other assets by the proprietor are not debited to an expense account. They are debited to an account known as a *drawing account*. Mr. Kelly's drawing account is entitled J. C. Kelly, Drawing.

Recording cash withdrawals by the proprietor. The check stub was the basis for the entry. The entry was recorded on the third line of the cash payments journal as shown below.

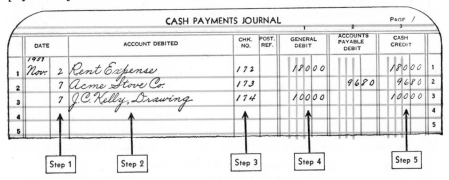

Analyzing the recording of cash withdrawals by the proprietor. The steps in recording the cash withdrawal by the proprietor were:

Step 1. The date was written in the usual manner.

Step 2. J. C. Kelly, Drawing was written in the Account Debited column. J. C. Kelly, Drawing was debited because the withdrawal of assets by the proprietor represents a decrease in proprietorship, and decreases in proprietorship are always debits.

Step 3. The check number, 174, was written in the Check No. column.

Step 4. The amount, $100.00, was recorded in the General Debit column. Withdrawals are not common enough to justify a special column for them.

Step 5. The amount, $100.00, was recorded in the Cash Credit column.

Step 6. A check mark was placed on the check stub to show that the check had been recorded.

Completed three-column cash payments journal. During the month of November, Mr. Kelly made a number of cash payments. Each of the transactions was recorded in the manner described for the first three transactions. The three-column cash payments journal of Kelly Appliances at the end of November appeared as shown on page 134.

CASH PAYMENTS JOURNAL

PAGE 1

DATE	ACCOUNT DEBITED	CHK. NO.	POST. REF.	GENERAL DEBIT	ACCOUNTS PAYABLE DEBIT	CASH CREDIT
1951						
Nov. 2	Rent Expense	172	64	180 00		180 00
7	Acme Stove Co	173	✓		96 80	96 80
7	J.C. Kelly, Drawing	174	32	100 00		100 00
7	Hills Electric Co	175	✓		714 20	714 20
8	Miscellaneous Expense	176	63	15 80		15 80
9	Rollo Manufacturing Co	177	✓		229 50	229 50
13	Delivery Expense	178	61	27 80		27 80
15	Salary Expense	179	65	100 00		100 00
16	Union Supply Co	180	✓		80 40	80 40
17	Miscellaneous Expense	181	63	10 00		10 00
25	Arco Atlas Co	182	✓		72 96	72 96
28	Delivery Expense	183	61	25 00		25 00
29	Bell Light Fixture Co	184	✓		88 74	88 74
30	J.C. Kelly, Drawing	185	32	100 00		100 00
30	Salary Expense	186	65	100 00		100 00
30	Totals			658 60	1282 60	1941 20
				(✓)	(21)	(11)

Three-column cash payments journal

The problems of recording withholding taxes and social security taxes when salaries are paid will be dealt with in a later chapter.

Proving the totals of the cash payments journal. At the end of the month, each column of the cash payments journal was footed with small pencil figures. The total of the Cash Credit column was proved to be equal to the total of the debit columns as follows:

Debits		*Credits*	
General.....................	$ 658.60	Cash.....................	$1,941.20
Accounts Payable..........	1,282.60		
Total.....................	$1,941.20		

Footing and ruling the cash payments journal. After the equality of debits and credits had been proved, the totals were recorded in ink. The page was then ruled. A single line was drawn across the amount columns to indicate addition. A double line was drawn across all columns except the Account Debited column to indicate the completion of the work.

Posting the first entry in the cash payments journal. Each entry in the General Debit column must be posted as a debit to an account in the general ledger.

The first entry is therefore posted as a debit to the account Rent Expense. This account, after the entry has been posted, appears as follows:

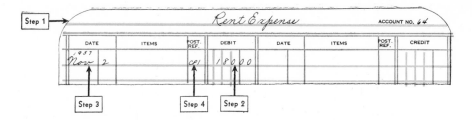

Step 1

Rent Expense   ACCOUNT NO. 64

DATE	ITEMS	POST. REF.	DEBIT	DATE	ITEMS	POST. REF.	CREDIT
1957 Nov 2		CP1	18000				

Step 3   Step 4   Step 2

Analyzing the posting of Rent Expense. The steps in posting the rent expense entry to the rent expense account were as follows:

Step 1. The title of the account, Rent Expense, and the account number, 64, were written at the top of the ledger page. (See page 229 for the explanation of account numbers and the chart of accounts.)

Step 2. The amount, $180.00, was posted to the Debit Amount column of the rent expense account.

Step 3. The year, 1957, was written at the top of the Date column. The date, Nov. 2, was written in the Date column.

Step 4. The source of the entry, CP1, was written in the Post. Ref. column. "CP1" shows that the entry was posted from the cash payments journal, page 1.

Step 5. The account number, 64, was written in the Post. Ref. column of the cash payments journal to show the completion of the posting.

The credit to the cash account will be posted at the end of the month as a part of the total of the Cash Credit column.

Posting additional entries in the General Debit column. Each entry in the General Debit column of the cash payments journal is posted to the debit of an account in the general ledger. The procedure of posting is the same as that used in posting the first entry to the debit of Rent Expense.

The items in the General Debit column of the cash payments journal are usually posted at intervals during the month. In this way the book-keeper keeps his work up to date and avoids having to do a large amount of posting at the end of the month.

Note that in the cash payments journal on page 134, the account number has been entered in the Post. Ref. column for each entry in the General Debit column. This shows that all of these items have been posted.

Posting cash paid on account. The entry on Line 2 of the cash payments journal on page 134 shows a payment on account to the Acme Stove Company. This amount must be posted to the debit of the creditor's account in the accounts payable ledger. The ledger account of the Acme Stove Company after the transaction has been posted is shown on page 136.

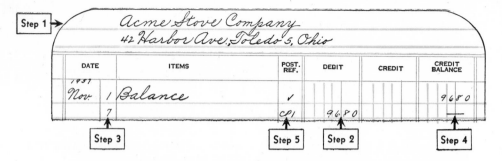

Analyzing the posting of cash payments to creditors' accounts. The steps in posting a cash payment to the Acme Stove Company account were:

Step 1. The Acme Stove Company account was located in the accounts payable ledger. The account was located quickly because the accounts in the accounts payable ledger are arranged in alphabetic order.

Step 2. The amount, $96.80, which was recorded in the Accounts Payable Debit column of the cash payments journal, was posted to the Debit column of the Acme Stove Company account.

Step 3. The date, 7, was written in the Date column.

Step 4. The debit amount, $96.80, was subtracted from the previous credit balance of $96.80. A short line was drawn in the Credit Balance column even with the debit to show that the account had no balance.

Step 5. The source of the entry, CP1, was written in the Post. Ref. column.

Step 6. A check mark was placed in the Post. Ref. column of the cash payments journal to show the completion of the posting. (Subsidiary ledger accounts are arranged alphabetically. The pages are not numbered. A check mark is used instead of page numbers to show posting.)

Posting additional cash payments on account. All other payments on account are posted in a similar manner. The check mark in the Post. Ref. column opposite each of the amounts in the Accounts Payable Debit column of the cash payments journal on page 134 shows that each has been posted.

Amounts are posted to creditors' accounts at frequent intervals during the month. When there are many such entries, the posting is often done daily. The bookkeeper thus avoids having much posting to be done at the end of the month. He may also find it useful to have the accounts payable ledger show the exact amount owed to any creditor at any time.

The accounts payable ledger of Kelly Appliances after the posting of the cash payments journal is illustrated on pages 137 and 138.

Acme Stove Company
42 Harbor Ave., Toledo 5, Ohio

DATE		ITEMS	POST. REF.	DEBIT	CREDIT	CREDIT BALANCE
1957						
Nov.	1	Balance	✓			9680
	7		CP1	9680		—
	29		P1		16000	16000

Alfred Supply Co.
4441 B Street, City

DATE		ITEMS	POST. REF.	DEBIT	CREDIT	CREDIT BALANCE
1957						
Nov.	11		J1		14400	14400

Arco Atlas Company
2424 State Street, City

DATE		ITEMS	POST. REF.	DEBIT	CREDIT	CREDIT BALANCE
1957						
Nov.	6		P1		25250	25250
	25		CP1	7296		17954

Bell Light Fixture Co.
424 Broadway, Cleveland 6, Ohio

DATE		ITEMS	POST. REF.	DEBIT	CREDIT	CREDIT BALANCE
1957						
Nov.	1	Balance	✓			8874
	25		P1		48150	57024
	29		CP1	8874		48150

Metals, Inc.
1296 Ash Street, Lansing 3, Michigan

DATE		ITEMS	POST. REF.	DEBIT	CREDIT	CREDIT BALANCE
1957						
Nov.	9		P1		4500	4500
	18		P1		15000	19500

Accounts payable ledger — Kelly Appliances

The posting of November 11 to the Alfred Supply Company account will be discussed in Chapter 15, "The General Journal."

Rollo Manufacturing Co
464 Belt Drive, Detroit 8, Michigan

DATE	ITEMS	POST. REF.	DEBIT	CREDIT	CREDIT BALANCE
1957 Nov. 4		P1		229 50	229 50
9		CP1	229 50		—

Union Supply Co
2964 State Street, Chicago 10, Illinois

DATE	ITEMS	POST. REF.	DEBIT	CREDIT	CREDIT BALANCE
1957 Nov. 1	Balance	✓			80 40
4		P1		125 00	205 40
9		P1		200 50	405 90
16		CP1	80 40		325 50

Wills Electric Co
44 Broadway, Grand Rapids 4, Michigan

DATE	ITEMS	POST. REF.	DEBIT	CREDIT	CREDIT BALANCE
1957 Nov. 1	Balance	✓			714 20
7		CP1	714 20		—
16		P1		120 00	120 00

Accounts payable ledger — Kelly Appliances (concluded)

Posting the totals of the cash payments journal. During the month the entries in the General Debit column have been posted to the accounts in the general ledger. The entries in the Accounts Payable Debit column have been also posted to the accounts in the accounts payable ledger. The posting of the totals of the cash payments journal was completed at the end of the month. The steps in posting the totals were:

Step 1. A check mark was placed in parentheses on the first line below the total of the General Debit column. This check mark shows that the posting of the individual items in the General Debit column has been completed. Each item in this column was posted to the debit of an account in the general ledger and therefore no further posting is required.

Step 2. The total of the Accounts Payable Debit column, $1,282.60, was posted to the debit of the accounts payable account in the general ledger. The source of the entry, CP1, was written in the Post. Ref. column of the accounts payable account.

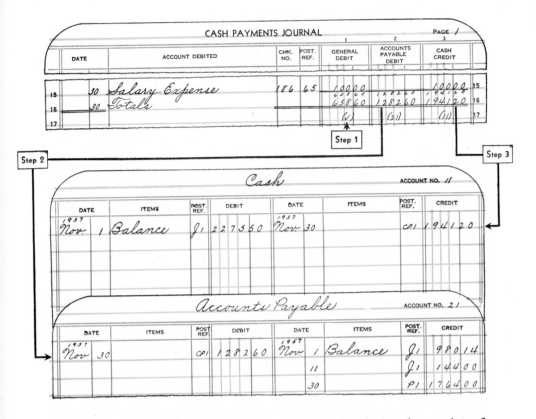

CASH PAYMENTS JOURNAL   PAGE /

DATE	ACCOUNT DEBITED	CHK. NO.	POST. REF.	GENERAL DEBIT	ACCOUNTS PAYABLE DEBIT	CASH CREDIT	
30	Salary Expense	186	65	100 00		100 00	15
30	Totals			658 60	1282 60	1941 20	16
				(✓)	(21)	(11)	17

Step 1

Step 2

Step 3

Cash   ACCOUNT NO. 11

DATE	ITEMS	POST. REF.	DEBIT	DATE	ITEMS	POST. REF.	CREDIT
1957 Nov. 1	Balance	J1	2275 50	1957 Nov. 30		CP1	1941 20

Accounts Payable   ACCOUNT NO. 21

DATE	ITEMS	POST. REF.	DEBIT	DATE	ITEMS	POST. REF.	CREDIT
1957 Nov. 30		CP1	1282 60	1957 Nov. 1	Balance	J1	980 14
				11		J1	144 00
				30		P1	1764 00

The completion of the posting was indicated by placing the number of the accounts payable account, 21, in parentheses on the line immediately below the total in the cash payments journal.

The accounts payable account in the general ledger has now been debited in one entry for the total amount debited to the creditors' accounts in the accounts payable ledger. The balance of the accounts payable account should therefore equal the sum of the balances of all of the accounts in the accounts payable ledger.

Step 3. The total of the Cash Credit column, $1,941.20, was posted to the credit of the cash account in the general ledger. The source of the entry, CP1, was written in the Post. Ref. column of the cash account.

The completion of the posting was indicated in the cash payments journal by placing the number of the cash account, 11, in parentheses immediately below the total.

Summary of the posting of the cash payments journal. Each item in the General Debit column was posted to the debit of an account in the general ledger. The total of the Accounts Payable Debit column was posted to the debit of the accounts payable account in the general ledger. The total debits posted to the general ledger were therefore as follows:

General Debit............ $ 658.60
Accounts Payable Debit...   1,282.60
                          _____
Total Debits............ $1,941.20

Note that the total debits are the same as the amount credited to cash, $1,941.20, the total of the Cash Credit column. Each individual amount in the Accounts Payable Debit column was also posted to the debit of the creditor's account in the accounts payable ledger. The total of the debits to the creditors' accounts in the accounts payable ledger is therefore equal to the one debit to the accounts payable account in the general ledger.

Proving the accounts payable ledger. In Chapter 11 creditors' accounts in the accounts payable ledger were credited when merchandise was bought on account. The accounts payable account was credited for the total of the purchases on account.

In this chapter creditors' accounts in the accounts payable ledger have been debited for the cash payments to the creditors. Also, the accounts payable account in the general ledger has been debited for the total amount paid to the creditors. If the work was done correctly, the total of the balances of the accounts with creditors should agree with the balance of the accounts payable account in the general ledger. In order to determine the correctness of the work, the following steps were taken:

Step 1. A list was prepared showing the balances of all the accounts in the accounts payable ledger that had credit balances at the end of the month. The complete accounts payable ledger from which this list was prepared is shown on pages 137 and 138 and the list itself is shown below.

Kelly Appliances Schedule of Accounts Payable November 30, 1957		
Acme Stove Company	1 6 0 0 0	
Alfred Supply Co.	1 4 4 0 0	
Arco Atlas Company	1 7 9 5 4	
Bell Light Fixture Co	4 8 1 5 0	
Metals, Inc.	1 9 5 0 0	
Union Supply Co.	3 2 5 5 0	
Wills Electric Co.	1 2 0 0 0	
Total Accounts Payable		1 6 0 5 5 4

Schedule of accounts payable

A list showing the account titles and the balances in the accounts payable ledger is known as a *schedule of accounts payable*.

Step 2. The accounts payable account in the general ledger was footed with small pencil figures. The debit total was subtracted from the credit total. The balance was written in the Items column on the credit side in small pencil figures. The accounts payable account with the footings and the balance is shown below:

DATE	ITEMS	POST REF	DEBIT	DATE	ITEMS	POST REF.	CREDIT
1957 Nov. 30		CP1	1 2 8 2 60	*1957* Nov. 1	Balance	J1	9 8 0 14
				11		J1	1 4 4 00
				30		P1	1 7 4 4 00

ACCOUNT NO. 21

Step 3. The balance of the accounts payable account was compared with the total of the balances of the creditors' accounts arrived at in Step 1 above. The balance of the accounts payable account, $1,605.54, was the same as the total of the schedule of accounts payable. This is evidence that the work has been done correctly.

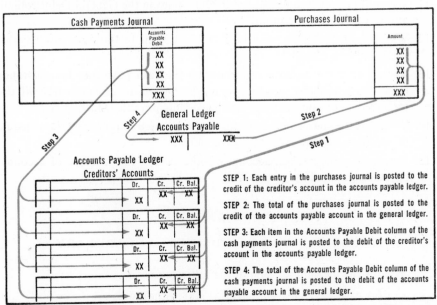

STEP 1: Each entry in the purchases journal is posted to the credit of the creditor's account in the accounts payable ledger.

STEP 2: The total of the purchases journal is posted to the credit of the accounts payable account in the general ledger.

STEP 3: Each item in the Accounts Payable Debit column of the cash payments journal is posted to the debit of the creditor's account in the accounts payable ledger.

STEP 4: The total of the Accounts Payable Debit column of the cash payments journal is posted to the debit of the accounts payable account in the general ledger.

Diagram of the posting of the purchases journal and the cash payments journal to the accounts payable account in the general ledger and to the creditors' accounts in the accounts payable ledger

1. What kinds of transactions are recorded in the cash payments journal?
2. When cash payments are made by check, what is the immediate record for entries in the cash payments journal?
3. Why is it important for the depositor to keep an accurate record of his checks and deposits on the check stubs?
4. Why should the check stub be filled out before writing the check?
5. How many lines in the cash payments journal are required to record a cash payment?
6. What account is debited and what account is credited for the payment of rent expense?
7. What account is debited and what account is credited when a cash payment is made to a creditor?
8. What is the name of the account used to record withdrawals by the proprietor?
9. Across what columns are the double ruled lines drawn to show the completion of the work in the cash payments journal?
10. What should be done before recording the totals of the cash payments journal in ink?
11. Why is it desirable to post the individual items in the General Debit column at intervals during the month?
12. Why is it desirable to post the individual items in the Accounts Payable Debit column often?
13. Assume that the purchases journal and the cash payments journal totals have been posted. With what account balance in the general ledger will the total of the account balances in the accounts payable ledger agree?
14. What was the source of the account balances used in preparing the schedule of accounts payable shown on page 140?
15. With what general ledger account was the total of the schedule of accounts payable compared?

INCREASING YOUR BUSINESS VOCABULARY

What is the meaning of each of the following:

(a) cash payments journal
(b) check
(c) drawer
(d) payee

(e) withdrawals
(f) drawing account
(g) schedule of accounts payable

CASES FOR DISCUSSION

1. Mr. Joseph L. Williams sometimes signs his checks J. L. Williams and sometimes Joseph L. Williams. When the checks are presented for payment at the bank, which checks will the bank pay?

2. Fred Atkins, who has never studied bookkeeping, does not understand why, when a cash payment entry is recorded in the cash payments journal, the name of the account debited and the name of the account credited are not both written. How would you explain the reason to him?

3. Mr. Jones, of the Jones Hardware Company, has a special column in his cash payments journal for rent expense. In the chapter you have just studied there is no special column for rent expense. Explain why the plan you have studied is a satisfactory plan.

DRILLS FOR UNDERSTANDING

Drill 12-A. The following cash payments were made by A. R. Baker for part of the month of November.

Instructions: 1. For each payment indicate (a) what account or accounts will be debited and (b) what account will be credited.

(1) Paid cash, $650.00, to Harmon and Company, a creditor, on account.
(2) Paid cash, $120.00, for advertising.
(3) Paid cash, $260.00, for salaries.
(4) Paid cash, $300.00, for rent.
(5) Paid cash, $200.00, for personal use.
(6) Paid cash, $140.00, for office equipment.
(7) Paid cash, $60.00, for repairs on delivery truck.
(8) Paid cash, $25.00, for cleaning windows.
(9) Paid cash, $300.00, to James C. Wilson, a creditor, on account.

Drill 12-B. *Instructions:* Answer the following questions:

(1) What was the total of the cash payments in Drill 12-A?

(2) What amount will be posted to the debit of Accounts Payable from Drill 12-A?

(3) How much was the proprietorship decreased by cash payments made in Drill 12-A?

APPLICATION PROBLEMS

Problem 12-1. Recording cash payments of a retail dress shop

The following cash payments were made by the Burch Dress Shop during March of the current year:

Mar. 1. Issued Check No. 210 for $621.25 to Parker Bros. on account.
2. Issued Check No. 211 for $200.00 to L. B. Harris for March rent.
9. Issued Check No. 212 for $125.00 to Sally M. Burch as a withdrawal in anticipation of profits.
12. Issued Check No. 213 for $1,480.30 to National Dress Co. on account.
13. Issued Check No. 214 for $335.00 to Hess Clothing Co. on account.
14. Issued Check No. 215 for $12.75 to the Bell Telephone Company for the March telephone bill. (Miscellaneous Expense)
15. Issued Check No. 216 for $1,095.00 to Burton & King on account.
19. Issued Check No. 217 for $781.50 to Adams & Lane on account.
25. Issued Check No. 218 for $789.10 to Todd Apparel Co. on account.
28. Issued Check No. 219 for $285.30 to Hess Clothing Co. on account.
30. Issued Check No. 220 for $250.00 for salaries.
30. Issued Check No. 221 for $100.00 to Sally M. Burch as a withdrawal in anticipation of profits.

Instructions: Record each of these cash payments transactions on page 3 of a cash payments journal similar to the one illustrated on page 134.

The cash payments journal for this problem will also be used in Problems 12-2 and 12-3.

Problem 12-2. Posting to creditors' accounts from the cash payments journal

This problem requires the accounts payable ledger used in Problem 11-3. If this ledger is not available, complete Exercise 12-A in the Appendix.

Instructions: Post the entries from the Accounts Payable Debit column of the cash payments journal prepared in Problem 12-1 to the creditors' accounts in the accounts payable ledger used in Problem 11-3.

The accounts payable ledger used in this problem will also be used in Problem 12-4.

Problem 12-3. Posting to general ledger accounts from the cash payments journal

This problem requires the general ledger used in Problem 11-4. If this ledger is not available, complete Exercise 12-A in the Appendix.

Instructions: 1. Post the amounts in the General Debit column of the cash payments journal prepared in Problem 12-1 to the appropriate accounts in the general ledger used in Problem 11-4.

2. Foot, prove, total, and rule the cash payments journal.

3. Post the totals of the special columns in the cash payments journal.

Problem 12-4. Proving the accounts payable ledger

Instructions: 1. Prepare a schedule of accounts payable from the accounts payable ledger in Problem 12-2. Your schedule should be similar in form to the one illustrated on page 140.

2. Compare the total of the schedule of accounts payable with the balance of the accounts payable account in the general ledger in Problem 12-3. If there is a difference, recheck your work until the error is found.

CHAPTER 13

Recording the selling of merchandise on account

Selling merchandise. Mr. Kelly, owner of Kelly Appliances, sells merchandise both for cash and on account. When cash is received at the time of a sale, the transaction is known as a *cash sale*. When merchandise is sold with an agreement that the amount is to be paid at some later date, the transaction is known as a *sale on account*. Other terms used to describe a sale on account are: *charge sale* or a *sale on credit*.

Mr. Kelly uses a special sales journal in which to record all sales on account. A journal in which sales on account, and only sales on account, are recorded is called a *sales journal*.

The immediate record — the sales slip. The most common immediate record of a sale on account by retail stores is a sales slip. A business form that shows all the details about a sale is called a *sales slip* or *sales ticket*.

In most stores in which sales are made on account, each salesclerk has his own sales slip book in which to record each sale as it is completed. Each sales slip in the book is numbered, and the salesclerk must account for each number. The original copy of the sales slip is usually kept by the store as a basis for its bookkeeping records.

The customer is often required to sign the original sales slip as a record that he approves the charge to his account. Usually one of the carbon copies of the sales slip is handed to the customer or is wrapped with the merchandise that is given or delivered to him.

Details of the sales slip. The form and the arrangement of items on sales slips vary with the particular needs of the business. The sales slip

SALES SLIP			No. 751
KELLY APPLIANCES			
289 MAIN STREET			
ANN ARBOR			
TERMS *On account* DATE *Nov. 2* 19 *52*			
SOLD TO *Frank Post* ✓			
1350 Long Street			
City			
QUANTITY	DESCRIPTION	PRICE	AMOUNT
1	*Rollo Pressure Cooker*	18 00	18 00
1	*Garbage Disposal*	127 00	127 00
			145 00
AMOUNT RECEIVED	CLERK *J.C.K.*		

Sales slip

145

shown on page 145 was prepared by the salesclerk for a sale made on account to Mr. Frank Post on November 2, 1957.

Analyzing the sales slip. The sales slip made out at the time of the sale to Mr. Post showed the following information:

1. The sales slip number.
2. The terms of the sale.
3. The date of the sale.
4. The name and the address of the customer.
5. The number and the description of each item.
6. The unit price of each item.
7. The total amount of the sale.
8. The amount of cash received at the time of the sale.
9. The salesclerk's number or initials.

If a business needs to record other information on its sales slips, additional space is provided. For example, a business with more than one department may provide space for the department name or number.

Recording sales on account. Two common methods of keeping records of sales on account are explained in this chapter. In the first method, the most important information on each sales slip is summarized in a book that is used only for that purpose. In the second method, the sales slips themselves are used as the journal.

The book in which all sales of merchandise on account are recorded is known by various names. It may be called the *sales journal*, the *sales book*, or the *sales register*. Regardless of the name of the book used for recording sales, the plan of recording sales is the same.

Each sales slip is summarized on a single line. The sales slips are entered in the order in which they are prepared. After each is recorded, it is filed by number or by customer's name so that it may be referred to readily when necessary.

The sales journal. The sales journal used by Kelly Appliances with the entry to record the sale on account to Frank Post is shown below.

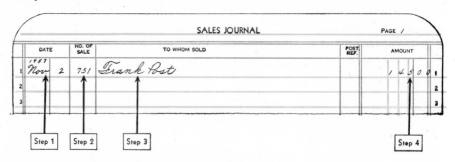

Analyzing the recording of a sale on account. The steps in recording Sales Slip No. 751 were as follow:

Step 1. The year, 1957, was written at the top of the Date column. Immediately below the year, on the first line, the date, Nov. 2, was written.

Step 2. The number of the sales slip, 751, was written in the No. of Sale column.

Step 3. The name of the customer was written in the To Whom Sold column.

Step 4. The amount of the sale was recorded in the Amount column.

Step 5. A check mark ($\sqrt{}$) was placed at the right of Frank Post's name on the sales slip to show that the sales slip had been recorded. (See the illustration on page 145.)

Accounts with customers. Kelly Appliances made a sale on account to Frank Post in the amount of $145.00. The business therefore has a claim against Mr. Post for that amount. Such claims are assets and are known as *accounts receivable*.

A business may refer to its customers who buy on account as *charge customers* or *debtors*. In order to know how much is due from each charge customer, it is necessary to keep a separate account with each one.

Accounts receivable ledger. As Mr. Kelly has a large number of charge customers, he finds it convenient to have the individual accounts with customers in a ledger separate from the other accounts. A ledger that contains accounts with customers only is known as an *accounts receivable ledger*.

Accounts receivable controlling account. If a business with many customers had an account in the general ledger for each customer, the ledger would be difficult to handle. The listing of each customer's name on the trial balance and on the balance sheet would also make these forms very long. For these reasons a single account in the general ledger is used to summarize all transactions with customers. The account that summarizes all transactions with customers is called a controlling account. The name of the controlling account for customers is *Accounts Receivable*.

The controlling account Accounts Receivable is debited for the total of the amounts posted to the debit of customers' accounts in the accounts receivable ledger. It is credited for the total of amounts posted to the credit of customers' accounts in the accounts receivable ledger. When all posting is completed at the end of a fiscal period, the balance of the controlling account agrees with the total of all of the balances of the customers' accounts in the accounts receivable ledger.

Posting to a customer's account in the accounts receivable ledger. Each entry in the sales journal is posted to a customer's account in the accounts receivable ledger. When the first entry in the sales journal was posted to the account with Frank Post, the account appeared as follows:

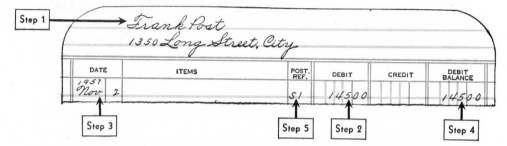

Balance-column ruling for customers' accounts. For customers' accounts Kelly Appliances uses a balance-column ledger that is ruled the same as the ledger used for creditors' accounts. The only difference is that for customers' accounts the balance column shows the heading *Debit Balance*. Customers' balances normally are debit balances.

The use of balance-column ruling for customers' accounts shows at any time how much is to be collected from each customer. The new balance due from a customer is shown after each posting from the sales journal.

Analyzing the posting to a customer's account. The steps in posting the sale on account to Frank Post were:

Step 1. The name and the address were written on the first two lines of the accounts receivable ledger page. As this was a new account, the address was obtained from the sales slip.

Step 2. The amount of the sale, $145.00, was recorded in the Debit amount column. Mr. Post's account was debited because Kelly Appliances has a claim of $145.00 against Mr. Post for the amount of the sale made to him. This claim is an asset because it gives the business the right to collect this amount of money. As all assets are debits, the amount was posted to the debit of Mr. Post's account.

Step 3. The year and the date were written in the Date column.

Step 4. The amount, $145.00, was written in the Debit Balance column.

Step 5. The posting reference, S1, was written in the Post. Ref. column to show that the item was posted from page 1 of the sales journal.

Step 6. A check mark was placed in the Post. Ref. column of the sales journal to indicate the completion of the posting. Page numbers are not used because the accounts in the accounts receivable ledger are arranged alphabetically and are not numbered.

Recording additional sales slips in the sales journal. Each sales slip for merchandise sold on account is recorded in the same manner as the Frank Post sales slip. All the essential information on each sales slip is summarized on one line of the sales journal. Entries in the sales journal are posted daily to the accounts receivable ledger in order to keep the individual accounts up to date.

Posting additional amounts to customers' accounts. The effect of posting additional entries in the sales journal to the customers' accounts in the accounts receivable ledger is shown in the following illustration:

Walter Love
360 Elm Street. City

DATE	ITEMS	POST. REF.	DEBIT	CREDIT	DEBIT BALANCE
1957 Nov. 1	Balance	✓			69 00
9		S1	295 40		364 40

The account of Walter Love had a balance at the beginning of November of $69.00. At that time the customer's name and address were written at the top of the account and the balance was entered in the manner shown above. The entry of November 9 in the sales journal was posted to Walter Love's account. This amount, $295.40, was entered in the Debit column of the customer's account and the new balance, $364.40, was entered in the Debit Balance column. The page of the sales journal from which this entry came, S1, was entered in the Post. Ref. column of the customer's account. The completion of the posting was indicated by placing a check mark in the Post. Ref. column of the sales journal.

Completed sales journal for November. During the month of November, Mr. Kelly made a number of sales on account. Each sale on account was recorded in the sales journal in the manner described for the sale to Frank Post. At frequent intervals during the month each entry was posted to the proper account in the accounts receivable ledger and check marks were placed in the Post. Ref. column of the sales journal to indicate that the transaction had been posted.

At the end of the month, the sales journal was totaled, ruled, and posted. The accounts to be debited and credited for the total of the sales journal were shown by writing *Accounts Receivable Dr./Sales Cr.* on the same line as the total. The completed sales journal for November is shown below.

	DATE	NO. OF SALE	TO WHOM SOLD	POST. REF.	AMOUNT	
	1957		SALES JOURNAL		PAGE 1	
1	Nov. 2	751	Frank Post	✓	1 4 5 0 0	1
2	4	752	W R James	✓	3 7 5 0 0	2
3	4	753	J. S. Martin	✓	1 1 7 0 0	3
4	8	754	L D Watts	✓	2 5 5 0 0	4
5	9	755	Walter Love	✓	2 9 5 4 0	5
6	13	756	Shepherd Young	✓	3 7 2 2 0	6
7	14	757	J C Miller	✓	1 5 0 0	7
8	16	758	J. C. Miller	✓	6 9 0 0	8
9	18	759	D C Walsh	✓	3 0 8 0 0	9
10	20	760	S. M. Shaw	✓	7 0 0 0	10
11	28	761	M R Cole	✓	9 8 0 0	11
12	30		Accounts Receivable Dr./Sales Cr.	12/41	2 1 1 9 6 0	12
13						13
14						14
15						15
16						16
17						17
18						18
19						19

Sales journal

Analyzing the posting of the total of the sales journal. The total of the sales journal showed the total increase for the month in accounts receivable, that is, the claims against customers for goods sold on account. Accounts receivable are an asset; increases in accounts receivable are therefore debits. The total of the sales journal is therefore debited to the asset account Accounts Receivable in the general ledger.

The total of the sales journal also shows the sales on account for the month. Sales are an income of the business. As increases in incomes are credits, Sales is credited for the total of the sales journal.

The steps followed in posting the total of the sales journal were:

Step 1. The total of the sales journal, $2,119.60, was posted to the debit of Accounts Receivable, Account No. 12 in the general ledger. The date, 30, was recorded in the Date column of the account.

Step 2. *S1* was written in the Post. Ref. column of the accounts receivable account to show that this entry came from page 1 of the sales journal.

Step 3. The accounts receivable account number, 12, was written in the left part of the Post. Ref. column.

Step 4. The total of the sales journal, $2,119.60, was also posted to the credit of Sales in the general ledger. The date, Nov. 30, 1957, was written in the Date column of the account.

Step 5. *S1* was written in the Post. Ref. column of the sales account to show that the entry came from page 1 of the sales journal.

Step 6. The sales account number, 41, was written in the Post. Ref. column and was separated from the other account number by a diagonal line.

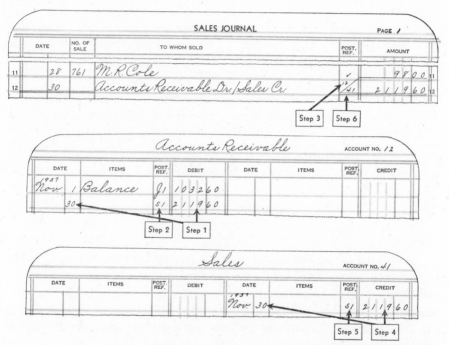

A second method — using sales slips as a sales journal. Some businesses file or bind the sales slips together and use them as a sales journal. When this method is used, the posting is done from the original sales slips and the sales journal is not used.

The method of using the sales slips for the sales journal is not the same in all businesses, but a satisfactory method is as follows:

Step 1. The sales slips are numbered consecutively as they are prepared and are placed in a file.

Step 2. The amount of each sales slip is posted directly to the customer's account in the accounts receivable ledger. The number of the sales slip is placed in the Post. Ref. column of the customer's account to show the source of the entry. A check mark is placed at the right of the customer's name on the sales slip to show that the slip has been posted.

Step 3. The amounts of all sales slips are added at the end of the month or at more frequent intervals if desired. Ordinarily an adding machine is used for this purpose.

Step 4. The total of the sales slips for the period is recorded in a two-column general journal as a debit to Accounts Receivable and a credit to Sales. Such an entry is illustrated below.

	GENERAL JOURNAL				PAGE *18*
DATE	NAME OF ACCOUNT	POST. REF.	DEBIT	CREDIT	
31	Accounts Receivable		2 1 9 6 1 0		
	Sales			2 1 9 6 1 0	
	Sales on account for				
	October				

The form of journal illustrated here is a two-column general journal. The use of this journal is discussed and illustrated in Chapter 15.

Step 5. The journal entry is posted to the debit of Accounts Receivable and to the credit of Sales in the general ledger.

CHAPTER QUESTIONS

1. What are some other terms that are used for "charge sales"?
2. What kind of sales are recorded in the sales journal?
3. What is the immediate record for entries in the sales journal?
4. What information is contained on the sales slip?
5. What are some other terms that are used in place of "sales journal"?
6. What important facts from the sales slip are summarized on one line in the sales journal?
7. How does the bookkeeper indicate on the sales slip that it has been recorded?
8. In which subsidiary ledger are the accounts with customers kept?
9. When merchandise is sold on account, what account is debited? What account is credited?
10. How often are sales journal entries posted to customers' accounts?
11. Why is an accounts receivable ledger used?
12. What is the difference between the headings of the amount columns of accounts receivable ledger accounts and those of accounts payable ledger accounts?
13. Explain in detail the relationship of the accounts receivable ledger and the accounts receivable account in the general ledger.

INCREASING YOUR BUSINESS VOCABULARY

What is the meaning of each of the following:

(a) cash sale

(b) sale on account

(c) sales journal

(d) sales slip

(e) accounts receivable

(f) charge customer

(g) accounts receivable ledger

(h) accounts receivable account

CASES FOR DISCUSSION

1. A grocer sold a typewriter that he had used in the store. He recorded this transaction in the sales journal. Why is this procedure incorrect?

2. Ronald Eastman makes 450 sales on account in an average month. He records each sale in the sales journal, from which he posts to the subsidiary and the general ledgers.

   (a) How much work might be saved by posting directly from the sales slips to the customers' accounts in the subsidiary ledger?

   (b) If this method were followed, how should he record the total sales for the month?

DRILL FOR UNDERSTANDING

Drill 13-A. Mr. Warren, of Warren's Hardware, keeps his customers' accounts in his general ledger. The debit column of his trial balance for the year ended December 31 of the current year is shown at the left.

Cash................	$2,275.00
Merchandise Inventory.	5,443.50
Frederick Adams......	132.00
M. R. Cole...........	146.90
W. R. James.........	86.50
J. M. Smith..........	70.30
K. R. Jones..........	246.20
Joseph Peart..........	80.00
J. W. Owens..........	72.80
M. W. Morrison......	150.00
B. J. Cutler..........	89.00
M. R. Abbott........	174.40
Supplies.............	104.60
Prepaid Insurance.....	96.00

Instructions: Answer the following questions:

(1) What was the total amount due from customers?

(2) If Mr. Warren had used an accounts receivable ledger:

   (a) What is the name of the controlling account that he would have used?

   (b) What would be the balance of this account on the trial balance of December 31?

   (c) How many lines would be saved on his trial balance?

APPLICATION PROBLEMS

Problem 13-1. Opening an accounts receivable ledger for a wholesale grocer

The names of the businesses to which Hoffman Wholesale Groceries sells on account and the amounts due from them on October 31 of the current year are:

Bard and Co., 20 Broadway, Hilton...........................	$624.75
M. E. Creager, 698 Railroad Street, City......................	342.25
Hull Grocery, 2932 Daly Avenue, City........................	221.30
J. B. Johnston, 598 June Street, City.........................	175.00
T. D. Shirk, 3625 Morton Street, City........................	272.60
Stambaugh Bros., 336 Main Street, City......................	352.72
R. K. Wise, Kingston..	125.00

Instructions: Open accounts in an accounts receivable ledger with balance-column ruling for the customers listed above. Allow five lines for each account. Record the balance in each account.

The ledger accounts opened in this problem will also be used in Problem 13-3.

Problem 13-2. Recording sales on account for a wholesale grocer

The following sales of merchandise on account were made by Hoffman Wholesale Groceries during November of the current year:

Nov.	1	M. E. Creager, $160.00	Nov.	19	M. E. Creager, $195.40
	3	Hull Grocery, $257.92		20	Stambaugh Bros., $116.03
	5	J. B. Johnston, $75.25		22	Hull Grocery, $210.88
	8	R. K. Wise, $201.00		25	J. B. Johnston, $150.90
	10	Stambaugh Bros., $389.95		26	Bard and Co., $85.00
	14	Bard and Co., $240.10		26	T. D. Shirk, $243.50
	17	T. D. Shirk, $160.46		29	R. K. Wise, $115.87
	17	R. K. Wise, $189.45			

Instructions: Record each of these transactions on page 11 of a sales journal similar to the one illustrated on page 150. The sales slips are to be numbered consecutively beginning with No. 101.

The sales journal prepared in this problem will also be used in Problems 13-3 and 13-4.

Problem 13-3. Posting to customers' accounts in the accounts receivable ledger

Instructions: Use the accounts receivable ledger accounts opened in Problem 13-1. Post the entries from the sales journal prepared in Problem 13-2.

The accounts receivable ledger prepared in this problem will be used also in Problem 14-2.

Problem 13-4. Totaling, ruling, and posting the total of the sales journal

Instructions: 1. In a general ledger open the following accounts. Record the balance for each account for which a balance is given. Date the balance October 31. Allow four lines for each account.

Acct. No.	Account Title	Balance
11	Cash	$2,197.10 (Dr.)
12	Accounts Receivable	2,113.62 (Dr.)
13	Office Supplies	235.75 (Dr.)
31	R. J. Hoffman, Capital	4,546.47 (Cr.)
41	Sales	

2. Total and rule the sales journal of Problem 13-2. Post the total to the sales account and to the accounts receivable account.

The general ledger prepared in this problem will be used also in Problem 14-3.

Recording cash receipts

Sources of cash receipts. Kelly Appliances receives cash from three sources: (1) from customers who are making payments on account, (2) from cash sales to customers, and (3) from miscellaneous sources. In all cases, the asset Cash is increased; therefore Cash is debited for the amount received.

The immediate record of cash receipts. A transaction in which cash is received or paid is known as a *cash transaction*. A bookkeeper needs a written form or record as a basis for recording each cash transaction.

When Mr. Kelly receives a check from a customer, the check is the basis for the entry. When he receives cash in the form of coins or bills, he records it on a machine known as a cash register. The cash register tape is the immediate record of such cash received.

By operating certain keys of the cash register, the clerk or the cashier records the amount of each cash receipt. The method of using the cash register in recording cash receipts is described and illustrated in a later chapter.

In some stores all cash receipts are recorded on a machine known as an autographic register. This machine records each transaction in duplicate. One copy is given to the customer and one copy is kept by the business as its immediate record.

Regardless of the exact form of the immediate record, the record must provide all the information needed for the bookkeeping entry.

The four-column cash receipts journal. Kelly Appliances records all cash receipts in a cash receipts journal. A special journal in which all cash receipts, but only cash receipts, are recorded is a *cash receipts journal*.

Mr. Kelly's cash receipts journal provides columns in which to record:

1. The date of the transaction.
2. The name of the account to be credited for each transaction.
3. The posting reference.
4. Debit and credit amounts.

The form of the cash receipts journal used by Kelly Appliances is illustrated on page 156.

				1	2	3	4	
DATE	ACCOUNT CREDITED	POST. REF.	GENERAL CREDIT	SALES CREDIT	ACCOUNTS RECEIVABLE CREDIT	CASH DEBIT		
1957 Nov 1	Balance on hand $2,275.50	✓						1
								2
								3
								4
								5
								6

Analyzing the cash receipts journal. Each transaction recorded in the cash receipts journal is an increase in the asset Cash. In each entry, therefore, Cash must be debited. A special Cash Debit column is provided.

Cash is received frequently from customers to apply on their accounts. Each such transaction decreases the value of the asset Accounts Receivable and is therefore credited to that account. Because such transactions occur frequently, a special column is provided for Accounts Receivable Credit. All amounts received from customers on account are recorded in this column.

Cash is also received frequently from cash sales. The sales are recorded on a cash register, and at intervals the total of the sales is entered in the cash receipts journal. As such entries are made frequently, a special Sales Credit column is provided for them.

Almost all cash receipts result from cash received on account from customers or from cash sales, but occasionally cash is received from other sources. All credits for which special columns are not provided are recorded in the General Credit column.

Typical entries will be discussed to explain the use of each of these columns.

Cash Receipts Entry No. 1 — Recording beginning cash balance

November 1. Cash on hand, $2,275.50.

The owner of a business may want to know the amount of cash on hand at any time. To avoid having to refer to the cash account in the general ledger to get the balance, the cash on hand at the beginning of each month is recorded. An entry that records information only but does not include debit or credit amounts to be posted is called a *memorandum entry.*

The first line in the cash receipts journal was used to record the memorandum entry of cash on hand on November 1. The cash account in the general ledger showed that the cash balance on November 1 was $2,275.50. The memorandum entry to record the November 1 cash balance is shown in the illustration above.

Analyzing the cash-on-hand entry. The year, the month, and the day were written in the Date column. *Balance on hand $2,275.50* was written in the Account Credited column. Nothing was written in the amount columns. A check mark (√) was placed in the Post. Ref. column to indicate that nothing was to be posted from this line.

Since the cash balance on hand, $2,275.50, had already been recorded in the cash account in the general ledger, the amount of this cash balance does not appear in any amount column in the cash receipts journal.

Cash Receipts Entry No. 2 — Receipt of cash on account

November 1. Received a check for $29.70 from J. S. Martin to apply on his account.

The check received from Mr. Martin was the basis for the cash receipts entry. This cash transaction was recorded on the second line of the cash receipts journal as follows:

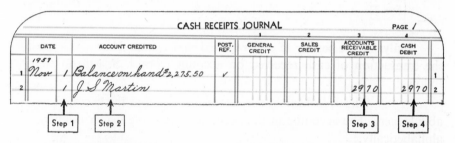

Analyzing the recording of cash received from a customer. The steps in recording the receipt of cash from a customer were as follows:

Step 1. The date was written in the Date column. Since the year and the month had already been written on this page, they were not repeated.

Step 2. The name of the customer, J. S. Martin, was written in the Account Credited column so that his account will be credited in the accounts receivable ledger.

Step 3. The amount, $29.70, was recorded in the Accounts Receivable Credit column. The amount was recorded in this column because the asset Accounts Receivable was decreased by the amount of the payment.

Step 4. The amount, $29.70, was also recorded in the Cash Debit column. Cash was debited because the receipt of cash increases this asset.

The check was then placed in the cash receipts file or drawer to be kept until deposited.

Posting the cash received on account. Mr. Kelly frequently wishes to know how much each customer owes the business so that he will know whether to permit further sales on account to a particular customer. For this reason, the amounts in the Accounts Receivable Credit column of the cash receipts journal are posted frequently to the credit of customers' accounts in the accounts receivable ledger.

The J. S. Martin account after the cash transaction of November 1 was posted is shown below.

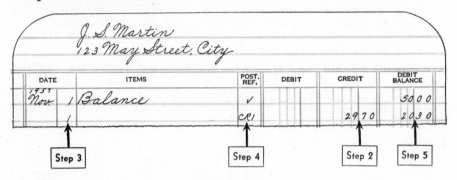

Analyzing the posting of cash received on account. The steps in posting the transaction of cash received on account from J. S. Martin were as follows:

Step 1. The J. S. Martin account was located in the accounts receivable ledger. The accounts in the accounts receivable ledger are arranged alphabetically.

Step 2. The amount, $29.70, which was recorded in the Accounts Receivable Credit column of the cash receipts journal, was posted as a credit to J. S. Martin's account.

Step 3. The date, 1, was written in the Date column. The account already had an entry with the year and the month; since neither had changed, it was not necessary to repeat them.

Step 4. The source of the entry, CR1, was written in the Post. Ref. column to show that the transaction was posted from page 1 of the cash receipts journal.

Step 5. The credit amount, $29.70, was subtracted from the previous debit balance, leaving a balance of $20.30. This balance, $20.30, was recorded in the Debit Balance column.

Step 6. A check mark was placed in the Post. Ref. column of the cash receipts journal to show the completion of the posting. Page numbers are not used when posting to customers' accounts because the accounts are arranged alphabetically and are not numbered. Each entry in the Accounts Receivable Credit column will be posted in the same way.

The cash receipts journal after this item was posted appears as follows:

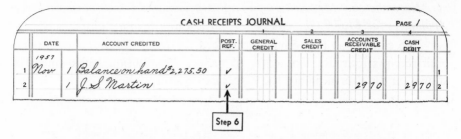

Step 6

Cash Receipts Entry No. 3 — Cash sales of merchandise

November 2. Cash sales as shown by cash register records, $442.50.

The recording of cash sales is shown on the third line of the cash receipts journal as follows:

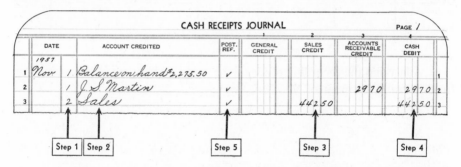

Step 1   Step 2   Step 5   Step 3   Step 4

Analyzing the recording of cash sales of merchandise. The steps in recording the entry for cash sales of merchandise were:

Step 1. The date, 2, was written in the Date column.

Step 2. The word *Sales* was written in the Account Credited column to show the source of the income.

Step 3. The amount, $442.50, was recorded in the Sales Credit column. Sales was credited because the amount represents an income to the business and all increases in income are credits.

Step 4. The amount, $442.50, was also recorded in the Cash Debit column because the asset Cash was increased.

Step 5. A check mark was placed in the Post. Ref. column of the cash receipts journal to show that the item was not to be posted as a separate item. At the end of the month the debit to Cash resulting from the cash sales will be posted as a part of the total of the Cash Debit column. The credit to Sales will be posted as a part of the total of the Sales Credit column.

Cash Receipts Entry No. 4 — Additional investment of cash

November 6. Mr. Kelly made out a personal check in favor of Kelly Appliances for $1,000.00 as an additional investment in the business.

The check was the immediate record for recording the entry in the cash receipts journal. The entry to record the additional investment is shown on the fourth line of the cash receipts journal below.

	DATE	ACCOUNT CREDITED	POST. REF.	GENERAL CREDIT 1	SALES CREDIT 2	ACCOUNTS RECEIVABLE CREDIT 3	CASH DEBIT 4	
	1957							
1	*Nov* 1	*Balance on hand $2,275.50*	✓					1
2	1	*J S Martin*	✓			29 70	29 70	2
3	2	*Sales*	✓		442 50		442 50	3
4	6	*J C Kelly, Capital*		1 000 00			1 000 00	4

CASH RECEIPTS JOURNAL — PAGE 1

Step 1   Step 2   Step 3   Step 4

Analyzing the recording of a general credit. The steps in recording the additional investment of Mr. Kelly were:

Step 1. The date, 6, was written in the Date column.

Step 2. *J. C. Kelly, Capital* was written in the Account Credited column. J. C. Kelly, Capital was credited because all increases in proprietorship are recorded as credits.

Step 3. The amount, $1,000.00, was recorded in the General Credit column. The account J. C. Kelly, Capital is in the general ledger. All transactions that cannot be recorded in special columns are recorded in the General Credit column.

Step 4. The amount, $1,000.00, was also recorded in the Cash Debit column because the asset Cash was increased.

Posting the additional investment of cash. At the end of the month the debit to Cash will be posted as a part of the total of the Cash Debit column.

Each item in the General Credit column must be posted separately. The cash receipts journal and the capital account after the posting of this transaction are shown on the opposite page.

When the transaction was posted to the J. C. Kelly, Capital account, the amount, $1,000.00, was entered in the Credit Amount column; the date of the transaction, 6, was entered in the Date column; and the source of the entry was indicated by writing *CR1* in the Post. Ref. column.

DATE	ACCOUNT CREDITED	POST. REF.	GENERAL CREDIT	SALES CREDIT	ACCOUNTS RECEIVABLE CREDIT	CASH DEBIT	
1957							1
Nov 1	Balance on hand $2,275.50	✓					1
1	J S Martin	✓			29 70	29 70	2
2	Sales	✓		442 50		442 50	3
6	J C Kelly, Capital	31	1000 00			1000 00	4
							5

J. C. Kelly, Capital   ACCOUNT NO. 31

DATE	ITEMS	POST. REF.	DEBIT	DATE	ITEMS	POST. REF.	CREDIT
				1957			
				Nov 1	Balance	J1	7972 06
				6		cr1	1000 00

The completion of the posting was then indicated by writing the account number, 31, in the Post. Ref. column of the cash receipts journal. All general credit items are posted in the same way.

Completed four-column cash receipts journal. During the month of November Mr. Kelly had a number of cash transactions similar to those described above. The complete cash receipts journal for the month of November is shown at the top of the following page.

Analyzing the completed cash receipts journal. The steps taken in completing the cash receipts journal were as follows:

Step 1. The columns were footed with small pencil figures.

Step 2. The equality of debits and credits was proved as follows:

Debits		Credits	
Cash Debit Total..........	$5,089.00	General Credit Total........	$1,000.00
		Sales Credit Total..........	2,396.00
		Accounts Receivable Cr. Total	1,693.00
Total Debits...............	$5,089.00	Total Credits..............	$5,089.00

The above calculations showed that the total of the Cash Debit column was equal to the sum of the totals of the three credit columns. This proved that the debits recorded in this journal were equal to the credits. This was a useful test of the accuracy of the work.

Step 3. The totals were written in ink and the columns were ruled in the usual manner as shown in the illustration.

DATE	ACCOUNT CREDITED	POST. REF.	GENERAL CREDIT	SALES CREDIT	ACCOUNTS RECEIVABLE CREDIT	CASH DEBIT	
1957							
Nov 1	Balance on hand $2,275.30	✓					1
1	J.S. Martin	✓			29 70	29 70	2
2	Sales	✓		442 50		442 50	3
6	J.C. Kelly, Capital	31	1000 00			1000 00	4
8	J.C. Miller	✓			80 00	80 00	5
9	Sales	✓		374 80		374 80	6
14	J.C. Miller	✓			375 00	375 00	7
15	L.O. Watts	✓			174 40	174 40	8
16	Sales	✓		669 74		669 74	9
20	Shepherd Young	✓			150 00	150 00	10
20	W.R. Moore	✓			117 00	117 00	11
23	Walter Love	✓			295 40	295 40	12
23	Sales	✓		473 36		473 36	13
25	W.R. Moore	✓			15 00	15 00	14
28	Walter Love	✓			69 00	69 00	15
29	S.M. Shaw	✓			70 00	70 00	16
29	J.C. Miller	✓			20 30	20 30	17
30	Frank Post	✓			145 00	145 00	18
30	S.M. Shaw	✓			152 20	152 20	19
30	Sales	✓		435 60		435 60	20
30	Totals		1000 00	2396 00	1693 00	5089 00	21
			(✓)	(41)	(12)	(11)	22

Cash receipts journal after footing, ruling, and posting

Posting the totals of the cash receipts journal. At the end of the month the steps in posting the cash receipts journal were:

Step 1. A check mark (√) was placed in parentheses on the first line below the total of the General Credit column to show that the items in this column had been posted to the individual accounts.

Step 2. The total of the Sales Credit column, $2,396.00, was posted to the credit of Sales in the general ledger. The posting was indicated by placing the sales account number, 41, in parentheses below the total.

Step 3. The total of the Accounts Receivable Credit column, $1,693.00, was posted to the credit of Accounts Receivable in the general ledger. The posting was indicated by placing the account number, 12, in parentheses below the total.

Step 4. The total of the Cash Debit column, $5,089.00, was posted to the debit of Cash in the general ledger. The posting was indicated by placing the account number, 11, in parentheses below the total.

General ledger accounts after posting sales on account and cash receipts. The sales account after posting sales on account and cash sales is shown below.

DATE	ITEMS	POST. REF.	DEBIT	DATE	ITEMS	POST. REF.	CREDIT
				1957 Nov. 30		S1	2 1 1 9 60
				30		CR1	2 3 9 6 00

Sales   ACCOUNT NO. 41

The sales account shows a credit of $2,119.60 resulting from posting the total of sales on account from the sales journal for the month. It also shows a credit of $2,396.00 resulting from posting the cash sales for the month, the total of the Sales Credit column of the cash receipts journal. This account then shows the total sales of Kelly Appliances for the month of November.

The accounts receivable account after the posting of cash received from customers and sales on account is shown below.

Accounts Receivable   ACCOUNT NO. 12

DATE	ITEMS	POST. REF.	DEBIT	DATE	ITEMS	POST. REF.	CREDIT
1957 Nov. 1	Balance	J1	1 0 3 2 60	*1957* Nov. 30		CR1	1 6 9 3 00
30		S1	2 1 1 9 60				

The accounts receivable account is the controlling account of the accounts receivable ledger. The accounts receivable account shows a debit balance on November 1 of $1,032.60, which was the amount due from customers on that date. It also shows a debit of $2,119.60 resulting from posting the total of the sales journal for the month.

The credit side of the account shows an amount of $1,693.00 resulting from posting the total of the Accounts Receivable Credit column of the cash receipts journal for the month. The balance of the account is the amount due from customers at the end of November. This balance should agree with the total of all the debit balances in the accounts receivable ledger.

The cash account after posting cash receipts for the month is shown on the following page.

				Cash			ACCOUNT NO. *11*	

DATE		ITEMS	POST. REF.	DEBIT	DATE		ITEMS	POST. REF.	CREDIT
1957 Nov.	1	Balance	J1	2 2 7 5 50	*1957* Nov.	30		CP1	1 9 4 1 2 0
	30		CR1	5 0 8 9 00					

The cash account had a debit balance of $2,275.50 on November 1. This was the amount of cash on hand at the beginning of the month. It also shows a debit of $5,089.00 resulting from posting the total of the Cash Debit column of the cash receipts journal for November.

The credit side of the cash account shows a credit of $1,941.20 resulting from posting the total of the Cash Credit column of the cash payments journal for November. The balance of the account represents the amount of cash on hand at the end of November.

Proving cash on hand. The cash on hand should be counted and proved at the end of each day. Counting the cash on hand and checking its accuracy with the bookkeeping records is known as *proving cash*. Proving cash serves as a frequent check on the accuracy of the work of the bookkeeper and the cashier. Proving cash also provides the owner of the business with day-to-day knowledge about the cash available for the operation of the business.

The formula for proving cash is as follows:

(Beginning Balance + Cash Receipts) − Cash Payments = Cash on Hand

The beginning balance and the receipts are shown in the cash receipts journal. Payments are shown in the cash payments journal. If the balance of cash shown by the amounts in the cash journals equals the amount of cash on hand, the accuracy of the records is said to have been proved.

In order to avoid the adding of long columns of figures, the bookkeeper may enter subtotals in pencil figures at intervals in the cash receipts journal and the cash payments journal. The cash receipts journal and the cash payments journal as they are footed after the proving of cash on December 7 are illustrated on the opposite page.

DATE	ACCOUNT CREDITED	POST. REF.	GENERAL CREDIT	SALES CREDIT	ACCOUNTS RECEIVABLE CREDIT	CASH DEBIT
1957 Dec. 1	Balance on hand $5,423.30	✓				
3	H. R. James	✓			375 00	375 00
4	J. S. Martin	✓			117 00	117 00
6	L. D. Watts	✓			255 00	255 00
7	Sales	✓		436 25		436 25

Subtotals and cash balance in cash receipts journal

DATE	ACCOUNT DEBITED	CHK. NO.	POST. REF.	GENERAL DEBIT	ACCOUNTS PAYABLE DEBIT	CASH CREDIT
1957 Dec. 2	Rent Expense	187	64	180 00		180 00
3	Union Supply Co.	188	✓		125 00	125 00
4	Purchases	189	51	16 33		16 33
6	Arco Atlas Company	190	✓		252 50	252 50
7	Miscellaneous Expense	191	63	7 50		7 50

Subtotals in cash payments journal

In each journal the equality of debits and credits in the column footings is proved in the same manner as it is proved at the end of the month. At the close of the day on December 7 the cash balance is found as follows:

Balance on hand December 1 (from cash receipts journal)......	$5,423.30
Total cash receipts (total of Cash Debit column in cash receipts journal)...	1,183.25
Total cash on hand and received...........................	$6,606.55
Less total cash payments (total of Cash Credit column in cash payments journal)....................................	581.33
Balance on hand December 7.............................	$6,025.22

This amount, $6,025.22, is the book record of the cash balance on hand on December 7. The actual cash on hand is found by adding the check stub record (cash in bank) and the amount of any undeposited cash. If this total of actual cash on hand agrees with the above book record, cash has been proved. This amount is then entered in small pencil figures in the Account Credited column of the cash receipts journal even with the column footings.

Chapter 14. Recording cash receipts   165

Cash short and over. If the cash on hand is less than the balance of the cash account, the cash is said to be *short*. If this error cannot be found or recalled, the shortage is debited to an account with the title *Cash Short and Over*. This entry is made in the cash *payments* journal. The amount of the shortage is recorded in the General Debit column and in the Cash Credit column.

If the cash on hand is more than the balance of the cash account, the cash is said to be *long* or *over*. If this error cannot be found or recalled, the amount that the cash on hand exceeds the account balance is credited to an account with the title *Cash Short and Over*. This entry is made in the cash *receipts* journal. The amount of the overage is recorded in the General Credit column and in the Cash Debit column.

The T account at the right shows the effect of cash short or cash over on the ledger account.

CASH SHORT AND OVER	
Debit this account for cash short.	*Credit* this account for cash over.

Proving the accounts receivable ledger. Chapter 13 discussed and illustrated transactions that dealt with selling merchandise on account. It illustrated the posting of transactions to the debit of customers' accounts and to the controlling account Accounts Receivable.

This chapter has discussed and illustrated transactions that dealt with cash receipts from customers. It has illustrated the posting of transactions

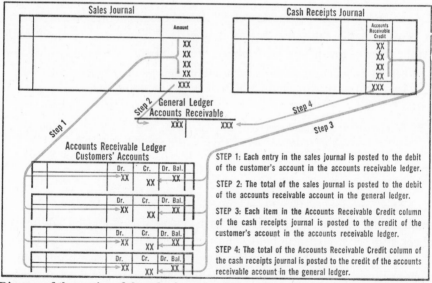

STEP 1: Each entry in the sales journal is posted to the debit of the customer's account in the accounts receivable ledger.

STEP 2: The total of the sales journal is posted to the debit of the accounts receivable account in the general ledger.

STEP 3: Each item in the Accounts Receivable Credit column of the cash receipts journal is posted to the credit of the customer's account in the accounts receivable ledger.

STEP 4: The total of the Accounts Receivable Credit column of the cash receipts journal is posted to the credit of the accounts receivable account in the general ledger.

Diagram of the posting of the sales journal and the cash receipts journal to the accounts receivable account in the general ledger and to the customers' accounts in the accounts receivable ledger

to the credit of customers' accounts and to the controlling account Accounts Receivable.

If the work has been done correctly, the total of the balances of the accounts with customers will agree with the balance of the accounts receivable account in the general ledger. In order to determine the correctness of the work, the following steps were taken:

Step 1. A list was prepared showing the balances of all the accounts in the accounts receivable ledger that had debit balances at the end of the month. The complete accounts receivable ledger from which this list was prepared is shown on pages 168, 169, and 170, and the list is shown below.

Kelly Appliances		
Schedule of Accounts Receivable		
November 30, 1957		
M. R. Cole	9 8 0 0	
W. R. James	3 7 5 0 0	
J. S. Martin	1 1 7 0 0	
J. C. Miller	8 4 0 0	
D. C. Walsh	3 0 8 0 0	
L. O. Watts	2 5 5 0 0	
Shepherd Young	2 2 2 0	
Total Accounts Receivable		1 4 5 9 2 0

Schedule of accounts receivable

A list showing the account titles and the balances in the accounts receivable ledger is known as a *schedule of accounts receivable*.

Step 2. The accounts receivable account in the general ledger was footed with small pencil figures. The credit total was subtracted from the debit total. The balance was written in the Items column on the debit side in small pencil figures.

		Accounts Receivable		ACCOUNT NO. 12				
DATE	ITEMS	POST. REF.	DEBIT	DATE	ITEMS	POST. REF.	CREDIT
1957 Nov 1	Balance	J1	1 0 3 2 6 0	1957 Nov 30		CR1	1 6 9 3 0 0
30	145920	S1	2 1 1 9 6 0				

Accounts receivable account with pencil footings and balance

Step 3. The balance of the accounts receivable account was compared with the total of the balances of the customers' accounts shown in the schedule of accounts receivable prepared in Step 1. The balance of the accounts receivable account, as shown by the small pencil figures on the debit side, was $1,459.20. This was the same as the total of the schedule of accounts receivable. This proves that the debits and the credits posted as totals to the controlling account are equal to the individual debits and credits posted to the customers' accounts.

M. R. Cole
121 West Third Street, City

DATE	ITEMS	POST. REF.	DEBIT	CREDIT	DEBIT BALANCE
1957 Nov. 28		S1	98 00		98 00

W. R. James
134 North Franklin Street, City

DATE	ITEMS	POST. REF.	DEBIT	CREDIT	DEBIT BALANCE
1957 Nov. 4		S1	375 00		375 00

Walter Love
360 Elm Street, City

DATE	ITEMS	POST. REF.	DEBIT	CREDIT	DEBIT BALANCE
1957 Nov. 1	Balance	✓			69 00
9		S1	295 40		364 40
23		CR1		295 40	69 00
28		CR1		69 00	—

Accounts receivable ledger — Kelly Appliances

J. S. Martin
123 May Street, City

DATE	ITEMS	POST. REF.	DEBIT	CREDIT	DEBIT BALANCE
1957 Nov. 1	Balance	✓			50 00
1		CR1		29 70	20 30
4		S1	117 00		137 30
27		J1		20 30	117 00

J. C. Miller
400 Laurel Street, City

DATE	ITEMS	POST. REF.	DEBIT	CREDIT	DEBIT BALANCE
1957 Nov. 1	Balance	✓			455 00
8		CR1		80 00	375 00
14		S1	15 00		390 00
14		CR1		375 00	15 00
16		S1	69 00		84 00
27		J1	20 30		104 30
29		CR1		20 30	84 00

W. R. Moore
4827 Cumberland Road, City

DATE	ITEMS	POST. REF.	DEBIT	CREDIT	DEBIT BALANCE
1957 Nov. 1	Balance	✓			132 00
20		CR1		117 00	15 00
25		CR1		15 00	—

Frank Post
1350 Long Street, City

DATE	ITEMS	POST. REF.	DEBIT	CREDIT	DEBIT BALANCE
1957 Nov. 2		S1	145 00		145 00
30		CR1		145 00	—

Accounts receivable ledger — Kelly Appliances (continued)

The postings of November 27 to the J. S. Martin and J. C. Miller accounts will be discussed and illustrated in Chapter 15, "The General Journal."

S. M. Shaw
635 Lee Street, Marion

DATE	ITEMS	POST. REF.	DEBIT	CREDIT	DEBIT BALANCE
1957 Nov. 1	Balance	✓			152 20
20		S1	70 00		222 20
29		CR1		70 00	152 20
30		CR1		152 20	—

D. C. Walsh
516 Jones Road, City

DATE	ITEMS	POST. REF.	DEBIT	CREDIT	DEBIT BALANCE
1957 Nov. 18		S1	308 00		308 00

L. D. Watts
310 Main Street, Brantford

DATE	ITEMS	POST. REF.	DEBIT	CREDIT	DEBIT BALANCE
1957 Nov. 1	Balance	✓			174 40
8		S1	255 00		429 40
15		CR1		174 40	255 00

Shepherd Young
503 Mill Road, Warren

DATE	ITEMS	POST. REF.	DEBIT	CREDIT	DEBIT BALANCE
1957 Nov. 13		S1	372 20		372 20
20		CR1		150 00	222 20

Accounts receivable ledger — Kelly Appliances (concluded)

Statement of account. A business form that shows the charges to a customer's account, the amounts credited to his account, and the balance is known as a *statement of account* or *statement*. It is customary for a business to send each charge customer a statement at intervals, usually monthly. When a customer receives his statement, he should compare it with the records in his own ledger. If his records do not agree with the statement, he should notify the creditor.

Kelly Appliances sends monthly statements to its customers and receives monthly statements from its creditors. One of the statements sent out by Kelly Appliances is illustrated on the following page.

KELLY APPLIANCES
289 MAIN STREET
ANN ARBOR

DATE Dec. 1, 1957

To   J. C. Miller
      400 Laurel Street
      City.

DATE	DEBITS	CREDITS	BALANCE
1957			
Nov. 1			455.00
8		80.00	375.00
14	15.00		390.00
14		375.00	15.00
16	69.00		84.00
27	20.30		104.30
29		20.30	84.00

Statement of account

CHAPTER QUESTIONS

1. From what sources does a retail business usually receive cash?

2. When cash is received, what account is always debited?

3. What are two common sources for the immediate record of cash received?

4. When cash is received for sales of merchandise, what account is credited?

5. What is the name of the journal in which all cash receipts are recorded?

6. Why is the amount of cash on hand recorded as a memorandum entry in the cash receipts journal?

7. Where does the bookkeeper get the amount that is entered as a cash balance at the beginning of a month?

8. Why should amounts received from customers be posted frequently to their accounts?

9. What is proved when the total of the debit column of the cash receipts journal equals the total of the three credit columns?

10. What do the numbers in parentheses below the totals of the cash receipts journal at the end of the month show?

11. With what does the balance of the accounts receivable account in the general ledger agree after all posting is completed?

12. Why is it important to prove cash each day?

INCREASING YOUR BUSINESS VOCABULARY

What is the meaning of each of the following:

(a) cash transaction
(b) cash receipts journal
(c) memorandum entry
(d) proving cash

(e) cash short
(f) cash over
(g) schedule of accounts receivable
(h) statement of account

CASES FOR DISCUSSION

1. R. A. Allison operates a retail radio and television shop. He uses a cash receipts journal with columns similar to those used by Kelly Appliances as shown on page 162. J. O. Jacks, who operates the same kind of store, uses a cash receipts journal without a special column for Sales Credit. What are the advantages of Mr. Allison's plan?

2. Hugh Hilts operates a retail shoe store and sells for cash only. What changes in the cash receipts journal used by Kelly Appliances as shown on page 162 would you recommend for Mr. Hilts and why?

3. The Crown Retail Store proves cash only once a week. What are the disadvantages of this plan as compared with the plan of a store that proves cash every day?

4. When Mr. Carter receives monthly statements from creditors, he does not compare the statements with his accounts payable ledger. Why is this not a good practice?

DRILL FOR UNDERSTANDING

Drill 14-A. The following are the cash receipts for the week of December 1-6:

Dec. 1.	Balance on hand..................................	$3,250.97
2.	Cash Sales......................................	270.00
3.	Accounts Receivable............................	425.50
	Cash Sales......................................	498.36

Dec.	4.	Accounts Receivable............................	$ 64.00
		Accounts Receivable............................	122.68
	5.	Cash Sales.....................................	722.38
		Accounts Receivable............................	68.21
	6.	Cash Sales.....................................	640.00
		Accounts Receivable............................	123.00
		Office Furniture................................	40.00

Instructions: Answer each of the following questions:

(1) In what journal should these transactions be recorded?
(2) What is the total of cash sales for the week?
(3) What is the total of cash received from charge customers?
(4) Will Cash be debited or credited for each cash receipt?
(5) What was the total amount of cash received during the week?
(6) Will Accounts Receivable be debited or credited? Why?
(7) If the owner has not paid out any cash during the week, how much cash should be on hand on December 6?
(8) In what column of a cash receipts journal will the credit amount for the sale of office furniture be recorded?

APPLICATION PROBLEMS

Problem 14-1. Recording cash receipts of a wholesale grocer

On November 1 of the current year, R. J. Hoffman, proprietor of Hoffman Wholesale Groceries, had a cash balance of $2,197.10. During the month of November he completed the following cash receipts transactions:

Nov. 1. Received $2,671.40 from cash sales of merchandise.
      4. Received $221.30 from Hull Grocery on account.
      7. Received $502.25 from M. E. Creager on account.
      8. Received $9,110.50 from cash sales of merchandise.
     11. Received $10.00 from the sale of office supplies to a neighboring merchant.
     14. Received $352.72 from Stambaugh Bros. on account.
     15. Received $7,125.80 from cash sales of merchandise.
     18. Received $257.92 from Hull Grocery on account.
     21. Received $250.25 from J. B. Johnston on account.
     22. Received $7,940.15 from cash sales of merchandise.
     25. Received $864.85 from Bard and Co. on account.
     27. Received $515.45 from R. K. Wise on account.
     29. Received $6,714.35 from cash sales of merchandise.

Instructions: Record each of these cash receipts transactions on page 11 of a cash receipts journal similar to the one illustrated on page 162 of this chapter.

The cash receipts journal prepared in this problem will also be used in Problems 14-2 and 14-3.

Problem 14-2. Posting to customers' accounts from the cash receipts journal

This problem requires the accounts receivable ledger used in Problem 13-3. 'If this ledger is not available, complete Exercise 14-A in the Appendix.

Instructions: Post the entries from the Accounts Receivable Credit column of the cash receipts journal prepared in Problem 14-1 to the customers' accounts in the accounts receivable ledger used in Problem 13-3.

The accounts receivable ledger used in this problem will also be used in Problem 14-4.

Problem 14-3. Posting to general ledger accounts from the cash receipts journal

This problem requires the general ledger used in Problem 13-4. If this ledger is not available, complete Exercise 14-A in the Appendix.

Instructions: 1. Post the amounts in the General Credit column of the cash receipts journal prepared in Problem 14-1 to the appropriate accounts in the general ledger used in Problem 13-4.

2. Foot, prove, total, and rule the cash receipts journal.

3. Post the totals of the special columns in the cash receipts journal.

Problem 14-4. Proving the accounts receivable ledger

Instructions: 1. Prepare a schedule of accounts receivable from the accounts receivable ledger in Problem 14-2. Your schedule should be similar in form to the one illustrated on page 167.

2. Compare the total of the schedule of accounts receivable with the balance of the accounts receivable account in the general ledger in Problem 14-3. If there is a difference, recheck your work until the error is found.

Need for a general journal. During the operation of any business, entries must be made that cannot be recorded in the purchases journal, the sales journal, the cash receipts journal, or the cash payments journal. Such entries are called *miscellaneous entries*. A journal that is used to record miscellaneous entries is usually known as a *general journal*. Examples of entries that are recorded in the general journal are:

1. An opening entry to record the beginning balance sheet of a business.
2. Entries made to record the purchase on account of any item other than merchandise.
3. Entries made at the end of a fiscal period to adjust and close accounts.
4. Entries made to correct errors.

Beginning balance sheet of Kelly Appliances. When Kelly Appliances installed a new bookkeeping system, the balance sheet prepared for the opening entry was as follows:

Assets		Liabilities	
Cash	2275 50	Accounts Payable	980 14
Accounts Receivable	1032 60		
Merchandise Inventory	5443 50	Proprietorship	
Supplies	104 60	J. C. Kelly, Capital	7972 06
Prepaid Insurance	96 00		
Total Assets	8952 20	Total Liabilities & Prop.	8952 20

Kelly Appliances
Balance Sheet
October 31, 1957

Beginning balance sheet of Kelly Appliances

Analyzing the balance sheet. The assets and the liabilities of Kelly Appliances include the following:

Cash — the amount of cash on hand.

Accounts Receivable — the amount due from customers.

Merchandise Inventory — the goods or merchandise on hand available for sale.

Supplies — materials, such as wrapping paper, twine, and stationery, used in operating the business.

Prepaid Insurance — the amount that has been paid for insurance for future months.

Accounts Payable — the amount owed to creditors.

Recording an opening entry in the general journal. Since the opening entry was a miscellaneous entry, it was recorded in the general journal as follows:

	DATE		NAME OF ACCOUNT	POST. REF.	DEBIT	CREDIT	
	1957						
1	Nov	1	Cash		2 2 7 5 5 0		1
2			Accounts Receivable		1 0 3 2 6 0		2
3			Merchandise Inventory		5 4 4 3 5 0		3
4			Supplies		1 0 4 6 0		4
5			Prepaid Insurance		9 6 0 0		5
6			Accounts Payable			9 8 0 1 4	6
7			J. C. Kelly, Capital			7 9 7 2 0 6	7
8			To record the October 31				8
9			balance sheet				9
10							10
11							11

GENERAL JOURNAL — PAGE 1

Opening entry in the general journal

Analyzing the opening entry. The balance sheet from which the opening entry was made was dated October 31. This balance sheet was prepared after all transactions for October 31 were completed. The opening entry was not recorded until the following day and was therefore dated November 1.

The asset accounts were listed in the Name of Account column in the same order in which they appeared on the balance sheet. The name of each asset account was written close to the line separating the Date column from the Name of Account column. The amount of each asset was recorded in the Debit column.

The names of the two accounts appearing on the right-hand side of the balance sheet were indented about one-half inch to indicate that they were credits. The amounts were recorded in the Credit column.

A brief statement was written below the last account to describe the entry.

Recording beginning balances in the accounts receivable ledger. After the journal entry on page 176 was posted, the accounts receivable account had a debit balance of $1,032.60. But this account did not show the amount to be received from each customer. An account with each customer was therefore opened in the accounts receivable ledger. The balance owed by each customer was recorded in the customer's account from the following schedule of accounts receivable:

Kelly Appliances Schedule of Accounts Receivable October 31, 1957		
Walter Love	69 00	
J. S. Martin	50 00	
J. C. Miller	455 00	
W. R. Moore	132 00	
S. M. Shaw	152 20	
L. O. Watts	174 40	
Total Accounts Receivable		1032 60

Schedule of accounts receivable

Recording beginning balances in the accounts payable ledger. After the journal entry on page 176 was posted, the accounts payable account had a credit balance of $980.14. But this account did not show the amount owed to each creditor. An account with each creditor was therefore opened in the accounts payable ledger. The balance owed to each creditor was recorded in the creditor's account from the following schedule:

Kelly Appliances Schedule of Accounts Payable October 31, 1957		
Acme Stove Company	96 80	
Bell Light Fixture Co	88 74	
Union Supply Co	80 40	
Wills Electric Co	714 20	
Total Accounts Payable		980 14

Schedule of accounts payable

The accounts receivable ledger on pages 168–170 and the accounts payable ledger on pages 137–138 show the beginning balances recorded in the customers' and the creditors' accounts.

Recording the buying of store supplies on account. Mr. Kelly buys supplies such as wrapping paper, twine, bags, and cleaning supplies for use in the store. These supplies are not purchases for sale and must not be debited to the purchases account. If the purchases of supplies are made for cash, they are recorded in the cash payments journal, where Supplies is debited and Cash is credited. If the purchases of supplies are made on account, they are recorded in the general journal.

On November 11, Mr. Kelly purchased supplies on account from the Alfred Supply Co. He received an invoice for $144.00. The general journal entry to record this invoice is shown below.

	DATE	NAME OF ACCOUNT	POST. REF.	DEBIT	CREDIT	
10	11	*Supplies*		144 00		10
11		*Accounts Payable-Alfred Supply Co*	/		144 00	11
12		*Invoice of Nov 11*				12
13						13
14						14
15						15

GENERAL JOURNAL — PAGE 1

Analyzing the recording of buying store supplies on account. The date, the name of the account to be debited, and the amount were recorded in the usual manner. The supplies account was debited because supplies are an asset of the business and all assets are recorded as debits.

The accounts to be credited, Accounts Payable-Alfred Supply Co., were written on the next line, indented about one-half inch. Two accounts were credited because (1) the liability account Accounts Payable was increased, and (2) the Alfred Supply Co. account in the accounts payable ledger was increased.

It is always advisable when an amount is to be posted to two accounts from an entry on one line to draw a diagonal line in the Post. Ref. column at the time the entry is made. This is a warning to the bookkeeper to post the item to two accounts.

The general journal after the posting of this entry has been completed is shown on the opposite page.

Analyzing the credit posting. The amount of the credit, $144.00, is posted to the credit of Accounts Payable in the general ledger and also to the credit of the account with the Alfred Supply Company in the accounts payable ledger. The posting to the general ledger is indicated by writing the number 21 in the Post. Ref. column of the journal. This number is

	DATE	NAME OF ACCOUNT	POST. REF.	DEBIT	CREDIT	
10	11	Supplies	14	1 44 00		10
11		Accounts Payable—Alfred Supply Co	✓		1 44 00	11
12		Invoice of Nov. 11.				12
13						13
14						14
15						15

Entry for supplies bought on account, after posting

the account number of the accounts payable account in the general ledger. The posting to the Alfred Supply Company account in the accounts payable ledger is indicated by a check mark in the Post. Ref. column.

Withdrawals by the proprietor. Assets taken out of the business by the proprietor for his personal use are known as *withdrawals*. When merchandise is withdrawn frequently by the proprietor, as it might be by a grocer or a druggist, the transaction may be recorded in the sales journal as a sale at cost price and the proprietor may be treated as an ordinary customer. In that case he may make settlement of his account at the end of a definite period just as a customer might.

When withdrawals of merchandise are relatively infrequent, each withdrawal is recorded in the general journal. The proprietor's drawing account is debited and the purchases account is credited for the cost price of the merchandise. Mr. Kelly's withdrawals of merchandise from the appliance business are relatively infrequent. He therefore records each withdrawal of merchandise for personal use in the general journal.

On November 23, Mr. Kelly took from stock for personal use an electric range with a cost price of $227.00. The entry in the general journal to record this transaction is given below.

	DATE	NAME OF ACCOUNT	POST. REF.	DEBIT	CREDIT	
13	23	J. C. Kelly, Drawing		2 27 00		13
14		Purchases			2 27 00	14
15		Electric range for				15
16		personal use				16
17						17
18						18

Entry for withdrawal of merchandise by proprietor

Chapter 15. The general journal   179

Correcting entries. An error in the books of account may be corrected by an entry in the general journal. Such an entry is often desirable if a number of postings have been made to the account before the error is discovered. Entries made in the general journal to correct errors in book-keeping records are known as *correcting entries*.

On November 27, J. S. Martin, a charge customer, reported to Mr. Kelly that merchandise amounting to $20.30 that he had not purchased and had not received was charged to him. The sales journal for the month of October showed that this sale should have been charged to J. C. Miller.

The general journal entry illustrated below was required to correct this error:

DATE		NAME OF ACCOUNT	POST REF.	DEBIT	CREDIT
	27	J. C. Miller		20 30	
		J. S. Martin			20 30
		To correct error in			
		posting sale of Oct. 29			

Correcting entry

The error occurred in the accounts receivable ledger only and did not affect the total of Accounts Receivable. Therefore, in the correcting entry a debit was made to one customer and a credit to another customer, but no entry had to be made in the accounts receivable account.

By posting the debit, the sale was charged to J. C. Miller, the customer who had purchased the merchandise and to whom it should have been charged. By posting the credit, the error in J. S. Martin's account was corrected; the debit entry of $20.30 in Martin's account was canceled.

General journal of Kelly Appliances. The general journal of Kelly Appliances after all the miscellaneous entries for the month of November were recorded and after the journal was posted is shown on the opposite page.

The posting of an item to the general ledger is indicated in the Post. Ref. column by an account number. The posting of an item to the accounts receivable ledger or to the accounts payable ledger is indicated in the Post. Ref. column by a check mark. When one amount is posted both to the

DATE	NAME OF ACCOUNT	POST. REF.	DEBIT	CREDIT	
1957					
Nov. 1	Cash	11	2 2 7 3 5 0		1
	Accounts Receivable	12	1 0 3 2 6 0		2
	Merchandise Inventory	13	5 4 4 3 5 0		3
	Supplies	14	1 0 4 6 0		4
	Prepaid Insurance	15	9 6 0 0		5
	Accounts Payable	21		9 8 0 1 4	6
	J. C. Kelly, Capital	31		7 9 7 2 0 6	7
	To record the October 31				8
	balance sheet.				9
11	Supplies	14	1 4 4 0 0		10
	Accounts Payable—Alfred Supply Co.	21✓		1 4 4 0 0	11
	Invoice of Nov. 11.				12
23	J. C. Kelly, Drawing.	32	2 2 7 0 0		13
	Purchases	51		2 2 7 0 0	14
	Electric range for				15
	personal use.				16
27	J. C. Miller	✓	2 0 3 0		17
	J. S. Martin	✓		2 0 3 0	18
	To correct error in				19
	posting sale of Oct. 29.				20

General journal of Kelly Appliances after miscellaneous entries for
November have been recorded and posted

general ledger and to the accounts receivable ledger or the accounts
payable ledger, the posting is indicated by an account number and a check
mark, as shown in the illustration.

Adjusting entries and closing entries. Entries that are made at the end
of a fiscal period to bring various accounts up to date are known as
adjusting entries. An example of an adjusting entry is one that is made to
bring the supplies account or the prepaid insurance account up to date.

Entries that are made at the end of a fiscal period to transfer the
balances of the sales, purchases, and expense accounts to the profit and
loss summary account are called *closing entries.*

The methods of making adjusting and closing entries in the general
journal will be discussed and illustrated in later chapters.

Order of posting from journals. Journals in which transactions are
recorded from the immediate records are called *books of original entry.*
Books of original entry may be posted to the ledgers in any order that is
desired.

As a general rule, all items affecting customers' and creditors' accounts are posted frequently so that the balances of these accounts will always be up to date. Items may be posted to general ledger accounts less often; but all such items, including the totals of special columns, must be posted each time a trial balance is to be taken. It is usually found satisfactory to post the special journals in the following order: (1) sales journal; (2) cash receipts journal; (3) purchases journal; (4) cash payments journal; and (5) general journal.

General ledger of Kelly Appliances. The general ledger of Kelly Appliances as it appears on November 30 after the completion of the posting of the five journals presented in Chapters 11–15, and after the accounts have been footed, is shown on pages 183 and 184.

Proving the posting. To prove the equality of debits and credits in the general ledger, Mr. Kelly prepared a trial balance of the ledger. The completed trial balance is shown below.

Kelly Appliances
Trial Balance
November 30, 1957

Account	No.	Debit	Credit
Cash	11	5423 30	
Accounts Receivable	12	1459 20	
Merchandise Inventory	13	5443 50	
Supplies	14	248 60	
Prepaid Insurance	15	96 00	
Accounts Payable	21		1605 54
J. C. Kelly, Capital	31		8972 06
J. C. Kelly, Drawing	32	427 00	
Sales	41		4515 60
Purchases	51	1537 00	
Delivery Expense	61	52 80	
Miscellaneous Expense	63	25 80	
Rent Expense	64	180 00	
Salary Expense	65	200 00	
		15093 20	15093 20

Trial balance of Kelly Appliances

Cash

ACCOUNT NO. 11

DATE	ITEMS	POST. REF.	DEBIT	DATE	ITEMS	POST. REF.	CREDIT
1957 Nov. 1	Balance	J1	2 2 7 5 5 0	1957 Nov. 30		CP1	1 9 4 1 2 0
30		CR1	5 0 8 9 0 0 (5413.30)				

Accounts Receivable

ACCOUNT NO. 12

DATE	ITEMS	POST. REF.	DEBIT	DATE	ITEMS	POST. REF.	CREDIT
1957 Nov. 1	Balance	J1	1 0 3 2 6 0	1957 Nov. 30		CR1	1 6 9 3 0 0
30		S1	2 1 1 9 6 0 (1459.20)				

Merchandise Inventory

ACCOUNT NO. 13

DATE	ITEMS	POST. REF.	DEBIT	DATE	ITEMS	POST. REF.	CREDIT
1957 Nov. 1	Balance	J1	5 4 4 3 5 0				

Supplies

ACCOUNT NO. 14

DATE	ITEMS	POST. REF.	DEBIT	DATE	ITEMS	POST. REF.	CREDIT
1957 Nov. 1	Balance	J1	1 0 4 6 0				
11		J1	1 4 4 0 0				

Prepaid Insurance

ACCOUNT NO. 15

DATE	ITEMS	POST. REF.	DEBIT	DATE	ITEMS	POST. REF.	CREDIT
1957 Nov. 1	Balance	J1	9 6 0 0				

Accounts Payable

ACCOUNT NO. 21

DATE	ITEMS	POST. REF.	DEBIT	DATE	ITEMS	POST. REF.	CREDIT
1957 Nov. 30		CP1	1 2 8 2 6 0	1957 Nov. 1	Balance	J1	9 8 0 1 4
				11		J1	1 4 4 0 0
				30		P1	1 7 6 4 0 0 (1605.04)

J. C. Kelly, Capital

ACCOUNT NO. 31

DATE	ITEMS	POST. REF.	DEBIT	DATE	ITEMS	POST. REF.	CREDIT
				1957 Nov. 1	Balance	J1	7 9 7 2 0 6
				6		CR1	1 0 0 0 0 0

General ledger after all journals have been posted and the accounts have been footed

J. C. Kelly, Drawing   ACCOUNT NO. 32

DATE	ITEMS	POST. REF.	DEBIT	DATE	ITEMS	POST. REF.	CREDIT
1957 Nov. 7		CP1	100 00				
23		J1	227 00				
30		CP1	100 00 / 427 00				

Sales   ACCOUNT NO. 41

DATE	ITEMS	POST. REF.	DEBIT	DATE	ITEMS	POST. REF.	CREDIT
				1957 Nov. 30		S1	2119 60
				30		CR1	2396 00 / 4515 60

Purchases   ACCOUNT NO. 51

DATE	ITEMS	POST. REF.	DEBIT	DATE	ITEMS	POST. REF.	CREDIT
1957 Nov. 30	1537.00	P1	1764 00	1957 Nov. 23		J1	227 00

Delivery Expense   ACCOUNT NO. 61

DATE	ITEMS	POST. REF.	DEBIT	DATE	ITEMS	POST. REF.	CREDIT
1957 Nov. 13		CP1	27 80				
28		CP1	25 00 / 52 80				

Miscellaneous Expense   ACCOUNT NO. 63

DATE	ITEMS	POST. REF.	DEBIT	DATE	ITEMS	POST. REF.	CREDIT
1957 Nov. 8		CP1	15 80				
17		CP1	10 00 / 25 80				

Rent Expense   ACCOUNT NO. 64

DATE	ITEMS	POST. REF.	DEBIT	DATE	ITEMS	POST. REF.	CREDIT
1957 Nov. 2		CP1	180 00				

Salary Expense   ACCOUNT NO. 65

DATE	ITEMS	POST. REF.	DEBIT	DATE	ITEMS	POST. REF.	CREDIT
1957 Nov. 15		CP1	100 00				
30		CP1	100 00 / 200 00				

General ledger after all journals have been posted and the accounts have been footed
(concluded)

CHAPTER QUESTIONS

1. What kinds of transactions are recorded in the general journal?
2. Give examples of entries that would be recorded in the general journal.
3. What is the immediate record for recording an opening entry in the general journal?
4. What is the basis for recording the beginning balances to the debit of customers' accounts in the accounts receivable ledger?
5. What is the basis for recording the beginning balances to the credit of creditors' accounts in the accounts payable ledger?
6. Why are supplies purchased on account for use in a business not recorded in the purchases journal?
7. Why is it advisable to draw a diagonal line in the Post. Ref. column of the journal at the time of making the entry when one amount is to be posted to two accounts?
8. Why is it important to post items to customers' and creditors' accounts frequently?
9. When must all items be posted to the general ledger?

INCREASING YOUR BUSINESS VOCABULARY

What is the meaning of each of the following:

(a) miscellaneous entries
(b) general journal
(c) merchandise inventory
(d) prepaid insurance
(e) withdrawals
(f) correcting entries
(g) adjusting entries
(h) closing entries
(i) books of original entry

CASES FOR DISCUSSION

1. On December 10, R. T. Bolton withdrew from his business for personal use merchandise valued at $35.00.
   (a) In what two ways may this transaction be recorded?
   (b) Describe the entry that is preferred if such transactions do not occur often.
2. On January 14, the Marion Grocery Company purchased on account from the Nord Paper Company $96.40 worth of supplies to be used in the store.
   (a) Describe the entry that should be made to record this transaction and the journal in which it should be made.

(b) Describe the method of posting the transaction.

(c) In what journal would the entry have been made if the purchase had been for cash?

3. On December 15, the Martin Supply Company purchased on account from the Acme Paper Company $48.50 worth of supplies to be used in the office. The bookkeeper entered the amount in the purchases journal.

(a) Why was this incorrect?

(b) Where should the entry have been made?

(c) What account should have been debited?

(d) What accounts should have been credited?

DRILL FOR UNDERSTANDING

Drill 15-A. The following are selected business transactions of the Fenton Grocery Company for the month of April. The business uses a purchases journal, a sales journal, a cash receipts journal, a cash payments journal, and a general journal.

Instructions: For each transaction, state:

(a) The journal in which the transaction would be recorded.

(b) The account or accounts that would be debited.

(c) The account or accounts that would be credited.

1. Purchased merchandise on account from Wholesalers Incorporated, $500.00.
2. Received cash, $400.00, from cash sales of merchandise.
3. Purchased office furniture on account from Ideal Furniture Company, $800.00.
4. Sold merchandise on account to J. R. Tomkins, $37.60.
5. Paid cash, $234.50, to Wholesalers Incorporated on account.
6. Received cash, $237.50, from W. L. Cody on account.
7. A. L. Fenton, the proprietor, withdrew merchandise from the business for personal use, $46.50.
8. Paid cash, $312.50, for cash purchase of merchandise.
9. Paid cash, $65.00, for store supplies.
10. Purchased supplies on account from Mason Supply Company, $136.80.
11. Paid cash, $360.00, for salaries.
12. Paid cash, $230.00, for insurance on merchandise for three years.
13. Paid cash, $200.00, for rent.
14. Paid cash, $45.00, to City Delivery Company for delivery service.
15. Paid cash, $15.00, for window cleaning service.

Problem 15-1. Recording an opening entry

F. H. Olsen, an auto supply dealer, decided to open a new set of books on April 1 of the current year. His balance sheet on March 31 was as follows:

F. H. OLSEN
Balance Sheet
March 31, 19--

Assets			Liabilities		
Cash........................	3,650	70	Accounts Payable..............	1,102	85
Accounts Receivable...........	1,118	50			
Merchandise Inventory.........	4,228	50			
Supplies.....................	76	90	Proprietorship		
Prepaid Insurance.............	88	00	F. H. Olsen, Capital..........	8,059	75
Total Assets.................	9,162	60	Total Liabilities & Prop.......	9,162	60

Instructions: Record the opening entry in the general journal.

Problem 15-2. Recording miscellaneous entries

The transactions given below are some of the transactions completed during the month of April by F. H. Olsen. Mr. Olsen records transactions in a purchases journal, a sales journal, a cash receipts journal, a cash payments journal, and a general journal.

Apr. 1. Paid $225.00 for the April rent (Check No. 45).
   3. Purchased office furniture on account from T. F. Rice Company, $618.40; invoice of April 2 (Invoice No. 33).
   5. Received $138.40 from F. W. Arden in full of April 1 balance.
   8. Sold merchandise on account to B. M. Bell, $116.80 (Sale No. 65).
   12. Paid $269.70 to the Kelton Manufacturing Co. in full of April 1 balance (Check No. 46).
   13. Sold merchandise on account to R. D. Thomas, $234.76 (Sale No. 66).
   15. Received $1,646.80 from cash sales for April 1 to 15.
   17. Took from stock for personal use a car radio costing $108.50.
   20. Paid $197.80 to the Gregory Manufacturing Co. in full of April 1 balance (Check No. 47).
   22. Purchased supplies on account from the Acme Supply Co., $64.80; invoice of April 20 (Invoice No. 34).
   24. Discovered that a March 22 sale of merchandise on account for $163.00 to F. W. Arden had been posted incorrectly to the account of F. V. Warden.
   28. Took $300.00 for personal use (Check No. 48).
   30. Paid $350.00 for clerks' salaries for the month (Check No. 49).
   30. Purchased merchandise on account from the Kelton Manufacturing Co., $569.74; invoice of April 29 (Invoice No. 35).
   30. Sold supplies on account as an accommodation to L. D. Toll, $13.30.
   30. Received $1,872.55 from cash sales for April 16 to 30.

Instructions: Select only those entries that should be made in a general journal and record them on two-column journal paper.

Bank deposits and

CHAPTER 16 **reconciliation of bank statements**

Protecting cash receipts. Business firms usually receive cash from customers in the form of coins, bills, checks, money orders, and bank drafts. The person who is responsible for the handling of cash and accounting for it is often the bookkeeper. A cashier may work with the bookkeeper in handling cash.

Whatever plan is used, the bookkeeping records must be kept so that the manager or owner knows the bank balance at all times. The books of the business must also agree with the bank's records.

Bank deposits. It is not safe to keep large amounts of cash at the store or the office. A checking account at a bank makes it possible to pay all bills by check. Checks provide good evidence that a bill has been paid. An individual or a business therefore usually deposits all receipts in a bank. They are safe in a bank, not only because they are protected by the bank, but also because in most banks each depositor's account is insured up to $10,000 by the Federal Deposit Insurance Corporation. The Federal Deposit Insurance Corporation is an agency of the Federal government.

Opening an account with the bank. Each new depositor is required to sign his name on a card so that the bank may verify his signature on all business papers that come to the bank. The card that a depositor signs to provide the bank with a copy of his authorized signature is known as a *signature card.*

Signature cards

Two signature cards are illustrated on page 188. The one at the left is the card for Kelly Appliances and shows that only J. C. Kelly, the proprietor, is authorized to sign checks for the business. The one at the right is the card of the Howard Hardware Store. It shows that either J. D. Howard or F. B. Fortney is authorized to sign checks for the business.

Signature cards are filed alphabetically by the bank for reference purposes in comparing the signatures of the depositors with their signatures on checks and other business papers that come to the bank. The signature card is therefore a safeguard established by the bank to protect the interests of its depositors. It is used to detect forgeries.

Endorsing a check for deposit. A depositor may deposit both cash and cash items. *Cash* includes coins and paper money. *Cash items* include business forms regarded as cash, such as bank checks, bank drafts, and money orders.

The depositor should write or stamp his name on the back of each cash item. The signature of the depositor on the back of a check is an *endorsement*. The act of signing is called *endorsing*.

The purpose of the endorsement is to transfer the title of the cash item to the bank. In addition, the depositor guarantees payment of the item by his endorsement.

An endorsement on the back of a check is written at a right angle to the writing on the front of the check. It often consists of the name of the depositor only. If the depositor wants to be certain that each endorsed item is deposited to his account, he may precede his signature with the words "For deposit."

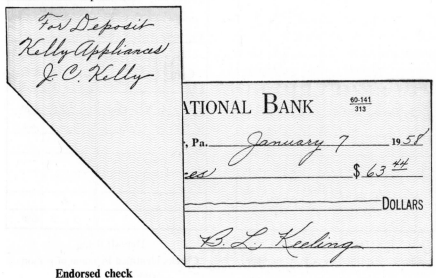

Endorsed check

The first endorsement is written near the *left end*. The endorsement should be made with a pen or with a rubber stamp. The illustration at the bottom of the preceding page shows the correct position of an endorsement.

Preparing the deposit ticket. The form provided by the bank on which the depositor lists all the cash and cash items that he wishes to deposit is called a *deposit ticket* or *deposit slip*. All paper money (bills) is listed in one amount. The total amount of cash represented by coins is listed on the next line. The amount of each cash item is listed separately.

Each check deposited may be identified by a number that is known as an A.B.A. number. The identification numbers assigned to banks by the American Bankers Association are called *A.B.A. numbers.* Any form, such as an express money order, that does not have an A.B.A. number may be listed by the name of the form.

If the bank does not care to have the A.B.A. numbers listed, the name of the person from whom the check was received may be used instead. This gives the depositor specific information about deposits that he may need if questions arise. Each depositor should ask his bank the method the bank prefers and then use that method.

SECOND NATIONAL BANK		
BROWNSVILLE, KENTUCKY		
Brownsville, Ky. December 20 1957		
PLEASE LIST WHERE PAYABLE		
BILLS	348	00
COIN	23	83
CHECKS 21-3	23	15
73-6	61	80
73-448	103	45
P. O. Money Order	15	00
	575	23
Kane's Hobby Shop		
NAME OF DEPOSIT ACCOUNT		

Deposit ticket
Checks identified by A.B.A. number

MERCHANTS NATIONAL BANK		
Ann Arbor		
Deposited for Account of		
Kelly Appliances		
289 Main Street		
Date December 12 1957		
	DOLLARS	CENTS
CASH { Bills	56	00
Coin	8	65
CHECKS:		
1 M. R. Cole	98	00
2 W. R. James	100	00
3		
4		
5		
6		
	262	65

Deposit ticket
Checks identified by name of person
from whom received

Some depositors prefer to make all deposit slips in duplicate so that they have a more complete record of each deposit. When this is done, the bank keeps the original and the teller signs the copy and returns it to the depositor as a receipt.

The total of all the cash and the cash items deposited is written at the bottom of the deposit ticket. The deposit ticket and the deposit are presented to the teller of the bank. The teller records the amount of the deposit and the date in a small book known as a *bank passbook* that is provided by the bank, or he gives the depositor a receipt.

A.B.A. numbers. There are two parts to each A.B.A. number. The first part refers either to a large city or to a state. The numbers 1 to 49 are assigned to the large cities, and the numbers 50 to 99 are assigned to the states. The second part of the number refers to a specific bank. For example, The First National Bank of Lancaster, Pennsylvania, is known as Bank 60-141, 60 referring to the state, Pennsylvania, and 141 referring to the number of the bank.

The A.B.A. number is printed on each bank check in the manner shown in the illustration below. It is the custom to print under the A.B.A. number the number of the Federal Reserve District. In the illustration below, this number is 3. The number of the Federal Reserve District may be followed by two other figures (in this illustration 13) that are used by the Federal Reserve Bank in routing checks.

Check showing A.B.A. number

Noting deposits in the cash receipts journal. Some businesses have a special bank column in the cash receipts journal in which to record all deposits. When this method is not used, it is a good practice when the deposit ticket has been prepared to place a check mark ($\sqrt{}$) in the cash receipts journal after each item deposited. This makes it possible for the bookkeeper to know which cash items have been deposited.

Bank service charges. Banks obtain income by using part of the funds deposited with them to purchase interest-bearing securities, such as government bonds. They also lend part of the funds deposited and charge interest on the loans. If a depositor has a rather large balance so that a considerable sum is available for investment, a bank will receive more than enough in interest to pay for all of the clerical work and supplies used in handling the customer's account.

If the balance of an account is small, the expense of handling the depositor's account may exceed the possible income to the bank. Banks therefore make a monthly charge, known as a *bank service charge*, whenever a depositor's balance is less than a fixed sum, such as $200.00, or whenever the balance is small compared to the number of checks written. Service charges vary in different communities.

The records of a bank. The bank keeps a ledger account for each of its depositors. Every time a bank receives a deposit or pays a check, the transaction is posted to the depositor's ledger account. The bank posts all deposits and checks of each depositor each business day.

The amount in a depositor's account after adding all deposits to the previous balance and subtracting the depositor's checks is known as the *bank balance*. Banks send each depositor at regular intervals or upon request a duplicate of his ledger account. A statement sent to a depositor showing all of the transactions in the depositor's account for the period is known as a *bank statement*.

The bank records of a depositor. A depositor who has a complete and accurate system of bookkeeping knows his bank balance at all times. The checkbook provided by the bank includes checks and a stub for each check. The check stub provides space for recording all deposits, withdrawals, and balances. If the stubs are kept properly, the depositor can refer at any time to the last check stub and determine his bank balance.

The bank records of a depositor when all cash has been deposited are proved as follows:

Beginning cash balance as shown in the cash receipts journal
   plus
the total of the Cash Debit column of the cash receipts journal
   minus
the total of the Cash Credit column of the cash payments journal
   equals
the check-stub balance.

Checking the accuracy of bank records. Although it is uncommon for banks to make errors in their records, there are instances when unavoidable errors do occur. For example, the bank may have accounts with several

John Smiths. Unless great care is used by the bank to compare the different signatures of these Smith accounts, a check may be charged to the wrong account or a deposit may be credited to the wrong account.

Another instance in which a bank may make a mistake is that of paying a check that has been forged. If a bank pays a forged check, the bank must stand the loss. When a depositor discovers the bank has made an error, he should notify the bank at once.

The depositor may also make errors in addition and subtraction on his own check stubs. He may locate the error when he proves cash or he may not locate it until he gets his bank statement at the end of the month.

In any of the above cases, the records of the bank and the records of the depositor would not agree. Good business practice, therefore, requires that the depositor compare his records with those of the bank immediately upon receipt of the bank statement.

The bank statement. A bank statement shows in detail (1) the balance the depositor had at the beginning of the month, (2) the checks paid by the bank, (3) service charges, if any, (4) the amounts deposited, and (5) the depositor's balance at the end of the month.

When a bank sends the bank statement to a depositor, it also returns each check paid by the bank during the month. The checks paid by the bank during the month are stamped or punched on a machine that shows the date they were paid by the bank. Checks returned to the depositor that the bank has paid are known as *canceled checks*. It is good business practice to keep all canceled checks because they are evidence of the payment of bills.

The bank statement for Kelly Appliances. On February 1, Kelly Appliances received its bank statement for the month of January. The bank returned with the statement the checks that it had paid for the business during January and a form showing that a service charge of $2.00 has been made. The bank statement is illustrated on page 194.

Analysis of the bank statement. The bank statement of Kelly Appliances illustrated on the following page shows:

1. The balance as of January 1, $1,863.90.
2. The checks paid by the bank during January as shown in the Checks column.
3. The charges made by the bank for services. The last item on the bank statement of $2.00SC is the service charge. Some banks make the service charge at the beginning of the month for services of the previous month.

MERCHANTS NATIONAL BANK

Kelly Appliances
289 Main Street
Ann Arbor, Michigan

REPORT PROMPTLY ANY
CHANGE IN YOUR ADDRESS

CHECKS			DEPOSITS	THE LAST AMOUNT IN THIS COLUMN IS YOUR BALANCE	
			BALANCE FORWARD	Jan. 1-58	1,863.90
116.25				2-58	1,747.65
			429.87	6-58	2,177.52
9.80	223.15	58.63		7-58	1,885.94
15.80			280.00	8-58	2,150.14
322.50	63.25			9-58	1,764.39
			174.61	10-58	1,939.00
27.80				13-58	1,911.20
100.00	150.00		549.40	15-58	2,210.60
15.00				16-58	2,195.60
			369.18	17-58	2,564.78
410.33			750.76	24-58	2,905.21
326.85				28-58	2,578.36
100.00	150.00	17.50		30-58	2,310.86
2.00SC	12.00		571.80	31-58	2,868.66

Bank statement

4. The deposits made during January as shown in the Deposits column.

5. The balances of the account for the various dates during the month.

Proving records with the bank statement. The bank statement at the end of the month is valuable proof of the accuracy of the bookkeeping records. When all cash receipts are deposited in the bank, the cash receipts as shown by the cash receipts journal must be the same as the deposits shown on the bank statement. When all cash payments are made by check, the bank statement must agree with the cash payments journal except for outstanding checks, for which the bookkeeper must account. A check that has been issued but not presented to a bank for payment is known as an *outstanding check*.

The process of bringing into agreement the bank balance as shown by the monthly bank statement and the balance as shown on the check stub is called *reconciling the bank statement*.

Reconciling the bank statement. When Mr. Kelly received the bank statement, he checked the balance as shown by his last check stub with the bank balance as shown on the bank statement. He found that the check stub showed the balance to be $2,234.16. The balance on the bank statement was $2,868.66. As the two balances were not equal, it was necessary to reconcile the bank statement. The following steps were taken:

Step 1. The checks received from the bank were arranged in order by check number.

Step 2. A check mark was placed on the stub of each check that had been returned.

Step 3. A bank reconciliation statement was prepared in the following form:

BANK RECONCILIATION, JANUARY 31, 1958

Balance on Check Stub, Jan. 31 . $2,234.16	Balance on Bank Statement, Jan. 31 . . . . $2,868.66
Deduct: Bank Service Charge . . 2.00	Deduct Outstanding Checks:

	Check No.	Amount
	871	$107.50
	874	339.00
	879	90.00
	880	100.00

	Total Outstanding Checks 636.50
Corrected Check-Stub Balance $2,232.16	Corrected Bank Balance $2,232.16

Analyzing the bank reconciliation statement. The following steps were taken to reconcile the bank statement:

Step 1. The last check stub in the checkbook was referred to. It showed a balance on January 31 of $2,234.16. This amount was recorded as shown above.

Step 2. The bank service charge, $2.00, as shown on the bank statement was deducted from the check-stub balance, giving a corrected check-stub balance of $2,232.16.

Step 3. The balance as shown on the bank statement for January 31, $2,868.66, was recorded as shown above.

Step 4. Each check stub that did not have a check mark on it was listed, together with the check number and the amount. The column was totaled and labeled "Total Outstanding Checks." The total was written under the bank statement balance to make subtraction easy.

Step 5. The total of the outstanding checks was deducted from the balance shown on the bank statement. This gave the corrected bank balance of $2,232.16.

The corrected check-stub balance and the corrected bank balance were the same. The bank statement was therefore said to be reconciled.

Recording service charges in the cash payments journal. When a service charge is made by a bank, the amount is deducted from the balance on the check stub. It is also necessary to record the service charge in the cash payments journal. This is done by a debit to Miscellaneous Expense in the General Debit column and a credit to Cash in the Cash Credit column. The entry in the cash payments journal is as follows:

	DATE	ACCOUNT DEBITED	CHK. NO.	POST. REF.	GENERAL DEBIT	ACCOUNTS PAYABLE DEBIT	CASH CREDIT	
4	3	*Misc.Exp.-bank service chg.*	✓		2 0 0		2 0 0	4
5								5
6								6
7								7

CASH PAYMENTS JOURNAL — PAGE 3

A check was not written for this entry; therefore a check mark (✓) was placed in the Check No. column. Since there was no check stub to provide an explanation of this entry, the words "bank service charge" were written after the name of the account debited.

CHAPTER QUESTIONS

1. What are the different forms in which a business usually receives cash from customers?
2. What are two important reasons for depositing all cash in a bank?
3. How much is a depositor's account insured for if he keeps his money in a bank that is insured by the Federal Deposit Insurance Corporation?
4. What is the reason for signature cards that the bank requires for each depositor?
5. What does a person guarantee when he endorses a check?
6. What is the advantage to the depositor of identifying checks on the deposit ticket by the name of the person from whom received instead of by the name of the bank or the A.B.A. number of the bank?
7. Why is it advisable for the cash receipts journal to show which cash items have been deposited?
8. What are the steps taken to prove the check-stub balance with the cash journals?
9. Why is it advisable to keep canceled checks?
10. What information does a bank statement contain?
11. With what amount does the corrected check-stub balance agree on the bank reconciliation statement?
12. What account is debited and what account is credited in the cash payments journal to record a bank service charge?

INCREASING YOUR BUSINESS VOCABULARY

What is the meaning of each of the following:

(a) signature card
(b) cash
(c) cash items
(d) endorsement
(e) endorsing
(f) deposit ticket
(g) A.B.A. numbers

(h) bank passbook
(i) bank service charge
(j) bank balance
(k) bank statement
(l) canceled checks
(m) outstanding check
(n) reconciling the bank statement

CASES FOR DISCUSSION

1. J. T. Zolla prefers to keep large sums of money in the store safe and to pay most of his bills by cash instead of by check. What are the disadvantages of this plan over depositing all cash and paying bills by check?

2. J. M. Ford receives his bank statement each month but does not reconcile his bank statement. What are some of the problems that might arise from this practice?

3. L. K. Dodge often writes checks without making out his check stubs. Why is this not a good practice?

DRILLS FOR UNDERSTANDING

Drill 16-A. Robert Wise has a checkbook balance of $223.00 at the end of January. His bank statement shows the balance to be $230.50. When he compared the stubs with the canceled checks, Mr. Wise discovered that he did not receive Check No. 4 for $7.50 presented to the Wilson Co. the day before. Reconcile Mr. Wise's bank statement.

Drill 16-B. Janet Emory received her bank statement, which showed a balance of $553.80. Janet's check stub showed a balance of $554.70. When Janet compared the canceled checks with her check stubs, she discovered that all checks written had been returned. She also noticed on the bank statement a service charge of 90 cents, which was not recorded on her check stubs. Reconcile Janet's bank statement.

Drill 16-C. Barbara Green has a check-stub balance of $345.10. The bank statement indicates Barbara's balance to be only $231.55. While Barbara was comparing the bank statement with her checkbook, she found that all checks written had been returned. She also noticed that a deposit of $113.00, made the day before, had not been recorded on the bank statement and that there was a service charge of 55 cents. Reconcile Barbara's bank statement.

Problem 16-1. **Preparing a deposit ticket**

On November 15 of the current year, B. L. Stewart, 917 Walnut Street, made a deposit consisting of the following items:

8 ten-dollar bills	9 half dollars	14 dimes
7 one-dollar bills	12 quarters	7 nickels

A check from Herman Dietz on the First National Bank, Chicago, Illinois, A.B.A. number 2-1.............................	$145.95
A check from Arthur Merton on the Citizens Bank, Troy, New York, A.B.A. number 50-65..............................	60.22
A check from J. D. Hancock on the Union Trust Bank, City, A.B.A. number 51-66....................................	114.10
A check from Duane Philips on the First State Bank, City, A.B.A. number 51-68....................................	75.00
A postal money order from Charles Benson...................	15.00

Instructions: Prepare a deposit ticket for the deposit, identifying checks by the A.B.A. numbers.

Problem 16-2. **Preparing a deposit ticket**

Instructions: Prepare a deposit ticket for the deposit given in Problem 16-1 but identify the checks and the money order by the name of the person from whom it was received.

Problem 16-3. Reconciliation of the bank statement of A. B. Norris

On July 1 of the current year, A. B. Norris received from the Citizens State Bank his bank statement for June, his canceled checks, and charge slips as follows: a service charge of 65 cents and a charge of $1.00 for collecting a note.

Instructions: 1. Record the two charge slips in the cash payments journal. In each case debit Miscellaneous Expense. After the first write the explanation "bank service charge"; after the second, "collection of note."

2. Prepare a reconciliation of Mr. Norris' bank statement in the same form as that on page 195. Additional data needed are:

(a) Mr. Norris' checkbook balance on June 30 was $613.45.

(b) The June 30 balance on the bank statement was $581.60. A deposit of $180.00 made on the evening of June 30 was not shown on the statement.

> Banks often provide a means whereby customers can make a deposit at the end of a business day or night. When a deposit is made after banking hours on the last day of the month, the amount of the deposit should be added to the balance shown on the bank statement before the outstanding checks are subtracted.

(c) When the canceled checks were compared with the check stubs, the following checks were found to be outstanding: No. 105, $18.95; No. 109, $54.85; and No. 120, $76.00.

Randall Wholesale Grocery

Recording, posting, and trial balance

Purpose of this practice set. This practice set illustrates the entire accounting process. It includes all the work of a fiscal period for the Randall Wholesale Grocery, which is operated by the proprietor, Mark Randall.

Only Part 1 will be completed at this time. Part 2, the work at the end of the fiscal period, will be completed after the class has studied Chapters 17, 18, and 19.

Although the records are those of a small wholesale grocery business, they illustrate the application of general principles of accounting that apply to all businesses.

Required materials. The transactions of this set may be recorded from the narrative of transactions given on pages 202 to 206 inclusive. They may be entered in bound books that may be obtained from the publishers or on unbound sheets of ruled paper. If the use of business papers is desired, a practice set containing business papers and bound books may be obtained from the publishers.

Model illustrations. The journals, ledgers, and forms used in this practice set are listed below. Also listed are the pages of this textbook on which similar books and forms are illustrated.

Books and Forms	*Models*
Purchases Journal	Page 121
Cash Payments Journal	Page 134
Sales Journal	Page 150
Cash Receipts Journal	Page 162
General Journal	Page 181
General Ledger	Pages 183 and 184
Accounts Receivable Ledger	Pages 168 to 170
Accounts Payable Ledger	Pages 137 and 138
Schedule of Accounts Receivable	Page 167
Schedule of Accounts Payable	Page 140
Trial Balance	Page 182

Chart of accounts. The general ledger accounts needed to record the transactions are listed on the inside front cover of the bound ledger provided for this practice set. They are also given in the following chart of accounts.

Randall Wholesale Grocery chart of accounts

BALANCE SHEET ACCOUNTS

(1) ASSETS

ACCT No.

11. Cash
12. Accounts Receivable
13. Merchandise Inventory
14. Supplies
15. Prepaid Insurance

(2) LIABILITIES

21. Accounts Payable

(3) PROPRIETORSHIP

31. Mark Randall, Capital
32. Mark Randall, Drawing
33. Profit and Loss Summary

PROFIT AND LOSS STATEMENT ACCOUNTS

(4) INCOME

ACCT. No.

41. Sales

(5) COST OF MERCHANDISE

51. Purchases

(6) EXPENSES

61. Delivery Expense
62. Insurance Expense
63. Miscellaneous Expense
64. Rent Expense
65. Salary Expense
66. Supplies Expense

Instructions for opening a set of books
for the Randall Wholesale Grocery

Instructions: 1. Open the necessary accounts in the general ledger by writing the account titles in the order in which they are given in the chart of accounts. Use the account numbers indicated.

If loose sheets (8½″ x 11″) are used, place four accounts on each sheet, but number each account with the account number shown on the chart.

Instructions: 2. Open all of the customers' accounts.

If the bound blanks available for this set are used, each customer's account is placed on a separate page. If loose sheets of ruled paper (8½″ x 11″) are used, three customers' accounts may be placed on each ledger sheet. The ledger paper should be ruled with a balance column similar to the accounts receivable ledger illustrated on page 168.

The accounts in the accounts receivable ledger are arranged in alphabetic order as they are in the loose-leaf ledgers commonly used for customers' accounts. The names and the addresses of the customers of the Randall Wholesale Grocery are given at the top of the following page.

Customers' names and addresses

Andrews Grocery, 1203 South Market St., City
Carter & Easton, Hamilton
Denton Grocery, 113 Center St., City
R. M. Evans, 433 West Third Street, City
J. B. Hampton, 2217 Main St., Lebanon
Knight & Lang, 14 Second St., Lebanon
L. J. Lewis Co., Warren
Madison Food Market, High St., Canton
E. M. Neal, 27 Seventh St., Lima
D. H. Rogers, 114 South St., City
Wagner Bros., 181 Hemlock Ave., Columbus

Instructions: 3. Open all the creditors' accounts.

If the bound blanks available for this practice set are used, each creditor's account is placed on a separate page. If loose sheets of ruled paper (8½″ x 11″) are used, three creditors' accounts may be placed on each ledger sheet. The ledger paper should be ruled with a balance column similar to the accounts payable ledger illustrated on page 137.

Creditors' names and addresses

Burton Supply Co., 496 Main Street, City
A. H. Crosby Co., 3127 Harding Ave., Marysville
Hartford Supply Co., Hartford
Jackson & Jackson, 187 South Juniper Ave., Trenton
Meyer, Inc., Youngstown
Nichols & Osborn, Fairview
Salem Grocery Co., 72 Highland, Ogden

Instructions: 4. Record the balance of each account in the general ledger under the date of October 1 using the balances given in the list of accounts below.

Acct. No.	Account Title	Balance
11	Cash	$ 3,072.10 (Dr.)
12	Accounts Receivable	4,701.00 (Dr.)
13	Merchandise Inventory	59,160.50 (Dr.)
14	Supplies	620.45 (Dr.)
15	Prepaid Insurance	750.00 (Dr.)
21	Accounts Payable	4,380.45 (Cr.)
31	Mark Randall, Capital	63,923.60 (Cr.)

Instructions: 5. Record the cash balance in the cash receipts journal in the manner in which this was done in the illustration on page 162.

6. Record each customer's balance in his account in the accounts receivable ledger. The amount of each customer's balance is shown in the following schedule of accounts receivable.

RANDALL WHOLESALE GROCERY
Schedule of Accounts Receivable
September 30, 19--

Andrews Grocery...	1,256 70	
Denton Grocery..	864 50	
R. M. Evans...	936 40	
Knight & Lang...	685 60	
Wagner Bros...	957 80	
Total Accounts Receivable..........................		4,701 00

Instructions: 7. Record each creditor's balance in his account in the accounts payable ledger. The amount of each creditor's balance is shown in the following schedule of accounts payable.

RANDALL WHOLESALE GROCERY
Schedule of Accounts Payable
September 30, 19--

A. H. Crosby Co...	1,182 20	
Jackson & Jackson...	1,033 50	
Nichols & Osborn..	989 50	
Salem Grocery Co..	1,175 25	
Total Accounts Payable..............................		4,380 45

Narrative of transactions for October

October 1
No. 1. Paid $450.00 for rent for October (Check No. 56).

October 2
No. 2. Purchased merchandise on account from Meyer, Inc., $9,110.50 (Invoice No. 1).

No. 3. Sold merchandise on account to Denton Grocery, $1,508.60 (Sale No. 1).

No. 4. Sold merchandise on account to R. M. Evans, $1,341.40 (Sale No. 2).

October 3
No. 5. Received $1,256.70 from Andrews Grocery on account.

No. 6. Paid $989.50 to Nichols & Osborn on account (Check No. 57).

No. 7. Sold merchandise on account to D. H. Rogers, $1,265.80 (Sale No. 3).

October 4
No. 8. Sold merchandise on account to Carter & Easton, $1,182.60 (Sale No. 4).

No. 9. The cash sales for October 1 to 4 were $8,943.30.

Cash proof. Prove the cash balance. The cash balance, ascertained by counting the cash on hand and by adding to this amount the bank balance on the check stub, is $11,832.60.

Posting. Post from each of the books of original entry the items that are to be posted individually. Column totals are not to be posted at this time but at the end of the month only.

October 6

No. 10. Paid, $1,033.50 to Jackson & Jackson on account (Check No. 58).

No. 11. Purchased merchandise on account from Nichols & Osborn, $8,629.60 (Invoice No. 2).

No. 12. Received $600.00 from Wagner Bros. on account.

No. 13. Sold merchandise on account to E. M. Neal, $1,792.75 (Sale No. 5).

October 7

No. 14. Sold merchandise on account to L. J. Lewis Co., $1,527.05 (Sale No. 6).

No. 15. Sold merchandise on account to Knight & Lang, $1,851.40 (Sale No. 7).

No. 16. Paid $1,175.25 to Salem Grocery Co. on account (Check No. 59).

October 8

No. 17. Paid $28.70 for telephone bill for September (Check No. 60).

> Minor expenses, such as those for telephone, electricity, and water, are charged to Miscellaneous Expense.

No. 18. Sold merchandise on account to J. B. Hampton, $1,297.35 (Sale No. 8).

No. 19. Purchased wrapping paper and cartons on account from the Burton Supply Co., $203.20 (Invoice No. 3).

> See page 178 for a discussion of purchases of supplies on account and an illustration of a general journal entry of this type.

October 9

No. 20. Sold merchandise on account to Andrews Grocery, $1,165.20 (Sale No. 9).

No. 21. Purchased merchandise on account from Nichols & Osborn, $8,735.75 (Invoice No. 4).

October 10

No. 22. Denton Grocery reported that they had been charged $119.70 on September 25 for merchandise that they had not received. This sale should have been charged to J. B. Hampton on September 25.

> See page 180 for a discussion and an illustration of a correcting entry of this type.

No. 23. Received $744.80 from Denton Grocery on account.

October 11

No. 24. Cash sales for October 6 to 11 were $12,675.75.

Cash proof. Prove the cash balance. The cash balance is $23,615.70.

Posting. Post the items that are to be posted individually from each of the books of original entry.

October 13

No. 25. Received $685.60 from Knight & Lang on account.

No. 26. Paid $8,629.60 to Nichols & Osborn on account (Check No. 61).

No. 27. Received $119.70 from J. B. Hampton on account.

No. 28. Purchased merchandise on account from A. H. Crosby Co., $8,970.10 (Invoice No. 5).

October 14

No. 29. Sold merchandise on account to R. M. Evans, $1,386.80 (Sale No. 10).

No. 30. Received $357.80 from Wagner Bros. on account.

No. 31. Paid $175.50 for miscellaneous supplies (Check No. 62).

October 15

No. 32. Mark Randall withdrew $300.00 for personal use (Check No. 63).

No. 33. Paid $1,462.50 for salaries for half of the month (Check No. 64).

October 16

No. 34. Sold merchandise on account to Madison Food Market, $2,039.40 (Sale No. 11).

No. 35. Sold merchandise on account to L. J. Lewis Co., $1,350.00 (Sale No. 12).

October 17

No. 36. Sold merchandise on account to Wagner Bros., $1,746.45 (Sale No. 13).

No. 37. Sold merchandise on account to Carter & Easton, $1,329.60 (Sale No. 14).

No. 38. Received $1,508.60 from Denton Grocery on account.

No. 39. Paid $265.80 to Rolf Trucking Company for delivery service for the first half of the month (Check No. 65). Debit Delivery Expense.

October 18

No. 40. Paid $8,735.75 to Nichols & Osborn on account (Check No. 66).

No. 41. Received a check for $1,265.80 from D. H. Rogers on account.

No. 42. Received a check for $1,182.60 from Carter & Easton on account.

No. 43. Cash sales for October 13 to 18 were $9,840.25.

Cash proof. Prove the cash balance. The cash balance is $19,006.90.

Posting. Post the items that are to be posted individually from each of the books of original entry.

October 20

No. 44. Paid $10,152.30 to A. H. Crosby Co. on account (Check No. 67).

No. 45. Purchased supplies on account from the Burton Supply Company, $142.60 (Invoice No. 6).

No. 46. Purchased merchandise on account from Nichols & Osborn, $9,145.20 (Invoice No. 7).

No. 47. Sold merchandise on account to Denton Grocery, $1,203.80 (Sale No. 15).

No. 48. Sold merchandise on account to Knight & Lang, $1,376.10 (Sale No. 16).

No. 49. Received $20.00 from the Rolf Trucking Company. The trucking company sent a letter with the check stating that in figuring the bill paid on October 17 there was an error of $20.00 and that a refund was therefore being made.

> Record this transaction in the cash receipts journal as a credit to Delivery Expense. Enter the amount in the General Credit column.

October 22

No. 50. Received a check for $1,851.40 from Knight & Lang on account.

No. 51. Purchased merchandise on account from Jackson & Jackson, $9,777.45 (Invoice No. 8).

No. 52. Sold merchandise on account to E. M. Neal, $1,325.80 (Sale No. 17).

October 23

No. 53. The proprietor, Mark Randall, took canned goods for personal use; cost price was $75.00.

> See the discussion of withdrawals by the proprietor on page 179. Since this is not a sale to a customer, credit the purchases account. (Record this transaction in the general journal.)

No. 54. Purchased merchandise on account from Hartford Supply Co., $8,900.80 (Invoice No. 9).

October 24

No. 55. Sold merchandise on account to R. M. Evans, $1,610.15 (Sale No. 18).

No. 56. Received $1,000.00 from E. M. Neal on account.

October 25

No. 57. Purchased merchandise on account from Salem Grocery Co., $8,488.00 (Invoice No. 10).

No. 58. Sold merchandise on account to J. B. Hampton, $2,856.40 (Sale No. 19).

No. 59. Paid $9,110.50 to Meyer, Inc., on account (Check No. 68).

No. 60. Received $936.40 from R. M. Evans on account.

No. 61. Cash sales for October 20 to 25 were $11,413.60.

Cash proof. Prove the cash balance. The cash balance is $14,965.50.

Posting. Post the items that are to be posted individually from each of the books of original entry.

October 27

No. 62. Sold merchandise on account to Madison Food Market, $1,479.55 (Sale No. 20).

No. 63. Paid $45.00 for miscellaneous supplies (Check No. 69).

October 28

No. 64. Received $1,165.20 from Andrews Grocery on account.

No. 65. Received $1,297.35 from J. B. Hampton on account.

October 29

No. 66. Received $2,039.40 from Madison Food Market on account.

No. 67. Paid $9,145.20 to Nichols & Osborn on account (Check No. 70).

No. 68. Paid $42.80 for electricity bill for October (Check No. 71).

No. 69. Paid $21.60 for water bill for October (Check No. 72).

October 30

No. 70. Received $1,527.05 from L. J. Lewis Co. on account.

No. 71. Mark Randall, the proprietor, withdrew $300.00 for personal use (Check No. 73).

No. 72. Paid $9,777.45 to Jackson & Jackson on account (Check No. 74).

October 31

No. 73. Paid $8,900.80 to Hartford Supply Co. on account (Check No. 75).

No. 74. Received $2,728.20 from R. M. Evans on account.

No. 75. Paid $1,462.50 for salaries for the last half of the month (Check No. 76).

No. 76. Paid $324.45 to Rolf Trucking Co. for delivery service (Check No. 77).

No. 77. The cash sales for October 27 to 31 were $10,986.10.

Cash proof. Prove the cash balance. The cash balance is $4,689.00.

Posting. Post the items that are to be posted individually from each of the books of original entry.

Completing and posting the journals

Instructions: *1.* Foot and rule the purchases journal. Post the total. Compare your work with the purchases journal shown on page 121.

2. Foot and rule the sales journal. Post the total. Compare your work with the sales journal shown on page 150.

3. Foot and rule the cash receipts journal. Post the totals of the special columns. Compare your work with the cash receipts journal on page 162.

4. Foot and rule the cash payments journal. Post the totals of the special columns. Compare your work with the cash payments journal on page 134.

Schedules and trial balance

Instructions: *5.* Prepare a schedule of the accounts receivable ledger and a schedule of the accounts payable ledger. Compare your work with the two schedules illustrated on pages 140 and 167. Prove the accuracy of the ledgers by comparing the totals of the schedules with the balances of the accounts receivable account and the accounts payable account in the general ledger.

6. Prepare a trial balance. Compare it with the model on page 182.

Work sheet with adjustments CHAPTER 17

Need for adjustments. The ledger accounts of Kelly Appliances on pages 183 and 184 show the results of all the transactions of the business. But these accounts do not show all the information needed for the preparation of the profit and loss statement and the balance sheet.

The account Merchandise Inventory shows the value of the goods on hand at the beginning of the month. This inventory has been changed during the month as a result of purchases and sales. If the true condition of the business is to be shown, the value of the goods on hand at the end of the month should be recorded.

The account Supplies shows the value of the supplies on hand at the beginning of the month plus the supplies purchased during the month. But some of these supplies have been used during the month. At the end of the month the expense resulting from the use of supplies should be recorded.

Similarly, the account Prepaid Insurance shows the value of the prepaid insurance at the beginning of the month. A part of the time for which this insurance was prepaid has expired. The expense resulting from the use of the insurance protection should be recorded.

Changes in accounts that are recorded at the end of a fiscal period to bring the accounts up to date are called *adjustments*. Journal entries to record adjustments are called *adjusting entries*.

Work sheet with columns for adjustments. The work sheet previously used had amount columns headed Trial Balance, P. & L. Statement, and Balance Sheet. When a business has to record adjustments, two additional columns for these adjustments are provided on the work sheet immediately after the Trial Balance columns. This form of a work sheet is used by Kelly Appliances. It has the following column headings:

		1	2	3	4	5	6	7	8
ACCOUNT TITLES	ACCT. NO.	TRIAL BALANCE		ADJUSTMENTS		P. & L. STATEMENT		BALANCE SHEET	
		DEBIT	CREDIT	DEBIT	CREDIT	DEBIT	CREDIT	DEBIT	CREDIT

The Adjustments columns of the work sheet are used by the bookkeeper to plan all of the adjusting entries *before* the adjusting entries are made in the journal. The planning of the adjusting entries on the work sheet provides proof of the accuracy of the work and helps to assure that no adjusting entry is overlooked.

Entering the trial balance on the work sheet. The trial balance of the general ledger of Kelly Appliances is entered in the Trial Balance columns of the work sheet as illustrated below.

Kelly Appliances
Work Sheet
For Month Ended November 30, 1951

	ACCOUNT TITLES	ACCT. NO.	TRIAL BALANCE DEBIT	TRIAL BALANCE CREDIT	ADJUSTMENTS DEBIT	ADJUSTMENTS CREDIT	P. & L. S DEBIT
1	Cash	11	5 4 2 3 30				
2	Accounts Receivable	12	1 4 5 9 20				
3	Merchandise Inventory	13	5 4 4 3 50				
4	Supplies	14	2 4 8 60				
5	Prepaid Insurance	15	9 6 00				
6	Accounts Payable	21		1 6 0 5 54			
7	J. C. Kelly, Capital	31		8 9 7 2 06			
8	J. C. Kelly, Drawing	32	4 2 7 00				
9	Sales	41		4 5 1 5 60			
10	Purchases	51	1 5 3 7 00				
11	Delivery Expense	61	5 2 80				
12	Miscellaneous Expense	63	2 5 80				
13	Rent Expense	64	1 8 0 00				
14	Salary Expense	65	2 0 0 00				
15			1 5 0 9 3 20	1 5 0 9 3 20			
16							
17							

Information needed for adjustments. Before adjustments can be recorded to show changes that have occurred in the merchandise inventory, supplies, and prepaid insurance accounts, three items of information are needed. These are: (1) an inventory of merchandise on hand at the end of the month; (2) an inventory of supplies on hand at the end of the month; and (3) the amount of insurance service that is to be charged to the operations of the business for the month.

When the end-of-month merchandise inventory was taken, it was found that merchandise worth $3,763.25 was on hand. The supplies inventory showed that supplies worth $123.60 were on hand. The insurance policies showed that $4.00 worth of insurance service was used during the month. These facts were not shown in the accounts or on the trial balance. Adjustments were therefore necessary to record the changes that have occurred during the month.

Adjustment for merchandise inventory. The merchandise inventory as shown on the trial balance, $5,443.50, was the value of the merchandise on hand on November 1. But a count of the merchandise on hand on November 30 showed it to be worth $3,763.25.

The beginning inventory is a part of the cost of merchandise sold. The ending inventory is a deduction from the cost of merchandise available for sale.

The debit side of the profit and loss summary account is used to summarize all costs and expenses. The credit side is used to summarize all income. In a merchandising business, the credit side of the profit and loss summary account is also used to show deductions from costs. The beginning inventory will therefore be debited to Profit and Loss Summary, and the ending inventory will be credited to Profit and Loss Summary.

Recording the adjustment for the beginning merchandise inventory. The entry on the work sheet to adjust the beginning merchandise inventory is shown in the partial work sheet below.

	ACCOUNT TITLES	ACCT. NO.	TRIAL BALANCE		ADJUSTMENTS	
			DEBIT	CREDIT	DEBIT	CREDIT
1	Cash	11	5423 30			
2	Accounts Receivable	12	1459 20			
3	Merchandise Inventory	13	5443 50			(a) 5443 50
14	Salary Expense	65	200 00			
15			15093 20	15093 20		
16	Profit and Loss Summary	33			(a) 5443 50	

Work sheet adjustment for beginning merchandise inventory

Analyzing the adjustment for the beginning merchandise inventory. The adjustment for the beginning merchandise inventory was made as follows:

Step 1. The amount of the beginning inventory, $5,443.50, was transferred to the debit of Profit and Loss Summary because it was a part of the cost of merchandise sold. This transfer was shown on the work sheet by writing the amount of the beginning inventory, $5,443.50, in the Adjustments Debit column on the line with Profit and Loss Summary.

The profit and loss summary account did not appear in the Account Titles column. The name of the account, Profit and Loss Summary, and the account number, 33, were therefore written on the first line below the totals of the trial balance.

Step 2. The amount of the beginning inventory, $5,443.50, was credited to Merchandise Inventory. This credit of $5,443.50 balanced the debit of $5,443.50 shown in the Trial Balance Debit column. Thus, the account was closed, showing that the balance of the account was transferred to the profit and loss summary account.

Step 3. The small letter "a" was written in parentheses before the amounts in the Adjustments columns to show the corresponding debit and credit. This method of identifying entries is desirable when a number of adjustments are recorded.

Effect of adjustment (a) on ledger accounts. The following illustration in T account form shows the accounts Merchandise Inventory and Profit and Loss Summary before and after adjustment (a) was journalized and posted:

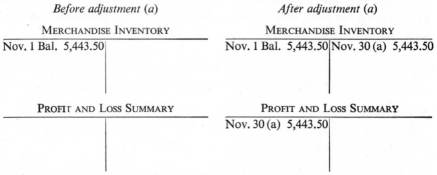

Before the adjustment was journalized and posted, the merchandise inventory account had a debit balance of $5,443.50, the value of the beginning inventory. The profit and loss summary account had no entries recorded in it.

After the adjustment was journalized and posted, the merchandise inventory account was in balance because the beginning merchandise inventory had been transferred to Profit and Loss Summary. The profit and loss summary account showed a debit of $5,443.50. This amount, the beginning inventory, was the first of the amounts in Profit and Loss Summary needed to find the cost of merchandise sold.

Recording the adjustment for the ending merchandise inventory. The adjustment to record the ending merchandise inventory is shown in the Adjustments columns of the partial work sheet below.

	ACCOUNT TITLES	ACCT. NO.	TRIAL BALANCE		ADJUSTMENTS	
			DEBIT	CREDIT	DEBIT	CREDIT
1	Cash	11	5 4 2 3 30			
2	Accounts Receivable	12	1 4 5 9 20			
3	Merchandise Inventory	13	5 4 4 3 50		(b) 3 7 6 3 25	(a) 5 4 4 3 50
14	Salary Expense	65	2 0 0 00			
15			1 5 0 9 3 20	1 5 0 9 3 20		
16	Profit and Loss Summary	33			(a) 5 4 4 3 50	(b) 3 7 6 3 25

Work sheet adjustment for ending merchandise inventory

Analyzing the adjustment for the ending merchandise inventory. The adjustment for the ending merchandise inventory was made as follows:

Step 1. The amount of the ending merchandise inventory, $3,763.25, was recorded in the Adjustments Debit column on the line with Merchandise Inventory. Merchandise Inventory was debited because the ending inventory is an asset.

Step 2. Profit and Loss Summary was credited in the Adjustments Credit column because the ending inventory was a deduction from cost of merchandise available for sale. All deductions from costs are recorded as credits to Profit and Loss Summary.

Step 3. The small letter "b" was written in parentheses before each amount to show the corresponding debit and credit.

Effect of adjustment (b) on ledger accounts. The following illustration in T account form shows the merchandise inventory account and the profit and loss summary account before and after the adjustment was journalized and posted.

Before adjustment (b)

MERCHANDISE INVENTORY

Nov. 1 Bal. 5,443.50	Nov. 30	5,443.50

After adjustment (b)

MERCHANDISE INVENTORY

Nov. 1 Bal. 5,443.50	Nov. 30	5,443.50
30 (b) 3,763.25		

PROFIT AND LOSS SUMMARY

Nov. 30	5,443.50	

PROFIT AND LOSS SUMMARY

Nov. 30	5,443.50	Nov. 30 (b) 3,763.25

Before adjustment (b) was made for the ending inventory, the merchandise inventory account was in balance. After the adjustment for the ending inventory was journalized and posted, the merchandise inventory account had a debit balance of $3,763.25. The merchandise inventory account then showed the value of the asset Merchandise Inventory as of the end of the month.

The profit and loss summary account before the adjustment for the ending inventory showed a debit balance of $5,443.50, which represented part of the cost of merchandise sold. After the adjustment for the ending inventory was journalized and posted, the profit and loss summary account also had a credit of $3,763.25. This amount was a subtraction from the cost of merchandise available for sale.

Adjustment for supplies used. At the end of the month the value of the supplies on hand was found to be $123.60. The debit balance of the supplies account was $248.60. The following calculation shows the cost of supplies used:

Supplies balance at the beginning of the month
    plus supplies bought during the month..... $248.60 (see the trial balance)
Supplies on hand at the end of the month...... 123.60 (inventory)
Cost of supplies used during the month....... $125.00

An adjustment is needed to correct the balance of the supplies account and to record the supplies expense. This adjustment is shown below.

ACCOUNT TITLES	ACCT. NO.	TRIAL BALANCE		ADJUSTMENTS	
		DEBIT	CREDIT	DEBIT	CREDIT
1 Cash	11	5423 30			
2 Accounts Receivable	12	1459 20			
3 Merchandise Inventory	13	5443 50		(b) 3763 25	(a) 5443 50
4 Supplies	14	248 60			(c) 125 00
14 Salary Expense	65	200 00			
15		15093 20	15093 20		
16 Profit and Loss Summary	33			(a) 5443 50	(b) 3763 25
17 Supplies Expense	66			(c) 125 00	

Work sheet adjustment for supplies and supplies expense

Analyzing the adjustment for supplies used. The adjustment to record the supplies used was made as follows:

Step 1. Supplies Expense was debited in the Adjustments Debit column for $125.00. Supplies Expense was debited because all expenses are recorded as debits. Supplies Expense did not appear in the Account Titles column. The name of the account and the account number, 66, were written on the next line below Profit and Loss Summary.

Step 2. The amount of supplies used, $125.00, was recorded in the Adjustments Credit column on the line with Supplies. Supplies was credited because the supplies used decreased the value of this asset.

Step 3. The small letter "c" was written in parentheses before each amount to indicate the corresponding debit and credit.

Effect of adjustment (c) on ledger accounts. The supplies and the supplies expense accounts before and after the adjustment was journalized and posted are shown in T account form below.

Before adjustment (c)		*After adjustment (c)*	
SUPPLIES		SUPPLIES	
Nov. 30 248.60		Nov. 30 248.60 | Nov. 30 125.00	
SUPPLIES EXPENSE		SUPPLIES EXPENSE	
		Nov. 30 125.00	

Before adjustment (c) was journalized and posted, the balance in the supplies account included the balance on hand at the beginning of the month plus the amount of supplies bought during the month. After the adjustment was made, the supplies account also showed a credit of $125.00. This amount, $125.00, when subtracted from the debit of $248.60, would leave a balance of $123.60, the value of the supplies on hand as shown by the inventory.

The supplies expense account before the adjustment had no balance. The debit of $125.00 after the adjustment was made shows the supplies expense incurred during the month.

Adjustment for insurance expense. Property insurance premiums are usually paid for two or three years in advance because the cost of the insurance is less than if the premiums are paid on a yearly basis. Insurance premiums paid in advance are known as *prepaid insurance*. Prepaid insurance is an asset of the business. As part of the protection is received each month, the value of the asset decreases monthly.

It was found that the value of the prepaid insurance of Kelly Appliances decreased $4.00 each month. This amount was recorded as an expense of the business.

The adjustment for insurance expense is shown in the Adjustments columns of the partial work sheet at the top of the following page.

ACCOUNT TITLES	ACCT. NO.	TRIAL BALANCE DEBIT	TRIAL BALANCE CREDIT	ADJUSTMENTS DEBIT	ADJUSTMENTS CREDIT
1 Cash	11	542330			
2 Accounts Receivable	12	145920			
3 Merchandise Inventory	13	544350		(b) 376325	(a) 544350
4 Supplies	14	24860			(c) 12500
5 Prepaid Insurance	15	9600			(d) 400
14 Salary Expense	65	20000			
15		1509320	1509320		
16 Profit and Loss Summary	33			(a) 544350	(b) 376325
17 Supplies Expense	66			(c) 12500	
18 Insurance Expense	62			(d) 400	

Work sheet adjustment for prepaid insurance and insurance expense

Analyzing the adjustment of the prepaid insurance account. The adjustment to record the insurance expense was made as follows:

Step 1. Insurance Expense was debited in the Adjustments Debit column for $4.00 because all expenses are recorded as debits. Insurance Expense does not appear in the Account Titles column. The name of the account and the account number, 62, were therefore written on the next line below Supplies Expense.

Step 2. Prepaid Insurance was credited in the Adjustments Credit column for $4.00 because this amount of insurance was used up.

Step 3. The small letter "d" was written in parentheses before each amount to indicate the corresponding debit and credit.

Effect of adjustment (d) on ledger accounts. The prepaid insurance and the insurance expense accounts before and after this adjustment was journalized and posted are shown below.

Before adjustment (d)	*After adjustment (d)*
PREPAID INSURANCE	PREPAID INSURANCE
Nov. 1 Bal. 96.00	Nov. 1 Bal. 96.00 Nov. 30 4.00
INSURANCE EXPENSE	INSURANCE EXPENSE
	Nov. 30 4.00

Before adjustment (d) was journalized and posted, the prepaid insurance account had a debit balance of $96.00. This was the value of the asset at the beginning of the month. After the adjustment was made, the prepaid insurance account also showed a credit of $4.00. The balance of the account, $92.00, was the amount of insurance service still to be furnished. This was the value of the asset Prepaid Insurance at the end of the month.

The insurance expense account had no entries before the adjustment was made. The debit of $4.00 after the adjustment was made showed the amount of insurance expense for the month.

Proving the Adjustments columns. To prove the accuracy of the adjustments on the work sheet, the Adjustments Debit and Credit columns were totaled. As the total debits equaled the total credits, the work was considered to be correct and the columns were ruled.

Kelly Appliances
Work Sheet
For Month Ended November 30, 1951

	ACCOUNT TITLES	ACCT. NO.	TRIAL BALANCE DEBIT	TRIAL BALANCE CREDIT	ADJUSTMENTS DEBIT	ADJUSTMENTS CREDIT	P. & L. STATE. DEBIT
1	Cash	11	5 4 2 3 30				
2	Accounts Receivable	12	1 4 5 9 20				
3	Merchandise Inventory	13	5 4 4 3 50		(b) 3 7 6 3 25	(a) 5 4 4 3 50	
4	Supplies	14	2 4 8 60			(c) 1 2 5 00	
5	Prepaid Insurance	15	9 6 00			(d) 4 00	
6	Accounts Payable	21		1 6 0 5 54			
7	J. C. Kelly, Capital	31		8 9 7 2 06			
8	J. C. Kelly, Drawing	32	4 2 7 00				
9	Sales	41		4 5 1 5 60			
10	Purchases	51	1 5 3 7 00				
11	Delivery Expense	61	5 2 80				
12	Miscellaneous Expense	63	2 5 80				
13	Rent Expense	64	1 8 0 00				
14	Salary Expense	65	2 0 0 00				
15			1 5 0 9 3 20	1 5 0 9 3 20			
16	Profit and Loss Summary	33			(a) 5 4 4 3 50	(b) 3 7 6 3 25	
17	Supplies Expense	66			(c) 1 2 5 00		
18	Insurance Expense	62			(d) 4 00		
19					9 3 3 5 75	9 3 3 5 75	

Section of work sheet showing trial balance and adjustments

Extending the balance sheet items to the Balance Sheet columns of the work sheet. The work sheet on page 217 shows the extension of the balance sheet items to the Balance Sheet Debit and Credit columns. The steps in extending these items were:

Step 1. The cash and the accounts receivable accounts were not adjusted. The balances of these accounts as shown in the Trial Balance Debit column were therefore extended into the Balance Sheet Debit column.

Step 2. The merchandise inventory account had a trial balance debit of $5,443.50 and an adjustment credit of the same amount. This debit and credit canceled each other. Therefore, only the adjustment debit of $3,763.25, the value of the merchandise inventory at the end of the month, was extended to the Balance Sheet Debit column.

Step 3. The supplies and the prepaid insurance accounts had debit balances in the Trial Balance Debit column and credits in the Adjustments Credit column. In each case the adjustment credit was subtracted from the trial balance debit to get the present value of these assets. Each balance was then extended to the Balance Sheet Debit column.

Step 4. The balance of the liability account Accounts Payable and the balance of the proprietorship account J. C. Kelly, Capital were extended from the Trial Balance Credit column to the Balance Sheet Credit column.

Step 5. The balance of J. C. Kelly, Drawing was extended from the Trial Balance Debit column to the Balance Sheet Debit column. This amount represented a deduction from proprietorship and therefore had to be shown as a debit.

Extending the profit and loss items to the P. and L. Statement columns of the work sheet. The work sheet on page 217 shows the extension of the income, cost, and expense items to the P. & L. Statement Debit and Credit columns. The steps in extending these items were:

Step 1. The credit balance of the sales account, $4,515.60, was extended to the P. & L. Statement Credit column. If there had been other income accounts, they also would have been extended to this column.

Step 2. The debit balance of the purchases account, $1,537.00, was extended to the P. & L. Statement Debit column because purchases made up a part of the cost of merchandise sold.

Step 3. All expense account balances from the Trial Balance Debit column and the Adjustment Debit column were extended to the P. & L. Statement Debit column.

Step 4. On the line with Profit and Loss Summary there were both a debit and a credit. As will be shown later, both items will be needed in the

Kelly Appliances
Work Sheet
For Month Ended November 30, 1957

	ACCOUNT TITLES	ACCT. NO.	TRIAL BALANCE DEBIT	TRIAL BALANCE CREDIT	ADJUSTMENTS DEBIT	ADJUSTMENTS CREDIT	P. & L. STATEMENT DEBIT	P. & L. STATEMENT CREDIT	BALANCE SHEET DEBIT	BALANCE SHEET CREDIT
1	Cash	11	542330						542330	
2	Accounts Receivable	12	145920						145920	
3	Merchandise Inventory	13	544350		(d)376325	(a)544350			376325	
4	Supplies	14	24860			(c)12500			12360	
5	Prepaid Insurance	15	9600			(e)400			9200	
6	Accounts Payable	21		160554						160554
7	J.C. Kelly, Capital	31		897206						897206
8	J.C. Kelly, Drawing	32	42700						42700	
9	Sales	41		451560				451560		
10	Purchases	51	153700				153700			
11	Delivery Expense	61	5280				5280			
12	Miscellaneous Expense	63	2580				2580			
13	Rent Expense	64	18000				18000			
14	Salary Expense	65	20000				20000			
			1509320	1509320						
15	Profit and Loss Summary	33			(a)544350	(d)376325	544350	376325		
16	Supplies Expense	66			(c)12500		12500			
17	Insurance Expense	62			(e)400		400			
18					933575	933575	756810	827885	1128835	1057760
19										
20	Net Profit						71075			71075
21							827885	827885	1128835	1128835

Eight-column work sheet

preparation of the profit and loss statement. For this reason, both amounts were extended into the P. & L. Statement columns. The debit amount represented the beginning inventory and was part of the cost of merchandise sold. This amount was extended to the P. & L. Statement Debit column. The credit amount represented the ending inventory and was a subtraction from the cost of merchandise available for sale. This amount was extended to the P. & L. Statement Credit column.

Calculating the net profit. The net profit was found from the P. & L. Statement columns. The two columns were totaled and ruled as shown in the illustration. The total of the P. & L. Statement Credit column, $8,278.85, was the sum of the income and the deduction from costs. The total of the P. & L. Statement Debit column, $7,568.10, was the sum of costs and expenses. Since the total of the P. & L. Statement Credit column exceeded the total of the Debit column, the difference was the *net profit*.

Total of the P. & L. Statement Credit column................ $8,278.85
Total of the P. & L. Statement Debit column................. 7,568.10

Net Profit... $ 710.75

Ruling and balancing the P. & L. Statement columns. To complete the P. & L. Statement columns, the amount of the net profit, $710.75, was written in the P. & L. Statement Debit column on the line immediately under the Debit column total. The two columns were then totaled and were ruled with a double line. The proof of the work was shown by the fact that the debit total was the same as the credit total.

Ruling and balancing the Balance Sheet columns. The Balance Sheet columns were totaled, and the totals were written on the same line with the first totals of the P. & L. Statement columns. The net profit for the period, $710.75, represented the increase in proprietorship. The amount of the net profit, $710.75, was therefore extended to the Balance Sheet Credit column so that it could be added to the total liabilities and proprietorship. The columns were then ruled, and the totals were written on the same line as the totals of the P. & L. Statement totals.

The fact that the Balance Sheet Debit total equaled the Balance Sheet Credit total proved that the calculations on the work sheet were correct.

Work sheet showing net loss. If the total of the P. & L. Statement Debit column exceeds the total of the P. & L. Statement Credit column, the difference is *net loss*. For example, assume that the footings of the P. & L. Statement columns and the Balance Sheet columns of the work sheet for J. L. Garrett are:

ACCOUNT TITLES	P. & L. STATEMENT		BALANCE SHEET	
	DEBIT	CREDIT	DEBIT	CREDIT
Net Loss.............	2,340 30	2,201 30	4,598 40	4,737 40
		139 00	139 00	
	2,340 30	2,340 30	4,737 40	4,737 40

The total of the P. & L. Statement Debit column, $2,340.30, is larger than the total of the P. & L. Statement Credit column, $2,201.30. This means that the cost of merchandise sold plus the expenses exceeds the total income. The difference between the two columns is always written under the smaller amount. The amount of the net loss, $139.00, is therefore written in the P. & L. Statement Credit column.

The amount of the net loss, $139.00, is also written in the Balance Sheet Debit column because it represents a decrease in proprietorship. If the amount of the net loss is correct, it represents the difference between the totals of the Balance Sheet columns of the work sheet. Therefore, to prove the accuracy of the work sheet, the net loss is added to the Balance Sheet Debit column.

CHAPTER QUESTIONS

1. What columns of the eight-column work sheet are used to plan the adjusting entries?
2. What information is needed (a) before the merchandise inventory account can be adjusted, (b) before the supplies account can be adjusted, and (c) before the prepaid insurance account can be adjusted?
3. What kinds of items appear on the debit side of the profit and loss summary account?
4. What kinds of items appear on the credit side of the profit and loss summary account for a merchandising business?
5. Why is the beginning inventory debited to Profit and Loss Summary in the Adjustments Debit column?
6. Where does the profit and loss summary account appear on the work sheet?
7. Why is the beginning inventory credited to Merchandise Inventory in the Adjustments Credit column?
8. Why is the ending inventory debited to Merchandise Inventory in the Adjustments Debit column?

9. Why is the ending inventory credited to Profit and Loss Summary in the Adjustments Credit column?
10. Why is it necessary to adjust the supplies account at the end of a fiscal period?
11. Why is Supplies credited for the amount of supplies used?
12. Why is Prepaid Insurance credited for the amount of insurance expense?
13. What accounts on the work sheet are extended to the Balance Sheet Debit column?
14. What accounts on the work sheet are extended to the Balance Sheet Credit column?
15. What do the items in the P. & L. Statement Debit column represent?
16. What do the items in the P. & L. Statement Credit column represent?
17. How is the net profit for the period determined?
18. What is the final proof of the correctness of the work sheet?

INCREASING YOUR BUSINESS VOCABULARY

What is the meaning of each of the following:

    (a) adjustments
    (b) adjusting entries
    (c) prepaid insurance

CASES FOR DISCUSSION

1. The net profit of Frank's Hardware Store at the end of December was determined to be $1,200.00. A later check showed that an error had been made in calculating the ending inventory. The inventory at first was calculated to be $6,000.00, but it should have been $5,000.00. How did this error affect the net profit?
2. The trial balance section of the work sheet of Hugh Moore on June 30 shows that Merchandise Inventory has a balance of $4,000.00. He has sold all of the beginning inventory and the merchandise purchased during the month. What adjustment will be made for the merchandise inventory account?
3. If the total of the Adjustments Debit column of a work sheet does not equal the total of the Adjustments Credit column, what kind of mistake has probably been made?
4. When J. R. Stone footed the P. & L. Statement columns of his work sheet, he obtained a debit footing of $6,000.00 and a credit footing of $5,000.00. Did the operation of the business result in a net profit or a net loss?

Drill 17-A. Beginning and ending inventories for four different businesses are given below.

Business 1
1. Beginning Inventory.... $6,000
   Ending Inventory....... 4,000

Business 2
2. Beginning Inventory.... $ none
   Ending Inventory....... 5,000

Business 3
3. Beginning Inventory........ $ 3,000
   Ending Inventory.......... none

Business 4
4. Beginning Inventory........ $ 7,000
   Ending Inventory.......... 10,000

Instructions: For each business state the adjustments needed for Merchandise Inventory.

Drill 17-B. The profit and loss summary account adjustments for merchandise inventory for a number of different fiscal periods are shown below as they appear on work sheets.

Merchandise Inventory Adjustments

	Debit	Credit
Work Sheet 1. Profit and Loss Summary	4,000	1,000
Work Sheet 2. Profit and Loss Summary	3,000	5,000
Work Sheet 3. Profit and Loss Summary	———	6,000
Work Sheet 4. Profit and Loss Summary	2,000	———

Instructions: Answer the following questions:

(a) What amounts represent the beginning inventories?
(b) What amounts represent the ending inventories?
(c) What does the blank in the Debit column for Work Sheet 3 indicate?
(d) What does the blank in the Credit column for Work Sheet 4 indicate?

Drill 17-C. *Instructions:* From the information given below, state (a) the amount of the adjustment needed to have the account show the actual value of the asset at the end of the period, (b) which adjustment column the amount would be recorded in, and (c) the amount that would be extended to the Balance Sheet Debit column:

Trial Balance Debit | *End-of-Period Information*
1. Supplies................. $300.00 — Supplies on hand............ $200.00
2. Supplies................. 600.00 — Supplies on hand............ none
3. Prepaid Insurance......... 120.00 — To be charged to each month.. 20.00
4. Prepaid Insurance......... 10.00 — Policy expires at end of this period

Chapter 17. Work sheet with adjustments 221

Problem 17-1. Work sheet for a clothing merchant

On May 31 of the current year, the end of a fiscal period of one month, the account balances in the general ledger of J. H. Royce, a clothing merchant and the list of inventories were as shown below.

Cash, $4,348.10
Accounts Receivable, $2,294.00
Merchandise Inventory, $20,236.76
Supplies, $208.00
Prepaid Insurance, $335.00
Accounts Payable, $3,710.00
J. H. Royce, Capital, $21,926.86

J. H. Royce, Drawing, $500.00 (Dr.)
Sales, $6,993.45
Purchases, $3,793.47
Delivery Expense, $117.38
Miscellaneous Expense, $160.10
Rent Expense, $250.00
Salary Expense, $387.50

Inventories, May 31
Merchandise inventory, $17,360.30
Supplies inventory, $170.00
Value of insurance policies, $295.00

Instructions: Prepare an eight-column work sheet similar to the model given in the illustration on page 217.

Problem 17-2. Work sheet for a furniture dealer

On December 31 of the current year, the end of a fiscal period of one year, the account balances in the general ledger of the Nelson Furniture Company and the list of inventories were as shown below.

Cash, $7,327.28
Accounts Receivable, $13,100.00
Merchandise Inventory, $26,001.06
Supplies, $976.78
Prepaid Insurance, $1,150.00
Accounts Payable, $11,130.00
M. E. Nelson, Capital, $44,722.08

M. E. Nelson, Drawing, $6,250.00 (Dr.)
Sales, $92,171.14
Purchases, $71,966.50
Delivery Expense, $2,438.00
Miscellaneous Expense, $1,313.60
Rent Expense, $6,000.00
Salary Expense, $11,500.00

Inventories, December 31
Merchandise inventory, $30,894.16
Supplies inventory, $281.13
Value of insurance policies, $918.75

Instructions: Prepare an eight-column work sheet similar to the model given in the illustration on page 217.

This problem will be continued in the next chapter. If it is collected by your teacher at this time, it will be returned to you before it is needed in Problem 18-1 in Chapter 18.

Financial reports

Relation of the work sheet and the reports. The work sheet summarizes all facts about the operations of a business for a fiscal period, but it does not provide this information in a convenient form for the use of the owner. As its title suggests, it is merely a working form that accumulates and classifies the information that is needed in making financial reports. After the work sheet is finished, reports are prepared from it. These reports are the profit and loss statement and the balance sheet.

Use of the profit and loss statement. The profit and loss statement contains information about the income, the costs, the expenses, and the net profit for the fiscal period.

At the end of each fiscal period, the proprietor may compare his profit and loss statement for that period with those prepared for other periods. From a comparison of the profit and loss statements for different periods, he can learn whether his income is increasing or decreasing. He can also learn whether the costs and the expenses are reasonable when compared with the income or whether some costs and expenses have been increasing more rapidly than they should. He can note any changes in his net profit and the reasons for these changes. By comparing carefully the profit and loss statement for one period with similar statements for other periods, he can obtain information that will assist him in the effective management of his business.

Use of the balance sheet. By studying the balance sheet, the proprietor can obtain information that is useful to him in the management of his business. He can observe whether he has sufficient cash on hand or will collect enough from his accounts receivable to enable him to pay his liabilities when they are due. By comparing the balance sheet with earlier balance sheets, he can observe whether his accounts receivable and his inventory are increasing more than they should, whether his liabilities are decreasing or increasing, and the extent of the change in his proprietorship. The comparison of several balance sheets provides much information about the soundness of the business by showing changes in assets, liabilities, and proprietorship.

The profit and loss statement. The P. & L. Statement columns of the work sheet, containing information needed in the preparation of the profit and loss statement, are shown below. The profit and loss statement prepared from this section of the work sheet is shown at the top of the opposite page.

	ACCOUNT TITLES	ACCT. NO.	TRIAL BALANCE		ADJUSTMENTS		P. & L. STATEMENT	
			DEBIT	CREDIT	DEBIT	CREDIT	DEBIT	CREDIT
9	Sales	41		4515 60				4515 60
10	Purchases	51	1537 00				1537 00	
11	Delivery Expense	61	52 80				52 80	
12	Miscellaneous Expense	63	25 80				25 80	
13	Rent Expense	64	180 00				180 00	
14	Salary Expense	65	200 00				200 00	
15			15093 20	15093 20				
16	Profit and Loss Summary	33			(a) 5443 50	(b) 3763 25	5443 50	3763 25
17	Supplies Expense	66			(c) 125 00		125 00	
18	Insurance Expense	62			(d) 4 00		4 00	
19					9335 75	9335 75	7568 10	8278 85
20	Net Profit						710 75	
21							8278 85	8278 85

Section of a work sheet including the profit and loss items

Analyzing the profit and loss statement. The first section of the profit and loss statement has the heading "Income," which was written beginning at the left margin. The only item recorded under this heading was Sales, which was indented about one-half inch. The amount of the sales, $4,515.60, was written in the second amount column so that the cost of merchandise sold may be readily subtracted from it.

It is customary to show on the profit and loss statement the calculation of the cost of merchandise sold. All of the information for this calculation is shown in the P. & L. Statement columns of the work sheet. The calculations and the sources of the amounts are shown below:

Beginning Merchandise Inventory, Nov. 1 (shown as a debit to Profit and Loss Summary)............................ $5,443.50

Purchases during November (shown as a debit to Purchases)..... 1,537.00

Total Cost of Merchandise Available for Sale.................. $6,980.50
Less Ending Inventory, Nov. 30 (shown as a credit to Profit and Loss Summary).................................... 3,763.25

Cost of Merchandise Sold................................ $3,217.25

Kelly Appliances
Profit and Loss Statement
For Month Ended November 30, 1951

Income:			
Sales			4515 60
Cost of Merchandise Sold:			
Merchandise Inventory, Nov. 1, 1951	5443 50		
Purchases	1537 00		
Total Cost of Mdse. Available for Sale	6980 50		
Less Merchandise Inventory, Nov. 30, 1951	3763 25		
Cost of Merchandise Sold			3217 25
Gross Profit on Sales			1298 35
Expenses:			
Delivery Expense	52 80		
Insurance Expense	40 0		
Miscellaneous Expense	25 80		
Rent Expense	180 00		
Salary Expense	200 00		
Supplies Expense	125 00		
Total Expenses			587 60
Net Profit			710 75

Profit and loss statement

The heading of the second section, "Cost of Merchandise Sold," was written beginning at the left margin. Each item that was entered under this heading was indented about one-half inch. Each amount was written in the first amount column so that the figures would not interfere with the calculations that must be made in the second amount column. Only the amount of the cost of merchandise sold was written in the second column.

The difference between the sales and the cost of merchandise sold is called the *gross profit on sales*. This title is a main heading and therefore begins at the left margin.

The next section of the profit and loss statement has the heading "Expenses," which was written beginning at the left margin. Each item listed under this heading was indented about one-half inch. The amount of each expense account balance was written in the first amount column. The accounts were listed in the order in which they appear in the ledger. The expenses may be arranged in any order desired. Kelly Appliances arranges them alphabetically.

The amount of the total expenses was written in the second amount column so that it could be easily subtracted from the amount of the gross profit on sales. The amount, $587.60, was subtracted from the gross profit on sales, $1,298.35, to get the net profit, $710.75.

Net loss on the profit and loss statement. If the expenses are greater than the gross profit, the difference between the gross profit and the expenses is the *net loss*. For example, J. L. Garrett, a part of whose work sheet was illustrated on page 219, suffered a loss in one fiscal period. The final part of his profit and loss statement appeared as follows:

Gross Profit on Sales.........................		464 50
Expenses:		
Delivery Expense..........................	32 50	
Insurance Expense.........................	15 00	
Miscellaneous Expense......................	57 60	
Rent Expense..............................	200 00	
Salary Expense............................	275 00	
Supplies Expense..........................	23 40	
Total Expenses............................		603 50
Net Loss.................................		139 00

The balance sheet. The Balance Sheet columns of the work sheet of Kelly Appliances used in preparing the balance sheet are shown below. The balance sheet of November 30 prepared from the figures in these columns is shown on the opposite page.

	ACCOUNT TITLES	7 DEBIT	8 CREDIT	
1	Cash	542 30		1
2	Accounts Receivable	1459 20		2
3	Merchandise Inventory	3763 25		3
4	Supplies	123 60		4
5	Prepaid Insurance	92 00		5
6	Accounts Payable		1605 54	6
7	J. C. Kelly, Capital		8972 06	7
8	J. C. Kelly, Drawing	427 00		8
19		11288 35	10577 60	19
20	Net Profit		710 75	20
21		11288 35	11288 35	21

Section of a work sheet including the balance sheet items

Assets				
Cash	5 4 2 3	30		
Accounts Receivable	1 4 5 9	20		
Merchandise Inventory	3 7 6 3	25		
Supplies	1 2 3	60		
Prepaid Insurance	9 2	00		
Total Assets			1 0 8 6 1	35
Liabilities				
Accounts Payable			1 6 0 5	54
Proprietorship				
J. C. Kelly, Capital	8 9 7 2	06		
Net Profit	7 1 0.7 5			
Less Withdrawals	4 2 7.0 0			
Net Increase in Capital	2 8 3	75		
J. C. Kelly, Present Capital			9 2 5 5	81
Total Liabilities and Proprietorship			1 0 8 6 1	35

Balance sheet in report form

Analyzing the balance sheet. In the assets section of the balance sheet, the amount of each asset was written in the first amount column and the total was placed in the second amount column.

In the liabilities section of this balance sheet, there was only one item, Accounts Payable. The amount of Accounts Payable was therefore written in the second amount column, because this amount represented the total of this section of the balance sheet.

In the proprietorship section, the calculation of the capital at the time of the balance sheet was shown. Note that the capital as reported on the work sheet was entered in the first amount column. The amount of the net profit and the amount of the withdrawals were then written at the left of the first amount column. The difference, which was the net increase in capital, could then be written under the amount of the capital and could be added to it. The three lines "Net Profit," "Less Withdrawals," and "Net Increase in Capital" were each indented about one-half inch. The calculation of the net increase in capital could then be readily distinguished from the remainder of the proprietorship section.

The capital account with the amount of net increase added to it (or the amount of net decrease subtracted from it) is called *present capital*. When the net increase in capital was added to the amount of the capital as shown on the work sheet, the present capital was extended into the second amount column. It was then added to the amount of the liabilities. The total of the liabilities and the proprietorship must equal the total of the assets. This proof may be stated in the form of the equation:

ASSETS $10,861.35 = LIABILITIES $1,605.54 + PROPRIETORSHIP $9,255.81

Net loss in the proprietorship section. When a business suffers a net loss, the proprietorship section of the balance sheet may be prepared in the manner shown below. The figures for this partial balance sheet were derived from the partial work sheet of J. L. Garrett on page 219.

PROPRIETORSHIP		
J. L. Garrett, Capital........................	6,000 00	
Net Loss........................ 139.00		
Add Withdrawals................. 300.00		
Total Decrease in Capital...................	439 00	
J. L. Garrett, Present Capital................		5,561 00
Total Liabilities and Proprietorship.............		7,615 00

The net loss and the withdrawals were added to show the total decrease in capital. This total decrease was subtracted from the capital at the beginning of the fiscal period to show the present capital.

Net profit with a decrease in proprietorship. When the withdrawals during the fiscal period exceed the net profit for the same period, the proprietorship section of the balance sheet appears as follows:

PROPRIETORSHIP		
D. O. Kane.................................	8,240 60	
Withdrawals...................... 600.00		
Less Net Profit.................... 410.00		
Net Decrease in Capital....................	190 00	
D. O. Kane, Present Capital.................		8,050 60
Total Liabilities and Proprietorship.............		11,231 10

Since the withdrawals exceeded the net profit, the net profit was subtracted from the withdrawals and the difference was called *net decrease in capital*. This amount was then subtracted from the capital at the beginning of the fiscal period to show the present capital.

Classification of accounts in the general ledger. The accounts in a ledger are arranged according to their location on the profit and loss statement and the balance sheet. The chart of accounts used by Kelly Appliances shows the account titles and the account numbers for all accounts. This chart of accounts is shown below.

CHART OF ACCOUNTS FOR KELLY APPLIANCES

BALANCE SHEET ACCOUNTS	PROFIT AND LOSS STATEMENT ACCOUNTS
(1) Assets	**(4) Income**
Acct.No.	Acct.No.
11. Cash	41. Sales
12. Accounts Receivable	
13. Merchandise Inventory	
14. Supplies	
15. Prepaid Insurance	**(5) Cost of Merchandise**
	51. Purchases
(2) Liabilities	
21. Accounts Payable	**(6) Expenses**
	61. Delivery Expense
	62. Insurance Expense
	63. Miscellaneous Expense
(3) Proprietorship	64. Rent Expense
	65. Salary Expense
31. J. C. Kelly, Capital	66. Supplies Expense
32. J. C. Kelly, Drawing	
33. Profit and Loss Summary	

Classified chart of accounts

Analyzing the chart of accounts. The first group of accounts is the *assets* group. The cash account is placed first and is followed by the other assets arranged in the order in which they can most quickly be converted into cash. The assets group is assigned account numbers 11 to 19.

The second group of accounts is the *liabilities* group, to which account numbers 21 to 29 are assigned.

The third group of accounts is the *proprietorship* group, to which account numbers 31 to 39 are assigned.

The fourth group of accounts is the *income* group, to which account numbers 41 to 49 are assigned.

The fifth group of accounts is the *cost of merchandise* group. This group is assigned account numbers 51 to 59. As Mr. Kelly buys and sells merchandise, his chart of accounts provides a section entitled "Cost of Merchandise." In this respect Mr. Kelly's chart of accounts differs from that of the Greene Realty Agency illustrated on page 51, which had only five groups of accounts.

The sixth group of accounts is the *expenses* group. This group is assigned account numbers 61 to 69.

Supplementary reports. The balance sheet lists the total amount of the accounts receivable and the total amount of the accounts payable. It does not, however, list the individual balances of accounts with customers and creditors. When these details are desired, it is customary to attach the schedule of accounts receivable and the schedule of accounts payable to the balance sheet. When the schedules of accounts receivable and accounts payable are used with the balance sheet as supplementary reports, they are commonly referred to as *supporting schedules*. The schedules of accounts receivable and accounts payable of Kelly Appliances are illustrated on pages 140 and 167.

CHAPTER QUESTIONS

1. What is the source of the information for preparing financial reports?
2. What is the purpose of a profit and loss statement?
3. How is the cost of merchandise sold determined?
4. What is the purpose of a balance sheet?
5. What are the three main sections of the balance sheet?
6. In what order are assets listed on the balance sheet?
7. In classifying the accounts in Mr. Kelly's ledger, for what is the first digit used?
8. Why does Mr. Kelly's chart of accounts have six groups of accounts when the Greene Realty Agency chart of accounts on page 51 had only five?

INCREASING YOUR BUSINESS VOCABULARY

What is the meaning of each of the following:

(a) gross profit on sales
(b) net loss
(c) present capital
(d) net decrease in capital
(e) supporting schedules

CASES FOR DISCUSSION

1. By analyzing his profit and loss statement for April and comparing it with the profit and loss statements for previous fiscal periods, O. J. Kerns notes that his total sales have been increasing. His net profit, however, has remained approximately the same. What could cause this situation?
2. The balance sheet of Fred Burk on June 30 showed his proprietorship to be $9,460.00. His balance sheet on July 31 showed the proprietorship to be $9,920.00. Name two probable causes of this change in proprietorship.

3. James Counts knows that his business has been making a net profit averaging $250 a month for six months. What other information is required to determine how sound his financial condition is?

DRILLS FOR UNDERSTANDING

Drill 18-A. The following are the accounts that appear in the ledger of the Trenton Radio Shop. Mr. Trenton has never classified his accounts.

Instructions: 1. For each account tell whether it is an asset, a liability, a proprietorship, an income, a cost of merchandise, or an expense account.

2. Draw up a chart of accounts similar in form to the one shown on page 229 by listing each of the following accounts on the chart with a proper account number.

T. R. Trenton, Capital	Accounts Payable	Salary Expense
Cash	Merchandise Inventory	Store Furniture
T. R. Trenton, Drawing	Insurance Expense	Profit and Loss Summary
Supplies Expense	Purchases	Sales
Supplies	Prepaid Insurance	Miscellaneous Expense
Accounts Receivable	Office Furniture	Rent Expense

Drill 18-B. The following items are found in the P. & L. Statement columns of the work sheets of several different businesses:

	P. & L. Statement Debit	Credit
Business No. 1:		
Purchases..............................	3,000	
Profit and Loss Summary..................	4,000	2,000
Business No. 2:		
Purchases..............................	6,000	
Profit and Loss Summary..................	.....	5,000
Business No. 3:		
Purchases..............................	7,000	
Profit and Loss Summary..................	8,000	.....

Instructions: Compute the cost of merchandise sold for each business.

Drill 18-C. The proprietorship sections of the balance sheets of several businesses are as follows:

	Business No. 1	Business No. 2	Business No. 3	Business No. 4
Capital.....................	$9,000.00	$10,000.00	$8,000.00	$5,000.00
Net Profit..................	1,000.00	1,500.00		
Net Loss...................			500.00	500.00
Withdrawals...............	500.00	none	700.00	none

Instructions: 1. Find the increase or decrease in capital for each business. *2.* Find the present capital of each business.

Problem 18-1. Financial reports for a furniture dealer

The work sheet completed in Problem 17-2 of the preceding chapter is required for this problem. If Problem 17-2 has not been returned to you, complete Exercise 18-A in the Appendix.

Instructions: 1. Prepare a profit and loss statement similar to the model given in the illustration on page 225.

2. Prepare a balance sheet in report form similar to the model given in the illustration on page 227.

Problem 18-2. An eight-column work sheet and financial statements

On June 30 of the current year, the end of a quarterly fiscal period, Peter Lowe, a clothing merchant, prepared the trial balance and the list of inventories shown below.

PETER LOWE

Trial Balance

June 30, 19--

Cash................................	11	3,723 58	
Accounts Receivable................	12	4,094 10	
Merchandise Inventory..............	13	9,605 33	
Supplies...........................	14	352 24	
Prepaid Insurance..................	15	234 08	
Accounts Payable...................	21		5,255 38
Peter Lowe, Capital................	31		11,990 80
Peter Lowe, Drawing................	32	1,260 00	
Sales..............................	41		17,008 25
Purchases..........................	51	11,751 73	
Delivery Expense...................	61	258 72	
Miscellaneous Expense..............	63	379 75	
Rent Expense.......................	64	840 00	
Salary Expense.....................	65	1,754 90	
		34,254 43	34,254 43

INVENTORIES, JUNE 30, 19--

Merchandise inventory, $9,982.84
Supplies inventory, $231.70
Prepaid insurance, $130.76

Instructions: 1. Prepare an eight-column work sheet similar to the model given in the illustration on page 217.

2. From the P. & L. Statement columns of the work sheet, prepare a profit and loss statement similar to the model given in the illustration on page 225.

3. From the Balance Sheet columns of the work sheet, prepare a balance sheet similar to the model given in the illustration on page 227.

Adjusting and closing entries

Need for adjusting entries. Adjustments made on the work sheet were illustrated and discussed in Chapter 17. But the work sheet is not a permanent part of the bookkeeping records. It is therefore necessary to record the adjustments that were made on the work sheet in the permanent records of the business.

Adjusting entries are recorded in the general journal. The posting of these entries brings the accounts in the general ledger up to date. The information for making adjusting entries is taken from the Adjustments columns of the work sheet.

The adjusting entry for the beginning inventory. The section of the work sheet with the adjustment for the beginning inventory is shown below. It is followed by the general journal entry to record this adjustment.

	ACCOUNT TITLES	ACCT. NO.	TRIAL BALANCE DEBIT	TRIAL BALANCE CREDIT	ADJUSTMENTS DEBIT	ADJUSTMENTS CREDIT
3	Merchandise Inventory	13	5443 50			(a) 5443 50
16	Profit and Loss Summary	33			(a) 5443 50	

GENERAL JOURNAL — PAGE 2

DATE	NAME OF ACCOUNT	POST. REF.	DEBIT	CREDIT
	Adjusting Entries			
1951 Nov 30	Profit and Loss Summary	33	5443 50	
	Merchandise Inventory	13		5443 50

Analyzing the adjusting entry for the beginning inventory. The general journal entry was made in the usual form. Instead of writing an explanation for each adjusting entry, the words "Adjusting Entries" were written above the first entry.

233

The merchandise inventory account shows a balance of $5,443.50 in the Trial Balance Debit column of the work sheet. The journal entry transferred this beginning inventory to the profit and loss summary account. Profit and Loss Summary was debited because this amount was a part of the cost of merchandise sold, and all costs and expenses are debits. Merchandise Inventory was credited because the balance has been transferred to Profit and Loss Summary.

The merchandise inventory account and the profit and loss summary account after this adjusting entry was posted are shown below.

			Merchandise Inventory					ACCOUNT NO. *13*
DATE	ITEMS	POST. REF.	DEBIT	DATE	ITEMS	POST. REF.	CREDIT	
1957 Nov. 1	Balance	J1	5 4 4 3 50	1957 Nov. 30		J2	5 4 4 3 50	

			Profit and Loss Summary					ACCOUNT NO. *33*
DATE	ITEMS	POST. REF.	DEBIT	DATE	ITEMS	POST. REF.	CREDIT	
1957 Nov. 30		J2	5 4 4 3 50					

The merchandise inventory account is now in balance. The profit and loss summary account shows the beginning inventory, $5,443.50, transferred to it as a debit. This is the first of the amounts used to determine the cost of merchandise sold.

The adjusting entry for the ending inventory. The ending inventory is an asset of the business. It must be recorded so that the merchandise inventory account will show the present value of the inventory. The section of the work sheet with the adjustment for the ending merchandise inventory and the general journal entry to record this adjustment are shown below.

			1	2	3	4
	ACCOUNT TITLES	ACCT. NO.	TRIAL BALANCE		ADJUSTMENTS	
			DEBIT	CREDIT	DEBIT	CREDIT
3	Merchandise Inventory	13	5 4 4 3 50		(b) 3 7 6 3 25	(a) 5 4 4 3 50
16	Profit and Loss Summary	33			(a) 5 4 4 3 50	(b) 3 7 6 3 25

DATE	NAME OF ACCOUNT	POST. REF.	DEBIT	CREDIT
30	Merchandise Inventory	13	3 7 6 3 2 5	
	Profit and Loss Summary	33		3 7 6 3 2 5

Merchandise Inventory was debited for \$3,763.25, the merchandise inventory at the end of the month, to record the value of this asset. Profit and Loss Summary was credited for the same amount because this amount was a subtraction from the beginning inventory, which was recorded as a cost or debit. The merchandise inventory account and the profit and loss summary account after this adjusting entry was posted are shown below.

Merchandise Inventory   ACCOUNT NO. 13

DATE	ITEMS	POST. REF.	DEBIT	DATE	ITEMS	POST. REF.	CREDIT
1957 Nov. 1	Balance	J.1	5 4 4 3 5 0	1957 Nov. 30		J2	5 4 4 3 5 0
30		J2	3 7 6 3 2 5				

Profit and Loss Summary   ACCOUNT NO. 33

DATE	ITEMS	POST. REF.	DEBIT	DATE	ITEMS	POST. REF.	CREDIT
1957 Nov. 30		J2	5 4 4 3 5 0	1957 Nov. 30		J2	3 7 6 3 2 5

The merchandise inventory account now has a debit balance of \$3,763.25, the amount of the ending inventory.

The profit and loss summary account has a debit of \$5,443.50, the beginning inventory. It has a credit of \$3,763.25, the ending inventory.

The adjusting entry for supplies. Supplies worth \$125.00 were used during the month. The part of the work sheet showing the adjustment to record this expense and the general journal adjusting entry made from the work sheet are shown below.

	ACCOUNT TITLES	ACCT. NO.	TRIAL BALANCE DEBIT	TRIAL BALANCE CREDIT	ADJUSTMENTS DEBIT	ADJUSTMENTS CREDIT
4	Supplies	14	2 4 8 6 0			(c) 1 2 5 0 0
17	Supplies Expense	66			(c) 1 2 5 0 0	

	DATE	NAME OF ACCOUNT	POST. REF.	DEBIT	CREDIT	
6	30	Supplies Expense	66	1 2 5 0 0		6
7		Supplies	14		1 2 5 0 0	7
8						8

Supplies Expense was debited to record the expense resulting from the use of supplies during the month. Supplies was credited to record the decrease in the value of this asset.

After the entry was posted, the supplies account and the supplies expense account appeared as follows:

Supplies   ACCOUNT NO. 14

DATE	ITEMS	POST. REF.	DEBIT	DATE	ITEMS	POST. REF.	CREDIT
1957 Nov. 1	Balance	J1	1 0 4 6 0	1957 Nov. 30		J2	1 2 5 0 0
11		J1	1 4 4 0 0				

Supplies Expense   ACCOUNT NO. 66

DATE	ITEMS	POST. REF.	DEBIT	DATE	ITEMS	POST. REF.	CREDIT
1957 Nov. 30		J2	1 2 5 0 0				

Analyzing the supplies and supplies expense accounts.

The supplies account has two debits. The debit of Nov. 1 is the amount of supplies on hand at the beginning of the month. The debit of Nov. 11 represents the purchases of supplies.

The credit to the supplies account on November 30, $125.00, represents the amount of supplies used. The balance, $123.60, represents the amount of supplies on hand as of November 30.

The supplies expense account shows a debit of $125.00. This amount represents the amount of supplies used during the month. Supplies used are an expense of the business.

The adjusting entry for prepaid insurance. Part of the insurance service represented by the premium that was paid for two years in advance was used during the month. The adjustment that was made on the work sheet must be recorded in order for the prepaid insurance account to show the present value of this asset. Insurance Expense must be debited to record this expense of the business.

The part of the work sheet showing the adjustment of Prepaid Insurance and the general journal adjusting entry made from the work sheet are shown below.

			1	2	3	4
	ACCOUNT TITLES	ACCT. NO.	TRIAL BALANCE		ADJUSTMENTS	
			DEBIT	CREDIT	DEBIT	CREDIT
5	Prepaid Insurance	15	96 00			(d) 4 00
18	Insurance Expense	62			(d) 4 00	

GENERAL JOURNAL   PAGE 2

	DATE	NAME OF ACCOUNT	POST. REF.	DEBIT	CREDIT	
8	30	Insurance Expense	62	4 00		8
9		Prepaid Insurance	15		4 00	9

The prepaid insurance account and the insurance expense account after this entry was posted are shown below.

Prepaid Insurance   ACCOUNT NO. 15

DATE	ITEMS	POST. REF.	DEBIT	DATE	ITEMS	POST. REF.	CREDIT
1957 Nov 1	Balance	J1	96 00	1957 Nov 30		J2	4 00

Insurance Expense   ACCOUNT NO. 62

DATE	ITEMS	POST. REF.	DEBIT	DATE	ITEMS	POST. REF.	CREDIT
1957 Nov 30		J2	4 00				

Analyzing the prepaid insurance and insurance expense accounts. The prepaid insurance account has a debit of $96.00, the value of the asset at the beginning of the month. It has a credit of $4.00, the decrease in the value of this asset during the month.

The insurance expense account has a debit of $4.00, the amount of expense for insurance during the month.

Adjusting entries in the general journal. The general journal with the four adjusting entries is shown at the top of page 238. The Post. Ref. column of the journal shows that the entries have been posted to the accounts in the general ledger.

DATE		NAME OF ACCOUNT	POST. REF.	DEBIT	CREDIT	
1957		*Adjusting Entries*				1
Nov	30	Profit and Loss Summary	33	5 4 4 3 5 0		2
		Merchandise Inventory	13		5 4 4 3 5 0	3
	30	Merchandise Inventory	13	3 7 6 3 2 5		4
		Profit and Loss Summary	33		3 7 6 3 2 5	5
	30	Supplies Expense	66	1 2 5 0 0		6
		Supplies	14		1 2 5 0 0	7
	30	Insurance Expense	62	4 0 0		8
		Prepaid Insurance	15		4 0 0	9
						10
						11
						12

Adjusting entries

Need for closing entries. Closing entries are needed at the end of each fiscal period to bring the proprietorship accounts up to date. Cost, expense, and income accounts need to be closed and the balances transferred to the profit and loss summary account. The balance of the profit and loss summary account needs to be closed and the balance transferred to the proprietor's drawing account. When these entries are made in the general journal and posted to the ledger, all cost, expense, and income accounts are in balance. The profit and loss summary account is also in balance. Entries to these accounts during the next fiscal period will thus be separated from those of the previous fiscal period. This is desirable so that records of one fiscal period can be easily compared with those of another.

Recording closing entries. Closing entries are recorded in the general journal. The three steps in recording closing entries are as follows:

Step 1. The balances of all income accounts are transferred to the credit of the profit and loss summary account.

Step 2. The balances of all cost and expense accounts are transferred to the debit of the profit and loss summary account.

Step 3. The balance of the profit and loss summary account is transferred to the proprietor's drawing account.

The P. & L. Statement columns of the work sheet provide the information needed to make the closing general journal entries. The P. & L. Statement section of the work sheet showing the income, cost, and expense accounts that are to be closed is as follows:

ACCOUNT TITLES	ACCT. NO.	P. & L. STATEMENT DEBIT	P. & L. STATEMENT CREDIT
9 Sales	41		4 5 1 5 6 0
10 Purchases	51	1 5 3 7 0 0	
11 Delivery Expense	61	5 2 8 0	
12 Miscellaneous Expense	63	2 5 8 0	
13 Rent Expense	64	1 8 0 0 0	
14 Salary Expense	65	2 0 0 0 0	
17 Supplies Expense	66	1 2 5 0 0	
18 Insurance Expense	62	4 0 0	

Section of work sheet showing income, cost, and expense items

From the information given in these columns, Mr. Kelly prepares the closing entries. The entire process of summarizing the income and the expense accounts and transferring the net profit or the net loss to the proprietor's drawing account is called *closing the ledger*.

The closing entries prepared from this section of the work sheet are shown below.

GENERAL JOURNAL   PAGE 2

	DATE	NAME OF ACCOUNT	POST. REF.	DEBIT	CREDIT
11		Closing Entries			
12	30	Sales	41	4 5 1 5 6 0	
13		Profit and Loss Summary	33		4 5 1 5 6 0
14	30	Profit and Loss Summary	33	2 1 2 4 6 0	
15		Purchases	51		1 5 3 7 0 0
16		Delivery Expense	61		5 2 8 0
17		Miscellaneous Expense	63		2 5 8 0
18		Rent Expense	64		1 8 0 0 0
19		Salary Expense	65		2 0 0 0 0
20		Supplies Expense	66		1 2 5 0 0
21		Insurance Expense	62		4 0 0
22	30	Profit and Loss Summary	33	7 1 0 7 5	
23		J. C. Kelly, Drawing	32		7 1 0 7 5
24					
25					
26					

Closing entries

Analyzing the closing entries. The words "Closing Entries" were written in the Name of Account column before the first closing entry was made. This heading explains the nature of the three closing entries, and therefore a separate explanation for each closing entry was not necessary.

The first closing entry transferred the credit balance of the sales account to the credit side of the profit and loss summary account. After this entry was posted, the sales account was closed and the credit side of the profit and loss summary account contained the total of the P. & L. Statement Credit column of the work sheet, $8,278.85. (See page 217.)

The second closing entry transferred the debit balances of the purchases account and the six expense accounts to the debit side of the profit and loss summary account. After this entry was posted, the purchases account and all of the expense accounts were closed. The debit side of the profit and loss summary account contained the total of the P. & L. Statement Debit column of the work sheet, $7,568.10. (See page 217.)

The third closing entry transferred the credit balance of the profit and loss summary account ($8,278.85 credit − $7,568.10 debit = $710.75 balance) to the credit side of J. C. Kelly's drawing account.

After these three entries were recorded and posted to the profit and loss summary account, the account appeared as follows:

Profit and Loss Summary ACCOUNT NO. 33

DATE	ITEMS	POST. REF.	DEBIT	DATE	ITEMS	POST. REF.	CREDIT
1957 Nov. 30		J2	5 4 4 3 50	1957 Nov. 30		J2	3 7 6 3 25
30		J2	2 1 2 4 60	30		J2	4 5 1 5 60
30		J2	7 1 0 75				

The third debit entry in Profit and Loss Summary, $710.75, showed the transfer of the balance to the proprietor's drawing account. The proprietor's drawing account after the posting of this entry is shown below.

J. C. Kelly, Drawing ACCOUNT NO. 32

DATE	ITEMS	POST. REF.	DEBIT	DATE	ITEMS	POST. REF.	CREDIT
1957 Nov. 7		CP1	1 0 0 00	1957 Nov. 30		J2	7 1 0 75
23		J1	2 2 7 00				
30		CP1	1 0 0 00				

The drawing account now shows a credit balance of $283.75 ($710.75 − $427.00 = $283.75). This amount was the net increase in proprietorship and could be transferred to the capital account if the proprietor desired to make this a permanent increase in his investment. Since Mr. Kelly planned to withdraw this amount in the near future, he left the net profit in his drawing account.

At intervals, probably once a year, the proprietor should decide whether the credit balance (or the debit balance) in the drawing account represents a permanent change in proprietorship. Whenever it is decided that the balance of the drawing account does represent a permanent change in proprietorship, the drawing account should be closed to the capital account.

After the posting of the closing entries, the accounts in the proprietorship section of the ledger of Kelly Appliances showed (1) the investment in the capital account and (2) the net increase in capital in the proprietor's drawing account. The sum of the balances of these two proprietorship accounts (J. C. Kelly, Capital and J. C. Kelly, Drawing) is the present capital, $9,255.81. The present capital on the balance sheet is also $9,255.81. The closing entries have therefore brought the proprietorship section of the ledger up to date.

General ledger of Kelly Appliances. The general ledger of Kelly Appliances as it appeared after the adjusting entries and the closing entries were journalized and posted is shown on pages 242 to 244. All income, cost, and expense accounts, as well as the profit and loss summary account, have been closed and ruled as explained in Chapter 10. All asset, liability, and proprietorship accounts that have both debits and credits have been balanced and ruled as was also explained in Chapter 10.

The asset, liability, and proprietorship accounts that have only debits or only credits are not balanced because the balance can be observed readily from the pencil footings. If, however, an account has a number of debits or credits, it might be balanced as a matter of convenience. For example, the capital account might be balanced once each year even though it was not considered necessary to balance it at the end of each monthly fiscal period.

The merchandise inventory account might have been balanced in the same manner as the cash account. As the first debit is exactly equal to the first credit and the second debit is therefore the balance of the account, it is satisfactory to draw the double lines directly under the first debit and the same first credit. The debit that remains below the double lines is the amount of the ending inventory.

Cash
ACCOUNT NO. 11

DATE		ITEMS	POST. REF.	DEBIT	DATE		ITEMS	POST. REF.	CREDIT
1957 Nov	1	Balance	J1	2 2 7 5 5 0	1957 Nov	30		CP1	1 9 4 1 2 0
	30	5433.30	CR1	5 0 8 9 0 0		30	Balance	✓	5 4 2 3 3 0
				7 3 6 4 5 0					7 3 6 4 5 0
1957 Dec.	1	Balance	✓	5 4 2 3 3 0					

Accounts Receivable
ACCOUNT NO. 12

DATE		ITEMS	POST. REF.	DEBIT	DATE		ITEMS	POST. REF.	CREDIT
1957 Nov	1	Balance	J1	1 0 3 2 6 0	1957 Nov	30		CR1	1 6 9 3 0 0
	30	145920	S1	2 1 1 9 6 0		30	Balance	✓	1 4 5 9 2 0
				3 1 5 2 2 0					3 1 5 2 2 0
1957 Dec.	1	Balance	✓	1 4 5 9 2 0					

Merchandise Inventory
ACCOUNT NO. 13

DATE		ITEMS	POST. REF.	DEBIT	DATE		ITEMS	POST. REF.	CREDIT
1957 Nov	1	Balance	J1	5 4 4 3 5 0	1957 Nov	30		J2	5 4 4 3 5 0
	30		J2	3 7 6 3 2 5					

Supplies
ACCOUNT NO. 14

DATE		ITEMS	POST. REF.	DEBIT	DATE		ITEMS	POST. REF.	CREDIT
1957 Nov	1	Balance	J1	1 0 4 6 0	1957 Nov	30		J2	1 2 5 0 0
	11		J1	1 4 4 0 0		30	Balance	✓	1 2 3 6 0
				2 4 8 6 0					2 4 8 6 0
1957 Dec.	1	Balance	✓	1 2 3 6 0					

Prepaid Insurance
ACCOUNT NO. 15

DATE		ITEMS	POST. REF.	DEBIT	DATE		ITEMS	POST. REF.	CREDIT
1957 Nov	1	Balance	J1	9 6 0 0	1957 Nov	30		J2	4 0 0
						30	Balance	✓	9 2 0 0
				9 6 0 0					9 6 0 0
1957 Dec.	1	Balance	✓	9 2 0 0					

General ledger closed, balanced, and ruled

Accounts Payable — ACCOUNT NO. 21

DATE	ITEMS	POST. REF.	DEBIT	DATE	ITEMS	POST. REF.	CREDIT
1957 Nov. 30		CP1	1 2 8 2 60	1957 Nov. 1	Balance	J1	9 8 0 14
30	Balance	✓	1 6 0 5 54	11		J1	1 4 4 00
				30	1605.54	P1	1 7 6 4 00
			2 8 8 8 14				2 8 8 8 14
				1957 Dec. 1	Balance	✓	1 6 0 5 54

J. C. Kelly, Capital — ACCOUNT NO. 31

DATE	ITEMS	POST. REF.	DEBIT	DATE	ITEMS	POST. REF.	CREDIT
				1957 Nov. 1	Balance	J1	7 9 7 2 06
				6		CR1	1 0 0 0 00
							8 9 7 2 06

J. C. Kelly, Drawing — ACCOUNT NO. 32

DATE	ITEMS	POST. REF.	DEBIT	DATE	ITEMS	POST. REF.	CREDIT
1957 Nov. 7		CP1	1 0 0 00	1957 Nov. 30		J2	7 1 0 75
23		J1	2 2 7 00				
30		CP1	1 0 0 00				
			4 2 7 00				
30	Balance	✓	2 8 3 75				
			7 1 0 75				7 1 0 75
				1957 Dec. 1	Balance	✓	2 8 3 75

Profit and Loss Summary — ACCOUNT NO. 33

DATE	ITEMS	POST. REF.	DEBIT	DATE	ITEMS	POST. REF.	CREDIT
1957 Nov. 30		J2	5 4 4 3 50	1957 Nov. 30		J2	3 7 6 3 25
30		J2	2 1 2 4 60	30		J2	4 5 1 5 60
30		J2	7 1 0 75				
			8 2 7 8 85				8 2 7 8 85

Sales — ACCOUNT NO. 41

DATE	ITEMS	POST. REF.	DEBIT	DATE	ITEMS	POST. REF.	CREDIT
1957 Nov. 30		J2	4 5 1 5 60	1957 Nov. 30		S1	2 1 1 9 60
				30		CR1	2 3 9 6 00
			4 5 1 5 60				4 5 1 5 60

General ledger closed, balanced, and ruled (continued)

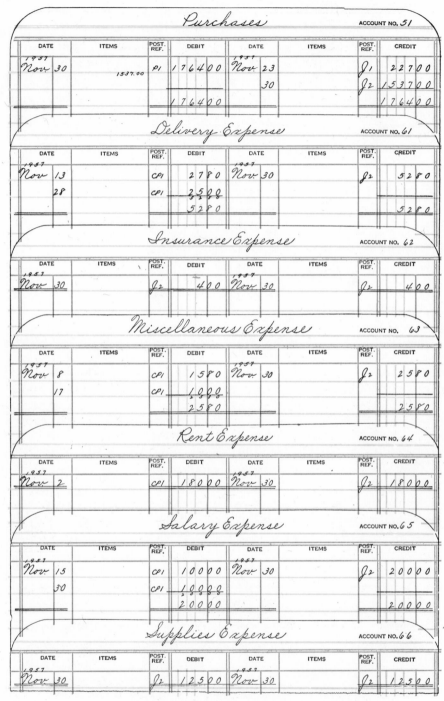

Purchases

ACCOUNT NO. 51

DATE	ITEMS	POST. REF.	DEBIT	DATE	ITEMS	POST. REF.	CREDIT
1957 Nov 30	1537.00	P1	1 7 6 4 00	1957 Nov 23		J1	2 2 7 00
				30		J2	1 5 3 7 00
			1 7 6 4 00				1 7 6 4 00

Delivery Expense

ACCOUNT NO. 61

DATE	ITEMS	POST. REF.	DEBIT	DATE	ITEMS	POST. REF.	CREDIT
1957 Nov 13		CP1	2 7 80	1957 Nov 30		J2	5 2 80
28		CP1	2 5 00				
			5 2 80				5 2 80

Insurance Expense

ACCOUNT NO. 62

DATE	ITEMS	POST. REF.	DEBIT	DATE	ITEMS	POST. REF.	CREDIT
1957 Nov 30		J2	4 00	1957 Nov 30		J2	4 00

Miscellaneous Expense

ACCOUNT NO. 63

DATE	ITEMS	POST. REF.	DEBIT	DATE	ITEMS	POST. REF.	CREDIT
1957 Nov 8		CP1	1 5 80	1957 Nov 30		J2	2 5 80
17		CP1	1 0 00				
			2 5 80				2 5 80

Rent Expense

ACCOUNT NO. 64

DATE	ITEMS	POST. REF.	DEBIT	DATE	ITEMS	POST. REF.	CREDIT
1957 Nov 2		CP1	1 80 00	1957 Nov 30		J2	1 80 00

Salary Expense

ACCOUNT NO. 65

DATE	ITEMS	POST. REF.	DEBIT	DATE	ITEMS	POST. REF.	CREDIT
1957 Nov 15		CP1	1 00 00	1957 Nov 30		J2	2 00 00
30		CP1	1 00 00				
			2 00 00				2 00 00

Supplies Expense

ACCOUNT NO. 66

DATE	ITEMS	POST. REF.	DEBIT	DATE	ITEMS	POST. REF.	CREDIT
1957 Nov 30		J2	1 2 5 00	1957 Nov 30		J2	1 2 5 00

General ledger closed, balanced, and ruled (concluded)

Post-closing trial balance. To prove the accuracy of the work at the end of the fiscal period, Mr. Kelly prepared a trial balance of his general ledger after posting the adjusting and closing entries. A trial balance made after the adjusting and closing entries have been posted is referred to as a *post-closing trial balance.* This proof of the equality of the debit balances and the credit balances in the general ledger shows that all the work of adjusting, closing, and balancing accounts has been done accurately and that all ledger accounts are ready for the next fiscal period.

The post-closing trial balance of the general ledger of Kelly Appliances is shown below.

Kelly Appliances Post-Closing Trial Balance November 30, 1957			
Cash	11	5 4 2 3 30	
Accounts Receivable	12	1 4 5 9 20	
Merchandise Inventory	13	3 7 6 3 25	
Supplies	14	1 2 3 60	
Prepaid Insurance	15	9 2 00	
Accounts Payable	21		1 6 0 5 54
J. C. Kelly, Capital	31		8 9 7 2 06
J. C. Kelly, Drawing	32		2 8 3 75
		1 0 8 6 1 35	1 0 8 6 1 35

Post-closing trial balance

Since all income, cost, and expense accounts have been closed into the proprietorship section of the ledger (drawing account), only the balance sheet accounts remain open. It is apparent, therefore, that the account balances shown on the post-closing trial balance should agree with the account balances shown on the balance sheet.

A comparison of the post-closing trial balance on November 30 with the balance sheet on November 30, page 227, shows that both are in agreement. This is proof that the ledger has been brought up to date. The entire ledger is represented by the following bookkeeping equation:

ASSETS $\quad$ = LIABILITIES + $\qquad\qquad$ PROPRIETORSHIP

$10,861.35 = $1,605.54 + Capital $8,972.06 + Drawing $283.75

CHAPTER QUESTIONS

1. In what journal are adjusting entries made?
2. What does the recording of adjustments do to accounts in the general ledger?
3. Where is the information for making adjusting entries in the general journal obtained?
4. What does the debit balance of each of the following accounts show after the adjusting entries have been journalized and posted:
   - (a) Merchandise Inventory
   - (b) Supplies
   - (c) Prepaid Insurance
   - (d) Supplies Expense
   - (e) Insurance Expense
5. What is the purpose of making closing entries?
6. In what journal are closing entries made?
7. What accounts will be in balance when all of the closing entries have been posted?
8. To what account are the balances of all cost and income accounts transferred?
9. What three entries are needed to close the ledger?
10. When all adjusting and closing entries have been posted, what three amounts will appear on the debit side of the profit and loss summary account?
11. What is the purpose of the post-closing trial balance?

CASES FOR DISCUSSION

1. At the end of a fiscal period, Paul Dawson, a shoe merchant, prepares a trial balance and the two financial reports, but he does not adjust and close the ledger. What effect will the omission of the adjusting entries and the closing entries have on the records at the end of the next fiscal period?
2. Louis Harmon's drawing account has a debit balance at the end of a fiscal period before the books are adjusted and closed. When the closing entries have been posted, under what conditions would his drawing account show (a) a debit balance? (b) a credit balance?
3. A. J. Smith, a retired businessman, owns and operates a farm. His bookkeeping records for the farm do not contain a drawing account. Mr. Smith permits each year's profit to remain in his farm business. If his farm showed a net profit of $3,500 for the current year, what would be his final closing entry?

Drill 19-A. At the end of a monthly fiscal period, three accounts of R. D. Quinn, a paint dealer, had the following balances:

Account Title	Debit Balance
Merchandise Inventory	$5,000.00
Prepaid Insurance	400.00
Supplies	200.00

The value of the merchandise inventory, the prepaid insurance, and the supplies at the end of the fiscal period were found to be:

Merchandise inventory.............	$4,800.00
Prepaid insurance.................	380.00
Supplies inventory................	156.00

Instructions: 1. Prepare the adjusting entries required to adjust the merchandise inventory account.

2. Prepare the entry required to adjust the prepaid insurance account.

3. Prepare the adjusting entry required to adjust the supplies account.

APPLICATION PROBLEMS

Problem 19-1. Adjusting and closing entries (net loss)

A partial work sheet of Kings Kandy Kitchen is illustrated below.

ACCOUNT TITLES	ACCT. No	ADJUSTMENTS DEBIT	ADJUSTMENTS CREDIT	P. & L. STATEMENT DEBIT	P. & L. STATEMENT CREDIT
Cash.....................	11				
Accounts Receivable.......	12				
Merchandise Inventory.....	13	(b) 4150 00	(a) 4602 50		
Supplies..................	14		(c) 58 50		
Prepaid Insurance.........	15		(d) 7 00		
Accounts Payable.........	21				
Kings Kandy Kitchen, Cap..	31				
Kings Kandy Kitchen, Draw.	32				
Sales....................	41				3280 90
Purchases...............	51			2175 50	
Miscellaneous Expense.....	61			57 10	
Rent Expense............	63			150 00	
Salary Expense...........	64			475 00	
Profit and Loss Summary...	33	(a) 4602 50	(b) 4150 00	4602 50	4150 00
Supplies Expense..........	65	(c) 58 50		58 50	
Insurance Expense........	62	(d) 7 00		7 00	

Instructions: Record in a general journal the adjusting entries and the closing entries required at the end of the fiscal period.

Problem 19-2. Work at the end of the fiscal period (net profit)

If you are not using the workbook correlating with this textbook, complete Exercise 19-B in the Appendix instead of this problem.

The ledger accounts of the Bowman Electric Shop are given in the workbook.

Instructions: 1. Foot the ledger accounts. Write the footings in very small figures with a sharp pencil and place each footing close to the last item. Compare your work with the ledger accounts on pages 242 to 244.

2. Prove cash. The cash on hand and in the bank on May 31, 19––, is $3,766.72, which should agree with the balance in the cash account.

3. Prepare a trial balance in the trial balance columns of eight-column work sheet paper. Compare your work with the illustration on page 217.

4. Complete the work sheet, using the following additional data as of May 31:

> Merchandise inventory, $11,487.86
> Supplies on hand, $227.50
> Prepaid insurance, $245.80

Compare your work with the work sheet illustrated on page 217.

5. Prepare a profit and loss statement from the information given on the work sheet. Compare your work with the profit and loss statement illustrated on page 225.

6. Prepare a balance sheet from the information given on the work sheet. Compare your work with the balance sheet illustrated on page 227.

7. Record in the general journal the adjusting entries shown in the Adjustments columns of the work sheet. Compare your work with the adjusting entries illustrated on page 238.

8. Record in the general journal the closing entries from the information shown in the P. & L. Statement columns of the work sheet. Compare your work with the closing entries illustrated on page 239.

9. Post the adjusting and closing entries.

10. Rule the accounts that balance. Balance each remaining account in the general ledger that has both debits and credits. Compare your work with the general ledger accounts illustrated on pages 242 to 244.

11. Prepare a post-closing trial balance. Compare your work with the post-closing trial balance illustrated on page 245.

PRACTICE SET 1 # Randall Wholesale Grocery

Part 2 ## Work at the end of the fiscal period

At this time you will complete the work at the end of the fiscal period for the Randall Wholesale Grocery for which you have recorded the transactions for the month of October.

In completing the work at the end of the fiscal period proceed as follows:

(1) Record the trial balance in the trial balance columns of a sheet of eight-column analysis paper.

(2) Record adjustments in the Adjustments column of the work sheet from the following data as of October 31:

> Merchandise inventory, $52,681.50
> Supplies on hand, $894.40
> Prepaid insurance, $623.25

(3) Complete the work sheet. Compare your work with the work sheet illustrated on page 217.

(4) Prepare a profit and loss statement from the information given on the work sheet. Compare your work with the profit and loss statement illustrated on page 225.

(5) Prepare a balance sheet from the information given on the work sheet. Compare your work with the balance sheet illustrated on page 227.

(6) Record in the general journal the adjusting entries shown in the adjustments columns of the work sheet. Compare your work with the adjusting entries illustrated on page 238.

(7) Record in the general journal the closing entries from the information shown in the profit and loss statement columns of the work sheet. Compare your work with the closing entries illustrated on page 239.

(8) Post the adjusting and closing entries and rule the accounts that balance. Compare your work with the general ledger accounts illustrated on pages 242 to 244.

(9) Balance each remaining account in the general ledger that has both debits and credits. Compare your work with the general ledger accounts illustrated on pages 242 to 244.

(10) Prepare a post-closing trial balance. Compare your work with the post-closing trial balance illustrated on page 245.

The combination journal and the petty cash fund

Need for different kinds of journals. The number and kinds of business transactions vary from business to business. It is not practical, therefore, for all businesses to use the same kind and the same number of journals. The books of original entry should be adapted to the needs of the business.

The combination journal. In earlier chapters we saw how a columnar journal may be used as the only book of original entry of a small service business. Later we used special journals as well as a general journal to record the transactions of a business buying and selling merchandise on account. Now we shall see how some small merchandising businesses can retain the benefits of special journals by combining several or all of their journals into one called a *combination journal* or *combined cash journal.*

In a combination journal similar types of transactions are sorted and summarized by columns as shown in the illustration on pages 252 and 253. Note that this journal is much the same as the columnar journal used in the first ten chapters, but columns have been added for accounts payable, accounts receivable, purchases, and sales.

Analyzing the combination journal. The use of the combination journal may be readily understood from a study of the recording of a few typical transactions. The transactions recorded on the first eight lines of the combination journal illustrated on pages 252 and 253 are therefore discussed in the following paragraphs.

Line 1 — May 1, sold merchandise on account to J. B. Wallace, $29.65.

The amount of the debit to Accounts Receivable, $29.65, is written in the Accounts Receivable Debit column. As this amount must also be posted to the account of the customer in the accounts receivable ledger, the name of the customer, J. B. Wallace, is written in the Name of Account column. The credit to Sales, $29.65, is recorded by writing the amount in the Sales Credit column.

Line 2 — May 1, purchased merchandise on account from Western Hardware Company, $329.62.

Purchases is debited by an entry in the Purchases Debit column, and Accounts Payable is credited by an entry in the Accounts Payable Credit column. In order that the credit may also be posted to the account of the creditor in the accounts payable ledger, the name of the creditor, Western Hardware Company, is written in the Name of Account column.

Line 3 — May 1, issued Check No. 127 for $269.75 to Franklin Mfg. Co. on account.

The amount of the debit, $269.75, is recorded in the Accounts Payable Debit column. To indicate that this amount is also to be debited to the creditor's account in the accounts payable ledger, the name of the creditor, Franklin Mfg. Co., is written in the Name of Account column. The amount of the credit to Cash, $269.75, is written in the Cash Credit column. The check number, 127, is written in the Check No. column.

Line 4 — May 1, issued Check No. 128 for $150 for the May rent.

A special column is provided only when it will be used frequently during the month. As Rent Expense is debited only once a month, a special column is not provided; instead the debit is recorded in the General Debit column. The title of the account debited, Rent Expense, is written in the Name of Account column. The amount credited to Cash is recorded in the Cash Credit column. The number of the check, 128, is written in the Check No. column.

Line 5 — May 2, received cash, $79.65, from Robert Norton on account.

The amount of the cash received, $79.65, is recorded in the Cash Debit column. The same amount is written in the Accounts Receivable Credit column. To show that Robert Norton's account in the account receivable ledger is to be credited, his name is written in the Name of Account column.

Lines 6 and 7 — May 3, purchased equipment on account from A. M. Allen, $125.

Since there is no special column for the equipment account, the debit amount must be recorded in the General Debit column. The title of the account to be debited, Equipment, is written in the Name of Account column.

The accounts payable account in the general ledger must be credited for $125, and the creditor's account, A. M. Allen, in the accounts payable ledger must also be credited for $125. The amount, $125, is therefore written in the Accounts Payable Credit column and the name of the creditor is written in the Name of Account column.

When the account titles for both the debit and the credit of a single transaction must be written in the Name of Account column, two lines are used. The account title for the debit is written on the first line. The account title for the credit is written on the next line and is indented about one-half inch.

Line 8 — May 3, total cash receipts for cash sales for May 1–3 were $289.77.

The amount of the debit to Cash is entered in the Cash Receipts Debit column, and the amount of the credit to Sales is entered in the Sales Credit column. The account title, Sales, is written in the Name of Account column to show the nature of this transaction.

Forwarding the combination journal totals. When a page of the combination journal is filled before the end of a month, the totals of the first page are forwarded to the second page. The bottom line in the illustration on page 252 shows how the "Totals" line is prepared for forwarding. The illustration on page 254 shows how the first line on a new page indicates the totals brought forward. The procedure in forwarding totals is:

Step 1. Each of the amount columns is totaled. The totals are entered in small pencil footings immediately below the line of the last entry.

Step 2. The equality of debits and credits is proved. This is done by adding on a separate sheet of paper the totals of all debit columns and the totals of all credit columns. The total debits should equal the total credits.

Step 3. When the total debits are found to equal the total credits, the column totals are entered in ink. A single line is drawn above the column

PAGE 10				COMBINATION JOURNAL		
CASH		CHK. NO.	DATE	NAME OF ACCOUNT	POST. REF.	
DEBIT	CREDIT					
			1957 May 1	1 J. B. Wallace	✓	1
			1	1 Western Hardware Co.	✓	2
	269 75	127	1	1 Franklin Mfg. Co.	✓	3
	150 00	128	1	1 Rent Expense	65	4
79 65			2	2 Robert Norton	✓	5.
			3	3 Equipment	16	6
				A. M. Allen	✓	7
289 77			3	3 Sales	✓	8
35 130	1 635 17		25	25 Sales	✓	35
1 884 83	1 635 17		25	25 Carried Forward	✓	36

Combination journal (left page)

totals to indicate addition and a double line is drawn below the totals in the manner shown in the illustration below.

Many printed forms provide single- and double-ruled lines at the bottom of each page. In such cases it is not necessary to rule lines.

Step 4. The date is entered in the Date column, "Carried Forward" is written in the Name of Account column, and a check mark is placed in the Post. Ref. column. None of these totals is to be posted, as these totals are to be included with the figures on the next page.

Step 5. The column totals are written on the first line of the next page.

Step 6. The date is written in the Date column and the words "Brought Forward" are written in the Name of Account column. A check mark is placed in the Post. Ref. column.

Any columnar or special journal might require more than one page for recording all the transactions for a month. The forwarding procedure described and illustrated above for the combination journal is the same procedure used for forwarding in any of these other journals.

Posting the individual items in the combination journal. Each amount in the General Debit column is posted to the debit of the account shown in the Name of Account column. Each amount in the General Credit column is posted to the credit of the account shown in the Name of Account column. The completion of the posting of each amount in the General columns is indicated by writing in the Post. Ref. column the number of the account to which the amount was posted.

FOR MONTH OF *May* 19 57   PAGE 10

| | GENERAL | | ACCOUNTS PAYABLE | | ACCOUNTS RECEIVABLE | | PURCHASES | SALES | |
	DEBIT	CREDIT	DEBIT	CREDIT	DEBIT	CREDIT	DEBIT	CREDIT	
1					29 65			29 65	1
2				329 62			329 62		2
3			269 75						3
4	150 00								4
5						79 65			5
6	125 00								6
7				125 00					7
8								289 77	8
35	521 38	169 10	1583 50	1624 80	460 33	226 80	159 4 93	2351 30	35
36	521 38	169 10	1583 50	1624 80	460 33	226 80	1594 93	2389 10	36

Combination journal (right page)

COMBINATION JOURNAL

	CASH		CHK. NO.	DATE	NAME OF ACCOUNT	POST. REF.	
	DEBIT	CREDIT					
1	1884 83	1635 17		*1957* May 25	*Brought Forward*	✓	1
2		81 77	143	27	*Reliable Tool Co.*	✓	2
3	90 18			28	*M. M. Stevens*	✓	3
12	2479 13	1828 31		31	*Western Hardware Co.*	✓	12
13	2479 13	1828 31		31	*Totals*		13
14	(11)	(11)					14

Combination journal footed, ruled, and posted (left page)

Each amount in the Accounts Receivable columns must be posted to a customer's account in the accounts receivable ledger. Each amount in the Accounts Payable columns must be posted to a creditor's account in the accounts payable ledger. The titles of the customers' and the creditors' accounts are given in the Name of Account column. The completion of the posting of each item is indicated by a check mark in the Post. Ref. column.

A check mark was also placed in the Post. Ref. column for each cash sales entry (see Lines 8 and 35 on page 252). This check mark indicates that neither the debit nor the credit is to be posted separately.

Posting the column totals of the combination journal. At the end of the month all columns of the combination journal are footed, proved, and ruled. The total of each special column is posted to the debit or to the credit of the account indicated by the column title. The posting of each column total is indicated by the number of the account written in parentheses below the column total. The totals of the General columns are not posted, since each amount in these columns is posted individually. To indicate that these totals are not to be posted, check marks are placed in parentheses under the totals of the General columns.

Variations in the use of the combination journal. Some small businesses make a combination journal their only book of original entry. More frequently, however, businesses that use a combination journal retain the general journal for recording special entries such as adjusting, closing, and correcting entries. Some businesses will also retain one or more of their special journals for recording sales, or purchases, or cash and then record only the summary totals from the special journal in the combination journal. For example, when invoices are filed or bound together and are

	GENERAL		ACCOUNTS PAYABLE		ACCOUNTS RECEIVABLE		PURCHASES	SALES	
	DEBIT	CREDIT	DEBIT	CREDIT	DEBIT	CREDIT	DEBIT	CREDIT	
1	52 38	169 10	1583 50	1624 80	460 33	226 80	1594 93	2389 10	1
2			81 77						2
3						90 18			3
12	727 88	169 10	1665 27	1850 30	540 18	458 60 25 50	1725 30	2831 45 25 50	12
13	727 88	169 10	1665 27	1850 30	540 18	458 60	1725 30	2831 45	13
14	(√)	(√)	(21)	(21)	(12)	(12)	(51)	(41)	14

Combination journal footed, ruled, and posted (right page)

used as the special sales journal, one entry would be made in the combination journal at the end of the month debiting Accounts Receivable and crediting Sales. Such a practice enables assistant bookkeepers to keep the subsidiary records, while the head bookkeeper controls the combination journal and the posting to the accounts in the general ledger.

Petty cash fund. A common business practice is to deposit *all* cash receipts in the bank and to make *all* withdrawals of such cash by writing checks. When this is done, bank statements show all cash receipts and all cash payments. The statements may then be used to prove the accuracy of the cash records of the business.

Most businesses, however, have small expenses for which it is not practical nor desirable to write a check. For example, the postman presents a letter or a package on which a few cents are due; the expressman delivers a collect package; the office boy is sent to the post office to send a registered letter. To pay for these expenses, a business may maintain a small cash fund. This fund of cash that is used for small payments is known as a *petty cash fund.*

Using the petty cash fund. The petty cash fund is established by drawing a check in favor of Petty Cash and by cashing this check. The amount of the check is often $50 or less. The money is kept separate from cash receipts. One person is usually responsible for making petty cash payments.

When cash is paid from the petty cash fund, a form is filled out to show to whom the cash was paid, what it was paid for, the amount spent, and the expense account to be debited. It may also show the signature of the person receiving the payment and the signature of the person making

Chapter 20. Combination journal and petty cash fund 255

or approving the payment. A form that provides written authority for a bookkeeping transaction is known as a *voucher*. One form of a petty cash voucher is shown in the illustration at the right.

| PETTY CASH VOUCHER |
| NO. 12   DATE July 8, 1957 |
| PAID TO Acme Typewriter Co.   AMOUNT |
| FOR Repairing typewriter   2 85 |
| CHARGE TO Miscellaneous Expense |
| PAYMENT RECEIVED: JACKSON SUPPLY COMPANY |
| Ralph Smith   APPROVED BY B. Jenson |

Petty cash voucher

Whenever a payment is made from the petty cash fund, the voucher for the payment is filled out and is placed in the petty cash drawer. The sum of the petty cash vouchers and the money in the drawer should equal the original amount of the petty cash fund.

At the end of each fiscal period and at any other time when the petty cash fund is low, a check made out to Petty Cash for an amount equal to the sum of the vouchers is written and cashed. At that time the vouchers are sorted according to the accounts to be debited. All amounts to be debited to one account are added together. An entry is then made in the combination journal debiting the various accounts for the proper amounts and crediting Cash for the total amount of the check.

Recording the transactions with petty cash in a combination journal. At the time the petty cash fund is established, the account Petty Cash is debited in the combination journal and Cash is credited. This entry is shown on Line 1 of the combination journal illustrated below. The effect of the transaction is to reduce the asset Cash and to set up a new asset, Petty Cash.

PAGE 16

COMBINATION JOURNAL

	CASH		CHK. NO.	DATE	NAME OF ACCOUNT	POST. REF.	GENERAL		
	DEBIT	CREDIT					DEBIT	CREDIT	
				1952					
1		50 00	114	July 1	Petty Cash		50 00		1
2		240 00	115	1	Globe Co.				2
22		48 53	125	31	Supplies		14 75		22
23					Delivery Expense		4 28		23
24					Miscellaneous Expense		29 50		24
25									25

Left-hand page of combination journal showing entries to establish and to replenish petty cash fund

On July 31 the petty cash fund was replenished. The following steps were made to bring the cash in the fund back up to $50:

Step 1. The petty cash vouchers were sorted and the amounts to be debited to individual accounts were added. This resulted in the following summary and proof:

Supplies............................. $14.75
Delivery Expense..................... 4.28
Miscellaneous Expense................ 29.50

Total............................. $48.53
Cash on Hand...................... 1.47

Proof............................. $50.00

Step 2. A check for $48.53 was then drawn to bring the petty cash fund up to its original amount. The check was made out to Petty Cash. The check stub from which the entry was made indicated that Supplies was to be debited for $14.75, Delivery Expense for $4.28, and Miscellaneous Expense for $29.50.

Step 3. The check for $48.53 was cashed and the cash was put into the petty cash drawer along with the remaining $1.47.

The entry to record the check that replenished the petty cash fund is shown on Lines 22, 23, and 24 in the combination journal illustrated on the preceding page. The titles of the accounts, Supplies, Delivery Expense, and Miscellaneous Expense, were written in the Name of Account column. The number of the check, 125, was written in the Check No. column on Line 22.

If this business used a cash payments journal instead of a combination journal, the entries to record petty cash transactions would be the same. The following illustration shows how these same entries for establishing and replenishing the petty cash fund would appear in a cash payments journal.

CASH PAYMENTS JOURNAL   PAGE 7

	DATE	ACCOUNT DEBITED	CHK. NO.	POST. REF.	GENERAL DEBIT	ACCOUNTS PAYABLE DEBIT	CASH CREDIT	
1	1957 July 1	Petty Cash	114		50 00		50 00	1
2	1	Globe Co.	115			240 00	240 00	2
12	31	Supplies			14 75			12
13		Delivery Expense			4 28			13
14		Miscellaneous Expense	125		29 50		48 53	14

Cash payments journal with entries for petty cash

Chapter 20. Combination journal and petty cash fund 257

CHAPTER QUESTIONS

1. Why is it that all businesses do not use the same kind and the same number of journals?
2. When is it necessary to use two lines, instead of one, in the Name of Account column of a combination journal for recording a business transaction?
3. When are the columns in the combination journal totaled?
4. How is the combination journal proved?
5. In the combination journal illustrated on pages 254 and 255, how is the posting of the column totals indicated?
6. What amounts in the combination journal illustrated on pages 252 and 253 are posted individually?
7. When a business uses a general journal as well as a combination journal, what kind of entries are usually recorded in the general journal?
8. Why do some businesses retain their special journals and record only the summary totals of these special journals in their combination journal once a month?
9. Why is it a good business practice to bank *all* cash receipts and to make *all* withdrawals of such cash by check?
10. What is the purpose of a petty cash fund?
11. In the combination journal illustrated on page 256, what entry is made to establish the petty cash fund?
12. When is the petty cash fund replenished?
13. When a check is drawn to replenish the petty cash fund, what entry is made?

INCREASING YOUR BUSINESS VOCABULARY

What is the meaning of each of the following:

(a) combination journal   (b) petty cash fund   (c) voucher

CASES FOR DISCUSSION

1. Assume that you are the only bookkeeper for A. J. Smith, the owner of a small toy shop. You have been using a columnar journal similar to that illustrated on page 44. Mr. Smith has asked you to suggest improvements in his bookkeeping system. Under what circumstances would you recommend shifting from this columnar journal to a combination journal with additional amount columns?
2. One high school bookkeeping student, when he first learned about forwarding, said that he did not see the need for it. He claimed that it would be

satisfactory to show the final total only for each column. Why is his suggestion a poor one?

3. Michael Rocco, a florist, deposited all cash receipts in the bank. All large payments were made by check. Small payments were made from a petty cash fund. Why was this method better than that of making small cash payments from cash receipts?

APPLICATION PROBLEMS

Problem 20-1. Recording transactions in a combination journal

Instructions: 1. Record on page 6 of a combination journal like the one illustrated on pages 254 and 255 the following transactions completed by John R. Richards during the month of June of the current year:

June 1. Issued Check No. 48 for $35 to establish a petty cash fund.
 1. Issued Check No. 49 for $200 for the June rent.
 2. Received $126.10 from Peter Potter on account.
 3. Purchased merchandise on account from Starrett Bros., $409.33.
 4. Sold merchandise on account to V. M. Moore, $88.20.
 5. Received $220.48 from Henry Jackson on account.
 5. Cash sales for June 1–5 were $293.85.
 8. Issued Check No. 50 for $269.75 to Bailey Manufacturing Company on account.
 9. Issued Check No. 51 for $73.88 for a cash purchase of merchandise.
 10. Purchased merchandise on account from Moss & Menke, $612.21.
 11. Received $15 for an old display case. (Store Equipment)
 12. Cash sales for June 7–12 were $375.57.
 14. Issued Check No. 52 for $168.90 to Starrett Bros. on account.
 17. Sold merchandise on account to J. M. Handy, $28.50.
 19. Cash sales for June 14–19 were $413.25.
 21. Received $41.80 from T. B. Dent on account.
 23. Issued Check No. 53 for $25 for newspaper advertising. (Advertising Expense)
 24. Purchased merchandise on account from The Wilson Company, $303.67.
 25. Issued Check No. 54 for $231.90 to the Hammitt Company on account.
 26. Issued Check No. 55 for $250 to Mr. Richards for a withdrawal for personal use.

Instructions: 2. Assume at this point of the problem that you have reached the bottom of the page. Total all columns and forward to the next page of the combination journal. Then continue to journalize the following transactions:

June 26. Cash sales for June 21–26 were $408.17.
 28. Sold merchandise on account to T. W. Baxter, $43.88.
 29. Issued Check No. 56 for $66.19 for utility bills for the month. (Miscellaneous Expense)

June 30. Issued Check No. 57 for $31.85 to replenish the petty cash fund. The petty cash payments were as follows: Supplies, $9.80; Advertising Expense, $2.50; Delivery Expense, $2.25; and Miscellaneous Expense, $17.30.

30. Issued Check No. 58 for $440 for the monthly payroll. (Salary Expense)

30. Cash sales for June 28–30 were $227.13.

Instructions: 3. Foot all columns of the combination journal and prove the equality of debits and credits.

4. Total and rule the combination journal.

Problem 20-2. Establishing, proving, and replenishing the petty cash fund

Instructions: 1. On June 1 of the current year, Marvin Chain drew and cashed Check No. 61 for $40 to establish a petty cash fund. Record this check in a combination journal like the model on page 256.

Mr. Chain paid cash from the petty cash fund as given below. The accounts to be charged are:

Supplies — for all supplies, such as ink, tape, wrapping supplies, and stamps.

Advertising Expense — for all advertising, such as newspaper advertisements.

Delivery Expense — for the delivery of goods sold.

Miscellaneous Expense — for all expenses not properly chargeable to Advertising Expense or Delivery Expense.

June 2. Paid $1.65 for a telegram.
4. Paid $1.25 for special delivery of a sale.
7. Paid 85 cents for ink and cellophane tape.
9. Paid $7 for having the office cleaned.
12. Paid $2.50 for a newspaper advertisement.
16. Paid $3.95 for wrapping supplies.
19. Paid $1.65 for two telegrams.
21. Paid $1.50 to himself for a luncheon purchased for a customer.
23. Paid $5 for having the office cleaned.
25. Paid $8 for postage stamps.
28. Paid $1 for immediate delivery of a sale.
29. Paid $3.25 for repairs to the typewriter.
29. At the close of this day, $2.40 remained in the petty cash fund.

Instructions: 2. On a separate sheet of paper, sort and summarize these transactions by accounts.

3. Prove the petty cash fund.

4. Check No. 88 was drawn to replenish the petty cash fund. Record in the combination journal the entry for replenishing the petty cash fund.

Problems relating to
sales and purchases

Granting credit for sales returns and allowances. A merchant may accept the return of goods previously sold to a customer. In such a case there is said to be a *sales return*. Or a merchant may give a customer credit for part of the sales price of goods that are in some way defective. There is then said to be a *sales allowance*.

Sales returns and sales allowances represent a decrease in sales. As a result, some businesses debit the amount of the sales returns and allowances to the sales account. It is recommended, however, that these debits be recorded in a separate account with the title *Sales Returns and Allowances*. A business can then readily see how large these sales returns and allowances are and whether they are increasing or decreasing from year to year. If the amounts are very large, one account may be kept for sales allowances and another account for sales returns. Usually it is satisfactory to combine the two into the same account.

The credit memorandum. A special business form that contains a record of the credit that the seller has granted for returns, overcharges, allowances, and similar items is known as a *credit memorandum*. A typical credit memorandum is shown at the right.

CREDIT MEMORANDUM	No. 16
	July 1, 1957
D. L. BOWMAN	C. M. Meadows
Book and Writing Papers	2016 State Street
HAMILTON	Gary, Indiana

WE CREDIT YOUR ACCOUNT AS FOLLOWS:

1 M Sheets 21 x 32-100# Posting Ledger	10.50

Credit memorandum

Recording sales returns and allowances. This credit memorandum shows that D. L. Bowman has given C. M. Meadows a credit of $10.50 for merchandise that Meadows has returned. The entry for this credit transaction is the first one shown in the combination journal on pages 262 and 263.

To record the debit to Sales Returns and Allowances, the account title was written in the Name of Account column and the amount of the debit, $10.50, was entered in the General Debit column.

To record the credit to the customer's account, the customer's name was written in the Name of Account column on the next line of the journal and was indented. The amount of the credit, $10.50, was entered in the Accounts Receivable Credit column.

The effect of this credit-granting transaction after posting to the proper accounts in the general and accounts receivable ledgers is shown in T account form below:

General Ledger

SALES RETURNS AND ALLOWANCES

7/1/57	10.50	

Accounts Receivable Ledger

C. M. MEADOWS

7/1/57 Bal.	186.60	7/1/57	10.50

ACCOUNTS RECEIVABLE

7/1/57 Bal.	4,310.14	7/1/57	10.50

The sales returns and allowances account, a minus sales account, has been debited for $10.50. The accounts receivable account has been credited for the same amount. Also, Mr. Meadows' account in the accounts receivable ledger has been credited for $10.50.

Receiving credit for purchases returns and allowances. The buyer of merchandise may be allowed credit by the seller for the return of part or

PAGE 17   COMBINATION JOURNAL

	CASH		CHK. NO.	DATE	NAME OF ACCOUNT	POST. REF.	GENERAL		
	DEBIT	CREDIT					DEBIT	CREDIT	
1				*1957* July 1	Sales Returns and Allow.		10 50		1
2					C. M. Meadows				2
3				1	Hudson Manufacturing Co.				3
4				2	Robert Smith				4
5		147 25	175	3	Transportation on Purchases		147 25		5
6				5	Johnson Manufacturing Co.				6
7					Purchases Returns & Allow.			16 50	7
15		456 29	191	11	Hudson Manufacturing Co.				15
16	294 00			12	Robert Smith				16

Combination journal with entries for returns and allowances (left page)

all of the merchandise purchased. He may also be allowed credit by the seller if the merchandise received was inferior in quality or was damaged in transit. In the latter case the merchandise is usually retained by the buyer. The credit received by the buyer because merchandise is returned is referred to as a *purchases return*. The credit received by the buyer because of inferior or damaged merchandise is referred to as a *purchases allowance*.

The buyer usually receives a credit memorandum from the seller showing the amount of the purchases return or the purchases allowance. As purchases returns and purchases allowances are ordinarily few in number, they are usually recorded in the same account with the title *Purchases Returns and Allowances*.

Recording purchases returns and allowances. A credit memorandum was received on July 5 from the Johnson Manufacturing Company for $16.50 worth of merchandise that had been returned. The entry on Lines 6 and 7 in the combination journal below shows this transaction recorded.

To record the debit to the creditor's account, the creditor's name was written in the Name of Account column and the amount of the debit, $16.50, was entered in the Accounts Payable Debit column.

To record the credit to Purchases Returns and Allowances, the account title was written in the Name of Account column on the next line of the journal and was indented. The amount of the credit was entered in the General Credit column.

FOR MONTH OF *July* 19 5 7 PAGE 17

	ACCOUNTS PAYABLE		DISCOUNT ON PURCHASES CREDIT	ACCOUNTS RECEIVABLE		DISCOUNT ON SALES DEBIT	PURCHASES DEBIT	SALES CREDIT	
	DEBIT	CREDIT		DEBIT	CREDIT				
1									1
2					10 50				2
3		465 60					465 60		3
4				300 00				300 00	4
5									5
6	16 50								6
7									7
15	465 60		9 31						15
16					300 00	6 00			16

Combination journal with entries for returns and allowances (right page)

The effect of this credit-receiving transaction after posting to the proper accounts in the general and accounts payable ledgers is shown in T account form below.

General Ledger

ACCOUNTS PAYABLE

7/5/57	16.50	7/1/57 Bal.	1,614.20

PURCHASES RETURNS AND ALLOWANCES

	7/5/57	16.50

Accounts Payable Ledger

JOHNSON MANUFACTURING CO.

7/5/57	16.50	7/1/57 Bal.	136.50

The accounts payable account has been debited for the amount of the credit received, $16.50. At the same time, the individual account in the accounts payable ledger has been debited for $16.50. The purchases returns and allowances account, a minus purchases account, has been credited for the amount of the purchases return.

Transportation on purchases. The buyer of merchandise is frequently required to pay the transportation charges on the merchandise received. These charges may include freight, express, or parcel post. All transportation charges should be included as a part of the cost of the merchandise.

The businessman ordinarily desires to know the part of the cost of the purchases that is represented by transportation charges; therefore the transportation charges are usually debited to a special account with the title *Transportation on Purchases*.

On July 3, D. L. Bowman paid the Crow Transportation Co. $147.25 for freight and drayage on purchases. Mr. Bowman then made the entry shown on Line 5 of the combination journal on pages 262 and 263.

If transportation charges on purchases are paid frequently, a special column may be provided for them.

Trade discount. In many lines of business, manufacturers and wholesalers print price lists and catalogs showing prices greater than those that the retailer will actually pay. These prices are known as *list prices*. The retailer receives a deduction from the list prices known as a *trade discount*.

When a retailer receives a purchase invoice, the invoice shows the actual amount charged him after the trade discount has been deducted. The invoice is recorded by the retailer at this amount. For this reason, the fact that a trade discount has been granted has no effect on the bookkeeping records.

Cash discount. When merchandise is bought on credit, the buyer is expected to pay the seller within the time agreed upon. To encourage the buyer to make payment before the end of the credit period, the seller may allow a deduction from the amount owed. A deduction that the seller allows on the amount of an invoice to encourage the purchaser to make prompt payment is known as a *cash discount*.

The cash discount on purchases taken by the buyer is called a *discount on purchases*. When the buyer takes advantage of this cash discount, he pays less than the purchase price recorded on his books. This cash discount is a deduction from purchases and is credited on the books of the buyer to an account with the title *Discount on Purchases*.

The cash discount on sales granted a customer is known as a *discount on sales*. When the customer takes advantage of a cash discount, the seller receives a sum less than the sales price recorded on his books. This cash discount is a deduction from sales and is debited on the books of the seller to an account with the title *Discount on Sales*.

Terms of sale. The understanding arrived at between the buyer and the seller as to payments for merchandise is called the *terms of sale*. If payment is to be made immediately, the terms are said to be "cash" or "net cash." When the buyer is allowed a period of time before payment, the sale is called a credit sale.

The period for a credit sale usually begins with the date of the invoice. It may extend to the end of the month in which the sale was made. It may extend for 30 or 60 days, or for any stipulated time agreed upon.

Invoices usually contain the terms of a credit sale. When a cash discount is included in the terms of a credit sale, it is usually expressed as a percentage of the amount of the invoice. The terms of a sale showing the rate of discount, the period in which the discount may be taken, and the time when full payment is due are shown on the invoice on page 266.

The terms of the invoice illustrated on page 266 are written 2/10, n/60. These cash discount terms, which are commonly read "two ten, net sixty," mean that the buyer may deduct 2% of the amount of the invoice if payment is made within 10 days from the date of the invoice. If he does not pay the invoice within 10 days, he may wait a total of 60 days and pay the face of the invoice with no discount allowed.

Other businesses may offer different terms. For example, the terms of one business may be 1/10, n/30 E.O.M. "E.O.M." means "end of month." If the terms are 1/10, n/30 E.O.M., a 1% discount may be taken if the invoice is paid within 10 days after the end of the month in which the

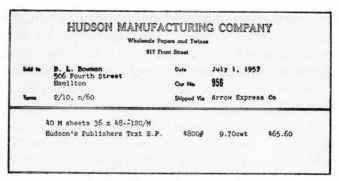

HUDSON MANUFACTURING COMPANY
Wholesale Papers and Twines
917 Front Street

Sold to	D. L. Bowman	Date	July 1, 1957
	506 Fourth Street		
	Hamilton	Our No.	956
Terms	2/10, n/60	Shipped Via	Arrow Express Co

| 40 M sheets 36 x 48-120/M | | | | |
| Hudson's Publishers Text E.F. | 4800# | 9.70cwt | 465.60 |

Invoice showing terms of payment

invoice was dated. The full amount of the invoice must be paid on or before 30 days after the end of the month.

Discount on purchases. On July 1, Mr. Bowman purchased merchandise amounting to $465.60 from the Hudson Manufacturing Company, terms 2/10, n/60. This invoice was paid on July 11. As payment was made within the discount period indicated in the terms, Mr. Bowman was entitled to take a discount of 2%. The calculations for the payment were: $465.60, total of invoice − $9.31, discount (2% of $465.60 = $9.31) = $456.29, the amount to be paid in cash.

The one debit and the two credits that result from this transaction are as follows:

	Dr.	Cr.
Accounts Payable — Hudson Mfg. Co. ...	$465.60	
Cash.............................		$456.29
Discount on Purchases..............		9.31

Recording discount on purchases. The entry on Line 3 in the combination journal illustrated on pages 262 and 263 shows the July 1 purchase transaction with the Hudson Manufacturing Company. The entry on Line 15 records the payment on July 11 for this purchase, with purchases discount taken. Observe in this payment transaction that the total of the invoice, $465.60, is recorded in the Accounts Payable Debit column; the amount of the cash paid, $456.29, is recorded in the Cash Credit column; and the amount of the discount on purchases, $9.31, is recorded in a special Discount on Purchases Credit column.

The debit and the two credits are all entered in special columns, but the debit to Accounts Payable must also be posted as a debit to the creditor's account in the accounts payable ledger. The title of the creditor's account, Hudson Manufacturing Co., is therefore entered in the Name of Account column.

When discounts on purchases or sales are recorded frequently, special columns in the combination journal are usually provided for them.

The effect of this discount-taking transaction after posting to the proper accounts in the general and subsidiary ledgers is shown in T account form below:

General Ledger

ACCOUNTS PAYABLE

1957		1957	
July 5	16.50	July 1	1,614.20
11	465.60		

CASH

1957		1957	
July 1	3,161.40	July 11	456.29

Accounts Payable Ledger

HUDSON MANUFACTURING CO.

1957		1957	
July 11	465.60	July 1	465.60

DISCOUNT ON PURCHASES

	1957	
	July 11	9.31

The accounts payable account in the general ledger has been debited for $465.60, the total amount of the July 1 invoice. Also, the individual account in the accounts payable ledger has been debited to show this account paid in full. Cash was credited for $456.29, the amount of cash actually paid. Discount on Purchases, a minus purchases account, was credited for $9.31, the amount of discount because of early payment within the discount period. The two credits in the general ledger, therefore, equal the one debit.

Discount on sales. On July 2, Mr. Bowman sold merchandise for $300 to Robert Smith, a charge customer. The terms of the invoice were 2/10, n/30. On July 12, Mr. Bowman received cash, $294, from Robert Smith in full payment of this invoice of July 2. The invoice was paid within the discount period; Mr. Smith was therefore entitled to a discount of 2% on the amount that he owed. The check that Mr. Bowman received was for $294 (the face of the invoice, $300, less the cash discount, $6). The two debits and the one credit that result from this transaction are as follows:

	Dr.	Cr.
Cash...	$294.00	
Discount on Sales.............................	6.00	
Accounts Receivable — Robert Smith...........		$300.00

Recording discount on sales. The entry on Line 4 in the combination journal illustrated on pages 262 and 263 shows the July 2 sale of $300 to Robert Smith. The entry on Line 16 records the receipt of $294 in payment of the invoice of $300 less a cash discount of $6.

Chapter 21. Problems relating to sales and purchases 267

Cash was debited in the Cash Debit column for the amount actually received, $294. Discount on Sales was debited in the Discount on Sales Debit column for $6. Accounts Receivable was credited in the Accounts Receivable Credit column for the full amount of the invoice, $300. The name of the customer was written in the Name of Account column so that the amount could be posted to the proper account in the accounts receivable ledger.

The effect of this discount-granting transaction after posting to the proper accounts in the general and subsidiary ledgers is shown in T account form below.

General Ledger		Accounts Receivable Ledger

CASH	ACCOUNTS RECEIVABLE	ROBERT SMITH

1957
July 1 3,161.40
   12   294.00
	1957
	July 1 4,310.14
		1957
		July 1 10.50
		    12 300.00
			1957
			July 2 300.00
				1957
				July 12 300.00

DISCOUNT ON SALES
1957 July 12   6.00

The cash account was debited for $294, the total amount of cash received. Discount on Sales, a minus sales account, was debited for $6, the amount of sales discount granted for early payment. The accounts receivable account was credited for $300, the total amount of the July 2 invoice. Also, Mr. Smith's individual account in the accounts receivable ledger was credited for $300 to show that his July 2 purchase was paid in full.

The work sheet. The work sheet of D. L. Bowman for the month ended July 31 is shown on page 269. This work sheet includes the five new accounts discussed in this chapter: Sales Returns and Allowances, Purchases Returns and Allowances, Transportation on Purchases, Discount on Purchases, and Discount on Sales. Of these new accounts, those having debit balances in the trial balance are extended into the P. & L. Statement Debit column. Those having credit balances in the trial balance are extended into the P. & L. Statement Credit column.

Accounts numbered with decimals. The account numbers 41.1 and 41.2 on Lines 11 and 12 of the work sheet indicate that these accounts are reported as deductions from the account numbered 41. Similarly, in this book any account that has a decimal in its number is a deduction from the account having the same number without the decimal. Many variations in the system of numbering accounts are used in business.

D. L. Bowman
Work Sheet
For Month Ended July 31, 1957

	ACCOUNT TITLES	ACCT. NO.	TRIAL BALANCE DEBIT	TRIAL BALANCE CREDIT	ADJUSTMENTS DEBIT	ADJUSTMENTS CREDIT	P & L STATEMENT DEBIT	P & L STATEMENT CREDIT	BALANCE SHEET DEBIT	BALANCE SHEET CREDIT
1	Cash	1.1	2,156.90						2,156.90	
2	Petty Cash	1.2	50.00						50.00	
3	Accounts Receivable	1.3	2,503.33						2,503.33	
4	Mdse. Inventory	1.4	6,346.95		(a)7,671.32	(b)6,346.95	6,346.95	7,671.32	7,671.32	
5	Supplies	1.5	1,487.31			(c)1,122.97			364.34	
6	Prepaid Insurance	1.6	1,008.00			(d)42.00			966.00	
7	Accounts Payable	2.1		5,286.06						5,286.06
8	D.L. Bowman, Capital	3.1		7,460.40						7,460.40
9	D.L. Bowman, Drawing	3.2	500.00						500.00	
10	Sales	4.1		13,419.26				13,419.26		
11	Sales Returns & Allow.	4.1.1	232.75				232.75			
12	Discount on Sales	4.1.2	78.52				78.52			
13	Purchases	5.1	12,907.07				12,907.07			
14	Purchase Returns & Allow.	5.1.1		235.41				235.41		
15	Discount on Purchases	5.1.2		273.00				273.00		
16	Transportation In	5.2	525.17				525.17			
17	Delivery Expense	6.1	642.30				642.30			
18	Miscellaneous Exp.	6.3	78.58				78.58			
19	Rent Expense	6.4	320.00				320.00			
20	Salary Expense	6.5	837.25				837.25			
21										
22	Profit & Loss Summary	3.3			(b)6,346.95 (a)7,671.32		6,346.95	7,671.32		
23	Supplies Expense	6.6			(c)1,122.97		1,122.97			
24	Insurance Expense	6.2			(d)42.00		42.00			
25			28,674.13	28,674.13	14,183.24	14,183.24	22,133.56	23,598.99	12,746.46	
26	Net Profit						1,465.43			1,465.43
							23,598.99	23,598.99	12,746.46	12,746.46

Work sheet of D. L. Bowman

The profit and loss statement. The profit and loss statement prepared from the work sheet on page 269 is shown below.

D.L.Bowman
Profit and Loss Statement
For Month Ended July 31, 1957

Income:			
Sales			1541926
Less: Sales Returns and Allowances		23275	
Discount on Sales		7852	31127
Net Sales			1510799
Cost of Merchandise Sold:			
Merchandise Inventory, July 1, 1957		634695	
Purchases	1290707		
Less: Purchases Returns and Allow. 23541			
Discount on Purchases 27300	50841		
Net Purchases	1239866		
Add Transportation on Purchases	52517		
Net Cost of Merchandise Purchased		1292383	
Total Cost of Mdse. Available for Sale		1927078	
Less Merchandise Inventory, July 31, 1957		767132	
Cost of Merchandise Sold			1159946
Gross Profit on Sales			350853
Operating Expenses:			
Delivery Expense		64230	
Insurance Expense		4200	
Miscellaneous Expense		7858	
Rent Expense		32000	
Salary Expense		83725	
Supplies Expense		12297	
Total Operating Expenses			204310
Net Profit			146543

Profit and loss statement

This profit and loss statement includes the two new accounts related to sales: Sales Returns and Allowances and Discount on Sales. Since both of these accounts are minus sales accounts, their amounts were totaled and then deducted from the total sales. The total sales less Sales Returns and Allowances and Discount on Sales is known as *Net Sales*.

This profit and loss statement also includes the three new accounts related to purchases: Purchases Returns and Allowances, Discount on Purchases, and Transportation on Purchases. Purchases Returns and Allowances and Discount on Purchases are both minus purchases accounts.

The amounts in these two accounts were totaled and then deducted from the total purchases. The total purchases less Purchases Returns and Allowances and Discount on Purchases is known as *Net Purchases*.

Transportation on Purchases should be included as a part of the cost of the merchandise. Transportation on Purchases was, therefore, added to the Net Purchases to secure the *Net Cost of Merchandise Purchased*.

Some businesses treat Discount on Sales as an expense account instead of a minus sales account and Discount on Purchases as an income account instead of a minus purchases account. When this is done, Discount on Sales is not considered to be a regular operating expense of the business. Neither is Discount on Purchases considered to be a part of the regular operating income of the business. These items are reported at the bottom of their profit and loss statements under the separate headings "Other Income" and "Other Expense." This procedure is becoming less common.

Closing entries. The closing entries made from the work sheet illustrated on page 269 are similar to those presented in earlier chapters. The five new accounts introduced in this chapter must, however, also be closed. The closing entries shown below include these new accounts.

| | CASH | | CHK. | DATE | NAME OF ACCOUNT | POST. | GENERAL | | |
	DEBIT	CREDIT	NO.			REF.	DEBIT	CREDIT	
10					*Closing Entries*				10
11				31	Sales		15419 26		11
12					Pur. Returns and Allow.		235 41		12
13					Discount on Purchases		273 00		13
14					Profit and Loss Summary			15927 67	14
15				31	Profit and Loss Summary		15786 61		15
16					Sales Returns and Allow.			232 75	16
17					Discount on Sales			78 52	17
18					Purchases			12907 07	18
19					Transportation on Pur.			525 17	19
20					Delivery Expense			642 30	20
21					Miscellaneous Expense			78 58	21
22					Rent Expense			320 00	22
23					Salary Expense			837 25	23
24					Supplies Expense			122 97	24
25					Insurance Expense			42 00	25
26				31	Profit and Loss Summary		1465 43		26
27					D. L. Bowman, Drawing			1465 43	27

PAGE 18 COMBINATION JOURNAL

Closing entries in the combination journal

Chapter 21. Problems relating to sales and purchases 271

CHAPTER QUESTIONS

1. What is the difference between a sales return and a sales allowance?
2. What common business form supplies the information for recording a transaction granting credit for allowances and returns?
3. In the combination journal on pages 262 and 263, what entry is required to record a transaction in which:
   (a) Merchandise is returned by a charge customer?
   (b) An allowance for returned merchandise is received from a creditor?
4. Why are transportation charges on merchandise received debited to the account Transportation on Purchases instead of to the purchases account?
5. Why does a trade discount have no effect on the bookkeeping records?
6. Why does the seller of merchandise often allow a cash discount if payment is made within a short time after the sale is made?
7. In the combination journal on pages 262 and 263, what four accounts are affected when a purchase on account is paid with a cash discount being taken? Which of these are general ledger accounts?
8. How does a business that has granted credit for sales returns and allowances and discount on sales determine its net sales for a fiscal period?
9. Under what divisional heading or section in the profit and loss statement is each of the following accounts reported:
   (a) Sales Returns and Allowances   (d) Discount on Sales
   (b) Purchases Returns and Allowances (e) Discount on Purchases
   (c) Transportation on Purchases

INCREASING YOUR BUSINESS VOCABULARY

What is the meaning of each of the following:

(a) sales return   (h) cash discount
(b) sales allowance   (i) discount on purchases
(c) credit memorandum   (j) discount on sales
(d) purchases return   (k) 2/10, n/30
(e) purchases allowance   (l) net sales
(f) transportation on purchases (m) net purchases
(g) trade discount   (n) net cost of merchandise purchased

CASES FOR DISCUSSION

1. Company X never recorded any purchases return transactions until it received a credit memorandum. Company Y recorded such transactions on the same day that the merchandise was shipped back. Which company followed the better plan?

2. On December 13 the bookkeeper for Charles Madison received a check for $196 dated December 11. This was in payment of a $200 invoice dated December 1 with the terms 2/10, n/60. Thus the payment was received two days after the discount-taking period. The envelope in which the check was mailed showed a December 11 postmark. If you were the bookkeeper for Mr. Madison, how would you handle this situation?

APPLICATION PROBLEMS

Problem 21-1. Recording transactions in a combination journal

Instructions: 1. Record the following selected transactions, which were completed by Richard Smart during the month of December, in a combination journal like the one on pages 262 and 263. All purchases and sales are made on account.

Dec. 1. Purchased merchandise amounting to $440.90 from Norton and Co.

     1. Received a check for $617.10 from D. T. Hamilton for our invoice of November 22 for $623.33 less a 1% discount of $6.23.

     4. Issued Check No. 316 for $123.16 to Brandon and Company in payment of their invoice of November 26 for $125.67 less a 2% discount of $2.51.

     5. Norton and Co. allowed us credit for $20 for defective merchandise.

     9. Sold merchandise amounting to $830.60 to B. F. Woolman.

     9. Issued Check No. 320 for $412.48 to Norton and Co. in payment of the balance of $420.90 on their invoice of December 1 less a 2% discount of $8.42.

> The amount of the invoice of December 1 was $440.90, but a credit of $20 was received on December 5. The balance of the invoice to which the discount applied was therefore $420.90, and the discount was 2% of this amount.

   13. Purchased merchandise amounting to $1,122.80 from Varden Bros.

   15. Issued a credit memorandum for $30 to B. F. Woolman for merchandise returned.

   19. Received a check for $792.59 from B. F. Woolman and gave him credit for that amount plus $8.01, a 1% discount.

> The amount of the invoice of December 9 was $830.60. A credit of $30 was given on December 15. The balance of the invoice to which the discount applied was therefore $800.60.

   20. Sold merchandise amounting to $527.70 to A. O. Prince.

   23. Issued Check No. 324 for $1,100.34 to Varden Bros. in payment of their invoice of December 13 for $1,122.80 less a 2% discount of $22.46.

   25. Received a credit memorandum for $13 from Mason Bros. for merchandise returned by us.

   26. Sold merchandise amounting to $450 to D. T. Hamilton.

Dec. 29. Received a check for $522.42 from A. O. Prince for our invoice of December 20 for $527.70 less a 1% discount of $5.28.
  30. Issued Check No. 326 for $60.50 to Arrow Trucking Company for freight and drayage on merchandise purchased.
  30. Issued Check No. 327 for $37.60 to replenish the petty cash fund. The expenses were: Supplies, $6.10; Miscellaneous Expense, $25; Delivery Expense, $2; and Transportation on Purchases, $4.50.

Instructions: **2.** Total the amounts in each column, prove the equality of debits and credits, and rule the journal.

Problem 21-2. Work at the end of a fiscal period

The trial balance of Ben Adamson, a retail merchant, on June 30 of the current year, the end of a quarterly fiscal period, was as follows:

BEN ADAMSON

TRIAL BALANCE

JUNE 30, 19--

Cash...............................	11	2,615 48	
Petty Cash...........................	12	45 00	
Accounts Receivable...................	13	1,963 75	
Merchandise Inventory.................	14	6,385 50	
Supplies.............................	15	478 63	
Prepaid Insurance.....................	16	250 00	
Accounts Payable.....................	21		2,036 45
Ben Adamson, Capital.................	31		7,100 00
Ben Adamson, Drawing................	32	900 00	
Sales................................	41		16,340 40
Sales Returns and Allowances...........	41.1	244 40	
Discount on Sales.....................	41.2	163 89	
Purchases...........................	51	10,680 30	
Purchases Returns and Allowances......	51.1		167 50
Discount on Purchases.................	51.2		138 10
Transportation on Purchases...........	52	301 75	
Miscellaneous Expense.................	62	303 75	
Rent Expense.........................	63	400 00	
Salary Expense.......................	64	1,050 00	
		25,782 45	25,782 45

Instructions: **1.** Prepare an eight-column work sheet for the quarterly fiscal period ended June 30 of the current year. The additional data needed at the end of the period are:

Merchandise inventory, June 30, $5,160.80
Supplies inventory, June 30, $208.03
Prepaid insurance, June 30, $165.00

2. Prepare a profit and loss statement and a balance sheet.

3. Record the adjusting entries and the closing entries.

Complete bookkeeping cycle using the combination journal

Norris Wholesale Toys, of which C. E. Norris is proprietor, uses as its book of original entry a combination journal with the same column headings as the one illustrated on pages 252 and 253. A general ledger, an accounts receivable ledger, and an accounts payable ledger are maintained.

Instructions: 1. Open the following accounts in the general ledger, using the account numbers given. If a workbook is not used, allow five lines in each account in the general ledger.

Norris Wholesale Toys chart of accounts

Acct. No.		Acct. No.	
	(1) Assets		**(4) Income**
11	Cash	41	Sales
12	Petty Cash	41.1	Sales Returns and Allowances
13	Accounts Receivable	41.2	Discount on Sales
14	Merchandise Inventory		
15	Supplies		**(5) Cost of Merchandise**
16	Prepaid Insurance	51	Purchases
		51.1	Purchases Returns and Allowances
		51.2	Discount on Purchases
	(2) Liabilities	52	Transportation on Purchases
21	Accounts Payable		
			(6) Expenses
		61	Insurance Expense
	(3) Proprietorship	62	Miscellaneous Expense
		63	Rent Expense
31	C. E. Norris, Capital	64	Salary Expense
32	C. E. Norris, Drawing	65	Supplies Expense
33	Profit and Loss Summary		

In recording transactions in the combination journal, charge to Miscellaneous Expense all expenses that cannot properly be charged to Insurance Expense, Rent Expense, and Salary Expense. Charge the purchases of supplies to the asset account Supplies, and charge the payment of transportation charges to the cost account Transportation on Purchases.

Instructions: 2. Record in the general ledger accounts under date of November 30 of the current year the account balances shown below:

NORRIS WHOLESALE TOYS
Trial Balance
November 30, 19--

Cash	11	3,293 20	
Petty Cash	12	50 00	
Accounts Receivable	13	1,578 40	
Merchandise Inventory	14	18,405 65	
Supplies	15	1,602 60	
Prepaid Insurance	16	465 00	
Accounts Payable	21		1,206 90
C. E. Norris, Capital	31		21,600 00
C. E. Norris, Drawing	32	7,000 00	
Sales	41		59,824 25
Sales Returns and Allowances	41.1	618 95	
Discount on Sales	41.2	168 60	
Purchases	51	39,441 20	
Purchases Returns and Allowances	51.1		567 20
Discount on Purchases	51.2		690 45
Transportation on Purchases	52	674 95	
Miscellaneous Expense	62	2,875 25	
Rent Expense	63	1,815 00	
Salary Expense	64	5,900 00	
		83,888 80	83,888 80

Instructions: 3. From the following list of accounts receivable on November 30, 19--, open accounts in the accounts receivable ledger for all customers and record the balance to be collected from each customer. If the workbook is not used, allow three lines for each account.

B. L. Benton, 165 Applegate Road, City............... $304.15
A. N. Harris, 1948 Sutton Street, City............... 379.60
David Meyers, 221 Oak Street, City............... ....
E. M. Rogers, 3470 Hillcrest Avenue, City............... 412.25
Barry L. Trent, 4221 Eileen Drive, City............... 482.40

Instructions: 4. From the following list of accounts payable on November 30, 19--, open accounts in the accounts payable ledger for all creditors and record the balance owed to each creditor. If the workbook is not used, allow four lines for each account.

Evans Bros., 735 Main Street, Cleveland............... ....
Hartman Toy Co., 1162 McMillan Street, Cincinnati........... $321.40
Jennings Plastic Toy Co., 1504 State Street, Dayton........... ....
Sheridan Toy Co., 2106 High Street, Hamilton............... 885.50

Transactions for December

Instructions: **5.** Record in the combination journal the following transactions completed by Norris Wholesale Toys during the month of December of the current year:

Dec. 1. Issued Check No. 231 for $165 for the December rent.

3. Issued a credit memorandum for $9 to E. M. Rogers for merchandise returned.

4. Received a check for $372.01 from A. N. Harris in payment of our invoice of November 26 for $379.60 less a 2% discount of $7.59.

4. Issued Check No. 232 for $876.64 to Sheridan Toy Co. in payment of their invoice of November 25 for $885.50 less a 1% discount of $8.86.

7. Received a check for $395.18 from E. M. Rogers and gave him credit for that amount plus a 2% discount of $8.07.

8. Hartman Toy Co. allowed us credit for $24 for defective merchandise.

9. Purchased merchandise on account from Jennings Plastic Toy Co., $868.25.

11. Sold merchandise on account to Barry L. Trent, $204.35.

12. Purchased merchandise on account from Evans Bros., $1,260.25.

14. Issued Check No. 233 for $25.50 for the telephone bill.

14. Sold merchandise on account to David Meyers, $335.75.

15. The cash sales for December 1 to 15 were $2,052.75.

> Post from the combination journal to the accounts receivable ledger and the accounts payable ledger.

17. Issued Check No. 234 for $25 for the electricity bill.

17. Received a check for $482.40 from Barry L. Trent in payment of our invoice of November 18 for that amount.

19. Issued Check No. 235 for $850.88 to Jennings Plastic Toy Co. in payment of their invoice of December 9 for $868.25 less a 2% discount of $17.37.

21. Received a check for $200.26 from Barry L. Trent in payment of our invoice of December 11 for $204.35 less a 2% discount of $4.09.

21. Issued Check. No. 236 for $1,235.04 to Evans Bros. in payment of their invoice of December 12 for $1,260.25 less a 2% discount of $25.21.

22. Sold merchandise on account to David Meyers, $441.15.

22. Sold merchandise on account to A. N. Harris, $263.35.

23. Issued Check No. 237 for $297.40 to Hartman Toy Co. on account.

24. Received a check for $329.03 from David Meyers in payment of our invoice of December 14 for $335.75 less a 2% discount of $6.72.

26. Purchased merchandise on account from Jennings Plastic Toy Co., $558.55.

Dec. 28. Purchased merchandise on account from Evans Bros., $695.

30. Jennings Plastic Toy Co. allowed us credit for $35 for shipment of wrong merchandise.

31. Issued Check No. 238 for $800 for the monthly payroll.

31. Issued Check No. 239 for $400 to the proprietor, C. E. Norris, for a personal withdrawal.

31. Issued Check No. 240 for $80 to Atlas Trucking Company for freight and drayage on merchandise purchased.

31. The petty cash vouchers were sorted and the petty cash payments for the month were found to be as follows: supplies, $13.30; miscellaneous expense, $20.10; transportation on purchases, $3.70. Issued Check No. 241 for $37.10 to replenish the petty cash fund.

31. The cash sales for December 16 to 31 were $1,241.90.

> Post from the combination journal to the accounts receivable ledger and the accounts payable ledger.

Work at End of Year

Instructions: **6.** Prove cash; the cash on hand and in the bank is $3,574.17.

7. Foot all columns of the combination journal and prove the equality of the debits and the credits. Total and rule the journal. Post.

8. Prepare schedules of accounts receivable and accounts payable.

9. Prepare an eight-column work sheet. Additional data for the adjustments are:

> Merchandise inventory, December 31, $19,530.70
> Supplies inventory, December 31, $188.90
> Prepaid insurance, December 31, $135.00

10. Prepare a profit and loss statement and a balance sheet for the year.

11. Record the adjusting and the closing entries. Post the entries to the general ledger and rule the accounts that balance. Balance each remaining account that has both debits and credits.

12. Prepare a post-closing trial balance.

Payroll records

The payroll. Employees are usually paid once a week. In some businesses, however, they are paid biweekly (once every two weeks), or semimonthly (twice a month), or monthly. Before these payments are made, a list of all employees entitled to pay, with the amounts due each, is prepared on a special form called a *payroll*. In large businesses, one or more clerks may spend all or most of their time keeping payroll records. These office workers are called *payroll clerks*. In smaller businesses the bookkeeper usually keeps the payroll records.

Payroll taxes. The trend of legislation, both federal and state, has been to place several kinds of taxes on a pay-as-you-go basis and to require employers to withhold these taxes from the wages of their employees. Not only must an employer withhold the amount of the taxes from the pay of each employee, but also he must keep a detailed record of the amounts, give reports to each employee, and send reports and payments to the government. For these taxes the employer serves as the government's collection agent and bookkeeper.

Income taxes withheld from employees by employer. A business is required to help the government in collecting the federal income taxes levied upon the employees of that business. The employer does this by withholding for income tax purposes a part of his employees' wages. The amounts withheld by the employer represent a liability for him until he makes payment to a district director of internal revenue or to a bank that is authorized to receive such funds.

Social security taxes. The social security laws of our federal government provide:
- (a) Old-age benefits for employees and their wives or husbands, and, under certain circumstances, benefits for the widow or widower, dependent children, and parents of the employee.
- (b) Grants to states that provide pay for persons who are temporarily unemployed and for certain relief and welfare purposes, such as aid to the blind.

A general term that is used to refer to taxes imposed under the terms of the social security laws is *social security taxes*.

One of the social security taxes is the *FICA tax*. FICA tax is the abbreviated name for Federal Insurance Contributions Act tax. This tax is frequently known as OAB tax or old-age benefits tax. It is based on the wages paid employees. Both the employer and the employee are required to pay this tax. The employee's tax is withheld from his wages by the employer and is paid, together with the employer's share, to the government.

Another social security tax is the *federal unemployment tax*. It is based on the wages paid employees. Only the employer pays this tax.

Each state also has a tax, known as the *state unemployment tax*, that is based on the amount of wages. In almost all states, this tax is paid solely by the employer.

FICA taxes are based on the first $4,200 paid to an employee during a calendar year. Federal and state unemployment taxes are based on the first $3,000 paid to an employee during a calendar year. These amounts may be changed by Congress, but the same principles of bookkeeping will apply regardless of changes in amounts.

Obtaining a social security card. Every employee in an occupation covered by the social security laws is required to have a social security card. This card is issued to anyone upon request without charge by the Social Security Administration. The application form may be obtained from any local post office. The application should be sent to the nearest field office of the Social Security Administration.

Any person may make application for a social security card even though he is not employed at the time. In fact, every person seeking a job

Application for social security account number

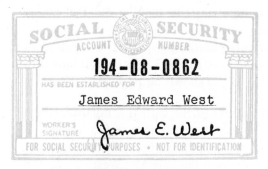

SOCIAL SECURITY

ACCOUNT NUMBER

194-08-0862

HAS BEEN ESTABLISHED FOR

James Edward West

WORKER'S
SIGNATURE *James E. West*

FOR SOCIAL SECURITY PURPOSES • NOT FOR IDENTIFICATION

Social security card

should obtain a social security card in advance of employment because having a card simplifies making application for employment. If a person is not employed at the time of making application for a social security card, he writes the word "Unemployed" in Item 12 on the application.

After filing an application, the employee will receive from the Social Security Administration a card showing the social security account number that has been assigned to him. If a person loses his social security card, he may apply for a new card. In this case he should write at the top of the application "Request for duplicate."

If an employee changes her name by marriage, she should notify the Social Security Administration of the change. A form for reporting the change may be obtained from the local Social Security field office.

Payroll time cards. The first requirement of an adequate payroll record system is an accurate record of the time each employee has worked. Time cards and a time clock are often used to obtain this information.

The Nolan Machine Shop uses a time clock to record the time of arrival and departure of each employee each day. Each employee has a card with his name on it in a rack beside the time clock. He "rings in" each morning and after lunch, and he "rings out" at noon and when he leaves at night. Each time an employee "rings in" or "rings out," the clock records the time on the

PAY ROLL NO.   37

NAME   James E. West

WEEK ENDING   September 21, 1957

MORNING		AFTERNOON		OVERTIME		HOURS
IN	OUT	IN	OUT	IN	OUT	
S 7:56	S 12:00	S 12:55	S 5:02			*8*
R 7:58	R 12:01	R 12:57	R 5:01			*8*
W 8:00	W 12:03	W 1:00	W 5:04			*8*
T 7:57	T 12:02	T 1:01	T 5:00	T 6:00	T 9:00	*3/8*
F 7:59	F 12:02	F 12:59	F 5:08			*8*

	HOURS	RATE	EARNINGS	
REGULAR	*40*	*2⁰⁰*	*80*	*00*
OVERTIME	*3*	*3⁰⁰*	*9*	*00*
TOTAL	*43*		*89*	*00*

Payroll time card

card. The payroll clerk uses the time cards in making out the weekly payroll record for each employee.

Mr. James E. West, a grinder in the finishing department, began work for the Nolan Machine Shop on September 16, 1957. His payroll time card for the week ended September 21, 1957, is shown on page 281.

Analyzing the time card. At the top of the card is a number, which is Mr. West's payroll number. The use of the number makes it easier to place each time card in the rack in its proper place than it would be if the cards were filed alphabetically. On the next lines are Mr. West's name and the payroll period.

For recording the time there are three sections — Morning, Afternoon, and Overtime — with an "In" and an "Out" under each section. When Mr. West reported for work on Monday, he dropped the card in the slot in the time clock and recorded his time of arrival as M7:56. The other entries on this line indicate that he checked out at lunch time at 12:00 and in at 12:55 and that he left for the day at 5:02. The entries following are for the remaining days of the week. On Thursday he worked three hours overtime. This is recorded as shown on the line for Thursday.

At the end of the week the payroll clerk entered the number of hours for each day in the right-hand column. Each firm has its own rules regarding deductions for tardiness. The payroll clerk must know these rules in order to make the proper deductions if employees are late.

Determining the employee's earnings. Each employee's hours of work and earnings are found as follows:

Step 1. The time card is examined for records of tardiness and early leaving, and notations are made.

Mr. West reported to work one minute late on Thursday afternoon. Deductions are not made by the Nolan Machine Shop for such short periods of time.

Step 2. The regular hours are extended into the Hours column.

The regular hours for Mr. West are 8 for Monday through Friday.

Step 3. The amount of overtime for each day is calculated and is entered above the regular hours for the day.

Mr. West worked from 6:00 p.m. to 9:00 p.m. on Thursday; hence the figure 3 is written above the figure 8 for that day.

Step 4. The regular hours and the overtime hours are added separately and are entered in the spaces provided at the bottom of the card.

Step 5. The rates for regular time and overtime are entered, and the earnings are computed.

Step 6. The Hours and the Earnings columns are then added to show the total hours and the total earnings.

After the payroll for the week is completed, the time cards are filed. Government regulations require that records concerning time worked and wages earned be kept for a period of at least four years.

Payroll register. Each week information about the entire payroll was entered in the payroll register. A part of the payroll register prepared for the week ended September 21 is shown below.

PAYROLL REGISTER

WEEK ENDED September 21, 1957   DATE OF PAYMENT September 23, 1957

NO.	EMPLOYEE'S NAME	NO. OF EXEMP-TIONS	TOTAL EARNINGS	DEDUCTIONS			NET PAY	
				FICA TAX	INCOME TAX	OTHER	AMOUNT	CHK. NO.
23	Arthur Andrews	2	99 70	2 24	13 20		84 26	690
11	Thomas Aylward	1	84 00	1 89	13 00		69 11	691
3	Richard Bradley	4	108 50	2 44	10 10		95 96	692
12	Alex M. Caldwell	2	99 70	2 24	13 20		84 26	693
6	Philip Dalton	1	75 00	1 69	11 20		62 11	694
22	Thomas Dover	3	99 70	2 24	10 90		86 56	695
15	John Engel	4	100 00	2 25	9 20		88 55	696
27	Edward Parker	1	75 00	1 69	11 20		62 11	724
9	William Parker	2	92 80	2 09	12 10		78 61	725
18	Howard Price	3	89 00	2 00	9 10		77 90	726
20	James Randolph	4	108 50	2 44	10 10		95 96	727
31	Allen J. Ross	2	92 50	2 08	12 10		78 32	728
16	Henry Stahl	4	75 00	1 69	4 30		69 01	729
37	James E. West	3	89 00	2 00	9 10		77 90	730
42	Walter Williams	2	106 50	2 40	14 70		89 40	731
	Totals		4000 00	90 00	382 50		3527 50	

Payroll register

Analyzing the payroll register. At the top of the payroll register the last day of the payroll week, September 21, and the date of payment, September 23, are entered.

A few days before the end of the payroll period, the time clock numbers, the names of the employees, and the number of their exemptions for income tax purposes were listed in the register.

An exemption is an amount of money on which a person does not have to pay income tax. Each person is allowed one exemption for himself, one exemption for his wife (or husband), and one exemption for each additional person who is dependent on him. The number of exemptions a worker declares affects the amount that is deducted each period for his income tax.

When the time cards for the week are computed, the total earnings figure from each card is written in the Total Earnings column of the payroll register opposite the employee's name.

The section headed "Deductions" is used to record the various amounts that are deducted from the employees' earnings. The column headed "FICA Tax" is used to record the amount that is deducted for old-age and survivors benefit taxes. Although this tax could be computed by multiplying $2\frac{1}{4}\%$ times each of the wages, the Nolan Machine Shop prefers to use a tax table furnished by the government to compute the tax. The FICA tax on the earnings of James E. West was $2.

> The tax rates used in this chapter were taken from laws in effect at the time this book was published. During the years 1960 through 1964 the FICA tax rate is to be $2\frac{3}{4}$ per cent. The rates may be changed by Congress, but the same principles will apply regardless of any changes in rates.

The column headed "Income Tax" is used to record the amount of income tax withheld from each employee's earnings. This amount is determined from a table furnished by the government that takes into account the amount of wages earned and the number of income tax exemptions claimed. James E. West has three exemptions. The income tax withheld from his earnings is $9.10.

The column headed "Other" is used to enter such items as deductions for purchases of United States Savings Bonds, deductions for union dues, and the like.

The section headed "Net Pay" is used to record the amount due each employee and the number of the payroll check issued to him.

After all the deductions have been computed and the net pay has been recorded for each employee, each of the amount columns is totaled. The accuracy of these additions is verified by comparing the total of the Total Earnings column with the sum of the totals of the Net Pay column and the Deductions columns.

Before checks are written for the net pay amounts, the manager or some person designated by him examines the payroll computations and approves the payroll.

Record of employee's earnings. A detailed account is kept of all items affecting the payments made to each employee. This record, known as the employee's earnings record, is kept on cards or sheets. A separate card or sheet is kept for each employee. The employee's earnings record for Mr. West is shown on the following page.

Analyzing the employee's earnings record. The illustration of the employee's earnings record provides information for thirteen weeks, a quarter of a year. The record is made with quarterly divisions because the employer is required to make reports on special forms for each quarter.

Mr. West's name is entered at the top of the card, together with his payroll number and his social security number.

Mr. West began work for the Nolan Machine Shop on Monday, September 16. The first entry in his earnings record is therefore made at the end of that week, September 21; hence there is no record before this date. The week ended September 21 is the twelfth week in the quarter; therefore the payroll clerk enters the information on the twelfth line. The date September 21 is entered on the twelfth line as 9/21.

The amount columns of the employee's earnings record are the same as the amount columns of the payroll register. The amounts opposite each employee's name in the payroll register are transferred to the corresponding columns of the employee's earnings record. The Nolan Machine Shop also records the number of the payroll check in the employee's earnings record.

The Quarterly Totals line provides space for the totals for the quarter. The form for the final quarter in the year also provides space for entering the totals for the year. These totals are needed in making reports to the government on both a quarterly and an annual basis.

The law requires that the employee's earnings record shall be kept on file for a period of at least four years. This is required in order to give the government time to check back on records of payments to employees and to audit the reports of employers.

EARNINGS RECORD FOR QUARTER ENDING Sept. 28, 1957

West — James — E. — 37 — 194-08-0862 — Sal.Exp

LAST NAME	FIRST	MIDDLE	TIME CLOCK NO.	SOC. SEC. NO.	ACCOUNT CHARGED

| PAY PERIOD | | TOTAL EARNINGS | DEDUCTIONS | | | NET PAY | |
WEEK NO.	WEEK ENDED		FICA TAX	INCOME TAX	OTHER	AMOUNT	CHECK NO.
1							
2							
11							
12	9/21	89 00	2 00	9 10		77 90	730
13	9/28	86 00	1 94	8 40		75 66	793
QUARTERLY TOTALS		175 00	3 94	17 50		153 56	

Employee's earnings record

Paying the payroll by check. The Nolan Machine Shop pays its employees weekly by check. It uses a special payroll check form that has a space in the upper left-hand corner to record amounts deducted from weekly earnings.

The payroll checks are drawn against a special payroll bank account. Each pay period a check for the total amount of the net pay is drawn on the regular checking account in favor of the payroll account and is deposited in the separate account against which the payroll checks are drawn. On September 23, the Nolan Machine Shop drew a check for $3,527.50 and deposited it in its payroll account, and then it drew payroll checks for each employee.

The check for Mr. West for the week ended September 21 appears below. The information for the check is taken directly from the payroll register.

DEDUCTIONS
FICA TAX ___2.00___
INCOME TAX ___9.10___
GROUP INS. _____
HOSPITAL CARE _____

NOLAN MACHINE SHOP

Cincinnati, _Sept. 23,_ 19_57_ No. _730_

PAY TO THE ORDER OF _James E. West_ _____ $77 90

Seventy-seven 90/100 _____ DOLLARS

NOLAN MACHINE SHOP
Payroll Account

ROCKY RIVER NATIONAL BANK
ROCKY RIVER, OHIO   6-107/410

Henry Johnson
TREASURER

Payroll check

Some firms make a carbon copy of the check containing all the information that is on the check with the exception of the signature of the employer and the name of the bank. The employee detaches the carbon copy and keeps it as his record of deductions and cash received.

Paying the payroll in cash. Some firms prefer to pay their employees in cash. This practice is usually followed when the employees find it difficult to get to a bank to have their checks cashed or when the employer is required by law to allow time off from work for the employees to deposit or cash their checks.

When the payroll is to be paid in cash, the payroll clerk must obtain the cash from the bank in the proper denominations so that he will have the necessary change when he distributes the money into the individual envelopes. In order to do this, he prepares a payroll change form similar to the following:

PAYROLL CHANGE SHEET

DATE Oct. 21, 1957

EMPLOYEE NO.	AMOUNT DUE	$20	$10	$5	$1	50¢	25¢	10¢	5¢	1¢
1	77 50	3	1	1	2	1				
2	84 26	4			4		1			1
3	84 88	4			4	1	1	1		3
4	61 21	3			1			2		1
75	67 06	3		1	2				1	1
76	78 61	3	1	1	3	1		1		1
77	57 33	2	1	1	2		1		1	3
78	84 12	4			4			1		2
TOTAL	4696 12	212	21	21	88	72	32	47	65	117

Payroll change sheet

From the employee's earnings record, each employee's number and the amount due him are entered in the first two columns of the payroll change sheet. Then the bills and the coins required for his pay envelope are listed in the columns at the right. For example, Employee No. 1 has $77.50 due him. To pay this amount, the payroll clerk needs three $20 bills, one $10 bill, one $5 bill, two $1 bills, and one 50-cent piece.

After the payroll change sheet is completed, all the columns are totaled and a payroll requisition form is prepared. This form shows the number of each denomination desired and the amount of each denomination. The total of the amounts must equal the total of the payroll shown on the payroll change sheet. A typical payroll requisition form is shown at the left.

PAYROLL REQUISITION

DENOMINATION	NUMBER OF EACH DENOMINATION	AMOUNT
$20.00	212	4240 00
10.00	21	210 00
5.00	21	105 00
1.00	88	88 00
.50	72	36 00
.25	32	8 00
.10	47	4 70
.05	65	3 25
.01	117	1 17
TOTAL PAYROLL		4696 12

Payroll requisition form

A check for the total amount of the payroll is then drawn. This check and the payroll requisition form are given to the bank clerk, who gives the payroll clerk the number of each denomination needed. The payroll clerk places the money in the envelopes for the employees.

Payroll receipt. A payroll receipt is prepared in duplicate for each employee. The receipt contains a summary of the earnings record showing the employee's name, his gross earnings, an itemized list of the deductions, and the net amount he receives. When the employee receives his pay envelope, he signs one copy of the payroll receipt, which the business keeps, and he retains the other copy as his record of earnings and deductions. An illustration of a payroll receipt is shown below.

PAYROLL RECEIPT

Name Mary F. Peters   Payroll No. 11   So. Sec. No. 408-06-7186

For Period Ended Oct. 19, 1957   Date of Payment Oct. 21, 1957

HOURS		GROSS EARNINGS		DEDUCTIONS			NET PAY	
REGULAR	OVERTIME			FICA TAX	INCOME TAX WITHHELD	OTHER		
40	5	76	00	1 71	9 20	GI 1 50	63	59

OTHER DEDUCTIONS:
GI- Group Insurance
HC- Hospital Care
SB- Savings Bonds
UD- Union Dues

Mary F. Peters
SIGNATURE

Payroll receipt showing the earnings, deductions, and net pay of an employee who is paid in cash

This payroll receipt shows that, for the week ended October 19, Mary F. Peters had gross earnings of $76. The deductions were: $1.71 for FICA taxes, $9.20 for income taxes withheld, and $1.50 for group insurance. The "Other" column under the heading "Deductions" is used for deductions that are not made every period. The various deductions that are entered in this column are identified by initials, which are keyed in the lower left corner of the receipt.

Where a time clock is not used. Firms employing a small number of persons usually do not find it economical to use a time clock. Employees are assumed to be present unless the payroll clerk is notified of absence. Also, many executives and junior executives do not use a time clock because they are paid at a certain rate a month and their pay is not affected by brief absences.

Even though a time clock is not used, an employee's earnings record must be kept for each employee. The method of paying the employee by check or by cash is similar to one of the methods discussed in this chapter.

CHAPTER QUESTIONS

1. Why must every employer keep accurate records of the wages or the salary paid to each employee?
2. What are the two principal types of taxes that the federal government requires employers to deduct from payrolls?
3. How is a social security card obtained?
4. What are the principal types of information recorded on the time card illustrated on page 281?
5. On what day did James West work overtime according to his time card on page 281?
6. What are the six steps commonly followed in determining each individual employee's earnings and the amount to be paid to each employee?
7. What are the principal types of information recorded in the payroll register illustrated on page 283?
8. What are the chief differences between the payroll register on page 283 and the employee's earnings record on page 285?
9. (a) What were James West's earnings for the week ended September 28? (b) How much did he actually receive?
10. How is the amount of income tax withheld from employees' wages determined?
11. On the employee's earnings record illustrated on page 285, what is the column headed "Other" used to record?
12. How is the payroll change sheet illustrated on page 287 prepared and used?

INCREASING YOUR BUSINESS VOCABULARY

What is the meaning of each of the following:

(a) payroll
(b) payroll clerks
(c) social security taxes
(d) FICA tax
(e) federal unemployment tax
(f) state unemployment tax

CASES FOR DISCUSSION

1. Lang's Music Shop pays its employees by check. Elmer Bantry pays his employees in cash. What are the advantages and the disadvantages of each method?
2. The Oakdale Manufacturing Company uses a time clock and time cards in recording employees' working time. Swain & Storey do not use a time clock, but the payroll clerk assumes that employees are present unless he is notified otherwise. What are the advantages and the disadvantages of each system?

3. The Meade Company requires each employee to sign a payroll receipt, similar to the one illustrated on page 288, each time wages are paid. The Standish Company, on the other hand, does not require employees to sign payroll receipts. What difference in payroll procedures might make payroll receipts desirable for one company but not for the other?

APPLICATION PROBLEMS

Problem 22-1. Application for social security account number

If the workbook correlating with this textbook is not available, this problem may be omitted.

Instructions: Fill in the application for a social security account number given in the workbook. Use your own personal data. Compare your application with the illustration on page 280.

Problem 22-2. Time cards

If the workbook correlating with this textbook is not available, complete Exercise 22-A in the Appendix instead of this problem.

Instructions: 1. Complete the time cards given in the workbook.

2. Record the time cards in a payroll register similar to the one on page 283 of the textbook. The date of payment is May 18.

3. Prepare a payroll change sheet similar to the one on page 287.

4. Prepare a payroll requisition form similar to the one on page 287.

Problem 22-3. Employee's earnings record

The total earnings of Janet Carter for the thirteen weeks in the quarterly period April through June of the current year are given below, together with the deductions for income tax, group insurance, and hospital care.

Week Ended	Total Earnings	Deductions Income Tax	Other
4/5	$60.00	$8.70	
4/12	64.50	9.40	
4/19	62.25	9.00	
4/26	60.00	8.70	
5/3	66.75	9.80	$4.50
5/10	64.50	9.40	
5/17	62.25	9.00	
5/24	60.00	8.70	
5/31	62.25	9.00	
6/7	66.75	9.80	
6/14	64.50	9.40	6.00
6/21	60.00	8.70	
6/28	60.00	8.70	

Instructions: Prepare an employee's earnings record, similar to the one on page 285, for Janet Carter for the second quarter of the current year. Additional data needed to complete the record are as follows:

(a) Miss Carter's time clock number is 57.
(b) Miss Carter's social security number is 268-05-9847.
(c) Miss Carter's earnings should be charged to Salary Expense.
(d) In addition to the deductions listed above, a deduction of 2¼% of her total earnings for each week is to be made for FICA taxes.

Problem 22-4. Cash payrolls

The Maxwell Company pays its employees in cash. For each pay period the payroll clerk prepares a payroll register showing the earnings, the deductions, and the net pay of each employee.

A part of the payroll register for the week ended June 21 of the current year, showing the number, the name, the number of exemptions, the total earnings, and the income tax deduction of each employee, is given below. An additional deduction of 2¼% of each employee's total earnings is to be made for FICA taxes.

PAYROLL REGISTER

WEEK ENDED   June 21, 19--   DATE

No.	Employee's Name	No. of Exemptions	Total Earnings	Deductions	
				FICA Tax	Income Tax
1	Wm. S. Baxter..........	5	$106 00		$7 80
2	John Bennett...........	1	95 00		14 80
3	Steven Cary...........	1	93 00		14 40
4	Ida M. Cook...........	2	75 00		8 90
5	Jean Denham...........	1	55 00		7 70
6	R. S. Foster...........	2	90 00		11 80
7	Ruth Horn.............	1	65)0		9 40
8	Sandra Klein...........	1	50 00		6 80
9	Mary Mitchell..........	1	55 00		7 70
10	C. F. Parks............	4	100 00		9 20
11	D. D. Porter...........	3	63 00		4 40
12	Paul Thorne...........	4	82 00		5 70
	Totals...............				

Instructions: *1.* Prepare a payroll register similar to the one illustrated on page 283. The date of payment is June 23.

2. Prepare a payroll change sheet similar to the one illustrated on page 287.

3. Prepare a payroll requisition form similar to the one illustrated on page 287.

CHAPTER 23

Taxes and reports

The payroll register illustrated in the previous chapter summarizes the payroll information for each pay period. This information must also be recorded in a journal and posted to the accounts.

A part of the payroll register of the Nolan Machine Shop for the week ended September 21 is illustrated below.

PAYROLL REGISTER

WEEK ENDED September 21, 1957 — DATE OF PAYMENT September 23, 1957

NO.	EMPLOYEE'S NAME	NO. OF EXEMP. TIONS	TOTAL EARNINGS	FICA TAX	INCOME TAX	OTHER	AMOUNT	CHK. NO.
23	Arthur Andrews	2	99 70	2 24	13 20		84 26	690
11	Thomas Aylward	1	84 00	1 89	13 00		69 11	691
20	James Randolph	4	108 50	2 44	10 10		95 96	727
31	Allen J. Ross	2	92 50	2 08	12 10		78 32	728
16	Henry Stahl	4	75 00	1 69	4 30		69 01	729
37	James E. West	3	89 00	2 00	9 10		77 90	730
42	Walter Williams	2	106 50	2 40	14 70		89 40	731
	Totals		4 000 00	90 00	382 50		3 527 50	

Debits and credits required in recording the payroll. The total of the Total Earnings column, $4,000, is the salary expense for the period. Salary Expense must therefore be debited for this amount.

The total of the FICA Tax column, $90, is the amount withheld from the salaries of employees for FICA taxes. Until this amount is paid to the government, it is a liability of the business. In order to record this liability, FICA Taxes Payable must be credited for $90.

The total of the Income Tax column, $382.50, is the amount withheld from salaries of employees for income taxes. Until this amount is paid to the government, it is a liability of the business. To record this liability, Employees Income Taxes Payable must be credited for $382.50.

The total of the Net Pay Amount column, $3,527.50, is the amount of cash actually paid to employees. To record the decrease in the asset Cash, the cash account is credited for this amount.

The debits and the credits based on the column totals of the payroll register are equal, as shown below:

SALARY EXPENSE DEBIT		FICA TAXES PAYABLE CREDIT		INCOME TAXES PAYABLE CREDIT		CASH CREDIT
$4,000.00	=	$90.00	+	$382.50	+	$3,527.50

Recording the payroll in the journal. The entry in the combination journal to record the totals of the September 21 payroll register of the Nolan Machine Shop is illustrated below:

	CASH DEBIT	CASH CREDIT	CHK. NO.	DATE	NAME OF ACCOUNT	POST. REF.	GENERAL DEBIT	GENERAL CREDIT	
11		3527 50	451	21	Salary Expense		4000 00		11
12					Employees Income Taxes Pay.			382 50	12
13					FICA Taxes Pay			90 00	13
14									14

PAGE 19 — COMBINATION JOURNAL

The credit to Cash, $3,527.50, is entered in the Cash Credit column. The amount of the Salary Expense, $4,000, is entered in the General Debit column. The amounts of the tax liabilities are entered in the General Credit column.

Payroll and tax liability accounts. After the above entry was posted, the two liability accounts, Employees Income Taxes Payable and FICA Taxes Payable, appeared as follows:

Employees Income Taxes Payable — ACCOUNT NO. 22

DATE	ITEMS	POST. REF.	DEBIT	DATE	ITEMS	POST. REF.	CREDIT
				1957			
				21		19	382 50

FICA Taxes Payable — ACCOUNT NO. 23

DATE	ITEMS	POST. REF.	DEBIT	DATE	ITEMS	POST. REF.	CREDIT
				1957			
				21		19	90 00

The credit of $382.50 in the employees income taxes payable account represents a liability of the business to pay the amount of income taxes withheld from the employees' salaries. The credit of $90 in the FICA taxes payable account represents a liability of the business to pay the amount of the FICA taxes withheld from the employees' salaries.

Recording the employer's share of FICA taxes. The FICA or old-age benefit taxes of the employer are the same as those of the employees. For the pay period ended September 21, 1957, the FICA taxes of the Nolan Machine Shop were therefore $90. To record this liability, the following entry was made in the combination journal of the Nolan Machine Shop:

Entry for employer's FICA taxes

FICA Taxes is debited to record the expense for the taxes. FICA Taxes Payable is credited to record the liability. After the entry was posted, these two accounts appeared as follows:

The FICA taxes payable account has two credits of $90 each. The first is the liability for the amount withheld from employees' wages for FICA taxes. The second is the liability for the employer's share of the tax.

The expense account FICA Taxes has a debit of $90, which is the employer's tax expense.

Recording the employer's state unemployment taxes. Under the provisions of the federal and the state unemployment insurance laws, employers are required to pay taxes that are used for the payment of unemployment compensation. Compensation is available under certain circumstances for those who are unemployed and who are unable to obtain employment. The taxes for unemployment purposes are based on the amount of the salaries and are, in most states, levied on the employers only.

The state unemployment tax on the salaries paid on September 21 by the Nolan Machine Shop, $4,000, was 2.7% of the salaries, or $108. To record this expense the following entry was made:

| | CASH | | CHK. | DATE | NAME OF ACCOUNT | POST. | GENERAL | |
	DEBIT	CREDIT	NO.			REF.	DEBIT	CREDIT
16				21	State Unemployment Taxes		108 00	
17					State Unemployment Taxes Pay.			108 00
18								
19								
20								
21								
22								
23								
24								

PAGE 19 — COMBINATION JOURNAL

Entry for state unemployment taxes

In a few states an unemployment tax is levied against the employee as well as against the employer. In these states the amount of the unemployment taxes withheld from employees is credited to the liability account State Unemployment Taxes Payable.

The expense account State Unemployment Taxes is debited for the amount of the tax expense, which is 2.7% of the total earnings, or $108. The amount of this tax is a liability until it is paid; therefore State Unemployment Taxes Payable is credited for $108.

After this entry was posted, the two accounts appeared as follows:

				State Unemployment Taxes Payable			ACCOUNT NO. 24	
DATE	ITEMS	POST. REF.	DEBIT	DATE 1957	ITEMS	POST. REF.	CREDIT	
				21		19	108 00	

				State Unemployment Taxes			ACCOUNT NO. 69	
DATE 1957	ITEMS	POST. REF.	DEBIT	DATE	ITEMS	POST. REF.	CREDIT	
21		19	108 00					

The credit of $108 in State Unemployment Taxes Payable is the employer's liability for the state unemployment tax for the week ended September 21. The debit of $108 in State Unemployment Taxes is the employer's expense for the state unemployment tax for the week of September 21.

Recording the employer's federal unemployment taxes. The federal unemployment tax on the salaries paid on September 21 by the Nolan Machine Shop, $4,000, was .3% of the wages, or $12. To record the expense the following entry was made:

PAGE 19				COMBINATION JOURNAL					
CASH		CHK. NO.	DATE	NAME OF ACCOUNT	POST. REF.	GENERAL			
DEBIT	CREDIT					DEBIT	CREDIT		
			21	*Federal Unemployment Taxes*		12 00			18
				Fed. Unemployment Taxes Pay.			12 00		19
									20
									21

Entry for federal unemployment taxes

The expense account Federal Unemployment Taxes was debited for the amount of taxes owed, .3% of the total earnings, or $12. The amount of this tax was a liability until it was paid; therefore, Federal Unemployment Taxes Payable was credited for $12.

After this entry was posted, the two accounts involved appeared as follows:

DATE	ITEMS	POST. REF.	DEBIT	DATE	ITEMS	POST. REF.	CREDIT
				1957			
				21		19	12 00

Federal Unemployment Taxes Pay ACCOUNT NO. 25

Federal Unemployment Taxes ACCOUNT NO. 64

DATE	ITEMS	POST. REF.	DEBIT	DATE	ITEMS	POST. REF.	CREDIT
1957							
21		19	12 00				

The credit of $12 in the account Federal Unemployment Taxes Payable is the employer's liability for the federal unemployment tax for the week of September 21. The debit of $12 in the account Federal Unemployment Taxes is the employer's expense for the federal unemployment tax for the week of September 21.

Paying the liability for employees income taxes and for FICA taxes. At the end of September the liability account Employees Income Taxes Payable had a credit balance of $1,530.50 and the liability account FICA Taxes Payable had a credit balance of $720. On October 14 the Nolan Machine Shop drew Check No. 489 for $2,250.50 in payment of these two liabilities. The entry to record this payment was as follows:

PAGE 21

COMBINATION JOURNAL

CASH DEBIT	CASH CREDIT	CHK. NO.	DATE	NAME OF ACCOUNT	POST. REF.	GENERAL DEBIT	GENERAL CREDIT	
	2250 50	489	14	Employees Income Taxes Pay.		1530 50		10
				F I C A Taxes Pay.		720 00		11
								12
								13
								14

Entry for payment of liability for employees income taxes and for FICA taxes

The liability accounts Employees Income Taxes Payable and FICA Taxes Payable were debited to record the decreases in these liabilities, and Cash was credited to record the decrease in the asset Cash.

After each quarter of the year, every employer must pay to the government the amount of the income tax withheld and the FICA taxes for which he is liable. If the total of these taxes for any month (except the third month of the quarter) exceeds $100, the employer is required to deposit these amounts in the Federal Reserve Bank that serves his district. Special rules apply for handling such taxes if the employees are household or agricultural workers.

Since the taxes for the Nolan Machine Shop exceeded $100 for both July and August, these taxes were deposited within 15 days after the close of each month. Then when the September payment was made, receipts for the deposits of the July and August taxes were attached to the quarterly report that accompanied the payment for September. The bookkeeping entries at the time the July and August taxes were deposited were similar to the one shown for the payment of the September taxes.

Paying the liability for state unemployment taxes. On October 28, the Nolan Machine Shop paid its liability for the state unemployment taxes for the three-month period ended September 30. The amount of this liability, $1,404, was obtained by adding the weekly credits in the account State Unemployment Taxes Payable. The entry to record this payment was as follows:

	CASH		CHK. NO.	DATE	NAME OF ACCOUNT	POST. REF.	GENERAL		
	DEBIT	CREDIT					DEBIT	CREDIT	
23		1404 00	501	28	State Unemployment Taxes Pay.		1404 00		23
24									24
25									25

PAGE 21 COMBINATION JOURNAL

Entry to record payment of liability for state unemployment taxes

This payment covered the state unemployment taxes based on the payrolls of July, August, and September.

Paying the liability for federal unemployment taxes. The federal unemployment taxes payable are paid by the Nolan Machine Shop at the end of the year. On December 31 the balance of the account Federal Unemployment Taxes Payable in the ledger of the Nolan Machine Shop was $624. On January 21 of the following year a check for this amount was sent to the District Director of Internal Revenue. To record the payment of the liability the following entry was made:

	CASH		CHK. NO.	DATE	NAME OF ACCOUNT	POST. REF.	GENERAL		
	DEBIT	CREDIT					DEBIT	CREDIT	
18		624 00	35	21	*Fed. Unemployment Taxes Pay*		624 00		18
19									19
20									20
21									21
22									22

Entry to record payment of liability for federal unemployment taxes

This payment covered the federal unemployment taxes based on the payrolls for 1957.

Reports to employees of taxes withheld. Every employer who is required to withhold taxes from employees' wages must furnish each of his employees with a statement showing the total earnings of the employee and the amounts withheld for taxes. This statement is made on a Form W-2 that is furnished by the District Director of Internal Revenue. The Form W-2 prepared for James E. West by the Nolan Machine Shop is illustrated below:

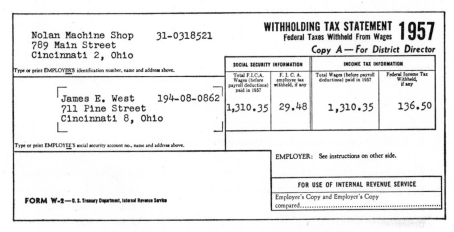

Nolan Machine Shop   31-0318521
789 Main Street
Cincinnati 2, Ohio

WITHHOLDING TAX STATEMENT 1957
Federal Taxes Withheld From Wages
Copy A — For District Director

Type or print EMPLOYER'S identification number, name and address above.

James E. West   194-08-0862
711 Pine Street
Cincinnati 8, Ohio

SOCIAL SECURITY INFORMATION		INCOME TAX INFORMATION	
Total F.I.C.A. Wages (before payroll deductions) paid in 1957	F.I.C.A. employee tax withheld, if any	Total Wages (before payroll deductions) paid in 1957	Federal Income Tax Withheld, if any
1,310.35	29.48	1,310.35	136.50

Type or print EMPLOYEE'S social security account no., name and address above.

EMPLOYER: See instructions on other side.

FOR USE OF INTERNAL REVENUE SERVICE

Employee's Copy and Employer's Copy compared..................

FORM W-2 — U. S. Treasury Department, Internal Revenue Service

Statement given to the employee for taxes withheld

When the employee files his income tax return, he must attach the original of this form to his income tax return. An employee should have a withholding statement from each employer for whom he worked during the taxable year.

CHAPTER QUESTIONS

1. The total earnings of the employees for the week ending September 21, 1957, as shown in the payroll register on page 292, amount to $4,000 and the total cash paid amounts to $3,527.50. What causes this difference?

2. What entry was made in the combination journal on page 293 to record the payment of the payroll and the amounts withheld from the employees' salaries?

3. What entry was made in the combination journal on page 294 to record the employer's share of the FICA taxes?

4. The FICA taxes payable account on page 294 has two credits. What do these amounts represent?

5. In most states who pays the unemployment tax?

6. What entry was made in the combination journal on page 295 to record the liability of the employer for state unemployment taxes?

7. What entry was made in the combination journal on page 296 to record the liability of the employer for federal unemployment taxes?

8. What entry was made in the combination journal on page 297 to record the payment of the liability for employees income taxes and for FICA taxes?

9. What entry was made in the combination journal on page 299 to record the payment of the liability for federal unemployment taxes?

10. What statement is the employer required to submit to each employee at the end of the year? What does it show?

CASES FOR DISCUSSION

1. R. L. King, the owner of a food-canning company, had a weekly payroll of $4,000, with the following deductions: employees income taxes, $400; FICA taxes, $2\frac{1}{4}\%$. Mr. King's liabilities for payroll taxes were as follows: FICA taxes, $2\frac{1}{4}\%$; state unemployment taxes, 2.7%; and federal unemployment taxes, .3%. What entry should Mr. King make in his combination journal each payday to record (a) the payment of wages and the amounts withheld and (b) the liability for his payroll taxes?

2. On January 8 of the current year, A. B. Kohl sent checks to the proper government authorities in payment of the following taxes previously recorded in his books: employees income taxes withheld, $264; FICA taxes, $76; federal unemployment taxes, $90; and state unemployment taxes, $202. What accounts should be debited and credited to record these payments?

Problem 23-1. Recording payrolls and payroll taxes

The payroll register totals of Excel Television Service for the week ended May 24 are given below:

No.	Employee's Name	No. of Exemptions	Total Earnings	FICA Tax	Income Tax	Other	Amount	Check No.
				Deductions			Net Pay	
	Totals..........		840 00	18 90	78 00		743 10	

The employer's liabilities for payroll taxes included the following:

FICA taxes   2¼%
State unemployment taxes   2.7%
Federal unemployment taxes   .3%

Instructions: 1. Make the entry in the combination journal to record the payroll and the withholdings. The payroll was paid by Check No. 482 on May 27.

2. Make the entries in the combination journal to record the employer's share of the payroll taxes.

Problem 23-2. Recording payroll transactions

F. O. Butler, owner of a stationery store, completed the payroll transactions given below.

Feb. 28. Issued Check No. 34 for $1,217.90 in payment of the monthly payroll of $1,400 less a deduction of $150.60 for income taxes and a deduction of $31.50 for FICA taxes.

28. Recorded the employer's payroll taxes at the following rates: FICA taxes, 2¼%; state unemployment taxes, 2.7%; federal unemployment taxes, .3%.

Mar. 10. Issued Check No. 43 for $213.60 in payment of the liabilities for payroll taxes and taxes withheld as follows: income taxes, $150.60; FICA taxes, $63.

31. Issued Check No. 56 for $1,174.62 in payment of the monthly payroll of $1,350 less a deduction of $145 for income taxes and a deduction of $30.38 for FICA taxes.

31. Recorded the employer's payroll taxes at the same rates as in February.

Apr. 10. Issued Check No. 69 for $205.76 in payment of the liabilities for payroll taxes and taxes withheld as follows: income taxes, $145; FICA taxes, $60.76.

10. Issued Check No. 70 for $111.35 in payment of the liability for state unemployment taxes.

Instructions: Record the transactions in a combination journal.

Problem 23-3. Recording and posting payroll transactions

The Curtis Appliance Shop completed the payroll transactions given below during the period January 1 to April 10. The Curtis Appliance Shop is liable for payroll taxes at the following rates: FICA taxes, $2\frac{1}{4}\%$; state unemployment taxes, 2.7%; and federal unemployment taxes, $.3\%$.

Jan. 10. Issued Check No. 15 for $335 in payment of the liabilities for employees income taxes and FICA taxes.

10. Issued Check No. 16 for $195.75 in payment of the liability for state unemployment taxes.

10. Issued Check No. 17 for $87.50 in payment of the liability for federal unemployment taxes.

31. Issued Check No. 29 for $2,096 in payment of the monthly payroll of $2,400 less a deduction of $250 for income taxes and a deduction of $54 for FICA taxes.

31. Recorded the employer's payroll tax liabilities.

Feb. 10. Issued Check No. 38 for $358 in payment of the liabilities for employees income taxes and FICA taxes.

28. Issued Check No. 61 for $2,008.25 in payment of the monthly payroll of $2,300 less a deduction of $240 for income taxes and a deduction of $51.75 for FICA taxes.

28. Recorded the employer's payroll tax liabilities.

Mar. 10. Issued Check No. 74 for $343.50 in payment of the liabilities for employees income taxes and FICA taxes.

31. Issued Check No. 88 for $2,271.50 in payment of the monthly payroll of $2,600 less a deduction of $270 for income taxes and a deduction of $58.50 for FICA taxes.

31. Recorded the employer's payroll tax liabilities.

Apr. 10. Issued Check No. 97 for $387 in payment of the liabilities for employees income taxes and FICA taxes.

10. Issued Check No. 98 for $197.10 in payment of the liability for state unemployment taxes.

Instructions: 1. Open the following accounts in the general ledger and record the balances as of January 1 of the current year:

Acct. No.	Account Title	Credit Balance
22	Employees Income Taxes Payable	$260.00
23	FICA Taxes Payable	75.00
24	State Unemployment Taxes Payable	195.75
25	Federal Unemployment Taxes Payable	87.50
63	Federal Unemployment Taxes	......
66	FICA Taxes	......
68	Salary Expense	......
69	State Unemployment Taxes	......

Instructions: 2. Record the transactions in a combination journal.

3. After each entry is journalized, post the items recorded in the General Debit and General Credit columns.

Depreciation of fixed assets

What is depreciation? Everyone knows that a bicycle worth $50 one Christmas is not worth that much the following Christmas. Similarly in a business, a delivery truck bought in January for $3,000 may not be worth more than $2,100 at the end of the year. This decrease in the value of the truck is the result of (a) wear and tear from use and from weather, and (b) the tendency of new models to replace old ones. This constant decrease in the value of an asset because of wear and of the passage of time is referred to as *depreciation.*

The amount by which an asset depreciates is an expense to the business. Depreciation expense is a constant expense occurring during the life of the asset. Like any other expense, depreciation expense must be subtracted from gross income each fiscal period in order for a business to arrive at its true net profit. If depreciation expense is ignored, the business is understating its expenses and overstating its profit.

Fixed assets. Assets that can be used for a number of fiscal periods in the operation of a business are known as *fixed assets.* Examples of fixed assets are equipment, machinery, buildings, and land.

Equipment includes such fixed assets as typewriters, desks, display cases, tables, and delivery trucks. In smaller businesses where only a few items of equipment are owned, these fixed assets are frequently recorded in a single account with the title Equipment. Other and larger businesses prefer to record them in separate accounts with such descriptive titles as Office Equipment, Store Equipment, and Delivery Equipment.

Recording the purchase of fixed assets. Fixed assets may be bought either for cash or on credit. When a fixed asset is purchased, it is recorded at the cost price.

For example, on July 1, 1957, D. A. Wirth, the proprietor of a feed and grain store, bought a typewriter for $180 in cash. Mr. Wirth recorded the purchase of the typewriter as a debit to Equipment and a credit to Cash. After the entry was posted, the equipment account in the assets section of the general ledger appeared as follows:

<table>
<tr>
<th colspan="5" style="text-align:center">𝓔𝓺𝓾𝓲𝓹𝓶𝓮𝓷𝓽</th>
<th colspan="5" style="text-align:right">ACCOUNT NO. 121</th>
</tr>
</table>

DATE	ITEMS	POST. REF.	DEBIT	DATE	ITEMS	POST. REF.	CREDIT
1957 Jan. 1	Balance	1	2 7 5 1 00				
Mar. 1		4	1 8 0 0 00				
July 1		9	" 1 8 0 00 " 4 7 3 1 00				

The total of the debit side of the equipment account, $4,731, showed the *cost price* of all equipment.

Calculating depreciation. Before a bookkeeper can record the depreciation expense of a fixed asset, he must know how to calculate that expense. The simplest way to calculate depreciation expense requires a knowledge of two things. These are: (1) the cost of the fixed asset and (2) its probable life. The typewriter that Mr. Wirth purchased on July 1, 1957, for $180 was estimated to have a life of 5 years. This meant that the estimated depreciation expense on this item of equipment for *each year* was $36 ($180 ÷ 5 years = $36).

The annual depreciation is frequently referred to as a percentage of the cost price. For example, a typewriter that depreciates ⅕ each year is said to depreciate at the rate of 20%.

The estimated present value of a fixed asset is known as *book value*. The original cost minus the recorded depreciation expense equals the book value.

The following table shows Mr. Wirth's estimate of depreciation expense and the book value of the typewriter for the years he plans to use it:

Typewriter	Recorded Depreciation for Each Year	Total Recorded Depreciation	Book Value
Cost at time of purchase, July 1, 1957.........................			$180
Last half of fiscal year ending 12/31/57.....................	$18	$18	162
Fiscal year ending 12/31/58........	36	54	126
Fiscal year ending 12/31/59........	36	90	90
Fiscal year ending 12/31/60........	36	126	54
Fiscal year ending 12/31/61........	36	162	18
First half of fiscal year ending 12/31/62.....................	18	180	0

Sometimes it is difficult for the businessman or the bookkeeper to estimate with reasonable accuracy how fast certain fixed assets will depreciate. Rates of depreciation approved by the Internal Revenue Service are available. These rates are based on the experience of business and industry and serve as excellent guides for estimating the life of fixed assets and the rates of depreciation.

Card record of fixed assets. When Mr. Wirth purchased the typewriter on July 1, 1957, he made out the card record shown below.

PERPETUAL RECORD OF EQUIPMENT								
Description Typewriter					Class Equipment			
Age when acquired New		Estimated life 5 years			Rate of annual estimated depreciation 20%			
COST				DEPRECIATION RECORD				
Date Purchased	Detailed Description and Name of Firm or Individual From Whom Purchased		Amount	Year	Rate	Amount		Total to date
1957				19 57	.20	18	00	18 00
July 1	Underwood Type-		180 00	19 58	.20	36	00	54 00
	writer #3979666			19 59	.20	36	00	90 00
	Office Equipment			19				
	Co., City			19				
				19				
				19				
				19				
				19				
				19				
				19				
				19				
SOLD, EXCHANGED OR DISCARDED				19				
Date	Explanation	Amount Realized	More than / less than \ Book Value	Debit Reserve	19			
					19			
					19			

Card record of a fixed asset

At the time the typewriter was purchased, Mr. Wirth recorded a complete description of the machine, including its serial number. He also recorded the date of purchase, the cost price, the estimated life, and the annual rate of depreciation. At the close of each fiscal period he brought the card up to date by recording the depreciation for that period. The card record shown below indicates how the record would appear at the close of the 1959 fiscal period.

Determining depreciation for the fiscal period. On December 31, 1957, the end of the annual fiscal year, Mr. Wirth referred to each of his card records of fixed assets and calculated the total amount of the depreciation. According to these card records, the total depreciation of equipment for this fiscal year was $312.60. This meant that during the fiscal year ended December 31 the equipment had decreased in value an amount estimated to be $312.60.

Valuation of fixed assets. The equipment account, like all fixed asset accounts, is debited for the cost price at the time of purchase. When a fixed asset, such as equipment, is discarded or sold, the fixed asset account is credited for the cost price. The balance, therefore, of the fixed asset account Equipment should always represent the cost price of the equipment on hand.

To determine the book value of equipment on hand, Mr. Wirth must subtract the total estimated depreciation of the equipment from the balance of the equipment account. The calculation is as follows:

Equipment....................................		$4,731.00
Less total depreciation:		
For previous years............................	$1,491.35	
For current year................................	312.60	1,803.95
Estimated book value of equipment on hand.........		$2,927.05

D.A.
Work
For Year Ended

	ACCOUNT TITLES	ACCT. NO.	TRIAL BALANCE		
			DEBIT	CREDIT	
1	Cash	111	1920 75		1
2	Accounts Receivable	112	185 68		2
3	Merchandise Inventory	113	3282 31		3
4	Supplies	114	264 50		4
5	Prepaid Insurance	115	128 75		5
6	Equipment	121	4731 00		6
7	Allowance for Depr. of Equip.	121.1		1491 35	7
21	Insurance Expense	65			21
22	Depreciation Expense	63			22
23					23
24	Net Profit				24
25					25

Work sheet with

Since the book value of equipment on December 31, 1957, was $2,927.05, that amount was the value which should be shown on the December 31 balance sheet.

Allowance for depreciation of equipment account. Depreciation cannot be credited to the equipment account, as that would indicate that some of the equipment had been sold or discarded. Whenever depreciation expense for equipment is recorded, the estimated amount of depreciation is credited to an account called *Allowance for Depreciation of Equipment*. The equipment account debit balance then continues to show the original cost of all equipment on hand. The credit balance in this new account, Allowance for Depreciation of Equipment, shows the estimated decrease in the value of the equipment because of depreciation. The difference between the balances of the two accounts is the estimated present value or book value.

Adjustment for depreciation on the work sheet. At the end of the fiscal year on December 31, Mr. Wirth made the adjustment for depreciation of equipment in the Adjustments columns of his work sheet. A partial work sheet is illustrated below.

Wirth
Sheet
December 31, 1957

		ADJUSTMENTS		P. & L. STATEMENT		BALANCE SHEET		
		DEBIT	CREDIT	DEBIT	CREDIT	DEBIT	CREDIT	
1						1920 75		1
2						185 68		2
3		(c) 2757 86	(b) 3282 31			2757 86		3
4			(d) 187 20			77 30		4
5			(e) 63 15			65 60		5
6						4731 00		6
7			(f) 312 60				1803 95	7
21		(e) 63 15		63 15				21
22		(f) 312 60		312 60				22
23		6603 12	6603 12	23234 56	25583 08	11753 71	9405 19	23
24				2348 52			2348 52	24
25				25583 08	25583 08	11753 71	11753 71	25

adjustment for depreciation

In the Trial Balance columns of the work sheet, Allowance for Depreciation of Equipment had a credit balance of $1,491.35, the sum of amounts credited to this account in previous fiscal periods. In the Adjustments columns, Allowance for Depreciation of Equipment was credited for $312.60 to record the decrease in the value of equipment as a result of the depreciation during the period. The credit of $312.60 to Allowance for Depreciation of Equipment was added to the credit balance of $1,491.35, and the total, $1,803.95, was extended to the Balance Sheet Credit column of the work sheet. This credit balance in the allowance for depreciation of equipment account will be deducted from the equipment account debit balance when the balance sheet is prepared.

The amount of the depreciation for the year, $312.60, was an expense and was debited to an expense account with the title *Depreciation Expense*. This amount, like the other expenses, was extended into the P. & L. Statement Debit column.

Adjusting entry in the journal to record depreciation. Mr. Wirth made the following adjusting entry in the combination journal from the Adjustments columns of his work sheet to record the depreciation:

PAGE 34				COMBINATION JOURNAL				
CASH		CHK. NO.	DATE	NAME OF ACCOUNT	POST. REF.	GENERAL		
DEBIT	CREDIT					DEBIT	CREDIT	
			31	Depreciation Expense		312 60		30
				Allow. for Depr. of Equip.			312 60	31
								32
								33
								34
								35
								36
								37
								38
								39
								40
								41

Entry to record depreciation

When the entry to record the depreciation of equipment was posted, the asset account, the allowance account, and the expense account appeared as shown on the opposite page.

Equipment — ACCOUNT NO. 121

DATE	ITEMS	POST. REF.	DEBIT	DATE	ITEMS	POST. REF.	CREDIT
1959 Jan. 1	Balance	1	2751 00				
Mar. 1		4	1800 00				
July 1		9	480 00				
			4731 00				

Allowance for Depreciation of Equip. — ACCOUNT NO. 121.1

DATE	ITEMS	POST. REF.	DEBIT	DATE	ITEMS	POST. REF.	CREDIT
				1959 Jan. 1	Balance	1	1491 35
				Dec. 31		34	312 60
							1803 95

Depreciation Expense — ACCOUNT NO. 63

DATE	ITEMS	POST. REF.	DEBIT	DATE	ITEMS	POST. REF.	CREDIT
1959 Dec. 31		34	312 60				

The debit balance of the equipment account, $4,731, showed the original cost of the equipment. The credit balance of the allowance account, $1,803.95, showed the total amount of the depreciation of all the equipment to date. The difference between these two balances, $2,927.05, was the book value, that is, the estimated present value. The debit balance of the depreciation expense account, $312.60, was the depreciation expense for the fiscal period.

Depreciation expense is a deductible expense in computing the state and federal income taxes of the business. Failure to record this $312.60 depreciation expense properly would result in an overstatement of the profit of the business for the period. It could also cause the business to pay higher taxes than it should.

Depreciation expense on the profit and loss statement. When Mr. Wirth prepared his profit and loss statement from the work sheet on December 31, he indicated the depreciation expense as an operating expense as shown below.

D. A. Wirth
Profit and Loss Statement
For Year Ended December 31, 1957

Gross Profit on Sales		8465 50
Operating Expenses:		
Delivery Expense	266 45	
Depreciation Expense	312 60	
F.I.C.A. Taxes	78 18	
Federal Unemployment Taxes	10 43	
Insurance Expense	63 15	
Miscellaneous Expense	430 14	
Rent Expense	1200 00	
Salary Expense	3475 00	
State Unemployment Taxes	93 83	
Supplies Expense	187 20	
Total Operating Expenses		6116 98
Net Profit		2348 52

Profit and loss statement showing depreciation expense

Equipment and allowance accounts on the balance sheet. When Mr. Wirth prepared his balance sheet from the work sheet on December 31, he indicated (a) the original cost of the equipment, (b) the decrease in value because of depreciation, and (c) the book value of the equipment. (See the balance sheet on page 311.)

The total cost of all equipment, $4,731, was shown in the first amount column on the line with Equipment. The depreciation of these fixed assets, $1,803.95, was placed immediately under the cost of the equipment and was subtracted from it. The difference between the two amounts, $2,927.05, was the book value of the equipment.

Classification of liabilities on the balance sheet. Liabilities that will be due within a relatively short time, usually within a year, are called *current liabilities*. Examples of current liabilities are Accounts Payable, Employees Income Taxes Payable, FICA Taxes Payable, State Unemployment Taxes Payable, and Federal Unemployment Taxes Payable.

Liabilities that do not have to be paid for a number of years in the normal operation of the business are known as *long-term liabilities* or *fixed liabilities*. An example of a long-term liability is Mortgage Payable.

A common order of arrangement for listing liability accounts on the balance sheet is the order in which they should be paid.

All of the liabilities of Mr. Wirth are current liabilities. He included on his balance sheet, shown on page 311, the heading "Current Liabilities" to show that all of these liabilities should be paid within a year.

CHAPTER QUESTIONS

1. Why are most fixed assets worth less than their purchase price after they have been used for a fiscal period?
2. If the expense of using a fixed asset is not recorded, how will this affect the total expenses of the business? How will this omission affect the net profit for the period?
3. What two things must a bookkeeper know about a fixed asset before he can calculate its depreciation expense?
4. Why is the amount of depreciation that is recorded an estimated amount?
5. Why is the amount of depreciation credited to the allowance for depreciation of equipment account rather than to the equipment account?
6. When is the depreciation of fixed assets recorded?
7. On the work sheet on pages 306 and 307, what accounts are debited and credited in making the adjustment for estimated depreciation?
8. Why is the allowance for depreciation of equipment called a valuation or minus asset account?
9. What is the difference between a current asset and a fixed asset? Between a current liability and a long-term liability?
10. What is a correct order for listing assets on the balance sheet? For listing liabilities on the balance sheet?

INCREASING YOUR BUSINESS VOCABULARY

What is the meaning of each of the following:

(a) depreciation	(f) minus asset
(b) fixed assets	(g) current assets
(c) equipment	(h) current liabilities
(d) book value	(i) long-term liabilities
(e) valuation account	(j) fixed liabilities

CASES FOR DISCUSSION

1. Suppose that Mr. Stone, the proprietor of a small business, maintains that since he makes no actual cash payments for depreciation he is not entitled to record depreciation as an expense. What is wrong with Mr. Stone's point of view?

2. When R. G. O'Grady purchased a new delivery truck, he told his bookkeeper to determine what the annual depreciation expense should be. What steps should be taken to determine what the annual depreciation expense should be?

3. C. W. Potter rents a typewriter for $6 a month. He can buy a new typewriter for $190. He estimates the life of a new typewriter to be 5 years. If interest and repair costs are ignored, how much would he save by buying the machine?

APPLICATION PROBLEMS

Problem 24-1. Calculating depreciation

Instructions: For each of the following fixed assets find the amount of annual depreciation.

Fixed Asset	Initial Cost	Estimated Life
1	$ 400	4 years
2	600	5 years
3	300	3 years
4	720	20 years
5	6,400	8 years
6	12,800	16 years

Problem 24-2. Finding book value

Instructions: For each of the following items of equipment find as of December 31, 1957, (a) the total amount of estimated depreciation and (b) the book value of each.

Fixed Asset	Date of Purchase	Initial Cost	Annual Rate of Depreciation
1	Jan. 1, 1955	$412.00	25%
2	July 1, 1956	360.00	20%
3	Jan. 1, 1957	972.36	5%
4	Nov. 1, 1957	150.00	8%

Problem 24-3. Recording depreciation

A. J. Smith purchased the following items of equipment during the first two years that he was in business:

Fixed Asset	Date of Purchase	Initial Cost	Annual Rate of Depreciation
1	January 1, 1956	$ 360	10%
2	July 1, 1956	50	25%
3	March 1, 1957	72	20%
4	July 1, 1957	470	8%
5	November 1, 1957	960	12%
6	December 1, 1957	16,000	5%

Instructions: 1. Record the adjusting journal entry for the total depreciation expense for the year ended December 31, 1956.

2. Record the adjusting journal entry for the total depreciation expense for the year ended December 31, 1957.

Problem 24-4. Work at the end of the fiscal period

The account balances in the general ledger of A. P. May, a dealer in building materials, on June 30 of the current year were as follows:

Cash, $1,300.20

Accounts Receivable, $319.97

Merchandise Inventory, $2,326.98

Supplies, $170

Prepaid Insurance, $223.65

Equipment, $2,750

Allowance for Depreciation of Equipment, $420

Accounts Payable, $1,267.20

A. P. May, Capital, $5,724.50

A. P. May, Drawing, $1,320 (Dr.)

Sales, $13,156.80

Sales Returns and Allowances, $160.30

Purchases, $10,067.40

Purchases Returns and Allowances, $170.50

Delivery Expense, $622.25

Miscellaneous Expense, $278.25

Salary Expense, $1,200

The additional data needed at the end of the annual fiscal period are: merchandise inventory, $5,238.65; supplies inventory, $58.45; prepaid insurance, $128.25; annual rate of estimated depreciation of equipment, 10%.

Instructions: 1. Prepare an eight column work sheet for the annual fiscal period ended June 30 of the current year.

2. Prepare a profit and loss statement and a balance sheet from the work sheet.

3. Record the adjusting and closing entries in a combination journal.

CHAPTER 25

Disposing of fixed assets

Ways of disposing of fixed assets. A fixed asset, such as a machine, a typewriter, or a desk, cannot be used forever. It may wear out, or the business may replace it with a newer model.

When a fixed asset is no longer useful to a business, it may be disposed of in any one of three ways: (1) it may be thrown away or discarded; (2) it may be sold; or (3) it may be traded in as part of the purchase price of a new asset.

Calculating loss or gain on the disposal of a fixed asset. A business will frequently experience a loss or a gain when one of its fixed assets is disposed of. This is so because depreciation is an estimate and the value of the fixed asset at the time it is discarded or sold will probably not equal its book value. For example, a fixed asset that cost $50 was estimated to have a useful life of 5 years. Thus it was estimated to depreciate 20% or $10 a year. The following outline shows the loss or the gain that would be experienced under different circumstances:

Situation	Description of Transaction	Cost Price	Allow. for Depr.	Book Value	Cash for Sale	Loss	Gain
1	Asset was discarded as worthless at the end of 4 years.	$50	$40	$10	..	$10	..
2	Asset was discarded as worthless at the end of 5 years.	50	50	..	..	..	..
3	Asset was sold for $15 at the end of 4 years.	50	40	10	$15	..	$5
4	Asset was sold for $10 at the end of 4 years.	50	40	10	10	..	..
5	Asset was sold for $10 at the end of 3½ years.	50	35	15	10	5	..
6	Asset was sold for $10 after 5 years.	50	50	..	10	..	10

Illustrations of loss or gain when a fixed asset is discarded or sold. As can be seen from the above illustrations, the book value of the fixed asset *at the time of its disposal* is necessary in determining loss or gain. It is important, therefore, that the depreciation expense be recorded at the time of disposal for that part of the final fiscal period during which the asset was used. Usually, the depreciation expense for this final period is considered sufficiently accurate if it is calculated to the nearest month. Thus an asset disposed of during the first half of a month need not have any depreciation expense charged to it for that month. Similarly, a fixed asset sold or discarded during the last half of a month would have a full month's depreciation expense recorded.

Discarding a fixed asset. On January 6, 1958, George Mott, a grocer, discarded a refrigerator. It had no trade-in or sale value. An analysis of the card record for this asset showed the following summary information:

Purchase price on January 5, 1949.............. $400
Total depreciation (9 yrs. @ 10%)............. 360
Book value, January 6, 1958.................. $ 40

At the time Mr. Mott purchased this refrigerator, he made a reasonable estimate that it would be used for 10 years and that it would depreciate 10% a year. As is frequently the case, his estimate did not prove to be correct. In this case the refrigerator lasted only 9 years and his books showed that it still had a value of $40. It would not have been practical to distribute this $40 expense back over the 9 years that the refrigerator was in use. Therefore, to record the discarding of the refrigerator and the loss from discarding an asset with a book value, Mr. Mott made the following entry in the combination journal:

CASH		CHK. NO.	DATE	NAME OF ACCOUNT	POST. REF.	GENERAL	
DEBIT	CREDIT					DEBIT	CREDIT
			1958 Jan. 6	Allow. for Depr. of Equip.		360 00	
				Loss on Fixed Assets		40 00	
				Equipment			400 00

PAGE 3 — COMBINATION JOURNAL

Entry to record the discarding of a fixed asset

Analysis of journal entry showing discarding of a fixed asset. The debit of $360 to Allowance for Depreciation of Equipment canceled the amount of the allowance previously recorded for the refrigerator.

The debit to Loss on Fixed Assets recorded the loss when a fixed asset with a book value of $40 was discarded. *Loss on Fixed Assets* is an expense account that is debited for the book value of any asset that is discarded.

The credit of $400 to Equipment canceled the debit to that account that was recorded when the refrigerator was purchased.

Selling a fixed asset. On January 11, 1958, Mr. Mott sold one of his display cases for $150 in cash. The card record for the display case showed the following summary information:

Purchase price on July 2, 1954................ $200
Total depreciation (3½ years @ 10%)..........   70
Book value, January 11, 1958................. $130

Mr. Mott, in receiving $150 for this used display case, sold it for $20 more than its book value ($150 − $130 = $20). To record this transaction he made the following entry:

CASH		CHK. NO.	DATE	NAME OF ACCOUNT	POST. REF.	GENERAL	
DEBIT	CREDIT					DEBIT	CREDIT
150 00			11	*Allow. for Depr. of Equip.*		70 00	
				Equipment			200 00
				Gain on Fixed Assets			20 00

Entry to record the sale of a fixed asset

Analysis of journal entry showing sale of a fixed asset. The debit to Cash, $150, was the amount actually received for the display case.

The debit to Allowance for Depreciation of Equipment, $70, canceled the amount of the allowance recorded for the used display case.

The credit to Equipment, $200, canceled the debit recorded in the equipment account when the display case was purchased.

The credit to Gain on Fixed Assets, $20, recorded the gain when a fixed asset with a book value of $130 was sold for $150. *Gain on Fixed Assets* is an income account that is credited for the gain that results when a fixed asset is sold for more than its book value.

> Fixed assets are sometimes sold for a price less than their book value. When such is the case, they are said to be sold at a loss. The journal entry to record such a transaction would be similar to the illustration above. Instead of crediting Gain on Fixed Assets, however, the expense account *Loss on Fixed Assets* would be debited for the difference between the selling price and the book value.

Trading in a fixed asset. According to income tax regulations, a loss or a gain is not recognized when one fixed asset of a business is traded in for another similar fixed asset. The new asset is recorded at a value equal to the sum of the cash actually paid plus the book value of the old asset.

On March 4, 1958, Mr. Mott purchased a new delivery truck and gave for it his old truck and $2,500 in cash. The fixed asset account for the truck and its valuation account, in T form, appeared as follows on March 4, 1958, immediately before the trade-in transaction was completed:

DELIVERY EQUIPMENT		ALLOWANCE FOR DEPRECIATION OF DELIVERY EQUIPMENT	
1/2/55 3,000		12/31/55	600
		12/31/56	600
		12/31/57	600

When the truck was purchased on January 2, 1955, it was estimated that it would have a useful life of 5 years and that it would therefore depreciate 20% or $600 each year. Since this old truck was used during the first 2 months of the 1958 fiscal period, it was necessary to record the depreciation expense for this time in order to bring the book value of the truck up to date. This was done with the following journal entry:

CASH				GENERAL	
DEBIT	CREDIT	CHK. NO.	DATE	NAME OF ACCOUNT	POST. REF.	DEBIT	CREDIT

PAGE 8   COMBINATION JOURNAL

						DEBIT	CREDIT	
10				4	Depreciation Expense		100 00		10
11					Allow. for Dept. of Equip.			100 00	11

Entry to record estimated depreciation for part of a fiscal period

After this entry was posted, the two balance sheet accounts showing the book value of the old truck appeared as follows:

DELIVERY EQUIPMENT		ALLOWANCE FOR DEPRECIATION OF DELIVERY EQUIPMENT	
1/2/55 3,000		12/31/55	600
		12/31/56	600
		12/31/57	600
		3/4/58	100
			1,900

Since the old truck was purchased for $3,000 and the total allowance for depreciation was $1,900, the old truck had a book value of $1,100 ($3,000 − $1,900 = $1,100) on March 4, 1958, the day it was traded in.

As Mr. Mott paid an additional $2,500 cash for the new truck, the value of this new truck to be recorded on the books in the delivery equipment account was $3,600. This amount was found as follows:

Original cost of old truck....................	$3,000
Less allowance for depreciation...............	1,900
Book value of old truck......................	$1,100
Add cash paid for new truck..................	2,500
Initial book value of new truck................	$3,600

The account Delivery Equipment should show the initial book value of the new truck, and the allowance account should be balanced. Mr. Mott made the following entry in his combination journal:

	CASH		CHK. NO.	DATE	NAME OF ACCOUNT	POST. REF.	GENERAL		
	DEBIT	CREDIT					DEBIT	CREDIT	
12		250000	133	4	Delivery Equipment		360000		12
13					Allow. for Depr. of Del. Equip.		190000		13
14					Delivery Equipment			300000	14
15									15

Entry to record trading in a fixed asset

Analysis of journal entry showing trading in of a fixed asset. The debit to Delivery Equipment, $3,600, for the new truck was considered the actual cost of the new truck and thus the new truck's initial book value. The debit to Allowance for Depreciation of Delivery Equipment, $1,900, canceled the amount of the allowance recorded for the old truck. The credit to Cash, $2,500, was the amount of cash actually paid. The credit to Delivery Equipment, $3,000, canceled the debit made in the delivery equipment account when the old truck was purchased.

The delivery equipment account and its valuation account, in T form, appeared as follows after posting, balancing, and ruling:

DELIVERY EQUIPMENT				ALLOWANCE FOR DEPRECIATION OF DELIVERY EQUIPMENT			
1/2/55	3,000	3/4/58	3,000	3/4/58	1,900	12/31/55	600
						12/31/56	600
3/4/58	3,600					12/31/57	600
						3/4/58	100
					1,900		1,900

The delivery equipment account now shows the initial book value of the new truck. The allowance account has been balanced and ruled so that future entries in this account will apply to the depreciation of the new truck only.

It should be observed that no record was made of the amount the dealer said the new truck was worth or the amount he said he was giving as an allowance for the old truck. These amounts were ignored, and the new truck was recorded at a value equal to the amount of cash paid plus the book value of the truck traded in.

Reporting gain and loss on fixed assets on the profit and loss statement. The profit and loss statement of Dudley Furniture is illustrated below. How this statement differs from statements illustrated heretofore is described on page 322.

	Dudley Furniture			
	Profit and Loss Statement			
	For Year Ended December 31, 1957			
1	Income from Sales:			
2	Sales			98 335 85
3	Less: Sales Returns and Allowances	1 034 50		
4	Discount on Sales	841 28	1 875 78	
5	Net Sales			96 460 07
6	Cost of Merchandise Sold:			
7	Mdse. Inventory, January 1, 1957		9 307 63	
8	Purchases	73 624 25		
9	Less: Pur. Ret. and Allow. 560 85			
10	Discount on Purchases 1 429 03	1 989 88		
11	Net Purchases	71 634 37		
12	Add Transportation on Purchases	456 14		
13	Net Cost of Mdse. Purchased		72 090 51	
14	Total Cost of Mdse. Available for Sale		81 398 14	
15	Less Mdse. Inventory, Dec. 31, 1957		8 159 66	
16	Cost of Merchandise Sold			73 238 48
17	Gross Profit on Sales			23 221 59
18	Operating Expenses:			
19	Delivery Expense	3 630 56		
20	Depreciation Expense	6 245 0		
21	Insurance Expense	2 400 0		
22	Miscellaneous Expense	653 11		
23	Rent Expense	2 400 00		
24	Salary Expense	7 350 15		
25	Supplies Expense	831 98		
26	Total Operating Expenses		15 730 30	
27	Net Profit from Operations			7 491 29
28	Other Income:			
29	Gain on Fixed Assets	220 40		
30	Other Expense:			
31	Loss on Fixed Assets	160 20		
32	Net Addition			60 20
33	Net Profit			7 551 49

Profit and loss statement showing Other Income and Other Expense sections

Line 1. The first heading is *Income from Sales* rather than *Income* as used previously. The more complete title is used to distinguish between income from sales reported at the beginning of the statement and income from gain on fixed assets reported near the end of the statement.

Line 27. In order to distinguish between profits that come from the regular operations of the business and profits that do not, the net profit obtained when the Total Operating Expenses are subtracted from the Gross Profit on Sales is called *Net Profit from Operations.*

Lines 28 and 29. A gain on the sale of a fixed asset is not considered to be a part of the regular operating income of the business. The income account Gain on Fixed Assets is therefore listed after Net Profit from Operations under the heading *Other Income.*

Lines 30 and 31. A loss on fixed assets is not considered to be one of the regular operating expenses of the business. The expense account Loss on Fixed Assets is therefore listed under the heading *Other Expense.*

Lines 32 and 33. The amount by which the gain on fixed assets exceeds the loss on fixed assets is labeled *Net Addition* and is added to the Net Profit from Operations. The sum is the Net Profit of the business for the period.

If the Other Income had been less than the Other Expense, the difference would have been entitled *Net Subtraction* and would have been subtracted from the Net Profit from Operations. The final lines of a profit and loss statement showing Other Income less than Other Expense is illustrated below:

Net Profit from Operations................			1,728 33
Other Income:			
Gain on Fixed Assets....................	116 50		
Other Expense:			
Loss on Fixed Assets....................	245 00		
Net Subtraction..........................			128 50
Net Profit...............................			1,599 83

CHAPTER QUESTIONS

1. What are the three ways of disposing of a fixed asset?
2. Why, at the time a fixed asset becomes worn out and worthless, do the bookkeeping records sometimes show that it has a book value?

3. Why, when a fixed asset is discarded, sold, or traded in, must the depreciation expense of that asset be recorded for the part of the final fiscal period that it was used?

4. What is meant by calculating depreciation expense "to the nearest month"?

5. When is it necessary in the disposal of a worthless fixed asset to debit the account Loss on Fixed Assets?

6. Under what circumstances could a worthless fixed asset be discarded without requiring an entry debiting the account Loss on Fixed Assets?

7. How does a bookkeeper determine whether a gain or a loss has been made on the sale of a fixed asset?

8. How does a bookkeeper determine the value to be recorded for a new fixed asset that is acquired by trading in a similar item?

9. How is the gain from the sale of a fixed asset shown on the profit and loss statement?

10. How is the loss from the disposal of a fixed asset shown on the profit and loss statement?

INCREASING YOUR BUSINESS VOCABULARY

What is the meaning of each of the following:

    (a) loss on fixed assets   (d) other income

    (b) gain on fixed assets   (e) other expense

    (c) net profit from operations

CASES FOR DISCUSSION

1. When A. J. Peters reported to his bookkeeper the discarding of a worthless file cabinet, its card record showed that it no longer had any book value. Mr. Peters then told his bookkeeper that since all possible depreciation expense had been recorded and no loss on the fixed asset had been incurred, no further bookkeeping entry was necessary. What was wrong with Mr. Peters' advice?

2. Suppose that one of your friends in the bookkeeping class made the mistake of assuming that an allowance account shows an amount of money set aside for use in the replacement of a fixed asset. How would you explain to him that this is not true?

3. When a new adding machine that cost $160 was purchased by Jones and Smith, partners in a lumber business, one thought they should estimate its useful life at 10 years and the other thought that 12 years would be a better estimate. Finally Mr. Jones stated, "Whether we decide on 10 years or 12 years will make little difference in the long run. The total expense to the business will be $160 in either case." Is there anything wrong with Mr. Jones's statement? Explain your answer.

Problem 25-1. Discarding fixed assets

H. M. Magee, an insurance agent, discarded as worthless the following items of office equipment:

Items	Date of Purchase	Initial Cost	Annual Rate Depreciation	Date of Disposal
#1	January 2, 1954	$400	25%	January 6, 1958
#2	June 2, 1949	160	10%	March 7, 1958
#3	July 5, 1952	500	20%	January 6, 1958
#4	April 28, 1940	180	5%	March 18, 1958

Instructions: 1. Calculate the book value and the amount of loss, if any, for each fixed asset.

2. Make the journal entries necessary to record depreciation for 1958 to the date of disposal of the assets. Calculate depreciation to the nearest month.

3. Make the journal entries necessary to record the discard of each item of office equipment.

Problem 25-2. Selling fixed assets

Fred Carr, a grocer, sold the following items of store equipment on December 1, 1957:

Item	Purchase Price	Book Value Dec. 1, 1957	Cash Received for Sale of Fixed Asset
Cash register	$600	$100	$130
Refrigerator	540	80	50

Instructions: Make the journal entries necessary to record the sale of these used fixed assets.

Problem 25-3. Trading in fixed assets

Assume that, instead of selling the items in Problem 25-2 for cash, Mr. Carr traded them in on December 1, 1957, for new and similar items of store equipment as follows:

(a) A new cash register for his old cash register plus $500 in cash.

(b) A new refrigerator for his old refrigerator plus $400 in cash.

Instructions: Make the journal entries necessary to record the trade-in of these fixed assets.

Problem 25-4. Purchase and disposition of equipment

R. J. Cole & Company maintains the following accounts that relate to fixed assets:

ACCT.
No.   ACCOUNT TITLE

121	Delivery Equipment
121.1	Allowance for Depreciation of Delivery Equipment
122	Office Equipment
122.1	Allowance for Depreciation of Office Equipment
123	Store Equipment
123.1	Allowance for Depreciation of Store Equipment
63	Depreciation of Delivery Equipment
64	Depreciation of Office Equipment
65	Depreciation of Store Equipment

Instructions: Record in a combination journal the following transactions selected from those completed during the current year.

Jan. 4. Issued Check No. 9 for $300 for cash purchase of office equipment.

Feb. 4. Bought store equipment on account from Carson Bros. for $750.

Mar. 4. Discarded office equipment for which there was no further use and which could not be sold. The office equipment cost $200 and had a book value of $15 at the time it was discarded.

Apr. 5. Sold old store equipment for cash, $20. The equipment cost $35 and had a book value of $10 when it was sold.

May 8. Bought a new delivery truck for $2,300 cash (Check No. 413) and the old truck. The old truck cost $2,000 and had a book value of $350 at the time of the trade-in.

June 1. Sold old office equipment for cash, $25. The equipment cost $80 and had a book value of $35 when it was sold.

June 30. Sold a truck for $900. The truck had been purchased two years ago on January 2 for $2,000. The depreciation rate was $500 a year. Allowance for depreciation for that amount was recorded at the end of the two previous years.

> (a) Record the depreciation for the current year to June 30.
> (b) Record the sale of the truck.

June 30. Office equipment costing $800, with depreciation at the rate of 10% a year, has a total allowance for depreciation of $440 on January 1 of the current year. On June 30 it is traded in on a new office machine. The cost of the new machine was the book value of the old machine plus $500 that was paid in cash (Check No. 554).

> (a) Record the depreciation for the current year to June 30.
> (b) Record the purchase of the new machine and the trade-in of the old.

Bad debts and accounts receivable

The importance of granting credit. Many businesses find that they can increase their volume of sales and thus their profit by selling on account. This practice of granting credit and allowing customers time in which to pay for their purchases is an added service that accommodates and thus draws more customers.

Most of the sales made by wholesale houses and manufacturers to retailers are credit sales. Many retail stores make sales to charge customers who pay at stated intervals, usually once a month. Federal statistics show that hundreds of the larger department stores throughout the United States report that less than 50% of their sales are cash sales.

Investigating customer credit. Before a business extends credit, it usually obtains information about the credit standing of the prospective charge customer. Retailers usually obtain the credit rating of a prospective charge customer from a local credit bureau. Wholesalers and manufacturers may obtain this information from the financial reports submitted by the prospective customer and from national credit agencies such as Dun & Bradstreet.

> Dun & Bradstreet, Inc. publishes a credit-rating book containing information about the financial condition of business houses throughout the United States. This reference book is available to businesses subscribing for it.

Uncollectible accounts. Even though a business is careful in extending credit to charge customers, there are usually some accounts that cannot be collected. These uncollectible accounts receivable are called *bad debts*. The expense caused by the uncollectible accounts is called *bad debts expense*. This bad debts expense, like any other expense of the business, must be subtracted from gross income in order to arrive at a true net profit. If this is not done, the business will be understating its expenses and overstating its profit.

An account receivable does not become a bad debt until it is known to be uncollectible. Sometimes this is several months or even a year or more after the date when the sale was made. During the time that this

326

account receivable which proved to be uncollectible was carried on the books, the value of the asset Accounts Receivable was overstated. Furthermore, the expense resulting from selling goods to a customer who did not pay was not recorded. It is desirable, therefore, for a business to make entries that will keep the accounts receivable account from being overstated and that will charge the bad debts expense to the period in which the sale was made.

Valuation of accounts receivable. The books of H. W. Wilcox, a wholesale hardware merchant, showed a balance of $5,515.77 in Accounts Receivable at the end of the quarterly fiscal period ended December 31, 1957. Mr. Wilcox knew from past experience that some of the individual accounts included in the balance of Accounts Receivable would eventually prove to be uncollectible. As a result, the $5,515.77 debit balance in Accounts Receivable was an overstatement of the value of this asset.

Mr. Wilcox had found from past records and experience that his uncollectible accounts usually amounted to about $\frac{1}{2}\%$ (.005) of his net sales for a fiscal period. Mr. Wilcox's net sales for the quarterly fiscal period ended December 31, 1957, were $22,064. He was therefore justified in *estimating* that $110.32 ($22,064 $\times$ .005 = $110.32) of his Accounts Receivable would be bad debts expense for this period.

In order for Mr. Wilcox to determine the estimated value of his accounts receivable on December 31, it was necessary to subtract the estimated amount of uncollectible accounts from the balance of the accounts receivable account. The following calculation shows this:

Accounts receivable............................	$5,515.77
Less estimated loss from bad debts..............	110.32
Estimated value of accounts receivable..........	$5,405.45

Some businesses find that they can secure their best estimate of bad debts expense by taking a percentage of their total *charge* sales for the period instead of a percentage of their total net sales. Others will take a percentage of the balance in the accounts receivable account at the end of a fiscal period. In any case, a business should use the method that results in the most accurate estimate. A change in credit granting policy or a change in economic conditions may cause a business to raise or lower its percentage figure so as to keep its estimate of bad debts as accurate as possible.

Establishing the allowance for bad debts account. Mr. Wilcox desired to have his ledger as well as his balance sheet show the estimated value of the accounts receivable. It was therefore necessary to record the estimated decrease in value of the accounts receivable because of uncollectible accounts.

Even though Mr. Wilcox estimated that accounts receivable to the amount of $110.32 would not be collected, he was not certain which of his customers would fail to pay. He could record the estimated loss by debiting an expense account; but without knowing which customers would not pay, he could not credit certain customers' accounts. Likewise, he could not credit the accounts receivable account in the general ledger because the balance of that account had to equal the sum of the balances of the customers' accounts. He therefore, by an adjusting entry, credited the estimated amount of the bad debts to an account with the title *Allowance for Bad Debts*. Since the loss from bad debts, $110.32, was one of the expenses of operating his business, he debited this amount to an expense account with the title *Bad Debts Expense*.

The entry in the combination journal to adjust the ledger record of accounts receivable and to show the estimated bad debts expense was as follows:

	CASH		CHK. NO.	DATE	NAME OF ACCOUNT	POST. REF.	GENERAL		
	DEBIT	CREDIT					DEBIT	CREDIT	
29				31	Bad Debts Expense		110 32		29
30					Allowance for Bad Debts			110 32	30

PAGE 24 — COMBINATION JOURNAL

Adjusting entry to establish allowance for bad debts

When the adjusting entry was posted, the accounts receivable account, the allowance for bad debts account, and the bad debts expense account in the general ledger appeared as follows:

Accounts Receivable — ACCOUNT NO. 12

DATE	ITEMS	POST. REF.	DEBIT	DATE	ITEMS	POST REF.	CREDIT
1957 Oct. 1	Balance	✓	3699 68	1957 Oct. 31		17	2855 50
31		17	3126 83	Nov. 30		22	3214 27
Nov. 30		22	3872 90	Dec. 31		24	3494 70
Dec. 31		24	4380 83				9564 47
		5515.77	15080 24				

Allowance for Bad Debts — ACCOUNT NO. 12.1

DATE	ITEMS	POST. REF.	DEBIT	DATE	ITEMS	POST. REF.	CREDIT
				1957 Dec. 31		24	110 32

Bad Debts Expense — ACCOUNT NO. 61

DATE	ITEMS	POST. REF.	DEBIT	DATE	ITEMS	POST. REF.	CREDIT
1957 Dec. 31		24	110 32				

The accounts receivable account has a debit balance of $5,515.77 and is classified as an *asset*. The Allowance for Bad Debts has a credit balance of $110.32 and is classified as a *minus asset*. Because Allowance for Bad Debts is used on the balance sheet in calculating the real value of Accounts Receivable, it is often called a *valuation account*. The bad debts expense account has a debit balance of $110.32 and is classified as an *operating expense*.

The debit balance of the accounts receivable account, $5,515.77, showed the total amount due from charge customers. The credit balance of the allowance for bad debts account, $110.32, showed the amount to be subtracted from the accounts receivable account because of estimated uncollectible accounts. The difference between these two balances, $5,405.45, was the estimated real value of the accounts receivable on December 31, 1957.

Until recent years valuation accounts were titled "Reserve for Bad Debts" and "Reserve for Depreciation." Today, however, the American Institute of Certified Public Accountants recommends the term *allowance* be used in preference to the term *reserve* in these account titles.

Adjustment of the allowance for bad debts account. Because new charge sales are made constantly, the amount of uncollectible accounts changes constantly. At the end of each fiscal period, Mr. Wilcox estimates his bad debts expense by taking ½% of the total net sales.

	ACCOUNT TITLES	ACCT. NO.	TRIAL BALANCE	
			DEBIT	CREDIT
1	Cash	11	2130 63	
2	Accounts Receivable	12	5872 15	
3	Allowance for Bad Debts	12.1		110 32
19	Bad Debts Expense	61		
20	Supplies Expense	69		
21	Insurance Expense	65		
22	Depreciation Expense	62		
23				
24	Net Profit			
25				
26				
27				
28				
29				
30				

Work sheet with

On March 31, 1958, the end of the quarterly fiscal period, Mr. Wilcox determined the total amount of net sales for January, February, and March. This total was $21,480. The estimated bad debts expense for the period was therefore ½% of this amount, or $107.40.

Bad debts on the work sheet. On March 31, 1958, Mr. Wilcox made an adjustment for bad debts expense in the Adjustments columns of his work sheet. In the illustration above, the waved lines indicate the omission of account titles and amounts not needed in this discussion.

The estimated bad debts expense, $107.40, was entered as a credit to Allowance for Bad Debts to record the additional allowance for bad debts for this fiscal period. The same amount was entered as a debit to Bad Debts Expense to record the estimated bad debts expense for the period.

Bad debts expense on the profit and loss statement. When Mr. Wilcox prepared his profit and loss statement from the work sheet on March 31,

		ADJUSTMENTS		P. & L. STATEMENT		BALANCE SHEET		
		3 DEBIT	4 CREDIT	5 DEBIT	6 CREDIT	7 DEBIT	8 CREDIT	
1						2130 63		**1**
2						5872 15		**2**
3			(a) 107 40				21 72	**3**

19	(a)	107 40		107 40				**19**
20	(d)	92 30		92 30				**20**
21	(e)	28 37		28 37				**21**
22	(f)	7 1 80		7 1 80				**22**
23		3901 8 10	3901 8 10	3522 6 18	3650 5 94	4044 4 72	3916 4 96	**23**
24				1279 76			1279 76	**24**
25				3650 5 94	3650 5 94	4044 4 72	4044 4 72	**25**
26								**26**
27								**27**
28								**28**
29								**29**
30								**30**

adjustment for bad debts

he indicated the bad debts expense as shown below. As Bad Debts Expense
is one of the expenses of operating the business, it is listed with the operating expenses.

H. W. Wilcox
Profit and Loss Statement
For Quarter Ended March 31, 1958

Operating Expenses:		
Bad Debts Expense	107 40	
Supplies Expense	92 30	
Total Operating Expenses		3952 34
Net Profit from Operations		1279 76

Bad Debts Expense on the profit and loss statement

Chapter 26. Bad debts and accounts receivable 331

Allowance for bad debts on the balance sheet. When Mr. Wilcox prepared his balance sheet from the work sheet on March 31, he indicated (1) the total amount due from charge customers, (2) the decrease in value because of estimated uncollectible accounts, and (3) the estimated real value of accounts receivable as follows:

H. W. Wilcox			
Balance Sheet			
March 31, 1958			
Assets			
Cash		2 1 3 0 63	
Accounts Receivable	5 8 7 2 15		
Less Allowance for Bad Debts	2 1 7 72	5 6 5 4 43	
Merchandise Inventory		2 8 8 0 3 41	
Total Assets			3 9 5 0 3 63

Allowance for Bad Debts on the balance sheet

The total amount due from charge customers, $5,872.15, was written on the line with Accounts Receivable. The estimated allowance for bad debts, $217.72, was placed immediately under the accounts receivable balance and was subtracted from it. The difference between these two amounts, $5,654.43, was the estimated real value of the accounts receivable. This amount was written in the first amount column so that it could be added with the other assets.

Adjusting entry for bad debts. Mr. Wilcox made the following adjusting entry in the combination journal from the Adjustments columns of his work sheet to record the estimated bad debts.

PAGE 37		COMBINATION JOURNAL							
CASH		CHK. NO.	DATE	NAME OF ACCOUNT	POST. REF.	**GENERAL**			
DEBIT	CREDIT					DEBIT	CREDIT		
			31	Bad Debts Expense		1 07 40			26
				Allowance for Bad Debts			1 07 40		27
									28

Adjusting entry for estimated bad debts

When this entry was posted, the accounts receivable account, the allowance for bad debts account, and the bad debts expense account in the general ledger appeared as follows:

Accounts Receivable — ACCOUNT NO. 12

DATE	ITEMS	POST. REF.	DEBIT	DATE	ITEMS	POST. REF.	CREDIT
1958 Jan. 1	Balance	✓	5515 77	1958 Jan. 31		29	6228 18
31		29	3260 66	Feb. 28		33	3256 09
Feb. 28		33	4927 26	Mar. 31		36	4524 19
Mar. 31		36	6176 92				14000 46
	5872.15		19180 61				

Allowance for Bad Debts — ACCOUNT NO. 121

DATE	ITEMS	POST. REF.	DEBIT	DATE	ITEMS	POST. REF.	CREDIT
				1957 Dec. 31		24	110 32
				1958 Mar. 31		37	107 40
							217 72

Bad Debts Expense — ACCOUNT NO. 61

DATE	ITEMS	POST. REF.	DEBIT	DATE	ITEMS	POST. REF.	CREDIT
1958 Mar. 31		37	107 40				

The debit balance of the accounts receivable account, $5,872.15, showed the total amount of the accounts due from charge customers. The credit balance of the allowance for bad debts account, $217.72, showed the amount to be subtracted from the accounts receivable account because of estimated uncollectible accounts. The difference between these two balances, $5,654.43, was the estimated real value of the accounts receivable on March 31.

Writing off uncollectible accounts. When it has been decided that a customer's account is uncollectible, the customer's account should be written off the books. To write off a customer's account, one account is

COMBINATION JOURNAL

CASH		CHK. NO.	DATE	NAME OF ACCOUNT	POST. REF.	GENERAL		
DEBIT	CREDIT					DEBIT	CREDIT	
			17	*Allowance for Bad Debts*		14 38		17
				M. C. Leonard				18
								19
								20
								21
								22
								23

Entry to write off an uncollectible

debited and two accounts are credited. The allowance for bad debts account in the general ledger is debited. The customer's account in the accounts receivable ledger and the accounts receivable account in the general ledger are credited.

On April 17, Mr. Wilcox decided that the past-due account of M. C. Leonard, with a debit balance of $14.38, was uncollectible. Mr. Wilcox therefore made the entry shown in the combination journal above.

The allowance for bad debts account in the general ledger was debited for $14.38 by writing the title of the account, Allowance for Bad Debts, in the Name of Account column and the amount, $14.38, in the General Debit column. This debit was made because an uncollectible account amounting to $14.38 covered by the allowance account was being eliminated from the accounts receivable ledger. The allowance for bad debts account must therefore be reduced by the amount of the customer's account written off. The debit entry to the allowance for bad debts account indicated this subtraction.

The M. C. Leonard account in the accounts receivable ledger was credited by writing his name in the Name of Account column and the amount of the credit, $14.38, in the Accounts Receivable Credit column. When this entry is posted, the credit to his account will close the account. His account will then be written off.

The accounts receivable account in the general ledger will be credited for $14.38 when this amount is posted as a part of the total of the Accounts Receivable Credit column at the end of the month. Whenever a customer's account is written off, the accounts receivable summary account in the general ledger must be reduced by the amount of the customer's account written off.

	5	6	7	8	9	10	11	12	
	ACCOUNTS PAYABLE		DISCOUNT ON PURCHASES	ACCOUNTS RECEIVABLE		DISCOUNT ON SALES	PURCHASES	SALES	
	DEBIT	CREDIT	CREDIT	DEBIT	CREDIT	DEBIT	DEBIT	CREDIT	
17									17
18					14 38				18
19									19
20									20
21									21
22									22
23									23

account when an allowance account is used

Posting the journal entry. After the debit to Allowance for Bad Debts was posted, the allowance for bad debts account appeared as follows:

Allowance for Bad Debts   ACCOUNT NO. *12.1*

DATE	ITEMS	POST. REF.	DEBIT	DATE	ITEMS	POST. REF.	CREDIT
1958 Apr. 17		38	14 38	1957 Dec. 31		24	1 10 32
				1958 Mar. 31		37	1 07 40

The corresponding credit to Accounts Receivable in the general ledger will be posted as a part of the column total at the end of the month.

When the credit to the customer's account in the accounts receivable ledger was posted, the account appeared as follows:

NAME *M. C. Leonard*
ADDRESS *504 Fifth Street, City*

DATE	ITEMS	POST. REF.	DEBIT	CREDIT	DEBIT BALANCE
1957 Oct. 18		15	14 38		14 38
1958 Apr. 17	Written off	38		14 38	— —

As a result of posting this amount to the customer's account, that account has been reduced $14.38, the same amount that the accounts receivable account in the general ledger will be reduced when the total of the Accounts Receivable Credit column is posted.

Chapter 26. Bad debts and accounts receivable   335

Recording bad debts expense at the time a debt becomes worthless. Most businesses and accountants prefer to follow the previously described method of estimating and recording bad debts expense. Some small businesses with relatively few uncollectible accounts do, however, record this expense at the time a debt is known to be worthless. This is done by debiting the account Bad Debts Expense and crediting Accounts Receivable and the customer's account for the amount of the debt.

This is a simple and acceptable method. It is not generally preferred because (a) it fails to charge the expense to the period in which the debt was incurred and (b) it can cause the accounts receivable account to have its value overstated on the balance sheet.

CHAPTER QUESTIONS

1. What is the major reason why some businesses sell on credit?
2. Why is the accounts receivable account evaluated at the end of a fiscal period?
3. Why is the amount of estimated uncollectible accounts receivable credited to the allowance for bad debts account rather than to the accounts receivable account?
4. Why is the allowance for bad debts account called a valuation account?
5. When are allowances for bad debts recorded?
6. How does a business estimate in advance what its bad debts expense will be?
7. In what section of the profit and loss statement on page 331 is the bad debts expense listed?
8. What entry was made in the combination journal on page 332 to record the estimated bad debts expense?
9. When is a customer's account written off the books?
10. In the combination journal on pages 334 and 335, what entry was made to write the customer's account off the books?
11. Why is the allowance for bad debts account debited when a customer's account is written off as uncollectible?
12. What simple method of recording bad debts expense is used principally by some small businesses with relatively few accounts receivable?

INCREASING YOUR BUSINESS VOCABULARY

What is the meaning of each of the following:

(a) bad debts   (b) bad debts expense   (c) allowance for bad debts

CASES FOR DISCUSSION

1. H. Q. Bunker and Son operate a garage. When their financial statements were compiled, no bad debts expense was included. How would this omission affect (a) the total value of the assets on the balance sheet and (b) the net profit or the net loss on the profit and loss statement?

2. B. M. Morton, a retail clothing merchant, credits Accounts Receivable for the amount of the estimated bad debts for each fiscal period. R. J. Pegolo, another retail clothing merchant, credits Allowance for Bad Debts for the amount of the estimated bad debts. What are the advantages of Mr. Pegolo's method?

APPLICATION PROBLEMS

Problem 26-1. Computing bad debts expense

The bookkeeping records of three different grocery stores showed the following summary information for the fiscal period ending December 31:

Grocery Store	Total Net Sales	Total Charge Sales	Balance in Accounts Receivable Account
#1	$28,604.48	$12,612.00	$1,984.60
#2	36,864.80	12,530.50	7,864.50
#3	28,111.00	14,211.21	2,160.00

Instructions: Compute the bad debts expense on December 31 for each of these stores under the following conditions:

(a) Store #1 estimated its bad debts would amount to ¼% (.0025) of its total *net sales.*

(b) Store #2 used 2% of its total *charge sales* as its estimate of bad debts.

(c) Store #3 used 3% of the *balance* in its accounts receivable account as its estimate of bad debts.

Problem 26-2. Recording transactions with bad debts expense

George Spear, proprietor of Spear's Specialty Store, records his transactions in a combination journal. In his general ledger he maintains accounts with Bad Debts Expense and Allowance for Bad Debts. At the beginning of the year the credit balance of the allowance for bad debts account was $126.36.

In this exercise you are given transactions taken from those completed by Spear's Specialty Store during the year. The selected transactions cover only uncollectible accounts, bad debts expense, and allowance for bad debts.

Instructions: Record in a combination journal all of the necessary entries for the following transactions:

Feb. 3. Decided that the past-due account of Carl Smith, $39.80, was uncollectible. Wrote off his account as a bad debt.

Mar. 31. (End of first quarterly fiscal period.) Increased the allowance for bad debts by making the necessary adjusting entry. The estimated bad debts expense for each quarterly fiscal period was 1½% of the total charge sales. The charge sales for the quarterly fiscal period ended March 31 were $8,880.40.

May 15. Henry Johnson, a charge customer, became insolvent. Wrote off his account of $35 as a bad debt.

June 30. The charge sales for the second quarterly fiscal period ended June 30 were $5,326.18. Increased the allowance for bad debts 1½% of that amount.

Aug. 11. Decided that the past-due account of R. H. Graham, $104.25, was uncollectible. Wrote off his account as a bad debt.

Sept. 30. The charge sales for the third quarterly fiscal period ended September 30 were $7,196.66. Increased the allowance for bad debts 1½% of that amount.

Dec. 31. Decided that the past-due accounts of the following charge customers were uncollectible:

> L. D. Smith, $50.66
> Estelle Edwards, $34.50
> E. H. Hoffman, $45

Wrote them off as bad debts in one combined entry, debiting Allowance for Bad Debts for the total.

Dec. 31. The charge sales for the fourth quarterly fiscal period ended December 31 were $6,422.30. Increased the allowance for bad debts 1½% of that amount.

Problem 26-3. Work at the end of the fiscal period

If you are not using the workbook correlating with this textbook, complete Exercise 26-B in the Appendix instead of this problem.

The ledger accounts of Stapp Feed Co., Wm. H. Stapp proprietor, are given in the workbook.

Instructions: 1. Foot the ledger accounts. Prove cash. The cash on hand and in the bank on December 31 is $7,087.22.

2. Prepare an eight-column work sheet for the annual fiscal period ended December 31 of the current year, using the following additional data as of December 31:

Additional allowance for bad debts, ½% of net sales
Merchandise inventory, $15,478.90
Supplies inventory, $195.88
Prepaid insurance, $240
Annual rate of estimated depreciation, 5%

3. Prepare a profit and loss statement and a balance sheet.

4. Record the adjusting entries and the closing entries.

5. Post the adjusting entries and the closing entries.

6. Rule the accounts that balance. Balance each remaining account in the general ledger that has both debits and credits.

7. Prepare a post-closing trial balance.

The use of the cash register

Need for recording transactions quickly. A retail store often makes hundreds of sales in a single day. The records of these sales must be accurate and complete in order to provide the manager with the information that he needs. A popular business machine that is used to record sales transactions is the *cash register*. Some form of cash register is commonly used wherever the customer deals directly with the cashier.

Use of the cash register. The cash register provides a convenient place for sorting and keeping the money used in the daily transactions. It also makes an immediate record of each transaction. A cash register of the type that is commonly used in retail stores is shown below.

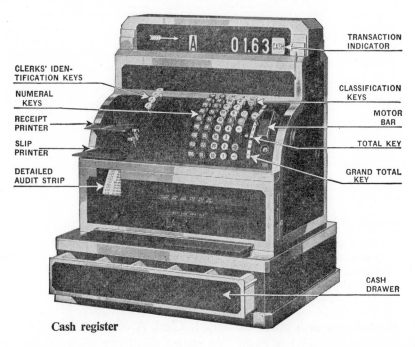

TRANSACTION INDICATOR

CLERKS' IDEN-TIFICATION KEYS

NUMERAL KEYS

RECEIPT PRINTER

SLIP PRINTER

DETAILED AUDIT STRIP

CLASSIFICATION KEYS

MOTOR BAR

TOTAL KEY

GRAND TOTAL KEY

CASH DRAWER

Cash register

There are many different types of cash registers. The one shown above records each transaction on a paper tape, supplies a receipt for the customer, and provides a convenient, organized money drawer.

Change fund. In the Allen Store, a retail clothing business, the amount of the petty cash fund was $100. This money was kept in the office safe. A definite amount, $20, was taken from the petty cash fund at the beginning of each day and was placed in the cash register for use in making change. At the end of the day this amount, $20, was taken out of the cash register and returned to the petty cash fund in the office safe.

Operating the cash register. The clerk operates the machine by pressing several of the keys and the motor bar. At the time the motor bar is pressed, the transaction is recorded on a paper tape in the machine. The transaction indicator in the illustration on page 339 shows that $1.63 was received for a cash sale. As this amount is recorded in full view of the customer, there is little likelihood that the clerk would intentionally record the wrong amount.

A diagram of the key arrangement of the register is shown below.

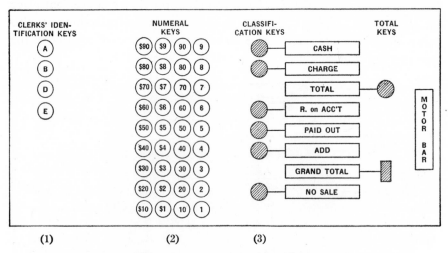

Key arrangement on a cash register

The groups of keys are as follows:

(1) The keys A, B, D, and E are used to identify the salesclerks handling the transactions. Each clerk is assigned one of these letters and uses exclusively the key assigned to him.

(2) The numeral keys record the amount of each transaction.

(3) The classification keys record the nature of each transaction.

Recording a cash sale. On July 1, Clerk A of the Allen Store sold merchandise for $1.63 in cash. To record this transaction on the cash register, Clerk A pressed the A key, the $1 key, the 60¢ key, the 3¢ key, the Cash key, and finally the motor bar. When the motor bar was operated, the complete transaction was shown in the transaction indicator at the top of the register and it was printed on a paper tape in the machine. At the same time the cash drawer came open so that the amount received could be placed in it.

ALLEN STORE

THANK YOU

JUL 1

−001 $ 01.63 Ca A

Receipt for a cash sale

When several items are sold to a customer, the amount of each item is recorded and the register operates like an adding machine to total the various items of the sale. Some types of cash registers will also compute the amount of change due.

When the motor bar was operated, the receipt shown at the left was automatically printed and was pushed out of the machine at the point marked "Receipt Printer." This receipt was given to the customer and was further proof that the transaction was properly recorded.

Recording a charge sale. On July 1, Clerk B of the Allen Store sold merchandise for $9.17 to Mrs. J. B. Arthur on account. He prepared the sales slip illustrated at the right. By using carbon paper, two copies were made. Each copy showed: the date; the name and the address of the customer; the clerk's initial or number; a description of the items sold, including the price of each item; and the total amount of the sale. He then inserted both copies of the sales slip in the slip printer of the cash register and recorded the charge sale on the machine.

To record the above transaction on the cash register, Clerk B pressed the B key, the $9 key, the 10¢ key, the 7¢ key, the Charge key, and finally the motor bar. The cash register made a perma-

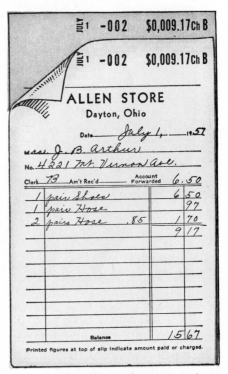

Sales slip in duplicate for a charge sale

nent record of the charge sale. It also printed the transaction number, the amount, and the clerk's letter, B, on both copies of the sales slip.

Analyzing the sales slip for a charge sale. The cash register did not record the name of the customer or a description of the items sold. The original copy of the sales slip was kept to show this information. The duplicate copy of the sales slip was given to Mrs. Arthur.

In order that the amount owed by the customer, Mrs. Arthur, might be readily observed, the balance owed was carried forward to each new sales slip and was added to the amount of the sale. Mrs. Arthur's balance was $6.50; the amount of the sale was $9.17; the new balance to be carried forward to the next sales slip was, therefore, $15.67.

Using sales slips as the accounts receivable ledger. In the Allen Store sales slips were filed alphabetically in a file cabinet kept near the cash register. This file cabinet served the purpose of an accounts receivable ledger. The Allen Store file for sales slips is illustrated below.

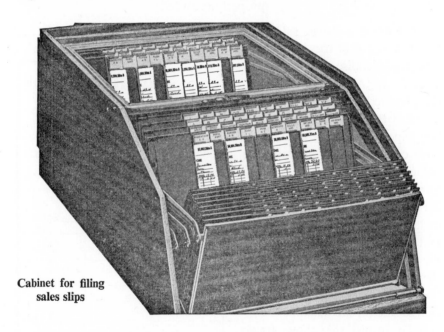

**Cabinet for filing
sales slips**

Each sale could have been posted from the sales slip to the customer's account in the accounts receivable ledger. The file cabinet, however, was a convenient method of keeping a record of the amount owed by each customer. Such a file cabinet is used by many small businesses in place of an accounts receivable ledger.

Recording cash payments. On July 1, Clerk B gave Mrs. A. L. James 50 cents, a cash refund for merchandise returned. He prepared a receipt that Mrs. James signed. The receipt was placed in the slip printer of the cash register. Clerk B then pressed the B key, the 50¢ key, the Paid Out key, and finally the motor bar. The receipt for this "paid out" transaction is illustrated at the right. Mrs. James's signature on the receipt was evidence that she received payment. This receipt was placed in the cash drawer.

Recording "no sale" transactions. A customer gave Clerk B a dollar bill and asked for change to make a pay telephone call. In order to open the cash drawer, Clerk B pressed the B key, the No Sale key, and the motor bar.

JULY 1 -003 $0,000.50Pd B

ALLEN STORE
Dayton, Ohio

PAID OUT

No. 25 DATE July 1, 1957
PAID TO Mrs. A. L. James
ADDRESS 917 Dexter Avenue
Account to be charged:
Sales Returns and Allowances
Explanation:
Refund for one apron returned.

Mrs. A. L. James
RECEIVED PAYMENT

Receipt for cash paid out

Recording cash received on account. When cash is received from a customer on account, the amount received must be entered in the cash register. A record must also be made on the customer's sales slip in the file cabinet to show the amount received and the remaining balance.

On July 1, Clerk D received $5 from Mrs. A. M. Thorne to apply on her account. Clerk D recorded this cash receipt on a sales slip. He also recorded this transaction in the cash register. The transaction was recorded in the same way as a charge sale, except that the Received on Account key was pressed instead of the Charge key. This sales slip after it was imprinted on the cash register is shown at the left.

To indicate that cash was received, the clerk wrote "Received on Account" in the explanation column of the sales

JULY 1 -005 $0,005.00Rc D

ALLEN STORE
Dayton, Ohio

Date July 1 1957
MRS. A. M. Thorne
No. 1345 Riverside Drive
Clerk D Am't Rec'd 5⁰⁰ Account Forwarded 17.65
Received on account 5 —

Balance 12 65
Printed figures at top of slip indicate amount paid or charged.

Sales slip for cash received
on account

slip. The amount received, $5, was deducted from the old balance, $17.65, and the remaining balance, $12.65, was recorded.

The amount of the cash received was recorded in the cash register and was printed on both copies of the sales slip. The original copy of the sales slip was filed on top of the other sales slips of Mrs. Thorne. The present balance, $12.65, written at the bottom of this slip indicated at a glance how much Mrs. Thorne still owed the Allen Store.

Detailed audit strip. Each of the transactions entered in the cash register was automatically printed on a paper tape known as the *detailed audit strip*. A section of the detailed audit strip showing the first five transactions completed by the clerks in the Allen Store is illustrated at the right.

The record on the detailed audit strip showed the number and the amount of each transaction. The nature of each transaction was indicated by the symbols *Ca* for a cash sale, *Ch* for a charge sale, *Pd* for an amount paid out, *NS* for no sale, and *Rc* for an amount received on account. The letters A, B, and D indicated the clerk who completed each transaction.

-005	$0,005.00Rc D
-004	$0,000.00NS B
-003	$0,000.50Pd B
-002	$0,009.17Ch B
-001	$0,001.63Ca A

Section of detailed audit
strip showing individual
transactions

Obtaining cash register totals. The cash register accumulated the total for each of the following types of transactions: (1) cash sales, (2) charge sales, (3) received on accounts, and (4) paid outs. At the end of each day the Total key was pressed and the totals for these groups of transactions were printed on the detailed audit strip. When these totals were printed, the cash register was automatically cleared so that none of the figures would be added to the transactions for the following day.

The section of the detailed audit strip of the Allen Store showing the totals at the end of the day, July 1, is shown at the left. The first column of numbers is the operation number, which is imprinted on the strip for each operation of the cash register. The second column shows the totals and the symbols. These symbols have the following meanings:

-086	$0,194.35GT
-085	$0,005.35Pd
-084	$0,030.00Rc
-083	$0,030.70Ch
-082	$0,164.35Ca

Section of the detailed audit
strip showing totals

GT, grand total, $194.35
Pd, paid out, $5.35
Rc, received on account, $30
Ch, charge sales, $30.70
Ca, cash sales, $164.35

Proving cash with the cash register totals. After the cash register was cleared and the total of each type of transaction was printed on the detailed audit strip, the strip was removed from the machine. The change fund of $20 was taken out of the cash register and was returned to the petty cash fund in the office safe. The money remaining in the cash drawer was then counted and entered on a daily balance slip similar to the one shown at the right. The total of each denomination of coin, the total paper money, and the total checks were listed in the spaces provided. The sum of all these items, $189, was the total cash in the drawer. To this amount was added the cash paid out, $5.35. The total, $194.35, was then the total cash received. The

DAILY BALANCE SLIP		
Denominations	Dollars	Cts.
Pennies		05
Nickels	1	55
Dimes	4	40
Quarters	2	50
Halves	1	50
Silver Dollars	—	
Paper Money	164	00
Checks	15	00
Total Cash in Drawer	189	00
Add Cash Paid Out	5	35
Total Cash Received	194	35
Total Cash Received on Detailed Audit Strip	194	35
Cash Short		
Cash Over		
No. of Paid-Out Slips	7	
No. of Charge Sales Slips	3	
No. of Rc. on A/c Slips	4	
Name C. J. Allen Date 7/1/57		

Cash proof on daily balance slip

total cash received as shown by the detailed audit strip was then entered on the daily balance slip. As the two amounts were the same, $194.35, the record of all the transactions in the cash register was considered to be correct.

Cash short and over. If the sum of the cash on hand at the end of the day plus the cash paid out during the day is less than the grand total recorded by the cash register, the cash is said to be *short*. If the sum of the cash on hand at the end of the day plus the cash paid out during the day is greater than the grand total recorded by the cash register, the cash is said to be *over*.

Whether the cash is short or over, the error is caused by mistakes in re-

DAILY BALANCE SLIP		
Denominations	Dollars	Cts.
Pennies		35
Nickels	1	15
Dimes	6	80
Quarters	4	50
Halves	12	00
Silver Dollars	—	
Paper Money	126	00
Checks	45	00
Total Cash in Drawer	195	80
Add Cash Paid Out	3	55
Total Cash Received	199	35
Total Cash Received on Detailed Audit Strip	198	85
Cash Short		
Cash Over		50
No. of Paid-Out Slips	4	
No. of Charge Sales Slips	7	
No. of Rc. on A/c Slips	3	
Name C. J. Allen Date 7/2/57		

Cash proof with cash over

cording transactions on the cash register or by mistakes in making change. If the error is large, the clerks should examine the detailed audit strip and try to recall the transaction that was recorded improperly or the transaction where a mistake was made in making change. If the error is small, usually no attempt is made to find the reason for it.

A record should be made of any error in the cash proof. If the cash is short, the amount of the shortage is entered on the daily balance slip on the line "Cash Short." If the cash is over, the amount of the overage is entered on the daily balance slip on the line "Cash Over" in the manner illustrated on page 345.

Cash short and over voucher. If the cash is short, the amount of the "cash short" is made up from the petty cash fund. A cash short and over voucher is filled out and is placed with the petty cash fund as a receipt for the amount taken out.

If there is too much cash on hand, the "cash over" is taken from the register and is placed with the petty cash. A cash short and over voucher is filled out and is placed with the petty cash as a receipt for the amount placed in the fund.

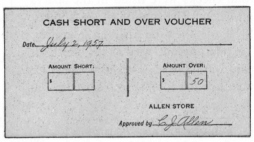

Cash short and over voucher for an overage

Paid-out slips and petty cash fund. In the Allen Store, all cash receipts were deposited in the bank. All large payments were made by check. Small cash payments, however, were made from the cash register. A paid-out slip was prepared for each of these transactions, and the amount was recorded by pressing the "Paid Out" key of the cash register. The paid-out slips were kept in the cash register.

At the end of the day, these paid-out slips were placed with the petty cash fund in the office safe, and an amount of cash equal to the total of the paid-out slips was taken from the fund. The cash taken from the petty cash fund was combined with the cash in the cash register, and the sum of these two amounts was proved with the grand total figure on the detailed audit strip (GT). This procedure made it possible to deposit in the bank an amount equal to the total cash receipts for the day.

The petty cash fund, then, was used for three purposes:

(1) To supply the cash register with an adequate amount of change at the beginning of the day.

(2) To adjust the amount of cash short or over each day.

(3) To replace the paid-out slips in the cash register with money.

Replenishing the petty cash fund. When the petty cash fund was running low, the paid-out receipts and the cash short or over vouchers kept with the fund were grouped together according to their nature. The amount of each group of payments was determined.

On July 31, the manager of the Allen Store grouped together the paid-out receipts and found that the various groups of payments were:

Sales Returns and Allowances..................................		$12.80
Salary Expense..		11.50
Miscellaneous Expense.....................................		17.84
Cash Short..	$2.76	
Less Cash Over..................................	2.30	
Net Cash Short..		.46
Total...		$42.60

As the total of all of the paid-out receipts plus the net cash shortage for the month was $42.60, a check was drawn for that amount. The check was cashed and the money was placed in the petty cash fund. The fund then had $100, the amount for which it was charged on the books. The entry to record this transaction is shown below. All the debits are recorded in the General Debit column, as special columns are not provided for any of these accounts.

Left-hand page of combination journal showing entry to replenish petty cash

Each time the petty cash fund is replenished, the cash short and over account is debited if cash short exceeds cash over. If cash over exceeds cash short, the cash short and over account is credited. In the entry recorded on Line 32 of the combination journal above, the total cash short for the period was larger than the total cash over.

If at the end of the fiscal period the cash short and over account in the ledger has a debit balance, it is listed on the profit and loss statement in the section with the heading "Other Expenses." If the cash short and over account in the ledger has a credit balance, it is listed on the profit and loss statement in the section with the heading "Other Income."

Sales returns and allowances for charge sales. When credit is given to a customer because merchandise is defective or is returned, a sales slip similar to the one at the left is made out in duplicate. The carbon copy is given to the customer. The original copy is used as the basis for an entry in the combination journal debiting Sales Returns and Allowances and crediting Accounts Receivable. This entry is illustrated on Lines 4 and 5 of the combination journal on pages 350 and 351.

The amount owed by the customer before the credit was given and the balance owed after the credit was given are entered on the sales slip. The slip is filed in the accounts receivable cabinet, illustrated on page 342, in the compartment containing the other sales slips for L. M. Wade. It is placed in front of the other sales slips and shows the new balance due from L. M. Wade.

ALLEN STORE
Dayton, Ohio

Date _July 2 1957_
Mr. _L. M. Wade_
No. _6301 Terrace Ave._
Clerk _13_ Am't Rec'd _____ Account Forwarded _14.59_

Credit for one scarf returned	1 69
Balance	12 90

Printed figures at top of slip indicate amount paid or charged.

Sales slip for a sales return or allowance

Recording purchases on account. When the merchandise represented by a purchase invoice was received, the merchandise was examined as to quality and was checked against the purchase invoice as to quantity. All calculations on the invoice were verified. If the purchase invoice was in agreement with the purchase order and the goods received, the purchase invoice was entered in the combination journal. The entry on Line 6 on pages 350 and 351 was an entry of this kind.

Purchases returns and allowances. If goods received were not satisfactory, omissions and errors were noted and reported to the seller. When a credit memorandum was received for merchandise returned or for an allowance granted, the transaction was recorded in the combination journal.

An entry of this kind is illustrated on Lines 12 and 13 of the combination journal on pages 350 and 351.

After the credit memorandum was used as the basis for the entry in the combination journal, it was filed with the invoice to which it applied so that only the balance due the creditor would be paid.

Payment of purchases invoices. The Allen Store did not use an accounts payable ledger. After each invoice was verified, it was placed in a file maintained for all unpaid purchases invoices. The purchases invoices were placed in the file in the order in which they were to be paid. In determining the date of payment, it was assumed that each invoice would be paid within the discount period. The file of unpaid invoices was examined each day to see if any invoices should be paid on that day.

All payments were made by check. An entry for each check stub was made in the combination journal. The entry of July 3 on Line 11 of the combination journal on pages 350 and 351 was an entry of this kind.

Paid invoices file. A folder for each creditor was maintained in the *paid invoices file.* As each purchase invoice was paid, it was filed in the folder labeled with the name of the firm from whom the purchase had been made. The folders were arranged in the file in alphabetic order.

The use of an unpaid invoices file and a paid invoices file made it unnecessary to maintain an accounts payable ledger. The unpaid invoices file showed at all times the total accounts payable. The paid invoices file was a record of completed purchases transactions.

The paid invoices file was consulted whenever the management desired information concerning past purchases. It was a convenient source of information on quantities and types of merchandise bought in the past from each creditor. From the contents of each folder it was possible to determine quickly any information desired with reference to the transactions completed with any creditor.

Recording transactions from the detailed audit strip. The Allen Store used a combination journal as its book of original entry. The transactions of July 1 to 3 as they are recorded in this combination journal are illustrated on the two following pages.

Analyzing the combination journal of the Allen Store.

Lines 1, 2, and 3. These three entries recorded the totals section of the detailed audit strip illustrated on page 344.

Line 1. Cash was debited and Sales was credited for the total of the cash sales (Ca), $164.35. The words "Sales for cash" were written in the

COMBINATION JOURNAL

	CASH		CHK. NO.	DATE	NAME OF ACCOUNT	POST. REF.	GENERAL		
	DEBIT	CREDIT					DEBIT	CREDIT	
1	164 35			*1957* July 1	Sales for cash				1
2				1	Sales on account				2
3	30 00			1	Received on account				3
4				2	Sales Returns & Allow.		1 69		4
5					L. M. Wade				5
6				2	Lincoln Mfg. Co.				6
7	152 30			2	Sales for cash				7
8				2	Sales on account				8
9	27 80			2	Received on account				9
10		150 00	108	2	Rent Expense		150 00		10
11		246 57	109	3	Jameson Bros.				11
12				3	Lincoln Mfg. Co.				12
13					Purchases Ret. & Allow.			10 00	13

Combination journal

Name of Account column to distinguish between this entry and the entry for sales on account given on the following line.

Line 2. Accounts Receivable was debited and Sales was credited for the total of the charge sales (Ch), $30.70. Since the sales slip file was used as the accounts receivable ledger, the amounts entered in the Accounts Receivable Debit column were not posted to customers' accounts. For this reason the customers' names were not given in the Name of Account column. The words "Sales on account" were written to indicate the nature of the transaction.

Line 3. Cash was debited and Accounts Receivable was credited for the total of the cash received on account (Rc), $30. Since the sales ticket file was used as the accounts receivable ledger, the customers' names were not given in the Name of Account column. The words "Received on account" were written to indicate the nature of the transaction.

Similar entries were made from the totals section of the detailed audit strip at the end of each day. Note the entries on Lines 7–9.

Lines 4 and 5. To record the debit resulting from the return by L. M. Wade, the account title, Sales Returns and Allowances, was written in the Name of Account column and the amount, $1.69, was entered in the General Debit column. To record the credit, the name of the customer,

	ACCOUNTS PAYABLE		DISCOUNT ON PURCHASES	ACCOUNTS RECEIVABLE		PURCHASES	SALES	
	DEBIT	CREDIT	CREDIT	DEBIT	CREDIT	DEBIT	CREDIT	
1							164 35	1
2				30 70			30 70	2
3					30 00			3
4								4
5					1 69			5
6		295 65				295 65		6
7							152 30	7
8				35 40			.35 40	8
9					27 80			9
10								10
11	251 60		5 03					11
12	10 00							12
13								13

of the Allen Store

L. M. Wade, was written in the Name of Account column in the indented position. The amount of the credit was entered in the Accounts Receivable column.

The name of the customer was not required for posting because the file of sales tickets was used instead of the accounts receivable ledger. The customer's name was written in the Name of Account column, however, so that reference could be made to the proper sales ticket if information about the transaction was desired.

Line 6. The purchase on account was recorded in the Purchases Debit column and the Accounts Payable Credit column. The file of unpaid invoices was used instead of the accounts payable ledger; nevertheless the name of the creditor was written in the Name of Account column so that further information could be obtained from the invoice if it was desired.

Lines 12 and 13. To record the debit resulting from the allowance for defective merchandise, the name of the creditor, Lincoln Manufacturing Co., was written in the Name of Account column and the amount, $10, was written in the Accounts Payable Debit column. To record the credit, the account title, Purchases Returns and Allowances, was written in the Name of Account column in the indented position. The amount of the credit was entered in the General Credit column.

The name of the creditor was not required for posting because the file of unpaid invoices was used instead of the accounts payable ledger; nevertheless the name of the creditor was written in the Name of Account column so that further information, if desired, could be obtained from the credit memorandum attached to the invoice.

CHAPTER QUESTIONS

1. What is the purpose of a cash register?
2. Why is a cabinet file for sales slips sometimes used in place of an accounts receivable ledger?
3. What is the meaning of each of the following symbols on the detailed audit strip on page 344: Ca, Ch, NS, Pd, and Rc?
4. How are the totals obtained for all the transactions entered on the cash register during the day?
5. How is the cash on hand proved each day?
6. What three entries were made in the combination journal on pages 350 and 351 at the end of each business day from the totals on the detailed audit strip?
7. In the Allen Store, what records were made to record (a) a cash shortage and (b) a cash overage?
8. How is a sales return for a charge sale recorded?
9. How is an allowance on a charge purchase recorded?
10. What system did the Allen Store use instead of an accounts payable ledger?

INCREASING YOUR BUSINESS VOCABULARY

What is the meaning of each of the following:

(a) cash register
(b) petty cash fund
(c) detailed audit strip
(d) grand total

CASES FOR DISCUSSION

1. J. A. Baker, a retail clothier, employs four salesclerks, who use a cash register that has the key arrangement shown on page 340. Describe how each of the following transactions would be recorded:

   (a) Clerk A sold merchandise for $4.50 in cash.
   (b) Clerk E received $12.75 to apply on account.
   (c) Clerk D paid out $2.50 for merchandise that was returned.
   (d) Clerk B gave a customer change for a dollar.
   (e) Clerk E sold merchandise for $13.98 on account.

2. C. F. Tennison, a retail druggist, makes purchases on account in small quantities from a number of wholesalers. He maintains an account for each of his creditors in an accounts payable ledger. Joseph Pine, another druggist, has the same type of transactions as Mr. Tennison. Mr. Pine does not maintain an accounts payable ledger; instead he keeps a file of all unpaid invoices. What are the advantages of each of these methods?

APPLICATION PROBLEMS

Problem 27-1. Proving cash

If you are not using the workbook correlating with this textbook, complete Exercise 27-A in the Appendix instead of this problem.

Instructions: 1. Fill in the daily balance slip given in the workbook and prove cash. The count of cash in the cash register, the detailed audit strip totals, and the cash register papers for February 20 are also given in the workbook.

2. Fill in the cash short and over voucher in the workbook for the cash shortage for the day.

Problem 27-2. Replenishing petty cash

If you are not using the workbook correlating with this textbook, complete Exercise 27-B in the Appendix instead of this problem.

On September 30 of the current year, the end of a monthly fiscal period, the petty cash fund of the Johnson Grocery Store contained the petty cash paid-out receipts and the cash short and over vouchers given in the workbook.

Instructions: 1. Detach the cash short and over vouchers and the petty cash paid-out receipts and separate them along the perforated lines.

2. Sort the cash short and over vouchers and the petty cash paid-out receipts into the following groups:

        (a) Cash short.
        (b) Cash over.
        (c) Delivery expense.
        (d) Miscellaneous expense.
        (e) Sales returns and allowances.
        (f) Supplies.

3. Find the net amount by which the cash is short or over.
4. Find the total amount in each group of petty cash paid-out receipts.
5. Record the entry to replenish the petty cash fund (Check No. 328).

Problem 27-3. Recording transactions from business papers

If you are not using the workbook correlating with this textbook, complete Exercise 27-C in the Appendix instead of this problem.

J. J. Todd, who operates an electrical appliance store, records his transactions in a combination journal like the one on pages 350 and 351. On June 27 of the current year, he finds that the page is filled.

Instructions: 1. Forward the following column totals on June 27 to a new page of Mr. Todd's combination journal:

Cash Debit, $3,138.72
Cash Credit, $2,364.53
General Debit, $826.00
General Credit, $24.85
Accounts Payable Debit, $5,059.12
Accounts Payable Credit, $4,317.28

Discount on Purchases Credit, $53.27
Accounts Receivable Debit, $260.75
Accounts Receivable Credit, $253.10
Purchases Debit, $4,553.85
Sales Credit, $6,825.41

Instructions: 2. Record in the combination journal the following transactions completed by Mr. Todd on June 27 to 30. The business papers referred to are numbered and given in consecutive order in the workbook.

June 27. (Business Paper 1.) Issued Check No. 406 in payment of the telephone bill.

27. (Business Paper 2.) Received a credit memorandum from King Bros. for returned merchandise.

27. (Business Paper 3.) Recorded the cash register totals for the day as shown on the detailed audit strip.

28. (Business Paper 4.) Recorded the cash register totals for the day as shown on the detailed audit strip.

30. (Business Paper 5.) Purchased merchandise on account from Osgood Mfg. Co.

30. Issued Check No. 407 for $337.46 in payment of the semimonthly payroll of $375 less a deduction of $29.10 for employees income taxes payable and a deduction of $8.44 for FICA taxes payable.

30. Recorded the employer's liability of $8.44 for FICA taxes, $10.13 for state unemployment taxes, and $1.13 for federal unemployment taxes.

30. (Business Paper 6.) Issued Check No. 408 in payment of Emery & Sons' invoice of June 21 less discount. This invoice was previously recorded as a debit to Purchases and a credit to Accounts Payable.

30. (Business Paper 7.) Issued Check No. 409 for $48.13 to replenish the petty cash fund.

30. (Business Paper 8.) Recorded the cash register totals for the day as shown on the detailed audit strip.

Instructions: 3. Foot, prove, and rule the combination journal.

Columnar special journals

CHAPTER 28

Planning books of original entry to meet the needs of the business. The books of original entry of a business should be planned to meet the special needs of the business. A business may use a combination journal in which is recorded all of its transactions as illustrated in the previous chapter. When the number of daily transactions of a business is large, it is often desirable to use separate journals with special columns.

The addition of special columns in a special journal saves time in making entries and in posting them. Saving time is important when there are many transactions of each kind every day.

Special columns in the cash receipts journal. When special columns are provided in the cash receipts journal, this book of original entry is known as a *columnar cash receipts journal*. The columnar cash receipts journal used during the month of May by the Miller Office Supply Company is shown below.

PAGE *12*

CASH RECEIPTS JOURNAL

DATE	ACCOUNT CREDITED	POST. REF.	GENERAL CREDIT	SALES CREDIT	ACCOUNTS RECEIVABLE CREDIT	DISCOUNT ON SALES DEBIT	CASH DEBIT	
1957 May 1	Balance on hand, $8314.52	✓						1
1	J. E. Walker	✓			246 30	4 93	241 37	2
1	Sales	✓		94 40			94 40	3
2	Store Supplies	15	4 95				4 95	4
29	Sales	✓		126 45			126 45	26
29	G. C. Jackson	✓			325 46		325 46	27
31	Sales	✓✓✓✓	96 54	69 85			69 85	28
31	Totals		96 54	1987 95	6842 42	128 10	8798 81	29
			(✓)	(41)	(13)	(412)	(11)	

Columnar cash receipts journal after posting

Analyzing the columnar cash receipts journal. This columnar cash receipts journal is similar to the one illustrated in Chapter 14 with the exception that a column has been added for discount on sales.

The amount of cash received in each transaction is recorded in the Cash Debit column. Accounts to be credited for which special columns are not provided are recorded in the General Credit column. Special columns are provided to record credits to sales and to customers' accounts because these transactions occur often.

Many charge customers pay their accounts within the discount period. A special column in which to record the discounts saves time in posting them individually. The transaction on Line 2 of the cash receipts journal on page 355 illustrates the use of the Discount on Sales Debit column. On May 1 a check for $241.37 was received from J. E. Walker in payment of an invoice for $246.30, less discount. Cash was debited for the amount of the check, $241.37. Accounts Receivable was credited for the amount of the invoice, $246.30. Discount on Sales was debited for the amount of the discount, $4.93. The two debits equal the amount of the credit.

Posting the columnar cash receipts journal. Amounts recorded in the Accounts Receivable Credit column are posted to the customers' accounts daily. Amounts recorded in the General Credit column are posted frequently to avoid too much work at the end of the fiscal period.

After cash has been proved and the equality of debits and credits has been verified, the totals of the special columns are posted to the accounts named in the headings of the columns. As each total is posted, the account number is placed in parentheses below the total.

The columnar cash payments journal. When special amount columns are provided in the cash payments journal, this book of original entry is known as a *columnar cash payments journal*. The columnar cash payments journal used during the month of May by the Miller Office Supply Company is shown on the opposite page.

Analyzing the columnar cash payments journal. The columnar cash payments journal is similar to the cash payments journal discussed in Chapter 12 except that special columns are provided in which to record transactions relating to payroll payments and discounts on purchases.

The amount of each cash payment is recorded in the Cash Credit column. Accounts to be debited for which special columns are not provided are recorded in the General Debit column as illustrated by the transaction on Line 2. Special columns are provided in which to record transactions with creditors and discounts on purchases as illustrated by the transaction on Line 3.

In the transaction on Line 3, an invoice amounting to $344 was paid, less the discount of $6.88. The amount of the invoice, $344, was re-

	DATE	CHK. NO.	ACCOUNT DEBITED	POST. REF.	GENERAL DEBIT	ACCOUNTS PAYABLE DEBIT	SALARY EXPENSE DEBIT	EMPLOYEES INCOME TAX. PAY. CREDIT	FICA TAXES PAY. CREDIT	DISCOUNT ON PURCHASES CREDIT	CASH CREDIT	
				1	2	3	4	5	6	7		
1	1957 May 1	114	Petty Cash	12	50 00						50 00	1
2	2	115	Rent Expense	67	200 00						200 00	2
3	2	116	H.B. Bickersons	✓		344 00				6 88	337 12	3
4	3	117	Miscellaneous Exp.	65	10 50						10 50	4
22	31	162	Salary Expense	✓			363 85	19 90	8 19		335 76	22
23	31	163	Store Supplies	15	8 60							23
24			Office Supplies	16	12 45							24
25			Miscellaneous Exp.	65	14 80							25
26			Trans. on Purchases	52	9 20							26
27			Advertising Exp.	61	3 75	6128 46	1819 25	99 50	40 93	89 80	48 80 9567 51	27
28	31		Totals		1850 03	6128 46	1819 25	99 50	40 93	89 80	9567 51	28
29					(✓)	(21)	(68)	(22)	(23)	(51.2)	(11)	29
30												30
31												31
32												32
33												33
34												34
35												35

Columnar cash payments journal after posting

corded in the Accounts Payable Debit column. The amount of the discount, $6.88, was recorded in the Discount on Purchases Credit column. The amount of the payment, $337.12, was recorded in the Cash Credit column. The two credits equaled the one debit.

The transaction on Line 22 illustrates the use of special columns relating to payroll payments. Salary Expense was debited in the Salary Expense Debit column for $363.85, which was the amount of the payroll. The credit of $19.90 in Column 4 recorded the employees' income taxes withheld. The credit of $8.19 in Column 5 recorded the FICA taxes withheld. The cash credit of $335.76 recorded the amount of the check that was cashed in order to pay employees. The three credits equal the debit.

Posting the columnar cash payments journal. Amounts recorded in the Accounts Payable Debit column are posted daily. Amounts recorded in the General Debit column are posted frequently to avoid too much work at the end of the fiscal period.

After cash has been proved and the equality of debits and credits has been verified, the totals of the special columns are posted to the accounts named in the headings of the columns. As each total is posted, the account number is placed in parentheses below the total.

Chapter 28. Columnar special journals   **357**

	DATE	ACCOUNT CREDITED	POST. REF.	GENERAL CREDIT	SALES CREDIT	ACCOUNTS RECEIVABLE CREDIT	DISCOUNT ON SALES DEBIT	CASH DEBIT	
1	1957 May 1	Balance on hand, $8314.52	✓						1
2	1	J. E. Walker	✓			246 30	4 93	241 37	2
3	1	Sales	✓		94 40			94 40	3
4	2	Store Supplies	15	4 95				4 95	4
26	29	Sales	✓		126 45			126 45	26
27	29	G. E. Jackson	✓			325 46		325 46	27
28	31	Sales	✓		69 85			69 85	28
29	31	Totals	1545.12	96 54	1987 95	6842 42	128 10	8798 81	29
30				(✓)	(41)	(13)	(412)	(11)	30
31	31	Balance, May 1	✓					8311 52	31
32								17113 33	32
33									33
34									34
35									35

Double-page cashbook (left page)

Double-page cashbook. Some businessmen prefer to keep the record of cash receipts and cash payments in one book known as the *cashbook*. If the two journals are brought together in one book, the cash receipts are recorded on left-hand pages and the cash payments are recorded on right-hand pages.

If the Miller Office Supply Company had kept its cash records in the double-page cashbook form, the cashbook would have appeared as shown above.

Posting the double-page cashbook. The double-page cashbook is posted in the same manner as are the separate cash receipts and cash payments journals.

In the cashbook all left-hand pages on which cash receipts are recorded have even numbers and all right-hand pages on which cash payments are recorded have odd numbers. Thus *C2*, or *C4*, or *C12*, etc., in the posting reference column of an account indicates that the item came from the cash receipts side of the cashbook. Similarly, *C3*, or *C5*, or *C13*, etc., in the posting reference column of an account indicates that the item came from the cash payments side of the cashbook.

Balancing and ruling the double-page cashbook. When a double-page cashbook is used, the cash on hand is proved each day in the same manner as when separate cash receipts and cash payments journals are used. (See page 164.) After the cash on hand has been proved at the end

DATE	CHK. NO.	ACCOUNT DEBITED	POST. REF.	GENERAL DEBIT	ACCOUNTS PAYABLE DEBIT	SALARY EXPENSE DEBIT	EMPLOYEES INCOME TAX. PAY. CREDIT	FICA TAXES PAY. CREDIT	DISCOUNT ON PURCHASES CREDIT	CASH CREDIT	
1957 May 1	114	Petty Cash	12	50 00						50 00	1
2	115	Rent Expense	67	200 00						200 00	2
2	116	H.C. Beckerson	✓		344 00				6 88	337 12	3
3	117	Miscellaneous Exp.	65	10 50						10 50	4
											26
26		Trans. on Purchases	52	9 20							26
27		Advertising Exp.	61	3 75						48 80	27
				1 850 03	*6 128 46*	*1 819 25*	*99 50*	*40 93*	*89 80*	*9 567 51*	
28	31	Totals		1850 03	6128 46	1819 25	99 50	40 93	89 80	9567 51	28
29				(✓)	(21)	(68)	(22)	(23)	(51.2)	(11)	29
30	31	Balance, May 31	✓							7545 82	30
31											31
32										17113 33	32
33											33
34											34
35											35

Double-page cashbook (right page)

of the month, the column totals are entered and posted. The double-page cashbook is then balanced as follows:

Step 1. The cash balance at the beginning of the month, $8,314.52, is written on the left-hand page in the Cash Debit column below the footing of the total cash receipts, $8,798.81. See Line 31 above.

Step 2. The cash balance at the end of the month, $7,545.82, is written on the right-hand page in the Cash Credit column below the footing of the total cash payments, $9,567.51. See Line 30 above.

Step 3. The proving totals at the end of the month, $17,113.33, are written on the same line of each page. See Line 32 above.

Step 4. Double lines are ruled to show that the cashbook is in balance. Note that the double lines cross both pages on the same line immediately under the two proving totals.

Forwarding the cashbook totals. When either page of the cashbook is full, the amount columns of both pages are totaled and the equality of debits and credits is proved. The totals of the amount columns on the cash receipts side are then forwarded to the top of the next left-hand page. The totals of the amount columns on the cash payments side are forwarded to the top of the next right-hand page. The words "Carried Forward" are written on each side of the cashbook on the line with the totals of the amount columns. The words "Brought Forward" are written on each side of the next two pages of the cashbook on the first line.

The columnar general journal. A general journal is used to record miscellaneous entries of all kinds. When special columns are provided in the general journal, this book of original entry is known as a *columnar general journal.* The Miller Office Supply Company has a number of miscellaneous transactions with customers and creditors that are recorded in the general journal. In order to make it easier to record and post miscellaneous transactions with customers and creditors, special columns are provided in the general journal for accounts receivable and accounts payable. The columnar general journal used by the Miller Office Supply Company is shown below:

GENERAL JOURNAL — PAGE 10

	ACCOUNTS PAYABLE DEBIT (1)	GENERAL DEBIT (2)	DATE	NAME OF ACCOUNT	POST. REF.	GENERAL CREDIT (3)	ACCOUNTS RECEIVABLE CREDIT (4)	
1		37 63	1957 May 3	Allowance for Bad Debts				1
2				L. B. Dawson			37 63	2
3				To write off an uncol-				3
4				lectible account.				4
5		10 00	3	Sales Returns and Allowances				5
6				C. L. Cotter			10 00	6
7				Credit Memo No. 18.				7
8		8 18	3	FICA Taxes				8
9		1 09		Federal Unemployment Taxes				9
10		9 82		State Unemployment Taxes				10
11				FICA Taxes Pay.		8 18		11
12				Fed. Unemployment Taxes Pay.		1 09		12
13				State Unemployment Taxes Pay.		9 82		13
14				To record employer's taxes.				14
15		150 75		C. A. Michael.				15
16				W. D. Murphy		150 75		16
17				To correct error in				17
18				posting sales invoice				18
19				No. 773				19
35	30 00		27	Curran & Curran				35
36				Purchases Returns & Allow.		30 00		36
37				Allowance for damaged				37
38				mdse.				38
39	685 00	22462 97	27	Carried Forward	✓	2 1954 26	1 1937 1	39

Miscellaneous entries in the columnar general journal

ACCOUNTS PAYABLE DEBIT	GENERAL DEBIT	DATE	NAME OF ACCOUNT	POST. REF	GENERAL CREDIT	ACCOUNTS RECEIVABLE CREDIT	
685 00	22462 97	1957 May 27	Brought Forward	✓	21954 26	1193 71	1
	9 63	27	Sales Returns and Allowances	41.1			2
			D. L. Logan	✓		9 63	3
			Credit Memo No. 26.				4
	3181 33	31	Purchases	51			20
			Accounts Payable	21	3181 33		21
			Total invoices for month.				22
	7531 90	31	Accounts Receivable	13			23
			Sales	41	7531 90		24
			Total invoices for month.				25
700 00	33521 87	31	Totals		32677 37	1544 50	26
(21)	(✓)				(✓)	(13)	27
							28

General journal after posting

Analyzing the columnar general journal. The debit amount columns in the columnar general journal were placed at the left of the Name of Account column. The credit amount columns were placed at the right of the Name of Account column. A journal in which the Name of Account column is placed between the debit amount columns and the credit amount columns is referred to as a *divided-column journal*.

The recording of transactions in a general journal was discussed and illustrated in Chapter 15. The difference between this columnar journal and the one in Chapter 15 is that this journal has columns for accounts payable and accounts receivable. Entries are recorded in the usual manner with the account to be credited indented slightly under the account to be debited.

When the journal page is filled, the columns are totaled and proved for equality of debits and credits. The totals are then forwarded to the next page.

Posting the four-column general journal. The individual amounts in the Accounts Payable Debit column were posted daily to the debit side of the appropriate creditors' accounts in the accounts payable ledger. A check mark was placed in the Post. Ref. column to indicate the completion of the posting. Similarly, the individual amounts in the Accounts Receivable Credit column were posted daily to the credit side of the appropriate customers' accounts in the accounts receivable ledger.

The individual amounts in the General columns that affected accounts in the general ledger were posted to accounts in the general ledger. The account number was written in the Post. Ref. column of the general journal to indicate the completion of the posting. When an amount was posted from the general journal, the letter *J* and the journal page number were written in the posting reference column of the account.

Posting the totals of the four-column general journal. At the end of the month the columns of the four-column general journal were totaled and proved. The sum of the totals of the debit columns, $34,221.87, was equal to the sum of the totals of the credit columns, $34,221.87. The records in the general journal were therefore assumed to be accurate.

The totals of the General columns were not posted because the items in these columns were posted individually to the general ledger accounts during the month. A check mark was placed below each of these columns to show that the total was not to be posted.

The total of the Accounts Payable Debit column, $700, was posted to the debit side of the accounts payable account in the general ledger and the account number, 21, was placed below the total to indicate that this amount had been posted. Similarly, the total of the Accounts Receivable Credit column, $1,544.50, was posted to the credit side of the accounts receivable account in the general ledger and the account number, 13, was placed below the total to indicate that this amount had been posted.

Recording purchases on account. The Miller Office Supply Company uses the purchases invoices as the purchases journal. The amount of each invoice is posted directly to the creditor's account in the accounts payable ledger. (See page 124.) A check mark is placed at the right of the name of the creditor printed at the top of the purchases invoice to show that the invoice was posted. The invoice is then placed in the unpaid invoices file, which is arranged according to due dates. The file of unpaid invoices is examined each day to determine what invoices should be paid.

As each purchases invoice is paid, an entry is made in the cash payments journal. The entry on Line 3 in the journal on page 357 is an entry of this kind. The purchases invoice is stamped "Paid" and is replaced in the file, where it remains until the end of the month.

At the end of the month, the amounts of all the purchases invoices for the month are added. The total of the invoices for the month is then recorded in the columnar general journal as a debit to Purchases and a credit to Accounts Payable. The entry on Lines 20–22 on May 31 in the journal illustrated on page 361 was an entry of this kind. All of the paid invoices for the month were then transferred to the "paid invoices file."

Recording sales on account. The Miller Office Supply Company uses duplicate copies of sales invoices as the sales journal. Each sales invoice is posted directly to the proper customer's account in the accounts receivable ledger. (See page 151.) The number of the sales invoice is placed in the posting reference column of the customer's account to show the source of the entry. A check mark is placed at the right of the customer's name on the sales invoice to show that the invoice was posted.

At the end of the month, the amounts of all the sales invoices for the month are added. The total of the invoices for the month is then recorded in the columnar general journal as a debit to Accounts Receivable and a credit to Sales. The entry on Lines 23–25 on May 31 in the general journal illustrated on page 361 was an entry of this kind. The sales invoices were then filed in numerical order.

The cash method of handling purchases on account. Some businesses prefer to handle all purchases on account as though they were cash purchases. This is done by recording the invoice in the cash payments journal only at the time it is paid. This method makes it unnecessary to maintain a purchases journal, accounts with creditors, or an accounts payable controlling account in the general ledger. Recording purchases only when they are paid is known as the *cash method of handling purchases*.

The steps in using the cash method of handling purchases on account are as follows:

Step 1. Each purchase invoice is verified and then is filed under the date it is to be paid.

Step 2. The bookkeeper examines the file each day, and checks are issued to the creditors in payment of the invoices due on that day.

Step 3. The amount of the check is recorded in the cash payments journal as a debit to Purchases and a credit to Cash. If the invoice is subject to a discount, only the amount of the check is recorded as a debit to Purchases.

Step 4. At the end of the month the total of the Purchases Debit column of the cash payments journal is posted to the debit of the purchases account in the general ledger.

CHAPTER QUESTIONS

1. When is it desirable to use special journals with special columns in which to record transactions?
2. What is the difference between a combination journal and a special journal?
3. What are the advantages of special columns in a journal?

4. What steps need to be taken before posting the totals of the cash receipts journal?
5. What do the numbers in parentheses below the totals of the cash receipts journal on page 355 show?
6. In which column of the cash payments journal, shown on page 357, are the amounts of cash payments recorded?
7. What was the amount of the invoice that was paid in the transaction on Line 3 of the cash payments journal shown on page 357?
8. What was the amount of cash withdrawn to pay the employees in the transaction on Line 22 of the cash payments journal on page 357?
9. What kinds of entries are recorded in the columnar general journal?
10. What should be done before the column totals of the general journal are forwarded to a new page?
11. Explain the procedure used when purchases invoices and sales invoices are used as the purchases journal and the sales journal.
12. Explain the procedure used when purchases on account are recorded only at the time of payment.

INCREASING YOUR BUSINESS VOCABULARY

What is the meaning of each of the following:

(a) columnar cash receipts journal
(b) columnar cash payments journal
(c) cashbook

(d) columnar general journal
(e) divided-column journal
(f) cash method of handling purchases

CASES FOR DISCUSSION

1. The Arrow Grocery Company uses a columnar cash receipts journal with the following headings:

(1) General Credit
(2) Sales Credit
(3) Accounts Receivable Credit

(4) Discount on Sales Debit
(5) Cash Debit

(a) From which of these columns are amounts posted individually?
(b) To what accounts are the individual amounts posted?
(c) Which column total of the cash receipts journal is not posted?

2. The Arrow Grocery Company also uses a columnar cash payments journal with the following column headings:

(1) General Debit
(2) Accounts Payable Debit
(3) Salary Expense Debit
(4) Employees Income Taxes Payable Credit

(5) FICA Taxes Payable Credit
(6) Discount on Purchases Credit
(7) Cash Credit

(a) From which of these columns are amounts posted individually?
(b) To what accounts are the individual amounts posted?
(c) Which column total of the cash payments journal is not posted?

Problem 28-1. Recording transactions in columnar special journals

Paul Denton, who operates the Denton Hardware Store, decided to open a new set of books on December 1 of the current year. The account balances in his ledger at the end of the fiscal period on November 30 were:

Cash, $1,605.84

Accounts Receivable, $516.75

Allowance for Bad Debts, $70.15

Merchandise Inventory, $6,821.50

Supplies, $119.60

Prepaid Insurance, $84

Equipment, $2,788.20

Allowance for Depreciation of Equipment, $242.85

Accounts Payable, $913.67

Employees Income Taxes Payable, $140

FICA Taxes Payable, $33.75

State Unemployment Taxes Payable, $36.45

Federal Unemployment Taxes Payable, $21.60

Paul Denton, Capital, $10,552.97

Paul Denton, Drawing, $75.55 (Dr.)

Instructions: 1. Record the following transactions completed by Mr. Denton during December in a cash receipts journal, a cash payments journal, and a general journal like those illustrated in this chapter.

Dec. 1. Recorded an opening entry from the account balances given above. Recorded the cash balance in the cash receipts journal.

1. Issued Check No. 1 for $50 to establish a petty cash fund.

1. Issued Check No. 2 for $125 for the December rent.

2. Received a check for $76.03 from Robert Fisher in payment of our invoice of November 22 for $76.80 less 77 cents discount.

3. Issued Check No. 3 for $10.50 in payment of the telephone bill. (Debit Miscellaneous Expense)

4. Issued Check No. 4 for $378.40 to Daniels Company in payment of their invoice of November 25 for $386.12 less $7.72 discount.

6. Issued Check No. 5 for $118.62 in payment of the weekly payroll of $150 less a deduction of $28 for employees income taxes payable and a deduction of $3.38 for FICA taxes payable.

6. Recorded the employer's liability of $3.38 for FICA taxes, $4.05 for state unemployment taxes, and 45 cents for federal unemployment taxes.

6. Cash sales for the week were $589.93.

8. Issued Check No. 6 for $162.50 in payment of the liability of $140 for employees income taxes payable and the liability of $22.50 for FICA taxes payable.

9. Received a check for $154.77 from E. C. Kemper in payment of our invoice of November 29 for $156.33 less $1.56 discount.

10. Wrote off the account of John J. Smith, $27.50, as a bad debt.

11. Issued Check No. 7 for $471.05 to Bagby Brothers in payment of their invoice of December 2 for $480.66 less $9.61 discount.

13. Issued Check No. 8 for $118.62 in payment of the weekly payroll of $150 less the same deductions as on December 6.

13. Recorded the employer's liability for social security taxes, which were the same as on December 6.

Dec. 13. Cash sales for the week were $726.48.

15. Issued Check No. 9 for $163.79 to Harry Moore in payment of his invoice of November 15.

16. Sold some wrapping supplies for $7.50 cash to accommodate a customer.

17. Issued Check No. 10 for $22.17 for supplies.

18. Received a credit memorandum for $12.50 from Tru-Steel Tool Company for merchandise returned to them.

19. Received a check for $100 from P. F. Parker on account.

20. Issued Check No. 11 for $118.62 in payment of the weekly payroll of $150 less the same deductions as on December 6.

20. Recorded the employer's liability for social security taxes, which were the same as on December 6.

20. Cash sales for the week were $684.23.

22. Issued Check No. 12 for $16.50 for the electricity bill. (Debit Miscellaneous Expense)

23. Issued Credit Memorandum No. 1 for $6.98 to Robert Fisher for merchandise returned.

24. Received a check for $116.62 from T. A. Benjamin in payment of our invoice of December 15 for $117.80 less $1.18 discount.

26. Issued Check No. 13 for $749.99 to Tru-Steel Tool Company in payment of their invoice of December 16 for $777.80 less the $12.50 credit, less $15.31 discount.

27. Issued Check No. 14 for $118.62 in payment of the weekly payroll of $150 less the same deductions as on December 6.

27. Recorded the employer's liability for social security taxes, which were the same as on December 6.

27. Cash sales for the week were $796.44.

29. Received a check for $42.07 from T. O. Reed in payment of our invoice of December 19 for $42.50 less 43 cents discount.

29. Issued Check No. 15 for $103.65 for transportation charges on purchases.

30. Received a check for $125.23 from Robert Fisher in payment of our invoice of December 20 for $133.48 less the $6.98 credit, less $1.27 discount.

30. Issued Check No. 16 for $377.40 to Birch & Company in payment of their invoice of December 20 for $385.10 less $7.70 discount.

31. Received a check for $50 from P. F. Parker on account.

31. Issued Check No. 17 for $156.82 for delivery service for the month. (Debit Delivery Expense.)

31. Issued Check No. 18 for $44.11 to replenish petty cash. The expenditures were as follows: Supplies, $5.95; Miscellaneous Expense, $12.66; Transportation on Purchases, $4.25; Delivery Expense, $2.50; and Sales Returns and Allowances, $18.75.

31. Cash sales for December 29 to 31 were $316.55.

Instructions: 2. Foot, total, and rule the columnar special journals.

Notes and interest

The use of notes. An unconditional written promise to pay a certain amount of money at a definite time signed by a person or persons agreeing to make payment is known as a *promissory note*, or, more briefly, as a *note*. When a person or a business borrows at a bank, the bank requires the borrower to sign a note. Notes are sometimes given to merchandise creditors when the buyer wants credit beyond the usual time for which credit is given.

Notes that a business receives, in which its debtors promise to pay, are known as *notes receivable*. Notes that a business gives creditors, in which it promises to pay, are known as *notes payable*. Notes receivable are assets. Notes payable are liabilities. A form of a note is shown below.

Note

Analyzing a promissory note. In the following table the terms used in connection with promissory notes are defined, and the applications of these terms to the foregoing illustration are shown.

Terms	Definitions	The Illustration
Maker	The one who signs the note and thus promises to make payment.	E. L. Cooper
Payee	The one to whom a note is payable.	Graham & Sons
Date	The day on which the note is issued.	October 24, 1957
Time	The days or months from the date of issue until the note is to be paid.	60 days
Maturity date	The date on which the note is due.	December 23, 1957
Principal	The amount the maker promises to pay.	$700
Interest rate	The rate paid for the use of the money.	4%

Interest on notes. A note that bears interest is said to be *interest-bearing*. If it does not bear interest, it is said to be *non-interest-bearing*. Interest is expressed as a percentage of the principal. This percentage is known as the *interest rate*. Interest at 6% means that 6 cents will be paid for the use of each dollar borrowed for a full year. When a note runs for less than one year, the amount of interest is found by determining what fraction of a year the time is. That fraction is then multiplied by the amount that would be charged for a full year. For example, if the time of a note is 6 months, which is one half of a year, the amount of interest would be one half the amount that would be paid for a full year.

When cash is paid for interest, the amount of the payment is debited to an expense account with the title *Interest Expense*. When cash is received for interest, the amount of the receipt is credited to an income account with the title *Interest Income*.

Computing interest using interest tables. Whenever a business has many calculations of interest, it commonly uses an interest table. Interest tables may be purchased at an office supply store or obtained from some banks. The illustration at the right shows an interest table for 6% on a monthly basis. Tables are available for almost any interest rate on both a monthly and a daily basis.

Analyzing the interest table. If a business has a note for $500 that is to run for 3 months, compute the interest as follows:

1. Follow down the interest table in the month column to the figure 3. The amount column on this line shows .015, which is the amount of interest for $1 for 3 months.

2. Multiply $500 by .015. The result is $7.50, which is the interest on $500 for 3 months.

INTEREST TABLE 6% for $1.00 on a Monthly Basis	
NUMBER OF MONTHS	AMOUNT OF INTEREST
1	.005
2	.01
3	.015
4	.02
5	.025
6	.03
7	.035
8	.04
9	.045
10	.05
11	.055
12	.06

Computing interest without interest tables. To compute the interest on a given amount for one year, the principal is multiplied by the interest rate. For example, the interest on $300 for 1 year at 5% is $15. The interest is computed as follows:

$$\$300 \times .05 = \$15$$

To calculate the amount of interest for a period of less than one year, the following formula is used:

PRINCIPAL $\times$ RATE $\times$ FRACTION OF YEAR = AMOUNT OF INTEREST

For example, to find the interest on $600 for 4 months at 5%, the following computation would be made:

$$\text{PRINCIPAL} \times \text{RATE} \times \text{FRACTION OF YEAR} = \text{AMOUNT OF INTEREST}$$

$$\$600 \times .05 \times \frac{4}{12} = \frac{\$120}{12} = \$10$$

For convenience in calculating, 360 days are commonly used as the number of days in a year. To find the interest on $400 for 90 days at 4% the following computation would be made:

$$\$400 \times .04 \times \frac{90}{360} = \frac{1440}{360} = \$4$$

Instead of multiplying the numbers and dividing by 360, the cancellation method can be used, as follows:

$$\$400 \times \overset{.01}{\cancel{.04}} \times \frac{\cancel{90}}{\underset{4}{\cancel{360}}} = \$4$$

Recording notes receivable. A business may accept a note from a charge customer as a means of granting an extension of time for the payment of an account. The note does not pay the amount the customer owes, but it does change the form of the asset from an account receivable to a note receivable.

On October 28, E. L. Cooper received from D. C. Walsh a 60-day, 5% note for $400 to apply on Mr. Walsh's account. Mr. Cooper recorded this transaction in a general journal with special columns for Accounts Payable Debit and Accounts Receivable Credit. The entry was made in a four-column general journal in the following manner:

			GENERAL JOURNAL			PAGE 22	
ACCOUNTS PAYABLE DR.	GENERAL DR.	DATE	NAME OF ACCOUNT	POST. REF.	GENERAL CR.	ACCOUNTS RECEIVABLE CR.	
	400 00	28	Notes Receivable				7
			D. C. Walsh			400 00	8
			Note Rec. No. 65				9
							10

Entry to record a note received from a customer

Notes Receivable was debited for $400 to record the increase in this asset. The amount of the debit was written in the General Debit column, and the title of the account to be debited, Notes Receivable, was written in the Name of Account column.

Accounts Receivable was credited to record the decrease in the value of this asset. The amount was written in the Accounts Receivable Credit column. The name of the customer, D. C. Walsh, was written in the Name of Account column so that this amount might be posted to the customer's account in the accounts receivable ledger.

Recording the collection of a note with interest. When cash is received in payment of a note and interest, a combined entry with two credits is made in the cash receipts journal. Cash is debited to record the increase in the asset Cash, Notes Receivable is credited to record the decrease in the asset Notes Receivable, and Interest Income is credited to record the increase in this type of income.

On December 27, E. L. Cooper received a check for $403.33 in payment of the note of October 28 with interest. The following entry was made in the cash receipts journal:

				1	2	3	4	5		
DATE		ACCOUNT CREDITED	POST. REF.	GENERAL CR.	SALES CR.	ACCOUNTS RECEIVABLE CR.	DISCOUNT ON SALES DR.	CASH DR.		
28	27	Notes Receivable		400 00				403 33	28	
29		Interest Income		3 33					99	
30									30	
31									31	
32									32	
33									33	

CASH RECEIPTS JOURNAL — PAGE 41

Entry to record the collection of a note and interest

Dishonored note receivable. When the maker of a note refuses or is unable to pay the note when it is due, the note is said to be *dishonored*. The notes receivable account should include only those notes that are not yet due. A dishonored note should therefore be removed from the notes receivable account. Such a note is usually debited to the customer's account so that the account will show the total amount owed by the customer, including the amount of the dishonored note. This information may be important if the customer requests credit in the future.

Mr. Cooper held a 60-day note, dated September 18, 1957, for $275.80, which the maker, L. C. Spence, was unable to pay when it came due on November 17. The entry made by Mr. Cooper to record this transaction, after posting, was as follows:

ACCOUNTS PAYABLE DR.	GENERAL DR.	DATE	NAME OF ACCOUNT	POST. REF.	GENERAL CR.	ACCOUNTS RECEIVABLE CR.	
9		275 80	17 Accounts Receivable—L.C. Spence √/				9
10			Notes Receivable	13	275 80		10
11			To charge the L.C. Spence				11
12			account for Note Rec. No. 64				12
13			dishonored today.				13
14							14
15							15
16							16
17							17
18							18
19							19
20							20

Entry to record a dishonored note receivable

The debit to Accounts Receivable, $275.80, was entered in the General Debit column, and the title of the general ledger account, Accounts Receivable, was written in the Name of Account column. As this amount also had to be debited to the account of L. C. Spence, the customer's name was also written in the Name of Account column. When the transaction was posted, the completion of the posting of the debit to the general ledger account was indicated by writing the account number in the Post. Ref. column. The completion of the posting to the customer's account was indicated by a check mark. The account number and the check mark were separated by a diagonal line in the manner shown in the illustration.

To record the decrease in the asset Notes Receivable, the account Notes Receivable was credited in the General Credit column and the title of the account was written in the Name of Account column.

If it is later decided that collection cannot be made from Mr. Spence, the balance of the account will be written off as a bad debt. At that time Allowance for Bad Debts will be debited and Accounts Receivable and L. C. Spence will be credited.

Recording notes payable. Not only may a business receive notes, but also it may issue them. It may issue them to those to whom it owes money in order to obtain additional time in which to pay some of its obligations. It may also issue them to a bank for the purpose of borrowing money. In either case a note issued by the business is a liability and is recorded in its books as a note payable.

For example, on October 24, E. L. Cooper gave a creditor, Graham & Sons, a 60-day, 4% note for $700 for the invoice of September 24 that was due on October 24. The entry made to record this transaction was as follows:

ACCOUNTS PAYABLE DR.	GENERAL DR.	DATE	NAME OF ACCOUNT	POST. REF.	GENERAL CR.	ACCOUNTS RECEIVABLE CR.	
			GENERAL JOURNAL			PAGE 22	
4 700 00		24	Graham & Sons				4
5			Notes Payable		700 00		5
6			Note Pay. No. 54				6

Entry to record a note issued to a creditor

As the liability Accounts Payable was decreased, it was debited for $700 in the Accounts Payable Debit column. The name of the creditor's account was written in the Name of Account column so that this amount could be posted to the creditor's account in the accounts payable ledger.

The liability Notes Payable was increased and therefore the notes payable account was credited in the General Credit column.

Recording the payment of a note with interest. When a business pays a note with interest, a combined entry with two debits is made in the cash payments journal. The debits are to the liability account Notes Payable and to the expense account Interest Expense.

On December 23, E. L. Cooper issued a check for $704.67 to Graham & Sons in payment of the note of October 24 with interest. The following entry was made in the cash payments journal:

DATE	CHK. NO.	ACCOUNT DEBITED	POST. REF.	GENERAL DR.	ACCOUNTS PAYABLE DR.	SALARY EXPENSE DR.	EMPLOYEES INCOME TAX. PAY. CR.	FICA TAXES PAY. CR	DISCOUNT ON PURCHASES CR.	CASH CR.	
			CASH PAYMENTS JOURNAL							PAGE 43	
32 23	185	Notes Payable		700 00						704 67	32
33		Interest Expense		4 67							33
34											34

Entry to record the payment of a note and interest

Both debits were entered in the General Debit column, as special columns were not provided for Notes Payable Debit or Interest Expense Debit. Cash was credited for $704.67 to record the amount of cash paid.

Borrowing money at a bank. If a businessman borrows money from a bank, he may give the bank an interest-bearing note and pay the interest at the maturity of the note. In that case he receives cash or credit for the face of the note, and at the maturity date he pays the face of the note plus the interest. If the note is a 60-day, 6% note for $1,000, he receives $1,000 when he issues the note, and at the maturity date he pays $1,010, the face of the note plus the interest.

The borrower may, however, be required to pay interest in advance. Interest charged in advance by a bank is referred to as *bank discount*. The amount received for a note after the bank has taken this discount is called the *proceeds*.

E. L. Cooper wished to borrow from his bank. It was the custom of his bank to charge interest in advance. On October 8, Mr. Cooper drew a 60-day, non-interest-bearing note for $1,000 in favor of his bank. The discount rate charged by the bank was 6%. The interest on $1,000 for 60 days at 6% was $10. The proceeds of the note, the amount received by Mr. Cooper, was therefore $1,000 minus $10, or $990.

When E. L. Cooper issued the note on October 8 and received credit for $990 from the bank, he recorded the transaction by the following entries in his general journal and in his cash receipts journal:

GENERAL JOURNAL — PAGE 21

ACCOUNTS PAYABLE DR.	GENERAL DR.	DATE	NAME OF ACCOUNT	POST. REF.	GENERAL CR.	ACCOUNTS RECEIVABLE CR.
21	990 00	8 Cash	✓			21
22	10 00	Interest Expense				22
23		Notes Payable		1000 00		23
24		Note Pay. No. 53.				24
25						25

CASH RECEIPTS JOURNAL — PAGE 33

DATE	ACCOUNT CREDITED	POST. REF.	GENERAL CR.	SALES CR.	ACCOUNTS RECEIVABLE CR.	DISCOUNT ON SALES DR.	CASH DR.
22	8 Notes Payable	✓	990 00				990 00	22
23								23

Entries to record the discounting of a note payable

The entry for the cash receipt must be recorded in the cash receipts journal, but the entry to record the debit to Interest Expense must be recorded in the general journal because the cash receipts journal of E. L. Cooper does not provide a General Debit column.

Whenever an entry must be made in more than one journal, the complete transaction is recorded in one place so that the transaction can be traced easily when the books are audited. The complete entry was therefore made in the general journal of E. L. Cooper. In this entry Cash was debited for $990, Interest Expense was debited for $10, and Notes Payable was credited for $1,000. In the cash receipts journal Cash was debited for $990 and the account title Notes Payable was entered in the Account Credited column.

The debit to Cash, $990, was posted from the cash receipts journal as a part of the total of the Cash Debit column; therefore a check mark was placed in the Post. Ref. column of the general journal on the line with Cash to indicate that this amount was not to be posted from this journal. The credit to Notes Payable, $1,000, was posted from the general journal; therefore a check mark was placed in the Post. Ref. column of the cash receipts journal on the line with Notes Payable to indicate that the credit was not to be posted from this journal.

As a result of these two entries, the debits and the credit posted to the accounts were as follows:

	DEBIT	CREDIT
Cash (posted from cash receipts journal)...........	$990	
Interest Expense (posted from general journal)......	10	
Notes Payable (posted from general journal)......		$1,000

Reporting interest income and interest expense. As interest income is not an income from selling merchandise, it is classified as *other income* and is placed in the Other Income section of the ledger.

As interest expense is not an expense from selling merchandise, it is classified as *other expense* and is placed in the Other Expense section of the ledger.

Interest on the work sheet. When E. L. Cooper prepared his work sheet from the ledger on December 31, the end of his semiannual fiscal period, the accounts with interest appeared at the end of the trial balance. Interest Income, which was a credit in the Trial Balance Credit column, was extended into the P. and L. Statement Credit column. Interest Expense, which was a debit in the Trial Balance Debit column, was extended into the P. and L. Statement Debit column.

The method of entering Interest Income and Interest Expense on the work sheet is shown in the following illustration:

	ACCOUNT TITLES	ACCT. NO.	TRIAL BALANCE			P. & L. STATEMENT	
			DEBIT	CREDIT		DEBIT	CREDIT
35	Salary Expense	68	990740			990740	
36	State Unempl. Taxes	69	26750			26750	
37	Interest Income	71		2714			2714
38	Interest Expense	81	4358			4358	
39	Loss on Fixed Assets	82	7680			7680	
40			422974	422974			

Interest on the work sheet

Interest on the profit and loss statement. The following illustration shows how E. L. Cooper reported interest income and interest expense on his profit and loss statement on December 31:

E. L. Cooper
Profit and Loss Statement
For Year Ended December 31, 1957

Income from Sales:			
Sales			2616843
Power Expense		7838	
Rent Expense		180000	
Salary Expense		990740	
State Unemployment Taxes		26750	
Supplies Expense		55957	
Total Operating Expenses			1707275
Net Profit from Operations			90303
Other Income:			
Interest Income		2714	
Other Expenses:			
Interest Expense	43.58		
Loss on Fixed Assets	76.80		
Total Other Expenses		12038	
Net Subtraction			9324
Net Profit			80979

Interest on the profit and loss statement

Interest Income is listed in the Other Income section. Interest Expense is listed in the Other Expenses section. Since the Other Expenses exceed the Other Income, the difference is called Net Subtraction and is deducted from the Net Profit from Operations to obtain the Net Profit.

CHAPTER QUESTIONS

1. When is a promissory note referred to as a note receivable?
2. When is a promissory note referred to as a note payable?
3. What is the person who signs a note called?
4. What does "6% interest" mean?
5. What are the three steps in computing interest when an interest table is not available?
6. What account is credited when cash is received for interest?
7. What accounts are credited when cash is received in payment for a note and interest?
8. Why is it important to record a dishonored note to the debit of the maker's account?
9. What account is debited when cash is paid for interest on a note?
10. What accounts are debited when cash is paid for the principal of a note and the interest?

INCREASING YOUR BUSINESS VOCABULARY

What is the meaning of each of the following:

(a) promissory note
(b) notes receivable
(c) notes payable
(d) maker of a note
(e) payee of a note
(f) maturity date of a note
(g) principal of a note

(h) interest rate
(i) interest-bearing note
(j) non-interest-bearing note
(k) dishonored note
(l) bank discount
(m) proceeds

CASES FOR DISCUSSION

1. George Lester, a dealer in farm equipment, receives a large number of notes. He has the Farmer's National Bank collect all of his notes for him. What special column would you advise Mr. Lester to add to his cash receipts journal?
2. D. T. Minor, a retail grocer, maintains a cash balance sufficient to pay all of his bills when they become due. J. E. Crane, another retail grocer, finds it necessary to borrow money from his bank at frequent intervals. Both merchants have an equal volume of sales. Which merchant is likely to have the smaller net profit from his business? Why?

Problem 29-1. Recording notes and interest

The transactions given below were selected from those completed by Thomas Lake, a used car dealer, during the months of April, May, and June of the current year.

Instructions: Record the following transactions, using a cash receipts journal, a cash payments journal, and a general journal.

April 1. Received from Henry Sanders a 60-day, non-interest-bearing note (Note Receivable No. 21) for $300, dated March 31, as a 60-day extension of the time of payment on the amount due for the sale of January 15.

3. Issued Note Payable No. 15 for $2,500 to Standard Motors Co. for an extension of time on account. The time was 60 days; the interest rate was 6%.

8. Received from Louis Wylie a 30-day, non-interest-bearing note (Note Receivable No. 22), dated today, for $595, in settlement of his account.

15. Issued Note Payable No. 16 for $3,600 to the Jet Manufacturing Co. for an extension of time on account. The time was 30 days; the interest rate was 6%.

28. Discounted at the First National Bank our 60-day, non-interest-bearing note (Note Payable No. 17). Face of note, $1,000; discount rate, 4%. Received credit for the proceeds, $993.33.

May 5. Discounted at the First National Bank our 30-day, non-interest-bearing note (Note Payable No. 18). Face of note, $5,000; discount rate, 3%. Received credit for the proceeds, $4,987.50.

8. Received a check for $595 from Louis Wylie in payment of his non-interest-bearing note (Note Receivable No. 22).

13. Received from Ernest Walters a 30-day, 5% note (Note Receivable No. 23) for $300 and a 60-day, 5% note (Note Receivable No. 24) for $500 in settlement of his account. Both notes were dated May 12. (Make a separate entry for each note.)

15. Issued Check No. 108 for $3,618 to the Jet Manufacturing Co. in payment of Note Payable No. 16 for $3,600 plus $18 interest.

31. Received notice from the bank that Henry Sanders had refused to pay his 60-day, non-interest-bearing note (Note Receivable No. 21) for $300 when it became due on May 30. Charged the note to the account of the maker.

June 2. Issued Check No. 156 for $2,525 to Standard Motors Co. in payment of Note Payable No. 15 for $2,500 plus $25 interest.

4. Issued Check No. 161 for $5,000 to the First National Bank in payment of Note Payable No. 18 for $5,000.

11. Received a check for $301.25 from Ernest Walters in payment of his note (Note Receivable No. 23) for $300 plus $1.25 interest.

June 19. Received from Joseph Benson a 90-day, 6% note (Note Receivable No. 25) for $1,750, dated today, in settlement of his account.

27. Issued Check No. 188 for $1,000 to the First National Bank in payment of Note Payable No. 17 for $1,000.

Problem 29-2. Calculating and recording interest and bank discount

Instructions: Using a general journal, a cash receipts journal, and a cash payments journal, record the following transactions selected from those completed by D. F. Turner, a dealer in farm implements, during October of the current year:

Oct. 3. Issued Check No. 172 to Ace Implement Co. in full payment of a 60-day, 5% interest-bearing note due today (Note Payable No. 41). Face of note, $600.

6. Discounted at the Farmers Bank his 30-day, non-interest-bearing note (Note Payable No. 45). Face of note, $400. Rate of discount, 6%. Received credit for the proceeds.

8. Received a check from L. D. Lyons in payment of the principal and interest on a 20-day, 5% interest-bearing note due today (Note Receivable No. 79). Face of note, $240.

10. Issued Check No. 178 to the City National Bank in payment of the principal and interest on a 90-day, 4% interest-bearing note due today (Note Payable No. 36). Face of note, $1,000.

15. Discounted at the Farmers Bank his 90-day, non-interest-bearing note (Note Payable No. 46). Face of note, $1,500. Rate of discount, 6%. Received credit for the proceeds.

17. Received a check from James Joyce in full settlement of his 180-day, 6% interest-bearing note due today (Note Receivable No. 61). Face of note, $500.

18. Issued Check No. 186 to Kent Manufacturing Co. in full payment of the principal and interest on a 60-day, 3% interest-bearing note due today (Note Payable No. 42). Face of note, $648.50.

24. Discounted at the Farmers Bank his 20-day, non-interest-bearing note (Note Payable No. 47). Face of note, $600. Rate of discount, 6%. Received credit for the proceeds.

25. Received a check from W. S. Slane in payment of the principal and interest on a 30-day, 5% interest-bearing note due today (Note Receivable No. 78). Face of note, $540.80.

27. Issued Check No. 195 to Acme Harvester Corporation in full payment of the principal and interest on a 90-day, 4% interest-bearing note due today (Note Payable No. 38). Face of note, $800.

28. Received a check from James Berry in full settlement of his 90-day, 6% interest-bearing note due today (Note Receivable No. 72). Face of note, $485.

Accrued expenses

Need for recording accrued expenses. At the end of each fiscal period the profit and loss statement should show all the expenses for the period even though some of them have not been paid. These unpaid expenses must be recorded before the reports are prepared at the end of the period in order that the profit and loss statement will be complete and accurate.

Expenses that are incurred in one fiscal period but not paid during that period are called *accrued expenses*. Two of the most common accrued expenses are salaries and interest on notes payable.

Salaries owed but not paid. L. A. Cole pays his employees at the end of each week. During December, 1957, he issued salary checks on the 6th, 13th, 20th, and 27th. The salaries for the last days in December were not paid until January 3, 1958. Therefore, on December 31, 1957, when the trial balance was prepared, Mr. Cole's salary expense account in the general ledger appeared as follows:

		Salary Expense					ACCOUNT NO. 68	
DATE	ITEMS	POST. REF.	DEBIT	DATE	ITEMS	POST. REF.	CREDIT	
1957 Dec. 1	Balance	✓	9308 50					
31		CP12	879 50					
			10,188 00					

The debit balance of December 1 was the total of the salary expense for the first eleven months of the year. The debit of December 31, $879.50, was the total of the Salary Expense Dr. column of the cash payments journal. It included the amounts paid on December 6, 13, 20, and 27.

On December 31, 1957 the amount that was earned by employees during the last days of the month, $110.40, is not shown in the salary expense account because the next payday is January 3, 1958. An adjusting entry is therefore necessary to record the salary expense for the last days in December that should be charged to the present fiscal year 1957.

Adjusting entry for accrued salaries. Mr. Cole made the following adjusting entry for accrued salaries on December 31, 1957.

ACCOUNTS PAYABLE DR.	GENERAL DR.	DATE	NAME OF ACCOUNT	POST. REF.	GENERAL CR.	ACCOUNTS RECEIVABLE CR.	
			GENERAL JOURNAL			PAGE 42	
			1 **2**	**3**		**4**	
15	110 40	31	Salary Expense				15
16			Salaries Payable		110 40		16
17							17

Adjusting entry for accrued salaries

The salary expense account was debited for $110.40 so that it would include the salary expense incurred but not paid during 1957. The liability account, Salaries Payable, was credited for $110.40, the amount that was owed to employees for the last days of December, 1957.

When this adjusting entry was posted, the salaries payable account and the salary expense account in the general ledger appeared as follows:

Salaries Payable ACCOUNT NO. 24

DATE	ITEMS	POST. REF.	DEBIT	DATE	ITEMS	POST. REF.	CREDIT
				1957 Dec. 31		J42	1 10 40

Salary Expense ACCOUNT NO. 68

DATE	ITEMS	POST. REF.	DEBIT	DATE	ITEMS	POST. REF.	CREDIT
1957 Dec. 1	Balance	✓	9 3 0 8 50				
31		CP12	8 7 9 50				
31		J42	1 1 0 40				

The credit balance of the salaries payable account, $110.40, showed the amount that was owed by Mr. Cole for salaries on December 31. The debit balance of the salary expense account, $10,298.40, showed the total amount of the expense for salaries for the fiscal year ended December 31, 1957. This total included salaries already paid during this period, $10,188, and the accrued salaries for the last days at the end of the fiscal period, $110.40.

Interest expense owed but not paid. Each day that an interest-bearing note payable is owed, the amount of interest expense that is incurred is increased. Even though the note and the interest will not be paid until a future fiscal period, the amount of the interest that was incurred during the current fiscal period should appear on the financial reports.

On December 31, 1957, Mr. Cole's interest expense account in the general ledger appeared as shown below.

DATE	ITEMS	POST. REF.	DEBIT	DATE	ITEMS	POST. REF.	CREDIT
1957 Dec. 6		CP12	9 00				

Interest Expense — ACCOUNT NO. 82

The debit to the interest expense account represents interest expense that was paid on December 6, 1957, on a 3-month note for $600 that became due on that date.

On November 1, Mr. Cole had issued another note for $4,000. The note was for 90 days, with interest at the rate of 6%, and was due on January 30. The interest expense on this note, $40, for the months of November and December, which were in the fiscal year ended December 31, 1957, should be debited to the interest expense account on December 31 by means of an adjusting entry. The profit and loss statement will then show all the interest expense for the fiscal year ended December 31, 1957, even though some of it has not been paid.

Adjusting entry for accrued interest expense. Mr. Cole made the following adjusting entry for interest expense on December 31, 1957:

	ACCOUNTS PAYABLE DR.	GENERAL DR.	DATE	NAME OF ACCOUNT	POST. REF.	GENERAL CR.	ACCOUNTS RECEIVABLE CR.	
23		40 00	31	Interest Expense				23
24				Interest Payable		40 00		24
25								25
26								26
27								27

GENERAL JOURNAL — PAGE 42

Adjusting entry for accrued interest expense

The interest expense account was debited for $40 so that it would include the interest expense incurred but not paid during 1957. The liability account, Interest Payable, was credited for $40, the amount that Mr. Cole owed for interest on notes payable on December 31, 1957.

When this adjusting entry was posted, the interest payable account and the interest expense account in the general ledger appeared as follows:

Interest Payable   ACCOUNT NO. 22

DATE	ITEMS	POST. REF.	DEBIT	DATE	ITEMS	POST. REF.	CREDIT
				1957 Dec. 31		J42	40 00

Interest Expense   ACCOUNT NO. 82

DATE	ITEMS	POST. REF.	DEBIT	DATE	ITEMS	POST. REF.	CREDIT
1957 Dec. 6		CP12	9 00				
31		J42	40 00				

The credit balance of the interest payable account, $40, showed the amount that was owed by Mr. Cole for interest on December 31, 1957. The debit balance of the interest expense account, $49, showed the total amount of the interest expense for the fiscal period ended December 31, 1957. This total included the interest expense already paid during the fiscal period, $9, and the accrued interest expense at the end of the fiscal period, $40.

Other accrued expenses. If there are other expenses (such as taxes and miscellaneous expenses for electricity, telephones, etc.) that have accrued but that have not been paid at the end of a fiscal period, an adjusting entry is made for each one. An appropriate expense account should be debited and a liability account (a "payable" account) should be credited in each adjusting entry.

Accruals on the work sheet. The preceding discussion and illustrations have shown: (a) the need for adjusting entries for accrued expenses, (b) the method of recording these adjusting entries in the columnar general journal, and (c) the effect of these entries on the accounts in the general ledger. Before the adjusting entries for accrued expenses are recorded and posted, the work sheet and the statements are prepared.

When Mr. Cole prepared his work sheet on December 31, 1957, he made the following adjustments for accrued expenses in the Adjustments columns:

	ACCOUNT TITLES	ACCT. NO.	TRIAL BALANCE		ADJUSTMENTS	
			DEBIT	CREDIT	DEBIT	CREDIT
23	Salary Expense	68	10188 00		(d) 110 40	
24	State Unemployment Taxes	69	275 08			
25	Interest Expense	81	9 00		(h) 40 00	
26			98693 47	98693 47		
27	Bad Debts Expense	61			(a) 210 83	
28	Salaries Payable	24				(d) 110 40
29	Supplies Expense	611			(e) 438 17	
30	Insurance Expense	64			(f) 240 00	
31	Depreciation Expense	62			(g) 325 50	
32	Interest Payable	22				(h) 40 00
33					8652 9 40	8652 9 40
34						
35						

Work sheet showing adjustments for accrued expenses

Effect of accrued expenses on the profit and loss statement. The adjusting entries for accrued expenses increase the balances of the expense accounts concerned. For example, the adjusting entry for accrued salary expense increases the balance of the salary expense account by $110.40, An accrued expense, therefore, appears on the profit and loss statement as a part of the balance of the expense account.

When Mr. Cole prepared his profit and loss statement on December 31, 1957, the balance of the salary expense account, which included the salary expense accrued on that date, was listed in the Operating Expenses section in the manner illustrated on page 310.

The balance of the interest expense account, which included the accrued interest expense, was listed in the Other Expenses section of the profit and loss statement in the manner illustrated on page 375.

Accruals on the balance sheet. When Mr. Cole prepared his balance sheet, the liabilities — Interest Payable and Salaries Payable — were listed in the Current Liabilities section of the balance sheet. This section of Mr. Cole's balance sheet for December 31, 1957, is shown in the illustration at the top of the following page.

Liabilities						
Current Liabilities:						
Notes Payable			4000 00			
Interest Payable			40 00			
Accounts Payable			2426 33			
Salaries Payable			110 40			
Employees Income Taxes Payable			113 40			
FICA Taxes Payable			114 62			
State Unemployment Taxes Payable			68 78			
Federal Unemployment Taxes Payable			30 56			
Total Current Liabilities					6904 09	

Current liabilities section of the balance sheet

Need for readjusting the salary expense account. When Mr. Cole makes the entry for the next payroll on January 3, 1958, he will debit the entire amount to Salary Expense in the same manner that he recorded the payment of each payroll in 1957. But the salaries for only the first days of January should be shown as an expense for the fiscal year 1958. This result can be obtained by recording a reversing entry at the beginning of the 1958 fiscal period. A journal entry made at the beginning of a new fiscal period to reverse an adjusting entry that was recorded at the end of the preceding period is called a *reversing entry.*

Reversing entry for accrued salaries. On January 2, 1958, Mr. Cole made the following entry to readjust the salary expense account:

	ACCOUNTS PAYABLE DR.	GENERAL DR.	DATE	NAME OF ACCOUNT	POST. REF.	GENERAL CR.	ACCOUNTS RECEIVABLE CR.	
1				Reversing Entries				1
2		110 40	1957 Jan. 2	Salaries Payable				2
3				Salary Expense		110 40		3

Reversing entry for accrued salaries

Through this entry Salaries Payable was debited for $110.40, the amount of the accrued salary expense for the preceding fiscal period, the year 1957. Salary Expense was credited for the same amount. This reversing entry is exactly the opposite of the adjusting entry for accrued salary expense recorded on December 31, 1957.

The reversing entry was posted to Salaries Payable and to Salary Expense. The salaries payable account was then in balance and was ruled. The accounts after the completion of this work appeared as follows:

Salaries Payable ACCOUNT NO. 24

DATE	ITEMS	POST. REF.	DEBIT	DATE	ITEMS	POST. REF.	CREDIT
1958 Jan. 2		J1	1 10 40	1957 Dec. 31		J42	1 10 40

Salary Expense ACCOUNT NO. 68

DATE	ITEMS	POST. REF.	DEBIT	DATE	ITEMS	POST. REF.	CREDIT
1957 Dec. 1	Balance	✓	930 8 50	1957 Dec. 31		J43	1 029 8 40
31		CP12	87 9 50				
			1 01 88 00				
31		J42	1 10 40				
			1 02 98 40				1 029 8 40
				1958 Jan. 2		J1	1 10 40

The salaries payable account was in balance. The salary expense account had a credit balance of $110.40, the amount of the salaries incurred but not paid in 1957.

During January, 1958, Mr. Cole paid salaries on January 3, 10, 17, 24, and 31. When the total of the Salary Expense Debit column in the cash payments journal was posted on January 31, the salary expense account in the general ledger appeared as follows:

Salary Expense ACCOUNT NO. 68

DATE	ITEMS	POST. REF.	DEBIT	DATE	ITEMS	POST. REF.	CREDIT
1957 Dec. 1	Balance	✓	930 8 50	1957 Dec. 31		J43	1 029 8 40
31		CP12	87 9 50				
			1 01 88 00				
31		J42	1 10 40				
			1 02 98 40				1 029 8 40
1958 Jan. 31		CP1	1 05 8 50	1958 Jan. 2		J1	1 10 40

The credit of $110.40 in the salary expense account is the part of the January salary payments that belongs to the preceding year. The balance of the salary expense account, $948.10, is the part of the January salary payments that is actually an expense for 1958.

Need for readjusting the interest expense account. The 90-day, 6% note for $4,000 issued by Mr. Cole on November 1, 1957, is due on January 30, 1958. When Mr. Cole pays this note and the interest on it, he will debit the entire amount of the interest to Interest Expense. But the interest for only one month, January, should be shown as an expense for

Chapter 30. Accrued expenses 385

the fiscal year 1958. This result can be obtained by recording a reversing entry at the beginning of the 1958 fiscal period.

Reversing entry for accrued interest expense. On January 2, 1958, Mr. Cole made the following reversing entry to readjust the interest expense account:

			GENERAL JOURNAL			PAGE 1	
ACCOUNTS PAYABLE DR.	GENERAL DR.	DATE	NAME OF ACCOUNT	POST. REF.	GENERAL CR.	ACCOUNTS RECEIVABLE CR.	
4		40 00	2 Interest Payable				4
5			Interest Expense		40 00		5

Reversing entry for accrued interest expense

Through this entry Interest Payable was debited for $40, the amount of the accrued interest expense for the preceding fiscal period, the year 1957. Interest Expense was credited for the same amount. This reversing entry is exactly the opposite of the adjusting entry for accrued interest expense recorded on December 31, 1957.

The reversing entry was posted to Interest Payable and to Interest Expense. The interest payable account was then in balance and was ruled. The accounts after the completion of this work appeared as follows:

Interest Payable — ACCOUNT NO. 22

DATE	ITEMS	POST. REF.	DEBIT	DATE	ITEMS	POST. REF.	CREDIT
1958 Jan. 2		J1	40 00	1957 Dec. 31		J42	40 00

Interest Expense — ACCOUNT NO. 82

DATE	ITEMS	POST. REF.	DEBIT	DATE	ITEMS	POST. REF.	CREDIT
1957 Dec. 6		CP12	9 00	1957 Dec. 31		J43	49 00
31		J42	40 00				
			49 00				49 00
				1958 Jan. 2		J1	40 00

The interest payable account was in balance. The interest expense account had a credit balance of $40, the amount of the interest expense incurred but not paid in 1957.

No additional notes payable were issued prior to January 30, 1958. On January 30, Mr. Cole issued a check for $4,060 in payment of his

$4,000 note and 90 days' interest, $60. This entry was recorded in the columnar cash payments journal as follows:

						1	2	3	4	5	6	7	
	DATE	CHK. NO.	ACCOUNT DEBITED	POST. REF.	GENERAL DR.	ACCOUNTS PAYABLE DR.	SALARY EXPENSE DR.	EMPLOYEES INCOME TAX PAY. CR.	FICA TAXES PAY. CR.	DISCOUNT ON PURCHASES CR.	CASH CR.	
30	30	85	Notes Payable		4000 00							4060 00	30
31			Interest Expense		60 00								31

CASH PAYMENTS JOURNAL — PAGE 1

Payment of a note payable and interest

After this entry was posted, the interest expense account appeared as follows:

Interest Expense — ACCOUNT NO. 82

DATE	ITEMS	POST. REF.	DEBIT	DATE	ITEMS	POST. REF.	CREDIT
1957 Dec. 6		CP12	9 00	1957 Dec. 31		J43	49 00
31		J42	40 00				
			49 00				
			49 00				49 00
1958 Jan. 31		CP2	60 00	1958 Jan. 2		J1	40 00

The debit entry in the interest expense account shows the interest expense, $60, that was paid on January 30. The credit entry in this account, $40, shows the part of this payment that belongs to the preceding fiscal year. The balance of the interest expense account, $20, represents the part of the $60 interest payment that belongs to the fiscal year 1958.

Accrued income. Income that is earned in one fiscal period but collected in a later fiscal period is called *accrued income*. Examples of accrued income are interest income and rent income. Each accrued income must be recorded before the reports are prepared at the end of the fiscal period so that the profit and loss statement will be complete and accurate.

The adjusting entry for any accrued income requires a debit to an asset account (a "receivable" account) and a credit to an income account. For example, an adjusting entry for interest accrued on notes receivable debits Interest Receivable and credits Interest Income.

The reversing entry for any accrued income requires a credit to an asset account (a "receivable" account) and a debit to an income account. For example, a reversing entry for interest accrued on notes receivable debits Interest Income and credits Interest Receivable.

CHAPTER QUESTIONS

1. Why should expenses that have been incurred but not paid be recorded before the reports are prepared at the end of the fiscal period?
2. What entry is made in the columnar general journal on page 380 to record the adjusting entry for accrued salaries?
3. What entry is made in the columnar general journal on page 381 to record the adjusting entry for accrued interest expense?
4. Under what heading of the profit and loss statement is the balance of the salary expense account listed?
5. Under what heading of the profit and loss statement is the balance of the interest expense account listed?
6. Under what heading of the balance sheet are the balances of the interest payable and salaries payable accounts listed?
7. Why is it desirable to record a reversing entry for salaries payable at the beginning of each fiscal period?
8. What reversing entry is made in the columnar general journal on page 384 to readjust the salary expense account?
9. What reversing entry is made in the columnar general journal on page 386 to readjust the interest expense account?
10. What adjusting entry is made to adjust an accrued income account?
11. What reversing entry is made to readjust an accrued income account?

INCREASING YOUR BUSINESS VOCABULARY

What is the meaning of each of the following:
(a) accrued expenses   (b) reversing entry   (c) accrued income

CASES FOR DISCUSSION

1. At the end of the fiscal period the bookkeeper for the Royal Manufacturing Company failed to record a liability of $200 arising from accrued salaries. What effect did this omission have (a) on the profit and loss statement and (b) on the balance sheet?
2. After L. C. Russell closed his books on March 31, his ledger included two liability accounts, Salaries Payable and Interest Payable. All of the salaries payable will be paid within three days after the beginning of the next fiscal period. The interest payable has accrued on five notes that will come due on different dates during the next period. For which of these two liabilities will a reversing entry be more beneficial?
3. Paul Robinson, the manager of a weekly newspaper, does not record accruals at the end of each fiscal period. He believes his method is satisfactory because receipts and payments are approximately uniform from year to year. What are the disadvantages of this method?

APPLICATION PROBLEMS

Problem 30-1. Adjusting and reversing entries for accrued interest and salaries

If you are not using the workbook correlating with this textbook, complete Exercise 30-A in the Appendix instead of this problem.

C. F. Archer is a wholesale plumbing supply dealer. His interest payable, salaries payable, salary expense, and interest expense accounts are given in the workbook as they appeared in his general ledger at the end of the fiscal year ended December 31, 1957, before the reports were prepared.

Instructions: 1. Record in a columnar general journal as of December 31, 1957, the adjusting entries for the following accrued expenses:

Accrued interest, $28.76   Accrued salaries, $216.90

2. Post the adjusting entries for accrued expenses. The accounts affected are Interest Payable, Salaries Payable, Salary Expense, and Interest Expense.

3. Record in the columnar general journal the entry required to close the expense accounts. The balances of the expense accounts are as follows:

Sales Returns and Allowances, $187.50   Salary Expense (see ledger account)
Discount on Sales, $163.48   State Unemployment Taxes, $120.04
Purchases, $40,639.67   Interest Expense (see ledger account)
Transportation on Purchases, $914.68   Bad Debts Expense, $117.50
FICA Taxes, $100.04   Supplies Expense, $931.06
Federal Unemployment Taxes, $13.34   Insurance Expense, $248
Miscellaneous Expense, $747.33   Depreciation Expense, $570
Rent Expense, $2,700

4. Post the closing entry recorded to close the expense accounts. Since only the accounts with interest expense and salary expense are given in the workbook, you will assume that all of the other parts of this entry have been posted.

5. Rule the expense accounts.

6. Record in the columnar general journal as of January 2, 1958, the reversing entries for the accrued interest expense and the accrued salary expense.

7. Post the reversing entries. The accounts affected are Interest Payable, Salaries Payable, Salary Expense, and Interest Expense.

8. Rule the liability accounts.

Problem 30-2. Work at the end of the fiscal period

The work sheet shown on the following page was prepared by Thomas Egan, proprietor of a retail dry goods store, on December 31 of the current year.

Instructions: 1. Prepare a profit and loss statement and a balance sheet from the work sheet.

2. Record the adjusting and the closing entries in a columnar general journal.

3. Record the reversing entries for accruals as of January 2 of next year in a columnar general journal.

THOMAS EGAN

WORK SHEET

FOR YEAR ENDED DECEMBER 31, 19--

	1	2	3	4	5	6	7	8
	TRIAL BALANCE		ADJUSTMENTS		PROFIT & LOSS STATEMENT		BALANCE SHEET	
ACCOUNT TITLES	DEBIT	CREDIT	DEBIT	CREDIT	DEBIT	CREDIT	DEBIT	CREDIT
Cash	4862 48						4862 48	
Accounts Receivable	8615 40						8615 40	
Allow. for Bad Debts		368 15		(a) 206 80				574 95
Merchandise Inv	22648 82		(c) 23906 19	(b) 22648 82			23906 19	
Supplies	2110 55			(d) 1549 70			560 85	
Prepaid Insurance	636 00			(e) 424 00			212 00	
Equipment	5137 50						5137 50	
Allow. for Depr. of Equip		613 49		(f) 256 88				870 37
Building	10000 00						10000 00	
Allowance for Depr. of Building		3400 00		(g) 200 00				3600 00
Notes Payable		4000 00						4000 00
Accounts Payable		5233 75						5233 75
Employees Inc. Taxes Payable		205 50						205 50
FICA Taxes Pay		122 85						122 85
State Unemp. Tax. Pay		76 14						76 14
Fed. Unemp. Tax. Pay		32 76						32 76
Thomas Egan, Capital		37505 93						37505 93
Thomas Egan, Draw	3600 00						3600 00	
Sales		71347 32				71347 32		
Sales Rets. and Allow	2755 84				2755 84			
Purchases	43061 36				43061 36			
Pur. Ret. and Allow		566 40				566 40		
Discount on Purchases		671 90				671 90		
Transportation on Pur	987 35				987 35			
Advertising Expense	1875 00				1875 00			
Delivery Expense	3710 60				3710 60			
FICA Taxes	245 70				245 70			
Fed. Unemp. Taxes	32 76				32 76			
Heat, Light, & Power	1953 27				1953 27			
Miscellaneous Expense	524 58				524 58			
Salary Expense	10920 00		(i) 120 00		11040 00			
State Unemp. Taxes	294 84				294 84			
Interest Expense	172 14		(h) 20 00		192 14			
	124144 19	124144 19						
Bad Debts Expense			(a) 206 80		206 80			
Profit & Loss Summary			(b) 22648 82	(c) 23906 19	22648 82	23906 19		
Supplies Expense			(d) 1549 70		1549 70			
Insurance Expense			(e) 424 00		424 00			
Depreciation of Equip			(f) 256 88		256 88			
Depreciation of Bldg			(g) 200 00		200 00			
Interest Payable				(h) 20 00				20 00
Salaries Payable				(i) 120 00				120 00
			49332 39	49332 39	91959 64	96491 81	56894 42	52362 25
Net Profit					4532 17			4532 17
					96491 81	96491 81	56894 42	56894 42

Partnerships

Purpose of a partnership. Many businesses require more capital than one individual is able to furnish. In such a case two or more persons may combine their assets to provide the necessary capital. Often the responsibility of managing a business may profitably be divided among two or more owners. The owners may then combine their skills as well as their assets under an agreement to share the profits and the losses.

When two or more persons combine their property or their skill or both in one business and agree to share in the profits or the losses, the business is referred to as a *partnership*. Each member of the partnership is known as a *partner*. Partnerships are common in retail stores, in personal services businesses, and among professional men such as lawyers, doctors, and accountants.

A partnership is similar to a single proprietorship, except that in the single proprietorship one person is the owner, while in the partnership two or more persons share in the ownership.

Organization of a partnership. A partnership is formed by an agreement or contract between the partners. This agreement may be oral, but it is desirable to have it in writing to avoid any misunderstandings that might arise from oral agreements. The written agreement by which a partnership is formed is commonly referred to as the *articles of copartnership*.

The articles of copartnership ordinarily show the names of the partners, the reasons for the formation of the partnership, the length of time that the partnership is to run, and the name and the location of the business. It is especially important that the agreement state clearly the amount of the investment of each partner, the part of the partnership property each partner owns, the duties of each partner, the limitations on each partner's activities, and the provisions for the distribution of profits and losses. The illustration on the next page contains the usual information included in a partnership agreement.

Partnership accounts. As in a single proprietorship, the number of accounts in the general ledger of a partnership depends upon the kind of

ARTICLES OF COPARTNERSHIP

THIS CONTRACT, made and entered into on the first day of November, 1957, by and between Arthur F. Poultney, of Butte, Montana, and David D. Duane, of the same city and state.

WITNESSETH: That the said parties have this day formed a copartnership for the purpose of engaging in and conducting a wholesale drug supply business in the city of Butte under the following stipulations, which are a part of this contract:

FIRST: The said copartnership is to continue for a term of ten years from November 1, 1957.

SECOND: The business is to be conducted under the firm name of Acme Drug Supply Company, at 827 Main Street, Butte, Montana.

THIRD: The investments are as follows: Arthur F. Poultney, cash, $15,000; David D. Duane, cash, $15,000. These invested assets are partnership property in which the equity of each partner is the same.

FOURTH: Each partner is to devote his entire time and attention to the business and to engage in no other business enterprise without the written consent of the other partner.

FIFTH: During the operation of this partnership, neither partner is to become surety or bondsman for anyone without the written consent of the other partner.

SIXTH: Each partner is to receive a salary of $3,000 a year, payable $250 in cash on the last business day of each month. At the end of each annual fiscal period the net profit or the net loss shown by the profit and loss statement, after the salaries of the two partners have been allowed, is to be shared as follows: Arthur F. Poultney, 60 per cent; David D. Duane, 40 per cent.

SEVENTH: Neither partner is to withdraw assets in excess of his salary, any part of the assets invested, or assets in anticipation of profits to be earned, without the written consent of the other partner.

EIGHTH: In case of the death or the legal disability of either partner, the other partner is to continue the operations of the business until the close of the annual fiscal period on the following December 31. At that time the continuing partner is to be given an option to buy the interest of the deceased or incapacitated partner at not more than 10 per cent above the value of the deceased or incapacitated partner's proprietary interest as shown by the balance of his capital account after the books are closed on December 31. It is agreed that this purchase price is to be paid one half in cash and the balance in four equal installments payable quarterly.

NINTH: At the conclusion of this contract, unless it is mutually agreed to continue the operation of the business under a new contract, the assets of the partnership, after the liabilities are paid, are to be divided in proportion to the net credit to each partner's capital account on that date.

IN WITNESS WHEREOF, the parties aforesaid have hereunto set their hands and affixed their seals on the day and year above written.

Arthur F. Poultney   (Seal)

David D. Duane   (Seal)

Articles of copartnership

business and the information desired. Since two or more persons share in the ownership of a partnership, separate capital accounts should be maintained for each partner. The capital account of each partner should show his share in the business, that is, the value of his ownership.

A separate drawing account should also be maintained for each partner in order to record the withdrawals of cash and merchandise by each partner. At the end of the fiscal period the drawing accounts should be debited for losses or credited for profits of the business in the manner stated in the partnership agreement.

Forming a partnership with cash investments. The opening entries of a partnership are similar to the opening entries of a single proprietorship. Ordinarily a separate entry is made to record the investment of each partner.

The illustration on the preceding page shows the articles of copartnership drawn up by A. F. Poultney and D. D. Duane when they formed a partnership to begin a wholesale drug supply business on November 1. Each partner invested $15,000 in cash. To record the investment of each partner, the following entries were made in the columnar cash receipts journal.

	DATE	ACCOUNT CREDITED	POST. REF.	GENERAL CR.	SALES CR.	ACCOUNTS RECEIVABLE CR.	DISCOUNT ON SALES DR.	CASH DR.	
				1	2	3	4	5	
1	1957 Nov. 1	A. F. Poultney, Capital		1500000				1500000	1
2		D. D. Duane, Capital		1500000				1500000	2

Cash investments of a partnership recorded in a cash receipts journal

Converting a single proprietorship business into a partnership. An established business operated by one owner may be converted into a partnership by a merger with another business or by the investment of cash or other assets by another person.

L. K. Holmes operated a supply business. On January 2 he formed a partnership with F. G. Harris. Mr. Holmes invested the assets of his business, and the partnership assumed the liabilities of his business. Mr. Harris invested $10,000 in cash.

The new partnership, Holmes and Harris, decided to open a new set of books. The investment of each partner was recorded with an opening entry in the columnar general journal. The two opening entries as they appeared in the columnar general journal on January 2, 1958, are shown at the top of the following page.

	ACCOUNTS PAYABLE DR.	GENERAL DR.	DATE	NAME OF ACCOUNT	POST. REF.	GENERAL CR.	ACCOUNTS RECEIVABLE CR.	
1		765 50	1958 Jan. 2	Cash				1
2		3422 00		Accounts Receivable				2
3		20885 00		Merchandise Inventory				3
4		450 00		Supplies				4
5		5300 00		Equipment				5
6				Accounts Payable		822 50		6
7				L. K. Holmes, Capital		30000 00		7
8				Investment.				8
9		10000 00	2	Cash				9
10				F. F. Harris, Capital		10000 00		10
11				Investment				11

Opening entries for a partnership recorded in a columnar general journal

The cash investments of the partners are not recorded in the cash receipts journal, as the amount of the cash is posted directly from the general journal. The amount of cash is, however, entered in the Account Credited column on the first line of the cash receipts journal as a balance for use in proving cash. The cash receipts journal of Holmes and Harris with the balance entered is shown below.

	DATE	ACCOUNT CREDITED	POST. REF.	GENERAL CR.	SALES CR.	ACCOUNTS RECEIVABLE CR.	DISCOUNT ON SALES DR.	CASH DR.	
1	1958 Jan. 2	Balance on hand, $10,765.50	✓						1

Beginning cash balance of a partnership recorded in a cash receipts journal

Recording an investment in a going concern. When a going concern of a single proprietorship is converted into a partnership, it may be agreed that the books of the original business are to be continued. It is only necessary then to record the investment of the new partner. This may be done by debiting the asset accounts for the assets invested, crediting the liability accounts for the liabilities assumed, and crediting the new partner's capital account for the net amount of his investment.

Partners' salaries. In the partnership of Holmes and Harris, Mr. Holmes had been operating a supply business for several years. Mr. Harris was a young man with no experience in the supply business. The articles of copartnership therefore provided that Mr. Holmes was to receive a monthly salary of $450 and Mr. Harris a monthly salary of $300.

The federal income tax and social security tax regulations do not recognize the salaries of partners as an expense of the business. The salaries are really withdrawals of profits. They should therefore be debited to the drawing account of each partner whenever they are taken from the business.

When the salaries were paid to Mr. Holmes and Mr. Harris at the end of January, L. K. Holmes, Drawing was debited for $450 and F. G. Harris, Drawing was debited for $300. Corresponding credits were made to Cash. The entries in the cash payments journal to record the payment of salaries are shown below.

CASH PAYMENTS JOURNAL PAGE 1

	DATE	CHK. NO.	ACCOUNT DEBITED	POST. REF.	GENERAL DR.	ACCOUNTS PAYABLE DR.	SALARY EXPENSE DR.	EMPLOYEES INCOME TAX PAY. CR.	FICA TAXES PAY. CR.	DISCOUNT ON PURCHASES CR.	CASH CR.	
28	31	28	L. K. Holmes, Drawing		450 00						450 00	28
29	31	29	F. G. Harris, Drawing		300 00						300 00	29
30												30
31												31
32												32
33												33
34												34

Payments of partners' salaries recorded in a cash payments journal

Similar entries were made at the end of each month when the salaries were paid to the partners. At the end of the year, therefore, the drawing account of Mr. Holmes showed a debit balance of $5,400, his total salary for the year. The drawing account of Mr. Harris showed a debit balance of $3,600, his total salary for the year. The net profit for the year was divided between the two partners and was credited to their drawing accounts.

Division of profits or losses. The articles of copartnership provided that the profits or the losses of the business after the salaries had been paid were to be shared in proportion to the partners' original investments. The total investment in the partnership was $40,000. Mr. Holmes had invested $30,000, or three fourths of the total; he was therefore entitled to three fourths of the profits (or the losses) after the partners' salaries had been paid. Mr. Harris had invested $10,000, or one fourth of the total, and was entitled to one fourth of the profits (or the losses) after the partners' salaries had been paid.

Partnership profits and losses may be divided in any way desired by the partners. The method of division is ordinarily stated in the articles of copartnership. If the partnership agreement does not state how the profits and the losses are to be divided, it is assumed by law that the profits and the losses are to be shared equally.

On December 31, the end of the fiscal year, the net profit earned by the partnership of Holmes and Harris was $12,000. Each partner's share of the profits was determined as follows:

Net profit..		$12,000.00
Less salaries of partners:		
L. K. Holmes...............................	$5,400.00	
F. G. Harris................................	3,600.00	9,000.00
Remainder of profits for distribution...............		$ 3,000.00

Division of remaining profit:
L. K. Holmes — ¾ of $3,000.00 = $2,250.00
F. G. Harris — ¼ of $3,000.00 = 750.00

Summary:	
L. K. Holmes — Salary.....................................	$ 5,400.00
¾ of remainder after salaries...............	2,250.00
Total.....................................	$ 7,650.00
F. G. Harris — Salary.....................................	$ 3,600.00
¼ of remainder after salaries...............	750.00
Total.....................................	$ 4,350.00

Profit and loss statement of a partnership. The profit and loss statement prepared by Holmes and Harris on December 31, 1958, showed the distribution of net profit to the partners. This profit and loss statement is illustrated on the next page.

Except for the Distribution of Net Profit section, the profit and loss statement of a partnership is similar to that of a single proprietorship. Note that the Distribution of Net Profit section of the profit and loss statement shows: (1) the salary of each partner for the year, (2) each partner's share of the remaining profits, and (3) each partner's total share of the net profit.

Balance sheet of a partnership. The balance sheet prepared by Holmes and Harris on December 31, 1958, showed the changes that took place in the proprietorship. This balance sheet is illustrated on page 398.

Note that the balance sheet of a partnership is similar to that of a single proprietorship except that the proprietorship of each partner is shown. The proprietorship section of the balance sheet shows: (1) the capital of each partner as it was before the report was prepared, (2) each partner's total share of the net profit less his withdrawals for the year, (3) each partner's net increase in capital, and (4) each partner's present capital as of the date of the report.

HOLMES AND HARRIS
Profit and Loss Statement
For Year Ended December 31, 1958

Income from Sales:
Sales $95,204.03
Less: Sales Returns and Allowances . $ 735.46
Discount on Sales 477.48 1,212.94
Net Sales $93,991.09

Cost of Merchandise Sold:
Merchandise Inventory, Jan. 1, 1958 . $21,432.25
Purchases $71,627.61
Less: Purchases Ret.& Allow.$ 740.82
Discount on Purchases. 1,196.87 1,937.69
Net Purchases. $69,689.92
Add Transportation on Purchases. . . 1,628.19
Net Cost of Merchandise Purchased . . 71,318.11
Total Cost of Mdse. Available for Sale. $92,750.36
Less Mdse. Inventory, Dec. 31, 1958 . 23,194.85
Cost of Merchandise Sold 69,555.51

Gross Profit on Sales. $24,435.58

Operating Expenses:
Bad Debts Expense . . . . $ 285.68
Delivery Expense. 1,600.82
Depreciation Expense 975.00
FICA Taxes. 158.89
Federal Unemployment Taxes 20.78
Insurance Expense 248.00
Miscellaneous Expense 832.69
Property Taxes 535.20
Salary Expense 7,061.75
State Unemployment Taxes 187.02
Supplies Expense. 356.29
Total Operating Expenses 12,262.12

Net Profit from Operations $12,173.46

Other Income:
Interest Income . . . . $ 72.16

Other Expense:
Interest Expense. 245.62

Net Deduction . . . 173.46

Net Profit $12,000.00

Distribution of Net Profit:
L. K. Holmes:
Salary . . . . $ 5,400.00
3/4 of Remaining Profit. . . . 2,250.00
Total Share of Profit . . . . $ 7,650.00

F. G. Harris:
Salary . . . . $ 3,600.00
1/4 of Remaining Profit. . . . 750.00
Total Share of Profit 4,350.00

Net Profit $12,000.00

Profit and loss statement of a partnership showing the distribution of profit

HOLMES AND HARRIS
Balance Sheet
December 31, 1958

Assets

Current Assets:

Cash		$ 3,983.22
Petty Cash		50.00
Notes Receivable		3,100.00
Accounts Receivable	$ 5,582.37	
Less Allowance for Bad Debts . .	267.37	5,315.00
Merchandise Inventory.		21,422.34
Supplies		459.58
Prepaid Insurance		376.00
Total Current Assets		$34,706.14

Fixed Assets:

Equipment.	$ 5,300.00		
Less Allow. for Depr. of Equipment	795.00	$ 4,505.00	
Building	$ 9,000.00		
Less Allow. for Depr. of Building.	180.00	8,820.00	
Total Fixed Assets.			13,325.00

Total Assets $48,031.14

Liabilities

Current Liabilities:

Notes Payable		$ 2,000.00
Interest Payable		18.00
Accounts Payable		2,562.12
Salaries Payable		135.25
Employees Income Taxes Payable. .		168.80
FICA Taxes Payable.		79.44
State Unemployment Taxes Payable .		46.75
Federal Unemployment Taxes Payable		20.78
Total Current Liabilities . . .		$ 5,031.14

Proprietorship

L. K. Holmes:

Capital		$30,000.00	
Share of Net Profit . .	$7,650.00		
Less Withdrawals . .	5,400.00		
Net Increase in Capital		2,250.00	
Present Capital.		$32,250.00	

F. G. Harris:

Capital		$10,000.00	
Share of Net Profit . .	$4,350.00		
Less Withdrawals . .	3,600.00		
Net Increase in Capital		750.00	
Present Capital.		10,750.00	

Total Proprietorship. 43,000.00

Total Liabilities and Proprietorship . . $48,031.14

**Balance sheet of a partnership showing the changes in proprietorship
during the preceding fiscal period**

Adjusting and closing entries for a partnership. The adjusting entries and the closing entries of a partnership are similar to those of a single proprietorship type of business. The adjusting entries are recorded in the columnar general journal. The Adjustments columns of the work sheet are used as the basis for the adjusting entries. The closing entries are also recorded in the columnar general journal. The P. & L. Statement columns of the work sheet are used as the basis for the closing entries.

In making the closing entries, it is customary to make separate entries for the partners' salaries and for the distribution of the remainder of the net profit (or loss). When the closing entries for the partnership are posted, each partner's drawing account will indicate the entire distribution of profits (or losses).

On December 31, 1958, the end of the fiscal year, the following entries were made to close the profit and loss summary account into the drawing accounts:

	ACCOUNTS PAYABLE DR.	GENERAL DR.	DATE	NAME OF ACCOUNT	POST. REF.	GENERAL CR.	ACCOUNTS RECEIVABLE CR.	
	1	2				3	4	
24		9000 00	31	Profit and Loss Summary				24
25				L. K. Holmes, Drawing		5400 00		25
26				F. G. Harris, Drawing		3600 00		26
27		3000 00	31	Profit and Loss Summary				27
28				L. K. Holmes, Drawing		2250 00		28
29				F. G. Harris, Drawing		750 00		29
30								30
31								31
32								32
33								33
34								34

GENERAL JOURNAL   PAGE *17*

Closing entries for a partnership recorded in a columnar general journal

When these entries were posted, the profit and loss summary account was closed. Mr. Holmes's drawing account had a credit balance of $2,250 and Mr. Harris' drawing account had a credit balance of $750. These two accounts then appeared as follows:

L. K. HOLMES, DRAWING		F. G. HARRIS, DRAWING	
5,400.00	5,400.00	3,600.00	3,600.00
	2,250.00		750.00

CHAPTER QUESTIONS

1. What is the purpose of a partnership?
2. Why should the partnership agreement be in writing?
3. What are the principal provisions of the partnership agreement on page 392?
4. How do the accounts in the general ledger of a partnership differ from those of a single proprietorship?
5. Why are not the salaries allowed each partner considered a business expense?
6. What accounts are debited in the cash payments journal on page 395 to record the payment of partners' salaries?
7. After partners' salaries are deducted, how may the remainder of the net profits be divided?
8. How does the profit and loss statement of a partnership differ from the profit and loss statement of a single proprietorship?
9. How does the balance sheet of a partnership differ from the balance sheet of a single proprietorship?
10. Why are two closing entries made to close the profit and loss summary account when the partners receive definite salaries?

INCREASING YOUR BUSINESS VOCABULARY

What is the meaning of each of the following:

(a) partnership   (b) partner   (c) articles of copartnership

CASES FOR DISCUSSION

1. The partnership of Nixon, Hakes, and Spears, dentists, allows each partner a monthly salary of $300. The salaries are debited to the drawing account of each partner when they are paid at the end of each month. Doctor Spears believes that the salaries should be considered an operating expense and should be debited to a partners' salaries account. Explain to Doctor Spears why his recommendation is not good accounting practice.

2. For the past thirty-five years Donald Powers has operated a large mercantile store. He has decided to offer a partnership to David Ambler, a young man without capital and without much store experience. How may the partnership profits be divided so as to recognize (a) differences in business experience and (b) differences in investment?

Problem 31-1. **Opening entries for investment of cash and other assets in a partnership**

On August 1 of the current year, Louis Harvey and Daniel Lynn formed a partnership for the purpose of continuing a retail music store that Mr. Harvey had been operating. The partnership, Harvey & Lynn, took over the assets of Mr. Harvey's business and assumed his liabilities. Mr. Lynn invested cash equal to Mr. Harvey's proprietorship. The balance sheet of Louis Harvey appeared as shown below.

LOUIS HARVEY

BALANCE SHEET

JULY 31, 19--

Assets			Liabilities		
Cash.................	3,633	60	Notes Payable...........	3,000	00
Notes Receivable........	560	00	Accounts Payable........	1,763	09
Accounts Receivable.....	2,126	75	Total Liabilities..........	4,763	09
Merchandise Inventory...	7,930	57			
Supplies...............	388	62			
Equipment.............	2,395	40	*Proprietorship*		
			Louis Harvey, Capital.....	12,271	85
Total Assets............	17,034	94	Total Liab. and Prop......	17,034	94

Instructions: Record the opening entry for each partner in a columnar general journal and record the cash balance in a columnar cash receipts journal.

Problem 31-2. Distribution of net profits of a partnership

R. Kirby, D. Tracy, and S. Holmes were partners engaged in operating a detective agency. The partners had invested in the business $8,000, $7,000, and $5,000 respectively.

According to the partnership agreement, each partner is to receive a salary of $3,000 a year, and all profits remaining after the salaries have been paid are to be divided according to the original investments of each partner.

At the end of the current fiscal period on December 31 the profit and loss statement showed that the net profit for the year had been $11,000.

Instructions: *1.* Prepare the portion of the profit and loss statement showing the distribution of the net profit.

2. Prepare the proprietorship section of the balance sheet, assuming that the partners withdrew their salaries but did not withdraw any additional amounts.

Problem 31-3. Opening entries for cash investments in a partnership

On May 1 of the current year, Henry Osborn and John Harmon formed a partnership to begin a haberdashery business. Each partner invested $5,000 in cash.

Instructions: Record the opening entry for each partner in a columnar cash receipts journal.

Problem 31-4. Work at the end of the fiscal period

The account balances in the general ledger of Grant and Grey, partners in a household furnishings business, on December 31 of the current year were as follows:

Cash, $2,448.18
Petty Cash, $50
Accounts Receivable, $3,505.66
Allowance for Bad Debts, $287.50
Merchandise Inventory, $14,961.49
Supplies, $293.60
Prepaid Insurance, $240
Equipment, $2,365.10
Allowance for Depreciation of Equipment, $581.80
Notes Payable, $1,000
Accounts Payable, $1,683.45
Employees Income Taxes Payable, $78.60
FICA Taxes Payable, $40.50
State Unemployment Taxes Payable, $24.30
C. A. Grant, Capital, $10,000

C. A. Grant, Drawing, $4,961.40 (Dr.)
J. N. Grey, Capital, $10,000
J. N. Grey, Drawing, $5,016.15 (Dr.)
Sales, $58,618.31
Sales Returns and Allowances, $396.14
Purchases, $40,665.07
Purchases Returns and Allowances, $185
Discount on Purchases, $423.82
Transportation on Purchases, $422.56
Delivery Expense, $1,380.48
FICA Taxes, $81
Miscellaneous Expense, $629.75
Rent Expense, $1,800
Salary Expense, $3,600
State Unemployment Taxes, $97.20
Interest Income, $9
Interest Expense, $18.50

Instructions: 1. Prepare an eight-column work sheet for the annual fiscal period ended December 31 of the current year. The additional data needed at the end of the annual fiscal period are:

Additional allowance for bad debts, 1% of charge sales of $20,731.16
Merchandise inventory, $16,723.40
Supplies inventory, $48.23
Prepaid insurance, $60
Annual rate of estimated depreciation of equipment, 5%
Accrued interest expense, $5
Accrued salary expense, $75

2. Prepare a profit and loss statement showing the distribution of profits. Mr. Grant receives a salary of $400 a month; Mr. Grey, $350 a month. Each partner shares equally in profits or losses after salaries have been taken out.

3. Prepare a balance sheet showing the changes in proprietorship.

4. Record the adjusting entries and the closing entries.

5. Record the reversing entries for the accruals as of January 2 of the next year.

Voss and Howard

Wholesale leather goods business

Purpose of this practice set. This bookkeeping practice set provides a review of the accounting principles discussed and illustrated in the preceding chapters. It includes all of the bookkeeping work for two months, November and December, of a wholesale leather goods business operated by John H. Voss and Charles R. Howard, partners.

Required materials. The records of this practice set may be completed from the *narrative of transactions* in this chapter or they may be made from the *business papers* that are available separate from the textbook. If the set with business papers is used, the transactions may be recorded in books that are provided with the papers. If the narrative of transactions in this textbook is used, the transactions may be recorded on loose sheets of ruled paper or in a set of bound blanks that may be obtained from the publisher.

The books and forms used in this practice set are as follows:

Books and Papers	*Models*
Cash Receipts Journal.............	Page 355
Cash Payments Journal...........	Page 357

The cash payments journal used in this set is exactly like the model on page 357 except that one additional column, Miscellaneous Expense Debit, is used immediately after the General Debit column.

General Journal..................	Page 360
Purchases Journal................	Page 121
Sales Journal....................	Page 150
General Ledger..................	Pages 242 to 244
Accounts Receivable Ledger........	Pages 168 to 170
Accounts Payable Ledger..........	Pages 137 and 138
Schedule of Accounts Receivable....	Page 167
Schedule of Accounts Payable.......	Page 140
Eight-Column Work Sheet..........	Pages 269, 306, 330, and 383
Profit and Loss Statement.........	Page 397
Balance Sheet....................	Page 398
Post-Closing Trial Balance..........	Page 245

General ledger. The general ledger accounts needed to record the transactions in this practice set are listed in the following chart of accounts:

Chart of Accounts for Voss and Howard

BALANCE SHEET ACCOUNTS

1 Assets

11 *Current Assets*
111   Cash
112   Petty Cash
113   Notes Receivable
114   Interest Receivable
115   Accounts Receivable
115.1 Allowance for Bad Debts
116   Merchandise Inventory
117   Supplies
118   Prepaid Insurance

12 *Fixed Assets*
121   Equipment
121.1 Allowance for Depreciation of Equipment

2 Liabilities

21 *Current Liabilities*
211   Notes Payable
212   Interest Payable
213   Accounts Payable
214   Employees Income Taxes Payable
215   FICA Taxes Payable
216   Federal Unemployment Taxes Payable
217   State Unemployment Taxes Payable
218   Property Taxes Payable

3 Proprietorship
311   John H. Voss, Capital
312   John H. Voss, Drawing
313   Charles R. Howard, Capital
314   Charles R. Howard, Drawing
315   Profit and Loss Summary

PROFIT AND LOSS STATEMENT ACCOUNTS

4 Operating Income

411   Sales
411.1 Sales Returns and Allowances
411.2 Discount on Sales

5 Cost of Merchandise

511   Purchases
511.1 Purchases Returns and Allowances
511.2 Discount on Purchases
512   Transportation on Purchases

6 Operating Expenses

611   Advertising Expense
612   Bad Debts Expense
613   Delivery Expense
614   Depreciation Expense
615   FICA Taxes
616   Federal Unemployment Taxes
617   Insurance Expense
618   Miscellaneous Expense
619   Property Taxes
6110   Rent Expense
6111   Salary Expense
6112   State Unemployment Taxes
6113   Supplies Expense

7 Other Income

711   Interest Income
712   Gain on Fixed Assets

8 Other Expense

811   Interest Expense
812   Loss on Fixed Assets

Instructions: 1. If you are using the blank books published for this set, the general ledger accounts are opened for you. Also the general ledger account balances are recorded.

If you do not have these blank books, proceed as follows:

(a) Write the account titles in the general ledger in the order in which they are given in the chart of accounts above. Use the account numbers indicated. If loose sheets (8½″ x 11″) are used, place two accounts on each page.

(b) Record the account balances shown on the trial balance below in the general ledger of Voss and Howard under date of October 31. A few accounts do not have balances, but they will be used in recording the transactions for the next two months.

VOSS AND HOWARD
Trial Balance
October 31, 19—

Cash	111	8652 18	
Petty Cash	112	100 00	
Notes Receivable	113	2600 00	
Accounts Receivable	115	4690 52	
Allowance for Bad Debts	115.1		476 30
Merchandise Inventory	116	39900 00	
Supplies	117	3104 10	
Prepaid Insurance	118	360 00	
Equipment	121	5500 00	
Allowance for Depreciation of Equip.	121.1		825 00
Notes Payable	211		1600 00
Accounts Payable	213		3988 92
Employees Income Taxes Payable	214		184 00
FICA Taxes Payable	215		90 00
Federal Unemployment Taxes Payable	216		51 48
State Unemployment Taxes Payable	217		54 00
John H. Voss, Capital	311		23400 00
John H. Voss, Drawing	312	8000 00	
Charles R. Howard, Capital	313		23400 00
Charles R. Howard, Drawing	314	7000 00	
Sales	411		236144 00
Sales Returns and Allowances	411.1	4122 00	
Discount on Sales	411.2	1570 00	
Purchases	511	177108 00	
Purchases Returns and Allowances	511.1		2133 00
Discount on Purchases	511.2		3165 80
Transportation on Purchases	512	2732 00	
Advertising Expense	611	2561 00	
Delivery Expense	613	1607 00	
FICA Taxes	615	386 10	
Federal Unemployment Taxes	616	51 48	
Miscellaneous Expense	618	1494 00	
Property Taxes	619	320 00	
Rent Expense	620	6000 00	
Salary Expense	621	17160 00	
State Unemployment Taxes	622	463 32	
Interest Income	711		183 80
Interest Expense	811	214 60	
		295696 30	295696 30

2. Enter the beginning cash balance in the Account Credited column of the cash receipts journal in the manner shown in the illustration on page 355.

This balance is not entered in an amount column of the cash receipts journal because it is not to be posted. It is, however, needed in the cash receipts journal for use in proving cash.

Accounts receivable ledger. A list of the customers of Voss and Howard is given below. This list contains (1) the name and the address of each customer and (2) the amount of each unpaid invoice.

Name and Address	Amount
Benton Gift Shop, 696 Erie Ave., Buffalo	
Ferris & Sutton, 2945 Elberon Ave., Dayton	
Gaynor Leather Shop, 3526 Broadway, Akron	
Haynes & Haynes, 5292 Walnut St., Erie	
Jackson & Potter, 2156 Main St., Pittsburgh	
Mitchell Luggage, 1492 Parkway, Grand Rapids	$1,243.60
R. C. Rigdon & Co., 2093 Elm Ave., Milwaukee	
Scott Sports Shop, 624 First St., Louisville	
Terrell Luggage Shop, 936 Madison St., Charleston	1,633.18
Tilford & Travis, 259 Fourth St., Athens	1,202.20
Vincent Sports Store, 1312 Ludlow Ave., Richmond	611.54

Instructions: **3.** Open accounts in the accounts receivable ledger with each of the customers by entering the names and the addresses given in the foregoing list.

4. For each account having an unpaid invoice, record the date of the entry, November 1, in the Date column, the word "Balance" in the Items column, and the amount of the invoice in the Debit Balance column.

Accounts payable ledger. A list of the creditors of Voss and Howard is given below. This list contains (1) the name and the address of each creditor and (2) the amount of each unpaid invoice.

Name and Address	Amount
Abbott Supply Co., 596 Main St., Springfield	
Bauer & Chandler, 1689 Front St., St. Louis	
Elliott Trunk Co., 1325 Clay St., Chicago	$1,770.80
Gardner & Sons, 2476 Cedar Road, New York	
Newman Luggage Mart, 3948 Marsh Ave., Cleveland	2,218.12
Porter Box Co., 1210 Broadway, Springfield	
L. H. Sheldon & Co., 967 Third St., Philadelphia	
Stevens Luggage, Inc., 2865 Sixth Ave., New York	
Ward & Stewart, 6724 River Road, St. Louis	

Instructions: **5.** Open accounts in the accounts payable ledger with each of the creditors by entering the names and the addresses given in the foregoing list.

6. For each account having an unpaid invoice, record the date of the entry, November 1, in the Date column, the word "Balance" in the Items column, and the amount in the Credit Balance column.

Narrative of transactions for November

November 1

No. 1. Issued Check No. 431 for $600 to Jeffers Realty Company in payment of the November rent.

No. 2. Sold merchandise on account to Tilford & Travis, $1,109.40 (Sale No. 345).

> Voss and Howard sell on the terms 2/10, n/30. As there is no variation in these terms, the terms are not mentioned for each sales transaction, and they need not be recorded by the bookkeeper. The bookkeeper must remember, however, that all sales are subject to a 2% discount if paid within 10 days.

No. 3. Sold merchandise on account to Scott Sports Shop, $1,176.30 (Sale No. 346).

November 2

No. 4. Issued Check No. 432 for $25.50 to the Citizens Telephone Company in payment of the November telephone bill, a miscellaneous expense.

No. 5. Sold merchandise on account to Haynes & Haynes, $1,169.10 (Sale No. 347).

No. 6. Purchased merchandise on account from Newman Luggage Mart; $2,417.50 (Invoice No. 221).

November 3

No. 7. Sold merchandise on account to Jackson & Potter, $1,172.40 (Sale No. 348).

No. 8. Purchased merchandise on account from Ward & Stewart, $1,422 (Invoice No. 222).

November 4

No. 9. Received a check for $1,600.52 from Terrell Luggage Shop for the sale of October 27, $1,633.18, less the 2% sales discount amounting to $32.66.

November 5

No. 10. Issued Check No. 433, payable to Cash, for $354.20 for the weekly payroll of $400 less the following deductions: employees income taxes withheld, $36.80; FICA taxes, $9.

No. 11. Issued Check No. 434 for $1,717.68 to Elliott Trunk Co. in payment of their invoice of October 27 less discount. The amount of the invoice was $1,770.80; the terms were 3/10, n/30; the amount of the purchases discount was therefore $53.12.

Voss and Howard keep a file of unpaid invoices. Each invoice is filed under the date on which it must be paid in order to receive the purchases discount. As business papers are not used in this practice set, the amount of the invoice and the terms are given each time a payment is made on account.

No. 12. Cash sales for the week were $2,030.70.

Cash proof and posting. Total all columns of the cash receipts journal and the cash payments journal, entering the totals in small pencil figures. Prove cash. The cash balance is $9,586.02.

Post the entries in the General columns of the various books of original entry. Post the individual entries in the Accounts Receivable columns and the Accounts Payable columns of the cash receipts journal, the cash payments journal, and the general journal and in the Amount columns of the purchases journal and the sales journal to the appropriate accounts in the accounts receivable ledger and the accounts payable ledger.

Do not post the totals of the columns until the end of the month.

November 7

No. 13. Purchased merchandise on account from **L. H. Sheldon & Co.**, $1,672.20 (Invoice No. 223).

No. 14. Sold merchandise on account to Terrell Luggage Shop, $1,159.80 (Sale No. 349).

No. 15. Sold merchandise on account to R. C. Rigdon & Co., $1,416.16 (Sale No. 350).

No. 16. Bought supplies on account from Abbott Supply Co., $76.06 (Invoice No. 224).

Record the entry in the general journal.

November 8

No. 17. Issued Check No. 435 for $274 to the First National Bank in payment of the liabilities for payroll taxes and taxes withheld as follows: income taxes, $184; FICA taxes, $90.

These amounts were shown as liabilities in the accounts Employees Income Taxes Payable and FICA Taxes Payable

No. 18. Issued Check No. 436 for $2,151.58 to the Newman Luggage Mart in payment of the invoice of October 30 less discount. The amount of the invoice was $2,218.12; terms, 3/10, n/30.

November 9

No. 19. Received a check for $1,152.77 from Scott Sports Shop for the sale of November 1, $1,176.30, less discount.

No. 20. Received from the Vincents Sports Store a 30-day, 6% interest-bearing note, dated today, for $611.54, for the sale of October 10.

November 10

No. 21. Issued Check No. 437 for $2,344.97 to Newman Luggage Mart in payment of the invoice of November 2 less discount. The amount of the invoice was $2,417.50; terms, 3/10, n/30.

No. 22. Issued Check No. 438 for $1,393.56 to Ward & Stewart in payment of the invoice of November 3. The amount of the invoice was $1,422; terms, 2/10, n/30.

No. 23. Received a check for $1,087.21 from Tilford & Travis for the sale of November 1, $1,109.40, less discount.

November 11

No. 24. Sold merchandise on account to Benton Gift Shop, $1,114.20 (Sale No. 351).

No. 25. Received a check for $1,148.95 from Jackson & Potter for the sale of November 3, $1,172.40, less discount.

No. 26. Purchased merchandise on account from Gardner & Sons, $2,804.40 (Invoice No. 225).

No. 27. Sold merchandise on account to Haynes & Haynes, $1,126.80 (Sale No. 352).

November 12

No. 28. Issued Check No. 439, payable to Cash, for $354.20 for the weekly payroll of $400 less the following deductions: employees income taxes withheld, $36.80; FICA taxes, $9.

No. 29. Cash sales for the week were $2,143.06.

Cash proof and posting. Total all columns of the cash receipts journal and the cash payments journal, entering the totals in small pencil figures. Prove cash. The balance is $8,599.70.

Post the entries in the General columns. Post the individual entries that affect accounts receivable and accounts payable to the appropriate accounts in the accounts receivable and accounts payable ledgers. Do not post the totals of the columns until the end of the month.

November 14

No. 30. Issued Credit Memorandum No. 42 for $110.70 to Benton Gift Shop for the return of merchandise included in the sale of November 11.

No. 31. Received a check for $1,136.60 from Terrell Luggage Shop for the sale of November 7, $1,159.80, less discount.

No. 32. Received from Mitchell Luggage a 90-day, 6% interest-bearing note, dated today, for $1,243.60, for the sale of October 17.

November 15

No. 33. Issued Check No. 440 for $9.80 to City Water Works in payment of the water bill of November 14, a miscellaneous expense.

No. 34. Issued Check No. 441 for $1,622.03 to L. H. Sheldon & Co. in payment of the invoice of November 7 less discount. The amount of the invoice was $1,672.20; terms, 3/10, n/30.

No. 35. Issued Check No. 442 for $400 to John H. Voss for his salary for the first half of November.

> According to the partnership agreement, each partner's salary is to be debited to his drawing account.

No. 36. Issued Check No. 443 for $350 to Charles R. Howard for his salary for the first half of November.

November 16

No. 37. Received a check for $1,387.84 from R. C. Rigdon & Co. for the sale of November 7, $1,416.16, less discount.

No. 38. Received a credit memorandum for $262.80 from Gardner & Sons for the return of merchandise included in our purchase of November 11.

November 17

No. 39. Sold merchandise on account to R. C. Rigdon & Co., $634.70 (Sale No. 353).

No. 40. Issued Check No. 444 for $138 to Lawton Motor Freight in payment of their invoice covering Transportation on Purchases, $117.50, and Delivery Expense, $20.50.

No. 41. Purchased merchandise on account from Stevens Luggage, Inc., $1,708.20 (Invoice No. 226).

November 18

No. 42. Issued Check No. 445 for $2,465.35 to Gardner & Sons in payment of the invoice of November 11 less the credit received on November 16 and less discount. The amount of the invoice was $2,804.40; the amount of the credit was $262.80; the terms were 3/10, n/30; the amount of the discount was $76.25.

No. 43. Sold merchandise on account to Mitchell Luggage, $1,070.10 (Sale No. 354).

November 19

No. 44. Issued Check No. 446, payable to Cash, for $354.20 for the weekly payroll of $400 less the following deductions: employees income taxes withheld, $36.80; FICA taxes, $9.

No. 45. Sold merchandise on account to Gaynor Leather Shop, $1,223.10 (Sale No. 355).

No. 46. Cash sales for the week were $2,095.20.

Cash proof and posting. Total all columns of the cash receipts journal and the cash payments journal, entering the totals in small pencil figures. Prove cash. The balance is $7,879.96.

Post the entries in the General columns. Post the individual entries that affect accounts receivable and accounts payable to the appropriate accounts in the accounts receivable and accounts payable ledgers.

November 21

No. 47. Purchased merchandise on account from Bauer & Chandler, $540 (Invoice No. 227).

No. 48. Sold merchandise on account to Jackson & Potter, $1,360.80 (Sale No. 356).

No. 49. Received a check for $1,104.26 from Haynes & Haynes for the sale of November 11, $1,126.80, less discount.

November 22

No. 50. Issued Check No. 447 for $163.50 to Moore and Sons for a cash purchase of merchandise.

No. 51. Charles R. Howard took from the store for his personal use one key and license case, cost price $7.20. (Credit Purchases.)

November 23

No. 52. Bought cartons to be used in the store on account from Porter Box Co., $213.60 (Invoice No. 228).

No. 53. Sold merchandise on account to Gaynor Leather Shop, $1,074.60 (Sale No. 357).

No. 54. Issued Check No. 448 for $26.50 to Lambert Glass Company for replacing a broken pane of glass, a miscellaneous expense.

November 24

No. 55. Received a check for $1,608 from Ferris & Sutton in payment of their note of October 25, $1,600, plus interest.

No. 56. Issued Check No. 449 for $1,674.04 to Stevens Luggage, Inc., in payment of the invoice of November 17 less discount. The amount of the invoice was $1,708.20; terms, 2/10, n/30.

November 25

No. 57. Received a credit memorandum for $57.60 from Bauer & Chandler for the return of merchandise included in our purchase of November 21.

No. 58. Received a check for $1,202.20 from Tilford & Travis for the sale of October 23.

No. 59. Issued Check No. 450 for $1,007.50 to Gardner & Sons for our Note No. 49 for $1,000, drawn on October 11, plus interest.

November 26

No. 60. Issued Check No. 451 for $472.75 to Bauer & Chandler in payment of the invoice of November 21 less the credit received on November 25 and less discount. The amount of the invoice was $540; the amount of the credit was $57.60; the terms were 2/10, n/30; the amount of the discount was $9.65.

No. 61. Issued Check No. 452, payable to Cash, for $370.15 for the weekly payroll of $420 less the following deductions: employees income taxes withheld, $40.40; FICA taxes, $9.45.

No. 62. Recorded the employer's payroll taxes for the month. These taxes were: FICA Taxes, $36.45; Federal Unemployment Taxes, $4.86; State Unemployment Taxes, $43.74.

No. 63. Cash sales for the week were $2,021.84.

Cash proof and posting. Total all columns of the cash receipts journal and the cash payments journal, entering the totals in small pencil figures. Prove cash. The cash balance is $10,101.82.

Post the entries in the General columns. Post the individual entries that affect accounts receivable and accounts payable to the appropriate accounts in the accounts receivable and accounts payable ledgers.

November 28

No. 64. Issued Check No. 453 for $142.50 to Allen J. Randall for making up circulars to be used for advertising purposes.

No. 65. Received a check for $600 from Benton Gift Shop to apply on the sale of November 11.

No. 66. Issued Check No. 454 for $24.30 to Green Supply Company for a carton of paper cups and a carton of paper towels, a miscellaneous expense.

No. 67. Purchased merchandise on account from the Newman Luggage Mart, $2,043.90 (Invoice No. 229).

No. 68. Bought supplies on account from Abbott Supply Co., $59.90 (Invoice No. 230).

No. 69. Received a check for $1,048.70 from Mitchell Luggage for the sale of November 18, $1,070.10, less discount.

November 29

No. 70. Purchased merchandise on account from Elliott Trunk Co., $2,526.60 (Invoice No. 231).

No. 71. Issued Check No. 455 for $606 to Bauer & Chandler for our Note No. 48 for $600, drawn on September 30, plus interest.

No. 72. Issued Check No. 456 for $213.60 to Porter Box Co. in payment of the invoice of November 23.

No. 73. Received a check for $1,333.58 from Jackson & Potter for the sale of November 21, $1,360.80, less discount.

No. 74. Received a check for $1,198.64 from Gaynor Leather Shop for the sale of November 19, $1,223.10, less discount.

No. 75. Issued Check No. 457 for $20.30 to City Gas and Electric Company in payment of the bill for gas and electricity, a miscellaneous expense.

No. 76. Purchased merchandise on account from Stevens Luggage, Inc., $1,222.20 (Invoice No. 232).

No. 77. Bought new equipment for $4,000 and issued in settlement our Note No. 50 for 4 months with interest at the rate of 3%.

Aldrich & Co., the seller of the equipment, agreed to accept a note with a low rate of interest as an inducement to us to purchase the equipment now rather than later.

November 30

No. 78. Issued Check No. 458 for $198.80 to Lawton Motor Freight in payment of their invoice covering Transportation on Purchases, $164.30, and Delivery Expense, $34.50.

No. 79. Issued Check No. 459 for $400 to John H. Voss for his salary for the second half of November.

No. 80. Issued Check No. 460 for $350 to Charles R. Howard for his salary for the second half of November.

No. 81. Issued Check No. 461 for $148.50 to Ideal Supply Co. for a cash purchase of supplies.

No. 82. Sold merchandise on account to R. C. Rigdon & Co., $535.90 (Sale No. 358).

No. 83. Issued Check No. 462 for $56.40 to replenish the petty cash fund. The petty cash vouchers showed that the payments made from the petty cash fund were as follows:

Supplies..	$ 9.00
Advertising Expense.......................................	15.00
Miscellaneous Expense.....................................	32.40
	$56.40

No. 84. Discarded equipment that originally cost $480. On January 1 of the current year this equipment had been depreciated for 6 years at the rate of 10% a year and therefore had an allowance for depreciation of $288.

Record the depreciation on this equipment for the 11 months of the current year at the rate of 10% a year. Then record the discarding of the fixed asset, charging Loss on Fixed Assets for the book value of the asset at the time it was discarded.

No. 85. Cash sales for November 28-30 were $707.26.

Cash proof and posting. Total all columns of the cash receipts journal and the cash payments journal, entering the totals in small pencil figures. Prove cash. The cash balance is $12,829.60.

Post the entries in the General columns. Post the individual entries that affect accounts receivable and accounts payable to the appropriate accounts in the accounts receivable and accounts payable ledgers.

Work at the end of the month

Instructions: **1.** Total and rule the columns of all books of original entry. Post the totals of the special columns (all columns except the General Debit and Credit columns) to the appropriate accounts in the general ledger.

2. Prepare schedules of the accounts receivable ledger and of the accounts payable ledger. Prove the accuracy of the ledgers by comparing the totals of the schedules with the balances of the accounts receivable account and the accounts payable account in the general ledger.

3. Prepare a trial balance.

Narrative of transactions for December

December 1

No. 86. Issued Check No. 463 for $600 to Jeffers Realty Company in payment of December rent.

No. 87. Sold merchandise on account to Vincent Sports Store, $1,107 (Sale No. 359).

December 2

No. 88. Sold merchandise on account to Scott Sports Shop, $1,152.90 (Sale No. 360).

No. 89. Purchased merchandise on account from Bauer & Chandler, $1,263.60 (Invoice No. 233).

December 3

No. 90. Issued Check No. 464, payable to Cash, for $370.15 for the weekly payroll of $420 less the following deductions: employees income taxes withheld, $40.40; FICA taxes, $9.45.

No. 91. Cash sales for December 1–3 were $1,104.74.

Cash proof and posting. Total all columns of the cash receipts journal and the cash payments journal, entering the totals in small pencil figures. Prove the cash balance, which is $12,964.19.

Post the entries in the General columns. Post the individual entries that affect accounts receivable and accounts payable to the appropriate accounts in the accounts receivable and accounts payable ledgers.

December 5

No. 92. Sold merchandise on account to Ferris & Sutton, $1,065.60 (Sale No. 361).

No. 93. Issued Check No. 465 for $5,850 to Bricker Leather Co. for the cash purchase of a job lot of merchandise.

No. 94. Issued Check No. 466 for $23.90 to Citizens Telephone Company in payment of December telephone bill.

No. 95. Sold merchandise on account to Terrell Luggage Shop, $961.20 (Sale No. 362).

No. 96. Received from Haynes & Haynes a 30-day, 6% interest-bearing note, dated December 1, for $1,169.10, in settlement of the sale of November 2.

December 6

No. 97. Issued Check No. 467 for $2,450.80 to Elliott Trunk Co. in payment of invoice of November 29 less 3% discount.

No. 98. Sold merchandise on account to Haynes & Haynes, $1,198.20 (Sale No. 363).

No. 99. Purchased merchandise on account from Stevens Luggage, Inc., $1,904.40 (Invoice No. 234).

No. 100. Received a check for $1,010 from R. C. Rigdon & Co. in payment of its note of October 6, $1,000, plus interest.

December 7

No. 101. Issued Check No. 468 for $76.06 to Abbott Supply Co. in payment of invoice of November 7.

No. 102. Bought supplies on account from Abbott Supply Co., $80.30 (Invoice No. 235).

December 8

No. 103. Sold merchandise on account to Tilford & Travis, $1,106.10 (Sale No. 364).

No. 104. Issued Check No. 469 for $1,982.58 to Newman Luggage Mart in payment of invoice of November 28 less 3% discount.

No. 105. Sold merchandise on account to R. C. Rigdon & Co., $1,242 (Sale No. 365).

No. 106. Issued Credit Memorandum No. 43 for $345.60 to Ferris & Sutton for return of merchandise included in sale of December 5.

December 9

No. 107. Issued Check No. 470 for $36.50 to McAlpin Company for relaying the linoleum in one section of the office, a miscellaneous expense.

No. 108. Received a check for $614.60 from Vincent Sports Store in payment of its note of November 9, $611.54, plus interest.

December 10

No. 109. Received a check for $1,129.84 from Scott Sports Shop in payment of sale of December 2 less discount.

No. 110. Received a credit memorandum for $110.70 from Stevens Luggage, Inc. for return of merchandise included in our purchase of December 6.

No. 111. Issued Check No. 471, payable to Cash, for $370.15 for the weekly payroll of $420 less the following deductions: employees income taxes withheld, $40.40; FICA taxes, $9.45.

No. 112. Cash sales for the week were $1,804.80.

Cash proof and posting. Total all columns of the cash receipts journal and the cash payments journal, entering the totals in small pencil figures. Prove the cash balance, which is $6,733.44.

Post the entries in the General columns. Post the individual entries that affect accounts receivable and accounts payable to the appropriate accounts in the accounts receivable and accounts payable ledgers.

December 12

No. 113. Issued Check No. 472 for $1,238.33 to Bauer & Chandler in payment of invoice of December 2 less 2% discount.

No. 114. Purchased merchandise on account from Gardner & Sons, $1,555.72 (Invoice No. 236).

No. 115. Sold merchandise on account to Scott Sports Shop, $1,097.10 (Sale No. 366).

December 13

No. 116. Sold merchandise on account to Vincent Sports Store, $1,015.20 (Sale No. 367).

No. 117. Issued Check No. 473 for $223.70 to First National Bank in payment of liabilities for payroll taxes and taxes withheld as follows: income taxes, $150.80; FICA taxes, $72.90.

No. 118. Purchased merchandise on account from L. H. Sheldon & Co., $2,966.40 (Invoice No. 237).

No. 119. Sold merchandise on account to Gaynor Leather Shop, $1,126.80 (Sale No. 368).

No. 120. Issued Check No. 474 for $60 to Charles R. Howard for a withdrawal of cash for personal use.

December 15

No. 121. Issued Check No. 475 for $1,757.83 to Stevens Luggage, Inc. in payment of invoice of December 6 less the credit of $110.70 received on December 10 and less purchases discount of $35.87.

No. 122. Purchased merchandise on account from Ward & Stewart, $1,917 (Invoice No. 238).

December 16

No. 123. Issued Check No. 476 for $12.30 to the City Water Works in payment of the water bill of December 13.

No. 124. Received from R. C. Rigdon & Co. a 30-day, 6% interest-bearing note, dated today, for $634.70, in settlement of the sale of November 17.

No. 125. Issued Check No. 477 for $400 to John H. Voss for his salary for the first half of December.

No. 126. Issued Check No. 478 for $350 to Charles R. Howard for his salary for the first half of December.

December 17

No. 127. Received a check for $1,217.16 from R. C. Rigdon & Co. for sale of December 8 less discount.

No. 128. Issued Check No. 479 for $161.20 to Lawton Motor Freight in payment of invoice of December 15 covering Transportation on Purchases, $119.90, and Delivery Expense, $41.30.

No. 129. Bought supplies on account from Abbott Supply Co., $122.50 (Invoice No. 239).

No. 130. Donated merchandise costing $93.60 as a door prize for the convention of the National Leather Manufacturers Association. (Debit Advertising Expense and credit Purchases.)

No. 131. Issued Credit Memorandum No. 44 for $66.60 to Vincent Sports Store for return of merchandise included in sale of December 13.

No. 132. Issued Check No. 480, payable to Cash, for $370.15 for the weekly payroll of $420 less the following deductions: employees income taxes withheld, $40.40; FICA taxes, $9.45.

No. 133. Cash sales for the week were $1,792.36.

Cash proof and posting. Total all columns of the cash receipts journal and the cash payments journal, entering the totals in small pencil figures. Prove the cash balance, which is $5,169.45.

Post the entries in the General columns. Post the individual entries that affect accounts receivable and accounts payable to the appropriate accounts in the accounts receivable and accounts payable ledgers.

December 19

No. 134. Received a check for $1,083.98 from Tilford & Travis for the sale of December 8 less discount.

No. 135. Sold merchandise on account to Ferris & Sutton, $1,148.40 (Sale No. 369).

No. 136. Purchased merchandise on account from Bauer & Chandler, $842.40 (Invoice No. 240).

December 20

No. 137. Received a credit memorandum for $102.60 from L. H. Sheldon & Co. for return of merchandise included in our purchase of December 14.

December 21

No. 138. Sold merchandise on account to Jackson & Potter, $1,125 (Sale No. 370).

No. 139. Purchased merchandise on account from Gardner & Sons, $1,659.60 (Invoice No. 241).

December 22

No. 140. Issued Check No. 481 for $1,509.05 to Gardner & Sons in payment of invoice of December 12 less 3% discount.

December 23

No. 141. Received a check for $929.63 from Vincent Sports Store for sale of December 13 less the credit of $66.60 given on December 17 and less sales discount of $18.97.

No. 142. Received a check for $1,074.60 from Gaynor Leather Shop for sale of November 23.

No. 143. Purchased merchandise on account from Elliott Trunk Co., $2,892 (Invoice No. 242).

December 24

No. 144. Issued Check No. 482 for $2,777.89 to L. H. Sheldon & Co. in payment of invoice of December 14 less the credit of $102.60 received on December 20 and less purchases discount of $85.91.

No. 145. Issued Check No. 483 for $1,878.66 to Ward & Stewart in payment of invoice of December 15 less 2% discount.

No. 146. Issued Check No. 484, payable to Cash, for $370.15 for the weekly payroll of $420 less the following deductions: employees income taxes withheld, $40.40; FICA taxes, $9.45.

No. 147. Cash sales for the week were $1,917.60.

Cash proof and posting. Total all columns of the cash receipts journal and the cash payments journal, entering the totals in small pencil figures. Prove the cash balance, which is $3,639.51.

Post the entries in the General columns. Post the individual entries that affect accounts receivable and accounts payable to the appropriate accounts in the accounts receivable and accounts payable ledgers.

December 27

No. 148. Received a check for $1,104.26 from Gaynor Leather Shop for sale of December 14 less discount.

No. 149. Issued Check No. 485 for $20.70 to City Gas and Electric Company in payment of bill for gas and electricity.

No. 150. Purchased merchandise on account from Newman Luggage Mart, $1,724.40 (Invoice No. 243).

No. 151. Sold merchandise on account to Mitchell Luggage, $2,185.30 (Sale No. 371).

December 28

No. 152. Issued Check No. 486 for $59.90 to Abbott Supply Co. in payment of invoice of November 28.

No. 153. Issued Check No. 487 for $150 to Allen J. Randall for making up circulars to be used for advertising purposes.

No. 154. Received a check for $70 from John Sanders in payment for old equipment that originally cost $240. On January 1 of the current year this equipment had been depreciated for 5 years at the rate of 15% a year and therefore had an allowance for depreciation of $180.
    Record the depreciation on this equipment for the 12 months of the current year at the rate of 15% a year.
    To record the sale of the equipment, proceed as follows:
    (1) Make the complete entry for the sale in the general journal.
    (2) Record the cash receipt in the cash receipts journal, debiting Cash and crediting Equipment for $70.
    (3) To avoid double posting to the cash account and to the equipment account, place a check mark in the Post. Ref. column after Cash in the general journal and a check mark in the Post. Ref. column after Equipment in the cash receipts journal. This method of checking to avoid double posting is illustrated on page 373 of the textbook.

No. 155. The balance of the account with Benton Gift Shop was found to be uncollectible. Wrote off the account as a bad debt.

December 29

No. 156. Sold merchandise on account to Scott Sports Shop, $253 (Sale No. 372).

No. 157. Received a check for $1,125.43 from Ferris & Sutton for sale of December 19 less discount.

No. 158. Issued our 60-day, 4% interest-bearing Note No. 51 for $1,222.20 to Stevens Luggage, Inc. in settlement of invoice of November 29.

No. 159. Issued Check No. 488 for $825.55 to Bauer & Chandler in payment of invoice of December 19 less 2% discount.

December 30

No. 160. Received a check for $1,102.50 from Jackson & Potter for sale of December 21 less discount.

No. 161. Issued Check No. 489 for $168.20 to Lawton Motor Freight in payment of invoice of December 30 covering Transportation on Purchases, $153.30, and Delivery Expense, $14.90.

No. 162. Received from Vincent Sports Store a 30-day, 6% interest-bearing note, dated December 28, for $1,107, in settlement of sale of December 1.

December 31

No. 163. Issued Check No. 490 for $1,609.81 to Gardner & Sons in payment of invoice of December 21 less 3% discount.

No. 164. Issued Check No. 491 for $87.40 to replenish the petty cash fund. The petty cash vouchers showed that payments made from the petty cash fund were as follows:

Supplies...	$38.70
Advertising Expense.......................................	12.50
Delivery Expense...	4.50
Miscellaneous Expense.....................................	31.70
	$87.40

No. 165. Issued Check No. 492 for $400 to John H. Voss for his salary for the last half of the month.

No. 166. Issued Check No. 493 for $350 to Charles R. Howard for his salary for the last half of the month.

No. 167. Issued Check No. 494, payable to Cash, for $433.95 for the weekly payroll of $500 less the following deductions: employees income taxes withheld, $54.80; FICA taxes, $11.25.

No. 168. Recorded the employer's payroll taxes for the month. These taxes were: FICA Taxes, $49.05; Federal Unemployment Taxes, $6.54; State Unemployment Taxes, $58.86.

No. 169. Cash sales for the week were $1,211.10.

Cash proof and posting. Total all columns of the cash receipts journal and the cash payments journal, entering the totals in small pencil figures. Prove the cash balance, which is $4,147.29.

Post the entries in the General columns. Post the individual entries that affect accounts receivable and accounts payable to the appropriate accounts in the accounts receivable and accounts payable ledgers.

Work at the end of the year

Instructions: 1. Total and rule the columns of all books of original entry. Post the totals of the special columns (all columns except the General Debit and General Credit columns) to the appropriate accounts in the general ledger.

2. Prepare schedules of the accounts receivable ledger and the accounts payable ledger. Prove the accuracy of the ledgers by comparing the totals of the schedules with the balances of the accounts receivable account and the accounts payable account in the general ledger.

3. Prepare an eight-column work sheet. The following additional data are needed at the end of the yearly fiscal period ended December 31:

Accrued interest income, $17.73
Allowance for bad debts, an additional ½% of charge sales of $180,530.45
Merchandise inventory, $45,331.60
Supplies inventory, $426.75
Prepaid insurance, $120
Estimated depreciation:
    Of new equipment purchased on November 29, depreciation for 1 month
      at rate of 15% a year
    Of old equipment on hand, depreciation for 12 months at 10% a year
Estimated property taxes payable, $320
Accrued interest expense, $10.94

4. Prepare a profit and loss statement. The net profit is divided as follows:
  (a) The partners receive amounts equal to their yearly salaries: Mr. Voss, $9,600; Mr. Howard, $8,400.
  (b) The remainder of the profit is divided equally.

5. Prepare a balance sheet.

6. Record the adjusting entries and the closing entries. The partners agree that each partner's increase in capital is to be transferred to his capital account;

therefore close each drawing account to the corresponding capital account. Post the entries to the general ledger and rule the accounts that balance.

7. Balance each remaining account in the general ledger that has both debits and credits, and prepare a post-closing trial balance.

8. Record the reversing entries for Interest Receivable and Interest Payable as of January 1 of the following year, post the entries, and rule the asset and the liability accounts.

Corporations and cooperatives

Nature of a corporation. Large businesses, such as factories and public utilities, usually require more capital than can be furnished by one individual or by several partners. With the growth of large business units has come a need for amounts of capital that may be obtained only from many individuals. A form of business organization that has the legal right to act as one person but that is owned by many is known as a *corporation*.

Most corporations are authorized by a state government. Some corporations are authorized by the federal government, such as national banks. Each corporation has legal authority to act as an individual. A corporation is an artificial person created by law.

Advantages of corporate organization. The corporate form of organization has many advantages over the single proprietorship and the partnership. Some of these advantages are:

(a) The investors are not responsible for the debts of a corporation.

(b) It permits many investors to combine their capital.

(c) It allows each investor to transfer his interest in the corporation without securing the consent of the other owners and without dissolving the corporation.

(d) It is not terminated by the death of the investors.

Ownership of a corporation. In a corporation there are ordinarily a number of owners, but the ownership of each person is not represented by a separate capital account for each investor as it is in a partnership. The ownership in a corporation is divided into units known as *shares*. All of the shares are referred to as the *capital stock*. The owner of one or more shares of the capital stock is known as a *stockholder*. The evidence of each stockholder's ownership in the corporation is a certificate known as a *stock certificate*. A typical stock certificate is illustrated on page 424.

Organization of a corporation. Corporations are organized through the authority provided by state and federal laws. The laws grant the right to incorporate a business and also prescribe the method of incorporation. Most states require that three or more individuals provide the assets with which to organize the corporation. The incorporators must

The Baker Manufacturing Company, Inc.
Incorporated Under the Laws of the
State of Delaware

This Certifies that --------------W. W. Woods----------------- is the owner of
------------One Hundred Thirty-------------- Shares of the Capital Stock of

THE BAKER MANUFACTURING COMPANY, INC.

transferable only on the books of the Corporation by the holder hereof in person, or by Attorney upon surrender of this Certificate properly endorsed.

IN WITNESS WHEREOF, the said Corporation has caused this Certificate to be signed by its duly authorized officers and its Corporate Seal to be hereunto affixed this ___tenth___ day of ___June___ A.D. 1957

A. J. Peters
Treasurer

E. C. Malone
President

--50--

Stock certificate

make written application to the proper state or federal officials. A written application to the state for permission to incorporate is known as a *certificate of incorporation.*

The certificate of incorporation usually contains: (1) the name under which the business is to be operated; (2) the location of the principal office of the corporation; (3) the object of the proposed corporation; (4) the amount of the capital stock, the kind of stock, and the number of shares; (5) the amount of capital with which the corporation will commence business; (6) the names and the addresses of the incorporators; and (7) the period for which the corporation is formed.

On June 2, 1957, E. C. Malone, F. E. Hill, A. J. Peters, and W. W. Woods decided to organize a corporation to manufacture and sell machinery used by bakers. They drew up the certificate of incorporation and filed it with the secretary of state of the state in which the corporation was to be formed. This certificate of incorporation is shown on page 425. The secretary of state furnished a certified copy of the certificate of incorporation to the organizers. This copy was recorded in the office of the recorder of the county in which the business was located. The certified copy of the certificate of incorporation is referred to as the *charter* of the corporation.

CERTIFICATE OF INCORPORATION

of

THE BAKER MANUFACTURING COMPANY, INC.

FIRST: The name of the corporation is The Baker Manufacturing Company, Inc.

SECOND: The principal office of said corporation is located at 105 West Tenth Street, in the City of Wilmington, County of New Castle, Delaware.

THIRD: The nature of the business, or objects or purposes to be transacted, promoted, or carried on are to engage in the business of manufacturing and selling machinery used by bakers and all business incidental to such manufacture and sale.

FOURTH: The total number of shares of stock that the corporation shall have authority to issue is Two Thousand (2,000) and the par value of each of such shares is Fifty Dollars ($50), amounting in the aggregate to One Hundred Thousand Dollars ($100,000).

FIFTH: The amount of capital with which the corporation will commence business is Thirty-three Thousand Dollars ($33,000).

SIXTH: The names and the places of residence of the incorporators are as follows:

E. C. Malone...... 1527 Vineyard Place, Dover, Delaware
F. E. Hill........ 3466 Trimble Avenue, Wilmington, Delaware
A. J. Peters..... 17 Beechcrest Road, Newport, Delaware
W. W. Woods...... 351 Park Avenue, New York, New York

SEVENTH: The corporation is to have perpetual existence.

WE, THE UNDERSIGNED, being each of the incorporators hereinbefore named for the purpose of forming a corporation to do business both within and without the State of Delaware, and in pursuance of the General Corporation Law of the State of Delaware, being Chapter 65 of the Revised Code of Delaware, and the acts amendatory thereof and supplemental thereto, do make this certificate, hereby declaring and certifying that the facts herein stated are true, and accordingly have hereunto set our hands and seals this second day of June, A. D. 1957.

In the presence of:

D. V. Price

R. E. Holt

E. C. Malone (SEAL)

F. E. Hill (SEAL)

A. J. Peters (SEAL)

W. W. Woods (SEAL)

State of Delaware
County of New Castle } ss.:

BE IT REMEMBERED, That on this second day of June, A. D. 1957, personally came before me, Matthew J. Moore, a Notary Public for the State of Delaware, all of the parties to the foregoing certificate of incorporation, known to me personally to be such, and severally acknowledged the said certificate to be the act and deed of the signers respectively and that the facts therein stated are truly set forth.

GIVEN under my hand and seal of office the day and year aforesaid.

Matthew J. Moore
Notary Public

Certificate of incorporation

Capital stock. The fourth paragraph of the charter on page 425 indicated that The Baker Manufacturing Company was authorized to issue capital stock in the amount of $100,000. The total amount of stock that a corporation is permitted by its charter to issue is known as the *authorized capital stock*.

According to the fourth paragraph of the charter, the total authorized capital stock of The Baker Manufacturing Company was divided into 2,000 shares, each share having a face value of $50. The face value of each share as stated on the stock certificate is known as the *par value* of the share.

If the face value of each share of stock is not stated on each certificate, the stock is said to be *no-par-value stock*. The charter of a corporation that has no-par-value stock states the number of shares of stock that may be issued.

When the capital stock is all of one kind, it is called *common stock*. If the capital stock is divided so that part of the stock carries special rights to the earnings and other preferences, the stock with the special preference is called *preferred stock*.

Stock subscriptions. Before application can be made for a charter, the organizers of a corporation must have definite promises from the incorporators to buy stock. Persons who promise to buy stock to organize a corporation are known as *subscribers*. The total amount of the stock subscribed before organization is listed in the application for the charter.

The Baker Manufacturing Company had 660 shares of stock subscribed before the charter was granted. Mr. Malone subscribed for 200 shares, Mr. Hill for 200 shares, Mr. Peters for 130 shares, and Mr. Woods for 130 shares at $50 for each share. As soon as the subscriptions were paid, therefore, they would have $33,000 in cash with which to begin operations.

Management of a corporation. A corporation ordinarily has a number of owners or stockholders. The stockholders hold an annual meeting to elect a group of persons who are given the power to manage the business. The group of persons elected to manage the business is known as the *board of directors*. Each stockholder is ordinarily entitled to one vote for each share of stock that he holds.

The board of directors controls the general policies of the corporation and elects the officers. These officers or their authorized agents carry on the business of the corporation. The officers are responsible to the board of directors, and the board of directors is responsible to the stockholders. All are governed by (a) the charter and (b) the bylaws adopted by the stockholders.

Opening entries for a corporation. The opening entry for a business operated by one person consists of debits to assets, credits to liabilities, and a credit to proprietorship. The opening entry for a partnership consists of debits to assets, credits to liabilities, and credits to the capital account of each partner. The opening entry for a corporation follows the same pattern as that for a single proprietor or for a partnership — assets are debited, liabilities that are assumed are credited, and an account called Capital Stock is credited.

The entry below illustrates the opening entry of a corporation where cash is the only asset and there are no liabilities.

	DATE	ACCOUNT CREDITED	POST. REF.	GENERAL CR.	SALES CR.	ACCOUNTS RECEIVABLE CR.	DISCOUNT ON SALES DR.	CASH DR.	
				1	2	3	4	5	
1	1957 June 10	Capital Stock		3300000				3300000	1
2									2
3									3
4									4
5									5
6									6

CASH RECEIPTS JOURNAL — PAGE 1

Entry to record the sale of capital stock

Analyzing the opening entry. The certificate of incorporation of The Baker Manufacturing Company provided that the corporation would commence business with a capital of $33,000. On the day the charter was received, the four incorporators purchased for cash 660 shares of stock for $33,000. A stock certificate was issued to each subscriber indicating the number of shares of stock that he owned. To record the receipt of cash by the corporation, the entry shown above was made in the cash receipts journal. The total amount of cash received was credited to one account, Capital Stock. Capital Stock was credited in the General Cr. column and Cash was debited in the Cash Dr. column.

Purchase of a business by a corporation. The Baker Manufacturing Company decided on June 10 to purchase the business of the partnership of C. J. Nelson and E. H. Tealy. In payment for their business, the partners agreed to accept shares of stock in the corporation. The balance sheet of the partnership showed that the difference between the assets and the liabilities amounted to $15,000. At $50 a share, the corporation would issue the partners 300 shares of stock for their interest in the business. The general journal entry to record this transaction is illustrated at the top of the next page.

ACCOUNTS PAYABLE DR.	GENERAL DR.	DATE	NAME OF ACCOUNT	POST. REF.	GENERAL CR.	ACCOUNTS RECEIVABLE CR.	
	584 38	1957 June 10	Cash				1
	1000 00		Notes Receivable				2
	575 62		Accounts Receivable				3
	10650 00		Merchandise Inventory				4
	121 50		Supplies				5
	250 00		Prepaid Insurance				6
	1000 00		Equipment				7
			Notes Payable		2500 00		8
			Accounts Payable		1281 50		9
			Capital Stock		15000 00		10
			Purchase of the business				11
			of Nelson and Tealey				12

Entry to record the purchase of a going business

Analyzing the entry for purchase of a going business. Each asset purchased was debited in the General Dr. column for the amount shown on the balance sheet of the partnership. The two liabilities taken over, Notes Payable and Accounts Payable, were credited in the General Cr. column for the amounts shown on the balance sheet. If cash had been paid to the partners, Cash would have been credited; but as the partners had agreed to accept stock in the corporation for their interest, Capital Stock was credited for the amount of their interest, $15,000.

When this entry and the entry in the cash receipts journal were posted, the capital stock account in the general ledger appeared as follows:

Capital Stock. ACCOUNT NO. 31

DATE	ITEMS	POST. REF.	DEBIT	DATE	ITEMS	POST. REF.	CREDIT
				1957 June 10		CR	33000 00
				10		J	15000 00

Financial statements of a corporation. At the end of the fiscal period on December 31, The Baker Manufacturing Company prepared its financial statements. During the fiscal period the corporation made a net profit of $3,913.66. The profit and loss statement was prepared in the same form illustrated previously for the single proprietorship and the partnership.

The assets and the liabilities of the corporation were shown on the balance sheet in the same manner as the assets and the liabilities of a single proprietorship or a partnership. The only difference in the statements was in the proprietorship section. The proprietorship section of the balance sheet prepared by The Baker Manufacturing Company on December 31 is shown below.

```
                      Proprietorship
Capital Stock  . . . . . . . . . .   $48,000.00
Earned Surplus . . . . . . . . . .     3,913.66
Total Proprietorship . . . . . . .                51,913.66
Total Liabilities and Proprietorship. . .         $86,982.19
```

Proprietorship section of a corporate balance sheet

The amount earned by a corporation and not distributed to the stockholders is known as *earned surplus, retained earnings,* or *earnings retained in the business.* If losses are greater than earnings, the net loss is known as a *deficit.*

The amount of profit earned by The Baker Manufacturing Company and not yet distributed to the stockholders, $3,913.66, was listed on the balance sheet under the title *Earned Surplus.* This amount was added to the amount of the capital stock to give the total proprietorship of the corporation, $51,913.66.

Closing entries for a corporation. The closing entries for the income, cost, and expense accounts of a corporation are the same as those of a single proprietorship or a partnership. Since there are no separate capital and drawing accounts for each owner in a corporation, the net profit of the corporation is credited to a separate account with the title *Earned Surplus.* The earned surplus account summarizes the changes in the proprietorship of the corporation.

When there is a net loss in a corporation, it is sometimes debited to a special account with the title *Deficit*; however a common procedure is to debit net losses to the earned surplus account.

When the closing entries were made for The Baker Manufacturing Company on December 31, the following entry was made in the general journal to close the profit and loss summary account:

	ACCOUNTS PAYABLE DR.	GENERAL DR.	DATE	NAME OF ACCOUNT	POST. REF.	GENERAL CR.	ACCOUNTS RECEIVABLE CR.	
26		3913 66	31	Profit and Loss Summary				26
27				Earned Surplus		3913 66		27

PAGE 14 — GENERAL JOURNAL

Entry to close the profit and loss summary account

Declaring dividends. The balance of the earned surplus account, $3,913.66, represents profits of the corporation that really belong to the stockholders of the corporation. The stockholders may not claim the profits, however, except by order of the board of directors. Corporations ordinarily wish to maintain a credit balance in the earned surplus account in the event that a coming fiscal period may not produce a profit. When the board of directors meets, it decides whether it is advisable to distribute all or part of the earnings to the stockholders.

When the board of directors of The Baker Manufacturing Company met on January 6, it decided that it should distribute $2 for each share of outstanding stock or a total of $1,920 of the earned surplus, to the stockholders. When the board of directors decides to distribute profits to stockholders, it is said to have *declared a dividend*. The amount of profits to be distributed is called the *dividend*. The amount of the dividend is usually expressed in terms of a certain amount **per share of outstanding stock.** For example, The Baker Manufacturing Company declared a dividend of $2 a share. The dividends are payable in cash by the corporation at the time fixed by the directors.

When the dividend was declared by the board of directors of The Baker Manufacturing Company, the earned surplus account was debited for $1,920, the amount of the net profits to be distributed to the stockholders. The liability account *Dividends Payable* was credited for $1,920 to show the amount owed to the stockholders by the corporation.

The declaration of the board of directors of The Baker Manufacturing Company provided that the dividend was to be paid on January 20. On that date a check was mailed to each of the stockholders for the total amount of the dividend due him.

The entry in the general journal to record the declaration of the dividend on January 6 was as follows:

	ACCOUNTS PAYABLE DR.	GENERAL DR.	DATE	NAME OF ACCOUNT	POST. REF.	GENERAL CR.	ACCOUNTS RECEIVABLE CR.	
18		1920 00	6	Earned Surplus				18
19				Dividends Payable		1920 00		19
20				To record Dividend No. 1 of				20
21				$2 a share.				21
22								22
23								23

Entry to record the declaration of a dividend

The entry in the cash payments journal to record the payment of the dividend on January 20 was as follows:

				CASH PAYMENTS JOURNAL						PAGE 3	
				1	2	3	4	5	6	7	
DATE	CHK. NO.	ACCOUNT DEBITED	POST. REF.	GENERAL DR.	ACCOUNTS PAYABLE DR.	SALARY EXPENSE DR.	EMPLOYEES INCOME TAX. PAY. CR.	FICA TAXES PAY. CR.	DISCOUNT ON PURCHASES CR.	CASH CR.	
12	20 23·28	Dividends Payable		1920 00						1920 00	12
13											13
14											14
15											15
16											16
17											17
18											18
19											19

Entry to record the payment of a dividend

Cooperatives. A business that is owned by its customers is known as a *cooperative*. A cooperative business is usually organized as a corporation.

One of the chief differences between a cooperative and an ordinary corporation lies in the power that each stockholder has in the stockholders' meetings. In the usual corporation each stockholder has one vote for each share of stock owned. It is possible, therefore, for a few large stockholders to have complete control of such a corporation. In the cooperative, however, each stockholder has one and only one vote, regardless of the number of shares of stock owned.

Earnings are distributed to the members of a cooperative in two ways: (a) participation dividends and (b) dividends on capital stock. The earnings distributed to each member in proportion to the amount of business that he has done with the cooperative during the fiscal period are known as *participation dividends*. The earnings distributed to each member in proportion to the amount of his investment in the cooperative are known as *dividends on capital stock*.

During the yearly fiscal period ended June 30, J. M. Tice, a member of the Lima Consumers Cooperative, bought merchandise totaling $2,500. On June 30 the board of directors of the cooperative declared a participation dividend of 2%. Mr. Tice therefore received a participation dividend of $50.

Mr. Tice owned shares of capital stock in the cooperative, for which he had paid $100. The cooperative declared a dividend on the capital stock of 4%. Mr. Tice's dividend was therefore $4.

CHAPTER QUESTIONS

1. What are the advantages of a corporation?
2. What is given as evidence of ownership in a corporation?
3. What information is given in the certificate of incorporation on page 425?
4. What entry was made in the cash receipts journal on page 427 to open the books of The Baker Manufacturing Company when stock was sold for cash?
5. What entry was made in the general journal on page 428 to record the purchase of the partnership of Nelson and Tealy?
6. How does the balance sheet of a corporation differ from the balance sheet of a partnership?
7. Who has the power to declare a dividend?
8. What entry is made in the general journal on page 430 to record the declaration of Dividend No. 1?
9. What entry is made in the cash payments journal on page 431 to record the payment of Dividend No. 1?
10. How does a cooperative differ from a corporation?
11. How are the earnings of a cooperative distributed to its members?

INCREASING YOUR BUSINESS VOCABULARY

What is the meaning of each of the following:

(a) corporation
(b) shares
(c) capital stock
(d) stockholder
(e) stock certificate
(f) certificate of incorporation
(g) authorized capital stock
(h) par value
(i) no-par-value stock
(j) subscribers
(k) board of directors
(l) earned surplus
(m) deficit
(n) dividend
(o) cooperative
(p) participation dividends

CASES FOR DISCUSSION

1. The Central Supply Company, Inc. declared a quarterly dividend of $1.25 a share on the 5,000 shares of outstanding capital stock. What entry was required to record (a) the declaration of the dividend and (b) the payment of the dividend?

2. E. S. Hayes owns 1 share of Elson Company common stock (par value $100). He also owns 10 shares of the local cooperative stock (par value $10). Mr. Hayes buys most of his groceries, gasoline, and oil from the local cooperative. On June 30 the Elson Company declared a 6% dividend on capital stock. The cooperative declared a 5% dividend on capital stock and a 1% participation dividend. On which investment will Mr. Hayes get the larger income on June 30? Why?

APPLICATION PROBLEMS

Problem 32-1. Opening entry for a new business organized as a corporation

The certificate of incorporation of The Doyle Lamp Company authorized a capital stock of $10,000 consisting of 200 shares (par value $50). On June 1 of the current year, the day the charter was received, the incorporators purchased 180 shares of stock for cash. A stock certificate was issued to each subscriber.

Instructions: Record the opening entry in a cash receipts journal.

Problem 32-2. Opening entry to incorporate a going concern

On January 2 of the current year a charter was granted to Porter-Pine, Inc. that authorized a capital stock of $50,000, consisting of 500 shares (par value $100).

This corporation had agreed to take over the hardware business owned by the partnership of Porter and Pine. On January 2 the corporation took over the assets and assumed the liabilities of the partnership shown in the following balance sheet:

PORTER AND PINE
BALANCE SHEET
DECEMBER 31, 19--

Assets			Liabilities		
Cash.................	729	34	Notes Payable..........	1,000	00
Accounts Receivable...	5,984	84	Accounts Payable........	3,745	72
Merchandise Inventory.	22,087	28			
Supplies.............	364	26	Total Liabilities..........	4,745	72
Equipment...........	1,580	00			
			Proprietorship		
			C. M. Porter,		
			Capital.... 16,000.00		
			J. S. Pine,		
			Capital.... 10,000.00		
			Total Proprietorship......	26,000	00
Total Assets...........	30,745	72	Total Liab. and Prop.....	30,745	72

On January 2, 160 shares of stock were issued to Mr. Porter and 100 shares of stock were issued to Mr. Pine for their equities in the partnership.

Instructions: Record the opening entry in a general journal.

Problem 32-3. Earnings and dividends of a corporation

The Hardy Corporation was organized with 500 shares of common stock, par value $100. During the first five years of operation, the net profits were $2,500, $8,000, $4,000, $3,600, and $9,000.

The dividends paid were ½ of the earnings in each year.

Instructions: 1. Find the dividend per share in each of the five years.

2. Find the balance of the earned surplus account at the end of the five-year period, assuming that all earnings were credited to Earned Surplus and that there were no charges to Earned Surplus other than dividends.

Problem 32-4. Declaring and paying a dividend

Instructions: Record in general journal form the following entries for The Hudson Company:

Dec. 31. The credit balance of the profit and loss summary account, $14,270, was transferred to Earned Surplus.

Jan. 6. A dividend of $6 a share was declared on the 1,000 shares of common stock outstanding.

Jan. 30. The dividend declared on January 6 was paid.

Problem 32-5. Balance sheet for a corporation

The Balance Sheet columns of the work sheet of Caldwell & Co. for the fiscal year ended December 31 of the current year are shown below.

Account Titles	Balance Sheet	
	Debit	Credit
Cash..	7,360 21	
Accounts Receivable...........................	8,187 25	
Allowance for Bad Debts.......................		106 84
Merchandise Inventory.........................	41,639 87	
Supplies......................................	872 45	
Equipment....................................	6,750 00	
Allow. for Depr. of Equipment................		562 50
Accounts Payable..............................		6,123 40
Taxes Payable.................................		385 60
Capital Stock.................................		50,000 00
Earned Surplus...............................		3,731 29
	64,809 78	60,909 63
Net Profit....................................		3,900 15
	64,809 78	64,809 78

Instructions: Prepare the balance sheet for Caldwell & Co. Add the net profit for the current fiscal period to the earned surplus account; do not report it separately.

Bookkeeping and budgeting for the family and the individual

Need for personal and family bookkeeping records. Bookkeeping records aid business in planning for more efficient operations. Bookkeeping records are also important for the individual or the family that wants to plan for more intelligent use of income. If systematic records are not kept, there is no basis upon which to plan for purchases of essentials, to provide adequately for savings, and to make funds available for recreation and some of the luxuries.

The Frank Terry family. Frank Terry has a wife and two children. For a number of years the Terry family has kept a set of books in which to record its income and expenditures. At the beginning of each year the family draws up a budget of its expected income and expenditures. Periodically during the year the expenditures are compared with the budget.

Terry family balance sheet. At the end of each year Mr. Terry prepares a balance sheet showing the assets, the liabilities, and the proprietorship of his family. The balance sheet on December 31, 1956, is:

THE FRANK TERRY FAMILY
Balance Sheet
December 31, 1956

Assets

Cash	$ 650.35	
Life Insurance Cash Value	845.00	
Furniture and Household Equipment	3,000.00	
Automobile	1,200.00	
House	14,650.00	
Social Security Deposits	390.00	
Total Assets		$20,735.35

Liabilities

IRC Savings and Loan Association	$ 9,276.62

Proprietorship

The Frank Terry Family, Capital	11,458.73
Total Liabilities and Proprietorship	$20,735.35

435

Analyzing the balance sheet.

Assets. Several of the assets are similar to those illustrated in other balance sheets. These are Cash, Furniture and Household Equipment, Automobile, and House. Two assets that have not been illustrated before are Life Insurance Cash Value and Social Security Deposits.

Life insurance policies provide for a cash surrender value. The amount the insurance company will pay a policyholder if he wishes to turn his policy in for cash is called the *cash surrender value.* This cash value is an asset. On December 31, 1956, Mr. Terry examined his policies and found that the cash surrender value totaled $845. This value was therefore listed on the balance sheet as an asset.

A tax of 2¼% on the first $4,200 of Mr. Terry's salary is withheld to provide for old-age and survivor benefits. These amounts are deposited to his credit with the Social Security Administration. The total of Mr. Terry's social security deposits on December 31, 1956, was $390. Social security deposits are considered to be an asset, because they provide an annuity for old age and benefits for survivors.

Liabilities. Mr. Terry owed $9,276.62 to the IRC Savings and Loan Association. This amount was the balance due on the mortgage the Association held on his home. Each month Mr. Terry makes to the Association a payment that both pays the interest due on the mortgage for the month and reduces the principal.

Proprietorship. By subtracting the total liabilities from the total assets, Mr. Terry found that his family proprietorship was $11,458.73.

Income and expense accounts.

Family and individual bookkeeping systems need to be as simple as possible and yet show all the important facts needed for making income tax returns and regulating expenditures.

An income account is maintained for Mr. Terry's salary. Other family income is recorded in the account Other Income. For each of the main types of expenses an account is kept. Income and expense accounts used by the Terry family are shown below.

Income Accounts:
  Salary
  Other Income

Expense Accounts:
  Automobile Expense — car insurance, repairs, oil, gas, and depreciation.
  Clothing Expense — all wearing apparel, including shoes and hats.
  Donations — church and charities.
  Food Expense — groceries, meat, and milk.
  Gifts — Christmas Club installments, birthday and personal gifts.

Household Expense — depreciation of house, depreciation of furniture and equipment, light, heat, water, electricity, telephone, cleaning, laundry.

Insurance Expense — life insurance and group insurance.

Interest Expense

Medical Expense — drugs, hospitalization insurance, dentist and doctor bills, hospital bills, etc.

Personal Expense — all amounts given to the members of the family for miscellaneous expenses for which no detailed record was kept.

Taxes — Federal Income

Taxes — Real Estate

Taxes — State Income

Vacation Expense — Vacation Club installments and additional vacation expenses.

Terry family budget. A family has the problem of distributing its income over all types of expenditures so that the greatest benefits will be received. Plans should be made in advance to show how much income may be received and how the available funds should be spent. A financial statement of estimated income and expenses for a period is called a *budget*. The Frank Terry family budget for 1957 is shown on the following page.

In preparing their 1957 budget, the family consulted their records for 1956 to determine how much was spent for each type of expense. They talked over changes they anticipated in their spending during the year of 1957 and decided upon an amount that was sufficient for each type of expense. The total of their estimated expense items was $5,171. They subtracted this amount from their estimated income, $6,035, to determine their estimated increase in proprietorship, $864.

Automobile Expense and Household Expense were divided into current expenses and depreciation expenses. This division was made so that Mr. Terry could estimate how much he had to pay out in cash in each pay period and how much his depreciation expenses would be.

A part of the money collected as life insurance premiums by the life insurance company is used to cover its operating costs and the benefits it must pay under some of its policies. This part of the premiums is an expense to the policyholder. The balance of the premiums accumulates as a cash value that may be withdrawn by the policyholder if he wishes to cancel his policy. This part of the premiums is an investment of the policyholder. The Terry family expected to pay $263 for insurance premiums during 1957. The expense part, $163, was listed in the expense section of the budget.

Mr. Terry was paid semimonthly. He had to decide how much of each pay check he should allot on each payday to the various types of expenditures. To determine these amounts he divided the yearly allotment for each expenditure by 24, the number of pay checks he received.

THE FRANK TERRY FAMILY
Budget
For 1957

	Yearly Estimates

Estimated Income:

Salary	$6,000.00	
Other Income	35.00	
Total Estimated Income		$6,035.00

Estimated Expenses:

Automobile Expense:		
Current $200.00		
Depreciation. 250.00	$ 450.00	
Clothing Expense	200.00	
Donations.	100.00	
Food Expense	1,080.00	
Gifts.	150.00	
Household Expense:		
Current $660.00		
Depreciation of Furniture		
and Household Equip-		
ment 150.00		
Depreciation of House . . . 300.00	1,110.00	
Insurance Expense.	163.00	
Interest Expense	460.00	
Medical Expense.	100.00	
Personal Expense	432.00	
Taxes--Federal Income.	570.00	
Taxes--Real Estate	146.00	
Taxes--State Income.	60.00	
Vacation Expense	150.00	
Total Estimated Expenses		5,171.00

| Estimated Increase in Proprietorship. . . . . | | $ 864.00 |

Budget of a family

Recording income and expenses. The Terry family uses a combination journal to record its income and expenses. The combination journal for the month of January is shown on pages 440 and 441.

Analyzing the combination journal. Special columns are provided in the combination journal for accounts that are frequently affected by transactions. General ledger columns are used to record transactions involving accounts for which there are no special columns.

Most of the transactions recorded in the combination journal of the Terry family involved the paying of cash for some purpose. These transactions were recorded in the manner explained in earlier chapters of the book. A few of the transactions recorded in Mr. Terry's journal were unusual and are explained in the following paragraphs.

Lines 8 and 9. On January 12, Mr. Terry paid the IRC Savings and Loan Association $90. Of this sum $51.67 was repayment of the principal and $38.33 was interest on the loan. The account IRC Savings and Loan Association was debited for $51.67 and Interest Expense was debited for $38.33.

Line 11. Mr. Terry's semimonthly salary was $250. From his salary the following deductions were made: federal income tax, $25.90; social security, $5.63. Cash was debited for the amount of the net pay received. Taxes — Federal Income and Social Security Deposits were debited for the amounts withheld for these purposes. Salary was credited for the salary earned.

Lines 12, 13, and 14. Mr. Terry deposits part of his salary check in a checking account and pays most of his bills by check. The cash not deposited is used for food, household, and personal allowances. Each payday Mrs. Terry receives an amount of money for the purchasing of food and the paying of miscellaneous household expenses. No record is kept in the family accounts of the details of these expenditures. Mrs. Terry carries over from month to month amounts remaining from her food and household allowances. In this way she is able to absorb heavy expenses incurred during one month with the balance from previous months.

Each payday each member of the family receives a personal allowance. No record is made in the family accounts of how personal allowances are spent.

The food allowance, the household allowance, and the personal allowances were established over a period of several years and were found to be adequate.

Line 15. In order to save systematically for the family vacation, Mr. Terry deposits $12.50 in a Vacation Club account at his bank each month. He considers this expenditure as an expense because the amount that he deposited in the Vacation Club account was used each year for vacations.

Lines 23 and 24. Occasionally Mr. and Mrs. Terry pay in cash from their personal funds amounts for items other than personal expenses. They make these payments in cash because it is not convenient for them to write many checks for small amounts. Very small expenditures of this type are paid from personal funds but are not recorded. If larger cash expenditures are made, Mrs. and Mrs. Terry record them in the combination journal and reimburse themselves at the time they receive their next allowances.

CASH DEBIT	CASH CREDIT	CHECK NO	DATE	NAME OF ACCOUNT	POST REF	GENERAL DEBIT	GENERAL CREDIT	
			1957 Jan 1	Balance on hand, $650.35	✓			1
	9 78	1	3	Briggs Garage				2
	26 00	2	3	Furniture and Household Equip.		26 00		3
	4 75	3	5	Telephone				4
	7 84	4	7	Gas and electric				5
	10 00	5	8	Medical Expense		10 00		6
	22 10	6	9	Oil Supply Co.				7
	90 00	7	12	IRC Savings and Loan Assn		51 67		8
				Interest Expense		38 33		9
	8 50	·8	14	Clothing				10
218 47			15	Salary			250 00	11
	45 00		15	Food allowance				12
	10 00		15	Household allowance				13
	18 00		15	Personal allowances				14
	12 50		15	Vacation Expense		12 50		15
	20 00	9	19	Insurance Expense		20 00		16
	5 95	10	22	Gifts		5 95		17
	4 25	11	28	Clothing				18
218 47			31	Salary			250 00	19
	45 00		31	Food allowance				20
	10 00		31	Household allowance				21
	18 00		31	Personal allowances				22
	3 75		31	Gasoline				23
	5 00		31	Donations		5 00		24
436 94	376 42		31	Totals 710.87		169 45	500 00	25

Combination journal of a family (left page)

During the latter half of January Mr. Terry paid in cash from his personal funds $3.75 for gasoline. He and Mrs. Terry made cash contributions to their church totaling $5. They reimbursed themselves by adding these amounts to the amounts they normally received for personal allowances. In this way they kept their personal funds from being depleted and maintained a record of nonpersonal expenditures.

	5 AUTOMOBILE EXPENSE DEBIT	6 CLOTHING EXPENSE DEBIT	7 FOOD EXPENSE DEBIT	8 HOUSEHOLD EXPENSE DEBIT	9 PERSONAL EXPENSE DEBIT	10 TAXES— FEDERAL INCOME DEBIT	11 SOCIAL SECURITY DEPOSITS DEBIT	
1								1
2	9 78							2
3								3
4				4 75				4
5				7 84				5
6								6
7				22 10				7
8								8
9								9
10		8 50						10
11						25 90	5 63	11
12			45 00					12
13				10 00				13
14					18 00			14
15								15
16								16
17								17
18		4 25						18
19						25 90	5 63	19
20			45 00					20
21				10 00				21
22					18 00			22
23	9 75							23
24	13 53	12 75	90 00	54 69	36 00	51 80	11 26	24
25	13 53	12 75	90 00	54 69	36 00	51 80	11 26	25
26								26
27								27
28								28
29								29

Combination journal of a family (right page)

Proving cash. At the end of each month Mr. Terry totals and proves the combination journal. Before he posts to the ledger, he compares the checkbook balance with the cash balance as reflected by the combination journal. Balances in the food, household, and personal allowances are carried over from month to month and are not included in the proving of cash.

Chapter 33. Bookkeeping for family and individual   441

Controlling expenditures. Mr. Terry divided his yearly budget into monthly allotments and entered these amounts on the heading line of the accounts. For example, the yearly allotment for current Automobile Expense was $200. Dividing this amount by 12, he entered the amount of the monthly budget, $16.67, in the heading of the Automobile Expense account as shown below:

DATE		ITEMS	POST. REF.	DEBIT	DATE	ITEMS	POST. REF.	CREDIT
Automobile Expense ACCOUNT NO. 51 — Monthly Budget: $16.67								
1957								
Jan.	31		1	1353				
Feb.	28		2	1646				
Mar.	31		3	2061				
Apr.	30		4	1593				
May	31		5	1788				
June	30		6	1884				

In order to control expenditures each month, Mr. Terry compared the totals of the accounts with the budget allotments. At the end of June when Mr. Terry checked the automobile account, he found the total for the first six months of the year was $103.25. The budget allotment for the same period was $100.02 ($16.67 × 6). From these figures Mr. Terry concluded that he was operating his automobile at about the budget figure.

Analyzing the year-end records. In order to prove the accuracy of the records for the year, a trial balance was taken of all the accounts in the ledger. Mr. Terry entered the trial balance in the first two columns of an eight-column work sheet so that he could make his adjusting entries and so that his expense and income analysis and his balance sheet for the year would all appear on one work sheet. The work sheet completed for the year ended December 31 is shown on the opposite page.

Adjusting entries. At the end of the year it is necessary that adjusting entries be made so that the asset and the expense accounts will reflect the correct values. Figures for the adjusting entries are taken from the Adjustments columns of the work sheet.

The value of the furniture and household equipment at the beginning of the year and all purchases of furniture and household equipment during the year were entered as debits in the furniture and household equipment account. This furniture and equipment has decreased in value because of depreciation. An entry must therefore be made to record the expense and

Work sheet for a family

The Frank Terry Family
Work Sheet
For Year Ended December 31, 1957

#	Account Titles	Acct. No.	Trial Balance Debit	Trial Balance Credit	Adjustments Debit	Adjustments Credit	Expense & Income Debit	Expense & Income Credit	Balance Sheet Debit	Balance Sheet Credit	#
1	Cash	11	135652						135652		1
2	Life Insurance Cash Value	12	84500		(a)10000				94500		2
3	Furniture & Household Equipment	13	314000			(d)15475			298525		3
4	Automobile	14	120000			(b)25000			95000		4
5	House	15	1465000			(c)30000			1435000		5
6	Social Security Deposits	16	48450						48450		6
7	Checking & Savings Accounts	21		865658						865658	7
8	The Frank Terry Family, Capital	31		1145873						1145873	8
9	Salary	41		630000				630000			9
10	Other Income	42		5000				5000			10
11	Automobile Expense	51	21590		(b)25000		46590				11
12	Clothing Expense	52	24293				24293				12
13	Donations	53	11000				11000				13
14	Food Expense	54	108000				108000				14
15	Gifts	55	14800				14800				15
16	Household Expense	56	67974		(e)15475 (c)30000		113449				16
17	Insurance Expense	57	26300			(a)10000	16300				17
18	Interest Expense	58	45996				45996				18
19	Medical Expense	59	14500				14500				19
20	Personal Expense	60	43200				43200				20
21	Taxes-Federal Income	61	62791				62791				21
22	Taxes-Real Estate	62	15500				15500				22
23	Taxes-State Income	63	6350				6350				23
24	Vacation Expense	64	16635				16635				24
25			2846531	2846531	80475	80475	539404	635000	2011531	2107127	25
26	Increase in Proprietorship						95596			95596	26
27							635000	635000	2107127	2107127	27

the decrease in the value of the asset. In order to simplify the records, the depreciation expense was debited to the account Household Expense; a separate account with depreciation was not set up. The decrease in value was credited directly to the account Furniture and Household Equipment; an allowance for depreciation was not set up.

The value of the automobile at the beginning of the year was shown in the asset account Automobile. The automobile has decreased in value during the year because of depreciation. The depreciation was recorded by debiting Automobile Expense and crediting Automobile.

The value of the house at the beginning of the year was shown in the asset account House. The house has decreased in value during the year because of depreciation. The depreciation was recorded by debiting Household Expense and crediting House.

During the year insurance premiums totaling $263 were debited to Insurance Expense, but this total was not all expense. With the payment of each premium the cash value of some of the life insurance policies was increased, and this increase was an asset.

The balance in the account Life Insurance Cash Value was not correct at the end of the year because, with the payment of premiums, the cash value of the policies had been increased. By checking the cash surrender tables printed on the policies, the ending cash value was determined to be $945. This amount was an increase of $100 over the beginning cash value of $845. To record the increase in the cash value, an adjusting entry was made debiting Life Insurance Cash Value and crediting Insurance Expense for the amount of the increase. When this entry was posted, the balance of the life insurance cash value account agreed with the cash surrender value stated on the policy and the balance of the insurance expense account represented the actual expense of insurance.

Closing entries. In order that the expense and the income accounts for one year could be easily compared with the expense and the income accounts for the following year, Mr. Terry closed each expense and each income account by transferring the balance of each account to an account entitled Expense and Income Summary. He made an entry in the combination journal from the information in the Expense and Income columns of the work sheet. The expense and income summary account was credited for the total of all the items in the Expense and Income Credit column, and each item was debited for its balance. The expense and income summary account was debited for the total of all the items in the Expense and Income Debit column, and each item was credited for its balance.

When these entries were posted, all expense and income accounts were in balance; each account was therefore ruled. The account Expense and Income Summary had a credit balance of $955.96. To close this account, an entry was made in the combination journal debiting Expense and Income Summary and crediting The Frank Terry Family, Capital. When this entry was posted, the expense and income summary account was in balance and the capital account had a credit balance of $12,414.69, which was the capital as of December 31, 1957.

Statement of income and expenses. In order to have a convenient means of comparing the operations of the family with the budget plan, Mr. Terry prepared a *statement of income and expenses.* This statement showed the amount and the source of income, the amount and the kind of each expense, and the amount of the increase in proprietorship. The statement of income and expenses prepared by Mr. Terry is shown below.

THE FRANK TERRY FAMILY
Statement of Income and Expenses
For Year Ended December 31, 1957

	Budget		Actual	
Income:				
Salary	$6,000.00		$6,300.00	
Other Income	35.00		50.00	
Total Income		$6,035.00		$6,350.00
Expenses:				
Automobile Expense . .	$ 450.00		$ 465.90	
Clothing Expense . . .	200.00		242.93	
Donations.	100.00		110.00	
Food Expense	1,080.00		1,080.00	
Gifts.	150.00		148.00	
Household Expense. . .	1,110.00		1,134.49	
Insurance Expense. . .	163.00		163.00	
Interest Expense . . .	460.00		459.96	
Medical Expense. . . .	100.00		145.00	
Personal Expense . . .	432.00		432.00	
Taxes--Federal Income.	570.00		627.91	
Taxes--Real Estate . .	146.00		155.00	
Taxes--State Income. .	60.00		63.50	
Vacation Expense . . .	150.00		166.35	
Total Expenses		5,171.00		5,394.04
Increase in Proprietorship.		$ 864.00		$ 955.96

Statement of income and expenses

The amounts in the Budget columns of the statement of income and expenses are based on the amounts in the family budget prepared at the beginning of the year. The amounts in the Actual columns are based on the amounts in the Expense and Income columns of the work sheet.

Balance sheet. In order to compare his assets and his proprietorship at the end of the year with those at the beginning of the year, Mr. Terry prepared the balance sheet shown below from the figures in the balance sheet columns of the work sheet.

THE FRANK TERRY FAMILY
Balance Sheet
December 31, 1957

Assets

Cash	$ 1,356.52	
Life Insurance Cash Value.	945.00	
Furniture and Household Equipment. . . .	2,985.25	
Automobile	950.00	
House.	14,350.00	
Social Security Deposits	484.50	
Total Assets		$21,071.27

Liabilities

IRC Savings and Loan Association	$ 8,656.58

Proprietorship

The Frank Terry Family, Capital.	$11,458.73	
Increase in Proprietorship	955.96	
The Frank Terry Family, Present Capital.		12,414.69
Total Liabilities and Proprietorship . .		$21,071.27

Balance sheet of a family

The asset Cash increased from $650.35 at the beginning of the year to $1,356.52 at the end of the year. A large part of this increase represented cash set aside in the budget each month to offset the depreciation of the automobile, the furniture and household equipment, and the house. Depreciation is included in the budget because it represents an expense. Depreciation, however, is not an immediate cash expense and, as a result, cash set aside for replacement of assets is accumulated in the checking account. Occasionally Mr. Terry uses a part of this cash fund when he trades in his car for a new one or when he replaces furniture or household equipment.

Revising the budget. In preparing the budget for 1958, Mr. Terry made use of the budget for 1957 and the actual income and expenses for 1957 shown in the statement on the preceding page. He compared the figures for each item of income and each item of expense.

The actual income was larger than the budget income because Mr. Terry received an increase in salary during the year. Some of the expenses exceeded the budget allowances, but the amount by which the actual expenses exceeded the budget was less than Mr. Terry's increase in salary. As a result, the actual increase in proprietorship was greater than the budgeted increase.

Mr. Terry and his family decided that their budget needed only a slight change for the coming year. On the basis of the actual expenses for the year 1957 and in the light of added income and expenses anticipated for the year 1958, the Terry family prepared a budget. Because the revised budget was based on well-kept records and on anticipated changes in spending, it was a sound one.

Income tax data. Mr. Terry kept a complete set of records. As a result, he found that he was able to fill out his income tax returns with a minimum of difficulty. Mr. Terry's records provided all the information he needed to prepare his returns.

From his two income accounts Mr. Terry obtained his yearly income as follows:

Salary	$6,300.00
Other Income	50.00
Total Income	$6,350.00

The instructions accompanying the income tax form showed that donations to charitable organizations, interest expense, and taxes could be subtracted from the amount on which federal income tax had to be paid. From a study of his accounts and check stubs, Mr. Terry found that the following amounts were allowable deductions under the law:

Donations	$110.00
Interest Expense	459.96
Taxes — Real Estate	155.00
Taxes — State Income	63.50
Taxes—State Gasoline	12.00
Automobile License	10.00
Total Deductions	$810.46

Mr. Terry kept his canceled checks on file and as a result could support the amounts he listed for each of his allowable deductions.

Bookkeeping for the individual. The advantages of keeping a budget are the same for the individual as for the family. The expenses of a family are generally more numerous than those of an individual, but the procedures for recording the expenses of one are essentially the same as for the other. From a periodic study of his records, an individual can determine how nearly his spending agrees with his spending plan.

CHAPTER QUESTIONS

1. Why is it important for a family to keep accurate records of its expenditures?
2. Why does Mr. Terry list among his assets the cash value of his life insurance policies?
3. Why does Mr. Terry list among his assets his social security deposits?
4. What procedure did the Terry family follow in setting up their budget for 1957?
5. Why were Automobile Expense and Household Expense divided on the budget on page 438 into current expense and depreciation expense?
6. On Lines 8 and 9 of the illustration on page 440, what entry was made to record the payment to the IRC Savings and Loan Association?
7. On Line 11 of the illustration on pages 440 and 441, what entry was made to record Mr. Terry's semimonthly salary?
8. What arrangement did the Terry family have for handling household and personal allowances?
9. Why did Mr. Terry record the amount $16.67 in the heading of the automobile expense account shown on page 442?
10. Which of Mr. Terry's accounts required adjustment at the end of the year?
11. What use is made of the comparison of budgeted and actual income and expenses in the statement of income and expenses?

INCREASING YOUR BUSINESS VOCABULARY

What is the meaning of each of the following terms:

(a) cash surrender value
(b) budget

(c) statement of income and expenses

CASES FOR DISCUSSION

1. The family bookkeeping system developed in this chapter illustrated the main books of account kept by the Terry family. In order to maintain control of household and personal allowances, what types of records would you recommend that the Terry family keep?
2. The Ray Brown family maintained a set of books similar to those illustrated in this chapter. All receipts and all payments were carefully recorded in the combination journal and were posted to the ledger. At the end of the year, however, no statements were made because the Brown family followed the same budget each year. What are the disadvantages of this system?
3. The Harold Attlee family maintains a record of cash income and expenditures but keeps no record of assets, depreciation, liabilities, or capital. What are the advantages of the Terry family's system in this chapter as compared with the Attlee family's system?

APPLICATION PROBLEMS

Problem 33-1. Recording the transactions of a family

The C. D. Green family has been keeping bookkeeping records similar to those of the Terry family illustrated in this chapter. The chart of accounts and the distribution of expenses are the same as those of the Terry family.

Instructions: 1. Record in a combination journal like the one on pages 440 and 441 the following transactions completed by Mr. Green during the month of April:

April 1. Balance of cash on hand, $452.80.

2. Issued Check No. 43 for $5.25 for the telephone bill.

3. Issued Check No. 44 for $26.95 for a floor lamp for the living room.

4. Issued Check No. 45 for $62.50 for a new suit.

5. Issued Check No. 46 for $87.50 in payment of the semiyearly taxes on the house.

8. Issued Check No. 47 for $24.60 for fuel oil.

10. Issued Check No. 48 for $9.45 for the gas and electric bill.

12. Issued Check No. 49 for $10 to the Community Chest.

15. Received his semimonthly salary of $225 less a deduction of $20.50 for income tax and a deduction of $5.06 for social security tax.

15. Gave Mrs. Green her $50 food allowance and her $10 household allowance.

15. Gave the members of the family their personal allowances, $16.

15. Reimbursed the personal allowances for the following cash expenditures:

> Gasoline and oil, $3.40
> Church donation, $3

15. Deposited $15 in the Vacation Club account.

15. Deposited $5 in the Christmas Club account.

20. Issued Check No. 50 for $12.50 for the monthly life insurance premium.

25. Issued Check No. 51 for $16.50 for automobile repairs.

27. Issued Check No. 52 for $80 to the Guaranty Savings and Loan Association. Of this amount $50 was repayment of the principal and $30 was interest on the loan.

30. Received his semimonthly salary of $225 less a deduction of $20.50 for income tax and a deduction of $5.06 for social security tax.

30. Gave Mrs. Green her $50 food allowance and her $10 household allowance.

30. Gave the members of the family their personal allowances, $16.

April 30. Reimbursed the personal allowances for the following cash expenditures:

> Gasoline and oil, $2.50
> Church donation, $3
> Gift, $3.50
> Clothing, $6.80

Instructions: 2. Total, prove, and rule the columns in the combination journal.

Problem 33-2. Work at the end of the fiscal period for a family

At the end of the fiscal year on December 31, the account balances in the ledger maintained by the C. D. Green family were as follows:

Cash, $1,331.85
Life Insurance Cash Value, $620.45
Furniture and Household Equipment,
  $2,784.60
Automobile, $1,050
House, $12,800
Social Security Deposits, $246
Guaranty Savings and Loan Association,
  $6,742.34
C. D. Green Family, Capital,
  $11,099.97
Salary, $5,400
Other Income, $19.84

Automobile Expense, $143.50
Clothing Expense, $340.25
Donations, $92
Food Expense, $1,200
Gifts, $122
Household Expense, $585.50
Insurance Expense, $243
Interest Expense, $352
Medical Expense, $122
Personal Expense, $432
Taxes — Federal Income, $470
Taxes — Real Estate, $175
Vacation Expense, $152

Instructions: 1. Prepare an eight-column work sheet for the year ended December 31 of the current year. Use the following data for adjustments:

(a) Estimated depreciation of furniture and household equipment, $139.
(b) Estimated depreciation of automobile, $250.
(c) Estimated depreciation of house, $250.
(d) Increase in life insurance cash value, $100.

2. Prepare a statement of income and expenses for the year.
3. Prepare a balance sheet for December 31, 19--.

CHAPTER 34

Bookkeeping and budgeting for school and social organizations

Need for organization records. Organizations such as clubs, lodges, associations, and churches are sometimes spoken of as social organizations, to distinguish them from business organizations. The business transactions of a social organization are usually handled or directed by an individual known as a *treasurer*.

The treasurer of any social organization finds it desirable to keep records of all transactions because:

(1) An organization needs to make plans so that its expenses will not exceed its income.

(2) The treasurer of any organization that collects dues needs to keep a careful record of the dues collected so that he will know, at all times, the amount paid and the amount owed by each member.

(3) The treasurer of a social organization receives and pays money that is not his own. His records should be kept in such a manner that their accuracy can be proved by an audit committee or an auditor. If a proof of the accuracy of the treasurer's record is not provided, there may be doubt as to whether the treasurer has properly accounted for all the receipts and all the payments of the organization.

(4) The members of social organizations are entitled to summary reports of the income and the expenditures of their treasurer as evidence of the manner in which their funds have been handled.

(5) The treasurer's financial reports are very helpful in the decisions made by the membership at business meetings of the organization.

Budgeting income and expenses. The planning of the activities of any social organization should include plans with reference to income and expenses, that is, the preparation of a *budget*. Usually this budget of estimated income and expenses is prepared by a committee — a special finance committee, an executive committee, or a committee of officers.

When a social organization has maintained records for several years, the first step in the preparation of a budget is an examination of these records. The income and the expenditures for several fiscal periods should be studied in detail. Estimates for the future can then be made with much greater accuracy.

When a new club is being formed, it is impossible to base the first budget upon past records. It becomes necessary then to rely on the judgment of one or more members of the organization or upon the experience and the records of other similar organizations.

Budget of a high school club. The Future Business Leaders of America Club of the Central High School is a school service organization that meets twice a month. The first official act of the officers and the sponsor was the planning of a financial budget for the school year of nine months. The membership at the beginning of the year was thirty-three. The constitution of the club stated that the dues were to be 25 cents a month for nine months.

Plans were made to have two candy sales and to arrange to sell tickets for a movie benefit. The proposal to spend $15 for additional clubroom equipment was approved. It was agreed that the club should provide a float for the homecoming parade, have a picture in the high school yearbook, send a delegate to the state convention, and have a Christmas party. The annual budget that was finally adopted was as follows:

FBLA Club

Budget

For School Year 1957-1958

Cash on Hand September 9, 1957			$ 14.50
Estimated Income:			
Dues from Members (33 @ $2.25). . . .		$ 74.25	
Profit from Candy Sales:			
October.	$10.00		
February	10.00	20.00	
Profit from Benefit Movie		25.00	
Total Estimated Income.			119.25
Total Estimated Cash Receipts.			$133.75
Estimated Payments:			
Christmas Party		$ 20.00	
Clubroom Equipment.		15.00	
Delegate Expenses		30.00	
Homecoming Float.		10.00	
Miscellaneous		6.00	
National Dues		16.50	
Picture in Yearbook		12.00	
Refreshments at Meetings.		8.00	
Total Estimated Payments.			117.50
Estimated Cash on Hand May 30, 1958. . . .			$ 16.25

Budget of a high school club

The immediate record of cash receipts. A bound book of blank receipt stubs with detachable blank receipts is known as a *receipt book*. Such a book is commonly used by the treasurer of a social organization as the immediate record of each cash receipt. A page of the receipt book of the FBLA Club is shown below.

Receipt and stub

The stub of the receipt should be filled out first and then the receipt should be prepared. The receipt is detached from the stub and is given to the individual from whom the money was received. The stubs in the receipt book then constitute a *continuous record* of all cash receipts.

Membership record book. A book that lists the names of all the members of an organization and shows the dues that have been collected from each member is a *membership record book*. The membership record book of the FBLA Club is illustrated below.

FBLA Club
Membership Record
For 1957-1958

	Sept.	Oct.	Nov.	Dec.	Jan.	Feb.	Mar.	Apr.	May
1. Aikman, Ernestine	.25	.25	.25	✓	.50	.25	.25	.25	.25
2. Batz, John	.25	.25	✓	✓	.75	.25	dropped		
3. Bear, Hilda	.50	✓	.25	.25	.25	.25	.25	.25	.25
4. Bower, Merton	✓	.75	✓	.25	.25	.25	.25	.25	
5. Carey, Catherine	.25	.25	.25	.25	.25	✓	✓	✓	1.00
6. Cebelin, Walter	.25	.25	.25	✓	.75	✓	.25	.25	.25
7. Daly, June	.25	.25	.25	.25	.25	.25	.25	.25	.25
8. Dosch, Ralph	.25	.50	✓	.25	✓	.50	.25		
9. Greene, Jane	.25	.25	.25	.25	1.25	✓	✓	✓	✓
32. Siaworth, Arthur	.25	.25	.25	.25	left school				
33. Stewart, Lucile	.25	.25	✓	.75	✓	.25	.25	.25	
Totals	8.75	8.25	7.75	7.00	9.75	9.00	7.50	7.25	6.75

Membership record book

At the time the dues are received from the members, they are recorded on the stubs in the receipt book. At intervals, usually at least once a week, these amounts are posted from the receipt-book stubs to the membership record. The posting is indicated on the stub by a small check mark, which is placed just at the right of the amount.

Each amount received from a member is entered in the membership record in the column for the month in which the payment is made. If dues are for more than one month, check marks are placed in the additional columns covered by the amount received so that anyone glancing at the record can readily see for which months each member has paid. Note that 50 cents was received from Hilda Bear in September. This amount was entered in the column for September and a check mark was placed in the column for October to show that the dues were received for this month also. Merton Bower made no payment in September but paid 75 cents in October. The amount received was entered in the October column and check marks were placed in the September and November columns.

Approval of bills. The treasurer of the FBLA Club maintains a file for unpaid bills. At intervals these bills are approved by the club president and the faculty sponsor. The bill is first stamped with a rubber stamp and the approval is indicated by the signatures of the president and the sponsor. After the bills have been properly approved, they may be paid by the treasurer. An invoice that has been approved by the student president of the FBLA Club and by the faculty sponsor is shown below.

ACME SUPPLY COMPANY

Complete Line of Office Supplies

596 Main Street
Springfield

Sold to	FBLA Club	Date	October 8, 1957
	Central High School		
	Springfield	No.	493
Shipped via		Terms	Net 10 days

12 rolls #36 Green Crepe Paper	.12	1.44
12 rolls #13 Yellow Crepe Paper	.12	1.44
3 balls #10 White Twine	.20	.60
		3.48

APPROVED
President Wm. Page
Sponsor Mary Janse

Invoice approved for payment

454   *20th Century Bookkeeping and Accounting*

Two-column cashbook. The records of the FBLA Club are kept on a cash basis; that is, only transactions involving the receipt and the payment of cash are recorded. The book of original entry is the two-column cashbook illustrated below.

Date		Explanation	Receipts		Payments	
1957 Sept.	9	Balance	14	50		
	9	Dues	3	75		
	10	Secretary's minute book				75
	10	Treasurers record books			1	50
	16	Dues	3	00		
	18	Banner for clubroom				89
	19	Refreshments at meeting of Sept. 9			1	80
	22	Get Well card — Jane Greene's mother				20
	25	Homecoming float expense			1	27
	30	Dues	2	00		
	30	Totals	23	25	6	41
	30	Balance			16	84
			23	25	23	25
1957 Oct.	1	Balance	16	84		

Cashbook of the FBLA Club

Analyzing the two-column cashbook. The first amount column, "Receipts," contains the balance at the beginning of the month and all receipts of cash. The second amount column, "Payments," contains all payments of cash. The date and the explanation of each transaction are given in the Date and the Explanation columns.

When the total of a cash record is not posted, it is desirable to record the cash balance in the cash receipts column. It is then possible to show the cash balance at the end of the period as the difference between the footings of the Receipts and the Payments columns without separate calculations at the bottom of the page.

At the end of the month the Receipts and the Payments columns are footed with small pencil footings and the balance (the difference between the totals of the Receipts and the Payments columns) is found. This balance should equal the cash on hand. In order to show that the total of the payments plus the balance on hand at the end of the month is equal to the total of the Receipts column, the new balance is added to the Payments column and the totals of the Receipts and the Payments columns are then brought down to the same line. The book is ruled with a double rule across all columns except the Explanation column, and the new balance is entered in the Receipts column with the date October 1.

Proof of accuracy of records. The faculty sponsor and an audit committee appointed by the president of the FBLA Club examine the treasurer's records at intervals to determine their accuracy. It is therefore necessary that the treasurer have his records in such a form that the accuracy can be proved.

The cash received from dues as recorded in the cashbook for each month must be equal (1) to the sum of the cash received from dues as shown on the receipts stubs for that month and (2) to the total of all the receipts entered in the column for that month in the membership record. For each cash payment the treasurer must have a bill or invoice that has been approved by the president and the sponsor to show that the payment was authorized. The invoice must also be receipted by the one to whom payment was made so that another claim for the payment of the same bill cannot be made. A bill that is correctly receipted is shown below.

ACME SUPPLY COMPANY
Complete Line of Office Supplies

596 Main Street
Springfield

Sold to	FBLA Club Central High School Springfield	Date	October 8, 1957
		No.	493
Shipped via		Terms	Net 10 days

12 rolls #36 Green Crepe Paper	.12	1.44
12 rolls #13 Yellow Crepe Paper	.12	1.44
3 balls #10 White Twine	.20	.60
		3.48

APPROVED

President: *Wm. Page!*

Sponsor: *Mary Vance.*

PAID
J.C.13.
Oct. 16, 1957.

Receipted invoice

Treasurer's report. A written report of cash receipts and cash payments that the treasurer of an organization prepares and submits to the membership is known as the *treasurer's report*. At the end of the month the treasurer classifies the receipts and the payments under the headings given in the budget so that comparisons may be made. The classification may first be made on a separate sheet of paper, but it is drawn up in a permanent form as a treasurer's report.

At the end of the year the items in each of the treasurer's monthly reports are combined into one report for the entire year. This report is most useful when it provides for a comparison of the budget and the actual income and expenses. The budget amounts may be entered in the first amount column and the actual amounts may be entered in the second amount column. Any difference between the actual amounts and the budgeted amounts can then be readily observed. This comparison of the budget amounts with the actual amounts will be useful in the preparation of the budget for the following year.

FBLA Club
Treasurer's Report
For School Year Ended May 30, 1958

	Budget	Actual
Cash on Hand September 9, 1957	$ 14.50	$ 14.50
Income:		
Dues from Members	74.25	72.00
Profit from Candy Sales	20.00	18.20
Profit from Benefit Movie	25.00	22.85
Homecoming Float Prize.		5.00
Total Cash Receipts and Beginning Balance.	$133.75	$132.55
Payments:		
Christmas Party	$ 20.00	$ 16.20
Clubroom Equipment.	15.00	19.18
Delegate Expenses	30.00	27.60
Homecoming Float.	10.00	8.43
Miscellaneous	6.00	6.90
National Dues	16.50	16.50
Picture in Yearbook	12.00	12.00
Refreshments at Meetings.	8.00	8.25
Total Payments.	$117.50	$115.06
Cash on Hand May 30, 1958.	$ 16.25	$ 17.49

Treasurer's report for a school club for a year

Records of other school organizations. The records of other high school organizations may be similar to the records of the FBLA Club, but some changes will be needed to adapt the records to the needs of each organization. For example, the high school athletic department of the Custer High School sponsors four major sports — football, basketball, baseball, and track. Arthur H. Jordan is the faculty manager of athletics. He has charge of all ticket sales and is responsible for the financial records of the high school athletic department.

At the end of the season of each major sport he prepares a treasurer's report, showing a comparison of cash receipts and cash payments with the budget set up for each sport, and a balance sheet.

Budgeting athletic department income and expenses. The athletic committee of the Custer High School prepared a budget of income and expenses for the entire school year covering all four major sports. This budget for the coming year was based upon a careful analysis of the income and the expenses of the last two years.

The annual budget was then divided into four budgets, one for each of the four major sports. The budget for the football season only is presented below.

CUSTER HIGH SCHOOL ATHLETIC DEPARTMENT
Budget
For Football Season Ending November 30, 1957

Cash on Hand Sept. 1, 1957		$ 125.80
Estimated Income:		
Season Tickets.	$1,100.00	
Home Game Receipts.	500.00	
Away-from-Home Guarantees	200.00	
Miscellaneous Income.	50.00	
Total Estimated Income.		1,850.00
Total Estimated Cash Receipts.		$1,975.80
Estimated Payments:		
Equipment	$ 500.00	
First Aid Supplies.	100.00	
Miscellaneous Expense	140.00	
Officials	175.00	
Traveling Expense	420.00	
Visiting Teams Guarantees	200.00	
Total Estimated Payments.		1,535.00
Estimated Cash on Hand Nov. 30, 1957 .		$ 440.80

Budget of a high school athletic department

Balance sheet of high school athletic department. At the close of each school year Mr. Jordan prepared a balance sheet for the athletic department. The balance sheet at the close of the 1957 school year was:

CUSTER HIGH SCHOOL ATHLETIC DEPARTMENT
Balance Sheet
June 30, 1957

Assets		Liabilities	
Cash	$ 125.80	Boles Sporting Goods Co. . . .	$ 82.50
Football Equipment	1,135.00	Davis Print Shop	44.60
Basketball Equipment	303.50		
Baseball Equipment	321.75	Total Liabilities.	$ 127.10
Track Equipment.	142.80		
		Proprietorship	
		Custer High School Athletic Department, Capital . . .	1,901.75
		Total Liabilities and Pro-	
Total Assets	$2,028.85	prietorship	$2,028.85

Balance sheet of an athletic department

The financial records of most athletic departments are kept on a cash basis; that is, no transactions are recorded in the bookkeeping system until cash is either received or paid. Unpaid bills and invoices are kept in a file, and supplementary records are kept of all equipment.

Equipment record. Edgar Hayes is the student athletic manager and is responsible for recording equipment issued to players and accounting for its return. This record of equipment is kept on mimeographed cards, one of which is illustrated in this paragraph. A card record that shows the equipment issued to and returned by each player is known as an

equipment record card. Some items of equipment are numbered and others are not. If an item is numbered, the number is written in the Issued column at the time the player is equipped. If the item is not numbered, a check mark is placed in this column. When the equipment is returned, check marks will be placed in the Returned column.

Name Paul Davis		
Type of Equipment	Issued	Returned
Football pants	22	
Game jersey	18	
Practice jersey	18	
Sweat jacket	18	
Shoulder pad	✓	
Headgear	27	
Shoes	✓	
Sweat socks	✓	
Regular socks	✓	
Ankle Wrap	✓	

Equipment record card

Combination journal. The combination journal used by the faculty manager, Mr. Jordan, is illustrated on the next two pages.

COMBINATION JOURNAL

	CASH		CHECK NO.	DATE	NAME OF ACCOUNT	SEASON TICKETS CREDIT	HOME GAME RECEIPTS CREDIT	
	DEBIT	CREDIT						
1				1957 Oct. 1	Cash balance, $134.60			1
2		18 50	22	2	Colored paper for advertising			2
3	265 00			2	Sales of season tickets	265 00		3
4		52 50	23	3	Equipment			4
5		24 60	24	3	Tickets			5
6		25 00	25	4	Season ticket books			6
7		31 20	26	4	First aid supplies			7
8	92 30			4	Gate receipts—Lincoln game		92 30	8
9		35 00	27	4	Officials for Lincoln game			9
10		50 00	28	4	Guarantee to Lincoln			10
18	102 70			18	Gate receipts—Riverside game		102 70	18
19		35 00	33	18	Officials for Riverside game			19
20	20 50			18	Candy sales, Riverside game			20
21		50 00	34	18	Guarantee to Riverside			21
22		87 50	35	22	Equipment			22
23		19 85	36	23	First aid supplies			23
24	205 50			24	Sales of season tickets	205 50		24
25	50 00			25	Guarantee from Racine			25
26		97 00	37	25	Transportation to Racine			26
27	1105 50	866 85		31	Totals	790 00	195 00	27

Combination journal

Analysis of the combination journal. Columns 1 and 2 are used in recording cash receipts and cash payments. Since the cash balance at the beginning of the month does not have a corresponding credit in the combination journal, it is not placed in the Cash Debit column but is written as a memorandum in the Name of Account column. If the cash balance were written in the Cash Debit column, the debit and the credit footings would not balance.

The next column is used for the check numbers. All payments are made by check. Recording the check number for each payment provides a useful cross reference between the combination journal and the canceled checks that are returned by the bank.

The next two columns are for the date and the description of each transaction.

Columns 3, 4, 5, and 6 at the right of the Name of Account column are income credit columns. All income is grouped under four headings — season tickets, home game receipts, away-from-home guarantees, and

	FOR MONTH OF *October* 1957						PAGE 1	
	5	6	7	8	9	10	11	12
	AWAY - FROM - HOME GUAR. CREDIT	MISC. INCOME CREDIT	EQUIPMENT DEBIT	FIRST AID SUPPLIES DEBIT	MISC. EXPENSE DEBIT	OFFICIALS DEBIT	TRAVELING EXPENSE DEBIT	VISITING TEAMS GUAR. DEBIT
1								
2					18 50			
3								
4			52 50					
5					24 60			
6					25 00			
7				31 20				
8								
9						35 00		
10								50 00
18								
19						35 00		
20		20 50						
21								50 00
22			87 50					
23				19 85				
24								
25	50 00							
26							97 00	
	100 00	20 50	365 00	51 05	85 80	70 00	195 00	100 00
27	100 00	20 50	365 00	51 05	85 80	70 00	195 00	100 00

for athletic department

miscellaneous income. If cash is received from any of these four sources, the amount is recorded as a debit in the Cash Debit column and as a credit in one of the four income credit columns.

Columns 7 to 12 are debit columns for recording expenditures. When a cash payment is made, the amount is recorded in the Cash Credit column and also is debited in one of the six debit columns.

Footing and proving the combination journal. At the end of the month Mr. Jordan foots each column of the combination journal. On a separate sheet of paper he adds the footing of the Cash Debit column and the cash balance at the beginning of the month. From this total he subtracts the footing of the Cash Credit column. The difference is the cash balance and should agree with the amount of cash on hand at the end of the month. After he has proved cash, he proves the entire combination journal by finding whether the sum of all debit footings is equal to the sum of all credit footings.

Proof of accuracy. Mr. Jordan's records are audited at intervals; he must therefore be able to prove their accuracy.

The receipts from the sale of season tickets, individual tickets to home games, and away-from-home guarantees can be proved with the record of ticket sales and guarantees in the principal's office. Miscellaneous income is more difficult to prove, as it comes from various sources; but often there is a record of this income in the principal's office.

For each payment recorded in the combination journal there must be on hand an invoice approved by the athletic director and the faculty manager. It is not necessary for these invoices to be receipted because all invoices are paid by check and the canceled checks are sufficient proof that the various invoices have been paid.

All receipts of cash are deposited in the bank and all payments are made by check. The bank's records must therefore agree with the record in the combination journal and in this way provide further proof of the accuracy of the combination journal.

Treasurer's report. At the end of each month Mr. Jordan prepares a statement of cash receipts and cash payments in the following form:

CUSTER HIGH SCHOOL ATHLETIC DEPARTMENT
Treasurer's Report
For Month Ended October 31, 1957

Cash on Hand October 1, 1957		$ 134.60
Income:		
Season Tickets.	$ 790.00	
Home Game Receipts.	195.00	
Away-from-Home Guarantees	100.00	
Miscellaneous Income.	20.50	
Total Income.		1,105.50
Total Cash Receipts and Beginning Balance.		$1,240.10
Payments:		
Equipment	$ 365.00	
First Aid Supplies.	51.05	
Miscellaneous Expense	85.80	
Officials	70.00	
Traveling Expense	195.00	
Visiting Teams Guarantees	100.00	
Total Payments.		866.85
Cash on Hand October 31, 1957.		$ 373.25

Treasurer's report for an athletic department for one month

This illustration is an example of the manner in which the reports of an organization are adapted to the needs of those using the reports. A profit and loss statment is not prepared for the Custer High School Athletic Department because those in charge of the athletic department are not primarily interested in the reasons for any change in proprietorship. They are, however, interested in knowing the sources of income and the reasons for which payments were made. This information is given in the statement of cash receipts and cash payments. A report of cash receipts and cash payments is also useful when the receipts and the payments are compared with the budget so that those controlling the organization can determine whether the budget is being followed.

Other financial reports. At the end of the season for each sport Mr. Jordan prepares a treasurer's report (statement of cash receipts and cash payments) and a balance sheet. The treasurer's report includes both the budget and the actual amounts so that the two may be compared readily.

CUSTER HIGH SCHOOL ATHLETIC DEPARTMENT

Treasurer's Report

For Football Season Ended November 30, 1957

	Budget	Actual
Cash on Hand September 1, 1957	$ 125.80	$ 125.80
Income:		
Season Tickets.	1,100.00	1,150.00
Home Game Receipts.	500.00	485.00
Away-from-Home Guarantees	200.00	200.00
Miscellaneous Income.	50.00	48.50
Total Cash Receipts and Beginning Balance.	$1,975.80	$2,009.30
Payments:		
Equipment	$ 500.00	$ 535.00
First Aid Supplies.	100.00	96.70
Miscellaneous Expense	140.00	88.95
Officials	175.00	180.00
Traveling Expense	420.00	430.00
Visiting Teams Guarantees	200.00	200.00
Total Payments.	$1,535.00	$1,530.65
Cash on Hand November 30, 1957	$ 440.80	$ 478.65

Treasurer's report for an athletic department for football season

1. Why should the treasurer of a school organization keep accurate records of all cash receipts and cash payments?
2. What types of records should a high school club keep?
3. What should be the first step of a club in planning the year's activities?
4. What two records should a club treasurer keep of the collection of dues from the members of the club?
5. Why do most school organizations require the president of the organization and the faculty sponsor to approve bills before the treasurer pays them?
6. How is the treasurer of an organization able to prove the payment of bills?
7. When is the use of a two-column cashbook preferable to the use of a multi-column combination journal?
8. When is an organization said to be keeping its record on the cash basis?
9. Where does the faculty manager of the athletic department get the information for the assets and the liabilities sections of the balance sheet?
10. What is the purpose of the equipment record?
11. How is a multicolumn combination journal proved?

INCREASING YOUR BUSINESS VOCABULARY

What is the meaning of each of the following:

(a) treasurer
(b) receipt book
(c) membership record book
(d) treasurer's report
(e) equipment record card

CASES FOR DISCUSSION

1. The treasurer of the Choral Club of the Westby High School reported that Alfred Welke had not paid his dues for October. Alfred claimed that he had paid. How could this difference be settled?
2. The FBLA Club cashbook shown on page 455 has only two money columns. Why does the faculty manager of the Custer High School Athletic Department use a combination journal with twelve money columns?
3. June Daly, the treasurer of the FBLA Club, is anxious to have all cash receipts and cash payments accounted for. What procedure does she follow to insure proof of accuracy in accounting for all the money she handles?
4. The athletic committee of the Custer High School prepared the budget for the football season that is illustrated on page 458. If you were the faculty manager, how would you use this budget to keep payments within income?

Problem 34-1. Records of a high school athletic department

Robert Mavis is faculty treasurer of the athletic department of the Monroe High School.

Instructions: 1. Record the following transactions completed by Mr. Mavis during the month of November of the current year. Use a combination journal similar to the one illustrated on pages 460 and 461. All payments were made by check. The first check for November was No. 37.

Nov. 1. Cash on hand, $410.80.
      1. Paid the Sullivan Printing Company $27.50 for printing season tickets and homecoming programs.
      1. Received $169.80, the final installment on the sale of season tickets.
      2. Paid a $50 guarantee to the Hamilton team.
      2. Paid $20 to officials for the Hamilton game.
      2. Received $87.65 from gate receipts for the Hamilton game.
      2. Received $24.50 from the sale of homecoming programs.
      4. Paid $15.37 for first aid supplies.
      6. Paid $62.75 for new football equipment purchased.
      9. Received a $50 guarantee from the Milford team.
      9. Paid $43.75 for traveling expenses to Milford.
     12. Paid $13.50 for an advertisement in the school paper.
     15. Paid $6.25 for candy to be sold at the game on Saturday.
     16. ᐟeceived $69.80 from gate receipts for the Loveland game.
     16. Received $11.85 from candy sale at game.
     16. Paid $20 to officials for Loveland game.
     16. Paid $50 guarantee to Loveland team.
     20. Paid $5.30 for washing jerseys.
     21. Paid $3.95 for first aid supplies.
     23. Received $50 guarantee from Newport team.
     23. Paid $46.45 for traveling expenses to Newport.
     26. Paid $48 for football banquet.
     27. Paid $43.85 for cleaning of all equipment.
     29. Paid $28.50 for football awards and letters.
     30. Cash on hand, $389.23.

Instructions: 2. Foot, prove, and rule the combination journal for November.

The combination journal prepared in this problem is needed for use in Problem 34-2. If it is collected by your teacher, it should be returned to you before Problem 34-2 is assigned.

Problem 34-2. Reports of a high school athletic department

The columnar footings of the combination journal of the athletic department of the Monroe High School for the month of November were found in the preceding exercise. The columnar footings of the combination journal for the months of September and October were:

	September	October
Cash Debit....................................	$555.25	$533.85
Cash Credit...................................	413.98	391.68
Season Tickets Credit..........................	520.50	228.20
Home Game Receipts Credit.....................	34.75	191.50
Away-from-Home Guarantees Credit...............	......	100.00
Miscellaneous Income Credit.....................	......	14.15
Equipment Debit...............................	271.90	34.38
First Aid Supplies Debit.........................	27.58	18.20
Miscellaneous Expense Debit......................	44.50	41.60
Officials Debit.................................	20.00	60.00
Traveling Expense Debit.........................	......	87.50
Visiting Teams Guarantees Debit..................	50.00	150.00

Instructions: Prepare a treasurer's report for the entire football season ended November 30 of the current year. Use as your guide the model illustration on page 463. The cash on hand on September 1 was $127.36. The budget figures for the football season were as follows:

MONROE HIGH SCHOOL ATHLETIC DEPARTMENT
BUDGET
FOR FOOTBALL SEASON ENDING NOVEMBER 30, 19--

Cash on Hand September 1, 19--..............		127 36
Estimated Income:		
Season Tickets............................	900 00	
Home Game Receipts.......................	400 00	
Away-from-Home Guarantees.................	200 00	
Miscellaneous Income.......................	50 00	
Total Estimated Income.....................		1,550 00
Total Estimated Cash Receipts..................		1,677 36
Estimated Payments:		
Equipment................................	370 00	
First Aid Supplies..........................	60 00	
Miscellaneous Expense......................	250 00	
Officials..................................	120 00	
Traveling Expense..........................	160 00	
Visting Teams Guarantees...................	300 00	
Total Estimated Payments...................		1,260 00
Estimated Cash on Hand November 30, 19--......		417 36

Bookkeeping for a professional man

CHAPTER 35

Need of records for a professional man. The keeping of adequate records by the professional man is not only desirable for efficient management of his affairs, but it is also necessary for tax purposes. The state and the federal income tax laws require the professional man to keep accurate records of his income and his expenses in order that he may make accurate tax returns and reports. Since the professional man derives his income primarily from fees for personal services, a few special records are needed.

Daily appointment book of a dentist. Dr. S. T. Stone is a dentist in a moderate-sized city. Virtually all of his work is done by appointment. His dental hygienist and secretary, Ruth Porter, keeps an *appointment book* that also serves as a record of daily charges to patients' accounts and cash collections from patients.

A page of the appointment book for a part of one day, April 1, 1957, is shown below.

APPOINTMENT AND DAILY RECORD				
HOUR	PATIENT	SERVICE RENDERED	FEES	RECEIPTS
8 00 / 30	Mrs. John L. Wilson	Denture - full upper	125 00	55 00
9 00 / 15 / 30 / 45	Mrs. D. L. Potter	Prophylaxis	5 00	5 00
10 00 / 15 / 30 / 45	Miss Mary Radford	Simple amalgam filling	4 00	
	Mr. E. L. Barrington	Compound inlay	16 00	5 00
	Miss Martha Walton	On account		27 00
	Mr. J. E. Johnson	On account		8 50
MONTH april DATE 1 YEAR 1957		TOTALS	205 00	190 50

Dentist's appointment book

Analyzing the appointment book. All appointments for the day were listed in the appointment book at the time the appointments were made.

467

Appointments were often recorded several weeks or months in advance. The name of each patient was recorded in the appropriate space to indicate the time of his appointment. On the day the work was done, the line was completed to show the type of service rendered, the charge for this service, and the amount collected if money was received.

Several lines at the bottom of the appointment sheet did not have any particular time apportioned to them. These lines were used for recording appointments outside of office hours and collections received from patients on their accounts when not received at the time of a regular appointment.

The appointment book illustrated on page 467 served also as a cash receipts journal. The first amount column, headed "Fees," was used to record the charges for the work. The second column, headed "Receipts," was used to record the amounts actually received. The first entry at the bottom of the page was an immediate record of $27 received on account on April 1 from Miss Martha Walton for work previously completed. The second entry at the bottom of the page was an immediate record of $8.50 received on account from Mr. J. E. Johnson. All of these entries were posted daily to the appropriate patients' record cards.

Patient's record and ledger account card. Dr. Stone used an individual card for each patient. The front of one of these record cards is shown below, and the reverse side is shown at the top of the following page.

NAME Miss Martha Walton		ADDRESS 1423 Center Street							
DATE	OPERATION	TOOTH No.	DR.	CR.	DATE	OPERATION	TOOTH No.	DR.	CR.
1957 Feb. 14	Prophylaxis		5 00						
14	Xray		5 00						
21	O. Alloy	19	5 00						
21	D. Syn. Porcel.	8	7 00						
Mar. 5	Extraction	17	5 00						
Apr. 1	On account			27 00					
16	M. O. Alloy	3	7 00						
16	C. Base		2 00	9 00					

Front of a patient's record card

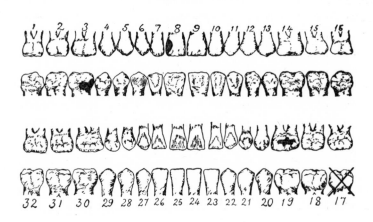

Back of a patient's record card

Analyzing the patient's record card. The patient's record card was an immediate record of the work done and was brought up to date each time the patient was in the dentist's chair. The front of the card was a complete ledger account of the patient. The back of the card had a chart of teeth that was marked by the dentist to supplement many of the entries on the front of the card.

Each entry on the front of the card showed the date the work was done, a description of the work done, the chart number of the tooth involved in the operation, and the amount of the charge for the work. As money was received from the patient, the amount received was credited to the patient in the Cr. amount column of his record card.

On the back of the card, the dentist shaded the diagram of the tooth to show the exact location of the work done. A cross marked through a tooth indicated extraction of that tooth.

Accounts receivable ledger. The patients' record cards were filed in a cabinet quickly accessible to the dentist, near the dentist's chair. This complete file of patients' record cards was Dr. Stone's accounts receivable ledger and also his individual patients' work completed file.

The combination journal of a dentist. All of the transactions completed by Dr. Stone were recorded in a combination journal similar to those developed in preceding chapters. Dr. Stone's combination journal for the month of April is illustrated in part at the top of the next two pages.

COMBINATION JOURNAL

	CASH		CHECK NO.	DATE	NAME OF ACCOUNT	POST REF.	GENERAL			
	DEBIT	CREDIT					DEBIT	CREDIT		
1		100 00	41	*1959* Apr. 1	Rent Expense	12	100 00			1
2		15 30	42	2	Burger Laboratories, Inc.					2
3	247 00			6	Professional Fees					3
28		18 20	51	30	To replenish petty cash fund					28
29		63 91	52	30	Salary Expense					29
30				30	FICA Taxes	57	1 69			30
31	1196 50	856 65		30	Totals		221 73	12 25		31
32	(11)	(11)					(✓)	(✓)		32
33										33

Combination journal

Analyzing the combination journal of a dentist. Special columns were provided in the combination journal for accounts that were frequently affected by transactions. The General Debit and Credit columns were used to record the transactions involving accounts for which there were no special columns.

Dr. Stone's secretary recorded in one entry in the combination journal the cash received for fees for an entire week. This entry was made at the close of business at the end of each week and on the last day of each month. The amount to be recorded was found by adding the totals of the Receipts column in the appointment book for the period for which the entry was made. Income from fees was recorded only when the cash had been received. The entry on Line 3 for April 6 illustrates the recording of fees received.

Dr. Stone made all large payments by check. He maintained a petty cash fund of $25 from which minor expenses were paid. Petty cash receipts were made out for each payment and were kept with the petty cash fund. Whenever the fund was running low, a check was drawn to replenish it. The entry for Check No. 51, Line 28, shows the entry to replenish the petty cash fund.

At intervals during the month Dr. Stone's secretary posted the items in the General Debit and Credit columns. On April 30 she totaled and ruled all of the amount columns of the combination journal. The sum of the totals of the debit columns was found to equal the sum of the totals of the credit columns. After this proof was made, the totals of all special columns were posted.

	PROFESSIONAL FEES CREDIT	DENTAL SUPPLIES EXP DEBIT	LABORATORY EXPENSE DEBIT	MISC. EXPENSE DEBIT	SALARY EXPENSE DEBIT	EMPLOYEES INCOME TAX PAY. CREDIT	FICA TAXES PAY CREDIT	DR. STONE DRAWING DEBIT	
1									1
2			15 30						2
3	247 00								3
28		8 20	6 20	3 80					28
29					75 00	9 40	1 69		29
30							1 69		30
31	1196 50	46 45	42 10	34 18	150 00	18 80	6 76	400 00	31
	1196 50	46 45	42 10	34 18	150 00	18 80	6 76	400 00	
32	(41)	(51)	(54)	(55)	(59)	(21)	(22)	(32)	32
33									33

of a dentist

Work at the end of the fiscal period. At the end of the year, December 31, 1957, Dr. Stone's secretary prepared an eight-column work sheet. From the work sheet, she prepared a statement of income and expenses. The statement is shown below:

```
                   DR. S. T. STONE
            Statement of Income and Expenses
            For Year Ended December 31, 1957
```

Professional Income:		
Professional Fees		$16,196.50
Professional Expenses:		
Dental Supplies Expense	$ 2,128.15	
Depreciation of Equipment . . .	360.88	
FICA Taxes.	67.50	
Insurance Expense	72.00	
Laboratory Expense.	850.32	
Miscellaneous Expense	228.26	
Office Supplies Expense	125.75	
Rent Expense.	1,200.00	
Salary Expense.	3,000.00	
Total Professional Expenses . .		8,032.86
Net Professional Income.		$ 8,163.64

Statement of income and expenses of a dentist

The information in the statement of income and expenses was used in the preparation of the income tax return.

A bookkeeping system for an attorney. The customer of a dentist is known as a *patient*; the customer of an attorney is known as a *client.* Unlike the dentist's patient, the attorney's client is seldom present while much of the work for him is being done. The work of an attorney in behalf of a client may be performed over a period of several weeks or months.

The attorney may keep an appointment book; but because of the nature of his work it will be supplemented by records with his clients that are best suited to the attorney's needs.

Collection docket of an attorney. The record kept by an attorney with clients who engage him to make collections for them is known as a *collection docket.* A page of the collection docket of Attorney Arthur Lambert is shown below.

ATTORNEYS' COLLECTION DOCKET No. 58

DEBTOR Henry Caldwell	DATE CLAIM REC'D Oct. 28, 1957
ADDRESS 1483 Langdon Avenue	DATE DISPOSED OF Dec. 2, 1957
BUSINESS	TOTAL AMOUNT $ 326.80
CREDITOR Crowell and Co.	AMOUNT COLLECTED $ 326.80
ADDRESS 210 West Main Street	FEES $ 81.70
REC'D CLAIM FROM	EXPENSE $
ATTORNEY FOR DEBTOR	AMOUNT REMITTED $ 245.10
CALLS ON DEBTOR	CHECK NO. 272

CORRESPONDENCE

RECEIVED FROM CREDITOR		
DATE	FOR	AMOUNT
Dec. 2	Commission	81 70

RECEIVED FROM DEBTOR				PAID TO CREDITOR			
DATE	AMOUNT	DATE	AMOUNT	CHECK NO.	AMOUNT	CHECK NO.	AMOUNT
Dec. 2 57	326 80			272	245 10		

REMARKS: Collection fee, 25%. No suit without further instructions.

Collection docket of an attorney

The collection docket contains space to record all the details relative to the case and to record all money collected and remitted to the client.

Case docket of an attorney. The record kept by an attorney with clients who engage him to represent them in law suits is known as a *case docket*. A page of Attorney Lambert's case docket is shown below.

ATTORNEYS' CASE DOCKET

IN THE *Common Pleas* COURT   COURT FILE NO. *a 11063*

COUNTY *Hamilton; State of Ohio*   OFFICE FILE NO. *128*

PARTIES	NATURE OF CASE
Reliable Motor Co., Inc.	ACTION *Lawsuit*
1233 Gilbert Avenue	
City	AMOUNT *Minimum fee $100 with costs*
PLAINTIFF	
VS. *Howard Orloff*	ATTORNEYS FOR PLAINTIFF
	ATTORNEYS FOR DEFENDANT
DEFENDANT	

DATE	PROCEEDINGS IN CAUSE AND DISPOSITION OF CASE
1957 Dec 4	*Suit filed*

DATE OF JUDGMENT   AMOUNT $

DATE	DESCRIPTION	✓	CHARGES	DATE	DESCRIPTION	✓	CREDITS
1957 Nov. 28	*Case received*		100 00	*1957 Nov. 28*	*Retainer*		50 00
Dec. 4	*Suit fee*		5 00	*Dec. 18*	*In full*		55 00

Case docket of an attorney

The case docket provides space for all the essential information relative to the case and space to record the financial transactions involved.

Combination journal of an attorney. Mr. Lambert maintained a combination journal similar to the one kept by Dr. Stone, the dentist. The combination journal kept by Mr. Lambert during the month of December is illustrated in part at the top of the next two pages.

	CASH		CHECK NO.	DATE	NAME OF ACCOUNT	POST. REF.	GENERAL		
	DEBIT	CREDIT					DEBIT	CREDIT	
1		100 00	271	1957 Dec 2	Rent Expense		100 00		1
2	326 80			2	Crowell & Co.			245 10	2
3		245 10	272	3	Crowell & Co.		245 10		3
4		5 00	273	4	Suit fee – J.C. Lancer				4
5		4 95	274	5	Telephone bill				5
6	387 50			6	Cash receipts for week				6
7	25 00			9	Mrs Edna Myer				7
8		150 00	275	12	Easton Johnson Drawing		150 00		8
9	421 50			13	Cash receipts for week				9
10									10
11									11

Combination journal

Analyzing the combination journal of an attorney. Mr. Lambert's combination journal contained two income columns. The column headed "Legal Fees" was used to record the income from representing clients in law suits. The column headed "Collection Fees" was used to record the income from collecting accounts for clients. Because of the difference in the type of work involved, it was desirable to separate these two most common sources of income.

Two columns headed "Advances for Clients" were used to record the expenses of a case that were paid by the attorney but that would later be collected from the client. It was desirable that a separate record be kept of these accounts receivable in order that the repayments would not be confused with income for services. The advances for clients and the repayment of the advances in no way affected the attorney's income.

Mr. Lambert made all large payments by check. He maintained a petty cash fund of $50 from which minor expenses were paid. Petty cash receipts were made out for each payment and were kept with the petty cash fund. Whenever the fund was running low, a check was drawn to replenish it.

At intervals during the month, Mr. Lambert posted the items in the General Debit and Credit columns. On December 31 he totaled and ruled all of the amount columns of the combination journal. The sum of the totals of all the debit columns was found to equal the sum of the totals of all the credit columns. After this proof was made, the totals of all special columns were posted.

	LEGAL FEES CREDIT	COLLECTION FEES CREDIT	ADVANCES FOR CLIENTS DEBIT	ADVANCES FOR CLIENTS CREDIT	MISC EXPENSE DEBIT	SALARY EXPENSE DEBIT	EMPLOYEES INCOME TAX PAY. CREDIT	FICA TAXES PAY CREDIT	
1									1
2		81 70							2
3									3
4			5 00						4
5					4 95				5
6	300 00			87 50					6
7	25 00								7
8									8
9	250 00	30 00		141 50					9
10									10
11									11

of an attorney

    Work at the end of the fiscal period. At the end of the year, December 31, 1957, Mr. Lambert prepared an eight-column work sheet. From the work sheet, he prepared the following statement of income and expenses:

ARTHUR LAMBERT
Statement of Income and Expenses
For Year Ended December 31, 1957

Professional Income:
    Legal Fees $11,970.00
    Collection Fees. 3,625.70
    Total Professional Income. . . . $15,595.70

Professional Expenses:
    Depreciation of Law Library. . . $ 205.30
    Depreciation of Office Equipment·   76.25
    FICA Taxes 97.88
    Miscellaneous Expense. 317.75
    Rent Expense 1,440.00
    Salary Expense 4,350.00
    Supplies Expense 165.20
    Traveling Expense. 56.83
    Total Professional Expenses. . .   6,709.21

Net Professional Income . . . . $ 8,886.49

Statement of income and expenses of an attorney

    The information provided by the statement of income and expenses was used in the preparation of the income tax return.

CHAPTER QUESTIONS

1. Why is it desirable for a professional man to maintain complete and accurate bookkeeping records?
2. What is the purpose of the appointment book of a dentist?
3. What information is shown on the patient's record card of a dentist illustrated on page 468?
4. What are the immediate records maintained by a dentist as presented in this chapter?
5. What are the immediate records maintained by an attorney as presented in this chapter?
6. How often were the cash receipts for fees entered in the dentist's combination journal?
7. How were petty cash payments handled by the dentist in this chapter?
8. What financial statement was prepared by the dentist in this chapter to aid him in making government reports and income tax returns?
9. What is the heading of the special column in the attorney's combination journal on pages 474 and 475 that is used to record the expenses of a case paid by the attorney in behalf of his client?
10. What entry was made in the combination journal of the attorney on pages 474 and 475 to record the collection of an account for a client?
11. What entry was made in the combination journal of the attorney on pages 474 and 475 to record the remittance to a client of a collection made in his behalf?

INCREASING YOUR BUSINESS VOCABULARY

What is the meaning of each of the following:

(a) appointment book
(b) patient's record card
(c) collection docket
(d) case docket

CASES FOR DISCUSSION

1. Dr. C. D. Meade is a dentist in a small town. He does not have a bookkeeper. He maintains a columnar cash record book and a summary page without a ledger. His accounts with patients are kept on individual cards. Do you consider this system satisfactory? Why?
2. R. F. Dale is a certified public accountant. Once each year he audits the books of five different manufacturing concerns in the city. During the rest of his time he does miscellaneous auditing work for other businesses. He does considerable consulting with individuals and businesses in filing income tax returns. What type of records is Mr. Dale likely to maintain?

APPLICATION PROBLEMS

Problem 35-1. Transactions of a dentist

Dr. Carl Payne, a local dentist, has employed you as a dental hygienist and secretary. He maintains a bookkeeping system like that used by the dentist in this chapter.

Instructions: 1. Record in a combination journal like the one on pages 470 and 471 the following transactions completed by Dr. Payne during the month of December of the current year. All cash payments are made by check.

Dec.
1. Paid the December rent, $140, with Check No. 227.
3. Paid American Dental Supply Co. $15 for laboratory expenses.
4. Paid the telephone bill, $7.50.
5. Paid X-ray Sales Company $135 for equipment. (Debit Dental Equipment.)
7. The cash receipts for the week were $415.
7. Withdrew $300 for personal use.
12. Paid Dental Service Supply Co. $50.30 for dental supplies.
14. The cash receipts for the week were $478.50.
14. Paid you your semimonthly salary of $140 less a deduction of $20.60 for income tax withheld and a deduction of $3.15 for FICA tax.
14. Recorded the employer's liability of $3.15 for his share of the FICA tax.
16. Paid Lanier & Co. $105 for three chairs for the waiting room. (Debit Office Equipment.)
17. Replenished the petty cash fund with a check for $19.25. The distribution was as follows: Dental Supplies Expense, $8.40; Laboratory Expense, $9.35; Miscellaneous Expense, $1.50.
20. Paid O. L. Kettwig $17.50 for washing the walls in the office.
21. The cash receipts for the week were $394.75.
23. Withdrew $200 for personal use.
24. Paid American Dental Supply Co. $50 for laboratory expenses.
28. The cash receipts for the week were $428.50.
31. Paid you your semimonthly salary of $140 less a deduction of $20.60 for income tax withheld and a deduction of $3.15 for FICA tax.
31. Recorded the employer's liability of $3.15 for his share of the FICA benefit tax.
31. Withdrew $300 for personal use.
31. Replenished the petty cash fund with a check for $23.95. The distribution of payments was as follows: Office Supplies Expense, $3.25; Dental Supplies Expense, $5.75; Laboratory Expense, $12.75; Miscellaneous Expense, $2.20.
31. The cash receipts for December 30 and 31 were $95.

Instructions: 2. Total, prove, and rule the combination journal.

Problem 35-2. Work at the end of a fiscal period for an attorney

At the end of the fiscal year on December 31 of the current year, the trial balance of the ledger maintained by John J. Bell, a local attorney, was as follows:

JOHN J. BELL

TRIAL BALANCE

DECEMBER 31, 19 __

Cash..	11	3,065 38	
Petty Cash.................................	12	75 00	
Advances for Clients......................	13	248 40	
Law Library...............................	14	595 00	
Allow. for Depr. of Law Library..........	14.1		142 50
Office Equipment..........................	15	1,250 00	
Allow. for Depr. of Office Equip.........	15.1		125 00
Employees Income Taxes Payable.........	21		93 40
FICA Taxes Payable......................	22		53 71
John J. Bell, Capital.....................	31		3,838 03
John J. Bell, Drawing....................	32	7,200 00	
Legal Fees.................................	41		12,420 00
Collection Fees...........................	42		7,587 12
FICA Taxes...............................	53	161 22	
Miscellaneous Expense...................	54	410 50	
Rent Expense..............................	55	3,600 00	
Salary Expense............................	56	7,165 30	
Supplies Expense..........................	57	193 75	
Traveling Expense.........................	58	295 21	
		24,259 76	24,259 76

Instructions: 1. Prepare an eight-column work sheet for the year ended December 31 of the current year, using the following data for adjustments:

Depreciation of law library, $71.25
Depreciation of office equipment, $62.50

2. Prepare a statement of income and expenses from the data given on the work sheet. Use as your guide the model statement of income and expenses on page 475.

3. Prepare a balance sheet from the data given on the work sheet. Use as your guide the model balance sheet illustrated on page 485.

Bookkeeping for a farmer

Need for records of a farmer. Farmers are engaged in the business of raising and selling farm products for a profit. Farming is therefore a business in the same sense that manufacturing and retailing are businesses. A farmer, like any other businessman, should have bookkeeping records that will show him whether or not he is making a fair return on his investment and how he can manage his business so that it will be increasingly profitable.

A farmer must make many decisions regarding what is to be produced on his farm, the amount of labor that is to be employed, the amount of fertilizer that should be used, and similar questions. Complete and accurate records are necessary in guiding a farmer in such decisions. Records are also needed in order that the farmer may make correct income tax reports.

The accrual basis and the cash basis of keeping records. The method of keeping records that shows (1) all income earned during a fiscal period even though the income is not yet received and (2) all expenses incurred during the fiscal period even though the expenses are not yet paid is known as the *accrual basis* of keeping records.

The method of keeping records that shows (1) only income actually received during a fiscal period and (2) only expenses paid during a fiscal period is known as the *cash basis* of keeping records.

Federal and state income tax laws permit the filing of income tax returns either on the accrual basis or the cash basis.

Mr. Thomas Burke, a farmer, keeps his bookkeeping records on a cash basis. He records income only when it is received. He records expenses, such as purchases of supplies, fertilizers, labor, and other items, only when he pays for them. He therefore makes no adjustments at the end of the fiscal period for any inventories on hand. In order that the fixed assets may show the true value on the books at the end of a fiscal period, he records depreciation on them at that time.

Balance sheet of a farmer. On January 1, 1957, Thomas Burke, a farmer, decided to open a new set of books. As a basis for his records he prepared the following balance sheet showing his assets, liabilities, and proprietorship as of December 31, 1956:

```
                      THOMAS BURKE
                      Balance Sheet
                   December 31, 1956
```

```
                          Assets

Cash . . . . . . . . . . . . . . . . . . $   789.00
Livestock. . . . . . . . . . . . . . $1,450.00
    Less Allowance for Depreciation
    of Livestock. . . . . . . . . . .      280.00   1,170.00
Machinery and Equipment. . . . . . . $5,282.50
    Less Allowance for Depreciation
    of Machinery and Equipment. . . .    2,178.00   3,104.50
Buildings. . . . . . . . . . . . . . $8,500.00
    Less Allowance for Depreciation
    of Buildings. . . . . . . . . . .    1,250.00   7,250.00
Land . . . . . . . . . . . . . . . . . . . . . .   15,000.00
Total Assets . . . . . . . . . . . . . . . . . .              $27,313.50

                        Liabilities

Notes Payable. . . . . . . . . . . . . . . . . . $   500.00
Mortgage Payable . . . . . . . . . . . . . . . .    7,500.00
Total Liabilities. . . . . . . . . . . . . . . .              $ 8,000.00

                       Proprietorship

Thomas Burke, Capital. . . . . . . . . . . . . .                19,313.50

Total Liabilities and Proprietorship . . . . . .              $27,313.50
```

Beginning balance sheet of a farmer

Analysis of the balance sheet of a farmer. The amounts on the balance sheet were determined from the records maintained by Mr. Burke and by an evaluation of his fixed assets.

As Mr. Burke operated on the cash basis, he did not record income until he had collected cash. Accounts receivable were therefore not listed on the balance sheet. A memorandum record was maintained for accounts receivable until they were collected. Similarly, inventories of things raised on the farm were not included on the balance sheet. When these products were sold, Cash was debited and an income account was credited. There were no supplies or prepaid insurance listed on the balance sheet, as such items were charged to expense accounts when they were paid.

The livestock account shown on Mr. Burke's balance sheet included the value of the dairy cattle and other livestock purchased. At the end of a fiscal period, the depreciation of this livestock was recorded the same as the depreciation of other fixed assets was recorded.

The value of livestock raised on the farm is not shown on the balance sheet because such livestock, like other farm products, is not entered on the books until it is sold and cash is received.

Occasionally Mr. Burke purchased livestock for resale that was fed for a few months only and was then sold. This livestock was an asset; but as its value would ordinarily increase during the time that it was kept, it was not subject to depreciation and was therefore not recorded in the fixed asset account Livestock. It was recorded in a special account entitled *Livestock Purchased Cost*. Whenever any of this livestock was on hand at the end of a fiscal period, it was recorded on the balance sheet as an asset at the cost price.

As the notes payable were given in return for cash or fixed assets, it was necessary to record the notes, because the assets should appear on the records. The mortgage payable was recorded for the same reason. No record was made of ordinary accounts payable until the accounts were paid; therefore no accounts payable were listed on the balance sheet.

The combination journal of a farmer. Thomas Burke recorded all of his transactions in a combination journal.

All payments recorded in the combination journal were made by check. Checks written for the purchase of farm assets and to pay farm business expenses were debited to the proper farm asset and expense accounts. Checks written to withdraw cash for personal use and to pay personal expenses were debited to the proprietor's drawing account.

Special columns were provided in the combination journal for accounts that were frequently affected by transactions. The General Debit and Credit columns were used to record the transactions involving accounts for which there were no special columns.

Since he completed relatively few transactions during a month, Mr. Burke did not feel that it was necessary to use two new pages of the combination journal for each month. He therefore recorded transactions until he filled a page. At that time the columns were totaled, the equality of debits and credits was proved, and the columnar totals were posted. The items in the General Debit and Credit columns were posted at intervals during the period. A part of Mr. Burke's combination journal is illustrated on pages 482 and 483. All of the transactions from January 1 through April 30 were recorded on these two pages.

Analyzing the combination journal, *Line 21.* On March 1, Mr. Burke received cash, $270, for corn that he sold. Cash was debited in the Cash Debit column. *Produce Sales* was credited in the Produce Sales Credit column.

Whenever both the debit and the credit parts of a transaction are recorded in special columns, a check mark is placed in the Post. Ref. column to indicate that no amount on this line is to be posted separately.

COMBINATION JOURNAL

	CASH	CHECK NO.	DATE	NAME OF ACCOUNT	POST. REF.	GENERAL		
DEBIT	CREDIT					DEBIT	CREDIT	
21	270 00			Mar 1	Sold corn	✓			21
22				5	Mdse. Received for Produce-eggs			3 75	22
23		56 00	7	12	Purchased seed corn	✓			23
24		225 00	8	19	For personal use	✓			24
25	92 00			30	Misc. Income-soil conservation payment			92 00	25
26		135 00	9	31	Hired labor	✓			26
27		43 25	10	Apr 2	Paris Department Store	✓			27
28		300 00	11	5	Livestock Purchased Cost		300 00		28
29	730 95			17	Sold hogs	✓			29
30		32 50	12	22	Mchry & Equip.-price transformer		32 50		30
31		9 28	13	26	Cox Refining Co.	✓			31
32		135 00	14	30	Hired labor	✓			32
33	2470 21	2967 66		30	Totals		33760 50	33568 50	33

Combination journal

Line 22. On March 5, Mr. Burke exchanged $3.75 worth of eggs for groceries for personal use. The federal income tax law provides that merchandise received in exchange for farm produce shall be reported as an income item separate from produce sales. Mr. Burke therefore maintained a special income account entitled *Merchandise Received for Produce*. This account was credited in the General Credit column. Since the groceries were for personal use, he debited his drawing account in the column headed *T. Burke, Drawing*.

Line 23. On March 12, Mr. Burke issued Check No. 7 for $56 in payment for seed corn. *Seeds, Plants, and Trees Purchased* was debited in the special column provided for that account and Cash was credited.

Line 24. On March 19, Mr. Burke wrote Check No. 8 for $225 to withdraw cash from the bank for his personal use. T. Burke, Drawing was debited and Cash was credited.

Line 25. On March 30, Mr. Burke received a check from the government for $92 in payment for conserving soil on part of his farm. Cash was debited for $92 and *Miscellaneous Income* was credited. Since this type of income is infrequent, no special column is provided for it. Miscellaneous Income was therefore credited in the General Credit column. Any income Mr. Burke receives from miscellaneous sources, such as for work away from his farm and for rental of his machinery and equipment to others, would be recorded as a credit to Miscellaneous Income.

	LIVESTOCK RAISED SALES CREDIT	PRODUCE SALES CREDIT	FEED PURCHASED DEBIT	FUEL AND OIL DEBIT	LABOR HIRED DEBIT	REPAIRS AND MAINTENANCE DEBIT	SEED, ETC., PURCHASED DEBIT	T. BURKE DRAWING DEBIT	
21		270 00							21
22								3 75	22
23						56 00			23
24								225 00	24
25									25
26					135 00				26
27								43 25	27
28									28
29	730 95								29
30									30
31				9 28					31
32	730 95	270 00	265 75	31 25	135 00	124 30	132 80	416 05	32
33	730 95	270 00	265 75	31 25	336 25	124 30	132 80	416 05	33

of a farmer

Line 26. On March 31, Mr. Burke issued Check No. 9 for $135 in payment for farm labor. *Labor Hired* was debited in the special column provided for that account and Cash was credited.

Line 27. On April 2, Mr. Burke issued Check No. 10 for $43.25 to the Paris Department Store for purchases made for the family. T. Burke, Drawing was debited and Cash was credited.

Line 28. On April 5, Mr. Burke issued Check No. 11 for $300 for livestock purchased for resale. The schedule of farm income and expenses for farmers' income tax returns, shown on page 487, requires a farmer to report livestock purchased for resale. The cost account *Livestock Purchased Cost* was debited for $300 in the General Debit column. Cash was credited.

When livestock purchased for resale is sold, the income account *Livestock Purchased Sales* is credited for the amount received. The difference between the cost of livestock and the sales price is the profit from livestock that has been purchased for resale.

Line 29. On April 17, Mr. Burke received cash, $730.95, for hogs sold. Cash was debited and *Livestock Raised Sales* was credited in the special column provided.

Line 30. On April 22, Mr. Burke issued Check No. 12 for $32.50 in payment for an electric fence transformer. *Machinery and Equipment* was debited in the General Debit column and Cash was credited.

Line 31. On April 26, Mr. Burke issued Check No. 13 for $9.28 to Cox Refining Co. for tractor fuel. *Fuel and Oil* was debited in the special column provided and Cash was credited.

Line 32. On April 30, Mr. Burke issued Check No. 14 for $135 for farm labor. This was recorded in the same manner as the transaction on Line 26.

Line 33. At the end of April, Mr. Burke totaled the columns of his combination journal, proved the equality of debits and credits, and ruled the journal. He then posted the totals of all the special columns to the proper ledger accounts. The items in the General Debit and Credit columns were posted at intervals during the period.

Work sheet and statements of a farmer. At the end of the annual fiscal year, on December 31, 1957, Mr. Burke prepared an eight-column work sheet. Since he kept his records on the cash basis, the only adjustments required were those for livestock purchased cost and for the depreciation of the fixed assets.

The amount paid for livestock that was sold during the year was no longer an asset. The cost of the livestock sold was therefore credited to

THOMAS BURKE
Profit and Loss Statement
For Year Ended December 31, 1957

Farm Income:

Livestock Purchased Sales	$ 1,862.25	
Livestock Raised Sales.	6,568.50	
Merchandise Received for Produce.	94.05	
Miscellaneous Income.	192.75	
Produce Sales	2,780.25	
Total Farm Income		$11,497.80

Farm Expenses:

Depreciation of Buildings	$ 170.00	
Depreciation of Livestock	145.00	
Depreciation of Machinery and Equipment	552.40	
Feed Purchased.	870.37	
Fertilizer and Lime	273.13	
Fuel and Oil (Farm Machinery)	233.25	
Insurance Expense	67.00	
Interest Expense.	375.00	
Labor Hired	1,020.00	
Machine Hire.	390.00	
Miscellaneous Expense	231.30	
Repairs and Maintenance	156.45	
Seeds, Plants, and Trees Purchased.	277.12	
Taxes	240.00	
Total Farm Expenses		5,001.02
Net Farm Profit.		$ 6,496.78

Profit and loss statement of a farmer

```
                         THOMAS BURKE
                         Balance Sheet
                       December 31, 1957
```

                              Assets

```
Cash . . . . . . . . . . . . . . . . . . .  $    794.20
Livestock. . . . . . . . . . . . . . $1,450.00
     Less Allowance for Depreciation
     of Livestock. . . . . . . . . . .    425.00   1,025.00
Machinery and Equipment. . . . . . . . $5,549.80
     Less Allowance for Depreciation
     of Machinery and Equipment. . . .  2,730.40   2,819.40
Buildings. . . . . . . . . . . . . . . $8,500.00
     Less Allowance for Depreciation
     of Buildings. . . . . . . . . . .  1,420.00   7,080.00
Land . . . . . . . . . . . . . . . . . . . . . . 15,000.00
Total Assets . . . . . . . . . . . . . . . . .            $26,718.60
```

                           Liabilities

```
Notes Payable. . . . . . . . . . . . . . . .  $    300.00
Mortgage Payable . . . . . . . . . . . . . .     6,000.00
Total Liabilities. . . . . . . . . . . . . .              $ 6,300.00
```

                          Proprietorship

```
Thomas Burke, Capital. . . . . . . . . . . . . . $19,313.50
     Net Farm Profit . . . . . . . . . $6,496.78
     Less Withdrawals. . . . . . . . .  5,391.68
     Net Increase in Capital . . . . . . . . .    1,105.10
Thomas Burke, Present Capital. . . . . . . . . .          20,418.60

Total Liabilities and Proprietorship . . . . . .          $26,718.60
```

Balance sheet of a farmer

Livestock Purchased Cost and was debited to Livestock Purchased Sales. The balance of the livestock purchased sales account then represented the gross profit on the livestock that was sold.

The depreciation of the fixed assets of a farmer varies with the type and the use of each asset. Typical depreciation rates are as follows: frame buildings, 2%; miscellaneous farm machinery, 10%; horses and cows, 10%; trucks, tractors, and combines, 10%.

In order to maintain an accurate record of his fixed assets, it was necessary for Mr. Burke to keep information about the date of purchase, the cost, and the annual depreciation of each fixed asset. He kept a separate card record for each fixed asset similar to the card shown on page 305.

From the data on the work sheet Mr. Burke prepared the profit and loss statement and the balance sheet illustrated.

Adjusting and closing entries for a farmer. From the data in the Adjustments columns of the work sheet that he prepared for the year ended December 31, 1957, Mr. Burke recorded the adjusting entries in the combination journal as shown below.

After the adjusting entries for livestock purchased cost and depreciation were posted, the income and expense accounts were closed into the profit and loss summary account. The credit balance of the profit and

	CASH		CHECK NO.	DATE	NAME OF ACCOUNT	POST. REF.	GENERAL		
	DEBIT	CREDIT					DEBIT	CREDIT	
1				1957	*Adjusting Entries*				1
2				Dec 31	Livestock Purchased Sales		1650 00		2
3					Livestock Purchased Cost			1650 00	3
4				31	Depreciation of Livestock		145 00		4
5					Allow. for Depr. of Livestock			145 00	5
6				31	Depr. of Machinery & Equip.		552 40		6
7					Allow. for Depr. of Mchy & Equip.			552 40	7
8				31	Depreciation of Buildings		170 00		8
9					Allow. for Depr. of Buildings			170 00	9
10					*Closing Entries*				10
11				31	Livestock Purchased Sales		1862 25		11
12					Livestock Raised Sales		6568 50		12
13					Mdse. Received for Produce		94 05		13
14					Miscellaneous Income		192 75		14
15					Produce Sales		2780 25		15
16					Profit and Loss Summary			11497 80	16
17				31	Profit and Loss Summary		5001 02		17
18					Feed Purchased			870 37	18
19					Fertilizer and Lime			273 13	19
20					Fuel and Oil (Farm Mchy)			233 25	20
21					Insurance Expense			67 00	21
22					Interest Expense			375 00	22
23					Labor Hired			1020 00	23
24					Machine Hire			390 00	24
25					Miscellaneous Expense			231 30	25
26					Repairs and Maintenance			156 45	26
27					Seeds, Etc. Purchased			277 12	27
28					Taxes			240 00	28
29					Depr. of Livestock			145 00	29
30					Depr. of Machinery & Equip.			552 40	30
31					Depr. of Buildings			170 00	31
32				31	Profit and Loss Summary		6496 78		32
33					Thomas Burke, Drawing			6496 78	33

Adjusting and closing entries for a farmer

loss summary account was then credited to Mr. Burke's drawing account. (If the profit and loss summary account had had a debit balance, it would have been debited to the drawing account.) The closing entries recorded by Mr. Burke in the General columns of the combination journal are shown on page 486.

Preparing income tax reports. Each farmer who is required to file an income tax return is required by the government to file a special form known as the *schedule of farm income and expenses.* The schedule of farm income and expenses prepared by Mr. Burke is shown below.

SCHEDULE F (Form 1040)	U. S. Treasury Department—Internal Revenue Service **SCHEDULE OF FARM INCOME AND EXPENSES** (For computation of Self-Employment Tax, see page 4) Attach this schedule to your Income Tax Return, Form 1040	1957

For Calendar Year 1957, or other taxable year beginning _____, 1957, and ending _____, 195__

Name and Address as shown on page 1, Form 1040

Thomas Burke
R. R. #1, Lafayette, Indiana

FARM INCOME FOR TAXABLE PERIOD COMPUTED ON THE CASH RECEIPTS AND DISBURSEMENTS METHOD
(See Instructions on Schedule D (Form 1040) for tax treatment of certain livestock held for draft, breeding, or dairy purposes)

1. SALE OF LIVESTOCK RAISED			2. SALE OF PRODUCE RAISED			3. OTHER FARM INCOME	
Kind	Quantity	Amount	Kind	Quantity	Amount	Items	Amount
Cattle	3	$1,125.00	Grain	1330bu	$2,262.00	Mdse. rec'd for produce	$ 94.05
			Hay	12 T	322.50	Machine work	55.00
Horses			Cotton			Breeding fees	
Mules			Tobacco			Wood and lumber	
Sheep			Vegetables	11bu	30.00	Other forest products	
Swine	139	4,585.05	Fruits and nuts			Agricultural program pay-	
Chickens	780	858.45	Dairy products			ments	137.75
Turkeys			Eggs	332dz	165.75	Patronage dividends, rebates	
Ducks			Meat products			or refunds	
Bees			Poultry, dressed			Other farm income (specify):	
Other (specify):			Wool				
			Honey				
			Sirup and sugar				
			Other (specify):				
Total		$ 6,568.50	Total		$2,780.25	Total	$ 286.80
		(Enter on line 1 of summary below)			(Enter on line 2 of summary below)		(Enter on line 3 of summary below)

4. SALE OF PURCHASED LIVESTOCK AND OTHER PURCHASED ITEMS

a. Description	b. Date acquired	c. Gross sales price	d. Cost or other basis	e. Profit (or loss)
18 feeder steers	2-6-57	$3,512.25	$1,650.00	$1,862.25
Total (enter on line 4 of summary below)				$ 1,862.25

SUMMARY OF INCOME AND DEDUCTIONS COMPUTED ON THE CASH RECEIPTS AND DISBURSEMENTS METHOD

1. Sale of livestock raised	$ 6,568 50	6. Expenses (from page 2)	$ 4,133 62
2. Sale of produce raised	2,780 25	7. Depreciation (from page 3)	867 40
3. Other farm income	286 80	8. Other deductions (specify):	
4. Profit (or loss) on sale of purchased livestock and other purchased items	1,862 25		
5. Gross Profits*	$11,497 80	9. Total Deductions	$ 5,001 02

10. Net farm profit (or loss) (line 5 minus line 9) to be reported on line 9, page 1, Form 1040 .... $ 6,496 78
* Use this amount for optional method of computing net earnings from self-employment. (See line 13, page 4.)

Schedule of farm income and expenses, page 1

The information reported on the schedule of farm income and expenses was obtained from the profit and loss statement prepared by Mr. Burke on December 31. (See illustration on page 484.) Because accurate records were maintained and the profit and loss statement was prepared, the preparation of the income tax return was simplified.

CHAPTER QUESTIONS

1. Why is it desirable for a farmer to maintain complete and accurate bookkeeping records of all of his farming operations?
2. When is income earned recorded when books are kept on the accrual basis?
3. When is income earned recorded when books are kept on the cash basis?
4. When are expenses recorded when books are kept on the accrual basis?
5. When are expenses recorded when books are kept on the cash basis?
6. Why do no accounts receivable appear on the balance sheet of a farmer who keeps his books on a cash basis?
7. Why do no accounts payable appear on the balance sheet of a farmer who keeps his books on a cash basis?
8. Why is a special account maintained for merchandise received for produce?
9. What adjusting entries should a farmer make at the end of the fiscal period if he keeps his books on the cash basis?
10. How does a farmer keep an accurate record of his fixed assets?
11. What is the source of the information used in preparing the schedule of farm income and expenses on the income tax return?

INCREASING YOUR BUSINESS VOCABULARY

What is the meaning of each of the following terms?

(a) accrual basis
(b) cash basis
(c) merchandise received for produce
(d) livestock purchased cost
(e) livestock purchased sales
(f) schedule of farm income and expenses

CASES FOR DISCUSSION

1. John Moland, a farmer, decided that he should keep his books on the accrual basis. In what respect would Mr. Moland's books differ from those kept by Mr. Burke in this chapter?
2. M. L. Johnson, a dairy farmer, received all of his income from the sale of milk, cream, and butter. He raised some of the grain fed to his cattle and purchased the remainder of it. He delivered his own products. In what ways would his records be likely to differ from those kept by Mr. Burke?

APPLICATION PROBLEMS

Problem 36-1. Recording transactions of a farmer

A. B. Williams, a farmer, maintained a set of books similar to those illustrated in this chapter.

Instructions: **1.** Record in a combination journal similar to the one shown on pages 482 and 483 the following transactions completed by Mr. Williams during October, November, and December of the current year. All payments were made by check, the first check for October being No. 63.

Oct.   2. Sold corn for cash, $287.50.
       7. Paid cash for seed for following year, $46.50.
       9. Paid wages for hired labor on the farm, $75.
     10. Received cash for use of tractor by neighbor, $20.
     14. Paid cash for insurance on house in which he lived, $17.35.
     17. Paid cash for gasoline and oil for farm machines, $14.30.
     20. Withdrew cash for personal use, $150.
     23. Paid cash for repairs to tractor and other farm machinery, $23.75.
     25. Received cash from sale of livestock that had been purchased as feeders, $590.25.
     28. Exchanged eggs worth $9.50 for groceries.
Nov.   1. Paid cash for feed for livestock, $83.75.
      7. Received cash from sale of livestock raised on farm, $384.20.
     12. Exchanged eggs and dairy products worth $15.60 for groceries.
     15. Paid $500 on the principal of the mortgage and $70 interest on the mortgage.
     18. Paid wages for hired labor on the farm, $25.
     19. Received $94.20 from sale of turkeys and chickens raised on farm.
     22. Paid for repairs on house in which he lived, $51.30.
     25. Received cash from sale of livestock raised on farm, $331.90.
     28. Paid cash for gasoline and oil for farm machines, $14.65.
     29. Paid note, $200, and interest on note, $3.
Dec.   5. Received cash from sale of corn and wheat, $351.45.
      6. Paid cash for feed for livestock, $65.75.
     12. Paid cash for seed for following year, $20.55.
     15. Withdrew cash for personal use, $250.
     17. Received cash from sale of livestock purchased as feeders, $688.30.
     22. Paid wages for hired labor on the farm, $18.50.
     27. Paid taxes, $107.66. (He estimated that $29.75 of this amount should be debited to his drawing account because it was taxes on the dwelling. Debit Taxes for the remainder.)

Instructions: **2.** Total, prove, and rule the combination journal.

Problem 36-2. Work at the end of a fiscal period for a farmer

At the end of the fiscal year on December 31, the trial balance of the ledger maintained by A. B. Williams was as follows:

A. B. WILLIAMS

Trial Balance

December 31, 19 _ _

Cash..........................	11	853 64	
Livestock......................	12	1,225 00	
Allow. for Depr. of Livestock......	12.1		280 00
Livestock Purchased Cost.........	13	656 00	
Machinery and Equipment........	14	2,187 50	
Allow. for Depr. of Mach. & Equip.	14.1		787 50
Buildings......................	15	4,375 00	
Allow. for Depr. of Buildings.....	15.1		655 50
Land..........................	16	12,000 00	
Notes Payable..................	21		350 00
Mortgage Payable...............	22		6,000 00
A. B. Williams, Capital..........	31		11,780 00
A. B. Williams, Drawing.........	32	3,618 75	
Livestock Purchased Sales........	41		1,333 20
Livestock Raised Sales...........	42		3,903 60
Merchandise Received for Produce.	43		122 40
Miscellaneous Income............	44		295 25
Produce Sales...................	45		1,198 25
Feed Purchased.................	54	367 14	
Fertilizer and Lime..............	55	93 90	
Fuel and Oil (Farm Machinery)...	56	115 15	
Insurance Expense...............	57	37 50	
Interest Expense.................	58	252 00	
Labor Hired....................	59	281 65	
Machine Hire...................	60	77 50	
Miscellaneous Expense...........	61	103 69	
Repairs and Maintenance.........	62	78 03	
Seed, Plants, and Trees Purchased.	63	188 25	
Taxes.........................	64	195 00	
		26,705 70	26,705 70

Instructions: 1. Prepare an eight-column work sheet for the annual fiscal period ended December 31 of the current year, using the following data for adjustments:

> All livestock purchased for resale has been sold
> Depreciation of livestock, $122.50
> Depreciation of machinery and equipment, $218.75
> Depreciation of buildings, $87.50

2. Prepare a profit and loss statement from the work sheet. Use as your guide the model on page 484.

3. Prepare a balance sheet from the work sheet. Use as your guide the model on page 485.

Appendix

Supplementary exercises

CHAPTER 1

Exercise 1-A. Balance sheet for an individual

Prepare a balance sheet, dated December 31, current year, for Edward Ellman. His assets and his liabilities are listed below.

Assets	*Liabilities*
Cash on hand, $421.00	Boles Grocery, $31.00
Government Bonds, $550.00	Crandall Bros., $61.00
Automobile, $925.00	Holden Dairy Co., $5.00
Furniture, $2,475.00	
House and Lot, $12,000.00	

Exercise 1-B. Balance sheet for a small business

Prepare a balance sheet, dated June 30, current year, for the Valley Theater. J. L. Tweedy is the proprietor and manager. The assets and the liabilities are:

Assets	*Liabilities*
Cash on hand, $1,495.60	City Light Co., $62.40
Furniture, $675.00	Films, Incorporated, $610.00
Equipment, $5,125.00	
Building, $10,000.00	

CHAPTER 2

Exercise 2-A. Opening entry for a professional man

Instructions: Record the balance sheet of Daniel M. Brown in a journal, using May 1 of the current year as the date of this opening entry. Compare the entry that you make with the model opening entry illustrated on page 12. The balance sheet of April 30 of the current year is given below.

DANIEL M. BROWN
BALANCE SHEET
APRIL 30, 19--

Assets			*Liabilities*		
Cash...................	612	25	Haynes Book Co..........	55	25
Supplies..............	37	50	Taylor Equipment Co......	465	00
Law Library..........	475	00			
Office Furniture.........	725	50	Total Liabilities..........	520	25
Office Equipment........	375	00			
			Proprietorship		
			Daniel M. Brown, Capital..	1,705	00
Total Assets............	2,225	25	Total Liab. and Prop.......	2,225	25

Exercise 2-B. Balance sheet and opening entry for a small service business

Instructions: 1. Prepare a balance sheet for the Scott Storage Garage, owned by Robert Scott. Date the balance sheet July 31 of the current year. Compare your balance sheet with the model balance sheet illustrated on page 9. On July 31, Mr. Scott's records showed the following assets, liabilities, and proprietorship:

(a) Cash, $497.85
(b) Garage Equipment, $3,250.00
(c) Office Equipment, $1,275.00
(d) Clark Motor Co. (creditor), $985.50
(e) Marsh Equipment Co. (creditor), $312.25
(f) Robert Scott's investment, $3,725.10

Instructions: 2. Record the balance sheet in the journal, using August 1 of the current year as the date of this opening entry. Compare your entry with the model opening entry illustrated on page 12.

CHAPTER 3

Exercise 3-A. Posting the opening entry of an accountant

> NOTE: *If Problem 3-1, page 25, is not used, the ledger for this exercise may be completed in the space in the workbook provided for Problem 3-1.*

The opening entry for David M. Spangler, an accountant, is given below:

JOURNAL   PAGE 1

Date	Name of Account	Post. Ref.	Debit	Credit
19--				
May 1	Cash...............................		981 24	
	Supplies.............................		67 50	
	Office Furniture.......................		375 00	
	Office Equipment......................		3,750 00	
	Dalton Equipment Co..............			812 50
	Eustis Brothers....................			34 20
	David M. Spangler, Capital.........			4,327 04
	To record April 30 balance sheet....			

Instructions: 1. Copy this opening entry on a sheet of paper.

2. Open the accounts in the ledger that are required for posting this opening entry. Allow one fourth of a page for each account. Number the accounts as follows: asset accounts, 11 to 14; liability accounts, 21 and 22; and capital account, 31.

3. Post the opening entry.

Exercise 3-B. Recording and posting the opening entry of a small business

The balance sheet of the Walsh Repair Shop, owned by M. R. Walsh, on July 31 of the current year is as follows:

WALSH REPAIR SHOP
BALANCE SHEET
JULY 31, 19--

Assets			Liabilities		
Cash...................	412	15	Kirk Equipment Co.......	197	50
Parts..................	375	20	Nelson & Son............	32	45
Office Equipment........	310	00			
Shop Equipment.........	3,500	00	Total Liabilities..........	229	95
			Proprietorship		
			M. R. Walsh, Capital......	4,367	40
Total Assets...........	4,597	35	Total Liab. and Prop......	4,597	35

Instructions: 1. Record this opening entry under the date of August 1 of the current year.

2. Post the opening entry to the ledger accounts. Allow one fourth of a page for each account. Number the accounts as follows: asset accounts, 11 to 14; liability accounts, 21 and 22; and capital account, 31.

CHAPTER 4

Exercise 4-A. Journalizing transactions of a dry cleaning shop

The Clean-Right Shop is owned and operated by Morris Burton.

Instructions: 1. Record in a five-column journal the selected transactions given below.

June 1. Paid $62.50 to R. E. Simmons & Co. on account (Check No. 1).
2. Received $25.00 for old office equipment (Receipt No. 1).
3. Paid $287.40 to Daniels Supply Company on account (Check No. 2).
4. Paid $15.00 for additional office equipment (Check No. 3).

Exercise 4-B. Journalizing transactions for an attorney

Instructions: Record in a five-column journal the following selected transactions completed during April by Charles A. Cochrane, an attorney.

April 1. Paid $150.00 for new law books (Check No. 52). The title of the account debited is Law Library.
2. Paid $25.00 to Knight Publishing Co. on account (Check No. 53).
3. Paid $250.00 to Samuel Irwin Company on account (Check No. 54).
4. Received $25.00 from the sale of old law books (Receipt No. 25).
4. Paid $35.00 for new law books (Check No. 55).

CHAPTER 5

Exercise 5-A. Journalizing income and expense transactions for a real estate business

Instructions: 1. Record the following selected transactions completed by the Martin Realty Agency in a five-column journal. In the Name of Account column of your journal, use the account titles listed below.

Cash   Automobile Expense   Miscellaneous Expense
Commissions Income   Entertainment Expense   Rent Expense
Advertising Expense

April 2. Received $400.00 as commission on the sale of a house (Receipt No. 33).
   4. Paid $65.00 for rent of office for April (Check No. 43).
   5. Paid $4.50 for entertaining a customer (Check No. 44).
   7. Received $60.00 as commission for serving as agent in securing a renter for a house (Receipt No. 34).
  12. Paid $7.75 for advertising (Check No. 45).
  13. Paid $10.00 to have the office cleaned (Check No. 46).
  15. Paid $8.35 for gas and oil used in operating the automobile on business (Check No. 47).
  16. Received $475.00 as commission on the sale of a house (Receipt No. 35).
  18. Received $45.00 as commission for serving as agent in securing a renter for a house (Receipt No. 36).
  19. Paid $3.60 for the water bill (Check No. 48).
  22. Paid $6.50 for entertaining a customer (Check No. 49).
  25. Paid $10.50 for advertising (Check No. 50).
  26. Paid $13.85 for gas and oil used in operating the automobile on business (Check No. 51).
  28. Received $37.50 as commission for serving as agent in securing a renter for a house (Receipt No. 37).
  30. Paid $8.15 for the electric bill (Check No. 52).
  30. Received $60.00 as commission for serving as agent in securing a renter for a house (Receipt No. 38).

Instructions: 2. Foot, prove, and rule the journal.

Exercise 5-B. Journalizing selected transactions of an attorney

David Wright is an attorney and obtains his income from legal fees for his professional services. The title he uses for his income account is *Fees Income*.

Instructions: 1. Record in a five-column journal the selected transactions given below. Use the following account titles:

Cash   Miscellaneous Expense
Office Furniture   Rent Expense
Anderson Publishing Company   Salary Expense
Fees Income   Stationery Expense

July 1. Paid cash, $125.00, for rent of the office for July. Issued Check No. 1.
   3. Received cash, $50.00, for legal services. Issued Receipt No. 1.
   5. Paid cash, $125.00, to the Anderson Publishing Company for amount owed on account. Issued Check No. 2.
   6. Received cash, $150.00, for legal services. Issued Receipt No. 2.
   9. Paid cash, $15.00, for stationery. Issued Check No. 3.
  12. Paid cash, $195.00 for a new desk. Issued Check No. 4.
  15. Received cash, $100.00, for legal services. Issued Receipt No. 3.
  17. Received cash, $75.00, for legal services. Issued Receipt No. 4.
  24. Paid cash, $12.50, for the telephone bill for July. Issued Check No. 5.
  27. Received cash, $145.00, for legal services. Issued Receipt No. 5.
  31. Paid cash, $250.00, for salary of the law clerk for month. Issued Check No. 6.

Instructions: 2. Foot, prove, and rule the journal.

CHAPTER 6

Exercise 6-A. Journalizing and posting the transactions of a doctor

You will need to prepare the ledger of James E. Vollmer, a doctor, before you can do the work in this exercise.

Instructions: 1. Open the twelve accounts in the ledger that will be needed for this exercise. Place four accounts on each page of your ledger. A list of the account titles with account numbers is given below.

Account Title	Acct. No.	Account Title	Acct. No.
Cash	11	James E. Vollmer, Capital	31
Automobile	12	Fees Income	41
Office Furniture	13	Automobile Expense	51
Equipment	14	Miscellaneous Expense	52
McClain Garage	21	Rent Expense	53
Glenn Company	22	Stationery Expense	54

Instructions: 2. Copy the balances given below in the proper accounts of the ledger prepared in Instruction 1. Date each account balance November 1 of the current year.

Assets (Debit Balances)
Cash, $1,275.00
Automobile, $3,100.00
Office Furniture, $525.00
Equipment, $5,685.00

Liabilities and Proprietorship (Credit Balances)
McClain Garage, $65.00
Glenn Company, $225.00

James E. Vollmer, Capital, $10,295.00

Instructions: 3. Journalize the transactions for November given below. Use journal paper similar to the model journal on page 58.

Nov. 1. Paid cash, $150.00, for rent for November. (Check No. 1)
2. Received cash, $50.00, for professional fees. (Receipt No. 1)
3. Paid cash, $17.00, for stationery. (Check No. 2)
5. Paid cash, $75.00, for office furniture (Check No. 3)
7. Paid cash, $65.00, to McClain Garage on account. (Check No. 4)
9. Received cash, $85.00, from sale of old office furniture. (Receipt No. 2)
11. Received cash, $35.00, for professional fees. (Receipt No. 3)
15. Paid cash, $7.50, for postage stamps, a miscellaneous expense. (Check No. 5)
17. Paid cash, $6.25, for gas and oil. (Check No. 6)
18. Paid cash, $8.25, for stationery. (Check No. 7)
24. Received cash, $150.00, for professional fees. (Receipt No. 4)
26. Received cash, $75.00, for professional fees. (Receipt No. 5)
30. Paid cash, $13.50, for telephone service for month. (Check No. 8)
30. Paid cash, $15.10, for electricity for month. (Check No. 9)
30. Received cash, $85.00, for professional fees. (Receipt No. 6)

Instructions: 4. Post the individual amounts in the General Debit and the General Credit columns to the accounts in the ledger.

5. Place a check mark in the Post. Ref. column for each entry crediting Fees Income to show that this entry is not posted individually.

6. Foot each amount column with small pencil figures. Prove the equality of debit and credits in your journal. The sum of the totals of the two debit columns should equal the sum of the totals of the three credit columns.

7. Draw single lines across all amount columns.

8. Write the column totals on the total line. Write the word "Totals" in the Name of Account column.

9. Rule your journal with double lines.

10. Post the totals of the three special columns. Place a check mark under the columns General Debit and General Credit to indicate that these totals are not posted.

CHAPTER 7

NOTE: *Exercises 7-A and 7-B may be used if the workbook pages are not available for Problems 7-1 and 7-2, page 77.*

Exercise 7-A. Trial balance for a personal service business

Mr. Guy B. Freeman is proprietor and manager of the Freeman Parcel Service. The footings in the accounts in his ledger on June 30 of the current year are as follows:

Account Numbers	Account Titles	Debit Footings	Credit Footings
11	Cash....................................	$4,216.24	$3,040.64
12	Delivery Equipment......................	6,175.00	....
13	Office Equipment........................	640.00	....
21	Glenway Gas & Oil Company..............	200.00	382.50
22	Haskins Automobile Company..............	600.00	1,920.00
31	Guy B. Freeman, Capital....................	....	4,420.01
41	Service Fees...............................	....	4,146.50
51	Heating Expense...........................	91.20	....
52	Labor Expense.............................	1,145.00	....
53	Miscellaneous Expense......................	81.40	....
54	Office Expense.............................	131.20	....
55	Rent Expense.............................	125.00	....
56	Truck Expense............................	504.61	....

Instructions: 1. Prove cash. The cash on hand on June 30 of the current year is $1,175.60.

2. Prepare a trial balance dated June 30 of the current year.

Exercise 7-B. Trial balance for a doctor

The footings in the ledger accounts of Dr. Rolland R. Bateman on January 31 of the current year are as follows:

Account Numbers	Account Titles	Debit Footings	Credit Footings
11	Cash....................................	$1,341.50	$ 662.78
12	Equipment...............................	4,125.00	....
13	Office Furniture...........................	1,216.00	....
21	Ransom Equipment Company..............	225.00	621.75
22	Helm Medical Supply Co....................	62.50	62.50
31	Rolland R. Bateman, Capital...............	....	5,205.45
41	Medical Fees..............................	....	792.80
51	Miscellaneous Expense......................	32.78	....
52	Rent Expense.............................	80.00	....
53	Salary Expense............................	262.50	....

Instructions: 1. Prove cash. The cash on hand on January 31 of the current year is $678.72.

2. Prepare a trial balance dated January 31 of the current year.

20th Century Bookkeeping and Accounting

CHAPTER 8

Exercise 8-A. Work sheet for a public accountant

The account balances in the ledger of M. A. Burnet, a public accountant, on October 31 of the current year, the end of a fiscal period of one month, were as follows:

Cash, $1,115.50

Automobile, $2,700.00

Office Furniture, $675.00

Professional Library, $350.00

Dennis Garage (creditor), $75.00

Meade-Lane (creditor), $127.50

M. A. Burnet, Capital, $2,751.70

Fees Income, $2,085.00

Automobile Expense, $37.50

Miscellaneous Expense, $41.20

Rent Expense, $120.00

Instructions: Prepare a six-column work sheet for Mr. Burnet, using the account balances given above.

Exercise 8-B. Work sheet for a doctor

The account balances in the ledger of Frank J. Ward, a doctor, on November 30 of the current year, the end of a fiscal period of one month, were as follows:

Cash, $1,078.50

Automobile, $2,950.00

Equipment, $5,275.00

Office Furniture, $987.10

Webber Company (creditor), $349.25

Harris Medical Supplies (creditor), $95.50

Frank J. Ward, Capital, $9,104.05

Medical Fees, $1,201.60

Miscellaneous Expense, $34.80

Rent Expense, $150.00

Salary Expense, $275.00

Instructions: Prepare a six-column work sheet for Dr. Ward, using the account balances given above.

CHAPTER 9

Exercise 9-A. Financial reports for an attorney

The work sheet of William T. Bailey, an attorney, for the month ended April 30 of the current year is given at the top of the following page.

Instructions: 1. Prepare a profit and loss statement.
2. Prepare a balance sheet in report form.

WILLIAM T. BAILEY
WORK SHEET
FOR MONTH ENDED APRIL 30, 19--

Account Titles	Acct. No.	Trial Balance Debit	Credit	P. & L. Statement Debit	Credit	Balance Sheet Debit	Credit
Cash...................	11	967 50	....	....	.. ...	967 50	....
Automobile............	12	3,250 00	....	....	.. ...	3,250 00	....
Office Furniture........	13	625 00	....	....	....	625 00	....
Professional Library.....	14	840 00	....	....	....	840 00	....
Dorton & Dorton.......	21	....	67 50	....	....	....	67 50
Hodson Company.......	22	....	132 10	....	....	....	132 10
William T. Bailey, Capital	31	....	4,841 65	....	....	....	4,841 65
Fees Income...........	41	....	886 60	....	886 60	....	....
Automobile Expense.....	51	45 50	....	45 50	....	....	....
Miscellaneous Expense...	52	31 10	....	31 10	....	....	....
Rent Expense...........	53	150 00	....	150 00	....	....	....
Stationery Expense......	54	18 75	....	18 75	....	....	....
		5,927 85	5,927 85	245 35	886 60	5,682 50	5,041 25
Net Profit.............				641 25	....	....	641 25
				886 60	886 60	5,682 50	5,682 50

Exercise 9-B. Financial reports for a public accountant

The work sheet of W. C. Corcoran, a public accountant, for the month ended October 31 of the current year is given below:

W. C. CORCORAN
WORK SHEET
FOR MONTH ENDED OCTOBER 31, 19--

Account Titles	Acct. No.	Trial Balance Debit	Credit	P. & L. Statement Debit	Credit	Balance Sheet Debit	Credit
Cash...................	11	1,110 50	....	....	....	1,110 50	....
Automobile............	12	2,750 00	....	....	....	2,750 00	....
Office Furniture........	13	725 00	....	....	....	725 00	....
Professional Library.....	14	350 00	....	....	....	350 00	....
C. W. Mattson Company.	21	....	57 50	....	....	....	57 50
Wallace Company.......	22	....	145 00	....	....	....	145 00
W. C. Corcoran, Capital..	31	....	4,122 75	....	....	....	4,122 75
Fees Income...........	41	....	857 00	....	857 00	....	....
Automobile Expense....	51	75 50	....	75 50	....	....	....
Miscellaneous Expense...	52	31 25	....	31 25	....	....	....
Rent Expense...........	53	140 00	....	140 00	....	....	....
		5,182 25	5,182 25	246 75	857 00	4,935 50	4,325 25
Net Profit.............		....	....	610 25	....	....	610 25
				857 00	857 00	4,935 50	4,935 50

Instructions: 1. Prepare a profit and loss statement.
2. Prepare a balance sheet in report form.

CHAPTER 10

Exercise 10-A. Closing entries for an attorney

A work sheet for William T. Bailey, an attorney, is given at the top of the preceding page.

Instructions: Record the closing entries in a journal.

Exercise 10-B. Closing entries for a public accountant

A work sheet for W. C. Corcoran, a public accountant, is given near the bottom of the preceding page.

Instructions: Record the closing entries in a journal.

CHAPTER 11

Exercise 11-A. Opening an accounts payable ledger for a book store

The creditors of Martha Walker, owner and manager of The Book Nook, and the amount owed to each creditor on October 1 of the current year are as follows:

Brant Book Company, Dayton......................	$42.25
Clayton Novelty Company, Chicago.................	22.40
Swift Publishing Company, Nashville..................	91.20
Wildman School Supplies, St. Louis...................	52.13

Instructions: Open accounts in an accounts payable ledger for Miss Walker's creditors. Enter the balance in each account. Allow three lines for each account.

The ledger accounts opened in this exercise will also be used in Exercise 11-B.

Exercise 11-B. Recording the purchases of a book store (based on Exercise 11-A)

Instructions: 1. Record each of the following purchases on account in a purchases journal similar to the one illustrated on page 121. The invoices are numbered consecutively beginning with No. 81 for the invoice from Wildman School Supplies.

2. As Miss Walker wishes her accounts payable ledger to show at all times the amount owed to each creditor, post to the individual accounts in the accounts payable ledger opened in Exercise 11-A immediately after you record the transactions for each day.

Oct. 1. Wildman School Supplies, $147.50.
    10. Brant Book Company, $49.80.
    10. Swift Publishing Company, $126.50.
    16. Wildman School Supplies, $51.85.
    16. Clayton Novelty Company, $62.40.
    24. Swift Publishing Company, $60.75.
    27. Brant Book Company, $75.60.

Instructions: 3. In a general ledger open Account No. 21 for Accounts Payable and Account No. 51 for Purchases. Allow four lines for each account. In the accounts payable account record the credit balance of $207.98, dating this balance October 1.

4. Total and rule the purchases journal. Post the total to the purchases account and the accounts payable account in the general ledger.

Exercise 12-A. Recording and posting the purchases and cash payments of a wholesale china dealer

The names of the businesses from which Richard Burton, a wholesale china dealer, buys on account and the amounts owed to them on September 30 of the current year are as follows:

	Account Balances
Lynn China Company, 347 State St., Weston..........	$215.30
Marshall Potteries, Charleston.......................	300.00
Monticello China Company, 7863 Marburg Ave., Clinton.	421.50
Zanesville Pottery Company, Zanesville..............	314.20

Instructions: 1. Open accounts in an accounts payable ledger with balance-column ruling for the creditors listed above. Allow five lines for each account. Record the balance in each account. Date the balance September 30 of the current year.

2. In a general ledger open the following accounts. Allow four lines for each account. Record the balance for each account for which a balance is given. Date the balance September 30 of the current year.

Acct. No.	Account Title	Balance
11	Cash	$4,235.60 (Dr.)
21	Accounts Payable	1,251.00 (Cr.)
31	Richard Burton, Capital	2,984.60 (Cr.)
32	Richard Burton, Drawing	
51	Purchases	
63	Miscellaneous Expense	
64	Rent Expense	
65	Salary Expense	

The cash payments transactions given below were made by Richard Burton during October of the current year.

Instructions: 3. Record the transactions in a cash payments journal similar to the one illustrated on page 134. All payments are made by check. Number the checks consecutively beginning with No. 110.

Oct. 2. Paid $125.00 for the November rent.

4. Paid $421.50 to Monticello China Company on account.

7. Paid $215.30 to Lynn China Company on account.

14. Paid $275.00 for semimonthly payroll.

17. Paid $314.20 to Zanesville Pottery Company on account.

21. Paid $14.20 for electricity bill. (Miscellaneous Expense)

23. Paid $300.00 to Marshall Potteries on account.

26. Paid $13.25 for November telephone bill. (Miscellaneous Expense)

28. Withdrew $300.00 for personal use.

31. Paid $275.00 for the semimonthly payroll.

The purchases journal of Richard Burton for the month of October is given below.

PURCHASES JOURNAL   PAGE 11

Date	No. of Invoice	From Whom Purchased	Post. Ref.	Amount
19-- Oct. 3	81	Monticello China Company............		682 50
5	82	Lynn China Company.................		814 10
15	83	Zanesville Pottery Company............		349 80
22	84	Marshall Potteries....................		519 25

Instructions: 4. Copy the purchases journal given above.

5. Post the entries from the purchases journal and the cash payments journal to the proper accounts.

6. Total and rule the purchases journal. Post the total to the purchases account and to the accounts payable account in the general ledger.

7. Foot, prove, total, and rule the cash payments journal.

8. Post the totals of the special columns in the cash payments journal.

9. Prepare a schedule of accounts payable from the accounts in the accounts payable ledger.

CHAPTER 13

Exercise 13-A. Opening an accounts receivable ledger for a furniture store

The customers of B. R. Turner, a retail furniture dealer, and the amount due from each customer on July 1 of the current year are as follows:

Stephen Corey, 2637 Bay Street, Milford..............	$207.50
L. A. Gaines, 675 Merritt Boulevard, City.............	300.40
Henry H. Newton, 1640 Hewitt Avenue, City..........	75.00
Roger Stimson, 241 River Road, City.................	457.90
D. E. Wilkes, 2730 Maple Park Avenue, City..........	128.80

Instructions: Open accounts in an accounts receivable ledger. Enter the balance in each account. Allow four lines for each account.

The ledger accounts opened in this exercise will also be used in Exercise 13-B.

Exercise 13-B. Recording sales on account for a furniture store (based on Exercise 13-A)

Instructions: 1. Record each of the following transactions in a sales journal similar to the one illustrated on page 150. The sales slips are to be numbered consecutively beginning with No. 76.

2. Post to the individual accounts in the accounts receivable ledger opened in Exercise 13-A immediately after you record the transactions for each day.

July 2. D. E. Wilkes, $274.80
    8. L. A. Gaines, $461.50
    8. Henry H. Newton, $105.32.
    17. Stephen Corey, $152.60.

July 17. L. A. Gaines, $75.
    25. Stephen Corey, $53.96.
    29. Roger Stimson, $109.60.
    29. L. A. Gaines, $113.50.

Instructions: 3. In the general ledger open Account No. 12 for Accounts Receivable and Account No. 41 for Sales. Allow four lines for each account. In the accounts receivable account record the debit balance of $1,169.60, dating this balance July 1.

4. Total and rule the sales journal. Post the total to the accounts receivable account and the sales account in the general ledger.

CHAPTER 14

Exercise 14-A. Recording and posting sales and cash receipts of a jewelry store

The names of the customers to whom Thomas Benton, a retail jeweler, sells on account and the amounts due from them on September 30 of the current year are:

	Account Balances
Daniel Cabot, 1472 Dreman Ave., Erie...............	$171.60
Susan Crane, 8584 Donegal, City.....................	50.00
George Graham, 4345 Michigan Ave., City............	100.00
M. E. Hedges, 2311 Lakewood Drive, City............	75.00
A. R. Kelley, 412 Salem Ave., City..................	62.25
Michael Murphy, 4340 Trenton St., City..............	200.00

Instructions: 1. Open accounts in an accounts receivable ledger with balance-column ruling for the customers listed above. Allow five lines for each account. Record the balance in each account.

2. In a general ledger open the following accounts. Allow four lines for each account. Record the balance for each account.

Acct. No.	*Account Title*	*Balance*
11	Cash	$1,314.20 (Dr.)
12	Accounts Receivable	658.85 (Dr.)
13	Office Supplies	177.60 (Dr.)
31	Thomas Benton, Capital	2,150.65 (Cr.)
41	Sales	3,412.50 (Cr.)

The cash receipts transactions given below were completed by Thomas Benton during October of the current year.

Instructions: 3. Record the transactions in a cash receipts journal similar to the one illustrated on page 162.

Oct. 1. Received $75.00 from M. E. Hedges on account.

4. Received $301.60 from cash sales of merchandise.

8. Received $62.25 from A. R. Kelley on account.

11. Received $910.20 from cash sales of merchandise.

11. Received $15.00 from the sale of office supplies to a neighboring merchant.

> Office supplies are not a part of the merchandise kept in stock for sale. For this reason, the sales account was not credited for this transaction; instead Office Supplies was credited.

15. Received $171.60 from Daniel Cabot on account.

18. Received $200.00 from Michael Murphy on account.

18. Received $412.60 from cash sales of merchandise.

23. Received $50.00 from Susan Crane on account.

25. Received $529.25 from cash sales of merchandise.

28. Received $100.00 from George Graham on account.

31. Received $476.20 from cash sales of merchandise.

The sales journal of Thomas Benton for the month of October is given below.

SALES JOURNAL PAGE 13

Date		No. of Sale	To Whom Sold	Post. Ref.	Amount	
19--						
Oct.	3	125	A. R. Kelley..........................		122	35
	9	126	Daniel Cabot........................		350	00
	14	127	Michael Murphy......................		75	00
	21	128	Susan Crane.........................		67	50
	26	129	George Graham......................		109	50

Instructions: 4. Copy the sales journal given above.

5. Post the entries from the sales journal and the cash receipts journal to the proper accounts.

6. Total and rule the sales journal. Post the total to the sales account and to the accounts receivable account in the general ledger.

7. Foot, prove, total, and rule the cash receipts journal.

8. Post the totals of the special columns in the cash receipts journal.

9. Prepare a schedule of accounts receivable from the accounts in the accounts receivable ledger.

CHAPTER 15

Exercise 15-A. Recording miscellaneous entries for a retail clothing store

George Beacom, a retail clothing merchant, decided to open a new set of books on July 1 of the current year. His balance sheet on June 30 was as follows:

GEORGE BEACOM
BALANCE SHEET
JUNE 30, 19--

Assets			*Liabilities*		
Cash....................	1,015	25	Accounts Payable.........	841	60
Accounts Receivable......	592	10			
Mdse. Inventory..........	2,140	60	*Proprietorship*		
Supplies................	91	45	George Beacom, Capital....	3,057	80
Prepaid Insurance........	60	00			
Total Assets............	3,899	40	Total Liab. and Prop.......	3,899	40

Instructions: 1. Record the opening entry in the general journal.

2. Record the following selected transactions in the general journal:

July 5. A. L. Benton reported that he was charged $51.90 for merchandise that he had not purchased. The sale was made to A. L. Bender.

12. Purchased supplies on account from the Wright Supply Co., $32.50; invoice dated July 11.

18. Took from stock for personal use one suit that cost $42.50.

25. Donald Marvin reported that he was charged $81.35 for merchandise he had not purchased. The sale was made to D. A. Martin.

CHAPTER 16

Exercise 16-A. Reconciliation of a bank statement

On August 1 of the current year, the Allen Hardware Store, owned and operated by M. A. Allen, received from the First National Bank the bank statement for July.

Instructions: Prepare a reconciliation of the bank statement using the following data:

(a) The checkbook balance on July 31 was $1,060.40.

(b) The July 31 balance on the bank statement was $1,169.98.

(c) Two charge slips accompanied the bank statement showing that the bank had made the following charges against the account of the Allen Hardware Store:

(1) A slip showing a service charge of 72 cents.

(2) A slip showing a charge of $1 for collecting a note for the Allen Hardware Store.

(d) The following checks were found to be outstanding: No. 91, $21.50; No. 93, $39.80; and No. 96, $50.

Exercise 16-B. Reconciliation of a bank statement

Instructions: Reconcile the bank statement of the Singer Appliance Company on December 1 of the current year. The following data are needed in preparing the reconciliation:

(a) The checkbook balance on November 30 was $1,395.39.

(b) The balance on the bank statement received by Mr. Singer on December 1 was $1,545.38.

(c) A comparison of the canceled checks with the stubs showed that the following checks had not been paid:

Check No. 180	$125.00
Check No. 182	25.30

(d) There was a service charge of 31 cents.

CHAPTER 17

Exercise 17-A. Work sheet for an automobile agency

On June 30 of the current year, the end of a fiscal period of one month, the account balances in the general ledger of the Langer Auto Sales Agency, owned and operated by R. A. Langer, and the list of inventories were as shown below.

Cash, $3,067.20
Accounts Receivable, $7,115.83
Merchandise Inventory, $21,640.82
Supplies, $428.10
Prepaid Insurance, $340.00
Accounts Payable, $7,108.03
R. A. Langer, Capital, $24,533.59

R. A. Langer, Drawing, $600.00 (Dr.)
Sales, $16,968.57
Purchases, $13,241.07
Gas and Oil Expense, $306.80
Miscellaneous Expense, $189.70
Rent Expense, $200.00
Salary Expense, $1,480.67

INVENTORIES, JUNE 30, 19--

Merchandise inventory, $22,141.72
Supplies inventory, $265.40
Value of insurance policies, $324.90

Instructions: Prepare an eight-column work sheet, similar to the model given on page 217.

CHAPTER 18

Exercise 18-A. Financial reports for a pharmacy (net profit with an increase in capital)

NOTE: If Problem 18-1, page 232, is not used, this exercise may be completed in the space in the workbook provided for Problem 18-1.

Instructions: 1. Prepare a profit and loss statement.
2. Prepare a balance sheet in report form.

HERMAN'S PHARMACY
WORK SHEET
FOR MONTH ENDED MARCH 31, 19--

Account Titles	Acct. No.	Trial Balance Debit (1)	Trial Balance Credit (2)	Adjustments Debit (3)	Adjustments Credit (4)	P. & L. Statement Debit (5)	P. & L. Statement Credit (6)	Balance Sheet Debit (7)	Balance Sheet Credit (8)
Cash	11	1584 23						1584 23	
Accounts Receivable	12	743 67						743 67	
Merchandise Inventory	13	4537 04		(b) 4044 72	(a) 4537 04			4044 72	
Supplies	14	304 59			(c) 61 56			243 03	
Prepaid Insurance	15	172 00			(d) 6 50			165 50	
Accounts Payable	21		1185 53						1185 53
H. J. Herman, Capital	31		5424 96						5424 96
H. J. Herman, Drawing	32	400 00						400 00	
Sales	41		3080 09				3080 09		
Purchases	51	1426 20				1426 20			
Delivery Expense	61	91 60				91 60			
Miscellaneous Expense	63	56 25				56 25			
Rent Expense	64	100 00				100 00			
Salary Expense	65	275 00				275 00			
		9690 58	9690 58						
Profit and Loss Summary	33			(a) 4537 04	(b) 4044 72	4537 04	4044 72		
Supplies Expense	66			(c) 61 56		61 56			
Insurance Expense	62			(d) 6 50		6 50			
				8649 82	8649 82	6554 15	7124 81	7181 15	6610 49
Net Profit						570 66			570 66
						7124 81	7124 81	7181 15	7181 15

CHAPTER 19

Exercise 19-A. Work at the end of the fiscal period (net profit with an increase in capital)

On January 31 of the current year, the end of a monthly fiscal period, the account balances in the ledger of Burton Electrical Supply, owned and operated by W. M. Burton, and the list of inventories were as shown below:

Cash, $3,022.80
Accounts Receivable, $1,920.48
Merchandise Inventory, $11,280.38
Supplies, $501.20
Prepaid Insurance, $530.20
Accounts Payable, $1,760.00
W. M. Burton, Capital, $14,511.96

W. M. Burton, Drawing, $400.00 (Dr.)
Sales, $8,357.22
Purchases, $4,860.80
Delivery Expense, $481.20
Miscellaneous Expense, $381.48
Rent Expense, $300.00
Salary Expense, $950.64

INVENTORIES, JANUARY 31, 19--

Merchandise inventory, $11,690.88
Supplies inventory, $260.60
Prepaid insurance, $513.80

Instructions: 1. Prepare an eight-column work sheet.
2. Prepare the profit and loss statement and the balance sheet.
3. Record the adjusting and the closing entries in the general journal.

Exercise 19-B. Work at the end of the fiscal period (net profit with a decrease in capital)

On June 30 of the current year, the end of a monthly fiscal period, the account balances in the general ledger of the Marshall Shoe Store, owned and managed by G. E. Marshall, and the list of inventories were as shown below:

Cash, $1,885.00
Accounts Receivable, $1,125.52
Merchandise Inventory, $6,852.60
Supplies, $376.30
Prepaid Insurance, $148.60
Accounts Payable, $1,884.30
G. E. Marshall, Capital, $9,286.82

G. E. Marshall, Drawing, $750.00 (Dr.)
Sales, $4,728.58
Purchases, $3,783.28
Miscellaneous Expense, $369.40
Rent Expense, $100.00
Salary Expense, $509.00

Additional data needed are:
Merchandise inventory, June 30, 19--, $7,467.80
Supplies inventory, June 30, 19--, $183.36
Insurance expired, $22.26

Note that in this exercise you are given the insurance expired during the period and not the value of the prepaid insurance at the end of the period.

Instructions: 1. Prepare an eight-column work sheet.
2. Prepare the profit and loss statement and the balance sheet.
3. Record the adjusting and the closing entries in the general journal.

CHAPTER 20

Exercise 20-A. **Recording transactions in a combination journal**

Instructions: 1. Record on page 6 in a combination journal like the one illustrated on pages 254 and 255 the following transactions completed by R. H. Holt during the month of May of the current year:

May 1. Issued Check No. 133 for $50 to establish a petty cash fund.

1. Received $78.67 from Paul Jones on account.

2. Issued Check No. 134 for $150 for the May rent.

3. Sold merchandise on account to Henry Jackson, $33.98.

3. Cash sales for May 1–3 were $206.80.

5. Purchased merchandise on account from Lamb & Sons, $361.25.

6. Issued Check No. 135 for $427.47 to Norton Manufacturing Co. on account.

7. Received $113.50 from Thomas Lucas on account.

9. Issued Check No. 136 for $75 for a cash purchase of merchandise.

10. Cash sales for May 5–10 were $488.55.

12. Received $25 for an old display table. (Store Equipment)

13. Sold merchandise on account to Fred Piper, $103.75.

15. Issued Check No. 137 for $141.36 to Baker Bros. on account.

16. Issued Check No. 138 for $300 to Mr. Holt for a withdrawal for personal use.

17. Cash sales for May 12–17 were $516.71.

19. Purchased merchandise on account from Beaver & Bent, $735.15.

21. Issued Check No. 139 for $33 for newspaper advertising. (Advertising Expense)

23. Sold merchandise on account to Robert Coyne, $45.

24. Cash sales for May 19–24 were $538.95.

26. Issued Check No. 140 for $67.89 for a cash purchase of merchandise.

Instructions: 2. Assume at this point of the problem that you have reached the bottom of the page. Total all columns and forward to the next page of the combination journal. Then continue to journalize the following transactions:

May 27. Issued Check No. 141 for $505.40 to The Boswell Company on account.

29. Issued Check No. 142 for $73.15 for utility bills for the month. (Miscellaneous Expense)

31. Issued Check No. 143 for $38.45 for delivery expense.

31. Issued Check No. 144 for $330 for the monthly payroll. (Salary Expense)

31. Issued Check No. 145 for $41.80 to replenish the petty cash fund. The petty cash payments were as follows: Supplies, $18.20; Advertising Expense, $7.50; Delivery Expense, $1.50; and Miscellaneous Expense, $14.60.

31. Cash sales for May 26–31 were $471.10.

Instructions: 3. Foot all columns of the combination journal and prove the equality of debits and credits.

4. Total and rule the combination journal.

Appendix 507

CHAPTER 21

Exercise 21-A. Recording transactions in a combination journal

Instructions: 1. Record the following selected transactions, which were completed by John Murphy during the month of June, in a combination journal like the one on pages 262 and 263. All purchases and sales are made on account.

June 2. Received a check for $174.54 from B. C. Porter for our invoice of May 23 for $176.30 less a 1% discount of $1.76.

3. Purchased merchandise amounting to $463.81 from McHenry Bros.

4. Sold merchandise amounting to $113.66 to T. B. Baxter.

6. McHenry Bros. allowed us credit for $11.50 for defective merchandise.

6. Issued Check No. 224 for $463.69 to Peyton & Co. in payment of their invoice of May 29 for $473.15 less a 2% discount of $9.46.

9. Issued a credit memorandum for $7.95 to T. B. Baxter for merchandise returned.

11. Issued Check No. 230 for $443.26 to McHenry Bros. in payment of the balance of $452.31 on their invoice of June 3 less a 2% discount of $9.05.

The amount of the invoice of June 3 was $463.81, but a credit of $11.50 was received on June 6. The balance of the invoice to which the discount applied was therefore $452.31, and the discount was 2% of this amount.

12. Sold merchandise amounting to $364.50 to A. D. King.

13. Issued Check No. 235 for $43.60 to Red Arrow Lines for freight and drayage on merchandise purchased.

14. Received a check for $104.65 from T. B. Baxter and gave him credit for that amount plus $1.06, a 1% discount.

The amount of the invoice of June 4 was $113.66. A credit of $7.95 was given on June 9. The balance of the invoice to which the discount applies was therefore $105.71.

17. Purchased merchandise amounting to $611.44 from the Clyde Co.

22. Received a check for $360.85 from A. D. King for our invoice of June 12 for $364.50 less a 1% discount of $3.65.

24. Sold merchandise amounting to $183.25 to B. F. Vance.

26. Issued Check No. 255 for $599.21 to the Clyde Co. in payment of their invoice of June 17 for $611.44 less a 2% discount of $12.23.

27. Purchased merchandise amounting to $534.65 from Knight & Sons.

30. Issued Check No. 264 for $51.80 to Red Arrow Lines for freight and drayage on merchandise purchased.

30. Received a credit memorandum for $21.30 from Knight & Sons for merchandise returned by us.

30. Issued Check No. 266 for $46.21 to replenish the petty cash fund. The payments were as follows: Supplies, $12.14; Miscellaneous Expense, $17.32; Delivery Expense, $4.50; and Transportation on Purchases, $12.25.

Instructions: 2. Foot, prove, and rule the combination journal.

CHAPTER 22

Exercise 22-A. Determination of earnings

The following table gives the hours worked and the hourly rate for ten employees. Each employee is paid his regular hourly rate for a maximum of 8 hours for Monday through Friday. If he works more than 8 hours on any of these five days, he receives time and a half for the overtime. He also receives time and a half for Saturday.

NAME	HOURS WORKED						HOURLY RATE
	M	Tu	W	Th	F	S	
Henry A. Abbott...............	8	8	8	8	8	4	$1.40
Robert C. Barton...............	8	8	8	8	10		1.60
Marvin Easton..................	8	10	8	8	8		1.70
Laurence Hershey...............	8	8	8	8	8	3	1.30
William Morton.................	8	8	8	0	8		1.95
Richard Parker.................	8	10	8	8	8		2.20
Raymond R. Ridge..............	8	8	8	8	10		2.00
Frank O. Sutton...............	8	8	8	8	8	4	2.00
Martin Tucker.................	8	8	8	8	8	2	1.80
David M. Weber................	8	10	8	8	8		2.10

Instructions: Determine the earnings for the week for each employee and the total earnings for all employees.

Exercise 22-B. Cash payrolls

The payroll register for the week ended March 8 of the current year, showing the number, the name, the number of exemptions, the total earnings, and the income tax deduction of each employee, is given below. An additional deduction of $2\frac{1}{4}\%$ of each employee's total earnings is to be made for FICA taxes.

PAYROLL REGISTER

Week ended March 8, 19 --   Date

No.	Employee's Name	No. of Exemptions	Total Earnings	Deductions	
				FICA Tax	Income Tax
1	Laura Cox.........................	1	45 00		5 90
2	Jean Dabney.......................	1	52 00		7 10
3	Clement Earle......................	4	95 00		7 90
4	J. G. Fisher.......................	3	85 00		8 40
5	Esther Harris......................	2	47 50		3 90
6	Walter Kern.......................	3	102 50		11 50
7	Mary Z. Long......................	2	61 25		6 40
8	Harriet Neyer.................... ..	1	48 00		6 40
9	Betty Pringle.....................	1	40 00		5 00
10	Ethel L. Stone.....................	2	72 50		8 50

Instructions: 1. Prepare a payroll register similar to the one illustrated on page 283. The date of payment is March 12.

2. Prepare a payroll change sheet similar to the one illustrated on page 287.

3. Prepare a payroll requisition form similar to the one illustrated on page 287.

CHAPTER 23

Exercise 23-A. Recording and posting payroll transactions

The Carter Company completed the payroll transactions given below during the period January 1 to April 10. The Carter Company is liable for payroll taxes at the following rates: FICA taxes, 2¼%; state unemployment taxes, 2.7%; and federal unemployment taxes, .3%.

Jan. 12. Issued Check No. 37 for $348.20 in payment of the liabilities for employees income taxes and FICA taxes.

     12. Issued Check No. 38 for $224.78 in payment of the liability for state unemployment taxes.

     12. Issued Check No. 39 for $97.43 in payment of the liability for federal unemployment taxes.

     31. Issued Check No. 81 for $2,241.76 in payment of the monthly payroll of $2,550.75 less a deduction of $251.60 for income taxes and a deduction of $57.39 for FICA taxes.

     31. Recorded the employer's payroll tax liabilities.

Feb. 8. Issued Check No. 125 for $366.38 in payment of the liabilities for employees income taxes and FICA taxes.

     28. Issued Check No. 188 for $2,433.48 in payment of the monthly payroll of $2,756.30 less a deduction of $260.80 for income taxes and a deduction of $62.02 for FICA taxes.

     28. Recorded the employer's payroll tax liabilities.

Mar. 11. Issued Check No. 223 for $384.84 in payment of the liabilities for employees income taxes and FICA taxes.

     31. Issued Check No. 262 for $2,428.02 in payment of the monthly payroll of $2,750 less a deduction of $260.10 for income taxes and a deduction of $61.88 for FICA taxes.

     31. Recorded the employer's payroll tax liabilities.

Apr. 10. Issued Check No. 298 for $383.86 in payment of the liabilities for employees income taxes and FICA taxes.

     10. Issued Check No. 299 for $217.54 in payment of the liability for state unemployment taxes.

Instructions: 1. Open the following accounts in the general ledger and record the balances as of January 1 of the current year:

ACCT. NO.	ACCOUNT TITLE	BALANCE
22	Employees Income Taxes Payable	$264.20
23	FICA Taxes Payable	84.00
24	State Unemployment Taxes Payable	224.78
25	Federal Unemployment Taxes Payable	97.43
63	Federal Unemployment Taxes	.....
66	FICA Taxes	.....
68	Salary Expense	.....
69	State Unemployment Taxes	.....

Instructions: 2. Record the transactions in a combination journal.

3. After each entry is journalized, post the items recorded in the General Debit and General Credit columns.

510   *20th Century Bookkeeping and Accounting*

CHAPTER 24

Exercise 24-A. Calculating depreciation, finding book value, and recording depreciation

Instructions: 1. Find the book value as of December 31, 1957, of each of the items of equipment given below.

2. Record the adjusting journal entry for the total depreciation expense (a) for the year ended December 31, 1956, and (b) for the the year ended December 31, 1957.

Fixed Asset	Date of Purchase	Initial Cost	Annual Rate of Depreciation
1	Jan. 1, 1956	$240	10%
2	July 1, 1956	300	15%
3	Apr. 8, 1957	640	25%
4	Aug. 26, 1957	840	5%
5	Nov. 12, 1957	72	12%

Exercise 24-B. Work at the end of the fiscal period

The account balances in the general ledger of C. M. Hurley, who operates a book shop, on December 31 of the current year were as follows:

Cash, $3,163.80

Accounts Receivable, $265.70

Merchandise Inventory, $4,833.35

Supplies, $267.25

Prepaid Insurance, $248

Office Equipment, $1,200

Allowance for Depreciation of Office Equipment, $445.80

Store Equipment, $2,600

Allowance for Depreciation of Store Equipment, $520

Accounts Payable, $355.27

C. M. Hurley, Capital, $7,680.30

C. M. Hurley, Drawing, $1,080 (**Dr.**)

Sales, $22,126.45

Sales Returns & Allow., $167.50

Purchases, $16,500

Purchases Returns & Allow., $137.50

Transportation on Purchases, $149.22

Miscellaneous Expense, $105.50

Rent Expense, $325

Salary Expense, $360

The additional data needed at the end of the annual fiscal period are: merchandise inventory, $2,427.62; supplies inventory, $59.80; prepaid insurance, $148; annual rate of estimated depreciation of office equipment, 10%; annual rate of estimated depreciation of store equipment, 8%.

Instructions: 1. Prepare an eight-column work sheet for the annual fiscal period ended December 31 of the current year.

2. Prepare a profit and loss statement and a balance sheet from the work sheet.

3. Record the adjusting and the closing entries in a combination journal.

CHAPTER 25

Exercise 25-A. Purchase and disposition of equipment

Joseph Egan, a retail shoe merchant, maintains in his general ledger accounts with Equipment, Allowance for Depreciation of Equipment, and Depreciation Expense.

Intsructions: 1. Record in a combination journal the following transactions selected from those completed by Mr. Egan during the current year.

Jan.   2. Issued Check No. 3 for $410 for a new electric typewriter.

Mar. 31. Recorded the estimated depreciation of equipment for the quarter ended March 31, $162.50.

Apr.   1. Discarded two chairs for which there was no further use and which could not be sold. The chairs cost $75 and had a book value of $10 at the time they were discarded.

June 30. Recorded the estimated depreciation of equipment for the quarter ended June 30, $165.30.

July   1. Sold an old office desk to a secondhand dealer for cash, $20. The desk cost $60 and had a book value of $12 when it was sold.

Aug. 15. Issued Check No. 261 for $125 for new display shelves.

Sept. 30. Recorded the estimated depreciation of equipment for the quarter ended September 30, $164.55.

Oct.   1. Bought a new typewriter for $155 cash (Check No. 301) and an old typewriter. The old typewriter cost $145 and had a book value of $50 at the time of the trade in.

Nov.   1. Sold an old adding machine for cash, $35. The adding machine cost $180 and had a book value of $46 after depreciation was recorded on September 30. The depreciation rate was $3 a quarter.

        (a) Record the depreciation for October.
        (b) Record the sale of the adding machine.

Dec. 31. Recorded the estimated depreciation of equipment for the quarter ended December 31, $164.12.

Instructions: 2. Foot, prove, and record the totals in the combination journal.

CHAPTER 26

Exercise 26-A. Recording transactions with bad debts expense

R. L. Fuller, a candy manufacturer, records his transactions in a combination journal. In his general ledger he maintains accounts with Bad Debts Expense and Allowance for Bad Debts. At the beginning of the year the balance of the allowance for bad debts account was $138.65.

In this exercise you are given transactions taken from those completed by Mr. Fuller during the year. The selected transactions in this exercise cover only uncollectible accounts, bad debts expense, and allowance for bad debts.

Instructions: 1. Record in a combination journal all of the necessary entries for the following transactions:

Feb. 18. Decided that the past-due account of Henry Jefferson, $45.25, was uncollectible. Wrote off his account as a bad debt.

Mar. 31. (End of first quarterly fiscal period.) Increased the allowance for bad debts by making the necessary adjusting entry. The estimated bad debts expense for each quarterly fiscal period was ½% (.005) of the total net sales. The net sales for the quarterly fiscal period ended March 31 were $17,472.10.

Apr. 9. C. B. Smith, a charge customer, became insolvent. Wrote off his account of $91.60 as a bad debt.

June 30. The net sales for the second quarterly fiscal period ended June 30 were $15,094.15. Increased the allowance for bad debts ½% (.005) of that amount.

July 23. Decided that the past-due account of B. F. Jackson, $77.50, was uncollectible. Wrote off his account as a bad debt.

Sept. 30. The net sales for the third quarterly fiscal period ended September 30 were $17,908.05. Increased the allowance for bad debts ½% (.005) of that amount.

Dec. 31. Decided that the past-due accounts of the following charge customers were uncollectible:

C. D. Lambert, $37.50
Elmer Madden, $50
S. T. Ruark, $49.85

Wrote them off as bad debts in one combined entry, debiting Allowance for Bad Debts for the total.

Dec. 31. The net sales for the fourth quarterly fiscal period ended December 31 were $16,620.30 Increased the allowance for bad debts ½% (.005) of that amount.

Instructions: 2. Foot, prove, and record the totals in the combination journal.

Exercise 26-B. Work at the end of the fiscal period

The account balances in the general ledger of Lintner's Wholesale Groceries on December 31 of the current year, the end of a quarterly fiscal period, were as follows:

Cash, $7,526.82
Petty Cash, $100
Accounts Receivable, $10,541
Allowance for Bad Debts, $202.32
Merchandise Inventory, $54,996.50
Supplies, $560.84
Prepaid Insurance, $696
Equipment, $6,380.80
Allowance for Depreciation of Equipment, $2,552.30
Accounts Payable, $5,723.10
Employees Income Taxes Payable, $252
FICA Taxes Payable, $216
State Unemployment Taxes Payable, $129.60
Federal Unemployment Taxes Payable, $57.60

Amos Lintner, Capital, $70,039
Amos Lintner, Drawing, $1,200 (Dr.)
Sales, $44,409.60
Sales Returns and Allowances, $652.20
Discount on Sales, $322.86
Purchases, $33,006.90
Purchases Returns and Allowances, $324.26
Discount on Purchases, $372.76
Transportation on Purchases, $457.06
FICA Taxes, $108
Federal Unemployment Taxes, $14.40
Miscellaneous Expense, $1,585.56
Rent Expense, $1,200
Salary Expense, $4,800
State Unemployment Taxes, $129.60

The additional data needed at the end of the period are:
Additional allowance for bad debts, 1% of total charge sales of $31,357.82.
Merchandise inventory, December 31, $59,530.68
Supplies on hand $254.32
Prepaid insurance, $565.60
Annual rate of estimated depreciation of equipment, 8%.

Instructions: 1. Prepare an eight-column work sheet for the quarterly fiscal period ended December 31 of the current year.

2. Prepare a profit and loss statement and a balance sheet.

3. Record the adjusting and closing entries in a combination journal.

CHAPTER 27

Exercise 27-A. Proving cash

Instructions: 1. Make a daily balance slip like the one on page 345. Fill in this form and prove cash from the information given below.

At the close of business on May 2 of the current year, the count of cash in the cash register drawer of Bette's Gift Shop was as shown in the tabulation at the left below. The detailed audit strip totals for May 2 were as shown at the right below.

Pennies..............	$	.35
Nickels..............		1.55
Dimes..............		4.40
Quarters............		12.75
Halves..............		15.50
Paper money........		191.00
Check..............		15.00

— 114	$0,248.50	GT
— 113	$0,007.75	Pd
— 112	$0,025.00	Rc
— 111	$0,028.25	Ch
— 110	$0,223.50	Ca

The cash register papers for May 2 were as follows:

(a) Sale on account to Mrs. C. O. Moore, $5.95.

(b) Received on account from Miss Irma Bath, $10.

(c) Paid out to Tom Jones for delivering orders, 60 cents.

(d) Sale on account to Mrs. David Payne, $16.50.

(e) Paid out to Mrs. A. B. Roth for merchandise returned, $4.50.

(f) Received on account from Mrs. L. D. Archer, $15.

(g) Sale on account to Mrs. Bessie Wilson, $5.80.

(h) Paid out to Larson Supply Co. for store supplies, $2.65.

Instructions: 2. Make a cash short and over voucher like the one on page 346. Fill in this voucher for the cash shortage for the day.

Exercise 27-B. Replenishing petty cash

On April 30 of the current year, the end of a monthly fiscal period, the petty cash fund of the Holt Haberdashery contained the following petty cash paid-out receipts and cash short and over vouchers:

	Paid-Out Receipts			*Cash Short and Over Vouchers*	
No.	*Account*	*Amount*	*Date*	*Classification*	*Amount*
26	Miscellaneous Expense........	$1.45	Apr. 4	Over...................	$1.00
27	Supplies...................	3.37	10	Short...................	.10
28	Sales Returns and Allow......	3.95	15	Short...................	.30
29	Miscellaneous Expense........	.35	23	Over...................	.20
30	Delivery Expense............	1.10	29	Short...................	.50
31	Sales Returns and Allow......	2.75			
32	Miscellaneous Expense........	4.15			
33	Delivery Expense............	.25			

Instructions: 1. Classify the paid-out receipts according to the accounts to be charged and find the total amount in each group.

2. Find the net amount by which the cash is short or over.

3. Record in a combination journal the entry to replenish the petty cash fund (Check No. 129).

Exercise 27-C. Recording transactions in a combination journal

W. C. Kaston, who operates a retail store, records his transactions in a combination journal like the one on pages 350 and 351.

Instructions: 1. Forward the following column totals on June 27 of the current year to a new page of Mr. Kaston's combination journal:

Cash Debit, $4,265.68

Cash Credit, $2,458.90

General Debit, $394.10

General Credit, $41.50

Accounts Payable Debit, $2,677.31

Accounts Payable Credit, $3,876.29

Discount on Purchases Credit, $34.26

Accounts Receivable Debit, $348.25

Accounts Receivable Credit, $287.50

Purchases Debit, $4,315.91

Sales Credit, $5,302.80

Instructions: 2. Record in the combination journal the following transactions completed by Mr. Kaston on June 27 to 30:

June 27. Purchased merchandise on account from Meyer Mfg. Co., $115.50.

27. The cash register totals for the day were as follows:

Sales for cash, $214.63

Sales on account, $21.75

Received on account, $20.00

28. Issued Check No. 165 for $306.23 to Henderson & Co. in payment of their invoice of June 19 for $312.48 less a 2% discount of $6.25.

28. Received a credit memorandum for $10 from Meyer Mfg. Co. for defective merchandise.

28. The cash register totals for the day were as follows:

Sales for cash, $231.95

Sales on account, $5.95

Received on account, $14.85

30. Issued Check No. 166 for $240.10 for the semimonthly payroll of $280 less a deduction of $33.60 for employees income taxes payable and a deduction of $6.30 for FICA taxes payable.

30. Recorded the employer's liability of $6.30 for FICA taxes, $7.56 for state unemployment taxes, and 84 cents for federal unemployment taxes.

30. Issued Check No. 167 for $150 to W. C. Kaston for a personal withdrawal.

30. The cash register totals for the day were as follows:

Sales for cash, $188.65

Sales on account, $30.15

Received on account, $45.25

30. Issued Check No. 168 for $37.80 to replenish the petty cash fund. The payments from this fund were as follows:

Sales Returns and Allowances, $12.90

Miscellaneous Expense, $22.70

Cash Short, $2.20

Instructions: 3. Foot, prove, and rule the combination journal.

CHAPTER 28

Exercise 28-A. Recording transactions in columnar special journals

George Newman, who owns and operates the Newman Electrical Supply House, completed the transactions given below during June of the current year.

Instructions: 1. Record the following transactions in a cash receipts journal, a cash payments journal, and a general journal like those illustrated in Chapter 28:

June 1. Issued Check No. 302 for $125 for the June rent.

    2. Received a check for $344.86 from Martin Lewis for our invoice of May 24 for $351.90 less $7.04 discount.

    2. Issued Check No. 303 for $180.70 in payment of the biweekly payroll of $200 less a deduction of $14.80 for employees income taxes payable and a deduction of $4.50 for FICA taxes payable.

    2. Cash sales for June 1 and 2 were $237.50.

    4. Wrote off the account of M. A. Stevens, $42.25, as a bad debt.

    6. Issued Check No. 304 for $809.72 to Dayton Electrical Co. in payment of their invoice of May 28 for $826.25 less $16.53 discount.

    8. Issued Check No. 305 for $9.75 in payment of the telephone bill.

    9. Cash sales for the week were $690.15.

  11. Sold some wrapping supplies for $5.25 cash to accommodate a customer. (Credit Supplies.)

  13. Issued Credit Memorandum No. 38 for $17.50 to William Walker for merchandise returned.

  14. Received $75 from H. R. Ward on account.

  15. Issued Check No. 306 for $375 for a new display case. (Debit Equipment.)

  16. Issued Check No. 307 for $180.70 in payment of the biweekly payroll of $200 less a deduction of $14.80 for employees income taxes payable and a deduction of $4.50 for FICA taxes payable.

  16. Cash sales for the week were $623.40.

  18. Received a credit memorandum for $12.75 from Dayton Electrical Co. for an allowance on defective merchandise.

  20. Received a check for $95.55 from T. H. Garland for our invoice of June 11 for $97.50 less $1.95 discount.

  21. Issued Check No. 308 for $231.67 to Randolph Corporation in payment of its invoice of June 12 for $236.40 less $4.73 discount.

  23. Cash sales for the week were $814.03.

  26. Received a check for $122.40 from D. D. Hauser for our invoice of June 16 for $124.90 less $2.50 discount.

  27. Issued Check No. 309 for $66.84 for transportation on purchases.

  28. Received a credit memorandum for $28.30 from Dawson & Co. for merchandise returned.

  29. Issued Check No. 310 for $138.05 for delivery service for the month. (Debit Delivery Expense.)

  30. Issued Check No. 311 for $180.70 in payment of the biweekly payroll of $200 less a deduction of $14.80 for employees income taxes payable and a deduction of $4.50 for FICA taxes payable.

  30. Recorded the employer's liability of $13.50 for FICA taxes, $16.20 for state unemployment taxes, and $1.80 for federal unemployment taxes.

  30. Issued Check No. 312 for $46.67 to replenish petty cash. The expenditures were as follows: Supplies, $5.20; Miscellaneous Expense, $15.85; Transportation on Purchases, $3.25; Delivery Expense, $4.20; Sales Returns and Allowances, $18.17.

  30. Cash sales for the week were $879.65.

Instructions: 2. Foot, prove, and rule the columnar special journals.

CHAPTER 29

Exercise 29-A. Recording notes and interest

The transactions given below were selected from those completed by Louis John-stone, who operates a furniture store, during September of the current year.

Instructions: Record the following transactions in a cash receipts journal, a cash payments journal, and a general journal.

Sept. 1. Received from James Parker a 60-day, 6% note for $400, dated today, as a 60-day extension of the time of payment on the amount due for the sale of August 15.

    6. Issued a 30-day, 4% note for $1,200 to Merrill Furniture Co. for an extension of time on account.

  10. Issued Check No. 315 for $402 to Superior Furniture Co. in payment of a 30-day, 6% interest-bearing note. Face of note, $400. Interest, $2.

  12. Discounted at the First National Bank his 90-day, non-interest-bearing note. Face of note, $2,000. Discount rate, 6%. Received credit for the proceeds, $1,970.

  15. Received a check for $421.40 from Steven Moore in full settlement of his 30-day, 4% interest-bearing note. Face of note, $420. Interest, $1.40.

  20. Received notice from the Central Trust Company that H. A. Gregory had refused to pay his 60-day, non-interest-bearing note for $500 when it became due on September 18. Charged the note to the account of the maker.

  22. Issued Check No. 330 for $500 to the Central Trust Company in payment of a 90-day, non-interest-bearing note due today.

CHAPTER 30

Exercise 30-A. Adjusting and reversing entries for accrued interest and salaries

On December 31 of the current year, before reports were prepared, the salary expense account of D. E. Wenzel had a debit balance of $8,245.67 and the interest expense account had a debit balance of $68.45. At the end of this yearly fiscal period, the following expenses had accrued: interest expense, $7.15; salary expense, $125.

Instructions: 1. Open the following general ledger accounts: Interest Payable, Account No. 22; Salaries Payable, Account No. 24; Salary Expense, Account No. 68; and Interest Expense, Account No. 82. Record the balances in the expense accounts.

2. Record in a columnar general journal as of December 31 of the current year the adjusting entries for the accrued expenses. Post to the ledger accounts.

3. Record the following partial closing entry in the columnar general journal: debit Profit and Loss Summary for $8,446.27; credit Salary Expense for $8,370.67; and credit Interest Expense for $75.60. Post the credits to the ledger accounts.

4. Rule the expense accounts.

5. Record in the columnar general journal, as of January 2 of the next year, the reversing entries for the accrued interest expense and the accrued salary expense. Post these entries to the ledger accounts.

6. Rule the liability accounts.

CHAPTER 31

Exercise 31-A. Opening entries for a partnership

On May 1 of the current year W. C. Bell and D. L. Hope, proprietors of separate retail groceries, formed a partnership. The partnership, Bell and Hope, took over the assets of the two proprietors and assumed their liabilities. Mr. Hope invested enough additional cash in the partnership to make his proprietorship equal to that of Mr. Bell. The balance sheets of Mr. Bell and Mr. Hope at the time the partnership was formed are shown below.

W. C. BELL

BALANCE SHEET

MAY 1, 19 --

Assets			Liabilities		
Cash.................	2,325	60	Notes Payable...........	1,500	00
Notes Receivable.......	200	00	Accounts Payable........	2,317	30
Accounts Receivable....	3,312	40			
Mdse. Inventory........	7,821	80	Total Liabilities..........	3,817	30
Supplies..............	157	50	*Proprietorship*		
Equipment............	3,200	00	W. C. Bell, Capital.......	13,200	00
Total Assets...........	17,017	30	Total Liab. and Prop.....	17,017	30

D. L. HOPE

BALANCE SHEET

MAY 1, 19 --

Assets			Liabilities		
Cash.................	1,210	65	Accounts Payable........	2,711	25
Accounts Receivable....	3,279	40			
Mdse. Inventory........	6,104	10	*Proprietorship*		
Supplies..............	101	10	D. L. Hope, Capital......	9,895	80
Prepaid Insurance.......	36	80			
Equipment............	1,875	00			
Total Assets...........	12,607	05	Total Liab. and Prop.....	12,607	05

Instructions: Record the opening entry for each partner in a columnar general journal. Assume that the cash balance has been entered in the Account Credited column of the cash receipts journal.

Exercise 31-B. Distribution of net profits of a partnership

John Marcus, David Newton, and George Olds were partners engaged in operating a restaurant. Each partner had invested $7,500 in the business. According to the partnership agreement, Marcus received a salary of $3,600 a year; Newton, $3,000; and Olds, $2,400. All profits remaining after the salaries have been paid are to be divided equally.

At the end of the current fiscal period on December 31, the profit and loss statement showed that the net profit for the year was $9,930.

Instructions: 1. Prepare the portion of the profit and loss statement showing the distribution of the net profit.

2. Prepare the proprietorship section of the balance sheet, assuming that the partners withdrew their salaries but no additional amounts.

CHAPTER 32

Exercise 32-A. Opening entry to incorporate a going concern

On March 1 of the current year a charter was granted to Nash & Kite, Inc., that authorized a capital stock of $50,000 consisting of 1,000 shares (par value $50). This corporation had agreed to take over the printing business owned by the partnership of Nash and Kite. On March 1 the corporation took over the assets and assumed the liabilities of the partnership shown on the following balance sheet:

NASH AND KITE

BALANCE SHEET

FEBRUARY 28, 19 --

Assets			Liabilities		
Cash..................	4,721	85	Notes Payable...........	1,875	00
Notes Receivable.......	900	00	Accounts Payable........	2,871	90
Accounts Receivable....	4,621	45			
Mdse. Inventory........	6,676	80	Total Liabilities.........	4,746	90
Supplies...............	716	40	*Proprietorship*		
Equipment.............	12,110	40	M. A. Nash, Capital.....	10,000	00
			J. S. Kite, Capital........	15,000	00
Total Assets...........	29,746	90	Total Liab. and Prop.....	29,746	90

On March 1, 200 shares of stock were issued to Mr. Nash and 300 shares were issued to Mr. Kite for their equities in the partnership.

Instructions: Record the opening entry in a general journal.

Exercise 32-B. Work at the end of the fiscal period

The account balances in the general ledger of The Erlanger Corporation on March 31 of the current year were as follows:

Cash, $6,819.86

Petty Cash, $100.00

Accounts Receivable, $8,112.46

Allowance for Bad Debts, $281.63

Merchandise Inventory, $22,410.50

Supplies, $381.10

Prepaid Insurance, $201.06

Equipment, $4,800.00

Allowance for Depreciation of Equipment, $560.00

Notes Payable, $2,000.00

Accounts Payable, $6,110.45

Employees Income Taxes Payable, $281.40

FICA Taxes Payable, $69.76

State Unemployment Taxes Payable, $125.55

Capital Stock, $30,000.00

Earned Surplus, $3,734.57

Sales, $27,876.12

Sales Returns and Allowances, $521.30

Discount on Sales, $194.10

Purchases, $23,671.54

Purchases Returns and Allowances, $161.57

Discount on Purchases, $295.65

Transportation on Purchases, $1,405.10

Delivery Expense, $610.20

FICA Taxes, $34.88

Miscellaneous Expense, $126.45

Rent Expense, $500.00

Salary Expense, $1,550.00

State Unemployment Taxes, $41.85

Interest Expense, $16.30

The additional data needed at the end of the monthly fiscal period are: additional allowance for bad debts, 1% of total charge sales of $11,463.80; merchandise inventory, $24,816.33; supplies inventory, $176.30; prepaid insurance, $176.90; annual rate of estimated depreciation, 10%; accrued salary expense, $62; accrued interest expense, $7.50.

Instructions: 1. Prepare an eight-column work sheet for the monthly fiscal period ended March 31 of the current year.

2. Prepare a profit and loss statement and a balance sheet from the work sheet.

3. Record the adjusting and closing entries in the general journal.

4. Record the reversing entries for the accruals in the general journal as of April 1 of the next period.

CHAPTER 33

Exercise 33-A. Personal records of an individual

Charles Richards, a single man employed as a bookkeeper, maintains bookkeeping records similar to those illustrated for a family in Chapter 33. He maintains a checking account, but he pays all small bills in cash.

Mr. Richards uses the following expense classification:

Board and Room — all regular meals and rent of room.

Clothing Expense — all wearing apparel.

Donations — church and charity.

Federal Income Tax — deductions from salary for income tax.

Insurance Expense — life insurance and group insurance.

Laundry and Dry Cleaning — washing, cleaning, and pressing.

Medical Expense — drugs, dentist and doctor bills, etc.

Miscellaneous Expense — toilet and shaving articles, barber service, gifts, newspapers, magazines, books, stationery, stamps, and other unclassified expenses.

Recreation — refreshments, movies, theaters, sports, social affairs, club dues, and vacation.

Transportation — streetcar, bus, taxi, train, and airplane fares.

Mr. Richards maintains a combination journal with the following money columns:

Cash Debit	Federal Income Tax Debit
Cash Credit	Laundry and Dry Cleaning Debit
General Debit	Miscellaneous Expense Debit
General Credit	Recreation Debit
Board and Room Debit	Transportation Debit
Donations Debit	Social Security Deposits Debit

Mr. Richards carries in his pocket a notebook in which he jots down each expenditure he makes. Each night he records in his combination journal the expenditures he has made during the day. He debits the individual expense accounts for the proper amounts and credits Cash for the total amount paid out.

CHAPTER 35

Exercise 35-A. Recording the transactions of a physician

Dr. J. H. Gordon, physician and surgeon, maintains a bookkeeping system like that used by the dentist in Chapter 35.

Instructions: 1. Open the following accounts in the ledger and record the balances indicated as of December 1 of the current year. Allow five lines for each account.

ACCT. No.	(1) ASSETS		ACCT. No.	(4) INCOME	
11	Cash................	$ 1,361.41	41	Professional Fees.....	$15,974.00
12	Petty Cash..........	50.00		**(5) EXPENSES**	
13	Automobile.........	2,850.00	51	Automobile Expense..	903.85
13.1	Allow. for Depr. of Automobile........	950.00	52	Depr. of Automobile..	......
14	Medical and Surgical Equipment........	5,533.88	53	Depr. of Medical and Surgical Equip......	......
14.1	Allow. for Depr. of Medical and Surgical Equipment........	608.25	54	Depreciation of Office Equipment.........	......
15	Office Equipment.....	1,693.50	55	FICA Taxes..........	74.36
15.1	Allow. for Depr. of Office Equipment.....	214.60	56	Insurance Expense....	84.00
			57	Laboratory Expense...	487.50
	(2) LIABILITIES		58	Medical Supplies Exp..	581.42
			59	Miscellaneous Exp....	276.55
21	Employees Income Taxes Payable......	88.00	510	Office Supplies Exp....	97.80
22	FICA Taxes Payable..	27.04	511	Rent Expense........	2,750.00
			512	Salary Expense.......	3,300.00
	(3) PROPRIETORSHIP				
31	J. H. Gordon, Capital.	7,682.38			
32	J. H. Gordon, Drawing (Dr.)..............	5,500.00			
33	Expense and Income Summary..........	....			

Instructions: 2. Record the following transactions in a combination journal having amount columns for Cash Debit; Cash Credit; General Debit; General Credit; Professional Fees Credit; Automobile Expense Debit; Medical Supplies Expense Debit; Miscellaneous Expense Debit; Salary Expense Debit; Employees Income Taxes Payable Credit; FICA Taxes Payable Credit; J. H. Gordon, Drawing Debit.

All payments were made by check, the first check for December being No. 205. The transactions completed by Dr. Gordon during December of the current year were:

Dec. 1. Paid the December rent, $250.

2. Paid Physicians' Linen Service Company for linen service, $6.75. (Charge to Miscellaneous Expense.)

3. Paid Puro Water Company for distilled water, $5. (Charge to Medical Supplies Expense.)

4. Paid the telephone bill, $7.25.

5. Paid Ericson's Garage for repairs to automobile, $16.85.

6. Deposited $367, the receipts for the past week.

9. Withdrew $200 for personal use.

12. Paid Johnson Drug Company for medical supplies, $31.83.

13. Deposited $462.50, the receipts for the past week.

Dec. 15. Paid Helen Cook, nurse-secretary, her semimonthly salary of $150 less deductions of $22 for income taxes withheld and $3.38 for FICA taxes.

15. Recorded the employer's liability of $3.38 for his share of the FICA taxes.

17. Replenished the petty cash fund with a check for $37.73. The distribution was as follows: Automobile Expense, $15.35; Medical Supplies Expense, $12.75; Miscellaneous Expense, $4.10; Office Supplies Expense, $5.53.

19. Paid Wilton Stationers for letterheads, $18.75. (Charge to Office Supplies Expense.)

20. Withdrew $125 for personal use.

20. Deposited $391.50, the receipts for the past week.

23. Paid Lang Medical Company for medical supplies, $16.09.

24. Paid Kramer Furniture Store for refinishing furniture, $35. (Charge to Miscellaneous Expense.)

26. Paid Holton Laboratories, Inc. for services rendered, $41.70. (Charge to Laboratory Expense.)

27. Deposited $275, the receipts for the past week.

30. Replenished the petty cash fund with a check for $42.33. The distribution was as follows: Automobile Expense, $13.87; Laboratory Expense, $4.50; Medical Supplies Expense, $21.15; Miscellaneous Expense, $2.81.

30. Withdrew $175 for personal use.

31. Paid Helen Cook her semimonthly salary of $150 less deductions of $22 for income taxes withheld and $3.38 for FICA taxes.

31. Recorded the employer's liability of $3.38 for his share of the FICA taxes.

Instructions: 3. Total, prove, and rule the combination journal.

4. Post the combination journal.

5. Prepare an eight-column work sheet for the annual fiscal period ended December 31, using the following data for adjustments:

> Depreciation of automobile, $950
> Depreciation of medical and surgical equipment, $275
> Depreciation of office equipment, $169.35

6. Prepare the statement of income and expenses and the balance sheet.

7. Record the adjusting and closing entries and post.

8. Balance and rule the ledger accounts and take a post-closing trial balance.

CHAPTER 36

Exercise 36-A. Recording the transactions of a farmer

William Peters, a farmer, maintains a set of bookkeeping records similar to those illustrated in Chapter 36. His trial balance on September 30 of the current year is given at the top of the following page.

Instructions: 1. Open ledger accounts for the accounts given in the trial balance of September 30 and enter the balances as of September 30 of the current year.

WILLIAM PETERS
TRIAL BALANCE
SEPTEMBER 30, 19 --

Cash....................................	11	821 35		
Livestock..............................	12	1,498 30		
Allowance for Depr. of Livestock.........	12.1		292 50	
Livestock Purchased Cost...............	13	733 00		
Machinery and Equipment...............	14	2,337 50		
Allowance for Depreciation of Machinery and Equipment.......................	14.1		785 75	
Notes Payable.........................	21		500 00	
William Peters, Capital.................	31		3,644 36	
William Peters, Drawing.................	32	1,895 50		
Profit and Loss Summary................	33	... ..	... ..	
Livestock Purchased Sales...............	41		1,281 80	
Livestock Raised Sales...................	42		2,476 50	
Merchandise Received for Produce........	43		77 15	
Miscellaneous Income...................	44		110 00	
Produce Sales.........................	45		1,868 90	
Depreciation of Livestock................	51	... ..	... ..	
Depr. of Machinery and Equipment.......	52	... ..	... ..	
Feed Purchased........................	53	244 33		
Fertilizer and Lime.....................	54	151 20		
Fuel and Oil (Farm Machinery)..........	55	91 25		
Interest Expense.......................	56	7 50		
Machine Hire..........................	57	61 50		
Miscellaneous Expense..................	58	123 10		
Rent Expense..........................	59	2,850 00		
Repairs and Maintenance................	60	108 45		
Seeds, Plants, and Trees Purchased........	61	113 98		
		11,036 96	11,036 96	

Instructions: 2. Record in a combination journal similar to the one shown on pages 482 and 483 the following transactions completed by Mr. Peters during the three-month period from October 1 to December 31. All payments were made by check, the first check for October being No. 52.

Oct. 1. Paid the fourth quarterly installment on the rent, $950.

3. Purchased feed for the livestock, $87.50.

4. Withdrew cash for personal use, $150.

8. Purchased fuel and oil for the farm machines, $23.25.

10. Received cash from the sale of livestock that had been purchased as feeders, $293.50.

15. Exchanged eggs and vegetables worth $15 for groceries.

16. Received cash from the sale of dairy products, $62.60.

22. Received cash from the sale of eggs and vegetables, $39.75.

25. Received cash from the sale of corn, $292.25.

27. Paid cash for repairs to the tractor, $12.50.

30. Received cash from the sale of livestock raised on the farm, $463.

Nov. 1. Received cash from the sale of corn, $151.20.
    5. Paid the note payable of $500, due today, and the interest on the note, $5.
    7. Received cash from the sale of livestock that had been purchased as feeders, $525.
    8. Withdrew cash for personal use, $125.
    11. Purchased feed for the livestock, $180.67.
    14. Purchased seed for next year, $55.70.
    18. Received cash from the sale of chickens and ducks raised on the farm, $58.05.
    21. Paid cash for repairs to the farm equipment, $10.50.
    26. Received cash from the sale of livestock raised on the farm, $174.60.
    29. Bought clothing, $29.75.

Dec. 1. Purchased a milk cow for $97.50. (Debit Livestock.)
    3. Received cash for helping a neighbor fill his silo, $15.
    5. Received cash from the sale of wheat, $245.
    6. Withdrew cash for personal use, $200.
    10. Paid cash for repairs to the barn, $75.
    15. Purchased fuel and oil for the farm machines, $19.50.
    20. Purchased seed for next year, $33.75.
    24. Received cash from the sale of livestock raised on the farm, $88.
    27. Received cash from the sale of cordwood, $30. (Miscellaneous Income.)
    30. Received $500 from the Farmers National Bank and gave the bank his 60-day 6% note for $500.
    30. Purchased a truck for farm use, $1,050.

Instructions: 3. Total, prove, and rule the combination journal. Post to the ledger accounts.

4. Prepare an eight-column work sheet for the annual fiscal period ended December 31 of the current year. The data needed for the adjustments are:

> All livestock purchased for resale has been sold
> Depreciation of livestock, $140.35
> Depreciation of machinery and equipment, $233.75

5. Prepare a profit and loss statement and a balance sheet from the work sheet.

6. Record the adjusting and the closing entries in the General columns of the combination journal. Post to the ledger accounts.

7. Rule the ledger accounts that balance, and balance and rule each remaining account that has both debits and credits.

8. Prepare a post-closing trial balance.

Index

closing the, 239; **defined,** 120; proving posting of, 182; relationship of purchases journal, accounts payable ledger, and, 123

Going business, purchase of a, by a corporation, 427

Gross profit on sales, 225

H

Heading, of balance sheet, 2, 91; of profit and loss statement, 88; of trial balance, 72; of work sheet, 82

High school athletic department, balance sheet of a, 459; budget of a, 458; combination journal of a, 460–461; equipment record of a, 459; other financial reports of a, 463; proof of accuracy of records of, 462; treasurer's report for, 462, 463

High school club, approval of bills of a, 454; budget of a, 452; immediate record of cash receipts of a, 452; membership record book of a, 453; proof of accuracy of records of a, 456; receipt book of a, 452; treasurer's report for a, 457; two-column cashbook of a, 455

I

Immediate record, of cash payments, 31, 41, 129; of cash receipts, 27, 155; of income transaction, 39; of purchases on account, 115; of sales on account, 145

In balance, trial balance, 73

Income, accrued, 387; **defined,** 39; from sales section on profit and loss statement, 321, 322; immediate record of, 39; increases in, 41, 61; interest, **see** Interest income; other, **see** Other income; section of profit and loss statement, 89; transaction, effect of, 41

Income account, 39, 229; closing, 97

Income and expenses, schedule of farm, 487; statement of, 445, 471, 475

Income tax, data for a family 447; reports for a farmer, preparing, 487

Income taxes, paying liability for employees, 297; withheld from employees by employer, 279

Incorporation, certificate of, 424, 425

Increase, in an account balance, 61; in an asset, 27, 30, 33, 41; in proprietorship, 39, 40

Individual, beginning balance sheet of a, 2; bookkeeping for the, 447

Insurance, cash surrender value of, 436; expense, adjustment for, 213; prepaid, **see** Prepaid insurance

Interest, on notes, 368; rate, 367, 368; recording collection of note and, 370; recording payment of note and, 372; computing, using interest tables, 368; computing, without interest tables, 368

Interest-bearing note, 368

Interest expense, classified as

other expense, 374; on profit and loss statement, 375; on work sheet, 374, 375; owed but not paid, 381; reversing entry for accrued, 386

Interest expense account, 368; need for readjusting, 385

Interest income, account, 368; classified as other income, 374; on profit and loss statement, 375; on work sheet, 374, 375

Interest tables, analyzing, 368; computing interest using, 368; computing interest without, 368

Inventory, **see** Merchandise inventory

Investment, additional, recording and posting an, 160; cash, forming a partnership with a, 393; in a going concern, recording an, 394

Invoice, approved for payment, 454; checking an, 116; **defined,** 115; **illustrated,** 115; payment of purchases, 349; receipted, 456; recording an, in a purchases journal, 117; showing terms of payment, 266; using, as purchases journal, 123; verifying extensions on an, 116

Invoices file, paid, 349, 362; unpaid, 349, 362

Items column in an account, use of, 19

J

Journal, 9; **see also** Cash payments journal, Cash receipts journal, Combination journal, General journal, Purchases journal, **and** Sales journal; after posting, **illustrated,** 58; after recording, **illustrated,** 44; checking accuracy of footings of, 44; columnar, 28; correcting errors in, **illustrated,** 45; **defined,** 9; divided-column, 361; five-column, 28; footing the four-column, 44; opening entry in a, 12; posting individual entries in General columns of four-column, 52–55; posting reference column in a, 20; posting totals of special columns in, 55; ruling the four-column, 9

Journal entry, date of, 10; opening, 10

Journalizing, **defined,** 28; summary of principles of, 34, 61, 62

L

Land, account, 312; depreciation of, 312

Ledger, **see also** Accounts payable ledger, Accounts receivable ledger, **and** General ledger; after posting, **illustrated,** 59–60; balance-column, ruling, 117; closed, balanced, and ruled, **illustrated,** 105–107; closing the, 95, 102, 103, 239; correcting errors in, 74; date of entry in, 19; **defined,** 17; footed, **illustrated,** 69–71; footing accounts in, 69; need for bringing proprietorship section up to date, 95; numbering accounts in, 51; proprietorship division of, 103; subsidiary, 120

Legal fees, 474

Liabilities, 2; balances of, 23; balancing, 104; classification of, on balance sheet, 313; current, 313; decreases in, 31, 32, 62; **defined,** 2; fixed or long-term, 313; group of accounts, 229; increases in, 61; section of balance sheet, 91

Life insurance, cash surrender value of, 436

List prices, 264

Livestock, 480; purchased cost, 481, 483; purchased sales, 483; raised sales, 483

Long-term liabilities, 313

Loss, net, 83

Losses, division of partnership, 395

Loss from bad debts, estimating the, 327

Loss on fixed assets, account, 318; on profit and loss statement, 321

M

Maker of a note, 367

Maturity date of a note, 367

Membership record book, 453

Memorandum, credit, 261; entry, 156

Merchandise, 115; buying, 115; cost of, sold, 224, 225; received for produce, 482; selling, 145; withdrawals of, by proprietor, 179

Merchandise inventory, 176; adjusting entry for beginning, 233; adjusting entry for ending, 234, 235; adjustment for beginning, 209; adjustment for ending, 211

Minus, assets, 311, 329; purchases accounts, 270; sales accounts, 270

Miscellaneous entries, 175; in columnar general journal, 360

Mortgage payable, 313

N

Net cost of merchandise purchased, 270, 271

Net loss, 83, 218; in proprietorship section of balance sheet, 228; on profit and loss statement, 226; work sheet showing, 219

Net profit, 83; calculating the, 84, 218; from operations, 322; on profit and loss statement, 90; where shown in ledger, 95; with decrease in proprietorship, 228

Net purchases, 270, 271

Net sales, 270

Non-interest-bearing note, 368

No-par-value stock, 426

"No sale" transactions, recording, on cash register, 343

Note, 367; analyzing, 367; **illustrated,** 367; interest-bearing, 368; interest on, 368; non-interest-bearing, 368; proceeds of a, 373; use of a, 367

Notes payable, 367; recording, 371; recording discounting of, 373; recording payment of, with interest, 372

Notes receivable, 367; dishonored, 370; recording, 369; recording collection of, with interest, 370; recording dishonored, 371

Number column in a columnar journal, 30